Canon Formation

Canon Formation

*Tracing the Role of Sub-Collections
in the Biblical Canon*

Edited by
W. Edward Glenny and Darian R. Lockett

t&tclark

T&T CLARK
Bloomsbury Publishing Plc
50 Bedford Square, London, WC1B 3DP, UK
1385 Broadway, New York, NY 10018, USA
29 Earlsfort Terrace, Dublin 2, Ireland

BLOOMSBURY, T&T CLARK and the T&T Clark logo are trademarks of
Bloomsbury Publishing Plc

First published in Great Britain 2023
Paperback edition first published 2024

Copyright © W. Edward Glenny, Darian R. Lockett, and contributors, 2023

W. Edward Glenny and Darian R. Lockett have asserted their right under the Copyright, Designs and Patents Act, 1988, to be identified as Editors of this work.

For legal purposes the Acknowledgments on p. xv constitute an extension of this copyright page.

Cover design: Charlotte James
Cover image: A page from Codex Alexandrinus, New Testament © INTERFOTO / Alamy

All rights reserved. No part of this publication may be reproduced or transmitted in any form or by any means, electronic or mechanical, including photocopying, recording, or any information storage or retrieval system, without prior permission in writing from the publishers.

Bloomsbury Publishing Plc does not have any control over, or responsibility for, any third-party websites referred to or in this book. All internet addresses given in this book were correct at the time of going to press. The author and publisher regret any inconvenience caused if addresses have changed or sites have ceased to exist, but can accept no responsibility for any such changes.

A catalogue record for this book is available from the British Library.

A catalog record for this book is available from the Library of Congress.

ISBN: HB: 978-0-5676-9208-5
PB: 978-0-5677-0917-2
ePDF: 978-0-5676-9207-8
eBook: 978-0-5676-9210-8

Typeset by RefineCatch Limited, Bungay, Suffolk

To find out more about our authors and books visit www.bloomsbury.com
and sign up for our newsletters.

Contents

List of Tables	vii
Foreword *Lee Martin McDonald*	viii
Acknowledgments	xv
Notes on Permissions	xvi
List of Abbreviations	xvii
Introduction *W. Edward Glenny and Darian R. Lockett*	1

Section One The Bible as a Whole and the Old and New Testament as Canonical Units

1	The Bible Canon and Its Significance: Textual Comprehensiveness, Function, Design, and Delimitation *Tomas Bokedal*	7
2	The Canonical Shape of the Hebrew Old Testament *Stephen G. Dempster*	33
3	The Canonical Shape of the Greek Old Testament *John D. Meade*	53
4	The Canonical Shape of the New Testament *Matthew Y. Emerson*	79

Section Two Old Testament Canonical Sub-Units

5	The Pentateuch as Canon *Stephen B. Chapman*	101
6	The Canon of Psalms *Nancy L. deClaissé-Walford*	121
7	The Canonical Role of Israel's Wisdom Collection *Craig G. Bartholomew*	139
8	The Macro-Structure of the *Megilloth* *Timothy J. Stone*	159
9	The Canonical Function of the *Nebi'im* *Christopher R. Seitz*	167
10	Prophetic Intentionality in the Twelve *Don C. Collett*	183
11	The Book of the Twelve in the Septuagint *W. Edward Glenny*	207

Section Three New Testament Canonical Sub-Units

12 The Four-Fold Gospel Collection *Gregory R. Lanier* 229

13 Corpus Apostolicum *Darian R. Lockett* 251

14 The Pauline Corpus *E. Randolph Richards* 271

15 Revelation as the Ending of the Canon *Külli Tõniste* 289

Section Four Hermeneutical Considerations of Canon

16 Hermeneutical Reflections on Canonical Sub-Collections: Retrospect and Prospect *Ched Spellman* 311

List of Contributors 333
Index of Biblical/Extra-Biblical References 337
Index of Ancient Sources 345
Index of Modern Authors 347

Tables

1.1	Significant Jewish and biblical symbolic numbers	20
2.1	Baba Batra 14b	47
2.2	Masoretes (Cairo [List], Aleppo, Leningrad)	47
2.3	Jerome—Prologus Galeatus	48
2.4	Josephus—Against Apion	48
3.1	Greek canon lists *ca.* 100–400	56
3.2	Greek canon lists *ca.* 401–850	58
3.3	Select Greek manuscripts 4th–16th	62
12.1	Dating and description of extra-Biblical "Gospels"	230
12.2	Dating and description of "Gospel" fragments	231
12.3	Dating and description of other attested "Gospels"	232
12.4	Questions at play for intrinsic vs. extrinsic canon paradigms	232
12.5	Early Greek papyri of the canonical Gospels (2–5 century)	235
12.6	Early manuscripts of select non-canonical "Gospels" (2–5 century)	235
12.7	Early references to canonical Gospels	236
12.8	Early references to non-canonical "Gospels"	236
12.9	Examples of scribal assimilation	239
12.10	Titles of non-canonical "Gospels"	241
12.11	*The Tetramorph* of Irenaeus	245

Foreword

I am honored to be invited to write the foreword to this volume. Most canon scholars acknowledge that the final word about the formation of the Bible has yet to be written, but most agree that recent scholarly contributions on this subject have moved us closer to understanding the origin of the biblical canon than was even possible just a few years ago. Useful and irenic interaction by scholars who have access to the same ancient sources allows for better results in our research, and we are the richer for it even when we disagree on how to interpret them.

Several earlier scholarly conclusions have been set aside, modified, or clarified because of multiple exchanges among current canon scholars. These include the dating of the formation of the Hebrew Bible or Old Testament canon to a much later time than some scholars earlier postulated anywhere from around 500 BCE to the Hasmonean period of around 160 BCE. Some are now suggesting a date from 200 even to 400 CE. This includes the tripartite divisions of the Hebrew Bible and the possibility of an earlier quadripartite division of the Hebrew Scriptures. There is also more focus on the significance of the Septuagint and its formation and textual reliability than was common in recent canon scholarship. In terms of the New Testament scholars are re-examining the dating of the Muratorian Fragment and recently new arguments of a later date have emerged based on actual examination of that document. Earlier, few scholars focused on the text-critical issues related to canon formation, but now this is common. Furthermore, we have more information on the ancient canon lists than was available earlier thanks to Ed Gallagher and John Meade and there is once again growing interest in the manuscript evidence as it influences our understanding of the development of the canon. Finally, there is greater familiarity with the church fathers and their assessments of ancient canonical and non-canonical writings. This is all encouraging and as a result we now have access to more informed conclusions than was possible earlier and that hopefully will continue in current and future canon inquiry.

The focus on sub-units of the biblical books in this volume is a most welcome focus that has not received adequate attention by earlier scholars or in my work on canon formation. This volume provides an important advance on canon formation in this often-neglected area. At some point in antiquity the books of both the Old and New Testaments were placed in groups of writings that had common features, but the sub-units varied in their contents and orders for centuries. It is interesting that the sub-units in the Hebrew Bible (HB) or Tanak are occasionally different from the ones in the church's Old Testament despite the eventual inclusion of the same HB books. Agreement on the chronological order of those books does not appear a factor in their formation and they were eventually placed together in sub-units in the HB and the church's Bible (Pentateuch, history, poetry and wisdom, and prophets) or in the Hebrew Bible (Torah, *Nevi'im* or Prophets whether former and latter that grouped the Twelve together early on, and finally the Writings). Later in rabbinic tradition and synagogue readings the *Hamesh Megillot* ("Five Scrolls" that include Song of Songs, Ruth, Lamentations, Ecclesiastes, and Esther) were read (and continue to be read) on special occasions in synagogues. The order of the Hebrew Scriptures by the combinations of books to arrive at the holy numbers of the twenty-two letter Hebrew alphabet or the twenty-four letter Greek alphabet varied for centuries. Even when some canonical books were doubted by some rabbinic sages or noncanonical books were later excluded (Sirach), the sacred numbers did not change, and combinations of books were made to adjust to those sacred numbers.

When I began seriously examining the origin of the Bible, I was largely dependent on the writings of James Sanders, Hans von Campenhausen, Brevard Childs, and Bruce Manning Metzger's earlier writings. Metzger, F. F. Bruce, and I all came out with books on the biblical canon within a few months of each other and I would have loved to have Metzger's and Bruce's work available before mine was published and I realized quickly that my work needed revisions in several places, but I also saw that I could not agree with them in some areas. As I continued investigating canon formation, I saw multiple differences among various scholars, especially between those who followed James Sanders and Brevard Childs. When I critiqued Childs' work on canon formation, I received a lot of negative responses and the second time I did it, I asked James Sanders, a former colleague with Brevard Childs, if I got it right and he said yes. Subsequently, I decided not to pursue that since I agreed largely with Childs' aim of preserving the Bible as the church's book and we agreed on that. I did notice that he cited my work in one of his last articles for another volume.

While much of this volume focuses on the importance of the sub-units of the books in the church's Bible, not much focus was given to it in antiquity whether among the Jews or the Christians. Perhaps as a result not much has been said about it in previous publications, including mine, but it does offer potential for greater understanding of how the biblical canon came together. Quite early (*ca.* 180–130 BCE) books in collections of Law and Prophets were circulating, but the precise contents of those collections are not clear until much later. Eventually there was greater clarity on the scope of those sub-units in later pandect collections of the church's Scriptures, especially in the *Ketuvim* (Writings) and in the order of the Twelve (Minor Prophets) and occasionally in the order of the Latter Prophets. That is understandable given the means of transmission of those units, namely on individual scrolls (rolls) for centuries.

The question about how the emergence of sub-units led to or were part of the processes that led to the formation of the Bible is the point in question here, but how significant is it that others in antiquity did not have strong arguments for the groupings or the order that now exist in the OT or NT? How do these sub-units clarify conclusions about the eventual scope of the two major collections (OT and NT) that make up the church's Bible? It is hoped that readers will find what follows in this volume helpful and that it will advance our understanding of several complex questions related to the formation of the church's Bible.

Below I will outline some of the many questions and issues that are still being examined by canon scholars. Regarding the NT, the groupings are mostly logical (Gospels and Letters), but the order varied in church collections for centuries.

Revelation is not always the last book in the NT collections, nor do Paul's writings always immediately follow Acts nor is Acts, always immediately after the Gospels. The four canonical Gospels are almost always in first place in the NT and almost always beginning with Matthew, but the letters vary in their locations in the collections of NT writings and where to place Acts, Hebrews, and Revelation varies in the surviving manuscripts. As in the case of the OT writings, the order varied until the manuscript technology increased the capacity of the codices that enable larger collections to be included in one volume of some 1,450–1,600 pages as we see in Codices Vaticanus, Sinaiticus, and Alexandrinus. By the twelfth century and the emergence of the compact Paris Bibles in smaller letters that were read with the aid of the magnifying glass and thinner pages, a whole Bible could be produced in one transportable volume that contained all the church's Scriptures. Then greater stability in the books and their order became more common. In what follows I will briefly consider first the shaping of the Hebrew/Tanak or Christian OT and then the shaping of the NT.

The shaping of the books in the Hebrew/Tanak or Christian OT varied for centuries, but the oldest collections appear to be grouped in the larger Torah and Prophets. The Writings do not appear as a group until the end of the second century CE and were earlier included among the Prophets. The same is true in the NT, and as late as the fourth century some rabbinic sages were still speaking of their Scriptures as Law and the Prophets. The contents of the Prophets are difficult to define until well into the early Christian era. They may well have included some noncanonical writings such as the 1 Enoch or Shepherd of Hermas. In the NT, "prophets" essentially included all the books that were not in "the laws of Moses" or Pentateuch. By the mid-second century CE, Justin identifies all of the church's "First" Scriptures as "prophets" and the others as "gospels" or "memoirs of the apostles" (1 Apology 67). The separation of the Writings from the Prophets in Judaism came later in the second century CE. Josephus listed four groupings of the Jewish Scriptures, but they did not conform clearly to the later tripartite collection of Hebrew Scriptures. In the NT there were only two groups of the Jewish Scriptures, "Law of Moses and the prophets," with only one exception in Luke 24:44 that also included "the psalms," but earlier in that chapter (24:27) "all the scriptures" were identified as "Moses and all the prophets." The Law and the Prophets comprised all of the church's first Scriptures and Luke 24:44 may indicate an emerging third division, but at that time only "psalms" and later the Prophets were divided into Prophets and Writings in the Hebrew Bible for some Jews. As late as the fourth century some rabbinic Jews were still referring to the Law and Prophets in reference to all of their Scriptures. The Writings (*Ketuvim*) are clearly a later development of the Jewish Scriptures, and most of the variations in the order or shape of those Scriptures is in the Writings. The internal order and content of these sub-collections were not always clear or distinct in the surviving ancient documents. This could be because of the physical transmission of the OT and NT writings, namely if initially in rolls or scrolls when the order could easily have varied, but later in codices in the fourth century when greater stability in order was possible and more likely.

The canonical shape of the NT writings varied for centuries also, but the Gospels were regularly (not always) placed at the beginning of the collections with Matthew, the most cited Gospel) in the lead in New Testament canon lists. The variances in the shape of the individual books of the New Testament continued for centuries in the surviving manuscripts and in some of the canon lists well into the time of the invention of the printing press, but there was more stability in their order after the formation of the Paris Bibles (twelfth to thirteenth century) and the emergence of several pandect collections in one or more volumes.

Scholars are well aware that the order of the New Testament varied especially in terms of the placing of the letters that followed Acts, namely whether Acts was followed by the Catholic Epistles or the Pauline Epistles, but also whether some of the New Testament letters were welcomed along with the majority of them, for example, the acceptance of the minor New Testament epistles (2 Peter, 2–3 John, and Jude, as well as the varied and challenging history of the acceptance of the book of Revelation). The Syrian Christians had a different gospel text for centuries (Diatessaron) and they also included 3 Corinthians in their Scripture collection for centuries until the Greek influence was more widely welcomed. The Ethiopian Christians whose churches were founded by Syrian missionaries were isolated from the rest of Christendom for almost a millennium, and the Ethiopian Christians had an even broader Old Testament and New Testament that continues to this day. How reflective is their collection of biblical books of the Syrian churches in the fourth and fifth centuries when their churches were established?

In conclusion, I will list below some of the continuing debatable issues in current canon formation inquiry. No one yet has answered all the questions listed below and that is often due to the lack of sufficient ancient primary sources that inform us on the questions we bring to canon examinations today. That is not a fault of our making, but it simply reflects that the earliest church fathers were not as interested in many questions we moderns have today. As a result, we today try to form a picture of the development of the Bible from multiple assessments of the same limited ancient sources. No one in antiquity wrote a book on how the church got the Bible! With that in mind, I close here with a list with a little comment in some places of some of the important questions and issues in contemporary canon formation inquiry that canon scholars will continue to address in future canon studies.

Some questions for Hebrew Bible/Tanak and Old Testament canon formation

1. What do we mean by "canon" and "Scripture" and when are these terms operative in early Christianity for both Hebrew and Christian writings? How are those terms different or the same?
2. Why is the Christian OT different from the Jewish HB/Tanak regarding its order and the books included in it for Christians?
3. Why are the Christian OT writings different in Orthodox, Catholic, and Protestant churches? There was a time when some of the Hebrew Old Testament books were questioned in early Christianity, such as Esther, but all of the major church bodies today welcome all of the books in the Hebrew Bible and some Christians welcome more.
4. How does the collection of Dead Sea Scrolls at Qumran and the Judean Desert add understanding to the shape of the Hebrew scriptures in the time of Jesus and before the separation of the Christians from Judaism?

5. Was the LXX Scriptures larger or smaller than the HB Scriptures or the same in the time of Jesus and the first century CE? Why were some non-HB texts found in the LXX found among the Dead Sea Scrolls and the Cairo Geniza? How relevant is that for understanding the formation of the Old Testament or the Hebrew Bible?
6. Was there a difference in the books in the Christian preserved LXX from the HB/Tanak? Why did some churches adopt a larger OT canon?
7. Were all the current sub-units in the HB present in the early churches or even in the multiple Judaisms in the centuries before and during the birth of the church? Were the scope and order of the Torah and the Twelve (Minor Prophets) settled before the time of Jesus and what relevance does that have for understanding canon formation before the birth of the church?
8. What comprised the Prophets before the separation of the *Ketuvim* (Writings)?
9. Why did some of the rabbinic sages initially accept Sirach as Scripture and for how long? Which canonical Hebrew Scriptures were doubted by some rabbinic sages and for how long?
10. What is the significance of the *Megilloth* and its order and location in the HB and Christian OT?
11. What is the significance of the numbers 22 and 24 for the books of the HB and what combinations were made to achieve those numbers?
12. What is the early evidence for the core elements of Jewish scriptural authority and when did that function as scripture in Israel and later Judaism, namely the Exodus, Wilderness Wanderings, and Entrance into Canaan?
13. When was the origin and order of the *Ketuvim* settled? Who in antiquity was interested in this question and why? When did they become a *separate* part of the HB/Tanak?
14. Why did some early churches welcome several books that were not later included in their OT or the Jewish HB?
15. What do the contents of the surviving Hebrew and Greek manuscripts of the HB/LXX tell us about the stability of the collections and texts of the HB/OT books?
16. What criteria were employed in the selection of the HB and LXX books? Why is there a difference and when did that difference begin?
17. Which of the HB books did the early churches initially welcome as Scripture, and how relevant is the NT citations of the HB scriptures (in Greek mostly) for determining the scope of the HB and later OT canon books?
18. Do the introductory scriptural formulae (e.g., "as it is written" or "as the scripture says") always identify *only* which texts the early Christians cited as Scripture? Are there exceptions in the NT and early church fathers?
19. Did the NT authors and early church fathers use or cite the "apocryphal" (or Deuterocanonical or pseudepigraphal) books *as scripture* or simply as illustrative material (e.g., Enoch, Wisdom of Solomon, Sirach, and others)?
20. How fluid was the collection of Hebrew Scriptures in the time of Jesus and before or even after? Despite considerable overlap in the books in canonical lists and surviving manuscripts of the Hebrew Scriptures and the LXX, what does it say about the fluidity of the HB and OT when those lists and manuscripts do not always include the same scriptural books?

21. Why and how do Protestants, Catholics, and Orthodox differ in the recognition of their OT books? They eventually, not initially, accepted the books in the HB/Tanak as Scripture, but why did Catholics accept the Deuterocanonical writings as Scripture, the Orthodox accepted them as "readable" but not "Scripture" and the Protestants rejected them altogether?
22. What role did Athanasius' *Thirty-Ninth Festal Letter* play in the formation of the church's OT in the East or West or the NT? Although his letter was read in both the eastern and western churches in 367, why did some churches in the east and west reject parts of it?
23. The Deuterocanonical or Apocrypha writings vary in their scope in the ancient manuscripts and in the canon lists. What does that say about the origin of those collections?
24. What does the presence of textual insertions and changes in the Hebrew and Greek canonical texts say about the notion of inspired Scripture in antiquity? Do these pseudonymous insertions help us understand the production and presence of pseudonymous writings circulating in Judaism and early Christianity?

Questions for New Testament Canon Formation

1. When were the NT writings acknowledged as Scripture? Since none are called Scripture in the first century, how did they function in churches before that recognition?
2. What role did the earliest sacred traditions and creeds play in the formation of the church's Bible?
3. Did the early use and citations of NT writings by the early church fathers always mean that they functioned as the sacred "Scripture"?
4. Was there a distinction between use, function, scriptural, and canonical in early Christianity?
5. How should the term canon be understood in relation to NT writings and non-NT writings in early Christianity?
6. How early and consistent was the notion of canon or rule applied to the church's NT scriptures in antiquity? Was that understanding uniform in most churches?
7. What was the focus of authority in the early churches *before* there was a New Testament canon of Scriptures? What authorities were operative in that "in between" time?
8. When was the Muratorian Fragment produced? Late second to early third century or late fourth or early fifth century? Did it influence anyone in the second century or anyone before the late fourth century? If earlier, does that necessarily mean that all churches at that time agreed with its assessment and list?
9. What can we learn from the surviving lists of the church's Scriptures? Since they are not the same in terms of their contents and were produced by the church's leaders or prominent teachers (Origen, Eusebius, Athanasius, Jerome, and others), do those lists reflect the Scriptures "on the ground" that were operative in the ancient local churches?

10. What can we learn from the surviving manuscripts with religious books that informed the faith of the early churches? Were they only illustrative material or Scripture or both?
11. To what extent were the ancient lectionaries in the churches their primary Scriptures that informed their faith? Since few churches had copies of all their Scriptures in early Christianity, what lectionaries circulating in the churches before the Bible informed their faith and would that faith have been different had they possessed all the Scriptures that are in Bibles today?
12. What does the textual evidence say about the sacredness of the biblical books when changes and additions were made in the biblical texts? Do the many textual variants in the NT texts reflect emerging views of their initially understood authority and inspiration?
13. To what extent were the early churches' beliefs informed by pseudonymous writings? Are there pseudonymous writings in the NT? What about pseudonymous texts later inserted in the NT writings, especially in the Gospels, Paul, and Catholic Epistles?
14. What does the presence of textual insertions and changes in the NT writings say about the early notion of inspiration in antiquity? Do these pseudonymous insertions help us understand the production and presence of pseudonymous writings circulating in early Christianity?
15. Did content or authorship of the NT writings eventually lead to their acceptance in the NT canon? Were apostolic names inserted as authors to obtain acceptance in the biblical canon or was the content in the books what made them useful in the churches and affected their decisions about those books regardless of authorship? In other words, was there an "irresistible momentum" by useful and acceptable content in many early churches that led to the inclusion of some books produced by pseudonymous authors? In other words, were all pseudonymous writings consciously rejected or were some of them welcomed and found useful? Were *all* pseudonymous writings eventually rejected by the ancient churches?
16. To what extent did church councils or leading church fathers influence the inclusion of the books in the church's OT and NT or did they simply reflect what was operative in the churches in their locations and at the times when the councils met?

The above questions and concerns indicate that we have a way to go before presenting the final answer to the question of how we got our Bible. There are, of course, more questions than those listed that are necessary to be answered before a full and final decision can be made about the origin of the Bible. These and other questions offer fruitful possibilities for a better understanding of the origin of the church's Bible as well as the Hebrew Bible. Some of the above questions will be addressed in what follows along with others that I have not included here. I commend the reading of the following chapters prepared by the authors who have carefully prepared their research for modern readers. Much of what they have to say will aid and advance future discussions of the formation of the Bible. I commend them for their contributions here.

Lee Martin McDonald

Acknowledgments

This book was conceived during a conversation Ed and Darian had over lunch in Berlin, Germany, on August 8, 2017, after a panel discussion at the International SBL meeting over Darian's book, *Letters from the Pillar Apostles*. Arising from Ed's comments on the panel, our lunch conversation focused on the need for a single volume covering each of the sub-collections of the Christian canon. We knew of no single resource that considered each of the major canonical sub-collections and so began to brainstorm what such a volume would look like. Now, several years later, we are grateful to see the seeds planted in that lunch in Berlin finally germinate into the present volume. There are many people who have helped us reach this point and would like to express our thanks here.

We are grateful for the valuable contributions from each of our authors. This volume was planned and initiated before, yet executed during, the world-changing events of the Covid-19 pandemic. Our contributors, living throughout the United States and Europe, experienced a variety of institutional challenges, delays, and extra demands during this period, and yet faithfully completed their work for this volume. We are truly grateful for their investment in and commitment to this project—their work has made this project a success.

Thanks are also due to Dominic Mattos and Sarah Blake at Bloomsbury who offered encouragement and ultimately a great deal of patience throughout the process of contracting, writing, and editing the volume. It was a particular delight to share our initial ideas about the volume with Dominic over a meal in Berlin (and we are grateful that Dominic also picked up the bill!).

Furthermore, the editors would like to thank student workers and TAs who helped with the final stages of proofreading and indexing. Thanks are due to Tori Hinsverk who compiled the indices and to Jacob Edwards for compiling the abbreviations list.

Finally, and most importantly, we both would like to thank our families for their patience and encouragement in the process. Darian would like to dedicate this volume to the memory of Steve Williams. A member of Trinity Presbyterian church, elder, and friend, Steve was a constant source of encouragement and endless interest in the canon. He passed suddenly in the late stages of this work and will be missed: we grieve in hope (1 Thess. 4:13).

Permissions

Nancy L. deClaissé-Walford. (2014), "The Canonical Shape of the Psalter," in *The Book of Psalms*, NICOT, 21–38, Grand Rapids: Eerdmans. Reprinted by permission of the publisher (Eerdmans); all rights reserved.

Christopher R. Seitz. (2018), "Prophets," in *The Elder Testament: Canon, Theology, Trinity* (chapter two), 139–60, Waco, TX: Baylor University Press. Reprinted by permission of the copyright holder, Baylor University Press.

Timothy Stone. (2016), "Macro-Structure of the Megilloth," in Brad Embry (ed.), *Megilloth Studies: The Shape of Contemporary Scholarship*, Hebrew Bible Monographs 78, 141–9; Sheffield: Sheffield Phoenix Press. Reprinted by permission of the copyright holder, Sheffield Phoenix Press.

Abbreviations

AB	Anchor Bible
ABG	Arbeiten zur Bibel und ihrer Geschichte
ANF	*Ante-Nicene Fathers*
ANTF	Arbeiten zur neutestamentlichen Textforschung
AT	Altes Testament
ATD	Das Alte Testament Deutsch
AYBRL	Anchor Yale Bible Reference Library
AYRL	Anchor Yale Reference Library
BBB	Bonner biblische Beiträge
BBR	Bulletin for Biblical Research
BBRS	Bulletin for Biblical Research Supplement
BCOTWP	Baker Commentary on the Old Testament Wisdom and Psalms
BdA	La Bible d'Alexandrie
BETL	Bibliotheca ephemeridum theologicarum lovaniensium
BJS	Brown Judaic Studies
BZAW	Beihefte zur Zeitschrift für die alttestamentliche Wissenschaft
CBET	*Contributions to Biblical Exegesis and Theology*
CBQ	*Catholic Bible Quarterly*
CTM	*Concordia Theological Monthly*
CTTS	*Current Trends in Technology & Sciences*
DJD	Discoveries in the Judean Desert (of Jordan)
DPL	*Dictionary of Paul and His Letters*. Edited by G. F. Hawthorne and R. P. Martin. Downers Grove, 1993
EC	*Early Christianity*
ECHC	Early Christianity in its Hellenistic Context
EJL	Early Judaism and Its Literature
ETR	*Etudes théologiques et religieuses*
ExpTim	*Expository Times*
FAT	Forschungen zum Alten Testament
GBS	Guide to Biblical Scholarship
HAR	*Hebrew Annual Review*
HBT	*Horizons in Biblical Theology*
Herm. *Vis.*	Shepherd of Hermas, Vision
HSCP	*Harvard Studies in Philology*
HTKAT	Herders Theologischer Kommentar Zum Alten Testament
HTR	*Harvard Theological Review*
HUCA	*Hebrew Union College Annual*
ICC	International Critical Commentary
IDBSup	*Interpreter's Dictionary of the Bible: Supplementary Volume*. Edited by K. Crim. Nashville, 1976
Int	*Interpretation*

ITC	International Theological Commentary
JBL	*Journal of Biblical Literature*
JBR	*Journal of Bible and Religion*
JECS	*Journal of Early Christian Studies*
JETS	*Journal of the Evangelical Theological Society*
JHS	*Journal of Hellenic Studies*
JPS	Jewish Publication Society
JSJSup	Supplements to the Journal for the Study of Judaism
JSNT	*Journal for the Study of the New Testament*
JSNTSup	Journal for the Study of the New Testament: Supplement Series
JSOT	*Journal for the Study of the Old Testament*
JSOTSup	Journal for the Study of the Old Testament: Supplement Series
JTI	*Journal of Theological Interpretation*
JTS	*Journal of Theological Studies*
LHBOTS	Library of Hebrew Bible/Old Testament Studies
LNTS	The Library of New Testament Studies
MSU	Mitteilungen des Septuaginta-Unternehmens
NA28	*Novum Testamentum Graece*, Nestle-Aland, 28th ed.
NGTT	*Nederduitse gereformeerde teologiese tydskrif*
NIGTC	New International Greek Testament Commentary
NovT	*Novum Testamentum*
NPNF[1]	Nicene and Post-Nicene Fathers, Series 1
NPNF[2]	Nicene and Post-Nicene Fathers, Series 2
NRSV	New Revised Standard Version
NTM	New Testament Monographs
NTS	*New Testament Studies*
NTTSD	New Testament Tools, Studies and Documents
OBO	Orbis biblicus et orientalis
OBT	Overtures to Biblical Theology
OS	Oudtestamentische Studiën
OTE	*Old Testament Essays*
PAST	Pauline Studies
PRS	*Perspectives in Religious Studies*
RC	Religion Compass
RevQ	*Revue de Qumran*
SAHS	Scripture and Hermeneutics Series
SBLDS	Society of Biblical Literature Dissertation Series
SBLSP	*Society of Biblical Literature Seminar Papers*
SBLSymS	Society of Biblical Literature Symposium Series
SBLRBS	Society of Biblical Literature Resources for Biblical Study
SEA	*Svensk exegetisk årsbok*
SEPT	Septuagint Commentary Series
SJ	Studia judaica
SJLA	Studies in Judaism in Late Antiquity
SJT	*Scottish Journal of Theology*
SNTMS	Society for New Testament Studies Monograph Series
SSEJC	*Studies in Early Judaism and Christianity*
STI	Studies in Theological Interpretation
STR	*Southeastern Theological Review*

SVigChr	Supplements to Vigiliae Christianae
TB	*Theologische Bücherei: Neudrucke und Berichte aus dem 20. Jahrhundert*
TCSt	Text Critical Studies
TENTS	Texts and Editions for New Testament Study
Them	*Themelios*
THGNT	*Tyndale House Greek New Testament*
TSAJ	Texte und Studien zum antiken Judentum
TU	Texte und Untersuchungn
TUGAL	Texte und Untersuchungen zur Geschichte der altchristlichen Literatur
TW	Theologisches Wörterbuch
TynBul	*Tyndale Bulletin*
UBS5	*The Greek New Testament*, United Bible Societies, 5th ed.
VC	*Vigiliae christianae*
VT	*Vetus Testamentum*
VTSup	Vetus Testamentum Supplements
WBC	Word Biblical Commentary
WTJ	*Westminster Theological Journal*
WUNT	Wissenschaftliche Untersuchungen zum Neuen Testament
ZAW	*Zeitschrift für die alttestamentliche Wissenschaft*
ZBK	Zürcher Bibelkommentare
ZNW	Zeitschrift für die neutestamentliche Wissenschaft und die Kunde der älteren Kirche
ZTK	*Zeitschrift für Theologie und Kirche*

Introduction

W. Edward Glenny and Darian R. Lockett

Several recent studies have shown that a crucial step in the process of canonization of the biblical texts was the coming together of discrete canonical sub-units. Examples include: (1) the relationship between the Torah and the Prophets as canonical units (Stephen B. Chapman), (2) the Book of the Twelve (James Nogalski, Don Collett, Christopher Seitz, and W. Edward Glenny), (3) Psalms (Gordon Wenham), (4) the Megilloth (Timothy Stone), (5) the Gospels (Francis Watson), (6) the Pauline Corpus (Stanley Porter, Brevard Childs), and (7) the Catholic Epistles (David Nienhuis, Robert Wall, and Darian Lockett). Brevard Childs argued that the "formation of the canon was not a late extrinsic validation of a corpus of writings, but involved a series of decisions deeply affecting the shape of the books" (Childs 1986: 59). The authoritative force that led to the formation of the Old and New Testaments was present at earlier stages in the process. Therefore, canonization was not a top-down judgment (stemming from a later reception, recognition, or declaration), but rather a judgment at work in the canonical process itself. Thus, Christopher Seitz recognizes a canon-consciousness within the formation of the literature (here speaking specifically of the Book of the Twelve): "order and association precede lists, and they are accomplishments of a deeply theological nature to begin with" (Seitz 2009: 45; see also Seitz 2011: 27–92).

For example, in the historical development of the New Testament canon, the four Gospels and the Pauline letters were received and recognized as distinct collections early in the process (see Trobisch 2000). Jens Schröter notes the "two most important collections, which stand at the beginning of the emergence of the New Testament" are "the four gospels and the Letters of Paul" while "Acts and the Catholic Letters, which are closely connected with Acts in terms of the history of the canon" came shortly after (Schröter 2013: 273). Many of the early codices specifically witness to the combination of Acts and the Catholic Epistles which forms a canonical link between the four-fold Gospels on one side and the Pauline Letter collection (including Hebrews) on the other.[1] An insight that underwrites these canonical sub-collections is the observation that most of the biblical texts made their way into the canon as part of a collection rather than as individual books. Evidence suggests that there was a method and strategy

---

[1] Some Greek New Testaments are now recognizing this fact and arranging the books of the New Testament accordingly; see the *Tyndale House Greek New Testament*.

to the way the books in the various collections were arranged and then to the way the collections were organized.

The above list of works demonstrates a growing awareness of the historical and theological importance of canon for understanding the Old and New Testaments. However, to date there has not been a single volume bringing together discussion of each of the canonical sub-units which eventually comprised the Old and New Testaments.

The present work aims to provide a state-of-the-question discussion of the various canonical sub-collections (touching on the development and significance of arrangement and association in each collection) while highlighting the historical and theological significance these collections have regarding the Christian canon as a whole. The essays are organized under four general headings. The first is "The Bible as a Whole and the Old and New Testaments as Canonical Units" which will include essays on the entire Bible Canon, the Old Testament/Hebrew Bible in its Hebrew and Septuagint form, and the New Testament. In the initial essay in this section Tomas Bokedal summarizes the early phase of Christian scriptural canon formation, dealing with the collection's textual comprehensiveness, development, design, and delimitation. Stephen Dempster follows with an essay on "The Canonical Shape of the Hebrew Old Testament," emphasizing its consistent tripartite structure. In his chapter on "The Canonical Shape of the Greek Old Testament" John Meade traces the historical development of the Septuagint's canonical shape through analysis of its early contents and arrangements. And Matthew Emerson's essay on "The Canonical Shape of the New Testament" completes the initial section of the volume; Emerson introduces different questions and methods concerning how to address the canonical shape of the New Testament, and, after describing the state of the question, he proposes paths forward where appropriate.

The next heading, "The Old Testament Canonical Sub-units" includes essays on the Torah, the Psalter, Wisdom writings, Prophets, and two essays on the Book of the Twelve (one considering the Hebrew and one the Greek text). In his essay on "The Pentateuch as Canon," Stephen Chapman discusses the importance of the five individual documents in this collection, their interrelationship with each other, and the interaction between the OT canon's three divisions. Writing on "The Canon of Psalms," Nancy deClaissé-Walford argues that the editors of MT Psalter shaped it to tell the story of Israel from the Davidic monarchy to the postexilic period and to celebrate God's sovereign reign over the people. Craig Bartholomew's essay on "The Canonical Role of Israel's Wisdom Collection" focuses on the sense of canon as authority, rather than collection, and applies this theological understanding of canon to the interpretation of Proverbs, Ecclesiastes, and Job. In "The Macro-Structure of the Megilloth," Timothy Stone contends that the arrangement of the books of the Megilloth highlights their diversity, and they need to be examined in relation with the other books of the Writings as a whole, with which they have their strongest connections, and which were all compiled in the same process. Christopher Seitz discusses the content and the logic of arrangement of the middle section of the Hebrew canon in his essay "The Canonical Function of the *Nebi'im*." Don Collett approaches the issue of "Prophetic Intentionality in the Twelve" from the perspective of canonical hermeneutics, emphasizing the shape of the individual books and the shape of the collection of books, and arguing that the two serve as the primary horizon for understanding Scripture's unity and its intentions. Edward Glenny's essay on "The Book of the Twelve in the Septuagint" concludes this section, arguing from LXX Twelve for the importance and value of including the Septuagint in the discussion of the Christian canon and canonical collections.

The third heading, "New Testament Canonical Sub-units," includes essays on the four-fold Gospel, Acts and the Catholic Epistles, the Pauline Corpus, and Revelation. In "The Four-Fold Gospel Collection," the first essay in this section, Gregory Lanier outlines the state of research on this sub-unit, especially as related to other "Gospel" writings, traces the emergence of a four-fold Gospel consciousness, and summarizes the implications of a four-fold Gospel. Darian Lockett examines the early evidence for the association of Acts and the Catholic Epistles in his chapter "Corpus Apostolicum." His essay first outlines the formation of the Catholic Epistles as an early canonical letter collection and then traces the evidence for the association of Acts and the Catholic Epistles in canon lists and manuscripts. Randolph Richards ("The Pauline Corpus") gives evidence from early lists, early writers, and manuscripts for a thirteen-letter Pauline collection (plus the early addition of Hebrews), which was published as a collection from the onset and was stable by at least the third century. In the final essay in this section, "Revelation as the Ending of the Canon," Külli Tõniste surveys the processes and circumstances by which Revelation came to be included at the end of the Christian canon and considers the contribution of Revelation to the canon.

The fourth and final heading, "Hermeneutical Considerations of Canon," includes one essay ("Hermeneutical Reflections on Canonical Sub-Collections: Retrospect and Prospect") by Ched Spellman. Spellman focuses on the significance of the canon for interpretation and examines several concepts native to canon studies, including the context of canon, the coherence of canonical intentionality, the notion of canon-consciousness, and the relevance of the biblical canon to the task of biblical theology.

To our knowledge there is no other collection of essays that so comprehensively introduces the reader to the details of canonical context for biblical interpretation. Whereas there are several monographs considering various canonical sub-collections (see above) and whereas there are several hermeneutical texts which consider a canonical approach to interpretation in general, no other text actually introduces the reader to the specific state of the question for each of the major canonical sub-collections. We hope this volume now fills this gap.

Bibliography

Childs, Brevard S. (1986), *Old Testament Theology in a Canonical Context*, Philadelphia: Fortress.
Schröter, Jens. (2013), *From Jesus to the New Testament: Early Christian Theology and the Origin of the New Testament Canon*. Baylor-Mohr Siebeck Studies in Early Christianity 1, Translated by Wayne Coppins, Waco, TX: Baylor University Press.

Seitz, Christopher R. (2009), *The Goodly Fellowship of the Prophets: The Achievement of Association in Canon Formation*, Grand Rapids: Baker Academic.
Seitz, Christopher R. (2011), *The Character of Christian Scripture: The Significance of a Two-Testament Bible*, Grand Rapids: Baker Academic.
Trobisch, David. (2000), *The First Edition of the New Testament*, Oxford: Oxford University Press.

Section One

The Bible as a Whole and the Old and New Testament as Canonical Units

1

The Bible Canon and Its Significance: Textual Comprehensiveness, Function, Design, and Delimitation

Tomas Bokedal

Apostolic address and authority

The gospel, in its written form, became a treasured resource in Irenaeus's presentation of the Christian faith in his five-volume work *Against Heresies*. At the beginning of the Third Book, the bishop of Lyons (*ca.* 120–202 CE) writes:

> For we have known the "economy" for our salvation (*dispositionem salutis nostrae*) only from those through whom the gospel came to us; and what they then first preached they later, by GOD's will, transmitted to us in the Scriptures so that would be the foundation and pillar of our faith (*fundamentum et columnam fidei nostrae futurum*; *Haer.* III, 1.1).[1]

In these introductory words Irenaeus reflects on the "apostolic" gospel being passed on and preserved in written form as part of the church's Scriptures. Also, elsewhere in his writings, he shows an interest in scriptural address and authority.[2] The above passage from *Adversus Haereses* might be inspired by Papias (cf. Iren. *Haer.* III, 1.1 with Euseb. *Hist. Eccl.* III, 39.1–2, 7, 14–16; Iren. *Haer.* V, 33.4) and the Lukan prologue, drawing lines of continuity between the audio-visually perceived, the orally proclaimed and the textually conveyed "apostolic" gospel (Luke 1:1–4; cf. 2:20; 7:22; 10:24; 24:25–27; and 1 John 1:1–4).

---

[1] Grant 1997: 123–24, modified, *nomina sacra* in small caps. As for Irenaeus's and/or his scribe's likely use of *nomina sacra* in his own writings (textual demarcations of sacred words—such as GOD, JESUS and SPIRIT—by contraction supplied with a horizontal supralinear line), see Bokedal forthcoming a.

[2] See Karl Barth's description of the function of biblical canonicity (the Scriptures set apart as canon) as address and criterion whereby the church, its faith and practice are to be largely recognized. (1936: 99–111). Cf. sub-heading below.

Following the reception of the gospel, the attentiveness towards the earliest Christian tradition that we see here in Irenaeus seems to be concentrated not least on its "apostolic" and, subsequently, scriptural character.[3] The blessed apostles, he states, "founded and built up the church" (*Haer.* III, 3.3).[4] Similar leanings, emphasizing apostolicity and/or scripturality, encounter the reader of yet earlier Christian literature from 2 Pet. 3:15–16 and Ignatius of Antioch onwards (see *Mag.* 13.1–2, *Tral.* 3.3, 7.1; *Rom.* 4.3: "I do not give you orders like Peter and Paul: they were apostles").[5] A comparable apostolic–canonical signal pertaining to eye-witness authority and Jesus's teachings is articulated by Luke (Luke 1:1–4; 10:16; Acts 1:1–3, see Bauckham, 2017: 116–24, esp. 124). More recent scholarly voices offer similar perspectives. Bruce Metzger, in his monograph on the New Testament canon, notes, as for the New Testament material in the nascent church,

> the remembered and transmitted words of Jesus were treasured and used, taking their place beside the Law and the Prophets and being regarded as of equal or superior authority to them. [...] At first Jesus' teachings circulated orally from hearer to hearer, becoming, so to speak, the nucleus of the new Christian canon. Then narratives were compiled recording the remembered words, along with recollections of his deeds of mercy and healing.
> Metzger 1987: 3; similarly, Harnack 1925: 7; regarding apostolicity as the basic canon criterion, see Bokedal 2014: 212–13, 339, 341–43, 347–51, 353–54

An alternative to Metzger's rendering of the story of New Testament Scripture formation surfaces in D. Moody Smith's presidential address delivered at the 1999 Annual Meeting of the Society of Biblical Literature: "Strangely, or not so strangely, the first and last books of the NT present themselves as scripture.... [I]t attests the existence of the idea of distinctively Christian scriptures before the end of the first century" (Smith 2000: 344; cf. Ashton 2007: 344; Deines 2013: 101–9; 2014: 3–12). A third scholarly voice, who has contributed significantly to our understanding of the emergence of the bipartite biblical canon also as an extended historical process, is Brevard Childs, who stresses that canonization (in the broad sense) is something inherent in the shaping on all levels of the biblical literature. Yet another influential scholar, Theodor Zahn, adds worship as an essential element in the canon formation: texts later named "canonical" were originally "read in corporate worship" (Childs 1979: 59, 1984 and 1992; Zahn 1889: 14; for ritual aspects of canon, see Bokedal 2014: 237–78).

Before elaborating further on some specifics of the emergent authoritative corpus of communal texts—such as textual–canonical *comprehensiveness, function, design* and *delimitation*—we may note a few additional points below in the present paragraph, summarizing the early phase of the Christian scriptural canon formation. As the

---

[3] See the Muratorian Fragment, 80, where Christian Scripture is divided into the two categories "the Prophets" and "the Apostles." For a brief overview of the meaning of "apostolic" and the various types of "apostleship," see Wolterstorff 1995: 288–96.
[4] In *Haer.* III, 3.3–4, Irenaeus uses the Greek word ἀπόστολος, "apostle," all in all fifteen times.
[5] Cited from the *Accordance 13* digital edition of Holmes 2007. The citation continues: "I am a convict; they were free, but I am even now still a slave."

significance of Jesus's person and work became fundamental for the primitive community, a new authoritative appeal was made also to "the Lord and the apostles," to which the church referred "in all matters of faith and practice" (Metzger 1987: 6). For Ignatius of Antioch and contemporary Christian leaders, the primary authority was the apostolic preaching—with its strong focus on the life, death and resurrection of Jesus (Metzger 1987, 49. Cf. Luke 24:25–27; and Acts 17:3)—which became fixed textually as the central part of the emerging canon, typically referred to as "the Scriptures, the Lord and the apostles." With this formula as its basis, primitive Christianity formed a closed literary fellowship by 70–120 CE (Bokedal 2014: 14; Theissen 2003: 171–74).

Comprehensiveness: appeal to the "full" apostolic text

Elsewhere in his writings, Irenaeus airs various aspects of what we could call his canon consciousness. He draws the reader's attention more specifically to distinct New Testament text units, such as Luke–Acts, the four-fold Gospel and the Pauline letter corpus. In order for readers to have access to the "complete" or "full" apostolic text, the Lyons bishop addresses those who study the Gospel of Luke to make sure that they also read the sequel, the Acts of the Apostles (*Haer.* III, 14.3–4; 15.1). Irenaeus admonishes those who accept only one of the Gospels—like Marcion adhering exclusively to Luke, or the Ebionites embracing only Matthew (*Haer.* I, 26.2)—to extend their scriptural repertoire to include all four Gospels. In comparable style, he reprimands the Ebionites for not using the Pauline letters (*Haer.* III, 15.1) and others for not accepting John's Gospel among their Scriptures (*Haer.* III, 11.9).

In line with his "canonical" concern for comprehensiveness, we may not be surprised to see that in his First Book (*Haer.* I, 3.6) he places "the writings of the evangelists and the apostles" on a par with "the law and the prophets" (Metzger 1987: 155) and that in other places he applies to the Scriptures the renowned canonical formula, "neither to add ... nor to withdraw" (see *Haer.* III, 11.8, cited below, and IV, 33.8, and Bokedal 2014: 293, 296–300). Scriptural canonicity, pertaining to canonical scope, here appears as a property of Sacred Scripture. Still, initial appropriation of the new apostolic writings as Scripture occurred prior to Irenaeus (2 Pet. 3:15–16; *Barn.* 4.14; *2 Clem.* 2.4; Tatian *Orat.* 13.1; Theoph. *Autolyc.* 3.2; see also Bokedal 2010: 48–52).

In summation, Irenaeus's stress on textual comprehensiveness applies not least to the various canonical sub-units: Luke–Acts, the four-fold Gospel, canonical inclusion of the Pauline epistles, and the placement of the writings of evangelists and apostles on a par with the Jewish Scriptures.

The NT canon—a collection of prior text collections

As for the wider question of New Testament canon formation, it is important to note that this appears to be an event taking place in discrete steps primarily during the first four Christian centuries (even if the case may be made that the canonical whole by some was envisioned already in the second century, or even earlier). The process of a growing New Testament being edited for, and gradually received among, the faith communities—as visible in Irenaeus—can, in a sense, be described as the emergence and recognition of a collection of prior text collections. The latter included the Pauline Corpus ascribed to the apostle Paul and the four-fold Gospel that from early on was associated with the names Matthew, Mark–Peter, Luke–Paul and John (*Haer.* III, 3.1; see Hurtado 2006b: 3–27).

In the next decades and centuries, a variety of writings that upfront emphasized apostolic origin (the Catholic Epistles)[6] and scripturality (2 Pet. 1:19–21; 3:15–16; Rev. 1:3; 22:7, 18–19; cf. Col. 4:16 and 2 Tim. 3:14–17; Keener 2020) were added to these earliest "apostolic" collections (Pauline writings and Gospels), bringing together both similar (1–3 John associated with John's Gospel) and less similar writings (Acts, Hebrews, James, Revelation). Around 200 CE, the collection as a whole was being referred to as the New Testament (ἡ καινὴ διαθήκη, Clem. *Strom.* I, 5.28.2), parallel to that of the Old Testament (ἡ παλαιὰ διαθήκη, Euseb. *Hist. Eccl.* IV, 26; V, 16.3).

In terms of the sequence of writings contained in the canonical sub-units, the arrangement of the emergent New Testament text corpus seemed to be focused more on the finalized number of writings included in each unit—four Gospels, seven Catholic epistles and thirteen or fourteen Pauline epistles—than a fixed sequence for the included writings (see Schmidt 2002 and Bokedal 2014: 138).[7] Before too long, however, a tendency towards standardization also regarding the sequence of books and canonical sub-unit collections materialized (as for characteristic title forms, see below). Similar to Melito of Sardis's approach towards the OT canon (*ca.* 175 CE), both the number of books and their order were noted ("πόσα τὸν ἀριθμὸν καὶ ὁποῖα τὴν τάξιν," Euseb. *Hist. Eccl.* IV, 26.13).

From the above brief account of the NT canon formation, we may note the discrete development towards a textual–canonical whole, where prior collections helped setting the agenda: from the emergence of the earliest sub-units—the four-fold Gospel and Corpus Paulinum and their association with apostolic names—to Acts, Catholic Epistles and Revelation and the increased awareness of canonical features, such as emphasized apostolicity, inspiration, scripturality, canonical delimitation and ordering.

Function: the Bible canon as intensified scriptural address and criterion

In its capacity as address to the faith community—and, indirectly, to the wider community—the Bible was present in the church as part of the continuous proclamation of the gospel (Bokedal 2014: 3; cf. McDonald 2017: 1, 358). This, too, is indicated by

---

[6] Note the emphasis on apostolicity through book titles with writings ascribed to James, Peter, John (the "pillars" according to Gal 2:9) and Jude, respectively.

[7] The arrangement of the Gospels occurs in twelve various sequences, and there are at least seven for the Catholic Epistles. For the Pauline writings, we note the placing of Hebrews early (after Romans in P46) or late in the collection; see further Laird 2016: 175–78.

Irenaeus in the introductory quote (*Haer.* III.1.1). In this opening line of Book Three, we can observe two key dimensions of scriptural authority, the Scriptures' basic function as *address* and *criterion*. As address, the Scriptures, read in public or in private, are to bring about the assent of faith ("we have known the 'economy' of our salvation only from those through whom the gospel came to us"). As criterion, the Scriptures are to judge other writings and teachings ("transmitted to us in the Scriptures so that would be the foundation and pillar of our faith").[8] Concerning the latter, we may notice the comparable phrasing, with a normative appeal, in the Gelasian Decree from the sixth century: "[It is] the prophetic, evangelical and apostolic Scriptures on which the catholic church by God's grace is founded" (*propheticae et evangelicae atque apostolicae scripturae, quibus ecclesia catholica per gratiam Dei fundata est*).[9] A similar understanding can be found in the scriptural appeal made by Irenaeus's contemporary, Clement of Alexandria (*ca.* 150–215 CE), who discusses the role of the emergent Scripture canon as first principle:

> For in the Lord we have the first principle of our teaching (ἀρχὴ τῆς διδασκαλίας), both by the prophets, the Gospel, and the blessed apostles, "in diverse manners and at sundry times," leading from the beginning of knowledge to the end. But if one should suppose that the first principle required something else, then it could no longer truly be preserved as a first principle.
> *Strom.* VII, 16.95–6; *ANF* 2: 550, modified; cf. the *Thirty-Nine Articles of Religion*, Articles 6–8; and *Formula of Concord*, Epitome 1–2

In Clement, Origen's teacher, as in Irenaeus, various aspects of intensified scriptural authority are voiced, such as the Scriptures' emphasized function as prophetic or apostolic address, and as criterion and first principle of Christian teaching.

Clement, too, we may notice, is well aware of the four-fold Gospel as a key scriptural text-unit (*Strom.* III, 13.93). Notably, in terms of canonical sub-unit delimitation, each respective unit has its own characteristic title forms: Gospels: ΕΥΑΓΓΕΛΙΟΝ ΚΑΤΑ …; Acts: ΠΡΑΞΕΙΣ ΑΠΟΣΤΟΛΩΝ; Catholic Epistles: ΙΑΚΩΒΟΥ ΕΠΙΣΤΟΛΗ, ΠΕΤΡΟΥ ΕΠΙΣΤΟΛΗ Α; Pauline Corpus: ΠΡΟΣ ΡΩΜΑΙΟΥΣ, ΠΡΟΣ ΚΟΡΙΝΘΙΟΥΣ Α, ΠΡΟΣ ΕΒΡΑΙΟΥΣ; Revelation: ΑΠΟΚΑΛΥΨΙΣ ΙΩΑΝΝΟΥ.

In early church teachers (Just. *1 Apol.* 67; Iren. *Haer.* III.1.1; Clem. *Strom.* VII, 16.95–96), the Gospels play a key role in establishing new authoritative s/Scripture, closely associated with the old Jewish Scriptures. Other well-defined canonical sub-units—each with characteristic titles allocated to the included writings—soon supplement the Gospels as foundational texts in the faith communities. As Irenaeus (*Haer.* III.1.1) and subsequent theology remind us, the authority of Scripture is a

---

[8] On scriptural address and criterion, Jenson (1999: 89) comments: "[w]hen a text is actually read, it is not merely text but in one way or another is living address." So, the "church reads Scripture, in expectation of faith." Jenson here recalls a distinction proposed in old Protestantism, namely that the authority of Scripture is a "double capacity: one to judge other writings and teachings [Scripture *as criterion*] … another to bring about the assent of faith … [Scripture *as address*]."

[9] *Decretum Gelasianum*, cap. 350–54, in Denzinger 1991: 162–65.

"double capacity: one to judge other writings and teachings [Scripture *as criterion*] ... another to bring about the assent of faith ... [Scripture *as address*]" (see note 8 above).

Delimitation and design: numerical appeal and the shaping of biblical canonicity

In the following, we shall explore a central, but neglected, aspect of the biblical canon formation, namely the broad, early appeal made to symbolical numerals, such as four, seven and twenty-two, when addressing the question of delimitation of the number of books in the canonical sub-units: the four Gospels, the seven Catholic Epistles and the twenty-two books of the Jewish Scriptures.

Four-Fold Gospel

Probably Irenaeus's most famous phrasing pertaining to canonicity is his fascination with the numeral four in his promotion of the four-fold Gospel. For Irenaeus, the four-fold Gospel indicated universality, renewed covenant and canonical sub-unit delimitation. Irenaeus argues:

> It is not possible that the Gospels can be either more or fewer in number than they are, since there are four directions of the world in which we are, and four principal winds.... The four living creatures [of Rev. iv. 9] symbolize the four Gospels.... and there were four principal covenants (καθολικαὶ διαθῆκαι) made with humanity, through Noah, Abraham, Moses, and Christ.
>
> Haer. III, 11.8[10]

To Irenaeus, as Metzger stresses, "the Gospel canon is closed and its text is holy" (Metzger 1987: 155, similarly, Origen, referenced by Eusebius, *Hist. Eccl.* VI, 25.3–14).

As indicated by the Muratorian Fragment,[11] for Irenaeus, Clement of Alexandria and others, the four-fold Gospel had been received by large portions of the church by the late second century.[12] Thus, from an early date, the symbolically significant numeral four became an unalterable standard associated with the ecclesial reception, production and dissemination of the Gospels: the Gospel must be four-fold. Interestingly, the British papyrologist T. C. Skeat has pointed out that Irenaeus bases his account of the mystical significance of the number four on an earlier source dated no later than 170 CE, or thereabout (Skeat 1992: 194–99). Larry Hurtado further notes that "several

---

[10] Cited from Metzger 1987: 154–55, who notes that "Irenaeus' words about the four Gospels have passed into the literature of the Church in the closest connection with the text of the Gospels, for they are used in a very large number of manuscripts as a brief preface to the Gospels."

[11] Material in the present paragraph, reused here with permission, from Bokedal, 2013: 67–68. For dating of the Muratorian Fragment to *ca.* 200 CE, see Verheyden 2003.

[12] See Hill, "The Four Gospel Canon in the Second Century" (http://youngadults.ccphilly.org/wp-content/uploads/2012/11/Four-Gospel-Canon-.pdf; accessed August 31, 2020).

recent studies agree in pushing back the likely origin of a four-fold Gospels collection to the earliest years of the second century" (Hurtado 2006b: 20). Charles Hill, for example, has argued that Papias knew the four canonical Gospels as a collection sometime around 125–135 CE; Theo Heckel places a four-fold Gospel collection sometime around 120 CE. Martin Hengel, too, defends an early date for the four-fold Gospel, and Graham Stanton, "[w]orking chronologically backwards from Irenaeus," concludes that a four-fold Gospels collection was being promoted from sometime shortly after 100 CE, "though it took time to win its well-known supremacy" (Hurtado 2006b: 20; Stanton 1997).

When discussing the Gospel tradition (*Haer.* III, 1.1; 11.8), Irenaeus's special emphasis on the number four—pertaining to the four cardinal directions and four divine covenants—helps to further substantiate the four-fold Gospel as the emerging ecclesial standard. Crucial additional support to Irenaeus's numerical emphasis can be found in the New Testament manuscript tradition. As Eldon Epp and Keith Elliott observe, "we have no manuscripts in which 'apocryphal' gospels were bound with any one or more of the 'canonical' Four" (cited from Epp 2002: 511, 487; Elliott 1996: 107, 110). As indicated above, the "apostolic" character of the Four—expressed through narratives of apostolic authorship—is further corroborated in terms of dating: the coming-into-being of the four-fold Gospel arguably emerged within close reach of the Apostolic Period.

Seven-church, seven-letter and fourteen-letter traditions

Also, in regard to other canonical sub-units in the New Testament manuscript tradition—such as the fourteen Pauline (including Hebrews) and seven Catholic Epistles, and Revelation with its address to seven churches (Rev. 1:4; 2:3–3:22)—the involvement of numerals becomes an integrated part of the appeal to canonical completion and function. Furthermore, use of the symbolical numbers four and seven to delimit canonical sub-units also adds to the notions of universality and fullness (Muratorian Fragment). Concerning the Pauline letter corpus, this is done in at least two major stages, when reference, from early on, is made to the so-called "seven-church tradition" and later to the fourteen-letter corpus as consisting of seven times two letters.[13] Amphilochius of Iconium (*ca.* 340–95) seems to relate to this tradition when he refers to the Pauline fourteen-epistle corpus as "twice seven epistles" (*Iambics for Seleucus*), a reference that Benjamin Laird argues suggests that Amphilochius was aware of the ancient seven-church tradition, which he thought was compatible with editions of the corpus containing fourteen epistles (Laird 2016: 219–24).

This early emphasis on significant numbers, such as four (four-fold Gospel) and seven (Pauline and Catholic Epistles), seems to have been a key element in the New Testament canon formation.

---

[13] See Laird 2016: 219–24. The tradition that Paul wrote to seven churches seems to be presupposed already in the Marcionite prologues, in the Muratorian Fragment, by Cyprian, Jerome, Victorinus of Pettau and others.

Twenty-two-book canon arrangements

Another indication of numerical importance to canon can be seen as several of the early church teachers adhere, in principle, to a twenty-two-book OT canon,[14] similar to that in Josephus's account in *Against Apion* (I, 41).[15] Moreover, there seems to be congruity between this numerical symbol indicating canonical completion (with reference to the twenty-two radicals of the Hebrew alphabet) and some early editions, or accounts, of the New Testament. Examples of this include the New Testament of the Syriac Peshitta and most likely John Chrysostom's New Testament, both of which represent twenty-two-book corpora, similar to that enlisted by Eusebius (twenty-two "recognized books," preceding his list of five "disputed books," *Hist. Eccl.* III, 25). Included among the Recognized Books (ἐν ὁμολογουμένοις) in Eusebius are the four Gospels, Acts, fourteen Pauline epistles, 1 Peter, 1 John and Revelation. On a related note, as we will see below, the New Testament twenty-seven-book arrangement is arguably a variant of the Hebrew alphabetical-related value twenty-two that indicates canonical completion.

Thus, in the aforementioned examples of canonical sub-unit closures, symbolically significant numbers (four, seven, twenty-two) turned out to be an integrated part of the literary outcome.

Paratextual arithmetical design patterns and the canonical text corpus

Arithmetically emphasized dimensions of the emerging second-century "canon consciousness" appear to be linked not least to the symbolical meaning of the numerals four and seven, implying universal address and fullness. Another key number, especially associated with the canonical shaping of the Jewish Scriptures, is the alphabetical number twenty-two, indicating textual completion. This alphabetical number indicating canonical completion was used to express Jewish religiosity more widely, for example through acrostic Hebrew poetry (Ps. 119, Lam. 1–4). For paratextual purposes pertaining to canonicity, numerals associated with the alphabet seem to have been employed also by early Christianity.

In the two centuries preceding the fourth-century Christian mega codices Vaticanus and Sinaiticus, the following arithmetical dimensions may be itemized as part of the emerging concept of a widely endorsed Scripture canon: (i) The twenty-two books of the Hebrew Bible/the Old Testament (to which later Augustine's forty-four-book

---

[14] A twenty-two-book OT canon is referred to, e.g., by Origen, Athanasius, Cyril of Jerusalem, the fathers of the Council of Laodicea, Gregory of Nazians, Amphiloch of Iconium, Epiphanius of Salamis, and Jerome.

[15] Josephus, at the end of the first century CE, had addressed the canon issues involved regarding the Jewish Scriptures. Brevard Childs, thus, can list indirect evidence for the existence of a rather stable Jewish canon (Childs 1992: 60; see Kooij 2003: 27–38) with reference to Josephus's treatise *Against Apion* (1, 37–43), in which he establishes the fixed number of the books of the Jewish Bible at twenty-two.

[2×22] OT also may have been linked), (ii) the quadriform Gospel (τετράμορφον τὸ εὐαγγέλιον, repeated twice in Iren. *Haer.* III, 11.8), (iii) the seven-/fourteen-letter structure (fourteen Pauline [2×7], seven Catholic, seven Asia Minor Epistles found in Rev. 2–3), and, in addition, (iv) the new-creation number eight, signaled by the eight alleged authors of the canonical New Testament (Matthew, Mark, Luke, John, Peter, James, Jude and Paul), the eight writings of the Praxapostolos (Acts and seven Catholic Epistles), and arguably also the eight occurrences in the New Testament of the Greek word for eight, ὀκτώ (cf. Trobisch 2000: 59). In these examples (i–iv), paratextual arithmetical features appear as tools to arrange and delimit the respective canonical sub-units.

Twenty-two-multiples linked to word-frequencies in the canonical sub-units

Though perhaps coincidental, we may note here as well the "alphabetical" word-frequency patterns embraced by various canonical sub-units, associated with the number twenty-two; for example, the twenty-two occurrences of the word λόγος, "word; message; computation" and the forty-four [2×22] of the expression Ἰησοῦς χριστός, "Jesus Christ," in the Catholic Epistles, and the twenty-two occurrences of the noun βασιλεύς, "king," in Matthew and Praxapostolos, respectively. These word patterns, linked to the numeral 22, might in fact be intended to relate to the Hebrew (and Greek) "alphabetical" notion of fullness and completion, from the first (letter) to the last (cf. Rev. 22:13).

Further examples of such word-frequency patterns, involving twenty-two-multiples, include:[16]

- the word πίστις occurring twenty-two times in Galatians; ἐκ πίστεως appearing twenty-two times in Corpus Paulinum; πιστεύω featuring 132 times [6×22; i.e., as a twenty-two-multiple] in the four-fold Gospel and 242 times [11×22] in the full New Testament (and the corresponding Hebrew verb אמן, "trust; believe," occurring twenty-two times in the Latter Prophets);
- the *nomen sacrum* ὁ πνεῦμα (τὸ πνεῦμα; το $\overline{\text{ΠΝΑ}}$) occurring eighty-eight times [4×22] in the four Gospels+Acts and 176 times [8×22] in the full New Testament (*THGNT*, NA28; the corresponding Hebrew word רוּחַ, "spirit; wind," similarly appearing 154 times [7×22] in the Latter Prophets; and the unpointed רוח forty-four times [2×22] in the Pentateuch and 154 times [7×22] in the Writings);
- the *nomen sacrum* combination Ἰησοῦς χριστός ($\overline{\text{ΙΣ}}$ $\overline{\text{ΧΣ}}$, which functions as a potential *inclusio* for three canonical sub-collections: Matt. 1:1–Acts 28:31, Jam. 1:1–Jude 25, and Rom. 1:1–Phlm 25) featuring forty-four times [2×22] in Praxapostolos (*THGNT*, NA28) and eighty-eight times [4×22] in the Pauline Corpus (*THGNT*); and χριστὸς Ἰησοῦς twenty-two times in 1–2 Timothy (*THGNT*, א);

---

[16] If not otherwise indicated, figures below and throughout the chapter are taken from the *Accordance 13* digital versions of the *Biblia Hebraica Stuttgartensia*, or *Tyndale House Greek New Testament* (hereafter *THGNT*).

- χριστός appearing twenty-two times in 1 Peter (*THGNT*, NA28, ℵ) and the Historical Books (LXX Rahlfs; hereafter LXXR), respectively; and χρι* 396 times [18×22; i.e., Greek words beginning with the three letters χρι] in Corpus Paulinum;[17] and
- Ἰησοῦς occurring twenty-two times in Philippians and 110 times [5×22] in Praxapostolos[18] (similar *nomina sacra* figures feature also in the Ignatian Corpus [*Accordance 13* digital edition of Holmes 2007]: πνεῦμα occurring twenty-two times in the seven-letter corpus; Ἰησοῦς twenty-two times in *Magnesians* and *Philadelphians*, respectively; and χριστός twenty-two times in *Magnesians*).

The above word-frequencies, which are all twenty-two-multiples, may be coincidental, that is, they may not be deliberately shaped at the compositional or editorial level and may thus be insignificant. However, to the extent that they have been used as a form of textual/paratextual arithmetical pattern, namely, textually helping to weave canonical sub-units together (not only externally through the new technology that the codex form offered, but also internally within the text), these figures could be potentially significant for canon studies. Below we shall return to the hypothetical possibility that alphabetical numerical patterns may be deliberate in more than one way when composing and editing the Old and New Testament material.

Canonical shaping and alphabetical all-comprehensiveness

Both the twenty-four letters of the Hellenistic Greek alphabet and the number of radicals in the Hebrew alphabet, twenty-two or twenty-seven (the five Hebrew "double letters" counted separately) may have been directly or indirectly influential when delimiting the number of books in the Hebrew Bible to twenty-two (Josephus and several early Church Fathers[19]), twenty-seven (an alternative figure), or twenty-four (the rabbinic canon); and the New Testament writings to twenty-seven.[20] Athanasius's Bible Canon presented in his 39th Festal Letter in 367 CE, accordingly, consisted of 22+27 books (omitting Esther from his list), that is forty-nine biblical books [7×7]; and the Ethiopic Bible Canon eventually tended to embrace eighty-one books [3×27].[21]

---

[17] "*χρι*" further occurs 616 times [2×14×22] (NA28), and χρι* 540 times [20×27], in the NT. See below regarding 27 as alphabetical numeral.

[18] The corresponding Hebrew name יְהוֹשֻׁעַ, "Joshua," occurs 168 times [7×24 = 12×14] in Joshua (cf. Table 1.1 below).

[19] See Athanasius, *Thirty-Ninth Festal Epistle* (Nicene and Post-Nicene Fathers 2.4:552): "There are, then, of the Old Testament, twenty-two books in number; for, as I have heard, it is handed down that this is the number of the letters among the Hebrews." Cf. note 14 above.

[20] See Lim 2013: 40–41: "Jerome considered the twenty-two-book canon to be the count of the majority ('by most people'); the twenty-four-book enumeration is a variant enumerated by 'some.' He also seems to know a twenty-seven-book count when he states that there are five letters of the Hebrew alphabet that are 'double letters' (*kaph, mem, nun, peh,* and *tsadeh*) that change shape depending on whether they are written at the beginning and in the middle (medial) or at the end (final). The canonical implication is that Samuel, Kings, Chronicles, Ezra, and Jeremiah with Kinoth (or Lamentations) are reckoned as double, thus increasing the total to twenty-seven."

[21] For references, see Mroczek 2016: 156–65. I am grateful to Matthew Novenson and Zachary Bradley for drawing my attention to the "symbolic" number 81, associated with the Ethiopic canon.

Moreover, a modern standard Protestant Bible, with its thirty-nine OT and twenty-seven NT books, includes altogether sixty-six writings [3×22], and may thus embrace potential arithmetical allusions to the Hebrew alphabetical figures twenty-seven and twenty-two.[22] That these alphabetical-related values, indicating canonical completion, were utilized more widely to indicate textual completeness can be seen as well in the Homeric works, both of which were divided into twenty-four books, apparently for no other reason than that of signaling Greek alphabetical all-comprehensiveness, alluding to the twenty-four letters, alpha to omega (cf. Rev. 1:8; 21:6; 22:13).[23] We may note as well that the expression τὸ βιβλίον, "the book, the scroll, the writing," occurs altogether twenty-four times in the NT, the root βιβ* occurs forty-eight times [2×24], and γραφ*, "writ-," twenty-four times in Luke and 240 times [10×24] in the NT. The Hebrew verb designating writing, כתב, "to write," moreover, occurs twenty-two times in Deuteronomy and eighty-one times [3×27] in the Writings. Both of these numbers are multiples of Hebrew alphabetical-related values (number of letters in the complete alphabet) arguably representing aspects of a completed or "closed" text.

Codicological design patterns: alphabetical paragraph division

The connection between these alphabetical figures and the biblical text may be further highlighted if we allow the old paragraph division of the Greek New Testament to be brought into our discussion. This paragraph division of the Greek NT is kept in the recently published *Tyndale House Greek New Testament* (*THGNT*),[24] in which Mark's Gospel includes altogether 192 paragraphs (including superscription and subscription) [8×24], i.e., a multiple of the alphabetical number twenty-four. Similarly, Matthew, with its 405 paragraphs [15×27], includes a multiple of another alphabetical number, namely twenty-seven. Gospels+Acts, here being viewed as a canonical sub-unit, further includes altogether 1,458 paragraphs [2×27×27]—which is a twenty-seven-multiple—again embracing potential references to alphabetical numerals (twenty-seven squared), representing completeness and holiness (see below). The same applies as well to the following canonical sub-units: 2 Corinthians with its fifty-four paragraphs [2×27], Philippians with twenty-four, 1 Thessalonians with twenty-four, and Revelation with altogether 120 paragraphs [5×24].

---

[22] Regarding the number 39, see Table 1.1 below.
[23] Gallagher (2012: 87), quotes Michael Haslam in this connection (1997: 58): "According to Michael Haslam, the scholars who divided Homer's two epics into 24 books each did so despite interrupting traditional episodic divisions and limiting the size of a book to much less than a scroll could actually contain. This they did specifically because they were concerned with the alphabet. 'It is not a numerical system but an alphabetical one, and the α–ω partitioning must have been devised for its symbolism, advertising Homer's all-comprehensiveness.'" See also Heiden 1998: 68.
[24] Due to variations in the manuscript tradition, the size and number of paragraphs may vary somewhat. The figures above are thus somewhat tentative. In the Introduction to *Tyndale House Greek New Testament* (Jongkind and Williams, eds. 2017: 512), we read the following on the principles used for the paragraph division: "Paragraphs are informed by manuscripts, in particular by those from the fifth century or earlier. We have not included every paragraph mark from these early manuscripts: we have included only divisions that occur in two such manuscripts (except in the Apocalypse where, due to more limited attestation, we have only required one)."

Codicological design patterns: alphabetical and divine-name figures

For similar arithmetical figures characterizing the broader codicological design, we shall now turn to the apparent use of alphabetical structures employed by the *scriptoria* responsible for producing some of our earliest Bible codices. In early Gospels manuscripts, the number of lines per column sometimes tends to converge toward multiples of one of the alphabetical numerals twenty-two, twenty-four or twenty-seven. This aesthetical–arithmetical tendency applies as well to the number of columns or pages used. An illustrative example of this is the four Gospels in Codex Sinaiticus (א). The number of lines per column, and the number of columns, used for the four Gospels are forty-eight [2×24] and 484 [22×22], respectively—with the alphabetical numeral twenty-four featuring together with the Hebrew alphabetical numeral twenty-two squared—arguably signifying fullness, on the one hand, and "pure holiness," on the other.[25] The geometrical square, or a squared number, in the Hebrew thought world, is often of primary symbolic significance. One important canonical implication from this "alphabetical multiple" is the presumably intended codicological–textual delimitation of the four Gospels in Codex Sinaiticus as a sacred canonical sub-unit—indicated by the alphabetical-related value 22, representing the total (number of letters). Perhaps even more significant in this regard is the number of columns used in Codex Sinaiticus for the rest of the NT. Here 578 [2×17×17][26] columns are used (excluding from the count the *Epistle of Barnabas* and *Shepherd of Hermas* after the Book of Revelation), where seventeen squared is a potential double reference to one of the sacred numerical values associated with the Tetragrammaton, YHWH/AHWH (which is either twenty-six or seventeen, or, alternatively, fifteen, for the short-form Yah/YH; see further Table 1.1 below). Moreover, the number of pages utilized for the four-fold Gospel in Codex Washingtonianus is 374 [17×22], which includes a potential aesthetical–arithmetical reference to alphabetical-related completeness (twenty-two = the total number of Hebrew consonants) as well as the divine Name (seventeen; cf. Rev. 1:8).

With regard to Codex Alexandrinus, we may note the following codicological figures linked to our two groups of numerals/multiples, alphabetical (twenty-two, twenty-four and twenty-seven) and divine-Name (fifteen, seventeen and twenty-six) multiples: Mark's fifty-one columns [3×17], Luke's eighty-eight [4×22], John's fifty-four [2×27], Acts' eighty-one [3×27], Romans' thirty [2×15], 1–2 Timothy's fifteen, Hebrews' twenty-four, Corpus Paulinum's 170 [10×17; my estimation, based on 1–2 Corinthians embracing forty-nine columns (7×7)], and, finally, the four-fold Gospel+Acts arguably using altogether 357 columns [3×7×17; my estimation; for corresponding figure for Praxapostolos, see below].

---

[25] Stevenson (1996: 34–35, 42, 47–58), for example, notes that in association with the Temple the square functions as a material representation of a theology of holiness. A perfect square in Ezekiel, accordingly, is the "shape" of pure holiness.

[26] Number of columns allocated to major canonical sub-units in Sinaiticus: the four Gospels (484 columns [22×22]); Pauline Epistles (298 columns), Acts (147 columns), Catholic Epistles (64 columns [2×32]), Revelation (69 columns [3×23]); regarding 17, 32 and 23, see Table 1.1. For images, see http://www.codex-sinaiticus.net/en/manuscript.aspx?book=37 (accessed August 28, 2020).

Additional examples from the manuscript tradition of what appears to be alphabetical arithmetical arrangement of the text includes the number of columns in the Great Isaiah Scroll (1QIsa^a) being fifty-four [2×27]; the number of pages in Codex Leningradensis being 240 [10×24] for the Torah and 945 [5×7×27] for Torah+Prophets+Writings+masorah (excluding the first introductory page); the number of lines per column and the number of leaves in the Gospels codex GA 2437 (eleventh–twelfth century) being twenty-four and 220 [10×22], respectively; corresponding codicological figures for GA 534 (thirteenth century) being twenty-two and 270 [10×27], for GA *Lect* 1627 (eleventh century), twenty-two and 168 [7×24]; for GA 2563 (eleventh century), twenty-four and 168 [7×24]; for GA 828 (twelfth century), twenty-seven and 176 [8×22]; for GA 260, twenty-four and 240 [10×24]; for GA 1443 (eleventh century), twenty-two and 308 [14×22]; and for GA 2252 (eleventh century), twenty-two and 308 [14×22].[27]

Codex Vaticanus, too, seems to have been designed in corresponding manner, with its forty-two lines [3×14; see Table 1.1 for potential significance of fourteen, the "Davidic" number] per column, its altogether (i) 572 columns [22×26] allocated to the four Gospels+Acts (and 343 columns [7×7×7] to the three Synoptic Gospels), (ii) 629 columns [37×17] to Gospels+Acts+Catholic Epistles, (iii) 234 columns [9×26 = 6×39] to the Pauline letters (regarding 39, see Table 1.1; cf also Praxapostolos in Codex Alexandrinus, containing 117 columns [3×39]), (iv) seventy-eight pages [3×26] to the Pauline letters (Romans to Hebrews), and (v) 288 pages [12×24] to the New Testament writings (Matthew to Hebrews).[28]

Name-related Numerals: alphabetical (22, 24 and 27) and divine-name numbers (15, 17, 26 and 39)

For an overview of the Jewish and Christian symbolic numbers used in this chapter—especially what I choose to call *Name-related Numeral(s)* (hereafter *NrN*), i.e., multiples of the alphabetical numbers 22, 24, 27 and the divine-Name numerals 15, 17, 26 (and 39)[29]—I refer the reader to the basic definitions provided in Table 1.1.

Creedal textual shaping: *nomina sacra* and possible inner-textual canonical shaping

As I have argued elsewhere (Bokedal 2014: 83–123), there seems to be a close connection between the Scripture canon formation and the special Greek *nomina*

---

[27] For images of the manuscripts, see http://www.csntm.org/Manuscript (accessed June 6, 2020).
[28] Heb. 1:1–9:13 + later scribal addition for the remaining part of the text. For images, see https://digi.vatlib.it/view/MSS_Vat.gr.1209 (accessed June 1, 2020).
[29] On early Jewish and Christian number symbolism/numerical theology, see Fletcher-Louis 2015: 39–49; Labuschagne 2016b; and Meyer and Suntrup 1987.

Table 1.1 Significant Jewish and biblical symbolic numbers

Jewish/biblical symbolic numbers	Basic symbolic meaning
4	Representing the horizontal dimension of the world, including the four cardinal directions (Rev. 7:1).
7 [3+4]	The frequently occurring number of fullness, abundance, and completeness, representing cosmic order (ἑπτά occurs eighty-eight times [4×22] in the NT (NA28)) (Labuschagne 2016b: 26–31).
8 [7+1]	Symbolizing resurrection and new creation in early Christianity (ὀκτώ occurs eight times in the NT (*THGNT*, NA28), fifty-four times [2×27] in the Historical Books (LXXR) and seventy-eight times [3×26] in LXX Rahlfs).
12 [3×4]	Signifying completeness, perfection (of the kingdom of God), and totality (the product of 3 and 4, representing God and the world, or the vertical and the horizontal dimensions of the world, respectively; δώδεκα occurs seventy-five times [5×15] in the NT [NA28]) (Labuschagne 2016b: 24).
11 [4+7]	The sum of 4 as the number of extensiveness and 7 as the number of fullness, 11 seems to have developed in the course of time a separate status as a number expressing fulfilment (Labuschagne 2016b: 70–73).
17	Representing one of the numerical values associated with the divine Name YHWH/AHWH: *yod* [1+0]/*aleph* [1]+*he* [5]+*waw* [6]+*he* [5] = 17 (according to Labuschange 2016a: 4; cf. Bauckham 2002).
26 15 23 32 13 39	Representing the numerical value of the divine Name YHWH, the Tetragrammaton: *yod* [10]+*he* [5]+*waw* [6]+*he* [5] = 26 = 15 [YH]+11 [WH]. Both 17 and 26 (and 15) represent, each in its own way, the presence of God through his name YHWH (Labuschagne 2016b: 89–90). Both also represent the Hebrew word *kabod*, "glory" (*kbd* = 17 or 26; or, when spelled *kbwd* = 23 or 32). *Kabod* symbolism in the Bible means that God and his glory are "regarded as belonging inextricably together" (cf. Exod. 33:17–23 [Labuschagne, 2016b: 90] and *Barn.* 12.7: "the glory of Jesus"). We may add here as well the numerical value for the Hebrew word for one (אחד, echad), which is 13; thus, YHWH [26]+*echad* [13], "The LORD is one" = 39.
as 22 [2×11] 24 [2×12] 27 [3×3×3]	The number of letters in the Hellenistic Greek (24) and Hebrew alphabets (22, or 27 when including the five end-consonant forms), representing completeness and totality.

sacra demarcations, which involve special highlighting by contraction of the Greek rendering of the divine name (κύριος, K̄C̄; θεός, Θ̄C̄) and related names in the Christian biblical manuscript tradition. By implementing a creedal–canonical function, the *nomina sacra* engraft onto the textuality of the Scriptures "what might be regarded as the embryonic creed of the first Church" (Roberts 1979: 46; Bokedal 2014: 91–93; Bokedal forthcoming a). I shall now take this argument a step further, by demonstrating the possible, or likely, connection between the appearance of *nomina sacra* and their rate of occurrences in the New Testament and other early Christian texts (Bokedal forthcoming b).

As already indicated, employment of alphabetical symbolism, to indicate fullness or completeness, may have attained significance even beyond the canonical and codicological shaping of the biblical text discussed above. Alphabetical structuring of the New Testament material may have played a role already at the level of textual composition and editing. Word-frequencies for the fifteen terms in the *nomina sacra* word-group[30] frequently feature as multiples of these alphabetical numerals (22, 24 and 27), as the following thirty-four examples from the twenty-seven-book New Testament corpus indicate (of which twenty-five are from *THGNT*). If we posit that these figures are not deliberate, the likelihood that an alphabetical *NrN* will occur is around twelve percent for each of the below examples:

- σταυρός, "cross," appears twenty-seven times in the twenty-seven-book NT corpus;
- σωτήρ, "saviour," twenty-four times; in addition, the letter combination "*σωτ*" appears eighty-one times [3×27] in the NT and twenty-four times in Praxapostolos. Similarly, מושיע, "deliverer, saviour," occurs twenty-seven times in the Hebrew Bible;
- κύριος Ἰησοῦς χριστός, "Lord Jesus Christ," twenty-four times (NA28);
- κύριος (forms in the singular), "Lord," 702 times [26×27] (NA28);
- ο κύριος (all cases; singular and plural forms) 351 times [13×27];
- ὁ κύριος (nominative singular) 110 times [5×22]; in addition, words beginning with the three letters κυρ* appear 744 times [31×24] in the NT;
- Ἰησοῦς χριστός, "Jesus Christ," 135 times [5×27] (NA28); we may note, as well, that Ἰησοῦς χριστός occurs eighty-eight times [4×22] in Corpus Paulinum (*THGNT*; NA28 eighty-three times), and forty-four times [2×22] in Praxapostolos; and χριστὸς Ἰησοῦς twenty-two times in 1–2 Tim.;
- $\overline{ΙΥ}$ $\overline{ΧΥ}$ (genitive singular) 120 times [5×24] (א); corresponding figures for the Pauline Epistles in א are: Rom. seventeen times, 1–2 Cor. fifteen times and Corpus Paulinum seventy-eight times [3×26] (cf. Table 1.1 above for potential significance of 15, 17 and 26); significantly, $\overline{ΙΥ}$ $\overline{ΧΥ}$ further serves as an *inclusio* for three major canonical text-units: Corpus Paulinum (Rom. 1:1–Phlm 25; א and A), Catholic Epistles (James 1:1–Jude 25; א, B, A, *THGNT*, NA28), and four Gospels+Acts (Matt. 1:1–Acts 28:31; B, *THGNT*, NA28, TR);
- $\overline{ΧΥ}$ $\overline{ΙΥ}$ (genitive singular) twenty-four times (א);
- $\overline{ΧΝ}$ (accusative singular) sixty-six times [3×22] (א); corresponding figure in א for Gospels+Acts is twenty-two times;
- τοῦ χριστοῦ (genitive singular) sixty-six times [3×22] (NA28); corresponding figure in NA28 for Corpus Paulinum is fifty-four times [2×27];
- τὸν χριστόν (accusative singular) twenty-two times (NA28);
- Ἰησοῦς 912 times [38×24];
- ἄνθρωπος, "human being," 550 times [25×22];
- ο ἄνθρωπος (forms in the singular) 162 times [6×27];
- ἀνθρώποις (dative plural) fourty-four times [2×22];

[30] For an introduction to *nomina sacra*, see Hurtado 2006a: 95–134; for discussion of fifteen/seventeen standard *nomina sacra* (Ιησοῦς, χριστός, θεός, πνεῦμα/πνευματικός, σταυρός/σταυρόω, πατήρ, ἄνθρωπος, υἱός, Ἰσραήλ, Ἰερουσαλήμ, οὐρανός, σωτήρ, Δαυείδ and μήτηρ), see Bokedal 2012: 263–95.

- α̅ν̅ο̅υ̅ (genitive singular) forty-eight times [2×24] (א);
- μήτηρ (forms in the singular), "mother," eighty-one times [3×27];
- οὐρανός (accusative case forms), "heaven," forty-eight times [2×24];
- τῷ οὐρανῷ (dative singular) twenty-four times;
- κύριος ὁ θεός, "Lord God," twenty-four times;
- θεὸς πατήρ, "God the Father," twenty-four times;
- πάτερ (vocative singular), "f/Father," twenty-four times;
- πατήρ (nominative singular) 110 times [5×22];
- ὁ πατήρ (nominative case forms) 108 times [4×27];
- ὁ πατήρ (dative case forms) twenty-four times;
- τὸν πατέρα (accusative singular) seventy-two times [3×24];
- πατέρες (nominative plural) twenty-four times; in the Pentateuch (LXX Göttingen), the following "alphabetical figures" for πατήρ are found: πατήρ (nominative singular) Genesis forty-eight times [2×24], πατρί Genesis twenty-seven times; πατήρ Leviticus twenty-four times; ὁ πατήρ Numbers twenty-four times, πατήρ (forms in the singular) Numbers twenty-two times; and τὸν πατέρα Pentateuch forty-four times [2×22];
- ὁ υἱὸς τοῦ θεοῦ, "the Son of God," twenty-seven times; in the NT ὁ υἱὸς τοῦ θεοῦ occurs 26 times in the singular (cf. Table 1.1); and once in the plural (Rom 8:19);
- υἱὸς τοῦ ἀνθρώπου (forms in the singular), "Son of Man," eighty-one times [3×27];
- υἱός, "s/Son," 378 times [14×27];
- υἱός (nominative case forms) 192 times [8×24];
- υἱός (dative case forms) twenty-four times; and
- ὁ πνεῦμα, "the Spirit," 176 times [8×22]; moreover, the letter combination "*πν*" occurs 486 times [18×27] in the NT (*THGNT*, NA28); in א, π̅ν̅ς̅ (genitive singular) features ninety-six times [4×24] in the NT, and π̅ν̅ι̅ (dative singular) fifty-four times [2 × 27] in Corpus Paulinum and twenty-two times in 1–2 Cor.

As an illustration of this form of alphabetical structuring by means of word-frequencies across various canonical sub-units, the *nomen sacrum* υἱός (υ̅ς̅), "son," provides a good example: υἱός occurs twenty-two times in 1 John, twenty-four times in 1–3 John (the first canonical sub-unit of which 1 John is part), twenty-seven times in the Catholic Epistles (the second canonical sub-unit of which 1 John is part), forty-eight times [2×24] in the Praxapostolos (Acts+Catholic Epistles; the third canonical sub-unit of which 1 John is part), and 378 times [14×27] in the twenty-seven-book NT corpus (the fourth canonical unit of which 1 John is part). In all five cases, across five canonical levels, the respective word-frequencies contain multiples of alphabetical numbers, namely, in order, 22, 24, 27, 24 and 27. A hypothesis endorsed by this chapter, and argued also elsewhere (Bokedal forthcoming a and Bokedal forthcoming b), is that these word frequencies—involving the term υἱός and other words[31]—were deliberately

---

[31] Another similar example is the word ἀνίστημι, "to stand up; to raise," occurring twenty-seven times in Luke, seventy-two [3×24] in Luke–Acts, forty-eight [2×24] in the Synoptics, and 108 [4×27] in the full NT; and the word ἀποθνῄσκω, "to die," appearing twenty-seven times in John, fifty-four [2×27] in the four Gospels+Acts, and 110 [5×22] in the full NT (see Bokedal forthcoming a).

shaped by those engaged in the composition and/or editing of the textual sub-units that make up the New Testament. Among other things, they may therefore potentially serve as means for determining the inner canonical shaping of these respective text units, where 1 John, 1–3 John, Catholic Epistles, Praxapostolos and the full NT appear to be inner-textually–canonically linked to one another by means of word-frequency patterns.

Outside the New Testament, we may notice that the Ignatian seven-letter corpus (*Accordance 13* digital edition of Holmes 2007), too, seems to embrace corresponding NrN for key *nomina sacra*: Ἰησοῦς χριστός 108 times [4×27], χριστός 130 times [5×26], κύριος thirty-four times [2×17], θεός 176 times [8×22] and πνεῦμα twenty-two times.

As for the Greek *nomen sacrum* θεός (Hebrew analogues listed below), we can further note the following NrN (if not deliberate, the likelihood that an NrN will occur is *ca.* 26 percent in each case—alternatively, 27 percent, if the number 39 is included):

- θεός in Romans: θεός 153 occurrences [9×17]; ο θεός 105 occurrences [7×15]; θεός* 154 occurrences [7×22] (θεός* = words beginning with the four Greek letters θεοσ, such as θεός and θεοστυγής); θε* 176 occurrences [8×22] (θε* = words beginning with the two Greek letters θε, such as θεός, θεοστυγής and θεάομαι); ο θε* 110 occurrences [5×22]; θ* 216 occurrences [8×27]; and ο θ* 130 occurrences [5×26].
- θεός in 1 Corinthians: θεός 105 occurrences [7×15]; θε* 130 occurrences [5×26]; ο θε* sixty-six occurrences [3×22]; θ* 154 occurrences [7×22]; and ο θ* seventy-eight occurrences [3×26].
- θεός in 1 and 2 Thessalonians: θεός in 1–2 Thess. fifty-four occurrences [2×27]; ο θεός 1 Thess. twenty-six occurrences; θε* 1 Thess. forty-four occurrences [2×22], 2 Thess. twenty-two occurrences, and 1–2 Thess. sixty-six occurrences [3×22]; ο θε* 1 Thess. twenty-six occurrences; θ* 1–2 Thess. seventy-eight occurrences [3×26]; ο θ* 1 Thess. twenty-seven occurrences, and 2 Thess. fifteen occurrences.
- θεός in the Twelve Prophets (LXX Göttingen; hereafter LXXG): θεός Hos. thirty-four occurrences [2×17], Am twenty-two occurrences, and Jon. seventeen occurrences; ο θεός Am twenty-two occurrences; θε* Twelve Prophets 168 occurrences [7×24], Mic. fifteen occurrences, Jon. seventeen occurrences, and Zech. fifteen occurrences; θ* Twelve Prophets 396 occurrences [18×22], Joel thirty-four occurrences [2×17], and Nah. seventeen occurrences.
- θεός in Ezekiel (LXXG): θεός forty-eight occurrences [2×24]; ο θε* thirty-nine occurrences; θ* 384 occurrences [16×24]; and ο θ* 182 occurrences [7×26].
- אֱלֹהִים, "God; god, deity": Masoretic Text 2600 occurrences [10×10×26], Num. twenty-seven occurrences, Deut. 374 occurrences [17×22], the Former Prophets 507 occurrences [13×39], 2 Sam. fifty-four occurrences [2×27], 1–2 Sam. 154 occurrences [7×22], 1–2 Kings 204 occurrences [12×17], Hos. twenty-six occurrences, Job seventeen occurrences, and Dan. twenty-two occurrences (the corresponding figure in the Mishnah (Kaufmann) is seventy-two occurrences [3×24]).
- *אלה: Pentateuch 1092 occurrences [3×14×26 = 2×14×39], Exod. 165 occurrences [11×15], Num. 104 occurrences [4×26], Deut. 429 occurrences [11×39], Ezek. 88

occurrences [4×22], Hos. thirty occurrences [2×15], Am. fifteen occurrences, Ps. 375 occurrences [5×5×15], and Neh. eighty-eight occurrences [4×22].
- שַׁדַּי, "*shaddai*, almighty": Masoretic Text forty-eight occurrences [2×24].
- יהוה, "YHWH": Pentateuch 1820 occurrences [70×26], Gen. 165 occurrences [11×15], Num. 396 occurrences [18×22], Deut. 550 occurrences [25×22], 2 Sam. 153 occurrences [9×17], Isa. 450 occurrences [2×15×15], Jer. 726 occurrences [3×11×22], Am. eighty-one occurrences [3×27], Jon. twenty-six occurrences, Zeph. thirty-four occurrences [2×17], the Writings 1,485 occurrences [9×11×15 = 5×11×27], Neh. seventeen occurrences, and 2 Chron. 384 occurrences [16×24].
- *הי: Pentateuch 1,914 occurrences [3×29×22], Josh. 420 occurrences [2×14×15], 1–2 Sam. 598 occurrences [23×26], 2 Kings 504 occurrences [3×7×24], Isa. 486 occurrences [18×27], Jer. 960 occurrences [4×10×24], Ezek. 450 occurrences [2×15×15], Am. eighty-five occurrences [5×17], Jon. twenty-six occurrences, Mic. forty-four occurrences [2×22], Esth. fifty-four occurrences [2×27], Neh. sixty occurrences [4×15], and 2 Chron. 646 occurrences [38×17].

Name-related Numerals (multiples of 15/17/26 and 22/24/27) for ἐγώ εἰμι, ἐγώ, etc.

As we look beyond the *nomina sacra* word-group, towards other seemingly related OT and NT terms, we may note that the expression ἐγώ εἰμι (forms in the singular, including "κἀγώ εἰμι" in Acts 26:29) appears twenty-four times in John and Leviticus (LXXR, LXXG), respectively, forty-eight times [2×24] in the New Testament— ἐγώ εἰμι (all forms) features ninety-six times [4×24] in the NT, the Pentateuch and the Historical Books (LXXR), respectively; these are all multiples of alphabetical numerals, as are the twenty-seven occurrences of the phrase in 1–2 Samuel and the twenty-two in Isaiah (LXXR).

Equally interesting are the NT word-frequencies for the pronoun ἐγώ, which can serve as illustration of the unexpectedly high presence of *NrN* in the New Testament, appearing as follows (*NrN* marked in boldface. Note that if these *NrN* figures were not deliberately designed—contrary to the argument in this chapter—the likelihood for an *NrN* to occur is c. 26 percent in each case):

ἐγώ (all forms):

- Matthew **270 occurrences [10×27]**
- Mark 129 occurrences/**130 occurrences [5×26]** (NA28)
- Luke **288 occurrences [12×24]**
- Synoptic Gospels 687 occurrences/**682 occurrences [31×22]** (א)
- John 541 occurrences/**525 occurrences [5×7×15]** (א)
- Four Gospels 1228 occurrences/**1,207 occurrences [71×17]** (א)
- Acts **312 occurrences [13×24 = 12×26]**
- Luke–Acts **600 occurrences [40×15]**
- Four Gospels+Acts **1,540 occurrences [70×22]**

The Bible Canon and Its Significance

- James twenty-three occurrences/**twenty-six occurrences** (א)
- 1–2 Peter **twenty-four occurrences/twenty-seven occurrences** (א)
- 1 John fifty-seven occurrences/**sixty occurrences** [4×15] (א)
- 1–2 John sixty-three occurrences/**sixty-six occurrences** [3×22] (א)
- 1–3 John sixty-nine occurrences [3×23]/**seventy-two occurrences** [3×24] (א)
- Catholic Epistles 123 occurrences/**132 occurrences** [6×22] (א)
- Praxapostolos 438 occurrences/**435 occurrences** [29×15] (NA28)
- Romans **150 occurrences** [10×15]
- 1–2 Corinthians **312 occurrences** [12×26]
- Ephesians forty-six occurrences [2×23]/**forty-five occurrences** [3×15] (NA28)
- Philippians **sixty occurrences** [4×15]
- Colossians **twenty-four occurrences/twenty-six occurrences** (א)
- 1 Thessalonians **fifty-one occurrences** [3×17]/**fifty-two occurrences** [2×26] (א)
- 2 Thessalonians **twenty-six occurrences/twenty-four occurrences** (א)
- 1 Timothy **fifteen occurrences**
- Philemon **twenty-two occurrences**
- Hebrews **sixty-six occurrences** [3×22]/**sixty-eight occurrences** [4×17] (א)
- Revelation **102 occurrences** [6×17] (*THGNT*, NA28, א)/**105 occurrences** [5×7] (TF35)/**110 occurrences** [5×22] (TR); corresponding LXXR figures for ἐγώ: Gen. **850 occurrences** [50×17], Num. **220 occurrences** [10×22], Judg. **289 occurrences** [17×17], Ruth **52 occurrences** [2×26], 1 Sam. **450 occurrences** [2×15×15], 1–2 Chron. **312 occurrences** [12×26], Neh. **187 occurrences** [11×17], Esth. **eighty-eight occurrences** [4×22], etc.

In addition to the aforementioned twenty-seven examples, *NrN* are found as well for the following seven forms of ἐγώ in the twenty-seven-book NT corpus:

- "ἐγώ" **340 occurrences** [20×17],
- "μου" **567 occurrences** [21×27],
- "μοι" **225 occurrences** [15×15],
- "ἐμοί" **ninety-six occurrences** [4×24],
- "με" **285 occurrences** [19×15],
- "ἐμέ" ninety-four occurrences/**ninety occurrences** [6×15] (NA28), and
- "κἀγώ" **seventy-eight occurrences** [3×26].

This is an unexpectedly high presence of *NrN* features for the above forms of ἐγώ involving the twenty-seven-book NT (six of the seven final examples, *THGNT*), Catholic Epistles (six interlinked canonical sub-units in א), Pauline Epistles (*THGNT*), and the four Gospels and Acts. The latter involve altogether four interlinked canonical sub-units, directly associated with *NrN*: Luke, Acts, Luke–Acts, and Gospels+Acts (*THGNT*), in addition to three further sub-units, namely Matthew, Mark and John.

Additional potentially significant *NrN* appearing in the OT and NT include the following word-frequency sums based on combinations of words appearing in the same verse/passage (e.g., the sum of the occurrences of the two words ἐγώ (1×)

and λέγω (3×) in Matt. 5:22 is four; search in *Accordance 13* on the form: εγω <AND> λέγω):

- εγω <AND> λέγω Matthew **330 occurrences** [15×22; involving **130 verses** [5×26]], John **450 occurrences** [2×15×15; involving **154 verses** [7×22]], Gospels+Acts **1,464 occurrences** [61×24; involving **552 verses** [23×24]], 1 Corinthians **24 occurrences**, Hebrews **44 occurrences** [2×22; involving **17 verses**].
- θεος <AND> λέγω Pentateuch (LXXG) **612 occurrences** [3×12×17; θεός **300 occurrences** [20×15], λέγω **312 occurrences** (12×26)], Luke **130 occurrences** [5×26], Acts **85 occurrences** [5×17], Praxapostolos **ninety-six occurrences** [4×24].
- χριστος <AND> λέγω NT **130 occurrences** [5×26], Gospels **90 occurrences** [6×15], John **thirty occurrences** [2×15], Synoptics **sixty occurrences** [4×15], Pauline Corpus **thirty occurrences** [2×15].
- Ἰησους <AND> λέγω NT **782 occurrences** [2×23×17], Matthew **216 occurrences** [8×27], Luke–Acts **153 occurrences** [9×17].
- εγω <AND> λέγω <AND> σύ Gospels **969 occurrences** [57×17], John **396 occurrences** [18×22], Gospels+Acts **1,104 occurrences** [2×23×24], Acts **135 occurrences** [5×27].
- εγω <AND> δε <AND> λεγω <AND> σύ Matthew **154 occurrences** [7×22], Mark **fifty-one occurrences** [3×17], Synoptics **364 occurrences** [14×26], Gospels+Acts **561 occurrences** [3×11×17].
- εγω <AND> δε <AND> λεγω <AND> σύ (NA28) Gospels **476 occurrences** [2×14×17], Gospels+Acts **576 occurrences** [24×24; involving **108 verses** [4×27]], NT **613** occurrences (commonly regarded as the number of laws in the Torah).
- εγω <AND> ο υιος ο ἄνθρωπος Gospels/NT **seventeen occurrences**.
- συ <AND> ειμι <AND> ο χριστός (cf. Mark 16:29) NT **seventy-eight occurrences** [3×26], Gospels **fifty-one occurrences** [3×17], Luke–Acts **seventeen occurrences**, Gospels+Acts **fifty-four occurrences** [2×27], Pauline Corpus **twenty-four occurrences**.
- "συ" <AND> "ει" <AND> "ο χριστός" NT **thirty-four occurrences** [2×17].
- "συ" <AND> "ει" <AND> "ο" <AND> "χριστός" Gospels **fifty-one occurrences** [3×17], Synoptics **thirty-four occurrences** [2×17], John **seventeen occurrences**.
- συ <AND> ειμι <AND> ο κύριος NT **seventy-eight occurrences** [3×26], Gospels **twenty-seven occurrences**, 1 Corinthians **seventeen occurrences**.
- συ <AND> ειμι <AND> ο υιος ο θεός Gospels/NT **thirty occurrences** [2×15].
- συ <AND> ειμι <AND> Δαυίδ NT **fifteen occurrences**.
- συ <AND> ειμι <AND> βασιλεύς Gospels/NT **thirty-nine occurrences**, John **twenty-four occurrences**.
- συ <AND> ειμι <AND> ο βασιλεύς Gospels/NT **twenty-seven occurrences**.
- συ <AND> ειμι <AND> ο ἅγιος NT **thirty-nine occurrences**, Synoptics **seventeen occurrences**, Gospels+Acts **twenty-six occurrences**.
- συ <AND> ειμι <AND> προφήτης John **twenty-two occurrences**, Gospels+Acts **fifty-one occurrences** [3×17], Acts **fifteen occurrences**.
- συ <AND> ειμι <AND> ο προφήτης Gospels+Acts **thirty-four occurrences** [2×17].

- συ <AND> ειμι <AND> Ἠλίας NT/Gospels **twenty-four occurrences**.
- κυριος <AND> ο θεός NT **165 occurrences [11×15]**, Gospels+Acts **sixty occurrences [4×15]**, Acts **twenty-seven occurrences**, 1–2 Thessalonians **twenty-two occurrences**.
- πνευμα <AND> ἅγιος (NA28) Gospels+Acts **136 occurrences [8×17]**, Praxapostolos **ninety occurrences [6×15]**, Pauline Corpus **fifty-two occurrences [2×26]**.
- λογος <AND> θεός NT **156 occurrences [6×26]**, Gospels **twenty-four occurrences**, Luke–Acts **forty-five occurrences [3×15]**, Pauline Corpus **sixty-six occurrences [3×22]**.
- ο λογος <AND> ο θεός Gospels+Acts **fifty-one occurrences [3×17]**, Luke–Acts **thirty-nine occurrences**, Revelation **twenty-two occurrences**.
- אלהים <AND> מֶלֶךְ Masoretic Text **456 occurrences [19×24]**, Pentateuch **twenty-six occurrences**, Isaiah **fifteen occurrences**, Writings **189 occurrences [7×27]**, Nehemiah **fifteen occurrences**.
- אלהים <AND> רוח Masoretic Text **108 occurrences [4×27]**, Pentateuch **twenty-four occurrences**, Latter Prophets **twenty-four occurrences**, Twelve Prophets **seventeen occurrences**.

Examples of Triune and Christological *NrN* Configurations

Basil the Great, *On the Holy Spirit* (Migne, Accordance 13)

- θεος <AND> πατηρ <AND> υιος <AND> πνεῦμα **136 occurrences [8×17]**.
- ο θεος <AND> ο πατηρ <AND> ο υιος <AND> ο πνεῦμα **twenty-two occurrences**.
- ονομα <AND> πατηρ <AND> υιος <AND> πνεῦμα **sixty occurrences [4×15]**.
- θεός <AND> χριστος <AND> πνεῦμα **130 occurrences [5×26]**.
- ο υιος <AND> ο θεός **fifty-two occurrences [2×26]**.
- θεός (**242 occurrences [11×22]**)+υἱός (183 occurrences) **425 occurrences [5×5×17]**.
- πνευμα <AND> ἅγιος **312 occurrences [12×26 = 13×24]**.

Athanasius (Migne, Accordance 13)

- ο πατηρ <AND> ο υιος <AND> ο πνεῦμα *Serapion* **675 occurrences [3×15×15 = 5×5×27]**.
- ο ονομα <AND> ο πατηρ <AND> ο υιος <AND> ο πνεῦμα *Serapion* **288 occurrences [12×24]**.
- ο θεος <AND> ο χριστος <AND> ο πνεῦμα *Serapion* **195 occurrences [13×15]**.
- θεος <AND> κυριος <AND> πνεῦμα *Arians* **352 occurrences [16×22]**.
- θεος <AND> Ἰησους χριστος <AND> πνεῦμα *Arians* **fifty-four occurrences [2×27]**, *Serapion* **308 occurrences [14×22]**.
- ο θεος <AND> Ἰησους χριστος <AND> ο πνεῦμα Athanasian Corpus (*Arians* and *Serapion*) **240 occurrences [10×24]**.
- ο υιος <AND> ο θεός *Serapion* **378 occurrences [14×27]**.

New Testament Nomina Sacra Configurations

- θεος <AND> υιος <AND> πνεῦμα NT **twenty-six occurrences** (*THGNT*, NA28, ℵ, Text Family 35 [hereafter TF35], Textus Receptus [hereafter TR]), Pauline Corpus **seventeen occurrences** (*THGNT*, NA28, ℵ, TF35, TR).
- θεος <AND> κυριος <AND> πνεῦμα Pauline Corpus **twenty-six occurrences** (*THGNT*, NA28, ℵ, TF35, TR).
- θεος <AND> χριστος <AND> πνεῦμα Pauline Corpus **thirty-nine occurrences** (*THGNT*, NA28, ℵ), Romans **seventeen occurrences** (*THGNT*, NA28, ℵ, TF35, TR).
- θεο* <AND> χρι* <AND> πνε* NT **sixty-eight occurrences** [4×17] (*THGNT*, NA28), Pauline Corpus 46 occurrences [2×23], Romans **seventeen occurrences**.
- θεος <AND> Ἰησους χριστος <AND> πνεῦμα NT **twenty-six occurrences** (alternatively, **thirty-four occurrences** [2×17] if Ἰησους and χριστος are counted separately)
- "πα*" <AND> "υι*" <AND> "πν*" NT **twenty-two occurrences** (*THGNT*, NA28, TF35, TR).
- πα* <AND> χρ* <AND> πν* NT **fifty-two occurrences** [2×26], Praxapostolos 21 occurrences (*THGNT*)/**twenty-two occurrences** (ℵ)/**twenty-seven occurrences** (TF35, TR).
- "πα*" <AND> "χρ*" <AND> "πν*" Praxapostolos **fifteen occurrences**.
- θε* <AND> υι* <AND> πν* NT **twenty-seven occurrences** (*THGNT*, NA28, ℵ, TF35, TR).
- "ιησ*" <AND> "χρι*" <AND> "υι*" <AND> "θεο*" NT **thirty-nine occurrences** (*THGNT*, NA28, TF35)/**thirty-four occurrences** [2×17] (ℵ).
- κυριος <AND> Ἰησους <AND> χριστός NT 266 occurrences (*THGNT*)/**264 occurrences** [12×22] (NA28; involving **eighty-five verses** [5×17])/**323 occurrences** [19×17] (TF35; κύριος **105 occurrences** [7×15], Ἰησοῦς **108 occurrences** [4×27], χριστός **110 occurrences** [5×22])/**338 occurrences** [13×26] (TR), Pauline Corpus 207 occurrences [3×3×23] (*THGNT*)/**240 occurrences** [10×24] (ℵ)/**264 occurrences** [12×22] (TF35)/**270 occurrences** [10×27] (TR), Romans **thirty-nine occurrences** (ℵ), Galatians **fifteen occurrences** (ℵ), 1–2 Corinthians **fifty-one occurrences** [3×17], Ephesians **twenty-two occurrences** (*THGNT*, NA28, ℵ), 1 Thessalonians **fifteen occurrences**, 1–2 Thessalonians **forty-four occurrences** [2×22], 1 Timothy **fifteen occurrences**, 1–2 Timothy **twenty-four occurrences** (ℵ).

The Bible Canon and its significance

In our discussion we have seen that the Christian Bible Canon is not merely a list of books, but that it from early on tended to embrace a number of key dimensions such as intensified scriptural address and normativity. Canonization (in the broad sense) was something inherent in the shaping of most, or all, levels of the biblical literature (Childs 1992)—from the remembered and transmitted words of Jesus, taking their place beside the Law and the Prophets, to the authoritative appeal to "the Lord and the

Apostles," to which the church referred "in all matters of faith and practice" (Metzger 1987). For regular practical purposes biblical canonicity implied that what was later named "canonical" was from early on "read in corporate worship" (Zahn 1889).

By way of summary, in terms of its significance, as *Urlitteratur*—as foundational religious text vis-à-vis the church—the Christian Bible Canon arguably operated, and kept operating, in the faith communities (and beyond) in a variety of ways. The normative corpus of Christian writings was perceived as Scripture with prophetic and apostolic address and authority (i). These writings soon appeared as quite well-defined canonical sub-units (ii), and as a text collection made up of prior collections (iii), supported by "canon formation narratives" (iv). When the notion of canon was used in this connection, it tended to be understood as a property of sacred Scripture (v), with the NT being placed on a par with the OT (vi). As compared to the earliest stages of its formation, this emergent Bible canon was increasingly functioning as (an) intensified scriptural address and criterion (vii)—as the sacred Scriptures, comprising a variety of literature, arranged into a textual whole (viii). To establish its status as a delimited scriptural corpus, appeal arguably was made to "fullness" numerals, the canonical formula, use of *inclusios*, and employment of canon lists (ix). Additionally, we noted two further dimensions integral to the Bible Canon as a delimited corpus, namely the apparent attention given to arithmetically designed text-units (codicological features, x) and inner-scripturally "weaved" canonical sub-units (word-frequencies linked to *Name-related Numerals*, xi). Last, we viewed the Bible Canon also as a creedally engrafted Scripture matrix (use of *nomina sacra* and word-frequencies linked to *Name-related Numerals*, xii); and as a continually received authoritative Scripture corpus in the church universal (xiii).[32]

Bibliography

Ashton, John. (2007), *Understanding the Fourth Gospel*, 2nd edn, Oxford: Oxford University Press.
Athanasius. (1857–66), *Against the Arians* and *Letters to Serapion*, edited by Jacques-Paul Migne, Paris: Patrologiae Graecae.
Athanasius. (1892), *Thirty-Ninth Festal Epistle*, The Nicene and Post-Nicene Fathers, second series, vol. 4, edited by A. Philip Schaff and Henry Wace, New York: The Christian Literature Company.
Barth, Karl. (1936–62), *Church Dogmatics*, vol. I/1, Edinburgh: T&T Clark.
Basil the Great. (1857–66), *On the Holy Spirit*, edited by Jacques-Paul Migne, Paris: Patrologiae Graecae.
Bauckham, Richard. (2002), "The 153 Fish and the Unity of the Fourth Gospel," *Neotestamentica* 36 (1.2): 77–88.
Bauckham, Richard. (2017), *Jesus and the Eyewitnesses: The Gospels as Eyewitness Testimony*, 2nd edn, Grand Rapids: Eerdmans.

---

[32] I would like to thank the editors of the present volume, Professors Ed Glenny and Darian Lockett, as well as my wife Anna Bokedal, for helpful feedback on an earlier draft of the manuscript.

Bokedal, Tomas. (2010), "Scripture in the Second Century," in M. Pahl and M. F. Bird (eds.), *The Sacred Text: Artefact, Interpretation and Doctrinal Formulation*, Gorgias Précis Portfolios 7, 43–61, Piscataway, NJ: Gorgias.

Bokedal, Tomas. (2012), "Notes on the *Nomina Sacra* and Biblical Interpretation," in H. Assel, S. Beyerle, and C. Böttrich (eds.), *Beyond Biblical Theologies*, WUNT 295, 263–95, Tübingen: Mohr Siebeck.

Bokedal, Tomas. (2013), "Canon Formation and Interpretation – Problems and Possibilities," in *CTTS Journal* 4: 9–75.

Bokedal, Tomas. (2014), *The Formation and Significance of the Christian Biblical Canon: A Study in Text, Ritual and Interpretation*, London: Bloomsbury T&T Clark.

Bokedal, Tomas. (forthcoming a), "But for Me, the Scriptures are Jesus Christ (IC XC; Ign. Phld. 8:2): Creedal Text-Coding and the Early Scribal System of *Nomina Sacra*," in S. E. Porter, D. I. Yoon, and C. S. Stevens (eds.), *Paratextual Features of New Testament Papyrology and Early Christian Manuscripts*, Text and Editions of New Testament Studies, Leiden: Brill.

Bokedal, Tomas. (forthcoming b), *Christ the Center: How the Rule of Faith, the* Nomina Sacra, *and Numerical Patterns Shape the Canon*, Studies in Scripture and Biblical Theology, Bellingham, WA: Lexham Press.

The Center for the Study of New Testament Manuscripts, http://www.csntm.org/Manuscript (accessed June 18, 2020).

Childs, Brevard S. (1979), *Introduction to the Old Testament as Scripture*, London: SCM.

Childs, Brevard S. (1984), *The New Testament as Canon: An Introduction*, London: SCM.

Childs, Brevard S. (1992), *Biblical Theology of the Old and New Testaments*, London: SCM.

Clement of Alexandria. (reprinted 1994), *The Stromata* or *Miscellanies*, The Ante-Nicene Fathers, vols 1 and 2, edited by A. Roberts and J. Donaldson, 299–568, Edinburgh: T&T Clark and Grand Rapids: Eerdmans.

Codex Sinaiticus. Available online: http://www.codex-sinaiticus.net/en/manuscript.aspx?book=37 (accessed July 8, 2020).

Codex Vaticanus. Available online: https://digi.vatlib.it/view/MSS_Vat.gr.1209 (accessed June 1, 2020).

Decretum Gelasianum. (1991), in Denzinger, *Enchiridion symbolorum definitionum et declarationum de rebus fidei et morum*, Freiburg im Breisgau: Herder.

Deines, Roland. (2013), "Did Matthew Know He was Writing Scripture? Part 1," *European Journal of Theology* 22 (2): 101–109.

Deines, Roland. (2014), "Did Matthew Know He was Writing Scripture? Part 2," *European Journal of Theology* 23 (1): 3–12.

Denzinger, see *Decretum Gelasianum*.

Elliott, J. Keith. (1996), "Manuscripts, the Codex and the Canon," *JSNT* 63: 105–23.

Epp, Eldon Jay. (2002), "Issues in the Interrelation of New Testament Textual Criticism and Canon," in L. M. McDonald and J. A. Sanders (eds.), *The Canon Debate*, 485–515, Peabody, MA: Hendrickson.

Eusebius. *Historia Ecclesiastica*. Available online: http://www.perseus.tufts.edu/hopper/text?doc=1.1&fromdoc=Perseus%3Atext%3A2008.01.0640 (accessed January 27, 2021).

Fletcher-Louis, Crispin. (2015), *Jesus Monotheism*, vol. 1: Christological Origins: The Emerging Consensus and Beyond, Eugene, OR: Cascade.

"The Formula of Concord". (1877 [1576]), in *The Creeds of Christendom, with a History and Critical Notes*, vol. 3, 93–180, New York: Harper & Brothers.

Gallagher, Edmon. (2012), *Hebrew Scriptures in Patristic Biblical Theory: Canon, Language, Text*, Supplements to Vigiliae Christianae, 63–104, Leiden: Brill.

Grant, Robert M. (1997), *Irenaeus of Lyons*, The Early Church Fathers, London and New York: Routledge.
Harnack, Adolf von. (1925), *The Origin of the New Testament and the Most Important Consequences of the New Creation*, trans. J. R. Wilkinson, London: Williams & Norgate.
Haslam, Michael. (1997), "Homeric Papyri and Transmission of the Text," in I. Morris and B. Powell (eds.), *A New Companion to Homer*, 55–100, Leiden: Brill.
Heiden, Bruce. (1998), "The Placement of 'Book Divisions' in the Iliad," *Journal of Hellenic Studies* 118: 68–81.
Hill, Charles. "The Four Gospel Canon in the Second Century" (http://youngadults.ccphilly.org/wp-content/uploads/2012/11/Four-Gospel-Canon-.pdf; accessed August 31, 2020).
Holmes, Michael W. (2007), *The Apostolic Fathers: Greek Texts and English Translations*, 3rd edn, Grand Rapids: Baker.
Hurtado, Larry W. (2006a), *The Earliest Christian Artifacts: Manuscripts and Christian Origins*, Grand Rapids: Eerdmans.
Hurtado, Larry W. (2006b), "The New Testament in the Second Century: Text, Collections, Canon," in J. W. Childers and D. C. Parker (eds.), *Transmission and Reception: New Testament Text-Critical and Exegetical Studies*, 3–27, Piscataway, NJ: Gorgias.
Irenaeus of Lyons. (1997), *Against Heresies*, trans. Robert Grant, London and New York: Routledge.
Jenson, Robert W. (1999), "The Religious Power of Scripture," *Scottish Journal of Theology* 52: 89–105.
Josephus. (1926), *Against Apion*, Loeb Classical Library 186, Cambridge, MA and London, UK: Harvard University Press.
Keener, Craig S. (2020), "Greek Versus Jewish Conceptions of Inspiration and 2 Timothy 3:16," *JETS* 63 (2): 217–31.
Kooij, Arie van der. (2003), "Canonization of Ancient Hebrew Books and Hasmonean Politics," in J.-M. Auwers and H. J. de Jonge (eds.), *The Biblical Canons*, 27–38, Leuven: Leuven University Press and Peeters.
Labuschagne, Casper J. (2016a), "General Introduction to Logotechnical Analysis (Rev.)" (University of Groningen). Available online: https://www.bing.com/search?q=general%20introduction%20to%20logotechnical%20analysis%20casper%20labuschagne%20pdf&pc=cosp&ptag=G6C999N1234D010517A316A5D3C6E&form=CONBDF&conlogo=CT3210127 (accessed October 26, 2020).
Labuschagne, Casper J. (2016b), *Numerical Secrets of the Bible: Introduction to Biblical Arithmology*, Eugene, OR: Wipf & Stock.
Laird, Benjamin P. (2016), *The Formation, Publication, and Circulation of the Corpus Paulinum in Early Christianity*, University of Aberdeen, Ph.D. thesis.
Lim, Timothy H. (2013), *The Formation of the Jewish Canon*, The Anchor Yale Bible reference library, New Haven: Yale University Press.
McDonald, Lee Martin. (2017), *The Formation of the Biblical Canon*, vol 2: *The New Testament: It's Authority and Canonicity*, London: Bloomsbury T&T Clark.
Metzger, Bruce M. (1987), *The Canon of the New Testament: Its Origin, Development, and Significance*, Oxford: Clarendon Press.
Meyer, Heinz and Rudolf Suntrup. (1987), *Lexikon der mittelalterlichen Zahlenbedeutungen*, Münstersche Mittelalter-Schriften 56, München: Wilhelm Fink Verlag.
Mroczek, Eva. (2016), *The Literary Imagination in Jewish Antiquity*, Oxford: Oxford University Press.

The Muratorian Fragment. (1987), trans. Bruce M. Metzger, in Metzger, *The Canon of the New Testament: Its Origin, Development, and Significance*, Oxford: Clarendon Press.
Roberts, C. H. (1979), *Manuscript, Society and Belief in Early Christian Egypt*, Oxford: Oxford University Press.
Schmidt, Daryl D. (2002), "The Greek New Testament as a Codex," in L. M. McDonald and J. A. Sanders (eds.), *The Canon Debate*, 469–84, Peabody, MA: Hendrickson.
Skeat, T. C. (1992), "Irenaeus and the Four-Gospel Canon," *Novum Testamentum* 34: 194–99.
Smith, D. Moody. (2000), "When Did the Gospels Become Scripture," *JBL* 119: 3–20.
Stanton, Graham. (1997), "The Fourfold Gospel," *NTS* 43: 317–46.
Stevenson, Kalinda Rose. (1996), *The Vision of Transformation: The Territorial Rhetoric of Ezekiel 40–48*, SBLDS 154, Atlanta: Scholars Press.
Theissen, Gerd. (2003), *The New Testament: History, Literature, Religion*, London: T&T Clark.
Thirty-Nine Articles of Religion. Available online: https://anglicancommunion.org/media/109014/Thirty-Nine-Articles-of-Religion.pdf (accessed January 27, 2021).
Trobisch, David. (2000), *The First Edition of the New Testament*, Oxford: Oxford University Press.
Tyndale House Greek New Testament. (2017), edited by Dirk Jongkind and Peter J. Williams, Wheaton, IL: Crossway and Cambridge: Cambridge University Press.
Verheyden, Joseph. (2003), "The Canon Muratori: A Matter of Dispute," in J.-M. Auwers and H. J. de Jonge (eds.), *The Biblical Canons*, 487–556, Leuven: Leuven University Press and Peeters.
Wolterstorff, Nicholas. (1995), *Divine Discourse: Philosophical Reflections on the Claim that God Speaks*, New York: Cambridge University Press.
Zahn, Theodor. (1889), *Einige Bemerkungen zu Adolf Harnack's Prüfung der Geschichte des neutestamentlichen Kanons*, I/1 Erlangen and Leipzig: A. Deichert'sche Verlagshandlung Nachf. [Georg Böhme].

2

The Canonical Shape of the Hebrew Old Testament

Stephen G. Dempster

The Hebrew Bible, the Bible of Judaism, is the origin and foundation of the first three quarters of the Christian Bible, and its content is found in the Bibles of the three major denominations of Christendom: Roman Catholicism, Greek Orthodoxy, and Protestantism. In Christianity it is called the Old Testament, and while it is the same as the content of the Protestant Old Testament, Roman Catholicism has added seven books and some additions to three other ones, and Eastern Orthodoxy has added four more to the Catholic list with other additions (for various canon lists see, Gallagher and Meade 2017: xxi–xxii; McDonald 2017: 498–99; Gillingham 1998: 61–66; and Beckwith 1985: 61–66, 500). The history of how these deutero-canonical books have been added to these two Old Testament canons is a complex development and cannot be considered here. Suffice it to say that these additional books, while often viewed as edifying literature in the synagogue and in many parts of the early church, were never viewed as canonical, i.e., part of the Jewish Bible by virtually all of Judaism.[1] And in the early church there was a significant group of eastern churches and scholars from the East, who accepted the Jewish view regarding the Hebrew "truth."[2] A significant number of other churches, mainly in the West, differed from this view because of the dint of popular practice, and it is quite clear that the post-Constantinian church had a group of books used for edification, and sometimes these books were confused with a narrower group that was used more authoritatively (Dempster 2016: 359–61). This concern is clearly shown in Athanasius's Easter Letter in 367 CE when he presents a canonical list to ensure congregations in his ambit distinguish between canonical books and others (Gallagher and Meade 2017: 118–26). Clarification was needed. Despite this complex development and some of its entailments for the Christian churches, it is clear that the Christian church was born with a Bible in its hands, and this Bible was received from the Synagogue (see the insightful comments of Gallagher and Meade 2017: 25–29). The content of that Bible is the irreducible core of the Old Testament of the major Christian denominations.

---

[1] The "canon" of the Qumran sect may represent an exception but for the arguments "pro" and "con" see Dempster 2009: 61–62. For the possible "canonicity" of Sirach (Ecclesiasticus) in some parts of Judaism see the incisive discussion in Beckwith: 1985: 435–450.
[2] See e.g. the Greek Christian lists in Gallagher and Meade 2017: 70–174; McDonald 2002: 585–86.

To speak of a Bible, one should not imagine one document as we have it in our culture today because the technical ability to put all the various texts of the Hebrew Bible into one document did not exist until the second century CE, long after the time the Hebrew Bible had been written. Before that time papyrus and parchment scrolls and clay tablets were used to produce written documents, and because of these mediums it was virtually impossible and certainly inconvenient to produce long texts on one scroll or tablet. This, of course, did not mean that a conceptual unity did not exist. For example, in other ancient cultures, texts like the Creation Story in Mesopotamia were written on seven clay tablets, and the Epic of Gilgamesh consisted of twelve tablets. Some of these texts date to the second millennium BCE. Technological limitation did not eliminate conceptual unity, and various means were developed to maintain that unity such as spatial proximity or numerical sequence in an archive or library (Pedersen 1998: 407–13).[3]

The fundamental shape of the Hebrew Bible

The earliest manuscript evidence for a complete Hebrew Bible comes from the tenth and eleventh centuries CE. The earliest complete codex is Leningradensis (1009 CE). There is an earlier codex that is missing quite a few pages, Codex Aleppo (930 CE), and a complete codex of the Prophets, Cairensis (890 CE), which has been redated by some to the twelfth century due to radiocarbon analysis. Since it was damaged in a fire in 1947 Codex Aleppo is missing all the Torah until Deut. 28:17; 2 Kgs 14:21-18:13; Jer. 29:9-33 and 32:2-4, 9-11, 21-24; Amos 8:12; Micah 5:1; Zeph, 3:20-Zech. 9:17; 2 Chr 26:19-35:7; Pss 15:1-25:2; Songs 3:11-8:14, Eccl, Lam, Esther, Dan and Ezra-Neh. The early codices present a clear picture. At this time the evidence is clear that the Jewish Bible had a tripartite structure, consisting of twenty-four books: The Torah (Law five books), the Nevi'im (Prophets eight books) and the Ketuvim (Writings eleven books). Even though Cairensis is a codex of the Prophets there is a list appended to the document with the books of the tripartite canon in the same sequence as Aleppo and Leningradensis. Thus, Jews use the acronym Tanak to designate their Bible. This tripartite structure is reflected in virtually all the many Jewish codices which follow from this earlier period, in eastern arrangements, western arrangements and later Rabbinic Bibles. While there is some diversity in the arrangement of the books in the second section, the Prophets, and considerable diversity in the third section, the Writings, the tripartite structure of the canon is a universal, consistent feature. Although Roger Beckwith notes nine variant orders in the Prophets and seventy-nine different orders in the Writings, these of course are mainly late medieval developments (1985: 202–11). Further, with printed Bibles there are some major deviations with the Megillot being printed after the Torah, as these are texts which would be read publicly in their entirety in the synagogue (Brandt 2001: 136-41).

---

[3] Even in the contemporary world there are multi-volume works which are produced because of technological limitation. One of the latest books on canon is an example, a two-volume work by McDonald 2017.

Jews were considerably late in adopting the codex format for their Bibles in contrast to the Christian churches, who quickly adopted it because its portability was an asset for evangelistic and mission purposes (Roberts and Skeat 1987 and Hurtado 2006). Jewish reluctance to accept the codex probably stemmed from the importance of tradition but this also meant that the individual books of the Tanak would have been written on separate scrolls. Some suggest that this meant that the exact order of the scrolls was not important as a result and any attempt to find meaning in the arrangement of the scrolls is the equivalent of a hermeneutical "wild goose chase" (Barton 2007: 82-91). But it is nonetheless clear that there was a very early concern for the tripartite structure and thus the grouping of documents into separate sub-collections. A baraita in the Talmud, i.e. a rabbinic tradition dated to the period of the Mishna but which was not included in it, presents a specific order for the scrolls following the *Torah*, whose existence and sequence are assumed: Genesis, Exodus, Leviticus, Numbers and Deuteronomy. The order of the two other divisions of the Bible are presented in two sequences: the *Prophets* consisting of Joshua, Judges, Samuel, Kings, Jeremiah, Ezekiel, Isaiah and the Twelve and the *Writings* consisting of Ruth, Psalms, Job, Proverbs, Ecclesiastes, Songs, Lamentations, Daniel, Esther, Ezra-Nehemiah, and Chronicles. While some date this evidence to the final formation of the Talmud (sixth to fifth centuries CE), it is clearly a baraita, an early saying of the rabbis from the time of the Mishnah. Thus, it should be dated at the latest to the time of the final compilation of the Mishna by Rabbi Judah (200 CE). Some would date it to the late second and first centuries BCE (Beckwith 1985).

In addition, there is evidence in the Talmud regarding debates for joining the various divisions on larger scrolls. This, as Haran observes, is largely ignored by paleographers. But according to the traditions such debates are around the same time as the baraita or earlier: Our Rabbis taught: it is permissible to fasten the Torah, the Prophets and the Hagiographa together (Baba Batra 13b; cf. Megillah 1:11, see Haran 1993: 60-61). This may well be the reason that an exact order is specified for the latter two divisions.

Evidence for such a tripartite structure is reflected in early Jewish sources dating to the late second century BCE. The grandson of Sirach (circa 130 BCE) writes a preface to his grandfather's work (circa 180 BCE) praising it for its use of Jewish scriptures which are three times identified as the "Law, Prophets and the other Writings." There are in fact three such uses of similar nomenclature for the Bible in quite close proximity: "the law, the prophets and other books which followed them"; "the law, the prophets and the other books of the fathers"; "the law, the prophecies and the rest of the books." While some scholars regard this as a bipartite nomenclature for the Jewish Bible (Law and Prophets) and a loose term describing other non-scriptural books, the most natural reading is to understand these three divisions as the three parts of the Hebrew Scriptures, now of course translated into Greek. Each of the three sections is described with a definite article, and moreover the content of the grandfather's work really consists in discussing and commenting on only the books of the Hebrew Bible. Indeed, the last section (Sir. 44:1-49:16) usually titled "In Praise of the Fathers," reads like a who's who of biblical characters from one end of the Hebrew Bible, starting with Adam, to the other, ending with Nehemiah, before returning back to Adam at the beginning.

But what is most significant is that the heroes in Sirach's praise parade do not need a formal introduction as they are household names to his audience. Indeed, it is clear that the Torah is distinguished from the rest of the books[4] and that the Twelve can be described as one authoritative book, not twelve prophets (Sir. 49:10). It may be also the case that Sirach himself described his Bible with tripartite nomenclature: The Law, Wisdom and Prophecies (Sir. 39:1–5) (Dempster 2001: 24–30).

Further corroborative evidence comes from Josephus, writing at the end of the first century CE (*Contra Apion* 1:8). He lists a Bible of twenty-two books, and although it is organized uniquely it still follows a tripartite pattern: five books of law, thirteen of prophets and four of hymns and precepts. This particular organization for the second and third divisions may be done to categorize the collections on the basis of genre in order to speak more relevantly to Greek and Roman readers of his work (Beckwith 1985: 118–27; Leimann 1989: 50–58). Though it may be the case that this order is a variant early work, nonetheless, while the arrangement of some of the individual books is unique, a tripartite structure arranges his Jewish Bible.

Evidence from early Christian sources confirms this tripartite division. Writing in the latter part of the fourth century CE, Jerome describes two possible orders for the Hebrew scriptures. In his Prologus Galeatus to his translation of the book of Samuel, he describes the Hebrews as having one collection of twenty-two books and another of twenty-four. But the first is an adaptation of the second by including two books as parts of other ones: Ruth with Judges and Lamentations with Jeremiah. Nevertheless, in both orders there is a strict tripartite structure: 5+8+9= 22 for the first one, and 5+8+11 for the second (Gallager and Meade 2017: 197–214).

There is further evidence from earlier Jewish and Christian sources for the numbers twenty-four (4 Ezra, circa 90 CE) and twenty-two (Origen, circa 220 CE; Melito, circa 160 CE), but there is no explicit identification of a tripartite structure.[5] However, such a structure is probably reflected in the common phrase "the Law and the Prophets" or "Moses and the Prophets" which is abundantly used in the New Testament and in other Jewish literature in the late pre-Common and early Common Eras.[6] In addition to these bipartite nomenclatures there is also one tripartite designation in the Gospel of Luke ("the Law of Moses, the prophets and the psalms"; 24:44) and possibly also at Qumran (Moses, the Prophets and David; 4QMMT). In Luke, this clearly functions as an alternative description for the entire collection of books, which are designated variously with correlative terms ("all the prophets have spoken" [24:25], "Moses and all the prophets" [24:27], "all the scriptures" [24:27], and "the scriptures" [24:32, 45]) and the law and the prophets. Some suggest this tripartite nomenclature in Luke 24:44

---

[4] Note the introduction of Joshua in 46:1 as a prophetic successor of Moses. Cf. the comments by Pancratius Bentjees: "The description of Joshua in 46:1 is strong evidence that in Ben Sira's time the later terminology of reckoning the books of Joshua, Judges, Samuel and Kings to the 'Former Prophets' was already in the air" (Bentjees 2000: 594).

[5] For Melito's comments and the possibility of the number "22" for his list see the discussion in Gallagher and Meade (2017), 81–83. Melito is one of the first to use the phrase "the books of the Old Covenant" and he also describes them with bipartite nomenclature: The Law and the Prophets.

[6] New Testament: Matt. 5:17, 7:12, 22:40, Luke 16:16, Acts 13:15, 24:14; Rom. 3:21; Qumran: CD 7:15-17; QS 1:1-3, 8:15-17. For a more comprehensive listing of evidence see Dempster 2008: 87–128.

indicates the emerging growth of a third section of the canon, but it more likely refers to a designation of the third section by a form of synecdoche, the part for the whole, since the Psalms comprised a very large scroll and it occurred at or near the beginning of the third division of the canon. Moreover, it is clear from other evidence in the New Testament, that the writers viewed other writings in the third division in addition to the Psalms as canonical (e.g. Daniel [cf. Matt. 24:15], Proverbs [Heb. 12:5–6], Job [1 Cor. 3:19], Ecclesiastes [Rom. 3:10]). Qumran may also have a similar tripartite designation, but this is based on the interpretation of a reading of a fragmentary text: "the book of Moses, the Prophets and David." In this letter (4QMMT), a bipartite designation for the scriptures is presented alongside this possible tripartite designation for the same literature. This letter seems to be addressed to a leader in order to impress upon him the fact that the scriptures were being fulfilled. As a result of recognizing this fact the leader, the letter says, will be able to understand "the Book of Moses and the Words of the Prophets and Dav[id.]" Later the fulfillment of the prophecies predicted "in the Book of Moses and the words of the Prophets" is regarded as coming true (Qimron and Strugnell 1994: 59 n. 10).[7]

So, it is clear that this tripartite division can be traced back to the earliest external evidence for the Hebrew Bible that is available. It is most likely that this arrangement was not haphazard, nor can it simply be tied to the evolution of the canon over a period of time.

The Arrangement of the books in the divisions

The Torah

Within the Jewish tradition the Torah is arranged chronologically: Genesis, Exodus, Leviticus, Numbers and Deuteronomy, yet in early lists there are a few deviations from this sequence. For example, the list of Melito, a Christian bishop who claims he received his knowledge from the East, has the sequence: Genesis, Exodus, Numbers, Leviticus and Deuteronomy. The chronological sequence starts with the beginning of the creation of the world and ends with the death of Moses. The story moves naturally and smoothly in chronological sequence for the most part. One exception is the numbering of the tribes and Aaron's benediction (Num. 1–6). Textually this precedes chapter 7 but would have followed it chronologically (cf. also 1:1 with 9:1).

A narrative genre provides the basic frame for the text, into which a block of law is inserted (Ex 25–Num. 10), followed by more narrative interspersed with legal material (Num. 11–36), concluding with a second rendition of law in homiletical and hortatory form (Deut. 1–33), culminating with a narrative report of the death of Moses (Deut. 34). Genesis begins with the creation of the world, the catastrophes of the flood and tower of Babel, the election of the fathers, and the transition of the family of Jacob to

---

[7] For strident reaction to this possibility see Ulrich 2003: 202–214. Timothy Lim does not question the reading "of David" but its interpretation as a reference to the writings: Lim 2013: 127–28. His argument that "David" refers to the historical "example" of David suggests in my judgment special pleading.

Egypt. Then Exodus narrates the Egyptian oppression, Israelite liberation and the Sinai Covenant, which occupies the last half of Exodus, the whole of Leviticus, and the first ten chapters of Numbers. Then the journey to the Promised Land begins and it ends with a new generation on the brink of entering the Land. Finally, Moses delivers his last charge to his people as they are perched to enter the land, before he transfers the mantle of leadership to Joshua.

This sequence is clearly chronological and even though the books were written on separate scrolls, syntactic links between the first four books show not only their conceptual unity but their grammatical cohesion. A syntactic break between Deuteronomy and the previous four works, as well as a syntactic link with the next book of the Prophets, Joshua, shows it functions as a type of Janus structure, looking back and concluding the Torah, while looking ahead to the Prophets (Dempster 2001: 19–56, esp. 44–49). In terms of broad topics, the monograph of David Clines is superb in its articulation of the major theme of the Torah (or Pentateuch) as the partial fulfillment of the promises to the patriarchs which are intended to reverse the curses of Genesis 3–11 (Clines 1997). Thus, the Torah can also be understood as two major sections: a primal history of Genesis 1–11 and a national history of Genesis 12–Deuteronomy 34. This relates to a broad genealogical theme beginning with a promise to the woman (Gen. 3:15) and narrowing down to a royal deliverer from the tribe of Judah in Gen. 49:8–12 (Alexander 1998: 191–21). The main hinge connecting these two histories and the theme of genealogy is the programmatic text of Gen. 12:1–3, positioned at the beginning of the national history, promising that Abram's seed is the instrument through which the entire world, which has been cursed, will be blessed.

The Prophets

This division consists of eight books, again with four books of narrative in chronological sequence and four others comprising collections of prophetic speeches. In the medieval period these clear thematic divisions were known as the Former and Latter Prophets. The Former Prophets begin with the conquest of Canaan and end with the destruction of Israel and its exile. Joshua presents the initial conquest followed by covenant renewal, Judges follows with the individual tribes taking up residence in Canaan and living with the remaining Canaanites with the attendant consequences of religious assimilation coupled with political chaos, Samuel subsequently introduces kingship and the reigns of Saul and David, while Kings narrates the breakup of the nation into rival kingdoms and the gradual destruction and exile of first, the northern kingdom, and secondly, the southern one.

But why is this narrative, the first half of this second canonical division, called prophecy (see Dempster 2018: 74–94)? There are probably three major reasons, the first being because it details the outworking in the life of the nation of the prophetic word of Deuteronomy, which foretold blessings for obedience and curse, including the climactic judgment of exile, for disobedience. In fact, it is no accident that the scroll of Deuteronomy is discovered in the last book of the Former Prophets (2 Kgs 22), and its discovery leads to the proclamation of final curse for the nation. The Former Prophets thus provide a dramatic witness of the fulfillment of the prophetic word in the life of the nation. But secondly, this history sketched out in Joshua-Kings is not an ordinary history but a history which details the power of the prophetic word in the life of the nation. At first sporadically, but then with a flurry, prophets arise in this history, and their predictions are noted in detail as are their fulfillments, whether those happen after a short period or a longer time span. These prophecies "change the gears of history with the Word of God" (von Rad 1962: 342). Finally, the core of the last book Kings (1 Kgs 17–2 Kgs 14), focuses on two prophets and their disciples as the real "movers and shakers" in Israel. The vast military power of the kings and their wealth and influence does not tell the real story of rule within the nation. Not just once but twice are heard epitaphs for these prophetic leaders: "My father, my father, the chariots of Israel and its horsemen!" (2 Kings 2:12, 12:14).

The order of the Former Prophets is consistent through all the traditions, and this is probably because of not only the syntactic links but the straightforward chronological sequence. On the other hand, there are a few variations in the arrangement of the Latter Prophets, the collections of prophetic speeches. The two major variations seem to be based on the difference between a literary order versus a chronological order. The order Jeremiah-Ezekiel-Isaiah-The Twelve may be based on decreasing order of size while the order Isaiah-Jeremiah-Ezekiel-The Twelve may be based on chronology with the first of the major prophets dating to the eighth century BCE and the last of the Twelve minor prophets dating to the post-exilic period (sixth to fifth century BCE). On the other hand, there may be a chronological reason for the Jeremiah-Ezekiel-Isaiah-Twelve sequence as well, as the books may be arranged chronologically according to the endings of their books. The Talmud, however, supplies theological reasons for the first order suggesting the following reasons:

> Now, Hosea came first, as it is written, "God first spoke to Hosea" (Hos. 1-2). But, did He first speak to Hosea? Were there not a number of prophets from Moses to Hosea? However, Rabbi Yohanan said that he was the first of four prophets who prophesied at that time, and these are they- Hosea, and Isaiah, Amos, and Micah. Then Hosea should have been placed first? Since his prophecies are written (in the collection together) with Haggai, Zechariah and Malachi, and Haggai, Zechariah, and Malachi were the last of the prophets, Hosea is considered together with them. Then it should have been written separately and placed earlier? Since it is small, it might have gotten lost. Now, Isaiah is before Jeremiah and Ezekiel, so Isaiah should have been placed first? Kings ends with an account of destruction, and Jeremiah is entirely an account of destruction, and Ezekiel begins with destruction and concludes with consolation, and Isaiah is entirely consolation. Thus, we adjoin destruction to destruction and consolation to consolation.
>
> Baba Batra 14b

It seems that the argument is being made that the Twelve should have begun first because Hosea represented the beginning of prophecy along with Amos, Isaiah and Micah. But since he is connected with the latest prophets (Haggai-Malachi), this affects the position of this prophetic text. And if Hosea was written on a separate scroll, and placed first, it might have gotten lost since the scroll would have been very small. This raises the question then as to why Jeremiah comes first instead of Isaiah. The reason is due to symmetry of theme: Kings ends with destruction and the same theme dominates Jeremiah, while Ezekiel begins with destruction and ends in consolation and Isaiah is all consolation. One wonders, though, if this is the same Isaiah! But perhaps the effect of the last half of Isaiah overwhelms the first half in the rabbinic mind.

As for the second arrangement of books—Isaiah-Jeremiah-Ezekiel-Twelve—it is clearly chronological and such an order may be possibly traced back to Sirach in which a chronological order is followed in the praise of the Fathers (Sir. 44–49). This is the order followed in Jerome (Prologus Galeatus) and in all the major early manuscripts (Cairensis, Aleppo, Leningradensis). There are some other variant orders in later manuscripts, but these are not dominant.

The hermeneutical function of the Prophets is clearly to reinforce and develop the themes of the Torah. At the beginning of the Prophets, all the promises to the Fathers are intact, and the future looks as bright as the promises of God. But at the end of the Former Prophets, which is really the midpoint of the Hebrew Bible, all these promises have been radically called into question. The Former Prophets described the growth of the nation, the beginning of a monarchy, the importance of the covenant with David, the construction of the temple, the journey into idolatry and the call for the nation to return to Yahweh by the prophets. But the call goes largely unheeded and the nation fractures into two states which are often at civil war, before the larger Northern Kingdom falls to the nation of Assyria and then the smaller Southern Kingdom of Judah is destroyed by Babylon. At the end of the Former Prophets the temple has been destroyed and Judah is in the dead end of exile. It seems as if the promise of Israel being a universal blessing is a cruel joke, and the Davidic scion with whom an everlasting covenant had been made is also dead. But the function of the Latter Prophets is to show how the nations were in fact responsible for their own fate with the violation of the Torah, as the speeches of various prophets provide the evidence of Israel being called into account by these prophets. But these particular prophets are unique in that their speeches were recorded and edited. They provide the hard evidence of a population that did not listen to the Torah. These prophets were also exceptional in providing hope for the nation, that beyond the judgment God was planning to keep the promises to the Fathers (Micah 7:18-20), and that a shoot would spring up from the stump of Jesse, bringing blessing to the world (Isa. 11). God would make a way through the dead end of exile just as he made a way through the Red Sea (Isa. 40–48). God would breathe new life into dead bodies which had decayed into dry bones (Ezek. 37). God would make a new covenant not like the old covenant at Sinai. He would write the Torah on the heart this time and give a complete amnesty for sin (Jer. 31:31–33).

Some would see the Torah as primary and the Prophets as secondary, others the Prophets as primary and the Torah as more or less background for God's "new work" that he was doing in Israel and the world (for an outline of some of the differences and discussion see Dempster 2006: 293–329, esp. 303–309). But according to Stephen Chapman they must both be seen as complementary. It is not law in addition to commentary (i.e. the prophets) or prophets plus background (i.e. the law) but the complete dialectical relationship between them both that reveals God (Chapman 2000).

The Writings

The earliest explicit evidence for the organization of this division of the Hebrew Bible is the baraita in the Talmud which arranges the books as follows: Ruth-Psalms-Job-Proverbs-Ecclesiastes-Song of Songs-Lamentations-Daniel-Esther-Ezra/Nehemiah-Chronicles. However, the order for Josephus, as mentioned previously (*Contra Apion* 1:8), would have been earlier but it has to be inferred, and since it is unique it may well have been the result of categorization according to genre for apologetic reasons. Then, Jerome's twenty-four book canon begins in the third section with Job and ends with Esther. The earliest complete manuscripts of Codex Aleppo and Leningradensis have the following sequence: Chronicles-Psalms-Job-Proverbs-Ruth-Song of Songs-Ecclesiastes-Lamentations-Esther-Daniel-Ezra/Nehemiah. But there are many deviations from this in the ensuing centuries in the Hebrew manuscript traditions. Roger Beckwith has enumerated at least seventy-nine different orders which he has grouped under three different categories: literary, chronological and liturgical (Beckwith 1985: 207–210). The order adopted by the Tiberian Masoretes, as indicated by the earliest manuscripts, groups the Megillot together chronologically (Ruth-Song of Songs-Ecclesiastes-Lamentations-Esther), while other orders often do this calendrically (Song of Songs-Ruth- Lamentations-Ecclesiastes-Esther). Probably the more ancient organization was the one preserved in the Talmud because the Megillot being grouped together is most likely due to later liturgical developments (for a different view see Stone 2013). The multiplicity of later orders suggests that within later Judaism there was a freedom to group the texts in various ways, not because there was no order but precisely because there was. Many of these orders can be explained as deriving from a few. As Steinberg and Stone have shown, variants are not to be counted but weighed. The orders which begin with Chronicles or end with Chronicles suggest that Chronicles could be added to the beginning or ending of the collection thus providing a frame (Steinberg and Stone 2015: 42–51). Clearly, in terms of age the closure with Chronicles is the earliest sequence.

The hermeneutical function of the Writings with its focus on more international dimensions such as found in Ruth, Daniel and Esther, and its more universally oriented wisdom literature (Job, Proverbs, Ecclesiastes, Song of Songs) has suggested a more "secular" outlook at times. Thus, a later term for this division was "Wisdom." In many ways this literature is a deep reflection on the universal implications of Torah. Having said this, it is important to recognize the Davidic-Jerusalem emphasis in this section as well, particularly in Ruth, the Psalter, the Solomonic works, Lamentations, and Chronicles. There have been a number of scholars who have made suggestions about the purpose of this section. There is no question that there is much more literary and theological heterogeneity in this division, as Morgan has noted the "incredible diversity of history, literature and theology in this canonical division" (Morgan 2018: 9). There is apocalyptic and wisdom literature, poetry and prose, lamentation and love poetry, psalmody and history. The fact that it is the third division of the canon, connected as it is to the Torah and the Prophets, is consistent with its wider more comprehensive view of the world in light of previous revelation. It is largely the Wisdom of the Sage, rooted in the Torah of Moses and the Word of the Prophets. In fact, Max Margolis has suggested that the three divisions of the canon have a biblical basis as they are rooted in three different institutions in Israel represented by three different individuals: the priest who instructed from the Torah, the prophet who proclaimed the Word, and the sage that used a sanctified reason (Margolis 1922: 54). There are a number of texts which suggest this. When Jeremiah was being persecuted, his enemies thought that they could eliminate him because they would still have access to the media of revelation: "Come and let us devise plans against Jeremiah. Surely the law is not going to be lost to the priest, nor counsel to the sage, nor the *divine* word to the prophet!" (Jer. 18:18). Similarly, in a time of judgment, Ezekiel proclaims that the people will lament that there will be no access to the media of revelation: "then they will seek a vision from a prophet, but the law will be lost from the priest and counsel from the elders" (Ezek. 7:26). Thus, this third dimension would allow for a much more diverse literature which stresses multiple theological issues such as address to God (Psalms, Lamentations), the question of theodicy (Job), seeking to understand natural revelation (Proverbs), the interpretation of dreams and visions (Daniel), the task of seeking to navigate one's way in a culture and time when God seems utterly absent (Esther), the difficult task of picking up the pieces and rebuilding (Ruth, Ezra-Nehemiah, Chronicles), and a final reflection on the meaning of it all (Ecclesiastes). In fact, some scholars argue that as the Torah and the Prophets deal with God's word to humanity in terms of legislation and prophecy, the Writings offer up the answering speech of Israel:

> Durch Gesang und Danksagung (Ps), durch Reflexion über das fromme Leben (WeisheitsLiteratur), durch Feieren (Megillot), durch den Ausblick (Daniel) und Rückbluck (Chronistisches Werk). Das Verbindende ist das dialogische Prinzip: Gott kommuniziert mit seinem Volk und mit dem Menschen, und er richtet es—oder ihn—in allem Scheitern immer neu auf.
>
> Jan Heller cited in Brandt 2001: 25

Nevertheless, the main threads sewn in the Torah and the Prophets—the promises to the Fathers, the Davidic covenant, and promise of universal blessing—are kept in view. While there can be complaint and lament to God and a wondering where his presence can be found, one does not read very far without realizing that God will set his King on Zion, his holy mountain and give him the entire earth as his inheritance (Ps. 2), and his reign will produce a new world in which justice will flourish and the Abrahamic promise of universal blessing will finally be achieved (Ps. 72:17). And if the genealogies begin the history in the first book of the Bible, tracing the line of blessing, the many genealogies at the end in Chronicles show the clear goal of history: the Davidic scion in a rebuilt temple in Zion. Indeed, the Writings help clarify the Torah and the Prophets. For example, there will be a long wait and much suffering—not just seventy years but seventy times seven years—before the exile is over and universal blessing arrives (Dan. 9; 2 Chr. 36:22-23). Thus, when the ending of Chronicles is read in the light of the earlier book of Daniel, there is an awareness that the eschatological clock is ticking.

The tripartite structure and theories of canonization

There are a number of theories which seek to explain the organization of the canon into three divisions. The first is tied to the gradual evolution of the canon (Ryle 1904). According to this view, initially the Torah was "canonized" around the fifth century BCE during the time of Ezra and Nehemiah and their reforms; then the prophets were distinguished in the second century BCE, and finally the Writings were sanctioned in approximately 90 CE at a rabbinic council at Yavneh in which the canonicity of certain books was discussed. Thus, the earliest date for the completion of the Bible was this council, the *terminus post quem*. The closing of the prophetic division was dated to the second century BCE because it is clear from Sirach that by his time they were viewed as a booked entity which was absolutely authoritative. Moreover, this explains why Daniel was not included in this division, since according to the modern consensus, it would have been written after the prophetic canon was closed. If it had been written before, it would have been included, given its prophetic stature. Finally, the terminus for the third division was finalized in 90 CE when the Rabbis met at Javneh and there discussed problems with some books being in the canon.[8] According to the theory these disputes were resolved, and the final canon was completed.

But this ship of a theory which sailed for a few generations in scholarship was shipwrecked in the 1960s by a number of observations (Lewis 1964 and now his own reflection on his essay: 2002). First, the evidence for the so-called council at Yavneh where certain books were supposedly finally included in the canon was virtually non-existent. There was simply a meeting (not a council) at which questions were raised about the canonical status of certain books. This implied that the books were already viewed as canonical and adds nothing about a process of canonization. Secondly, the fact that Daniel was not included in the prophets was also called into question since Daniel is more of a wise man, and he is never called a prophet in the book that bears his name. To be sure, despite the breakdown of this consensus, it lives on in attenuated form in recent canon studies in which the basic lines of the theory have been expanded. No longer is Yavneh given an important role, but the Writings are not viewed as closed until the second century CE or later (McDonald 2017: 373–77 cf. Lewis 2002: 150–52).

At the same time there are other interpretations of the evidence that have surfaced with the collapse of the evolutionary model. For example, some have suggested that the Maccabean crisis which led to the destruction of many holy books by Antiochus Epiphanes in his zeal to convert Judaism to Hellenism and resulted in the Maccabean revolt provoked a concern by the Jews to preserve their Scriptures. So, after victory there was a concerted effort to gather the holy books, much like Nehemiah who had purportedly gathered texts dealing with kings and prophets, the writings of David and letters and stored them in a library (2 Macc. 2:1-15). This evidence has been interpreted to suggest that there was already a Torah and another collection of literature which Judas subdivided into two sections, the Prophets and other writings, which are

---

[8] For example, *Yadayim* 3:5 in the Mishna where there is a discussion about the Song of Songs and Ecclesiastes.

indicated by the labels of their contents (kings and prophets, writings of David and letters; also from a more cultural perspective, cf. Davies 2010: 371–83).

Other scholars have recently turned their attention to the documents themselves for a canonical editing of the texts, which presupposes a robust canonical consciousness. In other words, there was an awareness within the biblical period itself that this literature was *sui generis*, and that canonicity was not finally a quality that was superimposed on the texts by an external authority but was an inherent quality of the texts themselves. Thus, a final redaction of the material demarcated the texts in number and structure. This coincided with a growing consciousness that the age of revelation was over, and thus steps were put in place to signify and highlight the importance of the canonical documents and emphasize the significance of memorization, reflection and wisdom.[9] Some of the evidence is as follows:

1. There is an extraordinary emphasis at the beginning of each major division on the biblical canon with a focus on the Word of God. For example, Genesis begins with the ten-fold repetition of "God said," the first of which creates light and establishes a rhythm between the day and night (Gen. 1:1-5). The second division begins with the importance of meditating on the divine Torah day and night (Josh. 1:8-9), and in the third division after the introductory Ruth, which essentially functions as a preface to the Psalter, the same expression occurs, i.e. to meditate on the Torah day and night (Ps. 1:2-3). Also, at the end of each division, the same feature appears. The Torah concludes with the death of Moses, the pre-eminent prophet of the Word of God (Deut. 24:10-12), the Prophets end with a call to remember the Torah of Moses and to prepare for the coming of Elijah before the day of Yahweh (Mal. 4:4-6, [3:22-24 Heb.]), and the Writings conclude with a word from both the Torah and the Prophets and the command to rebuild the temple being a fulfillment of Jeremiah's prophecy of seventy years of judgment for Sabbath neglect, which itself refers back to a prophecy in the Torah (2 Chr. 36:22-23; cf. Jer. 25, Dan. 9, and Lev. 26). This extraordinary emphasis on the Word of God suggests an awareness of the importance of the texts. These are not just ordinary documents. They are texts which produce life and light. It is as if the message of these texts is saying: Pay attention to these texts! Listen to them, get them into your heart. The Shema (Deut. 6:4–9) has now become the entire canon.
2. There is also in this tripartite structure an extraordinary eschatological emphasis. One of the key points in the literature has been the place of David. In the Torah there is the promise of a king from Judah who will rule the nations. It is no accident then that an eternal covenant is made with David from the tribe of Judah in the Former Prophets, and that hope is kept alive in the Latter Prophets when it seems as if it has almost become extinct. God was going to build for

---

[9] Some of the early scholarship stresses these redactions for the first two divisions and this has been followed by others more recently: see Blenkinsopp 1977; Chapman 2000. Others have expanded the domain to the entire canon: Dempster 1997: 23–56; Koorevaar 1997: 42–76. But it is important to note that a precursor for this view was Blau, 1901: 140-150.

David a house (dynasty) when he had desired to build for God a house (temple) (2 Sam. 7). The Writings focus on this Davidic figure at the beginning with the anticipation of David's birth and his genealogy (Ruth 4:17-22), and his virtual messianic status in the Psalter (Pss. 2, 72, 89, and 110). The conclusion with Chronicles has a long genealogical beginning which ends when David arrives on the historical scene. Indeed, the Chronicler seems to pin the hopes of the future on this figure and the temple. It is probably no accident then that this version of the Tanak which begins with Genesis and ends with Chronicles has as its midpoint that strange text about Jehoiachin being released from prison in Babylon and raised to a position of prominence. This is the mid-point of this Hebrew Bible. And thus, the endpoint is Cyrus' call for someone to go up and build a temple in Jerusalem. Here the Hebrew Bible brings the two houses together (dynasty and temple). This is clearly an eschatological emphasis, with the expectation of a Davidide to accomplish it all.

The focal points of ethics and eschatology are not incompatible with each other (cf. Koorevaar's insightful work who sees these themes at odds with each other, but this is unnecessary, Koorevaar 2014: 501-12). At the ending then of the first division, there is a focus on Israel outside the land; at the middle of the canon, Jehoiachin a Davidide in exile is outside the land; and at the end of the Prophets, even though Israel is in the land, it seems as if they are living under the threat of exile, while the closing of Chronicles emphasizes exile again. But the response for Israel is to wait for the salvation while meditating on the Torah and the Prophets and the Writings. As the first book ends with the hope that someday God would visit the Israelites in exile in Egypt and bring them up from there, the last book ends on the same note that God would visit them in Babylon and send them up to the land of promise. The call to return to the land at the end of Chronicles is laden with eschatological import, recalling the Torah (Deut. 30:1-19) and the Prophets (Isa. 40–55). The mourning and waiting of Israel in lonely exile will soon be over (Johnstone 2000).

3. Different tripartite models probably derived from this original exemplar which is reflected in the baraita preserved in the Talmud.[10] The example of Josephus is more easily explained as a deviation from this particular arrangement by moving all the historical books to the prophetic section and leaving the lyrical and proverbial literature to the third section. This would have pleased a Greek and Roman audience with their concern for symmetry and order, and the idea that there were twenty-two books in line with the letters of the Hebrew alphabet would have also been important for Jerome. This focus on genre may also have influenced the Septuagint, whose later codices have divided the books into four major categories: Law, History, Prophecy and Poetry.[11] The latter two categories

---

[10] I am indebted to Peter Gentry for some of the following discussion.
[11] Codex Vaticanus: Law, History, Poetry, Prophecy; Sinaiticus: [Law], History, Prophecy, Poetry; Alexandrinus: Law, History, Prophecy, Poetry, History. In the early Greek lists there are some similar orders. Bryennios: Law, History, Poetry, Prophecy, History; Melito: Law, History, Poetry, Prophecy +Esdras; Origen: Law, History, Poetry, Prophecy +Job, Esther.

may switch and there is some overlap in the books. But it is clear "That the Greek canon lists from the first four centuries attest a very stable collection that consistently mirrored the Jewish canon" (Gallagher and Meade 2017: 27). Secondly, the example of Jerome's list of twenty-four books, with Ruth and Lamentations included in the Writings, is arranged in chronological order. Finally, in the list appended to Cairensis, and in the Aleppo and Leningrad codices, the books are arranged chronologically, with the intent of beginning the writings with a book which begins with Adam, and placing the Megillot in chronological order and closing with Ezra-Nehemiah. These other orders blur some of the macro-structural significance found in the first explicit order recorded in the baraita in the Talmud.

Why there is no evidence of explicit lists and enumeration before the destruction of the temple is easily explained if the temple were a repository for the most holy books in Judaism. There is no question that sacred space and sacred text were coincidental from the beginning of Israel's history. The Ten Words, the first canon in ancient Israel, was placed in the holiest space in the sanctuary, in the immediate presence of God, in his throne room on earth. The scroll of Deuteronomy was laid up nearby as were other important documents throughout Israel's history. Consequently, it was no accident that a scroll was discovered in the temple during a dark period in the nation's history (see Beckwith 1985: 63–105; van der Toorn 2009; Gentry 2021). In a recent study Timothy Stone explains the importance of explicit lists and numeration of books after the destruction of the temple in 70 CE. In observing that meticulous precision and order was the hallmark of sacred space in the ancient world, never mind ancient Israel, Stone remarks:

> Imagine the temple without a collection of sacred documents or that they are haphazardly piled in a corner or on a shelf. In my judgment, this is unthinkable, whereas a temple collection gives a plausible answer to Kraft's doubts about canonical assumptions. In the cultural context of a temple collection, the boundaries and order of the canon may well be more—not less—important than they are today. To make lists of holy books while the temple remained standing would be superfluous. It is precisely this sacred *space*, and not some sacred *list*, that one would expect to be meaningful in the conceptual world of Judaism! Scholars' demand for a list may (ironically) betray an anachronistic appeal to the *formulation* of canons *as* lists in the second to fourth century CE in the church.
>
> Stone 2013: 70

It is no accident then that the synagogue and the early New Testament church inherited this tripartite canon. The late Brevard Childs wrote about the canon of the Old Testament that it "was not a late extrinsic validation of the corpus of its writings but involved a series of decisions deeply affecting the shape of its books . . . . Israel did not testify to its own self-understanding but by means of a canon bore witness to the divine source of its life" (Childs 1979: 59). The tripartite structure with its intentional symmetry, its contours and shape was not an arbitrary organization of ancient literature but had immense theological significance. Its final shape showed that the intention of the canon was that this source of life should be integrated into a person's consciousness repeatedly: the great word of God which created the world (Gen. 1) was made to be internalized by Israel's leadership (Josh. 1), be the continual source of delight for the people of Israelite (Ps. 1) and so inspire hope for the future in anticipation of a new world (2 Chr. 36:22–23).

Excursus

Comparison of arrangement in oldest orders

Table 2.1 Baba Batra 14b

Torah	Prophets	Writings
Genesis	Joshua	Ruth
Exodus	Judges	Psalms
Leviticus	Samuel	Job
Numbers	Kings	Proverbs
Deuteronomy	Jeremiah	Ecclesiastes
	Ezekiel	Song of Songs
	Isaiah	Lamentations
	Twelve	Daniel
		Esther
		Ezra – Nehemiah
		Chronicles

Table 2.2 Masoretes (Cairo [List], Aleppo, Leningrad)

Torah	Prophets	Writings
Genesis	Joshua	Chronicles
Exodus	Judges	Psalms
Leviticus	Samuel	Job
Numbers	Kings	Proverbs
Deuteronomy	Isaiah	Ruth
	Jeremiah	Song of Songs
	Ezekiel	Ecclesiastes
	Twelve	Lamentations
		Esther
		Daniel
		Ezra – Nehemiah

Table 2.3 Jerome—Prologus Galeatus

Torah	Prophets	Writings
Genesis	Joshua	Job
Exodus	Judges	Psalms
Leviticus	Ruth	Proverbs
Numbers	Samuel	Ecclesiastes
Deuteronomy	Kings	Song of Songs
	Isaiah	Daniel
	Jeremiah	Chronicles
	Lamentations	Ezra – Nehemiah
	Ezekiel	Esther
	Twelve	

Table 2.4 Josephus—Against Apion*

Torah	Prophets	Writings
Genesis	Job	Psalms
Exodus	Joshua	Proverbs
Leviticus	Judges-Ruth	Ecclesiastes
Numbers	Samuel	Song of Songs
Deuteronomy	Kings	
	Isaiah	
	Jeremiah-Lamentations	
	Lamentations	
	Ezekiel	
	Twelve	
	Chronicles	
	Ezra-Nehemiah	
	Esther	

*For this probable order see Beckwith 1985: 451, 457; Steinmann 1999: 116. For other possibilities see Lim 2013: 45.

Bibliography

Alexander, T. Desmond. (1998), "Royal Expectations in Genesis to Kings: Their Importance for Biblical Theology," *TB* 49: 191–212.

Barton, John. (2007), *Oracles of God: Perceptions of Ancient Prophecy in Israel after the Exile*, New York: Oxford University Press.

Beckwith, Roger T. (1985), *The Old Testament Canon of the New Testament Church and Its Background in Early Judaism*, Grand Rapids: Eerdmans.

Bentjees, P. (2000), "Canon and Scripture in the Book of Ben Sira," in M. Saebo et al. (eds.), *Hebrew Bible/Old Testament: History of Its Interpretation. From the Beginnings to the Middle Ages (until 1300)*, 2:591–605, Gottingen: Vandenhoeck & Ruprecht.

Blau, Ludwig. (1901), "Bible Canon," *Jewish Encyclopedia* 3:140–150.

Blenkinsopp, Joseph. (1977), *Prophecy and Canon: A Contribution to the Study of Jewish Origins*, Notre Dame: University of Notre Dame Press.

Brandt, Peter. (2001), *Endgestalten Des Kanons: Das Arrangement Der Schriften Israels in Der Jüdischen Und Christlichen Bibel*, Berlin: Philo.

Chapman, Stephen B. (2000), *The Law and the Prophets: A Study in Old Testament Canon Formation*, Forschungen Zum Alten Testament 27, Tübingen: Mohr Siebeck.

Childs, Brevard S. (1979), *Introduction to the Old Testament as Scripture*, Philadelphia: Fortress Press.

Clines, David J. A. (1997), *Theme of the Pentateuch*, 2nd edition, Sheffield: Bloomsbury T&T Clark.

Davies, Philip R. (2010), "The Nationalization of the Jewish Canon," *Cahiers Du Centre Gustav Glotz* 21: 371–83.

Dempster, Stephen G. (1997), "An 'Extraordinary Fact': 'Torah and Temple' and the Contours of the Hebrew Canon, Part 1," *TB* 48: 23–56.

Dempster, Stephen G. (2001), "From Many Texts to One: The Formation of the Hebrew Bible," in P. Michèle Daviau et al. (eds.), *The World of the Aramaeans I: Biblical Studies in Honour of Paul-Eugene Dion*, I:19–56, Sheffield: Sheffield Academic Press.

Dempster, Stephen G. (2006), "The Prophets, the Canon and a Canonical Approach: No Empty Word," in C. Bartholomew et al., *Canon and Biblical Interpretation*, Grand Rapids: Zondervan: 293–329.

Dempster, Stephen G. (2008), "Torah, Torah, Torah: The Emergence of the Tripartite Canon," in Emanuel Tov and Craig A. Evans (eds.), *Exploring the Origins of the Bible: Canon Formation in Historical, Theological and Literary Perspective*, Acadia Studies in Bible and Theology, 87–128, Grand Rapids: Baker Academic.

Dempster, Stephen G. (2009), "Canons on the Left and Canons on the Right: Finding a Resolution in the Canon Debate," *JETS* 52: 47–77.

Dempster, Stephen G. (2016), "The Old Testament Canon, Josephus, and Cognitive Environment," in D. Carson (ed.), *The Enduring Authority of the Christian Scriptures*, 321–61. Grand Rapids: Eerdmans.

Dempster, Stephen G. (2018), "The Tripartite Canon and the Theology of the Prophetic Word," in Andrew T. Abernethy (ed.), *Interpreting the Old Testament Theologically: Essays in Honor of Willem A. VanGemeren*, 74–94, Grand Rapids: Zondervan.

Gallagher, Edmon L., and John D. Meade. (2017), *The Biblical Canon Lists from Early Christianity: Texts and Analysis*, Oxford: Oxford University Press.

Gentry, Peter J. (2021), "MasPs^a and the Early History of the Hebrew Psalter: Notes on Canon and Text," in Gregory R. Lanier and J. Nicholas Reid (eds.), *The Books and Especially the Parchments: Studies on the Intersection of Text, Paratext, and Reception (Festschrift for Charles E. Hill)*. Texts and Editions for New Testament Study, Leiden: Brill.

Gillingham, Susan E. (1998), *One Bible, Many Voices: Different Approaches to Biblical Studies*, Grand Rapids: Eerdmans.

Haran, Menahem. (1993), "Archives, Libraries and the Order of Biblical Books," *Journal of Ancient Near Eastern Studies* 22: 51–61.

Hurtado, Larry W. (2006), *The Earliest Christian Artifacts: Manuscripts and Christian Origins*, Grand Rapids: Eerdmans.

Johnstone, William. (2000), "Hope for Jubilee: The Last Word in the Hebrew Bible," *Evangelical Quarterly* 72: 307–14.
Koorevaar, Hendrik J. (1997), "Die Chronik Als Intendierter Abschluss Des Alttestamentlichen Kanons," *Jahrbuch Für Evangelikale Theologie* 11: 42–76.
Koorevaar, Hendrik J. (2014), "The Exile and Return Model: A Proposal for the Original Macrostructure of the Hebrew Canon," *Journal for the Evangelical Society* 57: 501-12.
Leimann, Sid Z. (1989) "Josephus and the Canon of the Bible," in Louis H. Feldman and Gōhei Hata (eds.), *Josephus, the Bible, and History*, 50–58. Leiden: Brill.
Lewis, Jack P. (1964), "What Do We Mean by Jabneh?" *Journal of Bible and Religion* 32: 125–32.
Lewis, Jack P. (2002), "Jamnia Revisited." in Lee M. McDonald and James A. Sanders (eds.), *The Canon Debate*, 146–62, Peabody, MA: Hendrickson Publishers.
Lim, Timothy H. (2013), *The Formation of the Jewish Canon*, New Haven: Yale University Press.
Margolis, Max Leopold. (1922), *The Hebrew Scriptures in the Making*, Philadelphia: The Jewish Publication Society of America.
McDonald, Lee Martin. (2017), *The Formation of the Biblical Canon: Volume 1: The Old Testament: Its Authority and Canonicity*, London: Bloomsbury Publishing.
McDonald, Lee Martin and James A. Sanders (eds.). (2002), *The Canon Debate*, Peabody MA: Hendrickson Publishers.
Morgan, Donn F. (ed.). (2018), "Writings as Post-Exilic Literature and Canon," in *The Oxford Handbook of the Writings of the Hebrew Bible*. Oxford: Oxford University Press.
Pedersen, Olaf. (1998), *Archives and Libraries of the Ancient Near East 1500-300 B.C.*, Bethesda: CDL Press.
Qimron, E., and J. Strugnell, (1994), *Qumran Cave 4 V: Miqsat Ma'ase Ha-Torah.*, Discoveries in the Juadaean Desert 10, Oxford: Clarendon Press.
Roberts, Colin H., and T. C. Skeat. (1987), *The Birth of the Codex*, London: British Academy.
Ryle, Herbert Edward. (1904), *The Canon of the Old Testament: An Essay on the Gradual Growth and Formation of the Hebrew Canon of Scripture*, London: Macmillan and Co., Limited.
Sailhamer, John H. (1995), *Introduction to Old Testament Theology: A Canonical Approach*, Grand Rapids: Zondervan.
Sarna, Nahum M. (1971), "The Order of the Books." in Charles Berlin (ed.), *Studies in Honor of I. Edward Kiev*, 407–13, New York: Ktav.
Steinberg, Julius, and Timothy J. Stone. (2015), "The Historical Formation of the Writings in Antiquity," in Julius Steinberg and Timothy J. Stone (eds.), *The Shape of the Writings*, Siphrut: Literature and Theology of the Hebrew Scriptures 16, 1–58, Winona Lake, IN: Eisenbrauns.
Steinmann, Andrew. (1999), *The Oracles of God: The Old Testament Canon*, St. Louis: Concordia Publishing House.
Steins, Georg. (2015), "Torah Binding and Canon Closure," in Julius Steinberg and Timothy J. Stone (eds.), *The Shape of the Writings*, Siphrut: Literature and Theology of the Hebrew Scriptures 16, 238–80, Winona Lake, IN: Eisenbrauns.
Stone, Timothy J. (2013), *The Compilational History of the Megilloth: Canon, Contoured Intertextuality and Meaning in the Writings*, Tübingen: Mohr Siebeck.
Ulrich, E. (2003), "The Non-Attestation of a Tripartite Canon in 4QMMT," *Catholic Biblical Quarterly* 65: 202–14.

van der Toorn, Karel. (2009), *Scribal Culture and the Making of the Hebrew Bible*, Cambridge: Harvard University Press.

von Rad, Gerhard. (1962), *Old Testament Theology: The Theology of Israel's Historical Traditions*, translated by David Stalker, 2 Vols. New York: Harper and Row.

Morgan, Donn F. (ed.). (2018), "Writings as Post-Exilic Literature and Canon," in *The Oxford Handbook of the Writings of the Hebrew Bible*, Oxford: Oxford University Press.

3

The Canonical Shape of the Greek Old Testament

John D. Meade

Today's Hebrew Bible or Tanak contains twenty-four books in three divisions or in a tripartite shape: five books of the Torah, eight books of the Neviim (i.e. Prophets), and eleven books of the Ketuvim (i.e. Writings). The contents and structure (though not the precise order of books) is attested as early as the fourth-century CE testimony of Jerome (*Prologus Galeatus*), and perhaps earlier, depending on the date (*ca.* 200 CE?) of the list in the Babylonian Talmud (Baba Bathra 14b). Although not the purpose of this article, we must examine the putative, earliest evidence for this structure, paying attention to how these texts may or may not influence and shape the early Greek Old Testament.

Today's Christian Old Testament (Protestant, Catholic, Greek Orthodox) has the same basic quadripartite structure: Law (Gen.–Deut.), History (Josh.–Est.), Poetry (Job–Song), and Prophecy (Isa.–Mal.). These canons do not agree on the exact contents or the orders of books in each section. The Protestant canon mirrors the contents of the Jewish canon but in quadripartite arrangement according to literary genres. The Catholic canon includes Judith and Tobit among the History books, Wisdom of Solomon and Sirach/Ecclesiasticus among the Poetic books, Baruch among the Prophetic books, and 1–2 Maccabees at the very end of the Old Testament. The Greek Orthodox Bible includes 1 Esdras and adds 3 Maccabees to 1–2 Maccabees, retaining them at the end of the History books—not at the end of the Old Testament. This chapter will trace the historical development of the canonical shape of the Greek Old Testament through analysis of its early contents and arrangements.

Contents of the Greek Old Testament

Before describing the arrangement of the Greek Old Testament, defining its limits and contents is crucial. Surveying the evidence and views of the late Second Temple period up to the period of the Greek Christian canon lists and manuscripts will provide the necessary bearings for the discussion of the arrangement of the Greek Old Testament (for a more detailed treatment of the Biblical canon and its relationship to "the Septuagint," see Meade 2021).

Late Second Temple period

Evidence for a recognized, exclusive list of biblical books or a canon first appeared after 94 CE in Josephus' *Against Apion*, where he refers to "only twenty-two books," which he subsequently grouped into three sections: five of Moses, thirteen of prophets, and four remaining books (*A. Ap.* 1.37–42). Around 100 CE, *4 Ezra* 14:44–47 numbered the books published openly as twenty-four (Ossandón Widow 2018: 185–89), and *Gos. Thom.* 52 in the second half of the second century reveals that "twenty-four prophets have spoken in Israel, and they all spoke of you [i.e., Jesus]." The numbering of these books as twenty-two or twenty-four attests the narrow scope of the Jewish canon at that time and may indicate its closure at an earlier time, but the evidence for the earlier period is limited.

In the past, many scholars believed that around 90 CE at a council at Yavneh (or Jamnia) the Jews closed the books that filled the Writings, and therefore the Jewish tripartite canon that soon became the Rabbinic Bible or the Hebrew Bible was considered closed from the second century. However, most scholars now view Yavneh as only an assembly or a school, without authority, that discussed the scriptural status of Ecclesiastes and Song of Songs but made no official ruling. After the research of Lewis (1964), it became untenable to hold that this assembly was the occasion for the closing of the Jewish canon; the date of closing the Writings and therefore the close of the canon could be around 164 BCE (Beckwith 1985: 152) or in the second century CE (McDonald 2017: 484).

From the earlier period, six passages of the reputed Jewish tripartite canon consisting of Torah, Neviim, and Ketuvim have garnered attention because the putative three divisions were thought to include closed collections of books (below see discussion of *Prol. Sir.* 1–2, 8–10, 23–25; 4QMMT C 10–11; 2 Macc. 2:13–15; Philo *Vit. Cont.* 25; Luke 24:44; Josephus *Ag. Ap.* 1.39–40). However, the exact contents of the Neviim and its relationship to the third section, which still had no definite title by ca. 130 BCE, are still open to debate. John Barton (1986: 39–41) cautions against an entirely clear line separating "Prophets from Writings around the turn of the era." More than uncertainty of the contents within these sections, scholars now question whether any of these passages refer to the tripartite Jewish canon that would later be known from *b. Bat.* 14b, and therefore, they call the relative antiquity of the tripartite canon into question and favor an earlier quadripartite structure (McDonald 2018: 408–10).

These six passages along with the many bipartite references indicate a corpus of scripture with inviolable authority present within the diversity of Judaism, but they do not identify specific books (but see Hanhart 2002: 3; Beckwith 1985: 164–65), and whether they indicate the corpus is closed or open remains disputed (Barton 2013: 150). If the bipartite reference, "the Law and the Prophets," as Barton (1986: 44–55) posits, refers to Torah and non-Torah scripture, then the corpus of Scripture could still be quite wide. The debate over whether the compositions of the Second Temple period are proof of scripture proliferation (Mroczek 2016) or evidence of "revelatory exegesis" or modified modes of revelation (Jassen 2016: 368) continue unabated. In any case, VanderKam (2012: 55) concludes that there was "a limited set of books that was a functional collection of authoritative texts" on which Jewish groups could agree. Based on Qumran, Philo, NT, and Josephus, there probably was a Jewish canon in the late Second Temple period that consisted of the Torah, Prophets, Psalms, and other books. That is, a strong core canon had already been formed, but there probably was some uncertainty over some books at the edges as the varied reception of Esther and as the rabbinic statements on Ecclesiastes, Song of Songs, and Sirach show. Thus, the rabbis were defending a more-or-less defined canon (with some fuzziness around the edges) that they had received from the pre-70 CE period (Alexander 2007: 65). Researchers must confess that the paucity of evidence means that not all their questions of this early period will be answered.

This same paucity of evidence also poses a challenge for proving that Jews in Alexandria fixed a canon containing more books than Josephus' exclusive twenty-two books, which he claims all Jews regard (for the 'Alexandrian Canon Hypothesis,' see Swete 1900: 197). Since the work of Albert Sundberg (1964: 51), most scholars have abandoned this hypothesis of an expanded Alexandrian canon: "It is to be remembered that the hypothesis is built upon what is, at best, a tenuous foundation and is ... incapable of proof." Philo of Alexandria (*ca.* 20 BCE–40 CE) cited the Pentateuch numerous times and by comparison made minimal use of many of the other books that Josephus would later include in his twenty-two (Meade 2021: 209). Thus, some conclude that Philo esteemed only the Pentateuch as Scripture and the rest of the books as tradition (Lim 2013: 91, 183), while others maintain that Philo essentially held to "the Law and the Prophets" (Chapman 2000: 271–73). Furthermore, the New Testament's scriptural citations offer no evidence for the Alexandrian canon. Thus, if this canon existed, there is no early support for it, and we must wait for the fourth- and fifth-century magisterial codices to which we will return below.

Old Testament canon lists

The Greek canon lists present the clearest evidence of the situation (Gallagher and Meade 2017: 70–173). From around 100–400 CE, there are twelve OT canon lists (see Table 3.1). In approximate chronological order, they are as follows:

- The Bryennios List (*ca.* 100–150)
- Melito of Sardis (*ca.* 170)
- Origen (*ca.* 220; *apud* Eusebius)
- Cyril of Jerusalem (*ca.* 350)
- Athanasius (367)
- The Synod of Laodicea (before 380)
- Apostolic Canons (*ca.* 380)
- Amphilochius of Iconium (*ca.* 380)
- Gregory of Nazianzus (381–90)
- Epiphanius (three lists; *Panarion* in *ca.* 375; *On Weights and Measures* in 392).

After 400, there are at least seven more Greek canon lists of the OT up to *ca.* 850 (see Table 3.2):

Table 3.1 Greek canon lists *ca.* 100–400

Bryennios	Melito	Origen	Cyril of Jerusalem	Athanasius	Laodicea
Genesis–Leviticus	Genesis–Exodus	Genesis–Deuteronomy	**Historical Books** (*Five of Law*) Genesis–Deuteronomy	Genesis–Deuteronomy	Genesis–Deuteronomy
Joshua Deuteronomy	Numbers Leviticus	Joshua Judges-Ruth	Joshua Judges-Ruth	Joshua Judges Ruth	Joshua Judges-Ruth Esther
Numbers Ruth Job Judges Psalter	Deuteronomy Joshua Judges Ruth 1–4 Kingdoms	1–4 Kingdoms 1–2 Chronicles 1–2 Esdras Psalms Proverbs	1–4 Kingdoms 1–2 Chronicles 1–2 Esdras Esther **Poetic Books** Job	1–4 Kingdoms 1–2 Chronicles 1–2 Esdras Psalms Proverbs	1–4 Kingdoms 1–2 Chronicles 1–2 Esdras Psalms (150) Proverbs
1–4 Kingdoms 1–2 Chronicles Proverbs Ecclesiastes	1–2 Chronicles Psalms Proverbs Ecclesiastes	Ecclesiastes Song [The Twelve] Isaiah	Psalms Proverbs Ecclesiastes Song	Ecclesiastes Song Job	Ecclesiastes Song Job The Twelve
Song	Song	Jeremiah + Lamentations + Epistle of Jeremiah	**Prophetic Books** The Twelve	**The Prophets** The Twelve	Isaiah
Jeremiah The Twelve Isaiah	Job Isaiah **Prophets** Jeremiah The Twelve Daniel Ezekiel Esdras	Daniel Ezekiel Job Esther *Outside*: Maccabees	Isaiah Jeremiah+ Ezekiel Daniel+	Isaiah Jeremiah+ Ezekiel Daniel+ *To be read*: Wisdom Sirach Esther Judith Tobit	Jeremiah+ Ezekiel Daniel+
Ezekiel Daniel 1–2 Esdras Esther					

The Canonical Shape of the Greek Old Testament

Apostolic Canons	Gregory of Nazianzus	Amphilochius	Epiphanius 1	Epiphanius 2	Epiphanius 3
Genesis–Deuteronomy	Genesis–Deuteronomy	**Pentateuch** Genesis–Deuteronomy	Genesis–Deuteronomy	**Law Pentateuch** Genesis–Deuteronomy	Genesis–Deuteronomy
Joshua	Joshua	Joshua	Joshua	**Poetry Pentateuch** Job	Joshua
Judges	Judges	Judges	Judges	Psalter	Job
Ruth	Ruth	Ruth	Ruth	Proverbs	Judges
1–4 Kingdoms	1–4 Kingdoms	1–4 Kingdoms	Job	Ecclesiastes	Ruth
1–2 Chronicles	1–2 Chronicles	1–2 Chronicles	Psalter	Song	Psalter
1–2 Esdras	1–2 Esdras	1–2 Esdras	Proverbs	**Hagiographa Pentateuch** Joshua	1–2 Chronicles
Esther	Job	**Poetic Books** Job	Ecclesiastes	Judges + Ruth	1–4 Kingdoms
Judith	Psalms	Psalms	Song	1–2 Chronicles	Proverbs
1–4 Maccabees	Ecclesiastes	Proverbs	1–4 Kingdoms	1–2 Kingdoms	Ecclesiastes
Job	Song	Ecclesiastes	1–2 Chronicles	3–4 Kingdoms	Song
Psalms (151)	Proverbs	Song	The Twelve	**Prophecy Pentateuch** The Twelve	The Twelve
Five of Solomon	The Twelve	The Twelve	Isaiah	Isaiah	Isaiah
16 Prophets	Hosea	Hosea	Jeremiah+	Jeremiah+	Jeremiah+
	Amos	Amos	Ezekiel	Ezekiel	Ezekiel
	Micah	Micah	Daniel	Daniel	Daniel
	Joel	Joel	1–2 Esdras	**Remaining** 1–2 Esdras	1–2 Esdras
	Jonah	Obadiah	Esther	Esther	Esther
Outside:	Obadiah	Jonah			
Sirach	Nahum	Nahum			
	Habakkuk	Habakkuk			
	Zephaniah	Zephaniah	*Disputed*:	*Useful + Beneficial*:	
	Haggai	Haggai	Sirach	Wisdom	
	Zechariah	Zechariah	Wisdom	Sirach	
	Malachi	Malachi			
	Isaiah	Isaiah			
	Jeremiah	Jeremiah			
	Ezekiel	Ezekiel			
	Daniel	Daniel			
		? Esther ?			

Table 3.2 Greek canon lists *ca.* 401–850

Hypomnestikon	Dialogue of Timothy + Aquila	Ps.-Chrysostom 1	Ps.-Chrysostom 2	Ps.-Athanasius	John of Damascus	Nicephorus I
Genesis–Deuteronomy	Genesis–Deuteronomy	Genesis–Deuteronomy	Genesis–Exodus	Genesis–Deuteronomy	**Law Pentateuch** Genesis–Deuteronomy	Genesis–Deuteronomy
			Numbers–Deuteronomy Joshua		**Hagiographa Pentateuch**	
Joshua	Joshua	Joshua		Joshua	Joshua	Joshua
Judges	Judges-Ruth	Judges	Joshua	Judges	Judges + Ruth	Judges-Ruth
Ruth		Ruth	Judges	Ruth	1–2 Kingdoms	1–4 Kingdoms
			Ruth		3–4 Kingdoms	1–2 Chronicles
1–4 Kingdoms	1–2 Chronicles	1–4 Kingdoms	1–4 Kingdoms	1–4 Kingdoms	1–2 Chronicles	1–2 Esdras
1–2 Chronicles	1–4 Kingdoms	Esdras	Sirach	1–2 Chronicles	**Poetry Pentateuch**	Psalter (151)
					Job	
Esdras	Job	Proverbs	Isaiah	1–2 Esdras	Psalter	Proverbs
Psalms	Psalter of David	Sirach	Jeremiah	Psalter (151)	Proverbs	Ecclesiastes
Proverbs	Proverbs of Solomon	Ecclesiastes	Ezekiel	Proverbs	Ecclesiastes	Song
Ecclesiastes	Ecclesiastes with the Songs	Song	Daniel	Ecclesiastes	Song	Job
Song of Songs	The Twelve	16 Prophets	Hosea	Song	**Prophecy Pentateuch** Isaiah	
					The Twelve	
Twelve	Isaiah	Job	Joel	Job	Isaiah	Jeremiah
Isaiah	Jeremiah	David (= Ps.)	Amos	Twelve	Jeremiah+	Baruch
Jeremiah	Ezekiel		Obadiah	Hosea	Ezekiel	Ezekiel
Ezekiel	Daniel		Jonah	Joel	Daniel	Daniel
Daniel	Esdras		Micah	Amos	**Remaining**	The Twelve
					1–2 Esdras	
	Judith		Nahum	Obadiah	Esther	
Job	Esther		Habakkuk	Jonah	*Virtuous + Beautiful:*	*Antilegomena:*
			Zephaniah	Micah	Wisdom	1–3 Maccabees

Outside:	Apocrypha:	Haggai	Nahum		Wisdom
Esther	Tobit	Zechariah	Habakkuk		Sirach
Maccabees	Wisdom	Malachi	Zephaniah		Psalms + Odes of Solomon
					Esther
	Sirach		Haggai		Judith
			Zechariah		Susanna
			Malachi		Tobit and Tobias
			Isaiah		
			Jeremiah+		
			Ezekiel		
			Daniel		
			To be read:		
			Esther	Sirach	
			Judith		
			Tobit		
			Wisdom		
			Sirach		

- The *Hypomnestikon* or Joseph's Bible Notes (*ca.* 393–431; Menzies 1996: 86–87)
- *The Dialogue of Timothy and Aquila* (sixth century; Conybeare 1898: 66)
- Ps.-Chrysostom (two lists; *ca.* 400–450; Barone, forthcoming)
- Ps.-Athanasius (*ca.* 500; PG 28:284–99)
- John of Damascus (*ca.* 754; PG 94:1180)
- Nicephorus I (*ca.* 850; PG 100:1056–60).

The contents of the lists

The twelve Greek lists from the early period show remarkable unity in their contents, which largely overlap with the traditional Hebrew canon of twenty-two books. That is, in no uniform order, these lists include the five books of the Law of Moses, the Former and Latter Prophets, and the five Poetic books. Esther was normally included, but some lists—such as Melito, Athanasius, and Gregory—still excluded this book probably because of the earlier Jewish disputes over it. Jeremiah regularly encompassed not only Lamentations but also Baruch and the Epistle of Jeremiah. The title "Daniel" usually subsumed the works called Susanna and Bel and the Dragon. 1 Esdras is usually joined by the variant literary edition of 2 Esdras, which equals Ezra-Nehemiah. Joosten (2016: 699) suggests that the relationship between 1 and 2 Esdras is comparable to Old Greek (OG hereafter) Daniel and "Theodotion" Daniel, as two versions of the same book. Furthermore, most lists do not comment on whether the Psalter contained 150 or 151 Psalms (though see Laodicea [150] and Apostolic Canons [151]) or which forms of Esther and Daniel were intended. The ancients probably viewed these differences with the Jewish canon as matters of textual form and not of canon, which, as we will see, they consistently referred to as the Hebrew canon. The Africanus-Origen correspondence and later Jerome highlight differences of textual form between Jews and Christians, but most Christians from the middle of the second century believed their canon was equal to the Jewish canon. Of these twelve lists, only the Apostolic Canons, which has a complex textual history, includes the deuterocanonical books, but even some of its Greek witnesses preserve the narrower list of books.

The seven later lists from *ca.* 401–850 largely reflect the earlier ones (see Table 3.3). John of Damascus, following Epiphanius, includes Esther and does not include the deuterocanonical books (cf. Epiphanius *De Mens. et Pond.* 4–5). The *Hypomnestikon* and Ps.-Athanasius omit Esther and do not include deuterocanonical books. Ps.-Athanasius, however, does report an alternative numbering of the canonical books where "some of the ancients" say that Ruth is joined to Judges and Esther is included to maintain the twenty-two books of the Hebrews. The *Dialogue of Timothy and Aquila* includes Judith. Nicephorus excludes Esther and is the first to include Baruch independently of Jeremiah. Francesca Barone has edited the materials for the critical edition of the *Synopsis Scripturae Sacrae* of Ps.-Chrysostom (Barone, forthcoming). Her work has revealed that all the deuterocanonical books in the *Synopsis* included in Migne, except for Sirach, should be removed from the reconstructed archetype of this work. Therefore, this source reveals a list that includes Sirach but also omitted 1 Chronicles–Judith, Job, Wisdom, Proverbs, Ecclesiastes, Song of Songs, and Psalms, probably showing the incompleteness of the archetype. Perhaps, the original work contained these books, and they were omitted accidentally through transmission. The original author may have considered more books canonical than he finally commented on and listed. Barone's edition of the *Synopsis*' Protheoria has the reading ὁ Ἰώβ ("Job"), instead of Ruth, which is the reading in Migne's edition.

In summary, these nineteen canon lists from *ca.* 100–850 provide the most specific information on the contents of the Greek OT, and significantly, none of these lists represents what scholars today would refer to as the Jewish Alexandrian Canon or the Septuagint Canon. There is remarkable consistency across them, but minimal variation does occur over the status of Esther or a deuterocanonical book here or there. The cause of this consistency appears to be the Hebrew canon and to this matter we now turn.

The significance of the Hebrew canon

Of these nineteen canon lists from around 100–850, thirteen mention explicitly or imply that their twenty-two books correspond to the twenty-two letters of the Hebrew alphabet and consequently the twenty-two books of the Jewish canon. The Bryennios List does not have twenty-two books, but its Hebrew names for the books associate it with these lists. Melito mentions a search for an accurate number but his list does not have twenty-two books. Still, its contents largely agree with the Hebrew canon. Interestingly, Hilary, Jerome, and Rufinus also preserve the connection between the Hebrew alphabet and the Christian Old Testament in Latin (Gallagher and Meade 2017: 194–222). Those who mention or imply the connection between the Hebrew alphabet and the canon are as follows:

- Origen (*apud* Eusebius)
- Cyril of Jerusalem (implied)
- Athanasius
- Synod of Laodicea (implied)
- Gregory of Nazianzus
- Epiphanius (three lists)
- The *Hypomnestikon* (implied)
- *Dialogue of Timothy and Aquila*
- Ps.-Athanasius
- John of Damascus
- Nicephorus I (implied).

These early Greek Christians believed that their twenty-two-book canon was formed consciously according to the twenty-two-book Hebrew canon, which corresponded to the twenty-two letters of the Hebrew alphabet. They mostly included books that would correspond with the contents of Josephus and *b. Bat.* 14b.

However, mere mention of the Hebrew alphabet did not mean that these canon lists equaled Baba Batra or the later Hebrew codices in every detail as described above. But early patristic canon theory with its focus on the Hebrew alphabet and the twenty-two books of the Hebrews ensured that early Christians would form their OT according to

Table 3.3 Select Greek manuscripts 4th–16th

Vaticanus	Sinaiticus	Alexandrinus	Venetus	Ra 130	Ra 106	Ra 68 (= Ra 122)	Ra 46
Octateuch	Octateuch (Defective)	Octateuch	Octateuch (> Genesis + Exodus)	Octateuch	Octateuch	Octateuch	Octateuch
1–4 Kingdoms		1–4 Kingdoms	1–4 Kingdoms	1–4 Kingdoms	1–4 Kingdoms	1–4 Kingdoms	1–4 Kingdoms
1–2 Chronicles	1–2 Chronicles (Defective)	1–2 Chronicles	1–2 Chronicles	1–2 Chronicles	1–2 Chronicles	1–2 Chronicles	1–2 Chronicles
1–2 Esdras	2 Esdras (Defective)	The Twelve	Esther	1–2 Esdras	1–2 Esdras	Isaiah	1–2 Esdras
Psalms		Isaiah	1–2 Esdras	Esther	Tobit	Jeremiah + Baruch + Lamentations + Epistle of Jeremiah	Esther
Proverbs	Esther	Jeremiah + Baruch + Lamentations + Epistle of Jeremiah	Job	Judith	Judith	Ezekiel	Judith
Ecclesiastes	Tobit	Ezekiel	Proverbs	1–3 Maccabees	Esther	Susanna + Daniel + Bel	1–4 Maccabees
Song	Judith	Daniel	Ecclesiastes	Psalms + Odes	Job	The Twelve	Tobit
Job	1 Maccabees	Esther	Song	Job	Proverbs	Job	Isaiah
Wisdom	4 Maccabees	Tobit	Wisdom	Proverbs	Ecclesiastes	Psalms	Jeremiah + Baruch + Lamentations + Epistle of Jeremiah
Sirach	Isaiah	Judith	Sirach	Ecclesiastes	Song	Proverbs	Ezekiel
Esther	Jeremiah (Defective)	1–2 Esdras	The Twelve	Song	Wisdom	Ecclesiastes	Susanna + Daniel + Bel
Judith	The Twelve (Defective)	1–4 Maccabees	Isaiah	Wisdom	Sirach	1–2 Esdras	The Twelve
		Ep. Mar.	Jeremiah + Baruch + Sirach Lamentations + Epistle of Jeremiah		Isaiah	Esther	Proverbs

		Hypoth. Psalms	Ezekiel	Isaiah	Jeremiah + Baruch + Lamentations + Epistle of Jeremiah	Wisdom	Ecclesiastes
Tobit	Psalms	Psalms + Odes	Susana + Daniel + Bel	Jeremiah + Baruch + Lamentations + Epistle of Jeremiah Ezekiel		Sirach	Song
The Twelve	Proverbs	Job	Tobit	Susanna + Daniel + Bel and the Dragon	Susanna + Daniel + Bel	Judith	Job
Isaiah	Ecclesiastes	Proverbs	Judith	The Twelve	The Twelve	Tobit	Wisdom
Jeremiah + Baruch + Lamentations + Epistle to Jeremiah Ezekiel	Song	Ecclesiastes	1–4 Maccabees		1–2 Maccabees	1–3 Maccabees	Sirach
	Wisdom	Song	*Chronographion from Adam to Justinian*		Psalms + Odes	(1 Maccabees frag. in 122)	
Susanna + Daniel + Bel	Sirach	Wisdom					
Sirach							

the Hebrew canon though with slight variation at the edges of that canon, perhaps due to the earlier Jewish disputes over the book of Esther (e.g., *b. Meg.* 7a).

Albert Sundberg (1964: 146) supposed that the Eastern Christian fixation with the Hebrew canon developed in the fourth century and not before. However, the Bryennios List and Melito's list from the second century show that Christians had already accepted the more limited Jewish canon by excluding the deuterocanonical books except for a possible, but improbable, mention of the Wisdom of Solomon in Melito. Although debated, Origen's canon list probably does not represent his own canon list but only that of the Jews, despite how Eusebius understood it (see Gallagher 2012: 37–38; Gallagher and Meade 2017: 85). Origen mentions specifically how the churches use Tobit and Judith, while the Jews do not (*Ep. Afr.* 19.13–17), and therefore, his canon was probably wider than the Hebrew canon. The later fourth-century lists, however, are in continuity with the earliest lists of the Old Testament, which was formed consciously after the Jewish canon in the few centuries prior to the fourth century. These lists included the books of the Hebrew canon in Greek dress and they regularly excluded the deuterocanonical books.

Thus, we must be careful when calling the early Christian canon "The Greek Old Testament" or the "Septuagint canon," especially if by these terms, we mean the wider canon that included the deuterocanonical books, which would result among churches of North Africa. Primarily, early Christians would have called the scriptures leading up to Jesus "the Old Testament," and most of these early Christians would have identified their canon with the Hebrew canon. Some early Christians such as Tertullian (*Cult. fem.* 1.3), Origen (*Ep. Afr.* 19.13–17), and Augustine (*Doctr. chr.* 2.8.12.25) conceived that the church established its own wider canon with more books than the Hebrew canon, for edification. Thus, when we turn to consider the orders of the books of the Christian Old Testament, we should consider the church's Old Testament in relation to "the Hebrew canon."

Manuscripts of the Greek Old Testament

We turn now to the material evidence of the Greek manuscripts of the Old Testament to see what they reveal about the Greek Old Testament. Yet, we encounter another problem of method, for the scribes of these manuscripts did not leave comments on their estimation of individual books, and this has led to challenges in interpreting their significance for the canon. But fortunately, early Christians made clear statements for how they interpreted the complex situation. They described their religious and spiritual literature according to a three-part schema—canonical-useful-apocryphal—showing that their conception of scripture does not equal our own. These early Christians differentiated between "canonical" scripture as their authority and "useful" scripture as books having diminished authority in cases of ecclesiastical doctrine (cf. Athanasius, *Ep. fest.* 39; Amphilochius, *Iambi ad Seleucum* 251–60; Epiphanius, *De Mens. et Ponds.* 4; Jerome, *Praef. in Sol.*; and Rufinus, *Symb.* 36). Thus, they cite books not in their canon as scripture and include them in manuscripts but probably intend fine distinctions among them. In Brill's *Textual History of the Bible*, Armin Lange (2016: 74–75) says:

I have also referred repeatedly to the invention of the mega-codices as a catalyst in the development of the Christian canon. It was only the mega-codex format that made it possible to combine all biblical Scriptures (Old and New Testament) into one book. Consequently, the question of which books should be included in such a mega-codex as the one Bible will have brought the issue of canon to the attention of Christian thinkers and officials.... It is all the more interesting that none of the three preserved mega-codices corresponds precisely in its table of contents with any of the canon lists of the fourth century.

Lange concludes that the codex corresponds to the biblical canon, and proceeds to put the codices into tension with the extant canon lists. But a more consistent way forward is to interpret the canon lists as reflecting the canon, while the codex includes canonical books alongside other useful religious and spiritual literature. That is: codex does not correspond to canon. With that caveat, we still must investigate the contents of the full Greek bible manuscripts.

There are only seven full Greek bible manuscripts up to the fifteenth century: B (fourth), S (fourth), A (fifth), Ra 68 (fifteenth; Venice), Ra 106 (fourteenth; Ferrara), Ra 122 (fifteenth; Venice), Ra 130 (twelfth/thirteenth; Vienna). Furthermore, there are two complete Old Testament manuscripts: Codex Venetus (eighth) and Ra 46 (thirteenth/fourteenth; Paris; without Psalms). Table 3.3 contains a the contents of these manuscripts.

The three magisterial codices of Sinaiticus, Vaticanus, and Alexandrinus agree on the inclusion of Judith, Tobit, Wisdom, and Sirach, though not on their order and placement. They do not all contain the books of Maccabees with only two including 1 and 4 Maccabees and only Alexandrinus containing 2 and 3 Maccabees. Therefore, the material evidence of the codices is conflicted over the inclusion of the Maccabean literature. But what about the other four books that are included in all three? It is possible the compilers considered these books canonical because they chose to include them. However, we must avoid anachronism and not foist the concreteness of our modern Bible on top of the ancient codex. In the absence of explicit statements from the scribes of these codices, it is more consistent to conclude with most of the canon lists that these books are useful scriptures and were not considered to be authoritative in matters of doctrine.

The later minuscule manuscripts continue to exhibit flux on the books of Maccabees. Furthermore, Ra 68 and Ra 122 reveal a tendency to differentiate the canonical books from the deuterocanonical books by placing the latter between the Old and New Testament. That is, the deuterocanonical books are not integrated with the canonical books (cf. Table 3.3).

Summary conclusions

This brief survey of the chief evidences for the history of the Greek Old Testament shows that the canon of the early Christians was formed consciously according to the Hebrew canon. Thus, by the term "Greek Old Testament," we should not communicate that the canon's contents of early Christianity were significantly different from the Hebrew canon. The contents of the magisterial codices of the fourth and fifth centuries reflect the wider reading habits of early Christians, not their canon. The canon lists reveal the canon.

The early Greek Christian canon lists more or less reflect the contents of the Hebrew canon. Therefore, we should ask also what these lists and other patristic statements might tell us about the shape and structure of the Greek OT vis-à-vis the Hebrew.

Shape of the Greek Old Testament

The Jewish canon eventually achieved a tripartite structure to which Jerome, the early rabbis, and the Masoretes attest, even though they disagree among themselves in book orders and reckonings. We have seen that early Christian lists largely mirror the contents of the Hebrew canon, but the earliest evidence to the Christian OT does not reflect the structure of the Tanak. Brief examination of the evidence for book arrangement reveals that in the early period there was probably little concern about book order. If there was an order of individual books in the temple or Jewish libraries, it could not have been long established because when lists were eventually proliferated, a fluidity of orders obtained, while the contents of the canon remained more or less stable.

Early arrangements of Hebrew scriptures

In this period, any arrangement or structure of the scriptures would be best described as conceptual, not material, since the codex did not become widely used until Christians popularized it in the second century. Furthermore, examples of multiple books on one scroll are limited to cases of the Torah (4QpaleoGen-Exod[1]) and the Minor Prophets (e.g. 4QXII[c]). Some have hypothesized there was an arrangement of the biblical scrolls according to the three corpora of Torah, Neviim, Ketuvim in libraries (Sarna 2000) or in the temple itself as sacred space (Steinberg and Stone 2015: 38–40). But this is only a guess problematized by the lack of consensus among our sources. Thus, discussion of early arrangement of the collection of scriptures has usually focused on the bipartite and tripartite formulae.

There are six early references to a putative tripartite structure of the Jewish canon, but most references to the Jewish Scriptures in the Second Temple period are bipartite: Moses/the law and the prophets (e.g. 1QS 1.2–3; Matt. 5:17). Early rabbinic literature refers to the Scriptures with the bipartite formula more often than a tripartite one (Leiman 1976: 58–59; Barton 1986: 52–54). To what shape of the Jewish scriptures, if any, does "Law and the Prophets" or similar point?

Earlier scholars understood "the Law and the Prophets" to refer to the Scriptures in the first two divisions of the Hebrew Bible, since on this view the Writings were not closed until Jamnia/Yavneh around 90 CE (Ryle 1892). However, most scholars now view Yavneh as only an assembly or a school, without authority, that discussed the scriptural status of Ecclesiastes and Song of Songs but made no official ruling (Lewis 1964). Many now believe that a reference to "prophets" in this period does not indicate a canonical division ("the Prophets"). Some hold that the formula refers to any book written by an inspired successor of Moses, implying an open collection of Scriptures

(Barton 1986: 44–55; cf. Barton 2013: 150). Others, who recognize that "prophets" is not a canonical division at the time of the NT, contend that "the Law and the Prophets" was used as an "umbrella term for the totality of scripture" (Chapman 2000: 269) and that the term as used in the NT and Jewish sources does not refer to books outside of the Hebrew canon (Steinberg and Stone 2015: 24–25). On these latter views, not much can be learned about the exact contents of the collection or its structure other than the Torah was primary. But debate persists over whether six passages further illumine the situation.

Early tripartite structure of the Jewish canon?

From the early period, six passages of the putative, Jewish tripartite canon consisting of Torah, Neviim, and Ketuvim have garnered attention (*Prol. Sir.* 1–2, 8–10, 24–25; 4QMMT C 10–11; 2 Macc. 2:13–15; Philo *Vit. Cont.* 25; Luke 24:44; Josephus *Ag. Ap.* 1.39–40). Some believe the divisions have bearing on the identity of the books since set books fill each section. There is debate, however, about how fixed the books were in each section at this time, some considering them recently closed, while others considering them still open and fluid.

Of these six references to a putative tripartite canon, only the Sirach prologue finds general acceptance for a tripartite structure (Beckwith 1985: 112, 164; Steinberg and Stone 2015: 11–15; Dorival 2004: 98–99; 2014: 24; Kaestli 2007: 108), while other scholars are less convinced that this passage indicates the early existence of the shape of the rabbinic canon and understand "the Law and the Prophets" to refer to the Scripture of Ben Sira and the third part to refer to all other books, an undefined collection (Barton 1986: 47–48; Ulrich 2003: 212–13).

Three passages mention in the third place David/hymns/psalms (4QMMT C[?]; Philo; Luke 24:44), and some are confident that these or some of these passages refer to the Psalter and by extension represent the Ketuvim (Beckwith 1985: 111–18; Qimron and Strugnell 1994: 59n10; Dempster 2008: 114–16, 120–21). But others question whether "David" is in the text of 4QMMT C (Ulrich 2003: 211; Steinberg and Stone 2015: 15n61), or if the reconstruction is correct, perhaps it refers to the Psalms or an open or closed Ketuvim collection (Qimron and Strugnell 1994: 111–12), or to "the deeds of David" and thus no link to the Ketuvim (Lim 2001), or indicates four parts, not three (Dorival 2003: 92; 2014: 25). Most do interpret Philo's "hymns" and Luke's "psalms" as evidence for the Psalms but not as evidence for a fixed third division (Steinberg and Stone 2015: 25); instead, they understand them to be evidence of different literary forms in the Scriptures (Barton 1986: 58; Dorival 2014: 25–26).

In 2 Macc. 2:13-15, some understand the kings and the prophets (i.e. Neviim), the writings of David (i.e. Psalms at the beginning of Ketuvim), and letters of kings about votive offerings (cf. Ezra 6:3–12; 7:12–26 near the end of the Ketuvim) to refer to a tripartite structure (Beckwith 1986: 164–65; Dempster 2008: 116–17; and especially, Gentry 2021: 244–47). Trebolle Barrera suggested the passage could be understood as a reference to a tripartite arrangement before arguing against it (2002: 130), while Dorival suggests it is describing four or even five parts including the Law, the kings, the prophets, the books of David, and the royal letters (2014: 23; see below).

Josephus may in some way be adapting the tripartite canon (Beckwith 1985: 118–27; Lim 2013: 49; Chapman 2016: 41), but he also seems to be more concerned about using genre to structure his list (Barton 1986: 48; Mason 2002; Kaestli 2007: 109; Dorival 2014: 26; Steinberg and Stone 2015: 30–31).

Luke 11:51/Matt. 23:35 ("of the blood of Abel to the blood of Zechariah, who perished between the altar and the sanctuary") has been understood to refer to a canonical order of books at the time of Jesus; that is, the Pharisees are guilty of the blood of the martyrs in a canonical—not chronological—sense, from Genesis 4 to 2 Chronicles 24, the ordering of *b. Bat.* 14b (Beckwith 1985: 211–22). Not all are convinced this passage relates to a canonical order given the extreme paucity of external evidence for Chronicles as the conclusion to the Jewish canon, and because internally, Jesus appears to isolate Abel and Zechariah due to the similar nature of their martyrdoms "as two deeply incisive moments of an occurrence which has been going on for centuries and still continues in the present" and not due to a particular canonical arrangement (Peels 2001: 598–99; Steinberg and Stone 2015: 25–26).

Summary

Therefore, in the pre-rabbinic period, most Jews would have described their scriptures as "the Law and the prophets." A few other texts perhaps indicate that Jews considered that other literary genres were contained in the scriptures which did not neatly align with law or prophecy (Dorival 2004: 96–99; 2014: 23–27), or perhaps, a tripartite structure existed alongside other structures (Steinberg and Stone 2015: 12, 15). If these texts do not evince the tripartite arrangement, then other Jewish arrangements could have existed in the first century CE, which early Christians may have received instead of the later rabbinic arrangement which they never mention (McDonald 2018). It is difficult to say more.

The tripartite canon certainly existed for some Jews in Late Antiquity (Baba Bathra 14b), even though the sequence of books within the Neviim and especially the Ketuvim was in some flux (Jerome's *Prologus Galeatus*). This structure would eventually be received by the Masoretes, who did not adopt the same book order as the Talmud. In Late Antiquity, early Christian lists probably reflect other earlier or contemporary Jewish arrangements of the books.

The arrangement(s) of the Greek Old Testament

The contents of the Christian Old Testament among Greek fathers were quite similar to the contents of the Hebrew canon. Should one, therefore, explain the different arrangements between Tanak and Old Testament stemming from Jewish and Christian communities as Sweeney does (1997)? This conclusion presses the matter too far, since there were probably different Jewish arrangements of the same books now preserved only in the early Christian Old Testament lists. The fluctuation in book order at this time is expected since there was no physical or material way to guarantee a single order of books and the question remains whether there was a standard Jewish ordering of the books.

Evidence of unstructured arrangement in lists

The following sources have or imply a connection to the Hebrew canon but do not mark divisions between books in their lists: Bryennios, Origen, Athanasius, Synod of Laodicea, Epiphanius (*Pan.* 8.6; *Mens.* 22–23), *Hypomnestikon*, *Dialogue of Timothy and Aquila*, Ps.-Athanasius, and Nicephorus I. Although Melito does not imply a direct connection with the Hebrew canon, the contents of the list presuppose the Hebrew canon. Furthermore, Melito describes his extracts as taken from the "law and the prophets," a traditional designation for the Hebrew scriptures. Apostolic Canons 85 does not contain structural divisions, nor does it have strong connection to the Hebrew canon.

Minimal order can be discerned. All lists begin with the Law and tend to place the latter Prophets at or near the end. All lists end with either 1–2 Esdras/Esther/Job or one of the Prophets. The ones that end with 1–2 Esdras/Esther/Job are as follows:

- Bryennios
- Melito
- Origen
- Epiphanius (2 lists)
- *Hypomnestikon*
- *Dialogue of Timothy and Aquila*.

The lists that end with the latter prophets are as follows:

- Athanasius
- Synod of Laodicea
- Amphilochius
- Ps.-Athanasius
- Nicephorus I.

The lists that conclude with the Prophets find agreement with more lists that mark sections between books of the Old Testament (see below). But there are other lists that note an arrangement of books that end with Esther or Esdras, books that tend to be near or at the end of the Tanak. On the whole, the "latter Prophets" tend to be at or near the end of the collection (contra Seitz 2009: 93). The early Christians do not confess to modifying an established Jewish order of books to their own theology. The evidence shows that Christians had adopted other Jewish arrangements of the Hebrew canon (Dorival 2003: 90).

Evidence of structured arrangement in lists

As mentioned above, most early Christians transmit canon lists without any mention of an order or without signaling divisions. However, Melito of Sardis (Extracts *Preface apud* Eusebius *Hist. eccl.* 4.26.12–14) and Athanasius (*Ep. fest.* 39.16, 17) refer to an order of books before listing them. Examination of other early lists and notices shows that some early Christians conceived of an arrangement of the Old Testament and book order in tri- and quadripartite arrangements, but in none of these orders can the rabbinic tripartite canon be found except Jerome's *Prologus Galeatus* and Epiphanius' description of the Nazoraeans' scriptures (*Pan.* 29.7.2, 4).

Melito (Extracts Preface)

In his Extracts *Preface* preserved by Eusebius, Melito (170 CE) provides a canon list of the books of the Old Testament, "the Law and the prophets," which reflects the books of the Hebrew canon except for the omission of Esther. But before Melito presents his list of books, he reports that Onesimus desired to learn the facts (ἀκρίβεια "accuracy") of the old books, in regard to their number and their order (τάξις). Melito says he journeyed east (i.e. Palestine, "the place where these things were proclaimed and accomplished"), learned the books of the Old Testament accurately (ἀκριβῶς), appended (ὑποτάσσω) them, and sent them to Onesimus. Although the point is disputed, Melito probably sought out Christians in the east, for his native Sardis already had a flourishing Jewish community to consult, if that was his design (Gallagher and Meade 2017: 79). Since early Christians essentially adopted the Hebrew canon, which Melito's list attests, the exact source of the list is less significant. Thus, one should probably imagine that Melito's Christian source was based on a Jewish ordering of the books from the second century CE.

His ordering of the Pentateuch, Gen.–Exod.–Num.–Lev.–Deut., while not otherwise unknown (cf. Mommsen Catalogue), shows an order that was probably not widespread among Jews and Christians. However, the placement of Esdras (probably Ezra-Nehemiah) at the end of his list is unique among the Greek lists but is known from Jerome (*Epist.* 53.8) and some later Hebrew MSS including the Leningrad Codex (Ginsburg 1966: 6–7). Thus, Melito's list, while a Christian list, shows contact with the Hebrew canon (see Gallagher and Meade 2017: 80–81 for the interpretation of "Wisdom" in this list), and thus probably mirrors a Jewish order of books from the second century CE.

Athanasius (Ep. fest. 39.16, 17)

Athanasius (367 CE) says that he presents the canonical books in his list "in sequence" (ἑξῆς; *Ep. fest.* 39.16). He also mentions the total number of books of the Old Testament is twenty-two, "for, as I have heard, it has been handed down (παραδίδωμι) that this is the number of the letters of the Hebrew alphabet" (*Ep. fest.* 39.17), and immediately he gives his list of Old Testament books "in their order" (τάξις) and by name (ὄνομα). Athanasius passes down this tradition about the Hebrew alphabet as it was passed down (παραδίδωμι) to him. He also claims to set forth the Scripture, which he is convinced, the eyewitnesses or apostles handed down (παραδίδωμι) to their ancestors (*Ep. fest.* 39.16), who handed down this tradition to him (cf. *Ep. fest.* 39.20). Athanasius' "ancestors" are the link between himself and apostolic tradition. Thus, he claims his canon with its order goes back to the apostles (cf. Cyril of Jerusalem *Cat.* 4.35).

Athanasius does not mark any sections or divisions with titles except at the end when he signals the Prophets. For a list that depends on the Hebrew canon and focuses on order, it is surprising that Athanasius records no divisions, unless he did not receive an order with divisions from the ancestors. His list's order could be described according to genre: Law–History–Poetry–Prophecy. The first five books are set off from the historical books by marking Deuteronomy as the final (λοιπόν) book of the first section. But not all Christians who include divisions will make one between Law and History; rather, those sections are often combined under History. The poetic books are separated from the final section of the Prophets by the use of λοιπόν "finally," which leaves only the division between historical and poetic books unmarked but easily discerned from the transition between 1–2 Esdras to Psalms. This order matches Codex Vaticanus precisely, if one does not reckon Vaticanus' Wis.–Sir.–Est.–Jdt.–Tob. (books "to be read," not "canonical," according to Athanasius).

Eusebius (Extracts from the Prophets; PG 22:1021–1262)

In his *Extracts from the Prophets* from the first half of the fourth century, Eusebius surveys the passages that prophesy about Jesus Christ in the divine Scriptures. Thus, he does not list every book, and his placement of Isaiah at the end of "the prophetic scriptures" is suspicious, since it was probably his decision to treat this venerated book in the final place.

The first five books he surveys, he calls ἡ πεντάτευχος "the Pentateuch" (Gen.–Deut.), and from it, he transitions to αἱ ἑξῆς γραφαί "the following Scriptures," indicating a sequence between the Pentateuch and the Scriptures that come next (1.16). After selecting passages from Josh., 1–2 Kgdms., 3 Kgdms., 1–2 Chron., 2 Esd. (and noting he found nothing in Esther), he calls the whole section αἱ ἱστορικαὶ γραφαί "the historical scriptures" before transitioning to τὰ στιχήρη "the poetic books" (1.25; Pss., Prov., Eccl., Song, Job). Finally, after surveying the poetic books, he turns to αἱ προφητικαὶ γραφαί "the prophetic scriptures" beginning with the Twelve Prophets (3.10; Hos., [Joel], Amos, Aba., Jon., Mic., [Nah.], [Hab.], Sop., [Hag.], Zach., Mal., Jer.–Lam.–Bar., Ezek., Dan., Isa.). Eusebius does not leave comment on Joel, Nahum, Habakkuk, or Haggai (i.e., the books in brackets). Rather, he simply includes their place in the Twelve and adds a note "nothing is clear from x" (σαφὲς οὐδέν), presumably meaning "nothing is clear about Christ from these books." Thus, Eusebius furnishes a tripartite Old Testament: Historical–Poetic–Prophetic (Dorival 2003: 87) with what comes close to a quadripartite Old Testament: History–Pentateuch–Poetry–Prophecy. This tripartite structure does not resemble the rabbinic tripartite structure.

Cyril of Jerusalem (Cat. 4.35)

Around 350 CE, Cyril gave his fourth catechetical lecture which included a full canon list of the Old and New Testament Scriptures. After emphasizing that the new converts should read only the twenty-two books that the church reads publicly, he lists them according to three divisions having an established number of books: Historical(twelve)–Poetic(five)–Prophetic(five). As Eusebius before him, Cyril also separates the first five books of the Law of Moses from the other historical books coming close to four parts: History–Law–Poetry–Prophecy.

Gregory of Nazianzus (Carmen 12)

Around 390 CE, Gregory wrote a poem on the authentic books of divine Scripture. He also received the twenty-two books according to the Hebrew letters and divided them into three parts: Historical(twelve)–Poetic(five)–Prophetic(five). Gregory does not separate the Law from the historical books as Eusebius and Cyril had done.

Ps. John Chrysostom (Synopsis Scripturae Sacrae ln. 111–12)

There are two incomplete lists of books in this Antiochian work, one in the Protheoria and the other implied in the Synopsis. The textual history of this work is only now possible to trace due to the forthcoming critical edition, whose editor dates the work to 400–450 CE (Barone, forthcoming). In lines 111–112 of the Protheoria, the author summarizes the scriptures of the Old Testament under three divisions: Historical–Advisory–Prophetic. The first section includes the Octateuch (Gen.–Ruth) and the other historical books. The middle category is indicated by a new term τὸ συμβουλευτικόν that encompasses the three Solomonic books and Sirach, while the third division of the Prophets includes Psalms and Job after the sixteen prophets. This tripartite structure of the Old Testament parallels the one in Eusebius, Cyril, and Gregory of Nazianzus, although it has a different distribution of books. Sirach was added to the Solomonic books, while Psalms and Job no longer fit with the Solomonic books under the new rubric "Advisory" instead of "Poetic."

Epiphanius (Panarion 29.7.2, 4)

Epiphanius' *Panarion* contains a canon list (8.6), but the list contains no divisions between books. Nestled in his description of the heretical sect of the Nazoraeans, however, Epiphanius notes that they use not only the New Covenant but also the Old Covenant. They do not forbid "the legislation (νομοθεσία) and prophets (προφῆται) and the books called 'Writings' (γραφεῖα) by the Jews" (29.7.2). A little later, Epiphanius notes that this group is well trained in the Hebrew language, "[F]or all the Law (ὁ νόμος) and the Prophets (οἱ προφῆται) and the so-called Writings (τὰ γραφεῖα)—I indicate the poetic books and Kingdoms [Samuel or Kings or both?] and Chronicles and Esther, and all the others—are read in Hebrew among them, as of course also among the Jews" (29.7.4).

This text attests to the tripartite canonical structure among the Jews and the Nazoraeans. Epiphanius places "Kingdoms" (whether Kings or Samuel or both is not clear) in the Writings, a move unattested in Jewish sources. In *Mens.* 4 (see below), Epiphanius' division of "Writings" contains Joshua, Judges with Ruth, Chronicles, and 1–4 Kingdoms. The division in *Mens.* 4 does not neatly map to the "Writings" in *Pan.* 29.7. In *Pan.* 8.6, 1–4 Kingdoms and 1–2 Chronicles come after the poetic books and before the prophets. Given the close proximity to the poetic books there, Epiphanius may have simply lumped these history books with other books that the Jews would have considered part of the Writings. This text shows the macro Tanak order but demonstrates that the individual book order within the Writings was not fixed.

Jerome (Prologus Galeatus)

Although not a Greek father, Jerome's list provides necessary information for the shape of the rabbinic canon. Around 390 CE, Jerome uses the noun *ordo* "order" to describe sections of the Neviim and Ketuvim respectively. The usage of the term in these sections is unique among early Christian canon lists but perhaps it comes from Jerome's Jewish informants (Dorival 2003: 93). The Mishna and the Talmud were divided into six orders or *sedarim*, and *b. Bat.* 14b uses *sdr* to indicate the orders of the Neviim and Ketuvim (Alexander 2007: 75–76). There is no way to know whether the *baraita* or the canonizers of the Mishna used the term first and whether one is dependent on the other. But Jerome's *ordo* in *Prologus Galeatus* appears to be a Latin translation of the Hebrew term, which may have only relatively recently begun to be used for canon divisions.

Jerome presents two variations of the Jewish tripartite arrangement, neither one agreeing with the Talmud or Masoretes in every detail (Dorival 2003: 89–90) or the other Greek Christian tripartite arrangements. Jerome's first description enumerates the books as twenty-two and includes five double books (e.g. Jeremiah with Lamentations). He says the Jews join Ruth to Judges because the story is narrated as having happened in the days of the Judges. The second order has the same three divisions, but Ruth and Lamentations are reckoned as their own books and moved from the Prophets to the Writings resulting in twenty-four books. Jerome says the first scheme had been adopted by many Jews (*plerus*), while the second scheme had been adopted by some (*nonnullus*). His description perhaps indicates that the rabbinic tripartite Bible was relatively fluid, which could be better explained, if it was recently established rather than long standing (Dorival 2003: 90). Slightly later, Jerome drafted a second canon list of Old Testament books and did not include divisions between books (*Epist.* 53.8–9.4).

Epiphanius (Mens. 4) and John of Damascus (De Fide 4.17)

In 392 CE, Epiphanius wrote his *On Weights and Measures*, which is only incompletely preserved in Greek, but the Syriac version of the work appears to be complete. The work encompasses the antiquarian spirit and touches on many issues such as how the Hebrew scriptures were translated by the seventy-two translators, Origen's scholarly Greek editions of the Scriptures, the use of grammatical signs like the *asteriskos* (※), the list of Roman emperors, and two canon lists of the Old Testament.

After explaining how the books are reckoned according to the twenty-two letters of the Hebrew alphabet, Epiphanius describes the canon as arranged in four pentateuchs with two late books remaining: Law–Poetry–Writings or Hagiographa–Prophecy–Esdras-Esther. Epiphanius probably began with the Pentateuch and from there devised the rest of the arrangement. That he invented this arrangement (not the list of books) appears clear because the two remaining books could not be included in it, and more significantly, Epiphanius does not employ this arrangement for his two other canon lists (*Pan.* 8.6 and *Mens.* 22–23), which contain the books without divisions.

In the first half of the eighth century, John of Damascus transmits the same canon list as *Mens.* 4 but transposes the second and third Pentateuchs with the result: Law–

Writings or Hagiographa–Poetry–Prophecy–Esdras–Esther. He also puts Kingdoms before Chronicles.

Other than these two examples, a clear arrangement of the Old Testament scriptures according to four divisions is not mentioned among the early Greek fathers and synods. Although some have interpreted Amphilochius' list as quadripartite (Dorival 2003: 91), he did not indicate such a structure according to divisions. However, there are some lists such as Athanasius' and Amphilochius' that although they do not contain divisions, they can still be divided into three or four sections.

Summary

Early Greek Old Testament lists generally report the books of the Hebrew canon. The early lists reveal three arrangements: (1) simple list of books with no divisions, (2) tripartite arrangement of History–Poetry–Prophecy or Law–Prophets–Writings (Jerome's *Prologus Galeatus*), and (3) a quadripartite arrangement of Law–Writings–Poetry–Prophecy with other books. With relatively few exceptions, early Christians do not show great concern for the order of the books of the Old Testament. Early fathers like Epiphanius and Jerome transmit multiple, similar lists of the Old Testament books in different orders, showing little concern for a correct order of books. Those Christian lists which can be traced back to the Hebrew canon on the whole do not show the arrangement of books of the rabbinic canon. This fact has led some scholars to question the antiquity of the rabbinic canon or at least the divisions within it (Dorival 2003: 90).

Evidence of select Greek manuscripts

At the beginning, each Greek translation of a Hebrew book would have been copied in one scroll. Once codex technology developed, the books that shared the same genre were compiled and copied together in smaller codices. Alfred Rahlfs has identified seven such groupings and listed the manuscript evidence for them (1914: 373–439):

(1) Octateuch
(2) Kingdoms, Paraleipomena, Esdras
(3) Esther, Judith, Tobit
(4) 1–4 Maccabees
(5) Psalms-Odes
(6) Proverbs, Ecclesiastes, Canticum, Wisdom of Solomon, Sirach, Psalms of Solomon
(7) Sixteen Prophets.

Finally, when the codex was developed that could contain all these books in one cover, a Christian scribe would compile these seven codices or blocks of books into one mega codex or pandect Bible. The evidence of the colophon to the book of Esther in Codex Sinaiticus shows that its text was collated from Pamphilus' (martyred *ca.* 310) very old copy which began at the book of First Kingdoms and ended at Esther (Gentry 2016: 211). Furthermore, the manuscript layout and distribution of columns in Codex

Sinaiticus probably shows that the scribe copied separate codices according to their layouts in the creation of his own. The historical and prophetic books were copied in four columns per page, reflecting the scribe's exemplars, while the poetic books at the end of the Old Testament are represented in two columns, once again reflecting the layout of the smaller codex or exemplar from which the scribe collated and copied them (Gentry 2016: 211). Although the material evidence reflects seven book groupings, it is interesting that Christians conceptualized them only according to three or four genres as we have seen.

Manuscripts show the reading habits of early Christians—not the early Christian canon. The lists show the canon. But what do the early pandects reveal about book order? Codex Vaticanus has the same order of books in Athanasius' canon, if his books to be read (Wis.–Tob.) are omitted from analysis. In Vaticanus, these books come between the poetic and prophetic books and complete an early collection of scriptures, but they were not considered canonical by most early Greek fathers and synods. Thus, the order of books in Vaticanus comes close to agreeing with the modern four-part Old Testament: Law–History–Poetry–Prophecy, ending with Daniel before the first page of the Gospel according to Matthew.

Sinaiticus and Alexandrinus preserve still different orders of books. Though Sinaiticus is defective in much of its early contents, it is clear that it had Law–History–Prophets–Poetry, an order deviating from all Greek lists and arrangements. Alexandrinus has a similar ordering: Law–History–Prophecy–history–Poetry in which Esther–4 Maccabees comes between the prophetic and poetic books as a later history.

These manuscripts do not contain section divisions and therefore the scribe did not reveal his rationale. The three pandects show that scribes were settled on placing the Historical books first but there was still lack of fixity about the arrangement and order of the Prophetic and Poetic books.

Conclusions

In his essay, "Tanak versus Old Testament," Sweeney (1997: 360), says, "Although this [four-part] structure (and the order of the books therein) appears to have been set only after the widespread use of printed Bibles in the Western world, it is based on the order of books in the Latin Vulgate, and prior to that, the order of various Greek traditions." By now, it is clear that the arrangement of Pentateuch–History–Poetry–Prophecy in the Western Bible does not go back simply to Greek traditions through the Vulgate. Many arrangements were tripartite (History–Poetry–Prophecy) and several Greek lists end with history books. Although Sweeney follows Sundberg in calling the OT "a distinctly Christian canon" (Sweeney 1997: 358; Sundberg 1968: 155), the Greek lists depend on the Hebrew canon for their contents, and therefore, probably their arrangements. The drafters of these lists do not claim to have modified the contents or the order of the books they received to bridge to the New Testament. In the case of Epiphanius (*Mens.* 4), he probably created an order based on four pentateuchs or four groups of five books. But not only does this order appear artificial, Epiphanius does not promote it in his two other canon lists, showing its artificial nature.

Those Greek fathers who comment on arrangement and book order do not typically describe the Old Testament in the four parts of the modern, Western OT. Rather they appear to describe the arrangement according to the three dominant genres contained in the books in each section: books of Moses and subsequent books contain mostly history; the books of Solomon, Job, and Psalms contain mostly poetry; Isaiah, Jeremiah, Ezekiel, the Twelve, Daniel contain mostly prophecy.

Although some canon lists end with history (Esther/Esdras) and Sinaiticus and Alexandrinus end with poetic books, several Greek lists end with prophecy, specifically Daniel or the Twelve (Nicephorus I; also known from the Mommsen Catalogue). Perhaps, these arrangements of the Hebrew canon reflect a grand scheme of history to eschatology, from the creation of the world to Daniel's seventy weeks or to Elijah to return and the irruption of the Kingdom of God. Although this arrangement might appear to be a Christian invention, in the vacuum of a standard tripartite rabbinic canon in the first century CE, it is conceivable that at this time there were Jewish groups who read the prophets as the culmination of history in view of the coming Kingdom of God and that those canonical orders were received by early Christians.

Bibliography

Alexander, Philip S. (2007), "The Formation of the Biblical Canon in Rabbinic Judaism," in Philip S. Alexander and Jean-Daniel Kaestli (eds.), *The Canon of Scripture in Jewish and Christian Tradition*, 57–80, Prahins: Éditions du Zebre.

Barone, Francesca Prometea, ed. (forthcoming), Ps. Iohannis Chrysostomi *Synopsis Scripturae Sacrae*, Corpus Christianorum: Series Graeca. Turnhout: Brepols.

Barton, John. (1986), *Oracles of God: Perceptions of Ancient Prophecy in Israel after the Exile*, Oxford: Oxford University Press.

Barton, John. (2013), "The Old Testament Canons," in James Carleton Paget and Joachim Schaper (eds), *From the Beginnings to 600*. Vol. 1 of *The New Cambridge History of the Bible*, 145–64, Cambridge: Cambridge University Press.

Beckwith, Roger. (1985), *The Old Testament Canon of the New Testament Church*, Grand Rapids, MI: Eerdmans.

Chapman, Stephen B. (2000), *The Law and the Prophets: A Study in Old Testament Canon Formation*, Tübingen: Mohr Siebeck.

Chapman, Stephen B. (2016), "Collections, Canons, and Communities," in Stephen B. Chapman and Marvin A. Sweeney (eds.), *The Cambridge Companion to the Hebrew Bible/Old Testament*, 28–54, Cambridge: Cambridge University Press.

Conybeare, Fred C., ed. (1898), *The Dialogues of Athanasius and Zacchaeus and of Timothy and Aquila*, Oxford: Clarendon Press.

Dempster, Stephen G. (2008), "Torah, Torah, Torah: The Emergence of the Tripartite Canon," in Craig A. Evans and Emanuel Tov (eds.), *Exploring the Origins of the Bible: Canon Formation in Historical, Literary, and Theological Perspective*, 87–127, Grand Rapids: Baker.

Dorival, Gilles. (2003), "L'apport des Peres de l'Église a la question de la clôture du canon de l'Ancien Testament," in J.-M. Auwers and H. J. de Jonge (eds.), *The Biblical Canons*, 81–110, Leuven: Leuven University Press.

Dorival, Gilles. (2004), "La formation du canon biblique de l'Ancien Testament: Position actuelle et problems," in Enrico Norelli (ed.), *Recueils normatifs et canons dans l'Antiquité: Perspectives nouvelles sur la formation des canons juif et chrétien dans leur contexte culturel*, 83–112, Prahins: Zebre.

Dorival, Gilles. (2014), "La formation du canon des Écritures juives. Histoire de la recherché et perspectives Nouvelles," in Rémi Geounelle and Jan Joosten (eds.), *La Bible juive dans l'Antiquité*, 9–40, Lausanne: Zebre.

Gallagher, Edmon L. (2012), *Hebrew Scripture in Patristic Biblical Theory: Canon, Language, Text*, Leiden: Brill.

Gallagher, Edmon L. and John D. Meade. (2017), *The Biblical Canon Lists from Early Christianity: Texts and Analysis*, Oxford: Oxford University Press.

Gentry, Peter J. (2016), "Pre-Hexaplaric Translations, Hexapla, post-Hexaplaric Translations," in Armin Lange and Emanuel Tov (eds.), *Textual History of the Bible Vol. 1A*, 211–35, Leiden: Brill.

Gentry, Peter J. (2021), "MasPs^a and the Early History of the Hebrew Psalter: Notes on Canon and Text," in Gregory Lanier and Nicholas Reed (eds.), *The Books and the Parchments: Studies on the Intersection of Text, Paratext, and Reception*, 223–248, Leiden: Brill.

Ginsburg, Christian D. (1897, 1966), *Introduction to the Massoretico-Critical Edition of the Hebrew Bible*, reprint, New York: Ktav.

Grant, Robert M. and Glen W. Menzies, eds. (1996), *Joseph's Bible Notes (Hypomnestikon)*, Atlanta: Scholar's Press.

Hanhart, Robert. (2002), Introduction to *The Septuagint as Christian Scripture: Its Prehistory and the Problem of Its Canon*, by Martin Hengel, trans. by Mark E. Biddle, Grand Rapids: Baker.

Jassen, Alex P. (2016), "The Prophets in the Dead Sea Scrolls," in Carolyn J. Sharp (ed.), *The Oxford Handbook of the Prophets*, 353–72, Oxford: Oxford University Press.

Joosten, Jan. (2016), "The Origin of the Septuagint Canon," in Siegfried Kreuzer, Martin Meiser, and Marcus Sigismund (eds.), *Die Septuaginta—Orte und Intentionen: 5. Internationale Fachtagung veranstaltet von Septuaginta Deutsch (LXX.D), Wuppertal 24.-27. Juli 2014*, 688–99, Tübingen: Mohr Siebeck.

Kaestli, Jean-Daniel. (2007), "La formation et la structure du canon biblique: que peut apporter l'étude de la Septante?" in Philip S. Alexander and Jean-Daniel Kaestli (eds.), *The Canon of Scripture in Jewish and Christian Tradition*, 99–113, Prahins: Zebre.

Lange, Armin. (2016), "1.1.2 Canonical History of the Hebrew Bible," in Armin Lange and Emanuel Tov (eds.), *Textual History of the Bible Vol. 1A*, 35–81, Leiden: Brill.

Leiman, Sid Z. (1976), *The Canonization of Hebrew Scripture: The Talmudic and Midrashic Evidence*, Hamden, CT: Transactions of the Connecticut Academy of Arts and Sciences.

Lewis, Jack P. (1964), "What Do We Mean by Jabneh?" *JBR* (32): 125–32.

Lim, Timothy H. (2001), "The Alleged Reference to the Tripartite Division of the Hebrew Bible," *RevQ* (20): 23–37.

Lim, Timothy H. (2013), *The Formation of the Jewish Canon*, New Haven, CT: Yale University Press.

Mason, Steve. (2002), "Josephus and His Twenty-Two Book Canon," in Lee Martin McDonald and James A. Sanders (eds.), *The Canon Debate*, 110–27, Peabody, MA: Hendrickson.

McDonald, Lee Martin. (2017), *The Old Testament: Its Authority and Canonicity*. Vol. 1 of *The Formation of the Biblical Canon*, London: Bloomsbury.

McDonald, Lee Martin. (2018), "The Reception of the Writings and Their Place in the Biblical Canon," in Donn F. Morgan (ed.), *The Oxford Handbook of the Writings of the Hebrew Bible*, 397–413, Oxford: Oxford University Press.

Meade, John D. (2021), "The Septuagint and the Biblical Canon," in William A. Ross and W. Edward Glenny (eds.), *T&T Clark Handbook of Septuagint Research*, 207–28, London: T&T Clark / Bloomsbury.

Menzies, G. W. (1996), *Joseph Bible Notes (Hypomnestikon): Introduction, Translation, and Notes*, SBLTT 41.9, Atlanta: Scholars Press.

Mroczek, Eva. (2016), *The Literary Imagination in Jewish Antiquity*, Oxford: Oxford University Press.

Ossandón Widow, Juan Carlos. (2018), *The Origins of the Canon of the Hebrew Bible: An Analysis of Josephus and 4 Ezra*, Leiden: Brill.

Peels, H. G. L. (2001), "The Blood 'from Abel to Zechariah' (Matthew 23,35; Luke 11,50f.) and the Canon of the Old Testament," *ZAW* (113): 583–601.

Qimron, Elisha and John Strugnell, eds. (1994), *Qumran Cave 4, V: Miqṣat Ma'aśe Ha-Torah*, DJD 10, Oxford: Oxford University Press.

Rahlfs, Alfred. (1914), *Verzeichnis der griechischen Handschriften des Alten Testament*, MSU 2, Berlin: Weidmannsche Buchhandlung.

Ryle, Herbert Edward. (1892), *The Canon of the Old Testament: An Essay on the Gradual Growth and Formation of the Hebrew Canon of Scripture*, London: Macmillan.

Sarna, N. M. (2000), "Ancient Libraries and the Ordering of the Biblical Books," in *Studies in Biblical Interpretation*, 35–66, Philadelphia: Jewish Publication Society.

Seitz, Christopher R. (2009), *The Goodly Fellowship of the Prophets: The Achievement of Association in Canon Formation*, Grand Rapids: Baker.

Steinberg, Julius and Timothy J. Stone. (2015), "The Historical Formation of the Writings in Antiquity," in Julius Steinberg and Timothy J. Stone (eds.), *The Shape of the Writings*, Siphrut: Literature and Theology of the Hebrew Scriptures 16, 1–58, Winona Lake, IN: Eisenbrauns.

Sundberg, Albert C. (1964), *The Old Testament of the Early Church*, Cambridge, MA: Harvard University Press.

Sundberg, Albert C. (1968), "The 'Old Testament': A Christian Canon," *CBQ* (30): 143–55.

Sweeney, Marvin A. (1997), "Tanak versus Old Testament: Concerning the Foundation for a Jewish Theology of the Bible," in Henry T. C. Sun and Keith L. Eades (eds.), *Problems in Biblical Theology: Essays in Honor of Rolf Knierim*, 353–72, Grand Rapids: Eerdmans.

Swete, Henry Barclay. (1900, 1989), *An Introduction to the Old Testament in Greek*, Cambridge: Cambridge University Press; reprint, Peabody, MA: Hendrickson.

Trebolle Barrera, Julio. (2002), "Origins of a Tripartite Old Testament Canon," in Lee Martin McDonald and James A. Sanders (eds.), *The Canon Debate*, 128–45, Peabody, MA: Hendrickson.

Ulrich, Eugene C. (2003), "The Non-Attestation of a Tripartite Canon in 4QMMT," *CBQ* (65): 202–14.

VanderKam, James C. (2012), *The Dead Sea Scrolls and the Bible*, Grand Rapids, MI: Eerdmans.

4

The Canonical Shape of the New Testament

Matthew Y. Emerson

The question of the canonical shape of the New Testament is, to say the least, a contested and sometimes convoluted one. One complicating factor in addressing the topic is that many approaches to the canonical shape of the NT focus their attention on individual corpora rather than the NT canon as a whole.[1] These approaches are in some sense indebted to Harry Gamble's observation that the NT is "a collection of collections," and so many come to the question of canonical shape from within one of those collections (Gamble 2002/1985: 78). Some, but not all, then extrapolate to where the particular corpus might fit into the canonical shape of the entire NT. This latter step, however, is usually ancillary to the primary purpose of exploring the shape of individual corpora.

Another complicating factor in addressing the canonical shape of the NT is that, despite a number of works on canon and method, there appears to be no unifying approach to the question, whether from historical, literary, or theological perspectives. For some, to ask about the canonical shape of the NT is fundamentally an empirical and descriptive task. For others, it is more a literary exercise, while for still others it is primarily a historical and/or a biblical-theological question.

These same methodological fault lines exist in studies of individual NT (and OT) corpora as well, although they are exacerbated when moving from more manageable sub-units to the entire NT. For example, does one study the shape of the Catholic Epistles via consideration of the whole or through consideration of discrete units (i.e., the Petrine epistles)? Is "discrete unit," a term which usually refers to books with common authorship, even an appropriate way to analyze distinct parts of a particular corpus given the questions about authorship of, say, 2 Peter or 3 John?[2] Should we begin with reference to questions about authorship and background and audience, or with the literary connections between the seven letters commonly called "Catholic"? Again, as one might imagine, these kinds of questions are only amplified when we consider the NT canon as a whole.

---

[1] I have intentionally restricted my analysis below to studies of or comments on the shape of the NT as a whole, rather than on diving into the debates and issues related to particular corpora, since the remaining essays in this section of the volume deal with those distinct sections of the NT extensively.

[2] Throughout this essay I make reference to the views of others with respect to authorship of biblical books and to the potential for a final editor/redactor or set of editors/redactors for the NT canon. None of these should be taken necessarily as identical with my own views of authorship and/or the presence of post-compositional canonical editing and redaction. A *status quaestionis* essay is not the place to articulate my own views on those subjects.

The purpose of this essay is not necessarily to adjudicate between different views related to these questions, but instead to describe the state of the question accurately and to propose paths forward when appropriate. Regarding approaches to the shape of the NT, we will see that there are essentially three options: to see it as hermeneutically insignificant, to see it as hermeneutically significant only in a *post hoc* fashion, and to see it as hermeneutically significant because of its authorially- or editorially-intended compositional coherence. Again, there is variety even within these alternatives, and we will attempt to be as careful as possible in noting the different approaches from within this framework. Still, *status quaestionis* exercises must begin somewhere, and must do so in a heuristic fashion.

Regarding the methods by which scholars attempt to arbitrate between various historically attested canonical shapes for the NT and by which they attempt to understand its hermeneutical import, we will again employ a heuristic distinction between those who approach the question from empirical, historical, ecclesial, literary, and biblical-theological vantage points. In doing so, the goal is not to pit one approach against the other, or to suggest that those identified as models of a particular approach do not somehow also incorporate insights from these other areas. It is to suggest, however, that understanding the state of the question includes understanding the methodological differences that distinguish the key figures in the discussion.

Finally, we will see that there are a variety of approaches not only to the hermeneutical significance of the canon and to the methodology whereby it should be studied, but there is also significant variation in the ways in which canonical interpreters understand canonical shape. Some see it as simply a boundary setting mechanism for the process of interpretation, while others see canonical shape emphasizing some doctrine, theme, or biblical-theological connection between corpora or between the two testaments. We must begin, though, with the question of whether or not the shape of the NT is hermeneutically significant at all.

"A collection of collections"

Gamble's observation that the NT is "a collection of collections" might seem to be so obvious as to require no further comment or debate. After all, given what we now know about, for instance, the circulation of codices in the second century, to say that the NT is a collection of collections may be nearly tautological. But it is only pedantic if the phrase is used to describe the contents of the NT, rather than to posit some hypothesis or another about the NT's *shape*.

Canonical shape is hermeneutically and theologically insignificant

For some, the shape of the NT canon is of no real significance, in part due to the amount of fluctuation we see in the order of particular corpora. So, Bruce Metzger's comment that:

> The preceding survey of the very great variety in order, both of the several parts of the New Testament as well as of books within each part, leads one to conclude that

such matters were of no great significance for the ancient and medieval Church; they became an issue only with later editors and publishers.

Metzger 1987/2009: 300

Arthur Patzia comes to similar conclusions, saying, "*It is not clear whether any systematic theological presuppositions, or prejudices were used to determine the place of any books in the New Testament*. Because the order varies in so many lists, one is forced to assume that there were a number of different factors at work." Patzia goes on to list church usage in worship and liturgy and the change from roll to codex among these various factors. However, "Bound into codex form, these and/or other materials would be viewed as a unity." Patzia then argues that, "*These brief observations, though incomplete, show that there was no consistent or authoritative pattern employed by those who arranged all the books of the New Testament canon. The decision to include these twenty-seven books did not specify how they were to be arranged.*" The length of Paul's letters, as well as "authorship, apostolic primacy, ecclesiastical preferences, codex production, scribal errors and editorial decisions that may have been based on some theological grounds imperceptible to the modern reader" are identified by Patzia as potential criteria for arrangement. Patzia concludes, "*If anything, the forgoing discussion should prevent us from making any dogmatic statements and conclusive pronouncements about the order of the New Testament before the sixteenth century*" (Patzia 1995/2011: 182–83, emphases mine).

Of course, the most trenchant criticism of any sort of "canonical criticism," or even of canon as a concept of primary importance for biblical interpretation, comes from James Barr. He argues that, for instance, "canons are not particularly hermeneutical in their character. One of the deepest assumptions of modern canonical criticism is that canons give hermeneutical guidance and are intended to do so. This, however, is not their function" (Barr 1983, especially 160–61). Barr does not find the concept of "final form" compelling for the reason that each supposedly historically distinct unit of any given biblical book still has to be understood on its own (historical) terms. This same objection would obviously apply *mutatis mutandis* to the shape of the canon as a whole (Barr, 1983; see also Barr 1999: 378–438, along with 307–11). The proper focus of biblical interpretation is particular texts in particular books understood in their own individual historical and literary contexts.

In this view, then, while certain corpora are recognized as having been formed and circulated together, and while the NT as a unit is therefore accurately described as a collection of collections (see e.g. Niebuhr 2003: 578–81; and Parker 2008), the shape of both the collections and the NT are hermeneutically and theologically insignificant. Both the individual collections and the final NT canon are products of the various forces that Patzia mentions above, rather than some discernable overarching theological or hermeneutical concern. Thus, what is significant is the *fact* of canon, rather than the *shape* of it.

Canonical shape has *post hoc* significance

Returning to our introductory figure, Harry Gamble shares similar sentiments to the previous view, namely that "the NT acquired a relatively fixed content" only when the process of codex-making became sufficiently advanced in the fourth century to include larger amounts of material. For Gamble, then, both the content and the shape of the NT is a "merely technical factor" (Gamble 2002/1985: 67). Despite the similarities between Gamble's statements here and Metzger's and Patzia's, Gamble goes on to say, however, that the shape of the canon now has hermeneutical significance even if the process of its compilation was not entirely intentional with respect to shape.

Gregory Goswell, in an essay on the shape of the Hebrew Bible, refers to this *post hoc* hermeneutical significance as "paratext," and argues that,

> In some quarters there is a lack of recognition that the (differing) order of the biblical books is a paratextual phenomenon that cannot be put on the same level as the text itself. Whatever order is adopted as a starting point, it is a reading strategy and must be viewed as such. A prescribed order of reading the biblical books is in effect an interpretation of the text.
>
> Goswell 2008: 677

Goswell is clear in his introduction that text and paratext[3] are "conceptually differentiated," even if in practice they are nigh impossible to separate. While paratext is thus not an intrinsic feature of the text, it does have hermeneutical implications. For canonical shape, this means that "differing orders highlight different features of the books thus categorized, so that each order in its own way may be valid and useful to the reader" (Goswell 2008: 673–74). In a later article, he states the point even more starkly:

> The differing order of the biblical books is a paratextual phenomenon that cannot be put on the same level as the text itself. It is a post-authorial imposition on the text of Scripture, albeit an unavoidable one when texts of different origin are collected together in a canonical corpus. Where a biblical book is placed relative to other books inevitably influences a reader's view of the book, on the supposition that juxtaposed books are related in some way and therefore illuminate each other. A prescribed order of books is a *de facto* interpretation of the text.
>
> Goswell 2013: 459–60. See also Wall 2012: 111–30, with which Goswell interacts

Thus, in this view, canonical shape is a hermeneutical reality, but one that should be distinguished from the intentions of the biblical authors. Hermeneutically, one cannot help but read texts in context, and this includes the macro-level context of each book and its placement in the order of the NT canon.[4]

---

[3] Paratext includes but is not limited to the order of books.
[4] I would place my own meager attempt at a canonical approach to the NT in this category, although I would caution the reader unfamiliar with it that, if I were to write my dissertation again, it would not look like what is currently published. See Emerson 2013.

Canonical shape is compositional

Finally, there are those who view the shape not only of particular books but of the canon as a whole as compositional. That is, they posit that the shape of the books both within specific corpora and between all four major corpora is due to authorial, editorial, and/or redactional intention. For instance, this view would argue that the shaping both of an individual corpus, like that of Acts and the Catholic Epistles, matters for understanding the shape of the entire NT, as do any connections between that corpus and other parts of the NT. For some, this redactional intention to place certain books next to each other or in some other literary relation is identified as the intention of biblical authors, while for others the final redaction of individual corpora or of the NT as a whole is the intention of a later redactor who was not the author of a biblical book or set of books.[5]

Typically, one sees compositional approaches worked out especially in relation to individual corpora within the NT.[6] There are a few scholars, however, who apply a compositional approach to the entire NT. The seminal work in this regard is David Trobisch's *The First Edition of the New Testament*, although the groundwork is laid for it in some ways by Childs' suggestive comments in his *The New Testament as Canon*. Trobisch argues that there was, by the second half of the second century CE, a "final redaction" of the NT material, one he calls the "Canonical Edition of the New Testament" (Brodie 2004: 144, see also xxviii for his broader views regarding the literary connections within and the shape of the NT). This Canonical Edition, according to Trobisch, was produced by a final redactor or group of redactors who selected, edited, and arranged the material contained in the NT. The evidence Trobisch puts forth in defending this thesis is primarily literary: the presence of *nomina sacra*, the use of the codex form, the arrangement and number of writings, the titles of the various NT books and especially the continuity of them in distinct corpora, and the title of the Canonical Edition ("new covenant," Trobisch 2000: 8–44). These various pieces of evidence, according to Trobisch, demonstrate the *literary* unity of the NT achieved through final redaction.

Other compositional approaches include Ched Spellman's *Toward a Canon-Conscious Reading of the Bible* and Thomas Brodie's *The Birthing of the New Testament*. In these approaches, the key to the canonical shape of the NT is its intertextuality, both between NT books and between the OT and the NT (which is especially emphasized by Brodie). More than mere literary connections, though, these intertextual links between books and especially between significant portions of individual corpora provide clues as to the fabric of the canonical shape of the NT.

For instance, Thomas Brodie argues that Proto-Luke draws heavily on the Septuagint, and "particularly on the Elijah-Elisha narrative structure." Further, there is

---

[5] Although the book is primarily concerned with the Catholic Epistles corpus and not with the NT as a whole, see Nienhuis and Wall 2013: 17–69 for discussion of the concepts of composition, canonical redaction, and arrangement as they relate to the CE and subsequently to the entire NT.

[6] For examples of this approach with respect to individual corpora, see Lockett 2017; Trobisch 1994; and Watson 2013. On the textual processes related to the formation of the Christian canon and their connection to a compositional approach, see Bokedal 2014.

continuity between "Matthew's *logia*, 1 Corinthians, and Proto-Luke," along with the finalized version of Luke-Acts. This continuity draws together all three works' (and therefore also the Gospel of Luke's) use of the Old Testament, and especially the Torah and the Former Prophets. In this way, the Four-Fold Gospel corpus, Acts, and the Pauline epistles are shaped by common use of similar or identical OT material and therefore provide "radical reshaping" of the NT material, a reshaping that is oriented toward continuity with and the reinterpretation of the OT (Brodie 2004, esp. 147–89).

The curious case of Brevard Childs

In my estimation, it is unclear on whether Childs should be placed in the *post hoc* category or the compositional one. In this rubric Childs would fall into the latter category if we were discussing the shape of individual books; "canonical shape" for Childs in that regard just is the compositional final form of a particular book. But when we broaden the scope of the term "shape" to include macro-level canonical shape, the issue becomes less clear. In his last book, *The Church's Guide to Reading Paul*, Childs explicitly acknowledges what he understands to be an editor's shaping of the Pauline corpus (Childs 2008: 3–9, 73). This editorial act includes, for Childs, the selection and arrangement of books, and perhaps even the provision of intertextual ties between the books. This understanding of shape falls under the final category in our survey, that of a compositional approach to canonical shape.

But when Childs moves from discussing the shape of the Pauline corpus to the shape of the NT canon, his stance regarding whether the NT's shape is hermeneutically relevant in a *post hoc* or compositional fashion becomes less obvious. Various comments throughout demonstrate that Childs understood the NT's shape to have hermeneutical significance, but he does not ever state explicitly that this hermeneutical significance at the macro-canonical level arises from composition rather than simply from *post hoc* arrangement (for example, Childs 2008: 26). We find similarly ambiguous statements about shape in Childs' discussion of the place of Acts and Hebrews at the beginning and end, respectively, of the Pauline corpus. The verb of choice in these comments for describing the placement of these two books in the NT canon is "functioned." In other words, one could interpret Childs to be saying that their shape has a hermeneutical function but is not necessarily one that is authorially or editorially intended (Childs 2008: 226, 230, 249–50).

This ambiguity about the shape of the entire NT could be compared to stronger statements about the editorially-driven shape of the Pauline corpus. For instance, Childs states that, "Regardless of Paul's intention, the letter to the Romans has been heard in a particular way in the subsequent development of the Pauline corpus. Moreover, this was not an accidental construal, but one that found its warrant in the perspective of the prescript with its universal scope" (Childs 2008: 67). This sounds as though there was some kind of intentional canonical shaping happening at an editorial level that placed Romans purposefully and for thematic and hermeneutical reasons at the beginning of the Pauline corpus, a corpus that was (in this interpretation of Childs' statement) intentionally literarily brought together and shaped. Later in the same section he states that "the canonical shape of the corpus served to bear testimony to how the letters were received within a living tradition that culminated in the Pastoral Epistles" (Childs 2008: 68). Again, this could be read as Childs arguing for an intentional, editorial selection and arrangement of the Pauline corpus. Likewise, could he be read in his opening statement on the placement of the Pastoral Epistles: "Now we turn to *the end of the canonical process*, namely, to the function of the Pastoral Letters" (Childs 2008: 69). And he later says that "the canonical move [of finalizing the Pauline corpus with the inclusion of the Pastorals] sought to collect Paul's letters into a normative corpus of Scripture. The process of canonization, which was adumbrated long before the Pastorals, was now to encompass Paul's theology within the category of 'sound doctrine'" (Childs 2008: 73).

When we examine Childs' views on the entire NT, he affirms that the NT's canonical shape is *in some sense* compositional in a number of places (for example, Childs 1985: 21–22, 26–27). I qualify with "in some sense" because Childs is opaque as to whether or not the entire NT canon is compositionally shaped, rather than just the individual corpora of which it is comprised. We see this kind of ready admission of corpus-level compositional shaping combined with ambiguity about the means of canonical shaping with respect to the entire NT in Childs' introduction to the second testament: "By the collecting and reordering of once independent writings into an authoritative corpus of scripture, a new dynamic was established which profoundly influenced interpretation of the parts (cf. the analysis of the Pauline epistles as an example)" (Childs 1985: 38). Without the final clarifying parenthetical, this sentence could have been read as a reference to the compositional shaping of the entire NT, but as it stands with the final phrase, it can also be read as limiting compositional shaping to individual corpora. If the latter is Childs' position, then the combination of the four distinct corpora into one NT canon would have *post hoc* hermeneutical significance but not be compositional in nature.

This leads us back to the original question, then: is Childs' view of the canonical shape of the entire NT, and not just one particular corpus, a *post hoc* reality or a compositional one? He notes that the different NT corpora must be understood in relation to one another in a number of places; for example, he says, "Of course, ultimately the Pauline corpus will have to be related to the rest of the New Testament, especially to Acts, and to the Old Testament" (Childs 2008: 76; see also his comments in Childs 1986: 11–13). Is this required relation one of composition or *post hoc* hermeneutical significance, though? Ultimately, it is hard to say with Childs. With other canonical interpreters, the matter is much more clear—canonical shape is either a *post hoc* product of ecclesial reception or a compositional, intended feature of the text.

The matter is much clearer when we recall our previous discussions of the various categories. Brodie's and others' compositional approach could be described as a maximal approach to understanding the NT's canonical shape, whereas Metzger's and Patzia's could be described as minimalist with respect to the importance of canonical considerations. The mediating position, that canonical shape has *post hoc* hermeneutical significance, attempts to recognize the literary quality of the NT as a book without placing the hermeneutical import of such an acknowledgment at the level of textual composition. Regarding the maximalist and mediating positions, then, both agree that the NT's canonical shape is hermeneutically significant. Where disagreement remains is in which shape we examine, and by what method(s).

Which order? What shape?

If the shape of the NT canon carries hermeneutical significance, then the subsequent questions are, "which order do we consider as we take into account canonical shape?" and, "by what method do we study that particular shape?" While it is commonly acknowledged that the NT canon circulated in distinct codices by the end of the second century, the order of books within codices varied, as did the inclusion and exclusion of particular books. Further, the Western order of the Four Gospels and Acts, the Pauline Epistles, Hebrews and the Catholic Epistles, and Revelation, is not exactly what we find in the earliest circulating codices; there, most often Acts circulates with the Catholic Epistles and Hebrews is included in the Pauline corpus. If one were to put these distinct codices in an order similar to that of the West, from the Gospels to Revelation, then, you would have the Four Gospels, Acts followed by James through Jude, Paul with Hebrews included, and Revelation.

Given these differences in order (and there are more examples than just this one), which order "counts" when we attempt to interpret texts and books in light of canonical shape? More broadly, what about books that were included or excluded only in certain lists? This latter question is part of the discussion of canonical shape. In fact, in earlier uses of the term, "shape" is a consideration not only of order, but of the inclusion and exclusion of particular books from particular corpora and, by extension, the entire canon as a unit. If there are differences in shape with respect to both inclusion and order, how do we adjudicate between these variations in order to understand *the* canonical shape's impact on our interpretation of Scripture? In this section I want to highlight four approaches to these questions, although it is important to note that each approach is not isolated from the others. Most who address canonical questions take each of these categories into account; the difference between them is thus not based on excluding other approaches but on which approach is prioritized above the others. Like the categories in the previous section, and to some degree those in the following section, these are merely meant to be heuristic devices that introduce the reader to the basic questions of the field, not as, collectively, a totalizing schema.

Empirical

One approach to the question of "which shape?" is to base one's answer on a certain set of data, namely manuscripts, lists, and other attestations to canonical ordering. In this approach, the empirical data we have available is cited, compared, and analyzed, sometimes in order to conclude that one arrangement is the preferred one, at other times to say that there are too many possible arrangements to see any hermeneutical significance in canonical shape. The latter conclusion is that of Patzia and Metzger, but this is not necessarily the inevitable conclusion for those who take this approach. Sometimes, comparison of manuscripts, lists, and other attestations lead certain scholars to see a certain order as preferred. Again, there is variety here, as sometimes "preferred" means "most attested," at other times it means "earliest" (based on a certain set of criteria), and at other times it might mean "the dominant order in transmission or later reception." In any case, the choice of canonical shape on which to base a canonical interpretation, in this view, is derived primarily via empirical evidence.

In some respects, this approach is foundational to the rest. Each of the remaining approaches attempts to adjudicate between the different arrangements by prioritizing another set of criteria—historical, ecclesial, or literary. Again, this is not to say that each of the following approaches, or the empirical approach, excludes other approaches, but it is to say that each approach prioritizes a certain set of criteria in determining which canonical shape to consider.

Historical

Another approach that is related in many respects to the first asks, "what event(s) prompted the collection of various corpora or the writing of certain lists?" In this approach, the adjudication between various kinds of empirical evidence comes primarily through consideration of the socio-cultural factors that would have led to different orders in different regions at different times, and what socio-cultural factors would have led to a more universal canonical shape, whether for individual corpora or for the NT as a whole.

The most recent and explicit example of this approach is David R. Nienhuis's work on the Catholic Epistles. While his focus remains on the CE corpus, his thesis and methodology have implications for understanding the shape of the NT canon as a whole. For Nienhuis, the development of the CE collection, and specifically the authorship of James, crystallizes later than the rest of the NT and prompts the final form of the NT canon found in many early codices. According to Nienhuis, both the finalization of the CE collection and the subsequent crystallization of the NT canon as a whole are prompted by a number of historical factors in the late second and early third centuries (Nienhuis 2007). Nienhuis refers to his thesis as a "composition hypothesis" (22), but his methodology is one that requires historical reconstruction as the starting point for understanding canonical shape. This is stated explicitly throughout the book. His model is not the only example of this approach, though; one can detect it (as with the other approaches) in others, such as Trobisch,[7] although his concern is more literary in nature (see above). Kruger is perhaps an example of a theologically conservative approach in this regard, although he would argue that historical investigation into the canon's origins is not the ultimate criterion of canonicity (even if it is to be preferred over a community-oriented approach, which seems to be the case in his view). Rather, canon is "self-authenticating" as divine speech (see Kruger 2012,

---

[7] See Trobisch's suggestions about the Canonical Edition's "harmonizing tendency" with respect to the Jerusalem authorities and Paul, and about its "anti-Marcionite attitude," in Trobisch 2000: 80, 105 respectively. See also Wall's discussion of this feature of the canonical approach in Wall and Lemcio 1992: 17. Finally, see von Campenhausen (1972), for a widely influential work on the relation of canon formation to Marcion.

especially 27–124). Even so, in practice, Kruger seems primarily concerned with the historical defensibility of the Protestant canon, as the latter half of his *Canon Revisited* is taken up with empirical evidence to support an historical view of canonicity that maintains traditional views of date and authorship.

Ecclesial

A third approach to "which shape?" comes from Robert W. Wall and Eugene Lemcio, who emphasize communal reception. They take into account empirical, historical, and literary concerns (see Wall and Lemcio 1992: 15–25, especially 16–19), but at the foundation of their approach is a commitment to considering the NT's canonical shape from the perspective of reception history. Thus, Wall comments, "if canonical hermeneutics is centered by the ongoing relationship between canon and community, then the act of interpreting biblical texts must aim at the formation of a distinctively Christian people" (Wall and Lemcio 1992: 24). This ongoing relationship between canon and community is one that is embedded into the canonical process itself; that is, canonization is in large part a function of ecclesial reception via textual production. Notice how Wall describes the canonization process: "Different writings, first preserved and as 'scriptural', have been crafted together over time into a canonical whole in order to enhance the Bible's usefulness to the church as its rule of faith" (Wall and Lemcio 1992: 18, see also 110–28). Ultimately, this approach distinguishes between composition of individual books and canonization by the community of faith (see Lockett 2015: 127–36, especially 129–31 for this particular distinction).

Literary

Finally, there are literary-oriented approaches to answering the question of which shape. At the risk of multiplying categories, we should note that there are really two approaches within this last one—those who emphasize shape as a literary phenomenon that cannot be ignored, and those who emphasize shape as a compositional reality. The "order as unavoidable literary phenomenon" approach is characterized by Goswell's comments about "paratext" in the previous section of this chapter. One could also point to John Sailhamer's insights regarding "contextuality" (Sailhamer 1995: 213). Canonical shape in this approach exerts interpretive force, even if the shape of the canon is a *post hoc* phenomenon not intended by the original authors. This is true, for some, even if order, as a subset of shape, is considered an arbitrary factor. Childs, for example, in an interesting comment on the canonical shape of Acts, says, "The canonical significance of Acts lies elsewhere, regardless of its order within the New Testament collection," and specifically in its hermeneutical relation to the Pauline corpus.[8] A similar move is made when Childs connects e.g. the Catholic Epistles' and Revelation's canonical shapes

---

[8] Childs 1985: 239–40. He goes on to argue that its primary canonical purpose is to serve as an historical and theological interpretive foundation for reading Paul's letters.

specifically with their canonical titles. Regarding the former, the collection's title emphasizes their universal significance, even though they are titled with historical and geographical particularity (Childs 1985: 495). Regarding the latter, "The Revelation of John" is a title that connects the final book with the rest of the Johannine corpus (Childs 1985: 517).

The other kind of literary approach is compositional. Here, canonical shape is a feature of the text itself rather than some *post hoc*, ecclesially or communally produced aspect. The shapes of individual corpora and of the NT canon as a whole are determined primarily not by external historical forces or rather arbitrary factors like book length, but by intentional compositional features that are placed in the text. For some, these features are placed in the text by some of the biblical authors, while for others they are added by a later final redactor (which can be a community or an individual, depending on whose argument we consider). This approach can be seen, for example, in the works of Trobisch, Spellman, and Lockett, although each come at the question of canonical shape from slightly different angles and none of them arrive at exactly the same interpretive conclusions.

Interpreting the shape of the NT canon

If one determines that canonical shape has hermeneutical significance, and once one decides which shape will serve as the ground of canonical interpretation, the final and teleological question is, how is the canonical shape of the NT to be interpreted? Here, as above, there are a variety of approaches. I will highlight the four that are, in my estimation, most prominent: setting hermeneutical boundaries, the NT's relation to the OT, Paul's relation to other apostles, and thematic approaches.

Setting hermeneutical boundaries

Childs often refers to canonical shaping as boundary setting (see Childs 1985: 27). One example comes in his work on the Pauline corpus, where he says, "The structure of these books at the beginning and end of the corpus [Romans and Hebrews] sets the context for its interpretation. They address the crucial hermeneutical issue of the interpretation of Paul, namely, how are his letters in their highly particularized, time-conditioned, historical settings to be used by future generations of Christians?" (Childs 2008: 76). Similarly, in *The New Testament as Canon*, Childs begins his explanation of the methodology of canonical exegesis by claiming that, "The canonical form marks not only the place from which exegesis begins, but also the place at which it ends" (Childs 1985: 48). A few sentences later, Childs combines the canon's parameter-setting and hermeneutical functions when he states that, "The canon as a designation of the collection marks the parameters of the scriptures, but the canonical shaping of the text leads the interpreter to discern how the material within the canon was fashioned through a particular intertextuality to render its special message" (Childs 1985: 48, see also 42).

The New Testament kerygma and the Old Testament messianic hope

Childs does not limit the canonical shape's function to setting parameters and to merely generic notions of hermeneutical significance.[9] He and others argue that the shape of the NT canon is primarily interpreted as an affirmation of the Old Testament, or at least an exercise in reading it in light of the life, death, and resurrection of Jesus Christ (see Childs 1993: 70–79 and 1985: 31). There are various ways of stating this; for instance, Childs' repeated claim that the canonical shape of the NT is one which gives testimony to Jesus Christ should be understood in the context of Childs' insistence on a two testament canon and the NT's positive relation to the OT. "The interpreter enters into a dialogue with the text," argues Childs, "in an effort to discern how each writing within the New Testament canon construes its material in order to bear truthful witness to the gospel of Jesus Christ." Further, "The interpreter is reading the text toward a particular goal, namely, one which is congruent with the kerygmatic character *of the scriptures* in bearing testimony to God's redemption of the world in Christ" (Childs 1985: 48, emphasis mine). He also talks about canonical shape as a guide to understanding the gospel (Childs 1985: 40). Similarly, he says that "The function of canon is to assure its involving a received tradition which has been shaped toward the end of engendering faith in the Risen Lord of the Scriptures" (Childs 1985: 40). Ultimately for Childs the canonical function is Christological, in that it bears witness to the God-man, Jesus Christ, and sets the exegetical and theological boundaries for the church's understanding of his person and work (Childs 1985: 28–30, 44, see also Childs 2002 45).

Other examples of this interpretation of the NT's canonical shape include David Trobisch, who argues that the title of the New Testament, the selection and arrangement of books, and the use of *nomina sacra*[10] all are intended to "assert that the Jewish Bible is relevant to their audience" (Trobisch 2000: 76). Spellman notes that the compositional nature and structural placement of Revelation is intended to point to an ideal reader who understands the Old Testament "within the context of the entire Christian canon" (Spellman 2014: 215).[11] And not only does Revelation's compositional character and structural placement highlight the unity of the testaments in general; it also actually points to the fact, for Spellman, that, "The ideal reader of Revelation (and the Bible as a whole) is one who keeps and treasures it as a 'revelation' of the risen Lord" (Spellman

---

[9] Although there are a number of generic references to the hermeneutical function of canon. See e.g. Childs 1985: 37, 39.

[10] On the title of the NT and its relation to the OT, see Trobisch 2000: 62–63. On selection and arrangement of books, see 63–64 for a discussion which Trobisch concludes by saying, "The three parts of the Christian Old Testament may be reflected in the New Testament: the Gospels and Acts correspond to the historical books, the General Letters and the Letters of Paul to the poetic writings, and Revelation to the Prophets" (64). On the *nomina sacra* in relation to the OT, see 66–68.

[11] In discussing Revelation's placement in the canon, Spellman is one of the few who work with not only intertextual but also structural concepts of shape to interpret the canon's function and how the NT relates to the OT. For other examples of relating the NT's structure to the OT's, see Seitz's discussion of the Pauline corpus and the Book of the Twelve in Seitz 2009: 11–12, 33–35, 102; Seitz 2006: 76–84; Pennington 2012: 229–58, and, specifically his discussion of the Gospels as the "archway" of the canon; and also, Kruger 2012: 152–58.

2014: 219, see also Farkasfalvy 2006: 114). The canonical shape of the NT, with Revelation as its capstone, is for Spellman an indication of the unity of the testaments precisely because they together are the words of Christ.

Paul among the apostles

For some, the final shape of the NT canon is one which emphasizes historical and theological harmony between Paul and the other apostles (e.g. Gamble 2002/1985: 79). For instance, Wall states that Acts "provides the context within which the canonical conversation between the Pauline and non-Pauline collections is understood" (Wall and Lemcio 1992: 120; also ibid., 113–15; see also Bovon 2002).[12] The final shape of the CE collection—James, Peter, John, and Jude—is said to reflect Gal. 2:9, as well as the Jerusalem council in Acts 15 (see Wall and Lemcio 1992: 250–71). In certain iterations of this thesis, the apparent conceptual disunity between the letters of Paul and the letters included in the CE, as well as supposed historical evidences of disunity (e.g. Paul's confrontation of Peter in Galatians 2) are "harmonized" via their inclusion in the same NT canon, and especially by the narrative context set in Acts, as well as via the particular shape of the CEs. In some cases, this harmonization is explicitly tied to historical realities in the late second or early third centuries and is posited as a means of uniting a geographically disparate and, perhaps, theologically fragmented early church (e.g. Nienhuis 2007).

In other cases, there is still an emphasis on the united apostolic testimony of the NT, and particularly the combination of Paul and the apostolic attributions of authorship in the CE collection,[13] but there is much less attention paid to supposed disharmony between these individuals or the letters that bear their name.[14] In this approach, the interpretation of "Paul among the apostles" is not so much about legitimizing any particular letter in relation to other letters or about harmonizing supposed instances of disharmony between the corpora, but instead about having an "apostolic canon," one that is shaped by the inclusion of both the apostle to the Gentiles, Paul, and the apostle to the Jews, Peter (see e.g. Trobisch 2000: 59–62, 76–77). Peter's inclusion with the letter of James, the leader of the church at Jerusalem, the letters of John, another original Jewish disciple, as well as the letter of Jude, the Lord's (again, Jewish) brother, highlights the CE's function, in this interpretation, as a corpus focused on the Christian mission to the Jews. Alongside one another, the Pauline corpus and the CE collection give a holistic picture of the Christian mission to the entire world, Jew and Gentile. The

---

[12] But see Smith's critical comments about both Wall's and Childs' understanding of Acts in Smith 2002: 39–40. See also Goswell 2016: 67–82 on this interpretation of NT canonical shape.

[13] See e.g. Childs 1985: 28–29, where he says that "... sometimes a check was established to prevent a misreading of a witness, such as the function of James which guarded against a false reading of Paul." Notice that, for Childs, the diversity between James and Paul is not one of fundamental *disunity* at the historical level that is only subsequently harmonized via canonization but is rather complementary and intended to prevent false readings of one another. This is very different, as Childs himself points out (29), from the approach of James D. G. Dunn, where "diversity" equals "opposition."

[14] Lockett's *Letters from the Pillar Apostles* emphasizes the CE collection's relation to Paul's reference to the Jerusalem "Pillars" in Gal. 2:9 without pitting them against one another.

Gospel collection, as well as the structure of Acts with its movement from the mission to the Jews to the mission to the Gentiles, provides the narrative context for this globally oriented letter collection, and Revelation provides a fitting conclusion with its emphasis on the salvation of God's global people and the renewal of all creation.[15] A final note that must be included in this interpretation is that this holistic picture of Christ's church and the Spirit's mission, and in particular the harmony between Peter and Paul, is often tied, historically, to anti-Marcionism in the second century.[16]

Thematic

Finally, there are those who emphasize biblical theological themes in their understanding of the NT's canonical shape. Sometimes this thematic approach is taken on a structural level book by book, while at other times it is more author- or corpus-oriented. For some, this thematic approach means emphasizing the (enforced?) harmony that happens at a canonical level while study of the individual books demonstrates discord.[17] For others, a thematic approach is intended to highlight recurring concepts throughout the different parts of the canon and especially at structurally significant points (see Emerson 2013 for an example of this approach).

Moving forward

In order to move forward in the study of the shape of the NT canon, a number of questions have yet to be answered with any kind of scholarly consensus. First, what hermeneutical function does canonical shape have, if any? Why? From whence? This set of questions hinges upon two issues: the ability to prove or disprove canonically shaped textual features, and canonical shape's hermeneutical significance (or lack thereof). On the latter, it is possible, perhaps even probable, that consensus cannot be achieved. Barr's critique of Childs' canonical approach in *Holy Scripture* continues to resound with certain scholars. In other words, does "final form" really require us to downplay the historical context of particular pericopes or, in this case, particular books so that we can focus on the macro-level shape of the canon? Even if one does agree that

---

[15] Although I have included Wall and Lemcio as examples in the previous paragraphs, some of their comments about the NT's canonical shape are phrased in such a way that the "Paul v. Peter/James" conflict is minimized, and instead the emphasis is on the "catholicity" provided by the shape of the NT canon. See, e.g., *The New Testament as Canon*, 34–35, 145–47, 184–85. See, as well, Wall's comments about Revelation's structural suitability for the final book of the canon in ibid., 279–82.

[16] See, for example, Trobisch 2000: 82–89, 105–106; and Knox 1960. For a more recent essay on the relation between anti-Marcionitism and the formation of the NT canon, see Barton (2002); also, Nienhuis 2007: 236–38. On the Muratorian Fragment, see Hahneman (1992); and the response by Verheyden 2003: 487–556. See also Everett Ferguson's discussion in 2002: 309–320. On the influence of Montanism, see also Paulsen (1978).

[17] The paradigmatic example of this approach is James D. G. Dunn, especially exemplified in Dunn 2006. See also the famous comments of Ernst Käsemann concerning the diversity of the NT in, 1951–1952; see also Käsemann 1970: 124–33, especially 131. I am indebted to John Barton 2016: 268 n. 11 for these references. But see Childs' critique of Dunn's *Unity and Diversity*, and more broadly of the supposed discordant voices canonized in the NT, in Childs 1985: 29–30.

canonical shape is important, what kind of importance does it have? Is it merely functional, in that it sets the boundaries for what texts to interpret? Or is there some added significance related to literary sequence to which we must pay attention? These are not easy questions, and there are no easy answers, particularly given the variety of hermeneutical commitments among scholars interested in the issue of canon.

Second, what is the relationship between authorial intent of a biblical book and canonical shape? More particularly, when does authorship end and transmission begin? Perhaps this is not such a pressing question for those who do not insist on some kind of historically identifiable original author in order to tie authorial intent to either divine inspiration or, more particularly, inerrancy. But for those who do adhere to such doctrines, the question seems to become more urgent, at least in the sense of identifying what is text and what is (to use Goswell's term) paratext.[18]

Even for those who do not affirm theological doctrines like inspiration or inerrancy, or who wish to set them aside for the sake of empirical inquiry, this is still a rather pressing question, if only because the dividing line between canonical shaping and textual transmission determines in part what we can say about the proper interpretation(s) of the former. In other words, those who insist on either the empirical or historical approaches outlined above need to identify a place or multiple places in time and space in which various canonical shapes occurred. And, for the historical approach, this is especially pertinent for interpreting canonical shape, as, typically, one must identify the historical milieu for the specific shape the exegete references as the proper canonical context.

Thus, whether one takes a particular theological stance toward the canon or not, the ability to distinguish between text and paratext, or between canonical shaping and transmission, is tantamount to the canonical approach. A related question is, therefore, what criteria are available and appropriate to make such distinctions? This continues to be debated among both canonical interpreters and scholars of early Christianity interested in the development of the canon.

A third question relates to the previous in terms of the concept of authorial intent: Are intertextual links at important canonical points a product of authorial and/or editorial intent? Are they products of divine inspiration but not human intent? Or are they simply coincidental given commonalities in worldview? Again, for those who take a *post hoc* approach, whether on empirical, historical, ecclesial, or literary grounds, this may not matter all that much. What matters most is that the canon, including its intertextual connections, has *post hoc* hermeneutical significance. But for those who want to tie canonical shape more directly to compositional intent, (human or divine), or even to "canonical intent" (i.e. the interplay between author, editor/redactor, and compiler), the evidence for that intent is crucial. Thus, a further issue here, is, as above, the criteria by which one adjudicates whether supposed instances of canonical shaping are, in fact, intentional.

---

[18] For instance, if titles are added by later editors, but they are intended to canonically shape the NT, is that text or paratext? See, for instance, the discussion on the Gospels' titles in Goswell, (2017). Goswell notes that there is recent transatlantic interest in the question, pointing specifically to Petersen 2006.

Fourth, the question of whether the shape of the OT influences the NT is an increasingly common one, and one that has been relatively underexplored thus far. This will not be a pertinent question for those who see no or only *post hoc* hermeneutical significance in canonical shape. But for those who argue that canonical shape is intentional via categories like composition and intertextuality, this is an especially relevant question. We have seen above that "affirmation of the OT" is an important concept with which some canonical critics summarize their view of the hermeneutical significance of the canon. Perhaps the NT is an affirmation of the OT not only conceptually, but also structurally.[19]

A final and essential question that influences how one might answer the others is: what *is* the canon? This foundational query will necessarily impact how one views supposed evidence of canonical shape and the demarcation between composition and transmission, the relation between the intent of the human author(s) and/or editor(s) and the ecclesial reception of the text, and the like.

Conclusion

The *status quaestionis* for the shape of the NT canon is that it is still an open one. There is no real consensus in the field, either with respect to its hermeneutical significance or lack thereof, its static shape and the methods by which to determine such, its historical origins, or its meaning(s). With respect to hermeneutical significance, some scholars argue there is none at all; others argue that it has only a *post hoc* hermeneutical significance; and still others argue that canonical shaping is embedded in the text through compositional features. With respect to the proper shape of the canon to be considered when engaging in canonical criticism, as well as to its historical context, some scholars take an empirical approach, others an historical one, still others an ecclesial one, and others a variety of literary approaches. Finally, there are different understandings of the role and meaning of the shape of the NT, including setting hermeneutical boundaries, affirmation of Paul among other apostles, affirmation of the OT, and highlighting a specific theme or set of themes. Despite the fact that the *status quaestionis* remains open with respect to the shape of the NT canon, the fact remains that it is an established and important question, as demonstrated by the variety of essays and monographs dedicated to the subject. In order to move forward, then, those engaging in canonical criticism of the NT will need to come into closer proximity to one another in the areas of hermeneutics and methodology before there can be any kind of consensus established regarding the meaning of the NT's shape.[20]

---

[19] See the footnote at the end of the section on "The NT kerygma and the OT messianic hope" for examples.

[20] Many thanks to Darian Lockett, Ed Glenny, Brandon Smith, and Ched Spellman for their comments on an earlier version of this essay.

Bibliography

Barr, James. (1983), *Holy Scripture: Canon, Authority, Criticism*, Philadelphia: The Westminster Press.
Barr, James. (1999), *The Concept of Biblical Theology: An Old Testament Perspective*, Minneapolis: Fortress Press.
Bartholomew, Craig, Scott Hahn, Robin Parry, Christopher Seitz, and Al Wolters, eds. (2006), *Canon and Biblical Interpretation*, SAHS 7, Grand Rapids: Baker.
Barton, John. (2016), "James Barr and the Future of Biblical Theology," *Interpretation* 70 (3): 264–74.
Barton, John. (2002), "Marcion Revisited," in Lee Martin McDonald and James A. Sanders (eds.), *The Canon Debate*, 341–54, Peabody: Hendrickson.
Bokedal, Tomas. (2014), *The Formation and Significance of the Christian Biblical Canon: A Study in Text, Ritual and Interpretation*, London: Bloomsbury.
Bovon, François. (2002), "The Canonical Structure of Gospel and Apostle," in Lee Martin McDonald and James A. Sanders (eds.), *The Canon Debate*, 516–27, Peabody: Hendrickson.
Brodie, Thomas L. (2004), *The Birthing of the New Testament: The Intertextual Development of the New Testament Writings*, NTM 1, Sheffield: Sheffield Phoenix.
Childs, Brevard S. (1985), *The New Testament as Canon: An Introduction*, Minneapolis: Fortress.
Childs, Brevard S. (1986), *Introduction to Old Testament Theology in a Canonical Context*, Minneapolis: Fortress.
Childs, Brevard S. (1993), *Biblical Theology of the Old and New Testaments: Theological Reflections on the Christian Bible*, Minneapolis: Fortress.
Childs, Brevard S. (2002), *Biblical Theology: A Proposal*, Minneapolis: Fortress.
Childs, Brevard S. (2008), *The Church's Guide for Reading Paul: The Canonical Shaping of the Pauline Corpus*, Grand Rapids: Eerdmans.
Childs, Brevard S. (2011), *Introduction to the Old Testament as Christian Scripture*, Minneapolis: Augsburg Fortress, 1979, reprint Minneapolis: Fortress.
Dunn, James D. G. (2006), *Unity and Diversity in the New Testament: An Inquiry into the Character of Earliest Christianity*, 3rd edn, London: SCM.
Emerson, Matthew Y. (2013), *Christ and the New Creation: A Canonical Approach to the Theology of the New Testament*, Eugene: Wipf and Stock.
Farkasfalvy, Dennis. (2006), "The Apostolic Gospels in the Early Church," in Craig Bartholomew, Scott Hahn, Robin Parry, Christopher Seitz, and Al Wolters (eds.), *Canon and Biblical Interpretation*, 111–22, SAHS 7, Grand Rapids: Baker.
Ferguson, Everett. (2002), "Factors Leading to the Selection and Closure of the New Testament Canon," in Lee Martin McDonald and James A. Sanders (eds), *The Canon Debate*, 295–320, Peabody: Hendrickson.
Gamble, Harry Y. (2002), *The New Testament Canon: Its Making and Meaning; A Guide to Biblical Scholarship*, Minneapolis: Augsburg Fortress, 1985, reprint Eugene: Wipf and Stock.
Goswell, Gregory. (2008), "The Order of the Books in the Hebrew Bible," *JETS* 51 (4): 673–88.
Goswell, Gregory. (2013), "Two Testaments in Parallel: The Influence of the Old Testament on the Structuring of the New Testament Canon," *JETS* 56 (3): 459–60.
Goswell, Gregory. (2016), "The Place of the Book of Acts in Reading the NT," *JETS* 59 (1): 67–82.

Goswell, Gregory. (2017), "Authorship and Anonymity in the New Testament Writings," *JETS* 60 (4): 736–40.

Hahneman, Geoffrey M. (1992), *The Muratorian Fragment and the Development of the Canon*, Oxford: Clarendon Press.

Käsemann, Ernst. (1951–1952), "Begründet der neutestamentliche Kanon die Einheit der Kirche?" *Evangelische Theologie* 11: 13–21.

Käsemann, Ernst. (1970), *Das Neue Testament als Kanon: Dokumentation und kritische Analyse zur gegenwärtigen Diskussion*, Göttingen: Vandenhoeck & Ruprecht.

Knox, John. (1960), *Philemon Among the Letters of Paul*, London: Collins.

Kruger, Michael J. (2012), *Canon Revisited: Establishing the Origins and Authority of the New Testament Books*, Wheaton: Crossway.

Lockett, Darian R. (2015), "Not Whether, But What Kind of Canonical Approach: A Review Essay," *JTI* 9 (1): 127–36.

Lockett, Darian R. (2017), *Letters from the Pillar Apostles: The Formation of the Catholic Epistles*, Eugene: Pickwick.

McDonald, Lee Martin and James A. Sanders, eds. (2002), *The Canon Debate*, Peabody: Hendrickson.

Metzger, Bruce M. (2009), *The Canon of the New Testament: Its Origin, Development, and Significance*, Oxford: Clarendon Press, 1987; reprint.

Niebuhr, Karl-Wilhelm. (2003), "Exegese im kanonischen Zusammenhang: Überlegungen zur theologischen Relevanz der Gestalt des neutestamentlichen Kanons," in J.-M. Auwers and H. J. De Jonge (eds.), *The Biblical Canons*, BETL 163, Leuven: Peeters.

Nienhuis, David R. (2007), *Not by Paul Alone: The Formation of the Catholic Epistle Collection and the Christian Canon*, Waco: Baylor University Press.

Nienhuis, David R. and Robert W. Wall. (2013), *Reading the Epistles of James, Peter, John & Jude as Scripture: The Shaping and Shape of a Canonical Collection*, Grand Rapids: Eerdmans.

Parker, David C. (2008), *An Introduction to the New Testament Manuscripts and their Texts*, Cambridge: Cambridge University Press.

Patzia, Arthur G. (1995), *The Making of the New Testament: Origin, Collection, Text & Canon*, 2nd edn, reprint, Grand Rapids: IVP Academic, 2011.

Paulsen, Henning. (1978), "Die Bedeutung des Montanismus für die Herausbildung des Kanons," *VC* 32: 19–52.

Pennington, Jonathan T. (2012), *Reading the Gospels Wisely: A Narrative and Theological Introduction*, Grand Rapids: Baker Academic.

Petersen, Silke. (2006), "Die Evangelien uberschriften und die Entstehung des neutestamentlichen Kanons," *ZNW* 97: 250–74.

Sailhamer, John. (1995), *Introduction to Old Testament Theology: A Canonical Approach*, Grand Rapids: Zondervan.

Seitz, Christopher R. (2006), "The Canonical Approach and Theological Interpretation," in Craig Bartholomew, Scott Hahn, Robin Parry, Christopher Seitz, and Al Wolters (eds.), *Canon and Biblical Interpretation*, 58–110, SAHS 7, Grand Rapids: Baker.

Seitz, Christopher R. (2009), *The Goodly Fellowship of the Prophets: The Achievement of Association in Canon Formation*, Acadia Studies in Biblical Theology, Grand Rapids: Baker Academic.

Smith, David E. (2002), *The Canonical Function of Acts: A Comparative Analysis*, Collegeville: The Liturgical Press.

Spellman, Ched. (2014), *Toward a Canon-Conscious Reading of the Bible: Exploring the History and Hermeneutics of the Canon*, NTM 34, Sheffield: Sheffield Phoenix.

Trobisch, David. (1994), *Paul's Letter Collection: Tracing the Origins*, Minneapolis: Augsburg Fortress.
Trobisch, David. (2000), *The First Edition of the New Testament*, Oxford: Oxford University Press.
Verheyden, Joseph. (2003), "The Canon Muratori: A Matter of Dispute," in J.-M. Auwers and H. J. De Jonge (eds.), *The Biblical Canons*, 487–556, BETL 163, Leuven: Peeters.
von Campenhausen, Hans. (1972), *The Formation of the Christian Bible*, Philadelphia: Fortress.
Wall, Robert W. (2012), "The Canonical View," in Stanley E. Porter and Beth M. Stovell (eds.), *Biblical Hermeneutics: Five Views*, 111–30, Downers Grove: InterVarsity.
Wall, Robert W. and Eugene E. Lemcio. (1992), *The New Testament as Canon: A Reader in Canonical Criticism*, JSNTSup 76, Sheffield: Sheffield Academic.
Watson, Francis. (2013), *Gospel Writing: A Canonical Perspective*, Grand Rapids: Eerdmans.

Section Two

Old Testament Canonical Sub-Units

5

The Pentateuch as Canon

Stephen B. Chapman

Pentateuchal scholarship, like biblical scholarship more widely, is routinely described as currently split between diachronic and synchronic approaches (Moor 1995; Roux and Otto 2007). The debate tends to be framed as a cultural divide between historically reconstructive approaches at home in European scholarship and the more reader-oriented treatments produced in North American scholarship, and there is truth in that characterization. However, critical scholars in North America can be just as historically reconstructive (e.g., Friedman 1987; Van Seters 1994; Carr 1996; Baden 2012; Blenkinsopp 2012) and European scholars have become increasingly interested in the "final form/s" of the Pentateuch (e.g., Jonker 2004; Beck and Schorn 2006; Römer and Schmid 2007; cf. Clines 1998).[1]

The more important difference, I would like to suggest, is therefore between two basic models of diachronic investigation, which I will term "latitudinal" and "longitudinal."[2] This distinction is my own, but it is similar to one made by Konrad Schmid between an older diachronic approach focused on "horizontal text divisions" and a newer approach centering on "vertical block divisions" (2010: 16), as well as the distinction drawn by Rainer Albertz between a "highway model" and an "island-bridge model" (2018: 73). With my latitudinal–longitudinal comparison, I aim to contrast the "latitudinal" source-critical approach to pentateuchal formation in North America with the "longitudinal" European initiative to combine the documentary, supplementary, and fragmentary hypotheses of pentateuchal formation going back to the nineteenth century (Römer 2013; Kratz 2016).

It seems that biblical scholarship in the United States has never really gotten over the Documentary Hypothesis.

---

[1] I employ the conventions "final form/s" and "received text/s" to signal that the final version of the Pentateuch did not in fact take one single text form, often assumed to be the MT. See Blum 1991.

[2] For an engaging study of longitude as a technical achievement and conceptual marker of the modern era, see Sobel 2019. Longitude and latitude are geographical coordinates for determining locations on the Earth's surface, measured in degrees. Longitude lines or "meridians" run pole-to-pole and determine east–west locations. Latitudes lines or "parallels" run equidistant to the Equator (0° latitude) and fix north–south locations.

Latitude versus Longitude

In its classic nineteenth-century form, the Documentary Hypothesis envisioned four discrete pentateuchal sources (commonly known by their abbreviations J, E, D, and P), each of which recounted its own version of Israel's origins from beginning to end (even if the beginnings and endings of the four sources were not identical). Each source was thus "latitudinal" in that it extended throughout the Pentateuch as a whole, with the result that the Pentateuch in its present shape is the literary equivalent of a braided rope. (D was a special case. Its tradition was usually confined to Deuteronomy and not thought to be identifiable in the other books of the Pentateuch, and yet Deuteronomy was also held to offer its own version of a pentateuchal story. See Ausloos 2015; Otto 2000.) These four pentateuchal sources were entirely hypothetical in the sense that no extant manuscript provided the text of only one source apart from the rest. The sources were reconstructed from the received text/s of the Pentateuch on the basis of their differences from each other and their distinctive vocabularies, motifs, and themes.

By contrast, the form-critical approach of Hermann Gunkel and the "history of religions" school focused on specific genres and narrative cycles (*Erzählkränze*) within the Pentateuch and attempted to trace their individual histories of development (Lüdemann 1996; Buss 1999; Waschke 2013). This scholarship was "longitudinal" in the sense that it was less concerned to read across the books of the Pentateuch and instead investigated the local coherence of the Pentateuch's major components, such as the primeval history in Genesis 1–11, the ancestor narratives in Genesis 12–36, the Joseph cycle in Genesis 37–50, and so on. It was just as diachronic, just as concerned to chart growth and development over time. But because its primary focus was on an earlier, oral stage of the biblical traditions, it did not necessarily presume a unified story of origins behind each individual cycle or narrative complex within the Pentateuch.

For most of the twentieth century, these two main approaches to the Pentateuch coexisted uneasily. The working assumption, not always articulated, was that form criticism reconstructed the oral prehistory of the biblical narratives and then source criticism explained their formulation and combination as written texts. However, in 1977 Rolf Rendtorff exposed the fundamental incompatibility of the two models. The direct target of his critique was the notion of pentateuchal sources extending throughout the various books of the Pentateuch, with each source telling its own version of the whole (Rendtorff 1977).[3]

Rendtorff drew on Gunkel's legacy. He also built on Martin Noth's approach to the history of Israel, in which five thematic complexes (Promise to the Ancestors, Guidance Out of Egypt, Guidance in the Wilderness, Revelation at Sinai, Guidance into the Arable Land) were viewed as coming together relatively independently at an oral stage of transmission prior to being combined into a single pentateuchal story (Noth 1960;

---

[3] The English translation by John J. Scullion, under the cumbersome title *The Problem of the Process of Transmission in the Pentateuch*, did not appear until 1990. For an evaluation of Rendtorff's accomplishments, see Oeming 2019.

see further Dozeman 2017: 98–110). Rendtorff similarly imagined multiple written stories at an early stage of pentateuchal formation rather than written versions of the same story. Ever since this rejection of the Documentary Hypothesis, European scholarship has increasingly viewed the idea of latitudinal sources with great suspicion (see Römer 2013: 9–14 on "die Frage eines durchgehenden Erzählfadens"), replacing the idea of the Pentateuch as a braided rope with that of the Pentateuch as a patchwork quilt. In this longitudinal model, the individual literary cycles within the Pentateuch largely have their own developmental histories and the editorial stitching between them mostly occurred late in the process of the Pentateuch's formation.[4]

Why North American scholarship has resisted this shift from the latitudinal to the longitudinal is an intriguing question. Surely the fact that key works of European scholarship (e.g., Blum 1984; 1990) were never translated into English has played a role. It is also the case that pentateuchal scholarship has become the technical province of specialists, who often do not write broadly enough for non-specialists and whose research has never produced a clear consensus, let alone a new paradigm for the field (Hagedorn 2007; Schmid 2014: 239–40). Usually unacknowledged, however, is how ideological factors are also at work in this North American preference.

Undisclosed commitments

One such ideological factor relates to the model's pedagogical rationale. The Documentary Hypothesis maintains its dominance in numerous English-language textbooks and course lectures because, as one colleague who teaches in the Bible Belt said to me, "It's such an effective way to convince students they can't be fundamentalists." What teachers like this colleague have experienced is how the Documentary Hypothesis carries within it a high degree of internally consistent logic and can therefore go toe to toe successfully with the culturally transmitted assumptions of biblical literalism.

These teachers of course know that the Documentary Hypothesis in its classic form has all sorts of problems and that scholarship has moved on, but they also feel the lack of a new paradigm for similar use in their classrooms. So, they continue to teach the Documentary Hypothesis, fearing that nothing else will persuade their students as well to think critically about the OT. Ironically, the usefulness of the Documentary Hypothesis for this purpose may also signal its closeness to literalistic ways of thinking, with students in the end only exchanging one form of literalism for another.

---

[4] In this description I am favoring the block model advanced by scholars who now work primarily with a version of the old fragmentary hypothesis. There are also "neo-documentarians" who subscribe to a renewed documentary hypothesis and scholars who favor a supplementary hypothesis. These scholars might not envision multiple stories of origin to the same extent. But according to Kratz 2016: 553, "The narrative of the Pentateuch ... cannot have occurred independently in the three literary strata D, P, and non-P, irrespective of whether one adopts the documentary, fragmentary, or supplementary hypothesis or a combination of all three hypotheses." Cf. Schmid 2014: 264–65.

Nevertheless, pedagogical and ideological concerns in this fashion fuel the continued hegemony of the Documentary Hypothesis in North America.[5]

Another ideological motivation for the Documentary Hypothesis is that it actually funds a discernible biblical theology for those who want one (not everyone does), even though this theology is not always spelled out and is more often implied rather than stated openly. Because the source-critical, "latitudinal" approach exemplified in the Documentary Hypothesis treats the Pentateuch's four sources as four versions of the same basic story of Israel's origins, the Pentateuch is viewed less as a single composite narrative and more as four related narratives, in rough parallel to how the NT begins with four versions of the life of Jesus.[6] Even as exegetical work on the Gospels frequently modulates into research on the historical Jesus, pentateuchal exegesis then easily turns into a reconstruction of the history of ancient Israel.

A theological approach to the Pentateuch as a collection of versions correspondingly takes shape as an assemblage and recital of Israel's story of origins behind the versions, yielding a salvation-historical character and theme for the Pentateuch as a whole (e.g., Wright 1952; Wright and Fuller 1957; cf. Schmid 2014: 242–43). This historicized theology of the Pentateuch becomes something like a gospel *diatesseron*, a harmonization of the events and accents of the individual sources and traditions into one consistent story (cf. Kratz 2016: 536–37). Yet in doing so this history also substitutes itself to some degree for the Bible (Lockett 2017). Here again there is a closeness between this kind of theological thinking and biblical literalism, with its intolerance of ambiguity, difference, and multivocality (cf. Morgan 1979). Contemporary advocates of the Documentary Hypothesis can even be antagonistic toward the Pentateuch as it stands: the Pentateuch is said to resemble a "sick" patient that remains "incoherent" and "unreadable" without the critical "surgery" that source criticism provides (Baden 2016: 250–51).

The more interesting question is why ancient Israel did not insist on absolute consistency and uniformity within its narrative of origins, just as the early church did not insist on a single gospel but recognized four. Or, to put the point positively, why variant traditions were preserved within the Pentateuch and left to stand despite their differences. Was it a historical accident, a custodial concern for compiling all available tradition, or a midrashic disregard for systematization? These rationales have all been suggested. But perhaps the Pentateuch's ancient editors had another idea about what constituted the Pentateuch's coherence. In correspondence with NT references like John 20:30–31 and 21:24–25 (Söding 1996), the possibility emerges that comprehensive, fully consistent historiography was ultimately less important for the Pentateuch's

---

[5] Whenever I teach the core OT class at Duke Divinity School, I detail the Documentary Hypothesis, its problems, and newer critical alternatives to it. Some students are always upset—not because of the challenge to Mosaic authorship, but because they took an entire course on the OT in college and never heard that there were criticisms of the Documentary Hypothesis, not to mention newer theories on offer. "I went to a good school. Why didn't I ever hear anything about this?" they ask me. Sometimes they add that the Documentary Hypothesis was really the only thing they were taught in their undergraduate course on the OT.

[6] This perspective leads to accounts of the "theology of J" and the "theology of P," just as we have treatments of the "theology of Matthew" or the "theology of Q." E.g., Brueggemann and Wolff 1975.

tradents than the articulation and inculcation of religious faith. The OT is *scripture* rather than history or historiography *per se*, and it was molded and arranged to be the means of gaining, strengthening, and maintaining that faith.

Canonical context

How then is a theology of the Pentateuch to be pursued in a descriptive, historically sensitive manner if the Pentateuch's literary development cannot be traced in detail or with confidence? (I presume that most of those who are interested in a theology of the Pentateuch would want such a theology to be descriptive and historically sensitive, although with this stance I do not mean to exclude constructive and normative dimensions from the task; cf. de Pury and Knauf 1995; Witte 2016.) A theology of the Pentateuch must begin with the received literary shape of the Pentateuch rather than a reconstruction of the Pentateuch's constituent sources. This starting point is actually *more historical* than beginning with reconstructed sources—not simply because those sources are hypothetical, but because those sources, while apparently real, were not historically preserved as such and *became in time* the received text/s of the Pentateuch now familiar to us. Not to connect earlier sources with the received text/s of the Pentateuch is to introduce an unhistorical gap between one stage of the biblical tradition and another.

Historical criticism scored a crucial point in the early modern era by confronting the anachronistic conflation of the "is" with the "was" in religious traditions: things were not always the way they are now, critical scholars insisted, they have a history. Yet historical criticism would proceed to overcompensate by engaging in its own anachronistic conflation of the "was" with the "is": how things were before, that remains their true and unchanging essence. Later changes were either inconsequential or degenerative. So, for example, historical critics tend to insist that there *are* two creation accounts in the Bible, even though it is abundantly evident that what once *were* two creation accounts in Genesis 1–3 have been combined into one (Levin 2005: 112). Or the predictive aspect of biblical prophecy is held to be illegitimate because in some reconstructions early prophecy lacked this element (e.g., Schmid 2012: 387), even though prediction is clearly now a vital aspect of the Bible's portrayal of prophecy (*pace* Van Seters 2013).

Canonical criticism[7] offers its own crucial intervention right at this point, insisting not only on specified historical connections between antecedent sources and final text/s, but also a more careful disambiguation between the prehistory of a text and the text itself. Brevard Childs identified this problem almost fifty years ago by describing it as a "grievous error for Christian scholars to assume that the reconstruction of the

---

[7] I am fully aware of Brevard Childs' objection to the term "canonical criticism" because it might be heard as merely one more historical-critical method rather than challenging historical criticism in precisely the way that I have just outlined. But used loosely, and in parallel with historical criticism, the term seems serviceable. After all, historical criticism is not a "method" either.

literature's historical development can now replace the study of the canonical shape of the Pentateuch." Childs proposed a major course-correction: "Rather, the present shape of the Pentateuch offers a particular interpretation—indeed confession—as to how the tradition was to be understood by the community of faith. Therefore it seems to me important first of all to describe the actual characteristics of the canonical shape and secondly to determine the theological significance of that shape" (Childs 1972: 715). Unlike purely synchronic or intertextual approaches, such a canonically oriented form of criticism continues to concern itself with the prehistory of the biblical text. However, it approaches the text's prehistory through the present shape of the text, which serves as the ultimate contextualization for earlier reconstructed traditions.

As Christopher Seitz has put it, the received shape of the biblical text is "a kind of commentary on the text's prehistory." He explains further:

> Through the arrangement and sequencing of the material as we now have it, [the text's final-form presentation] is a theological statement made by allowing certain aspects of the prehistory to receive prominence and clarity, and other aspects of that prehistory to recede in importance ... [W]hile historical analysis may lay bare levels of tradition ..., it will not have adequate theological or literary warrant for determining which level is to have exegetical priority. It will either conclude that the biblical text is a container of competing and incongruent theological claims, or it will wittingly or unwittingly give precedence to one such claim over another.
>
> Seitz 2005: 100

Precisely because most historical approaches to biblical interpretation wrench the Bible's individual traditions apart in order to examine them more closely and in isolation, such approaches are at a loss when it comes to assessing those traditions in relation to each other. The typical move is to imagine controversy and compromise leading to the biblical literature's present form/s (e.g., Blenkinsopp 2004: 206; Nihan 2010: 357–58; Schmid 2014: 269), but social reconstructions like this never quite touch how a resultant (combined) form of that literature was actually, which is to say historically, understood by the community for which it then functioned as scripture. Even if the biblical literature was created through conflict and compromise, it was no longer read that way when it was read as a new unity. To read the biblical literature as "about" the circumstances of its production leads to a historicist variety of modern allegory (see Römer 2016a: 363–64 on "allegorical dating"), as opposed to reading the biblical literature as realistic depiction, as it was traditionally, which is to say historically, read (Frei 1974).

Crucially, historical indices for how the composite biblical literature was to be understood have been provided by the literature's tradents in their editorial work on the text, which thereby contextualizes the traditions it transmits (Childs 1979: 60; 1995: 10). In this regard it might be helpful to think of canonical criticism in parallel with a newer type of redaction criticism which operates "by a movement backwards from a critical reading of the finished text" (Williamson 2002: 96). Canonical criticism probes into the depth dimension of the biblical witnesses from the standpoint of their definitive contextualization, rather than anachronistically isolating and reifying them apart from that contextualization. That is why canonical criticism is not an exclusively synchronic type of interpretation but of necessity entails diachronic investigation. But unless a reconstruction of prior traditions and stages is connected with and contextualized by the Bible's literary shape, the reconstruction remains incomplete and potentially misleading.

In the case of the Pentateuch, to begin with its received shape means to take the Pentateuch's book-units with full seriousness. Their integrity and order are finally even more important to the tradition than their number (five). This is partly because the Jewish and Christian traditions have preserved these book-units with great fidelity even when their interpreters have neglected to explore questions about the holistic meaning of these books or pursued more oracular styles of interpretation focused on single verses or words without regard to their literary context (cf. Sommer 2016). While there are some exceptions, the norm already at Qumran was for each book to be written on its own scroll (Schmid 2010: 23–25; cf. Haran 1990: 165–76).

Even more important, however, is the fact that cross-references at the beginnings and endings of the pentateuchal books reflect the Pentateuch's present book divisions, which means that the book-units are older than, and have been incorporated into, "the last redactional shaping of the text" (Schmid 2010: 27; cf. Childs 1972: 716: "it is quite clear that the five books were seen as separate entities by the final Biblical editor"). These cross-references have a geographical emphasis, but they also refer to key figures and motifs, and they highlight significant narrative threads in moving from one book to the next (cf. Schmid 2010: 26). Genesis 50 thus presents an evident narrative conclusion with its report of Joseph's death, along with his dying wish for his bones to be carried from Egypt when Israel enters the land promised to Abraham, Isaac, and Jacob. Yet these threads resume later. Not only is Joseph's wish partially fulfilled in Exod. 13:19, it is further fulfilled in Josh. 24:32 (Witte 2006).

The first chapter of Exodus recapitulates the basic scenario from Genesis 50,[8] especially the location of Israel in Egypt, and does so using language from the first chapter of Genesis: "they multiplied and grew exceedingly strong" (Exod. 1:7; cf. Gen. 1:28).[9] Joseph's death is reiterated (Exod. 1:6). As in Genesis, the final chapter of Exodus has conclusive force in relation to the proceeding narrative, especially with its reference to Moses finishing his work (Exod. 40:33) and its dramatic description of the glory of the LORD filling the tabernacle in the tent of meeting (Exod. 40:34–39). But Leviticus 1:1 then refers to the same tent of meeting and the same central characters: the LORD, Moses, and the Israelites. Leviticus likewise features a concluding colophon ("These are the commandments" Lev. 27:34). Language similar to the end of Leviticus appears in Num. 1:1, including a reference to the tent of meeting and Israel's location at Sinai. Numbers finishes in turn with a colophon of its own ("These are the commandments" Num. 35:13), which also underscores Israel's new location "in the plains of Moab."

---

[8] My colleague Brent Strawn has reminded me of the text-critical debate concerning the initial *waw* in Exod. 1:1, which does not appear in the LXX (Wevers 2004). But at least in the MT the *waw* signals that Exodus is a continuation of the Genesis narrative (Dohmen 2015: 90).

[9] For convenience, I employ the NRSV for biblical translations in this essay.

Deuteronomy begins with the same location as the ending of Numbers, although now describing it in greater detail (Deut. 1:1–5). Deuteronomy ends with the death of Moses and a colophon about his lasting significance (Deut. 34:10–12). Joshua 1:1 begins "After the death of Moses" and highlights Joshua's role as Moses' successor with language echoing Deut. 31:7–8 about being strong and bold because the LORD is with him (Josh. 1:7–9). Thus, the effect throughout the Pentateuch is one of narrative imbrication, with the end of each book tucked into the beginning of the next, as if they were tiles on a roof.

To emphasize the key point, these common features at the book-seams of the Pentateuch are not only synchronic reference points but book-conscious indices. They exist in the way they do in order to give assistance in reading across the book divisions of the Pentateuch *because those book divisions already existed* when the seams were edited into their present literary format (Schmid 2010: 27). This insight provides the strongest possible warrant for privileging these books *as books* within a canonical approach to the Pentateuch. (Of course, "book" here does not mean codex but literary "work" or simply "scroll"; see Chapman 2016: 36–43). Moreover, as sketched, the transition between Deuteronomy and Joshua is not different in kind from the other book transitions within the Pentateuch, suggesting that the scope of the Pentateuch resulted secondarily from its delimitation within a larger group of texts, most likely Genesis–2 Kings (Schmid 2010: 16).

Although numerous scholars continue to interpret the epilogue to Deuteronomy (Deut. 34:10–12) as a "neutralization" or "subordination" of prophetic claims to religious authority in favor of Mosaic revelation (e.g., Blenkinsopp 2004: 204–6; Nihan 2013), Deut. 34:10–12 celebrates Moses *as a prophet* even as it establishes his non-repeatable priority. The prophets who come after Moses will continue his work, with his authority (cf. Deut. 18:15). Revelation is not being claimed for the Pentateuch alone (Chapman 2020: 113–31). Indeed, the present form of the Pentateuch anticipates future action by God (Schmitt 1982: 188–89). By excluding Israel's entry into the land, the Pentateuch becomes "prophetic" rather than "historical" in the sense that it looks ahead to its own fulfillment (Schmid 2006).

The most obvious evidence for not seeing the conclusion to the Pentateuch as absolute is that Israel's story continues, and one of the reasons that some critical scholars work with the notion of a Hexateuch rather than a Pentateuch is the use of priestly language and motifs closely resembling the pentateuchal P source in Joshua 13–21/22 (e.g., Petersen 1980; Cortese 1989; Knauf 2008: 19–21). By contrast, Thomas Römer (2016b) views these motifs in Joshua as later priestly additions to the Deuteronomistic History rather than continuations of the pentateuchal P source. Yet the links are real, whether they are conceived in historical terms as primary or secondary. In addition to the previously mentioned reference to Joseph's bones in Josh. 24:32, the motif of "subduing the land" in Gen. 1:28 and Josh. 18:1 is particularly striking (Blenkinsopp 1976).

So, the boundary of the Pentateuch, as well as its status as a distinct grouping within the canon, is "softer" than commonly thought, with Deuteronomy 34 serving as much as a bridge as a conclusion (Schmid 2006: 13 n. 69).

Pentateuchal privilege

The idea of a "hard" boundary between the Pentateuch and the Prophets has emerged in part from the assumption that the Pentateuch always possessed the hermeneutical privilege it later holds in Jewish tradition (McDonald 2017: 394–96; Kazen 2019; but see Collins, Evans, and McDonald 2020: 54). This view must be questioned due to its likely anachronism. It is true that the Pentateuch receives pride of place in the work of some early Jewish interpreters like Philo (Sterling 2011, but cf. Cohen 2007). One passage in the Mishnah implies that Torah scrolls have greater value than scrolls of the Prophets or the Writings (m. Meg. 25b–26a). Yet official religious instruction (*halakah*) was not restricted to pentateuchal interpretation at Qumran or in early rabbinic traditions (Chapman 2020: 279–82), as it comes to be in medieval Judaism—although even in later Judaism this restriction is less absolute and more nuanced than often assumed (Routtenberg 1979/80; Robinson 1984; Neusner 2014; Taubes n.d.). References to "the law of Moses" are not limited to pentateuchal books in the NT or early rabbinic writings. So, for example, John 10:34 quotes Ps. 82:6 and 1 Cor. 14:21 quotes Isa. 28:11–12 as from the "law." Cited as "torah" are also 1 Sam. 1:34 in b. Ḥul. 17b, Isa. 59:13 in b. Šabb. 119a, and Prov. 5:8 in b. 'Abod. Zar. 17a (Bronznick 1967). Naomi Janowitz concludes that "equation of the term Torah with five books written by Moses ... is surprisingly late in the history of Judaism" (1991: 131). Lawrence Schiffman discusses "the *growing* centrality of the 'Torah' to Judaism" during the Tannaitic and Amoraic periods (2012: 182, my emphasis).

Not even references within the Hebrew Bible to "the torah of Moses" line up neatly with pentateuchal legislation as we now know it (Shaver 1989; Pakkala 2011). Moreover, "law" is sometimes credited to prophets rather than priests or Moses. For example, in 2 Chron. 29:25 new cultic instructions are attributed to David, Gad, and Nathan, "for the commandment was from the LORD through his prophets" (cf. Steins 2010: 125–26). Similar attributions are made in Ezra 9:10–11; Dan. 9:10; and Ps. 78:1. Even though the exact phrase "the law and the prophets" does not appear in the Hebrew Bible (but see 2 Macc. 15:9 and 4 Macc. 18:10), appeals to the "law of Moses" are sometimes accompanied by a concomitant appeal to "the words of the prophets" or "the words" (e.g., Jer. 26:4–5; Zech. 7:12), suggesting that the "law of Moses"—whatever its textual scope—was not seen as a self-sufficient scriptural authority (Chapman 2000).

The anachronism of essential and unchanging pentateuchal priority is also the basis of the common presumption that the Samaritan community, from the very beginning of its existence, considered only the Pentateuch to be authoritative. Indirect evidence for this scholarly view has been claimed for the "Moses layer" of redaction on the pre-sectarian Samaritan Pentateuch (Kartveit 2009: 280–81). By elevating Moses' status, so the theory goes, the Samaritan community maintained a resistance to the prophetic tradition, which was increasingly understood as competing with Moses for authority (Anderson and Giles 2012: 68–90).

Yet explicit historical evidence for a Torah-only Samaritan canon does not come earlier than Origen in the first half of the third century CE (*C. Cels.* 1.49, *Hom. in Num.* 25.1; *Comm. in Joh. fragm.* 57, *Comm. in Joh.* 13.26.154; *Comm. in Rom.* 2.14). While routinely excused from consideration, Justin Martyr in the mid-second century CE refers to "the Jews and Samaritans, having the word of God delivered to them *by the prophets*" (*1 Apol.* 53, my emphasis). Justin was a Gentile Christian and not a Samaritan in religious terms, but he considered himself a Samaritan geographically as a native of Flavia Neapolis. Although his knowledge of Samaritan religious practices was imperfect (Rebrik 2006), it seems odd that he would not have known the Samaritans of his day refused to recognize the biblical prophets. Nevertheless, scholars regularly make the opposite judgment: namely, that since the Samaritans of course would have only recognized the Pentateuch, Justin must have been mistaken (e.g., Hall 1987: 250–51).

Given the evident interest of Josephus even earlier in differentiating the Jewish and Samaritan communities, it is noteworthy that he mentions nothing about a contrasting scope to their scriptures (cf. Pummer 2009; Lim 2017: 94–95). Moreover, recent scholarship has emphasized how Samaritan culture in the Hellenistic period "was to a large extent indistinguishable from that of Jews" (Pummer 2018: 77; Hensel 2019). Is it likely that competing biblical canons existed within the two communities when their worship practices did not exhibit significant differences? At the very least, it must be admitted that no direct evidence concerning the scope of the Samarian/Samaritan biblical canon exists for the Second Temple period. Indeed, Pseudo-Tertullian (third century CE) explicitly describes the narrower scope of the Samaritan canon as an innovation of "Dositheus the Samaritan, who first dared to reject the prophets as not having spoken with the Holy Spirit" (*Adversus omnes haereses* 11, as cited in Pummer 2002: 36). Dositheus is usually dated to the first century CE (Isser 1976).

For all these reasons, it is more likely that the Samaritans later rejected scriptural writings that they had earlier regarded as authoritative (Kartveit 2009: 295).

Canonical format

Additional canonical insights emerge from the Pentateuch's internal organization. As Schmid has detailed (2010: 28), the word counts of the Pentateuch's five books are not closely equivalent: 20,611 words in Genesis, 16,712 words in Exodus, 11,950 words in Leviticus, 16,413 words in Numbers, and 14,294 words in Deuteronomy. Such an imbalance immediately underscores how Genesis and Deuteronomy exist as relatively self-standing units within the overall structure, and how they embrace a central panel consisting of Exodus–Leviticus–Numbers (Childs 1986: 53). This conclusion based on respective length is reinforced by the narrative character of the five books. Genesis appears to be only loosely connected to the central panel, which consists of books sharing a closer relationship to each other in terms of their respective characters and themes, not least because of their common focus on Sinai and Mosaic legislation (Childs 1979: 130). Deuteronomy similarly is not integrated into the Sinai panel either but recapitulates and extends it. Its narrative setting is forty years after Sinai, as Israel, now in Moab, is poised to enter the land.

One consequence of this organizational format is to highlight the place of Leviticus in the middle of the structure (cf. Leder 2010: 33–35 on the "concentric organization of the Pentateuch"), a conclusion that tallies nicely with the focus on Leviticus in traditional Jewish pedagogy (Marcus 1996: 38–39). Here it is crucial to see how

Leviticus ritually enacts the Sinai legislation by effectively pausing the action of the wider narrative in order to depict an almost timeless mini-world of priestly activity (Milgrom 1976: 541), like a snow globe at the Pentateuch's core. From this perspective, the shape of the Pentateuch does not exclusively unfold as a sequential narrative but is instead an envelope structure in which pre- and post-Sinai panels surround the Sinai event (Balentine 1999: 127; Hamm 2019). Genesis has been shaped in such a way as to gesture continually ahead to the future by use of its promise motif (not yet fulfilled in Gen. 50:24) and its foreshadowing of exile (e.g., Gen. 12:10–20; 15:12–16). Deuteronomy rehearses and interprets the Sinai event by emphasizing Israel's need to remember it. Sinai itself occurs within time and yet transcends time, especially in its ongoing priestly implementation.

The centrality of Leviticus endorses a more "longitudinal" theology of the Pentateuch, in which the focus will be less on reading across the books for their "latitudinal," salvation-historical story and instead on attending to the Pentateuch's mandates with regard to vital worship and a sustainable form of communal life. The Pentateuch is not a story; it is an abiding pattern of life set within a story. The way to understand the Pentateuch is accordingly not merely to reconstruct it as a story (or history) but to read it as showcasing and conveying a divinely given polity. The prophetic dimension of Israel's faith has already been incorporated into the Pentateuch internally through editorial shaping (Schmitt 1982). The Pentateuch does not oppose the prophetic impulse but understands it to consist precisely in the way that the pattern of life graciously given by God in Torah confronts and challenges competing patterns of life.

A perennial pitfall within Christian, especially Protestant, scholarship has been to overemphasize the ethical aspect of the Pentateuch at the expense of the sacramental (Brueggemann 1997: 590). But renewed appreciation for the centrality of Leviticus within the canonical shape of the Pentateuch can help to balance the Pentateuch's ethical demands, which are real, with its simultaneous call to the holy and joyful service of God within a worshiping community.

It is no accident that Jewish and Christian traditions have identified the Pentateuch with Moses, whose depiction within the Pentateuch is much more than that of religion-founder, political leader, or scribe. Moses is the Israelite everyman, the paradigmatic figure representing what it means to live a faithful and just life in community, the ideal spiritual mediator before God on Israel's behalf. For this reason, he is just as much a touchstone for Israelite faithfulness as the Pentateuch itself (Exod. 14:31). Schmid contends that Deut. 34:7 alludes to Gen. 6:3, portraying Moses' life as lasting the divinely ordained maximum of 120 years (2014: 269). As such, this link would be one of many editorial signs indicating that the canonical shape of the Pentateuch is closely aligned with the persona of Moses (Matthews 2012).

The voice of the Pentateuch is thus a Mosaic voice, even if that voice is more of a literary achievement than a historical legacy. To this extent, there is an essential logic to the tradition of the Pentateuch's Mosaic authorship, which expresses the conceptual coherence of the Pentateuch as well as its authority. As Childs concluded, "Mosaic authorship of the Pentateuch is an important theological affirmation which is part of the canonical witness" (1979: 135).

The Law, the Prophets, and the Writings

The Pentateuch never existed by itself. This judgment should be beyond dispute, since "the narrative threads of the Pentateuch continue into the Former Prophets" (Schmid 2010: 17). Yet the idea of a Pentateuch-only scripture within Persian-era Israel has had a long shelf life in critical scholarship. Standard treatments of the OT canon since the end of the nineteenth century have reconstructed a linear, three-stage process of expansion in which the Pentateuch was first "canonized" around the time of Ezra (*ca.* 444 BCE), followed by the addition of the prophetic corpus at the beginning of the second century BCE, and then by the rest of the OT Writings toward the end of the first century CE (e.g., Ryle 1892).

However, this theory has never been able to explain adequately how the Prophets and the Writings were preserved and transmitted during the period prior to their canonization, when they supposedly lacked scriptural status. The argument that they were not yet fully canonical because they had not been finalized textually has become increasingly difficult to sustain as it has become more and more clear that significant post-priestly redaction of the Pentateuch took place after the time of Ezra (Grabbe 2001; De Troyer 2010; Schmid 2011: 159–84; Römer 2014; Giuntoli and Schmid 2015). Still, scholars continue to believe that while references to the "law of Moses" are found within the rest of the canon, references to other books of the canon are not evident in the Pentateuch.

Nonetheless, the hermeneutical flow between the Pentateuch and the other two canonical divisions is not unidirectional. An awareness of the prophetic tradition is registered by multiple pentateuchal texts (e.g., Genesis 20; Exodus 7–11; Numbers 11–12; Deuteronomy 18). Scriptural traditions about wisdom and the scribes have also exercised an influence on the Pentateuch (e.g., Genesis 2–3; 18:22–33; 37–50; see further Berge 2010; Lundbom 2010). It is not convincing to say that these features of the Pentateuch stem from exclusively oral or not-yet-scriptural traditions. One suggestive possibility of an intertextual, interscriptural allusion occurs in Gen. 6:13, in which Amos 8:2 might be quoted (Smend 1981). On the basis of this and other potential examples, Schmid concludes: "Taken together, there is a historical realm of possible mutual influence reaching from approximately the eighth to the fourth centuries. It is likely not only that the Pentateuch influenced the prophets but that influences ran in the other direction as well" (Schmid 2016: 848). Such a possibility underscores how the Pentateuch was never Israel's sole "Bible," even if its text did stabilize somewhat earlier than the texts of the other canonical divisions.[10]

This literary-historical situation suggests that whatever the Pentateuch "means," it means in relation to the rest of the biblical canon, and not in isolation (cf. the call within Orthodox Judaism for "the entire Bible" to "assume primacy as a central religious text" in Levy 1996). A common way of viewing the Pentateuch within the context of the

---

[10] However, this last point should not be conceded too quickly. Trebolle Barrera 2002: 145 finds that "the Pentateuch, Isaiah, the Minor Prophets, and Psalms exhibit similar histories of literary formation, textual transmission, transmission of manuscripts, and of authorized interpretation which identify them as the nuclear components of the biblical canon."

canon, in Christian as well as Jewish scholarship, is to see the Pentateuch as setting out the basic story of Israel, followed by the other portions of the canon, which illustrate and extend the message of the Pentateuch but, by virtue of a canonically imposed hierarchy, do not challenge or correct it (e.g., Schmid 2014: 266). Missing in such an understanding is the radicality of the prophetic and wisdom writings, an independence that is sustained rather than harmonized away in the canonical form of their witnesses.

Early Jewish tradition displays a more supple awareness of interaction between the biblical canon's three divisions. In the famous words of Ben Azzai (second century CE): "I thread the words of the Torah onto the Prophets and the words of the Prophets onto the Writings, and the words of the Torah are as joyful as when they were given at Sinai" (Lev. Rabb. 16:4). Sometimes in rabbinic debates an appeal is made to other portions of the canon in order to qualify or even negate a pentateuchal injunction (e.g., m. Yad. 4:4). Indeed, rabbinic traditions demonstrate a consistent appreciation for the threefold form of scripture (b. B. Bat. 14b), often supporting a particular judgment by citing a biblical passage from each of the three divisions of the canon rather than only one (Chapman 2015; cf. Trebolle Barrera 2002: 142). While not as pronounced in Christian tradition, a sense of the OT as a triple authority is likewise evident, including already in the NT (e.g., Luke 24:44; for other examples, Chapman 2015: 298–303).[11]

In their present canonical form, the Pentateuch, the Prophets, and the Writings represent three related but distinctive theological witnesses, each one implicated in and supported by the other. The significance of this tripartite structure for biblical theology, especially because of the way it reorients a salvation-historical approach, was highlighted by Claus Westermann (1979: 12):

[T]he structure of the Old Testament in its three parts indicates that the narrative of the Old Testament is determined by the word of God occurring in it and by the response of those for whom God acts and with whom [God] deals. It is the canon of the Old Testament itself which shows us the structure of what happens in the Old Testament in its decisive elements. We have thus found an objective starting point for an Old Testament theology which is independent of any preconceptions about what the most important thing in the Old Testament is and independent of any other prior theological decisions. If one asks what the Old Testament says about God, this threefold structure shows us the way to the answer.

The tripartite structure of the canon alters the historical unfolding of the biblical witnesses by emphasizing certain aspects of Israel's history and de-emphasizing others, pushing certain things into the foreground and others into the background (Childs 1986: 13). This tripartite structure is itself an expression of Israel's hard-won theological perspective on its identity and purpose within the world.

---

[11] Both early Judaism and early Christianity could also view the HB/OT as unitary (Law/Torah) or bipartite (the Law and the Prophets). These various canon concepts appear to have coexisted for some time rather than only succeeding each other within a rigid sequence. The concepts also emerged prior to an absolute determination of their contents (i.e., exactly which books were contained in the designated canonical units).

Israel's fullest apprehension of God cannot therefore be satisfied with only the Pentateuch but requires all three canonical voices in order to testify most clearly and comprehensively to the reality it confesses as God (cf. Witte 2016: 1119). Rather than a soloist with two backup singers, a canonical OT theology is a trio in which each voice joins the others without losing its own melody. Only a chorus could ever hope to praise God fittingly.

Bibliography

Albertz, Rainer. (2018), "The Recent Discussion of the Formation of the Pentateuch/Hexateuch," *HS* 59: 65–92.

Anderson, Robert T., and Terry Giles. (2012), *The Samaritan Pentateuch: An Introduction to Its Origin, History, and Significance for Biblical Studies*, SBLRBS 72, Atlanta: Society of Biblical Literature.

Ausloos, Hans. (2015), *The Deuteronomist's History: The Role of the Deuteronomist in Historical-Critical Research into Genesis–Numbers*, OS 67, Leiden: Brill.

Baden, Joel. (2012), *The Composition of the Pentateuch: Renewing the Documentary Hypothesis*, AYRL, New Haven, CT: Yale University Press.

Baden, Joel. (2016), "Why is the Pentateuch Unreadable? Or, Why Are We Doing This Anyway?" in Jan C. Gertz et al. (eds.), *The Formation of the Pentateuch: Bridging the Academic Cultures of Europe, Israel, and North America*, FAT 111, 243–51, Tübingen: Mohr Siebeck.

Balentine, Samuel E. (1999), *The Torah's Vision of Worship*, OBT, Minneapolis: Fortress.

Beck, Martin, and Ulrike Schorn, eds. (2006), *Auf dem Weg zur Endgestalt von Genesis bis II Regum: Festschrift Hans-Christoph Schmitt zum 65. Geburtstag*, BZAW 370, Berlin: de Gruyter.

Berge, Kåre. (2010), "Was There a Wisdom-Didactical Torah-Redaction in the Exodus Story?" *SEA* 75: 57–75.

Blenkinsopp, Joseph. (1976), "The Structure of P," *CBQ* 38 (3): 275–92.

Blenkinsopp, Joseph. (2004), *Treasures Old & New: Essays in the Theology of the Pentateuch*, Grand Rapids: Eerdmans.

Blenkinsopp, Joseph. (2012), *The Pentateuch: An Introduction to the First Five Books of the Bible*, AYRL, New Haven: Yale University Press.

Blum, Erhard. (1984), *Die Komposition der Vätergeschichte*, WMANT 57, Neukirchen-Vluyn, Neukirchener.

Blum, Erhard. (1990), *Studien zur Komposition des Pentateuch*, BZAW 189, Berlin: de Gruyter.

Blum. Erhard. (1991), "Gibt es die Endgestalt des Pentateuch?" in J. A. Emerson (ed.), *Congress Volume: Leuven 1989*, VTSup 43, 46–57, Leiden: Brill.

Bronznick, Norman M. (1967), "Qabbalah as a Metonym for the Prophets and Hagiographa," *HUCA* 38: 285–95.

Brueggemann, Walter. (1997), *Old Testament Theology*, Minneapolis: Augsburg Fortress.

Brueggemann, Walter, and Hans Walter Wolff. (1975), *The Vitality of Old Testament Traditions*, Atlanta: John Knox.

Buss, Martin J. (1999), *Biblical Form Criticism in Its Context*, JSOTSup 274, Sheffield: Sheffield Academic.

Carr, David M. (1996), *Reading the Fractures of Genesis: Historical and Literary Approaches*, Louisville: Westminster John Knox.

Chapman, Stephen B. (2000), "'The Law and the Words' as a Canonical Formula within the Old Testament," in Craig A. Evans (ed.), *The Interpretation of Scripture in Early Judaism and Christianity: Studies in Language and Tradition*, JSPSup 33, SSEJC 7, 26–74, Sheffield: Sheffield Academic.

Chapman, Stephen B. (2015), "'A Threefold Cord Is Not Quickly Broken': Interpretation by Canonical Division in Early Judaism and Christianity," in Julius Steinberg and Timothy J. Stone (eds.), with the assistance of Rachel Marie Stone, *The Shape of the Writings*, Siphrut 16, 281–309, Winona Lake, IN: Eisenbrauns.

Chapman, Stephen B. (2016), *1 Samuel as Christian Scripture: A Theological Commentary*, Grand Rapids: Eerdmans.

Chapman, Stephen B. (2020), *The Law and the Prophets: A Study in Old Testament Canon Formation*, Grand Rapids: Baker Academic.

Childs, Brevard S. (1972), "The Old Testament as Scripture of the Church," *CTM* 43 (11): 709–22.

Childs, Brevard S. (1979), *Introduction to the Old Testament as Scripture*, Philadelphia: Fortress.

Childs, Brevard S. (1986). *Old Testament Theology in a Canonical Context*, Philadelphia: Fortress.

Childs, Brevard S. (1995), "On Reclaiming the Bible for Christian Theology," in Carl E. Braaten and Robert W. Jensen (eds.), *Reclaiming the Bible for the Church*, 1–17, Grand Rapids: Eerdmans.

Clines, David J. A. (1998), "Beyond Synchronic/Diachronic," in *On the Way to the Postmodern: Old Testament Essays I, 1967–1998*, JSOTSup 292, 68–87, Sheffield: Sheffield Academic.

Cohen, Naomi. (2007), *Philo's Scriptures: Citations from the Prophets and Writings; Evidence for Haftarah Cycle in Second Temple Judaism*, JSJSup 123, Leiden: Brill.

Collins, John J., Craig A. Evans, and Lee Martin McDonald. (2020), *Ancient Jewish and Christian Scriptures: New Developments in Canon Controversy*, Louisville: Westminster John Knox.

Cortese, Enzo. (1989), *Josua 13–21: ein priesterschriftlicher Abschnitt im deuteronomistischen Geschichtswerk*, OBO 94, Freiburg: Universitätsverlag.

De Troyer, Kristin. (2010), "When Did the Pentateuch Come into Existence? An Uncomfortable Theory," in Wolfgang Kraus and Martin Karrer (eds.), *Die Septuaginta – Texte, Theologien, Einflüsse*, WUNT 219, 269–86, Tübingen: Mohr Siebeck.

Dohmen, Christoph. (2015), *Exodus 1–18*, HTKAT, Freiburg: Herder.

Dozeman, Thomas. (2017), *The Pentateuch: Introducing the Torah*, Minneapolis: Fortress.

Frei, Hans W. (1974), *The Eclipse of Biblical Narrative*, New Haven, CT: Yale University Press.

Friedman, Richard Elliott. (1987), *Who Wrote the Bible?* San Francisco: HarperOne.

Giuntoli, Federico, and Konrad Schmid, eds. (2015), *The Post-Priestly Pentateuch: New Perspectives on Its Redactional Development and Theological Profiles*, FAT 101, Tübingen: Mohr Siebeck.

Grabbe, Lester L. (2001), "The Law of Moses in the Ezra Tradition: More Virtual than Real?" in James W. Watts (ed.), *Persia and Torah: The Theory of Imperial Authorization of the Pentateuch*, SBLSymS 17, 91–113, Atlanta: Society of Biblical Literature.

Hagedorn, Anselm C. (2007), "Taking the Pentateuch to the Twenty-First Century," *ExpTim* 119 (2): 53–8.

Hall, Bruce W. (1987), *Samaritan Religion from John Hyrcanus to Baba Rabba: A Critical Examination of the Relevant Material in Contemporary Christian Literature, the Writings of Joseph, and the Mishnah*, Studies in Judaica 3, Sydney (Australia): University of Sydney/Mandelbaum.

Hamm, Allison K. (2019), "The Speaking Text: Leviticus as Generative Discourse," ThD diss., Duke University, Durham, NC.

Haran, M. (1990), "Book-Size and the Thematic Cycle in the Pentateuch," in Erhard Blum et al. (eds.), *Die Hebräische Bibel und ihre zweifache Nachgeschichte: Festschrift für Rolf Rendtorff*, 167–76, Neukirchen-Vluyn: Neukirchener, 1990.

Hensel, Benedikt. (2019), "On the Relationship of Judah and Samaria in Post-exilic Times: A Farewell to the Conflict Paradigm," *JSOT* 44 (1): 19–42.

Isser, Stanley Jerome. (1976), *The Dositheans: A Samaritan Sect in Late Antiquity*, SJLA 17, Leiden: Brill.

Janowitz, Naomi. (1991), "The Rhetoric of Translation: Three Early Perspectives on Translating Torah," *HTR* 84 (2): 129–40.

Jonker, Louis C. (2004), "Winds of Change? Recent Developments in Exegetical Methodology in Germany," *NGTT* 45.3: 599–608.

Kartveit, Magnar. (2009), *The Origin of the Samaritans*, VTSup 128, Boston: Brill.

Kazen, Thomas. (2019), "The Role of Law in the Formation of the Pentateuch and the Canon," in Pamela Barmash (ed.), *The Oxford Handbook of Biblical Law*, 257–74, New York: Oxford University Press.

Knauf, Ernst Axel. (2008), *Josua*, ZBK, AT 6, Zurich: Theologischer Verlag.

Kratz, Reinhard G. (2016), "The Analysis of the Pentateuch: An Attempt to Overcome Barriers of Thinking," *ZAW* 128 (4): 529–61.

Leder, Arie C. (2010), *Waiting for the Land: The Story Line of the Pentateuch*, Phillipsburg, NJ: P & R Publishing, 2010.

Levin, Christoph. (2005), *The Old Testament: A Brief Introduction*, trans. Margaret Kohl. Princeton, NJ: Princeton University Press.

Levy, B. Barry. (1996), "The State and Directions of Orthodox Bible Study," in Shalom Carmy (ed.), *Modern Scholarship in the Study of Torah: Contributions and Limitations*, 39–80, Northvale, NJ: Jason Aronson.

Lim, Timothy L. (2017), "The Emergence of the Samaritan Pentateuch," in Andrew B. Perrin, Kyung S. Baek, and Daniel K. Falk (eds.), *Reading the Bible in Ancient Traditions and Modern Editions: Studies in Memory of Peter W. Flint*, EJL 47, 89–104, Atlanta: Society of Biblical Literature.

Lockett, Darian. (2017), "Limitations of a Purely Salvation-Historical Approach to Biblical Theology," *HBT* 39 (2): 211–31.

Lüdemann, Gerd, ed. (1996), *Die "Religionsgeschichtliche Schule": Facetten eines theologischen Umbruchs*, Studien und Texte der religionsgeschichtliche Schule 1, Frankfurt: Lang.

Lundbom, Jack R. (2010), "Wisdom Influence in the Book of Deuteronomy," in K. L. Noll and Brooks Schramm (eds.), *Raising Up a Faithful Exegete: Essays in Honor of Richard D. Nelson*, 193–209, Winona Lake, IN: Eisenbrauns.

Matthews, Danny. (2012), *Royal Motifs in the Pentateuchal Portrayal of Moses*, LHBOTS 571, New York: T&T Clark.

McDonald, Lee Martin. (2017), *The Formation of the Biblical Canon, Volume 1: The Old Testament, Its Authority and Canonicity*, London: Bloomsbury T&T Clark.

Milgrom, Jacob. (1976), "Leviticus," in *IDBSup*, 54–55, Nashville: Abingdon, 1976.

Marcus, Ivan G. (1996), *Rituals of Childhood: Jewish Acculturation in Medieval Europe*, New Haven, CT: Yale University Press.
Moor, Johannes C. de, ed. (1995), *Synchronic or Diachronic? A Debate on Method in Old Testament Exegesis*, OS 34, New York: Brill.
Morgan, Robert. (1979), "The Hermeneutical Significance of Four Gospels," *Int* 33 (4): 376–88.
Neusner, Jacob. (2014), "The Rabbis and Prophecy," *Review of Rabbinic Judaism* 17 (1): 1–26.
Nihan, Christophe. (2010), "The Emergence of the Pentateuch as 'Torah,'" *RC* 4 (6): 353–64.
Nihan, Christophe. (2013), "The 'Prophets' as Scriptural Collection and Scriptural Prophecy during the Second Temple Period," in Philip R. Davies and Thomas Römer (eds.), *Writing the Bible: Scribes, Scribalism and Script*, 67–85, Durham, UK: Acumen, 2013.
Noth, Martin. (1960), *The History of Israel*, 2nd edn, New York: Harper.
Oeming, Manfred, ed. (2019), *Im Spannungsfeld von Universität und Politik, Kirche und Israel: Studien zu Leben, Werk und Wirkungen von Rolf Rendtorff*, Biblisch-theologische Studien 179, Göttingen: Vandenhoeck & Ruprecht.
Otto, Eckart. (2000), *Das Deuteronomium im Pentateuch und Hexateuch: Studien zur Literaturgeschichte von Pentateuch und Hexateuch im Lichte des Deuteronomiumrahmens*, FAT 30, Tübingen: Mohr Siebeck.
Pakkala, Juha. (2011), "The Quotations and References of the Pentateuch Laws in Ezra-Nehemiah," in Hanne von Weissenberg, Juha Pakkala, and Marko Marttila (eds.), *Changes in Scripture: Rewriting and Interpreting Authoritative Traditions in the Second Temple Period*, BZAW 410, 193–221, Berlin: de Gruyter.
Petersen, John E. (1980), "Priestly Materials in Joshua 13–22: A Return to the Hexateuch?" *HAR* 4: 131–46.
Pummer, Reinhard. (2002), *Early Christian Authors on Samaritans and Samaritanism: Texts, Translations and Commentary*, TSAJ 92, Tübingen: Mohr Siebeck.
Pummer, Reinhard. (2009), *The Samaritans in Flavius Josephus*, TSAJ 129, Tübingen: Mohr Siebeck.
Pummer, Reinhard. (2018), "Samaritan Studies – Recent Research Results," in Magnar Kartveit and Gary Knoppers (eds.), *The Bible, Qumran, and the Samaritans*, SJ 104, 57–77, Berlin: de Gruyter, 2018.
Pury, Albert de, and Ernst Axel Knauf. (1995), "Le théologie de l'Ancien Testament: kérygmatique ou descriptive?" *ETR* 70 (3): 323–34.
Rebrik, Viktor. (2006), "Justin the Martyr and Samaritans," in Haseeb Shehadeh and Habib Tawa (eds.), with Reinhard Pummer, *Proceedings of the Fifth International Congress of the Société d'Études Samaritaines, Helsinki, Aug 1–4, 2000*, 223–6, Paris: Geuthner.
Rendtorff, Rolf. (1977), *Das überlieferungsgeschichtliche Problem des Pentateuch*, BZAW 147, Berlin: de Gruyter = (1990), *The Problem of the Process of Transmission in the Pentateuch*, trans. John J. Scullion, JSOTSup 89, Sheffield: JSOT.
Robinson, Ira. (1984), "Torah and *Halakha* in Mediaeval Judaism," *SR* 13 (1): 47–55.
Römer, Thomas. (2013), "Zwischen Urkunden, Fragmenten und Ergänzungen: zum Stand der Pentateuchforschung," *ZAW* 125 (1): 2–24.
Römer, Thomas (2014), "The Pentateuch," in Rudolf Smend et al. (eds.), *Die Entstehung des Alten Testaments*, 5th edn, TW 1/1, 53–166, Stuttgart: Kohlhammer.
Römer, Thomas. (2016a), "How to Date Pentateuchal Texts: Some Case Studies," in Jan C. Gertz et al. (eds.), *The Formation of the Pentateuch: Bridging the Academic Cultures of Europe, Israel, and North America*, FAT 111, 357–70, Tübingen: Mohr Siebeck.

Römer, Thomas. (2016b), "The Problem of the Hexateuch: Pentateuch, Hexateuch, Enneateuch," in Jan C. Gertz et al. (eds.), *The Formation of the Pentateuch*, FAT 111, 813–27, Tübingen: Mohr Siebeck.

Römer, Thomas, and Konrad Schmid, eds. (2007), *Les dernières rédactions du Pentateuque, de l'Hexateuque et de l'Enneateuque*, BETL 203, Leuven: Leuven University Press.

Routtenberg, Hyman. (1979/80), "Prophecy and Halacha," *Dor le Dor* 8 (2): 61–69.

Roux, Jurie le, and Eckart Otto, eds. (2007), *South African Perspectives on the Pentateuch Between Synchrony and Diachrony*, LHBOTS 463, New York: T&T Clark International.

Ryle, H. E. (1892), *The Canon of the Old Testament: An Essay on the Gradual Growth and Formation of the Hebrew Canon of Scripture*, New York: Macmillan.

Schiffman, Lawrence H. (2012), "The Term and Concept of Torah," in Karin Finsterbusch and Armin Lange (eds.), *What is Bible?*, CBET 67, 173–91, Leuven: Peeters.

Schmid, Konrad. (2006), "Buchtechnische und sachliche Prolegomena zur Enneatuchfrage," in Martin Beck and Ulrike Schorn (eds.), *Auf dem Weg zur Endgestalt von Genesis bis zum II Regum: Festschrift Hans-Christoph Schmitt zum 65. Geburtstag*, BZAW 370, 1–19, Berlin: de Gruyter.

Schmid, Konrad. (2010), *Genesis and the Moses Story: Israel's Dual Origins in the Hebrew Bible*, Siphrut 3, trans. James D. Nogalski, Winona Lake, IN: Eisenbrauns.

Schmid, Konrad. (2011), *Schriftgelehrte Traditionsliteratur: Fallstudien zur innerbiblischen Schriftauslegung im Alten Testament*, FAT 77, Tübingen: Mohr Siebeck.

Schmid, Konrad. (2012), "The Canonical Prophets: Isaiah to Malachi," in Jan Christian Gertz et al. (eds.), *T & T Clark Handbook of the Old Testament: An Introduction to the Literature, Religion and History of the Old Testament*, 385–400, New York: T&T Clark.

Schmid, Konrad. (2014), "Der Pentateuch und seine Theologiegeschichte," *ZTK* 111 (3): 239–70.

Schmid, Konrad. (2016), "The Prophets after the Law or the Law after the Prophets? Terminological, Biblical, and Historical Perspectives," in Jan C. Gertz et al. (eds.), *The Formation of the Pentateuch: Bridging the Academic Cultures of Europe, Israel, and North America*, FAT 111, 841–50, Tübingen: Mohr Siebeck.

Schmitt, Hans-Christopher. (1982), "Redaktion des Pentateuch im Geiste der Prophetie: zur Bedeutung der 'Glaubens'-Thematik innerhalb der Theologie des Pentateuch," *VT* 32 (2): 170–89.

Seitz, Christopher. (2005), "Canonical Approach," in Kevin J. Vanhoozer (ed.), *Dictionary for Theological Interpretation of the Bible*, 100–102, Grand Rapids: Baker Academic.

Shaver, Judah R. (1989), *Torah and the Chronicler's History Work: An Inquiry into the Chronicler's References in Laws, Festivals, and Cultic Institutions in Relation to Pentateuchal Legislation*, Atlanta: Scholars Press.

Smend, Rudolf. (1981), "'Das Ende ist gekommen': ein Amoswort in der Priesterschrift," in Jörg Jeremias and Lothar Perlitt (eds.), *Die Botschaft und die Boten: Festschrift für Hans Walter Wolff zum 70. Geburtstag*, 67–74, Neukirchen-Vluyn: Neukirchener.

Sobel, Dava. (2019), *Longitude: The True Story of the Lone Genius Who Solved the Greatest Scientific Problem of His Time*. New York: Bloomsbury.

Söding, Thomas. (1996), "Die Schrift als Medium des Glaubens: zur hermeneutischen Bedeutung von Joh 20:30f.," in Knut Backhaus and Franz Georg Untergassmair (eds.), *Schrift und Tradition: Festschrift für Josef Ernst zum 70. Geburtstag*, 343–71, Paderborn: Schöningh.

Sommer, Benjamin D. (2016), "Book or Anthology? The Pentateuch as Jewish Scripture," in Jan C. Gertz et al. (eds.), *The Formation of the Pentateuch: Bridging the Academic Cultures of Europe, Israel, and North America*, FAT 111, 1091–1108, Tübingen: Mohr Siebeck.

Steins, Georg. (2010), "Mose, dazu die Propheten und David: Tora, Torauslegung und Kanonstruktur im Lichte der Chronikbücher," in Georg Steins and Johannes Taschner (eds), *Kanonisierung—die Hebräische Bibel im Werden*, Biblisch-theologische Studien 110, 107–31, Neukirchen-Vluyn: Neukirchener, 2010.

Sterling, Gregory E. (2011), "The Interpreter of Moses: Philo of Alexandria and the Biblical Text," in Matthias Henze (ed.), *A Companion to Biblical Interpretation in Early Judaism*, 415–35, Grand Rapids: Eerdmans.

Taubes Michael. (n.d.), "Torah, Nevi'im, and Kesuvim: How are They Different, How are they Similar?" Available online: https://download.yutorah.org/2019/1053/Shavuot_To-Go_-_5779_Rabbi_Taubes.pdf, (accessed June 7, 2020).

Trebolle Barrera, Julio. (2002), "Origins of a Tripartite Old Testament Canon," in Lee Martin McDonald and James A. Sanders (eds.), *The Canon Debate*, 128–45, Peabody, MA: Hendrickson.

Van Seters, John. (1994), *The Life of Moses: The Yahwist as Historian in Exodus–Numbers*, Louisville: Westminster John Knox.

Van Seters, John. (2013), "Prophecy as Prediction in Biblical Historiography," in Mark J. Boda and Lissa M. Wray Beal (eds.), *Prophets, Prophecy, and Ancient Israelite Historiography*, 93–103, Winona Lake, IN: Eisenbrauns.

Waschke, Ernest-Joachim, ed. (2013), *Hermann Gunkel (1862–1932)*, Biblische-theologische Studien 141, Neukirchen-Vluyn: Neukirchener.

Westermann, Claus. (1979), *What Does the Old Testament Say About God?* Atlanta: John Knox.

Wevers, J. W. (2004), "Two Reflections on the Greek Exodus," in J. H. Ellens et al. (eds.), *God's Word for Our World: Biblical Studies in Honor of Simon John De Vries*, 1:21–37, London: T&T Clark.

Williamson, H. G. M. (2002), "Biblical Criticism and Hermeneutics in Isaiah 1:10–17," in Christoph Bultmann, Walter Dietrich, and Christoph Levin (eds), *Vergegenwärtigung des Alten Testaments: Beiträge zur biblischen Hermeneutik; Festschrift für Rudolf Smend zum 70. Geburtstag*, 82–96, Göttingen: Vandenhoeck & Ruprecht.

Witte, Markus. (2006), "Die Gebeine Josephs," in Martin Beck and Ulrike Schorn (eds.), *Auf dem Weg zur Endgestalt von Genesis bis II Regum: Festschrift Hans-Christoph Schmitt zum 65. Geburtstag*, BZAW 370, 139–56, Berlin: de Gruyter.

Witte, Markus. (2016), "Methodological Reflections on a Theology of the Pentateuch," in Jan C. Gertz et al. (eds.), *The Formation of the Pentateuch: Bridging the Academic Cultures of Europe, Israel, and North America*, FAT 111, 1109–20, Tübingen: Mohr Siebeck.

Wright, G. Ernest. (1952), *God Who Acts: Biblical Theology as Recital*, London: SCM.

Wright, G. Ernest, and Reginald H. Fuller. (1957), *The Book of the Acts of God: Christian Scholarship Interprets the Bible*, Garden City, NJ: Doubleday.

6

The Canon of Psalms

Nancy L. deClaissé-Walford

The book of Psalms is a rich collection of poetry from the life of ancient Israel. The psalms express a wide range of emotions and feelings: joys, sorrows, fears, hurts, amazements, and yearnings; and they address a wide variety of topics: interpersonal relationships, enemies, illnesses, national crises, the splendor of creation, the goodness of God, and human sinfulness. The Psalter is arguably the most-loved book of the Old Testament. The New Testament contains allusions to and quotes from no less than 129 psalms—attesting to its tremendous popularity with and influence on the New Testament writers.[1] Martin Luther captured how central the psalms are to the life of faith, when he wrote that the Psalter "might well be called a little Bible. In it is comprehended most beautifully and briefly everything that is in the entire Bible" (Luther 1960: 254). Furthermore, Nahum Sarna observes: "In the Psalms, the human soul extends itself beyond its confining, sheltering, impermanent house of clay. It strives for contact with the Ultimate Source of all life. It gropes for an experience of the divine Presence. The biblical psalms are essentially a record of the human quest for God" (Sarna 1993: 3).

In this chapter I will briefly discuss the traditional understanding of the origins and authorship of the Psalter, summarize critical approaches to the text of Psalms in the classical and modern periods, and then discuss the shape, story, and shaping of the Psalter, and their relationship to the compilation of the Psalter and its inclusion in the canon.

Origins and authorship

The origins of individual psalms are buried deep within the history of ancient Israel. Many appear to have oral origins—words repeated again and again throughout the generations. Others appear to have written origins—poetry composed specifically for cultic and didactic functions. Assigning a precise date to most of the psalms in the

---

[1] E.g., Matt. 5:5 = Ps. 37:29; Matt. 27:46 = Ps. 22:8; Mark 12:10–11 = Ps. 118:22–23; Luke 12:24 = Ps. 147:9a; John 6:31 = Ps. 78:24; Acts 2:25–28 = Ps. 16:8–11; 1 Cor. 15:27 = Ps. 8:5; Heb. 1:8–9 = Ps. 45:6–7.

Psalter is extremely difficult, since a part of their beauty is their timelessness. A few psalms do evince clues to general time frames for their compositions. Psalm 45, for instance, was most likely composed in the preexilic period as a royal wedding song (Kraus 1988: 453 and Craigie 1983: 338). Some scholars maintain that Ps. 81 originated in the northern kingdom of Israel between 950 and 722 BCE (Craigie 1983: 322 and Dahood 1968: 263). Psalms 74 and 79 appear to come from the exilic period (Dahood 1968: 199 and 250, and Tate 1990: 299), and Ps. 137 can be placed in the exilic or postexilic period. Additionally, the concept of authorship was vastly different in the ancient world than it is today. In many cases an "author" was designated to lend prestige or authority to a work rather than to name the actual composer or collector of the work (for example, the comments of Kraus 1988 and Craigie 1983). The book of Psalms is traditionally associated with David, based on the occurrence of l^{e}david in the superscriptions of seventy-two of the 150 psalms in the MT form of the book.[2] The sixth-century CE Babylonian Talmud Tractate 14b states:

> Who wrote the Scriptures? — Moses wrote his own book and the portion of Balaam and Job. Joshua wrote the book which bears his name and [the last] eight verses of the Pentateuch. Samuel wrote the book which bears his name and the Book of Judges and Ruth. David wrote the Book of Psalms, including in it the work of the elders, namely, Adam, Melchizedek, Abraham, Moses, Heman, Yeduthun, Asaph, and the three sons of Korah. Jeremiah wrote the book which bears his name, the Book of Kings, and Lamentations. Hezekiah and his colleagues wrote Isaiah, Proverbs, the Song of Songs and Ecclesiastes. The Men of the Great Assembly wrote Ezekiel, the Twelve Minor Prophets, Daniel and the Scroll of Esther. Ezra wrote the book that bears his name and the genealogies of the Book of Chronicles up to his own time.

The *Midrash Tehellim*, which contains materials that dates to as early as the first century BCE, states in its commentary on Ps. 1:

> As Moses gave five books of laws to Israel, so David gave five Books of Psalms to Israel, the Book of Psalms entitled *Blessed is the man* (Ps. 1:1), the Book entitled *For the leader: Maschil* (Ps. 41:1), the Book, *A Psalm of Asaph* (Ps. 73:1), the Book, *A Prayer of Moses* (Ps. 90:1), and the Book, *Let the redeemed of the Lord say* (Ps. 107:2). Finally, as Moses blessed Israel with the words *Blessed art thou, O Israel* (Deut. 33:29), so David blessed Israel with the words *Blessed is the man*.
>
> Braude 1959: 5

Thus, although the Psalms have been traditionally associated with David, for scholars today the question of the origin of individual psalms is more difficult and often unclear.

---

[2] The Hebrew preposition l (l^e) can mean, among other things, "of," "to," or "for."

Critical approaches to the text—Classical period

From the time of the Enlightenment to the mid-twentieth century, scholars studying the biblical text gave the majority of their time to the disciplines of textual, source, form, and redactional criticism. Hermann Gunkel applied the form-critical method to the psalms, categorizing each by its *Gattung* and *Sitz im Leben* (Gunkel 1967). Gunkel's form-critical method has had a lasting impact on psalm studies, allowing those studying the psalms to group them together for comparison. A simplified form of Gunkel's *Gattungen* follows:

Major types

Four major types of psalms appear in the Psalter, classified according to their form (*Gattung*) and literary type.

Hymns

1. Hymns of the Community (e.g., Pss. 15, 29, 46, 67, 76, 81, 105, 107, 113, 125, 129, 147, 150) include a number of themes, including praising God for all that God does on behalf of the people and for God's presence among the people.
2. Thanksgiving Hymns of the Individual (e.g., Pss. 23, 34, 66, 87, 91, 111, 121, 139, 146) are sung by single voices, praising God for goodness to or on behalf of individuals, usually for deliverance from some trying situation.
3. Community Laments (e.g., Pss. 12, 44, 53, 74, 83, 85, 90, 106, 126, 137) are sung by the assembled people, protesting and grieving the tragedies and injustices in and threats to their communities. Community laments consist of the peoples' appeals to God and their confidence that God has or will respond.
4. Individual Laments (e.g., Pss. 3, 9, 10, 11, 27, 36, 51, 59, 71, 88, 102, 120, 141, 143) are sung by single voices, appealing to God for deliverance from life threatening situations.

Minor types

In addition to the four major types of psalms are a number of minor but significant types. These psalms are categorized, for the most part, by subject matter rather than by form (*Gattung*).

1. Creation Psalms (e.g., Pss. 8, 19, 65, 104) celebrate God's sovereignty over the created world and the place and role of human beings in the world.
2. Wisdom Psalms (e.g., Pss. 1, 32, 37, 49, 73, 78, 112, 119, 127, 128, 133, 145) provide instruction in right living and right faith in the tradition of the other wisdom writings of the Hebrew Bible. In most of these psalms, the path to wisdom is through adherence to the Torah, the instruction of the Lord.
3. Enthronement Psalms (e.g., Pss. 47, 95, 96, 97, 98, 99) celebrate the enthronement of God as sovereign in the midst of the people of God. The "kingship of God" is a dominant theme in the book of Psalms.

One other minor type of Psalms that can be classified according to its subject matter is Royal Psalms (e.g., Pss. 2, 21, 45, 72, 89, 110, 144), which speak of God's provision for the Israelite kings who reigned in Jerusalem during the period of the monarchy.

Critical approaches to the text—the Modern period

The foundations are laid

An emphasis on textual, source, form, and redaction criticism of the biblical text dominated scholarship well into the twentieth century. But change was coming in the form of James Muilenberg's 1968 Society of Biblical Literature meeting's presidential address entitled "Form Criticism and Beyond" (Muilenberg 1969). The impact of that presidential address was immense. John Barton wrote this about Muilenberg's presidential address:

> There are not many movements in biblical study whose beginning can be exactly dated, but such is the case with the movement known as "rhetorical criticism." Muilenberg took it as a given that form criticism was the dominant mode of study then adopted by American scholars. He argued that form criticism was perfectly valid and satisfactory, but that it might be time to move on from its competence in studying individual pericopes and return to the project of trying to understand texts in their entirety. What was needed, Muilenberg suggested, was a close attention to the articulation of biblical texts, so that one might see how *the argument* of chapters and books is constructed and thus how it is that chapters and books have persuasive ("rhetorical") force with their readers.
>
> Barton 1996: 199

Muilenburg's address ushered in a new era of biblical scholarship, moving well beyond the approaches that had dominated biblical studies up to that time to a new era in the study of the biblical text.

Another voice of change came in the form of Robert Polzin's 1975 article, in *Semeia*, who echoed the sentiments of Muilenburg. Polzin argues: "Traditional biblical scholarship has spent most of its efforts in disassembling the works of a complicated watch before our amazed eyes without apparently realizing that similar efforts by and large have not succeeded in putting the parts back together again in a significant or meaningful way" (Polzin 1975: 82). Polzin invites us to picture a magnificent timepiece made up of cogs and wheels, springs and tiny mechanisms, and delicate hands, each with its own place in the dance of the whole. Source, form, and redaction criticism dissected it and laid it out before us, piece by piece for study and examination. But when asked what are the intricate pieces for, in their original configuration, what purpose did these elements serve, these analytical tools were unable to give the simple answer—to keep time. Muilenburg and Polzin recognized the need to not only analyze the text, but also to synthesize the larger whole.

Brevard S. Childs was another voice calling for change. He championed what came to be known as the canonical approach to the text of the Old Testament. In a 1976 essay titled "Reflections on the Modern Study of the Psalms," and in his 1979 *Introduction to the Old Testament as Scripture*, Childs encouraged scholars to move away from dissecting the text of the Old Testament and move toward examining the text in the form in which it was preserved for us, i.e., as a whole.

James Sanders concurred with Childs but maintained that an understanding of the communities of faith who shaped the biblical texts was crucial to understanding the texts as they were preserved for and transmitted to future generations. He writes: "The text cannot be attributed to any discreet genius, such as author or editor or redactor, in the past. It can only be attributed to the ancient communities which continued to find value in the received traditions and scriptures, generation after generation, passing them on for the value they had found in them" (Sanders 1984: 29). He further states: "There had been a relationship between tradition written or oral, and community, a constant, ongoing dialogue, a historical memory passed on from generation to generation in which the special relationship between canon and community resided" (Sanders 2000: 164).

A new era in the study of the Psalter

Gerald H. Wilson, in his 1985 work, *The Editing of the Hebrew Psalter*, argues two points: first, that "there is evidence within the Hebrew Psalter itself of an editorial movement to bind the whole together"; and second, "that the unity achieved by this process is not merely a convenient combination of disparate items into an 'accidental' formal arrangement, but represents the end result of purposeful, editorial organization" (Wilson 1985: 4). As a result of Wilson's ground-breaking work, a new era of psalm studies began.

In 1989, a full session of the Book of Psalms section of the Society of Biblical Literature was devoted to questions of the shape and shaping of the book. Out of that session came a volume titled *The Shape and Shaping of the Psalter*. In 1992, an entire issue of the journal *Interpretation* (46/2) was devoted to the topic. In the last thirty years, numerous books and articles have been published, and many doctoral dissertations have been written, that address issues of the shape and shaping of the Psalter, both the overall story (the metanarrative), and the connectedness between psalms (the micro or local narrative, for example, Jacobson 2017; James 2017; Tucker 2014).

Following the calls of Childs and Sanders to take the canonical text seriously, but preceding the work of Wilson, Claus Westermann noted in 1962 a movement in the Psalter from lament (at its beginning) to praise (at its end), and identifies royal psalms as an important aspect of the Psalter's framework (Westermann 1962). Furthermore, Gerald Sheppard observed in a 1980 work, first, that Pss. 1 and 2 act as prefaces to the Psalter; second, that close lexical ties exist between the two psalms; and third, that David's identification with Ps. 2 demonstrates his full embrace of the ideals of Ps. 1 (Sheppard 1980: 142). Michael Goulder observed in 1982, "it is entirely proper to begin the study of the Psalter with the expectation that it will be an ordered and not an assorted collection; or, at the very least, that it will contain elements that were rationally ordered" (Goulder 1982: 8).

Lest we think, however, that twentieth-century scholars are the first to grapple with the question of the "shape" of the book of Psalms, in its commentary on Ps. 3 the *Midrash Tehellim*, which contains material dating to as early as the first century BCE, states:

> As to the exact order of David's Psalms, Scripture says elsewhere: *Man knoweth not the order thereof* (Job 28:13). R. Eleazar taught: The sections of Scripture are not arranged in their proper order. For if they were arranged in their proper order, and any man so read them, he would be able to resurrect the dead and perform other miracles. For this reason the proper order of the sections of Scripture is hidden from mortals and is known only to the Holy One, blessed be He, who said, "*Who, as I, can read and declare it, and set it in order?*".
>
> Isa. 44:7
>
> When R. Joshua ben Levi sought to arrange the Psalms in their proper order, a heavenly voice came forth and commanded: "Do not rouse that which slumbers!" (Braude 1959: 49–50).

The Shape of the Psalter

Many of the psalms in the book of Psalms appear to have been part of smaller, already-existing collections before they were incorporated into the Psalter. Some of the collections that can be identified are:

the Davidic Collections	Pss. 3–41; 51–72; 108–110; 138–145
the Korahite Collections	Pss. 42–49; 84–85; 87–88
the Elohistic Collection	Pss. 42–83
the Asaphite Collection	Pss. 73–83
the Enthronement Psalms	Pss. 93–99
the Songs of Ascents	Pss. 120–134
the Hallelujah Psalms	Pss. 111–118; 146–150

The five-book division of the Psalter is an early tradition. The Psalm scrolls found at the Dead Sea are divided into five books, even though the individual psalms included within the five books differ from the Hebrew Bible book of Psalms (Sanders 1967 and Flint 1997). The Septuagint divides its Psalter into five books as well. As stated earlier, the *Midrash Tehellim* likens the five-book division of the Psalter to the five books of the Torah: "As Moses gave five books of laws to Israel, so David gave five Books of Psalms to Israel" (Braude 1959: 5). Book I consists of Pss. 1–41; Book II of Pss. 42–72; Book III of Pss. 73–89; Book IV of Pss. 90–106; and Book V of Pss. 107–150. Doxologies divide the books, appearing at 41:13; 72:18–19; 89:52; and 106:48. The similarities among them ("Blessed be the LORD") and that the word "amen" occurs in the Psalter only in the doxologies strongly suggest that they were purposefully shaped and added to the Psalter at about the same time, although there is no evidence of when this may have been.

Psalm types and superscriptions within the Psalter also provide clues to the shape of the book. First, with regard to psalm types, recall that Claus Westermann observed that there is a "movement" from lament psalms in the first portion of the Psalter to hymnic psalms in the latter portion (Westermann 1967). The distribution is as follows:

- In Book I, twenty-four of the forty-one psalms (59%) are laments, while eight (20%) are hymns.[3]
- In Book II, twenty of the thirty-one psalms (65%) are laments, while six (19%) are hymns.
- In Book III, eight of the seventeen psalms (47%) are laments, and six (35%) are hymns.
- In Book IV, only four of the seventeen psalms (24%) are laments, while five (29%) are hymns.
- And in Book V, ten of the forty-four psalms (23%) are laments, and twenty-three (52%) are hymns.

Second, the superscriptions of the psalms may help us understand the shape and shaping of the Psalter. The number of psalms with superscriptions is significantly higher in the first three books of the Psalter than in the last two, suggesting that the psalms in the first three books represent a more deliberate collecting of pre-existing psalm collections:

- In Book I, thirty-seven of the forty-one psalms have superscriptions (93%).
- In Book II, thirty of the thirty-one psalms have superscriptions (97%).
- In Book III, all seventeen psalms have superscriptions (100%).
- In Book IV, only six of the seventeen psalms have superscriptions (35%).
- And in Book V, twenty-six of the forty-four psalms have superscriptions (59%).

Psalms attributed in their superscriptions to David are greater in number in Books I, II, and V than in Books III and IV, suggesting that Davidic attribution in the Psalter may be a key to understanding its shaping.[4]

- In Book I, thirty-seven of the forty-one psalms are attributed to David (93%).[5]
- In Book II, eighteen of the thirty-one psalms are attributed to David (58%).
- In Book III, only one of the seventeen psalms is attributed to David (6%).
- In Book IV, two of the seventeen psalms are attributed to David (12%).
- And in Book V, fourteen of the forty-four psalms are attributed to David (32%).

Gerald Wilson examined the superscription attributions of the psalms, their genre, and the occurrence of superscriptions and concluded that the Psalter narrated a story of

---

[3] The remaining percentages of psalms within each of the five books are psalms that are classified as other than lament or hymn, i.e., wisdom, royal, enthronement, and creation. For a full discussion of psalm types, see deClaissé-Walford (2004: 19–29).
[4] See below for more on the "storyline of the Psalter."
[5] Psalm 10 does not have a superscription, but is firmly linked to Psalm 9. See Kraus (1988: 188–89), and Holladay (1993: 77). Psalm 33 has solid linguistic links to Psalm 32. See Wilson (1985: 174–75).

the rise of ancient Israel under the leadership of kings David and Solomon in Books I and II; the demise of the northern kingdom of Israel and the destruction of Jerusalem by the Babylonians in Book III; the exile in Babylon in Book IV; and the return from exile, the rebuilding of the temple, and the restoration of worship in Book V. In the next section we will explore how the superscriptions are related to this implicit narrative running throughout the Psalter.

The "story" of the Psalter

Book I—the reign of David

Book I opens with words encouraging fidelity to the Torah (Ps. 1:2). It continues with words of warning to the nations and their rulers to recognize the God of Israel as king over all (Ps. 2:10–11). Readers thus enter the Psalter with two admonitions: diligently study and delight in the Torah and acknowledge God as sovereign.

Thirty-nine psalms "of David" make up Book I. The overwhelming majority of them are laments and provide insight into every facet of David's life—the king, the human being, the warrior, the parent, the servant of the Lord. David's life was fraught with conflict and oppression from without and within the nation state he founded—the Philistines, Saul, David's own family (see 1 Sam. 19:11; 29:1; 31:1; 2 Sam. 3:1; 5:22; 15:6, 10; 20:1; 1 Kgs 1:24–25).

Book II—the succession of Solomon

Book II, like Book I, contains many laments. But not all are attributed to David. The Korahites, who were, according to the book of Chronicles, temple singers during the reigns of David and Solomon (see 1 Chron. 6:31–37 and 9:19), mix their voices with David in singing the Book's opening laments (Pss. 42–49). But, interestingly, fifteen psalms of David appear in the middle of Book II (Pss. 51–65), fourteen of which are laments and eight of the fourteen are connected in their superscriptions to particular events in the life of David. These psalms remind readers once again that David's life was one of turmoil and strife, but they also depict a person who loved God and strove to serve God with fervor.

Psalm 72, the closing psalm of Book II, is one of only two psalms in the Psalter ascribed to Solomon (the other is one of the Songs of Ascents, Ps. 127). H.-J. Kraus describes Ps. 72 as a collection of wishes and prayers for the well-being of the king, likely used at an enthronement ceremony for a king in Jerusalem (Kraus 1989: 76–77). Childs suggests that the canonical placement of Ps. 72 indicates that the psalm "is 'for' Solomon, offered by David" (Childs 1979: 516). Book II ends with the words, "The prayers of David son of Jesse are ended" (72:20).

Book III—the divided kingdoms

Book III opens with "A Psalm of Asaph" (Ps. 73). Like the sons of Korah, Asaph was, according to the book of Chronicles, a temple singer during the reigns of David and

Solomon.⁶ Fifteen of the seventeen psalms in Book III are attributed to Asaph and the sons of Korah. Only one psalm, Ps. 86, is attributed to David. With the close of Book II, David moves into the background. The focus is now on David's descendants, who will determine the future of ancient Israel.

In Ps. 73, the psalm singer looks at the world and sees the wicked prospering while the righteous suffer, and he questions whether conventional theology and mores still hold true in life.⁷ There seems to be no reasoned connection between righteousness and reward, wickedness and punishment. In despair, the psalm singer enters the sanctuary of the Lord and there finds order in the seeming chaos of life (Ps. 73:17).

Psalm 73 is a turning point, signaling a new chapter in the Psalter's story. David's reign has come to an end and Solomon's reign will conclude with the nation divided into two kingdoms that will be in constant conflict with one another and with the nations around them. Community laments and community hymns dominate Book III. The voice of David, the individual, gives way to the voices of the communities of faith, who are attempting to make sense of all the turmoil, internal and external, political and religious, that is taking place.

Psalm 88, placed at the end of Book III, is an individual lament like no other in the Psalter. Psalms of lament in the Hebrew Psalter typically consist of five elements: (1) an Invocation, in which the psalmist calls on the name of God; (2) a Complaint, in which the psalmist tells God what is wrong; (3) a Petition, in which the psalmist tells God what the psalmist wants God to do; (4) Words of Trust, in which the psalmist outlines the reasons for trusting that God can and will answer the psalmist's petition; and (5) Words of Praise, in which the psalmist celebrates the goodness and sovereignty of God (deClaissé-Walford 2004: 23–25). Psalm 88 is almost wholly composed of the element of Complaint. Invocation and Petition are brief lines within the psalm, and Words of Trust and Words of Praise are missing completely.

Psalm 89 follows. It begins, in vv. 1–37, with praise to God for the good provisions to David, the king of God's choosing. But the psalm takes a sudden turn in v. 38, asking God why God has "spurned and rejected," "renounced the covenant," "removed the scepter from his hands" (vv. 38, 39, 44). In 722 BCE, the Assyrians destroyed the city of Samaria and scattered the population of Israel. In 587 BCE, the Babylonians destroyed Jerusalem and took a major portion of its population into captivity in Babylon. The nations of Israel and Judah were no more; Davidic kingship was ended; the people were exiled from their homeland. Book III of the Psalter ends with the community of faith lamenting and asking God, "LORD where is your steadfast love of old . . .?" (v. 49).

---

6   First Chronicles 6:39 and 25:1, 2 and 2 Chron. 5:12 state that Asaph was a descendant of Levi, part of one of the great families or guilds of musicians and singers in preexilic Israel, see Nasuti 1988.
7   Humankind in the ancient Near East believed in a basic moral governance of the world. Act and consequence were connected. Thus, the good prospered and the wicked perished. Sages and wisdom teachers taught that there was a fundamental order in the world which could be discerned by experience, that the gods had established the order, and that all of humanity was bound by the rules governing that order. For a detailed treatment, see Gammie and Purdue 1990.

Book IV—in exile in Babylon

Book IV opens with "A Prayer of Moses, the Man of God." It is the only psalm in the Hebrew Psalter so designated. The whole of Book IV of the Psalter is dominated by the person of Moses. Outside of Book IV, Moses is mentioned only once in the Hebrew Psalter (Ps. 77:21); in Book IV, he is mentioned seven times (Pss. 90:1; 99:6; 103:7; 105:26; 106:16, 23, 32).[8]

The Israelites in exile in Babylon cannot affect a return to the days of King David. They can only move forward. Moses intervenes with God on behalf of the people just as he did in the time of the wilderness wandering (Ps. 90:13; see Exod. 32:12), and he points the way forward (see Freedman 1985: 59). Enthronement psalms, celebrating God as sovereign over the people rather than a king of the Davidic line, occur at the center of Book IV (Pss. 93–99). At the Book's end, two psalms recount the history of God's dealings with the community of faith throughout its long history. Psalm 105, a Community Hymn, recalls God's provision, protection, and sustenance for the people throughout their history. Psalm 106 recounts that same history, but it is a community lament, reminding the people of their repeated unfaithfulness to God, despite God's good provisions to them.

While Ps. 89 at the end of Book III directs questions to God about why Israel is suffering in its present situation, the end of Book IV offers a simple petition to God to "save us and gather us" (106:47). In 539 BCE, the Persian army, under the leadership of Cyrus II, defeated the Babylonians. In the following year, Cyrus issued a decree allowing captive peoples to return to their homelands, to rebuild, and to resume their religious practices. But the repatriated peoples would remain part of the vast Persian Empire, subject to Persian law. Cyrus's decree meant that the Israelites could rebuild their temple and continue their religious practices, but they could not restore their nation-state under the leadership of a king of the line of David.

Book V—return from exile

Book V opens with Ps. 107, a hymn celebrating God's deliverance of the community of faith from perilous circumstances. Verses 33–41 outline the beneficence that God bestows upon the people, and the psalm closes with an admonition to "the wise" to heed God's good provisions. Beginning with Ps. 108, David, who has been virtually absent from the Psalter (in its superscriptions) since his final words in Book II (Ps. 72:20), returns.[9] Psalms 108–110, 122, 124, 131, and 138–145 are "of David," and in them David leads the people in praise of God as sovereign. In the middle of the book, with psalms of David forming an inclusio around them, are psalms used in various celebrations and commemorations in Jewish life:

---

[8] Marvin Tate describes Book IV as a "Moses Book" (Tate 1990: xxvi).
[9] Recall that in Book III, only one psalm is "of David" (Ps. 86); and in Book IV, only two psalms are "of David" (Pss. 101 and 103).

- Pss. 113–118, the Egyptian Hallel, recited during Passover
- Pss. 119, a wisdom acrostic about Torah piety, recited during the Feast of Pentecost
- Pss. 120–134, the Songs of Ascents, recited during the Feast of Booths (Tabernacles or Sukkoth).

David leads and the people join him to praise and give thanks to the God who sustained, protected, and guided them throughout their history. The last psalm of David in Book V, Ps. 145, is a masterful alphabetic acrostic that celebrates the sovereignty of God over the community of faith and over all creation. The Hebrew Psalter closes with a five-fold doxology of praise to the God who calls on "all that have breath" to praise him. Thus, the five books of the Psalter narrate the history of ancient Israel, the very history recorded in the books of Samuel, Kings, Chronicles, Ezra, Nehemiah, and a number of the prophets.

Craigie (31) suggests the Psalter had substantially reached its present form "by the fourth century B.C." He suggests a four-step process from composition to compilation involving: (1) composition of individual psalms; (2) formation of small collections; (3) gathering of several small collections into larger units; and (4) the emergence of a "collection of collections," the Book of Psalms, which included the addition of several individual psalms along with the collections (see Craigie 1983: 27–31 for more details on this process).

The shaping of the Psalters

The book of Psalms in the Hebrew Bible is not the only collection of psalms from the life of ancient Israel. In the Septuagint (LXX) translation of the Psalms, undertaken at least by 200 BCE, the psalms are presented in the same order as they are in the Hebrew Bible, but the manner in which they are presented and numbered differs.

MT	LXX
1–8	1–8
9–10	9
11–113	10–112
114–115	113
116:1–9	114
116:10–19	115
117–146	116–145
147:1–11	146
147:12–20	147
148–150	148–150

Superscriptions are longer in the LXX and occur more often than in the Masoretic Text (MT).[10] Of particular interest is the occurrence of Davidic ascriptions. In Pss. 3–89, every psalm lacking a superscription in the MT is provided with a Davidic superscription (MT Pss. 10 and 33 in Book I and MT Pss. 43 and 71). In Pss. 90–150 (Books IV and V), the LXX assigns Davidic authorship to many psalms that do not have superscriptions (MT Pss. 91, 93–99, 104, 137 = LXX Pss. 90, 92–98, 103, 136) (Willgren 2016: 175). In addition, the LXX includes Ps. 151, a celebration of David's victory over Goliath (1 Sam. 17). The psalm's superscription introduces it as a "genuine psalm of David" (ἰδιόγραφος εἰς Δαθιδ), but one that is "outside the number" (ἔξωθεν τοῦ ἀριθμοῦ). Thus, while there seems to have been some measure of fixedness of the psalmic contents in the second century BCE, there was still a considerable amount of fluidity between Hebrew texts.

Forty-two psalm scroll fragments have been identified among the Dead Sea Scrolls. By far the largest of the scrolls is 11QPs^a, followed by 4QPs^a, 5/6HavPs, 4QPs^b, 4QPs^c, and 4QPs^e (Flint 2013: 61). 4QPs^a, which dates to the second century BCE, contains portions of Pss. 5–69 in the following order:

5:9–13; *6*:2, 4, 6; *25*:8, 10, 12, 15; *31*:23–24; *33*:2, 4, 5, 6, 8, 10, 12, 20, 21; *34*:1, 21–22; *35*:2, 13–18, 20; 26–27; *36*:1, 3, 5–7, 9; *38*:2, 4, 6, 8–10, 12, 14,16–23; *71*:1–14; *47*:2; *53*: 2, 4–5, 7; *54*:2–3, 5–6; *56*:4; *62*:13; *63*:2, 4; *66*:16, 18–20; *67*:1–2, 4–8; *69*:1–19.[11]

11QPs^a, which dates from the late first century BCE to the first century CE, includes psalms in the following order on its readable, undamaged portions:

101; *102*:1–2, 18–29; *103*:1; *109*:21–31; *118*:25–29; *104*:1–6, 21–35; *147*:1–2, 18–20; *105*:1–11, 25–35, 38–39, 41–42, 44–45; *146*:9–10; *148*:1–13; *121*; *122*; *123*:1–2; *124*:7–8; *125*; *126*; *127*:1; *128*:3–6; *129*; *130*; *131*:1; *132*:8–18; *119*:1–6, 15–28, 37–49, 59–72, 82–96, 105–120, 128–142, 150–164, 171–176; *135*:1–9, 17–21; *136*:1–26; *118*:1, 15–16, 8–9, 29; *145*:1–7, 12–21; *Apocryphal Psalm 154*:3–19; *Non-canonical Psalm "Plea for Deliverance"*; *139*:8–24; *137*:1, 9; *138*; *Ben Sirach 51*:13–23, 30; *Non-canonical Psalm "Apostrophe to Zion"*; *93*:1–3; *141*:5–10; *133*:1–3; *144*:1–7, 15*; *Apocryphal Psalm 155*; *142*:3–7; *143*:1–8; *149*:7–9; *150*; *Non-canonical Psalm "Hymn to the Creator"*; *2 Samuel 23*:7*; *Non-canonical prose section "David's Compositions"*; *140*:1–4; *134*:1–3; *Apocryphal Psalm 151a*; *Apocryphal Psalm 151b:1*.[12]

11QPs^a contains portions of thirty-nine MT psalms and ten other compositions, six of which were previously known to scholars (Pss. 151A, 151B, 154, and 155; 2 Sam. 23; and Sir. 51) and four previously unknown (Plea for Deliverance; Apostrophe to Zion; Hymn to the Creator; and David's Compositions).

---

[10] LXX Ps. 70 = MT Ps. 71 is superscripted in the LXX "of David of the sons of Ionadab and the first ones taken captive." LXX Pss. 146–148 are attributed to Haggai and Zechariah. See Willgren (2016: 175).
[11] http://dssenglishbible.com/scroll4Q83.htm. Accessed June 8, 2020.
[12] http://dssenglishbible.com/scroll1Q10.htm. Accessed June 8, 2020.

While the deterioration of the bottom portion of 11QPs^a renders determining the superscriptions of many psalms on the scroll problematic, a considerable number have been discerned and, according to Gerald Wilson, numerous others have been restored based on spatial considerations (Wilson 1997: 456). In summary, 11QPs^a opens with Ps. 101, ascribed to David, and ends with Pss. 151A and 151B, both ascribed to David, and 31.1% of the psalms in 11QPs^a are attributed to David in comparison to 27.8% in Books IV and V of the MT Psalter (Wilson 1997: 454).

Concluding remarks

The Masoretic Text (MT), the Dead Sea Scrolls (DSS), and the Septuagint (LXX) indicate that a number of "editions" of psalm collections circulated in the life of ancient Israel and early Judaism. The superscription of LXX Psalm 151 suggests that by the time of the Psalter's translation into Greek (most likely at least a century before the common era) the canonical number of 150 had been fixed for the Psalter, but that the internal order and division of the psalms was still fluid. The various psalm manuscripts discovered at the Dead Sea support a conclusion that the internal order and even the content of the Psalter was not fixed until a relatively late date. The consensus of many scholars is that the "final" form of the 150-psalm Psalter was fixed sometime in the early Christian era (first century CE).

This fluidity is especially apparent in the Books IV and V, when comparing the MT "shaping" with that of the DSS. Peter Flint observed that for Pss. 1–89, no deviations in content and only two deviations in arrangement have been discovered in the DSS documents. "But for Psalms 90 and beyond disagreements with the Received Text are far more extensive, both in terms of the ordering of material and the presence of compositions not found in the MT-150 Psalter" (Flint 1997: 141). Wilson convincingly argues that Books I–III of the MT-Psalter were stabilized earlier than Books IV and V (Wilson 1985 and deClaissé-Walford 1997 and 2004). The findings among the Dead Sea Scrolls, particularly 4QPs^a and 11QPs^a, were significant parts of the formulation of his argument. The overwhelming preponderance of MT psalms found among the Dead Sea psalm scrolls (123 of the 150 MT psalms), however, indicates a strong tradition of psalms circulating in the second and first centuries, BCE.

The community that composed or preserved the Dead Sea Scrolls apparently considered the psalms a key component of their authoritative texts. 4QMMT states, "to you we have wr[itten] that you must understand the book of Moses [and the words of the] prophets and of David [and the annals] [of eac]h generation" (Flint 1998: 467). The War Scroll (4QM^a) refers to the Psalter as a book (*spr*) (Flint 1998: 468). A major question in psalm studies, however, has to do with the "canonicity" of the Dead Sea psalm scrolls, particularly 11QPs^a, the largest of the psalm scrolls. James Sanders argues that all of the MT "Psalter material" in 11QPs^a comes from Books IV and V of the MT Psalter and "while it is certainly not in traditional order, its fluidity is amenable to more than one explanation ... either as unique and at some limited variance with a generally accepted order; or as a 'local text,' representing a limited but valid Psalter tradition" (Sanders 1966: 88–89). Further, he maintained that the order of psalmic texts on another scroll discovered in Cave 11 (11QPs^b) was evidence of an established Qumran Psalter tradition (Sanders 1968: 287). Sanders concluded, "All in all, it seems best . . . to think of the Psalms Scroll [11QPs^a] not as a deviation from a rigidly fixed canon of the latter third of the Psalter, but rather as a sign-post in the multi-faceted history of the canonization of the Psalter" (Sanders 1966: 89). Shemaryahu Talmon and Moshe Goshen-Gottstein maintained that 11QPs^a, with its "unorthodox arrangement of the canonical psalms" and "numerous noncanonical interpolations," resembles not so much a canonical book of Psalms as "a synagogue Psalter, [or] an incipient prayerbook" (Yarkin 2015: 777). Patrick Skehan described 11QPs^a as a "library edition" of psalms arranged after the fixing of the MT Psalter sometime in the fourth century BCE (Skehan 1978: 172). Emmanuel Tov maintains that multiple text forms existed alongside the proto-MT Psalter prior to the time it was fixed in form, and states that the eventual priority of the MT Psalter was "merely the result of historical events" (Tov 2012: 179).

William Yarkin articulates well the major issue surrounding the question of the status of 11QPs^a and, indeed, all of the Dead Sea psalms scrolls. He writes:

> Scholarly debate over the question has proceeded on the assumption that there exists a standard 150-psalm *seper tehillim* of the configuration found in the Second Rabbinic Bible and reproduced in all subsequent printings of the Hebrew Bible to the present day. The question about scrolls from Qumran containing psalms, then, has been framed with reference to this presumed standard Hebrew Psalter.
>
> Yarkin 2015: 775

Another issue in the study of the MT, LXX, and DSS forms of the Psalter is the role of and emphasis on David. In the MT, as stated above, David is ever-present in Books I and II, is virtually absent in Books III and IV, and reappears in Book V.[13] David's presence in Book V, however, is tempered by the Enthronement psalms in Book IV (Pss. 93–99) that celebrate God as sovereign and by Psalm 145, the closing psalm of David in Book V, in which David celebrates God as "the king" (*hmlk*, v. 1).

The LXX version of the Psalter, however, places David in a more prominent position in every book. As stated earlier in the chapter, in Pss. 3–89, every psalm lacking a superscription in the MT is provided with a Davidic superscription in the LXX (MT Pss. 10 and 33 in Book I and MT Pss. 43 and 71 in Book II). In Psalms 90–150 (Books IV and V), the LXX assigns Davidic authorship to many psalms that do not have superscriptions (MT Pss. 91, 93–99, 104, 137 = LXX Pss. 90, 92–98, 103, 136). In addition, the LXX concludes with Psalm 151, a celebration of David's victory over Goliath (1 Sam. 17).

11QPs^a evinces a marked emphasis on David by its arrangement of the psalms that differs from the MT in "a new and unexpected order," and includes a number of non-MT Psalter compositions (Wilson 1997: 449). First, while all of the MT psalms found in 11QPs^a are found in Books IV and V of the MT Psalter, many psalms from those

---

[13] In Book I, the superscriptions attribute 37 out of the book's 41 psalms to David, in Book II, in 18 out of the 31 psalms; in Book III, in 1 of 17; in Book IV, in 2 of 17, and in Book V, in 14 out of 44.

books are not included. 11QPs^a includes Ps. 93 (an Enthronement Psalm) but does not include the remaining Enthronement Psalms (94–99), which Wilson has argued form the "editorial heart" of the final form the MT Psalter (Wilson 1985: 214–19, and 1997: 453). Further, 11QPs^a does not include Pss. 90–92, with their focus on Moses and the rule of God rather than a human king during the premonarchic period of ancient Israel, and it does not include Pss. 106–108, which, according to Wilson, address the failure of the Davidic monarchy (Wilson 1997: 453).

The subject matter of the non-MT Psalter compositions included in 11QPs^a is David and his wisdom, his prophetic character, and his role as sovereign ruler. 11QPs^a ends with four of these compositions: 2 Sam. 23, "David's Compositions," Ps. 151A, and Ps. 151B, all of which focus on the person of David. Additionally, "by dispersing titled Davidic Psalms among untitled ones, the compiler of 11QPs^a has succeeded in permeating the entire collection with a Davidic character and in giving 'orphan' Psalms a Davidic home" (Flint 1997: 194), and this partially explains the difference in the order of psalms in 11QPs^a compared to the MT. Gerald Wilson offers these summary words: "It seems difficult to escape the conclusion that the intent of the editors was to cast an aura of Davidic authority over the whole text by expanding Davidic superscriptions, by distributing Davidic psalms throughout the collection, and above all by including the prose composition praising David's role as psalmist extraordinary" (Wilson 1997: 456).

Thus, in examining the three versions of the Psalter extant in ancient Israel and early Judaism, we conclude the following. First, there existed a strong tradition of psalms circulating in the second and first centuries, BCE. Second, there is evidence that the MT Psalter was shaped to tell the story of ancient Israel from the time of the Davidic monarchy to the postexilic period and celebrates the reign of God as sovereign over the people. Third, while the order of the psalms in the LXX Psalter is the same as the MT Psalter, the addition of Davidic superscriptions and Ps. 151 place a greater emphasis on the person of David. And finally, the strategic placement of psalms attributed to David and the inclusion of four psalms celebrating David's wisdom, prophetic character, and kingship gives 11QPs^a a distinct Davidic character, and reflects perhaps the hope for the restoration of a Davidic kingship.

Bibliography

Alexander, Joseph A. (1865), *The Psalms*, 6th ed., 3 vols, New York: Scribner.

Barton, John. (1996), *Reading the Old Testament: Method in Biblical Study*, rev. and enlarged edn, Louisville: Westminster John Knox Press.

Braude, William G. (1959), *The Midrash on Psalms*, vol. 1, New Haven: Yale University Press.

Childs, Brevard S. (1976), "Reflections on the Modern Study of the Psalms," in *Magnalia Dei: The Mighty Acts of God*, edited by F.M. Cross et. al., 377–88, Garden City NY: Doubleday.

Childs, Brevard S. (1979), *Introduction to the Old Testament as Scripture*, Philadelphia: Fortress Press.

Childs, Brevard S. (2005), "The Canon in Recent Biblical Studies: Reflections on an era," *Pro Ecclesia* 14: 26–45.

Craigie, Peter C. (1983), *Psalms 1–50*, Word Biblical Commentary 19, Waco TX: Word Books, Publisher.
Dahood, Mitchell. (1968), *Psalms II: 51–100*, The Anchor Bible, New York: Doubleday.
deClaissé-Walford, Nancy L. (1997), *Reading from the Beginning: The Shaping of the Hebrew Psalter*, Macon, GA: Mercer University Press.
deClaissé-Walford, Nancy L. (2004), *Introduction to the Psalms: A Song from Ancient Israel*, St. Louis: Chalice Press.
Delitzsch, Franz. (1846), *Symbolae ad Psalmos illustrados isogogicae*, Leipzig.
Delitzsch, Franz. (1881, repr. 1975), *Biblical Commentary on the Psalms*, 3 vols, Grand Rapids: Eerdmans.
Flint, Peter W. (1997), *The Dead Sea Psalms Scrolls and the Book of Psalms*, Studies in the Texts of the Desert of Judah, vol. 17, Leiden: E. J. Brill.
Flint, Peter W. (1998), "The Book of Psalms in Light of the Dead Sea Scrolls," *Vetus Testamentum* 48/4: 453–72.
Flint, Peter W. (2013), *The Dead Sea Scrolls*, Core Biblical Studies, Nashville: Abingdon.
Freedman, David Noel. (1985), "Other than Moses . . . Who Asks (or Tells) God to Repent?" *Bible Review* 1/4: 56–59.
Gammie, John G. and Leo G. Perdue, eds. (1990), *The Sage in Israel and the Ancient Near East*, Winona Lake, IN: Eisenbrauns.
Goulder, Michael. (1982), *The Psalms of the Sons of Korah*, JSOT Supplement Series 20, Sheffield: JSOT Press.
Gunkel, Hermann. (1967), *The Psalms: A Form-Critical Introduction*, Facet Books Biblical Series 19, translated by Thomas M. Horner, edited by John Riemann, Philadelphia: Fortress Press.
Holladay, William L. (1993), *The Psalms Through Three Thousand Years: Prayerbook of a Cloud of Witnesses*, Minneapolis: Fortress Press.
Howard, David M. (1989), "Editorial Activity in the Psalter: A State-of-the-field Survey," *Word and World* 9: 274–85.
Jacobson, Karl N. (2017), *Memories of Asaph: Mnemohistory and the Psalms of Asaph*, Minneapolis: Fortress Press.
James, Joshua T. (2017), *The Storied Ethics of the Thanksgiving Psalms*, London: Bloomsbury, T&T Clark.
Kraus, Han-Joachin Kraus. (1988), *Psalms 1–59: A Commentary*, Minneapolis: Augsburg Publishing House.
Kraus, Han-Joachin Kraus. (1989), *Psalms 60–150: A Commentary*, Minneapolis: Augsburg Publishing House.
Luther, Martin. (1960), "Preface to the Psalter," in *Luther's Works*, translated by C. M Jacobs, Philadelphia: Muhlenberg Press.
McCann, J. Clinton, Jr., ed. (1993), *The Shape and Shaping of the Psalter*, Journal for the Study of the Old Testament, Supplement Series 159, Sheffield: JSOT Press.
Nasuti, Harry P. (1988), *Tradition History and Psalms of Asaph*, Society of Biblical Literature Dissertation Series 88, Atlanta: Scholars Press.
Polzin, Robert E. (1975), "'The Ancestress of Israel in Danger' in Danger," *Semeia* 3: 81–98.
Sanders, James A. (1966), "Variorum in the Psalms Scroll (11QPs[a])," *Harvard Theological Review* 59/1: 83–94.
Sanders, James A. (1967), *The Dead Sea Psalms Scroll*, Ithaca, NY: Cornell University Press.
Sanders, James A. (1968), "Cave 11 Surprises and the Question of Canon," *McCormick Quarterly Review* 21: 284–98.

Sanders, James A. (1984), *Canon and Community: A Guide to Canonical Criticism*, Guides to Biblical Scholarship, edited by Gene M. Tucker, Philadelphia: Fortress Press.

Sanders, James A. (2000), "Canonical Context and Canonical Criticism," in *From Sacred Story to Sacred Text: Canon as Paradigm*. Eugene, OR: Wipf & Stock.

Sarna, Nahum N. (1993), *On the Book of Psalms: Exploring the Prayers of Ancient Israel*, New York: Schocken Books.

Sheppard, Gerald T. (1980), *Wisdom as a Hermeneutical Construct: A Study in the Sapientializing of the Old Testament*, New York: de Gruyter.

Skehan, Patrick. (1978), *Qumran: sa piété, sa théologie t son milieu*, Paris: Louvain.

Talmon, Shemaryahu. (1966), "Pisqah Be'emsaʿ Pasuq and 11QPs[a]," *Textus* 5: 12–13.

Tate, Marvin E. (1990), *Psalms 51–100*, Word Biblical Commentary 20, Waco, TX: Word Books, Publisher.

Tov, Emmanuel. (2012), *Textual Criticism of the Hebrew Bible*, 3rd and exp. edn, Minneapolis: Fortress Press.

Tucker, W. Dennis Jr. (2014), *Constructing and Deconstructing Power in Psalms 107–150*, Atlanta: Society of Biblical Literature.

Westermann, Claus. (1962), "Zur Sammlung des Psalters," *Theologia Viatorum* 8: 278–84.

Willgren, David. (2016), *The Formation of the Book of Psalms: Reconsidering the Transmission and Canonization of Psalmody in Light of Material Culture and the Poetics of Anthologies*, Forschungen zum Alten Textament 2, Reihe 88, Tübingen: Mohr Siebeck.

Wilson, Gerald H. (1985), *The Editing of the Hebrew Psalter*, SBLDS 76, Chico, CA: Scholar's Press.

Wilson, Gerald H. (1997), "The Qumran *Psalms Scroll* and the Canonical Psalter: Comparison of Editorial Shaping," *Catholic Biblical Quarterly* 59: 448–64.

Yarkin, William. (2015), "Were the Psalm Collections at Qumran True Psalters?" *Journal of Biblical Literature* 134 (4): 775–89.

7

The Canonical Role of Israel's Wisdom Collection

Craig G. Bartholomew

Canon as applied to the Bible has more than one meaning (see Metzger 1987: 289–94).[1] It refers, on one hand to the *list* of books the Christian church regards as authoritative. On the other hand, it refers to the *authoritative nature* of the books in this list, namely, canon as rule. This distinction is important as we consider the canonical role of Israel's wisdom collection. Some canonical readings of the Bible arise from *the order of books in the list*.[2] One thinks, for example, of the four Gospels in the New Testament or the Book of the Twelve in the OT. In theory—and in practice—canonical readings of such collections can be done without any commitment to the books being authoritative in the second sense of canon.

Canon as list and the OT wisdom books

Proverbs, Job, and Ecclesiastes are all found in the third major division of the Hebrew Bible, namely the *Ketuvim* or Writings. However, whereas the order of the lists is canonically significant for some sections of the Bible, when it comes to the OT wisdom books, namely Proverbs, Job, and Ecclesiastes, this "list approach" is of little help (on the formation of the canon of the OT see Beckwith 1985; Carr 2011; Lim 2013). Childs (1979: 501–503) points out of the Writings that

- Nearly every aspect about how the Writings were formed is contested.
- The relationship of the Writings to the Law and the Prophets is also contested.
- There is major disagreement about the order of the books constituting the Writings.

Childs concludes that "the sequence of the books within the canonical division had little significance and no normative order was ever established by the synagogue" (Childs 1979: 503). If this is correct then there is little value in focusing a canonical

---

[1] Metzger notes that the word canon is "used in a kaleidoscopic variety of senses" (289).
[2] Sailhamer 1995: 213–15, refers to this as "con-textuality." He discusses the con-textual links between Proverbs and Ruth and notes (214), that "A canonical order insures that the books of the OT are read in a predetermined context." However, he acknowledges that there are several contending orders for the OT.

reading of Proverbs, Job, and Ecclesiastes on such questions as the relationship between Psalms and Proverbs, the relationship between Job and Song of Songs, and so on. Of course, within the Writings Ecclesiastes is part of the Megilloth, namely Song of Songs, Ruth, Lamentations, Ecclesiastes, Esther, and it is certainly worth exploring the interrelationship between Ecclesiastes and the other books of the Megilloth, a subject covered in another chapter of this volume.[3]

Canon as authority

It is the second sense of canon as authority that will therefore be our major concern in this chapter. This, we might say, is the *theological* understanding of canon. John Webster points out that to understand the Bible as canon theologically means swimming against powerful streams. The first is *historical critical* investigation of the canon. The effect is to historicize and secularize our understanding of the canon. A second is the articulation of canon in terms of *religious history*. From this perspective canon is a socio-cultural concept with the result that canon is not an inherent property of a text/s but the relation of a text/s to a religious community,[4] so that no account needs to be given of God's action in the production of the canon. A third is *socio-political* theories of canon according to which the development of the canon is investigated in terms of power relationships and ideological critique. A fourth is postmodern analyses: "If ideology critics dissolve the canon's givenness into strategies of power, postmodern repudiations of textual determinacy dissolve the canon into acts of reading" into setting the text in play (Webster 2001: 15). A fifth is the dogmatic mislocation of the canon introduced by Post-Reformation theology through which the canon is required to be the foundational doctrine. Webster does not regard this as a natural result of Reformation theology but rather as an abstraction of *sola Scriptura* from the other *solas*. For Webster this fifth point is related to the other four: it is "as the canon is lifted out of the network of doctrines within terms of which it makes sense it becomes patent of naturalistic explanations, whether of the more traditional historical-critical variety or of a socio-political cast" (Webster 2001: 10).

Webster argues rightly that our view of the Bible as canon needs to be relocated within the divine economy, a context in which full account is taken of divine action. "Scripture has its being in its reference to the activity of God. If that reference is damaged or distorted, its true character is obscured" (Webster 2001: 28). Webster is at pains to emphasise the humanity and human production of the books of the canon and proposes that a way to avoid the false distinction between their humanity and inspiration is to speak of them as means of grace or as witness. "In short: the texts of the canon are human communicative acts which are assumed into the economy of revelation and reconciliation" (Webster 2001: 31).

Webster's language of "assumed" reminds one of Wolterstorff's use of speech act theory and God appropriating human texts to address us as a way of accounting for the

---

[3] See Melton 2018 and the chapters by Dell, Steinberg, Gerstenberger, and Stone in Morgan 2019.
[4] For major sources see Webster 2001: 12, fn. 2. In particular he refers to Smith 1993.

Bible's authority (Wolterstorff 1995). A concern here is that a gap is potentially opened up between the message of the texts and God's address through them. In my view the way to respond to this is that not only the Bible as canon must be understood within the context of the divine economy but so too must the human production of the texts that make up the canon. In this respect Webster rightly moves on to discuss the role of the Spirit noting that "An account of the canon and canonization is therefore an account of the extension of Christ's active, communicative presence through the commissioned apostolic testimony.... The role of pneumatology is primary to 'de-centring' the church's act of canonization" (Webster 2001: 36). As I have explored elsewhere, Christoph Schwöbel provides, in my view, a fine account of the relationship between revelation, experience, and Scripture (Bartholomew 2020a: 183–87, see also Schwöbel 1992). It is best to regard the production of the canon as a very particular case of *concurrence*, in which the Spirit supervises the production of the texts so that, to allude to Augustine, what Scripture says, God says. *Sola Scriptura* needs to be held in close company with *tota Scriptura*. It is in its totality that the Bible is God's Word written which is why the topic of this chapter and the theme of this book is so very important.

Canon—not as authority—and the OT wisdom books

Of the five approaches to canon that we need, according to Webster, to be careful of if we are to attend to the Bible as authoritative canon, the first four are well documented in the history of modern study of the OT wisdom books. Historical criticism came late to OT wisdom but come it did, and a developmental approach to OT wisdom as well as the application of source, form, redaction, and tradition criticism to the OT wisdom books ensued (see Bartholomew 2016: 3–33).

Gunkel with his form criticism played an important role in bringing OT wisdom back into focus. He argued that, especially in Proverbs, the form of OT wisdom is so distinctive that it cannot be late and derived from law and prophecy. Its *Sitz im Leben* should rather be located in a class of wise men in Israel. That such wise men or sages were in touch with ANE wisdom was soon confirmed by the discovery of the "Instruction of Amenemope" (Hallo 1997: 1.47). The final form of the OT wisdom texts could well be late but a long oral and written process of development pushing back into the origins of Israel underlies them. This process lent itself to tradition historical analysis, pursued with vigour by Hugo Gressmann (see Gressmann 1924; 1925), as well as an analysis of how wisdom developed into the texts we have. For Gunkel the original form was the pithy didactic saying of the proverb. Over time this developed into expansive forms and later wisdom was more overtly religious.

Through historical criticism the history of composition of the wisdom books became a major concern. In Proverbs different collections are clearly evident and analysis focused on the date, history, and development of the collections. Solomonic authorship was increasingly rejected. F. Delitzsch noted of Proverbs that "Critical analysis resolves it into a colourful market of the most manifold intellectual products of at least three epochs of proverbial poetry" (Delitzsch 1873: 3). Proverbs also came to be dated late.

As it became apparent that wisdom literature was widespread across the ANE the question of the relationship between OT and ANE wisdom moved to the fore. A developmental approach also meant that some argued that the earliest Israelite wisdom was secular and that only later was the religious, Yahwistic dimension introduced. Attention to composition history resulted in the unity of the wisdom books increasingly being questioned. For example, by the middle of the twentieth century Marvin Pope articulated the consensus view that "the Book of Job in its present form can hardly be regarded as a consistent and unified composition by a single author" (Pope 1965: xxviii).

As concerns *tradition history*, views differed as to whether or not ancient OT wisdom was distinctive theologically. Preuss is an extreme example of such a view (see Murphy 1992: lxi). For Preuss,

1. Wisdom is marginal to Israel's faith.
2. The God of wisdom is not Yahweh.
3. Wisdom concentrates on the orders in reality.
4. The sages sought to discover the mechanical correspondence between action and consequence, as reflected in Proverbs.
5. A deed-consequence viewpoint is the basic dogma of early wisdom.

This type of approach had a major influence on how Job and Ecclesiastes were read. They came to be seen as representing a crisis in the mechanical view of wisdom embodied in Proverbs. Crüsemann, for example, maintains that "[t]his difference between Koheleth and his predecessors must be taken as the starting point for understanding Koheleth" (Crüsemann 1984: 57–77, at 61). Murphy points out that this idea of a crisis in wisdom came to overshadow analysis of OT wisdom almost as much as the influence of the exile in OT studies (Murphy 1992: lxi, see also Gese 1983: 141–53). OT wisdom came to be seen as a separate tradition in Israel with little awareness of the other major traditions. Only late in its development was wisdom thought to have been brought into dialogue with torah and prophecy.

Redaction criticism can be seen as something of a bridge between historical criticism and literary approaches, with its investigation of how books were edited into wholes. However, redactional criticism still depends on identifying stages in the composition of the wisdom books. Childs' canonical approach which works with historical criticism is an example. He sees the older collection of Prov. 10 forwards, for example, as "left largely in an unedited stage, that is to say, there has been no attempt to interject the later developments upon the earlier stage" (Childs 1979: 555).

Historical criticism has brought far too many gains simply to be rejected and to revert to pre-critical interpretation. However, from a theological perspective it is not hard to see that there is a tremendous shadow side to such gains. Any unity of the wisdom books is shredded as layer after speculative layer is unearthed. When the books are read to an extent as wholes they are set against each other, embodying radically different approaches to wisdom, indeed worldviews. Not surprisingly the huge amount of work done by historical critics did not, on the whole, lend itself to rich theological readings. The major exception to this is Gerhard von Rad's *Wisdom in Israel*, which remains a fecund resource for the study of OT wisdom (von Rad 1972).

From the 1970s onwards we witnessed *the literary turn* in biblical studies, and this had major implications for historical criticism and the OT wisdom books. If ever we needed evidence that *theory is underdetermined by the facts* this was it. Where repetition had been a sign of a different source we now discovered that repetition is at the heart of literature. Contradictory views could now be read as deliberate juxtapositions. Where Ecclesiastes had been carved up into multiple sources we ended up with Michael Fox's analysis of Qoheleth in terms of the different voices and their interrelationships (Fox 1993: 115–31). His work ushered in a veritable paradigm shift in studies of Ecclesiastes. And just as we discovered signs of the Psalter being a literary whole and not just 150 disparate psalms, so too the argument developed that Proverbs was a literary whole moving from the major wisdom insight in 1:7 to its climax in Prov. 31 with the embodiment of wisdom in the valiant woman. Multiple studies also showed how Job could be read as a complex literary whole. Recently there has been close attention to intertextuality and the OT wisdom books, another fertile area of exploration (Dell and Kynes 2013; 2014; 2020).

Childs denies that his final form approach is literary, but in my view there is a close relationship between his approach and the literary one. Indeed, "form" is a literary word, and, from a literary perspective "final form" is tautologous since what other form of a literary text do we have than the one we receive? Final form implies that there are other forms, but of course they are almost always never other forms of *this* text, but rather different literary texts. The difference between Childs' canonical hermeneutic and literary approaches is that his final form reading depends upon being able to reconstruct stages in the redaction of the text into its "final form." By comparison, a literary approach generally reads the text as we receive it synchronically.

The literary turn leaned towards a reading of the Bible as authoritative canon because it moved biblical studies toward reading books as unified wholes, an indispensable move if we are ever to read the canon as a unified whole. Of course, many who engaged in literary readings had little or no interest in the canon as authoritative, but, nevertheless, in terms of canon as a rule this was a positive move.

It was especially Jewish literary scholars such as Meir Sternberg and Robert Alter who did the extraordinary and wonderfully creative heavy lifting in establishing a literary approach to the HB/OT. However, an effect of the resultant openness of biblical studies toward literary theory was that once postmodernism developed out of literary theory and began to colonize the disciplines, the route to the OT was already well established. Indeed, before the literary turn could be fully appropriated and its challenge to historical criticism fully explored, the wild pluralism of postmodernism was upon us. David Clines, for example, one of the leading postmodern OT scholars in the UK, provided a series of postmodern readings of Job (Clines 1998). Postmodernism radically destabilized the OT text—is there a text?—and nowadays we even have talk of postmodern textual criticism, with the fluidity of the text going all the way down, as it were. In my view postmodernism, a working out of the unstable DNA of modernity, was ever deconstructive, but never constructive in opening a fresh way forward and beyond modernity. As its demise has begun, an effect is that historical criticism remains the default mode of much OT and OT wisdom scholarship.

Amidst the pluralism of postmodernism, a positive move in terms of canon as rule has been the minority revival of so-called *theological interpretation* (see Bartholomew and Thomas 2016). Karl Barth, Childs, and others are the fathers of this movement. As it has developed it has become clear that it is a broad church with many different groupings within it. Central to theological interpretation is a desire to recover a way of reading the Bible for the church as Scripture, and this does indeed beckon well for canonical reading of OT wisdom.

Canon as rule and the OT wisdom books

Child writes of Proverbs that,

> my criticism arises from the hermeneutical assumptions which seem to dominate, often uncritically, much of modern biblical study. Specifically in terms of wisdom, one is left in the end without a clear description of how the canonical book of Proverbs functioned as sacred scripture within the community of faith which caused the book to be treasured.
>
> Childs 1979: 551

With Childs I would argue that this is a serious deficit. In contrast with Childs I would argue that there are reasons why historical criticism is so often deficient in this area and that we need a stronger, critical engagement with historical criticism. The OT wisdom books are part of the canon as authoritative rule, and our most rigorous scholarship falls short if it is not oriented toward hearing God's address to us today through these books. I agree with Childs that we need to respect and attend to the discrete witness of the OT, even as we take seriously the ways in which the explosion of good news in the Christ event casts its light backwards and forwards.

An insight of modern OT study is the recognition of wisdom as a distinct genre.[5] Debate continues as to whether or not there were wisdom schools in Israel, but clearly there were sages who specialized in this type of literature. Below we will explore the question of how wisdom relates to other genres within the OT. For now our focus is on how to read the three major OT wisdom books and their interrelationship so that we are most likely to hear God's address through them.

Proverbs: the foundational wisdom book

Childs rightly observes that "Clearly the book of Proverbs remains the basic source for the study of biblical wisdom to which Job and Ecclesiastes are secondarily related" (Childs 1979: 547). This—however obvious—is a tremendously important point if we are to access the canonical voice/s of OT wisdom. The truth of Childs' statement has become clearer as we have discovered that Proverbs is designed as a literary whole. From headings within the book it is quite clear that pre-existing collections underlie

---

[5] See Kynes 2019 for a critical overview of this development. Kynes argues for retaining wisdom as a concept but foregoing wisdom as a genre. In my view this is an unhelpful dichotomy.

the form of the book as we have received it but such sources—which we do not have—even if they can be speculatively reconstructed, are never an earlier version of "the final form" of Proverbs, as discussed above.

This is not to argue that connections between individual proverbs and sections of proverbs are always discernible from Prov. 10 and following. However, recent investigations of the proverbial sayings in 10–31 have shown that again and again many individual proverbs are not context-less, as earlier scholars had assumed, but there are signs of editing of sections of proverbial sayings.[6] If this development has taken place at the micro-level, at the macro-level there has been an emerging sense of the literary shape of Proverbs as a whole (see for example, Ansberry 2011). This parallels developments in the study of books such as Isaiah, Psalms, Job, and Ecclesiastes. Narrative readings of Ecclesiastes as a whole are turning out to be remarkably fertile, and a growing body of literature has emerged on the Psalter as a whole (see McCann 1993; Bartholomew and West 2001).

Studies of the Psalter provide a useful parallel to Proverbs. Recognition that the Psalms has an introduction (Pss. 1–2) and a conclusion (Pss. 145–50), is divided into five books mirroring the Pentateuch, and has a high point in the kingship psalms of Book Four, does not mean that every psalm is clearly and deeply interwoven into the integrated whole. Research in this area continues and it seems to me that in the context of the overarching shape of the whole, each Psalm retains a relative autonomy. However, it is important to note that once such oral compositions as the psalm and the proverb are reduced to writing and placed in a book, they inevitably develop a context, whether intentional or not, and connections begin to appear, again, whether intentional or not. In other words, they take on a somewhat different life. This is simply how literature works, and it may often produce effects not originally seen or intended by the author/editor. Failure to recognize this has led some scholars to oppose reading Proverbs as a whole. They are of the view that a proverb only thrives in a living, oral context, and that when it is reduced to writing it dies. However, as Van Leeuwen, for example, points out in his detailed study of Prov. 25–27, the authors have through careful editing created literary contexts for individual sayings which compensate for the loss of their life-context. These are elaborate enough to provide clues for our interpretation of them which the life-situation would have provided (Van Leeuwen 1988: 30–31). Prov. 26:1–12 is an excellent example in this respect.

Clearly the dominant motif in Proverbs is the fear of the LORD as the beginning (starting point and foundation) of wisdom or knowledge. Indeed, it functions amongst other ways as an inclusio for the book as whole (Prov. 1:7; 31:30), in contrast to Job and Ecclesiastes. Job (1:1) begins with the fear of the LORD and Ecclesiastes ends with it (12:13–14) but neither is contained with an inclusio of the fear of the LORD as is Proverbs. This clues us in to the foundational nature of Proverbs in OT wisdom. We have come to realize that wisdom is grounded in a theology of creation and this comes to clear expression in Prov. 3:19–20 and especially in the delightful passage in

---

[6] See Whybray 1995, chapter 2, for a description of these developments; Van Leeuwen 1988; Heim, 2013.

Prov. 8:22–31. Little wonder then that with the fear of the LORD as the starting point thematically Proverbs ranges across creation, identifying wisdom in all areas of life.

Prov. 1–9 is the first major section of the book made up largely of speeches. A focus is avoiding sexual temptation which we would expect for an adolescent male but more important is the variety of strategies employed to urge the reader to seek wisdom rather than folly. In this way 1–9 open up for the reader in front of the text a world in which humans are drawn either by the love of wisdom or of folly, the doctrine of two ways which is comparably how the Psalter (Pss. 1–2) begins. Proverbs 1–9 creates through vivid metaphors a world for the reader that functions as the interpretive key for the book as a whole (see Keefer 2020; Zabán, 2012; Reichenbach 2011). Metaphor is the building block of such world construction, and in Prov. 1–9 a worldview is evoked through the repetition of strong, evocative metaphors: two types of love, two paths or ways, two women, Lady Folly and Lady Wisdom, and the climax of 1–9 in the two houses (Prov. 9) with two invitations and two meals.

This type of world or worldview construction generally functions with a basic or root metaphor (see Pepper 1970, especially chapter V). The root metaphor provides the substrate in which the surface metaphors cohere. OT wisdom scholars disagree about the root metaphor: Camp (1987: 45–67) suggests that Lady Wisdom is the root metaphor in 1–9, and for Habel it is the two ways, the way of wisdom and the way of folly (Habel 1972). Van Leeuwen is, I think, right that

> underlying the contrasting metaphors ... is a yet more basic reality which these surface metaphors portray. The surface metaphors build a world for the reader which is at base ordered by God. God's world is the context for human life and as such it has two characteristics. First, as creation it has boundaries or limits. Second, human life in God's world is characterised by two possibilities. Either it is drawn towards Wisdom, who prescribes life within God-given limits, or toward Folly, who offers counterfeit delights in defiance of created limits.... The socio-ethical order of Proverbs 1–9 is grounded in the creation order revealed by Wisdom who accompanied God as he set the cosmic boundaries.
>
> Van Leeuwen 1990: 116–17

At root, Proverbs is grounded in the view of *creation ordered by God's wisdom*. In this world there exists a life–death struggle between wisdom and folly, a battle in which love of wisdom, her path, her house, and her feast stand for true life and are the means to blessing.

In this masterful way 1–9 establish the basic contours or what we might call the A, B, Cs of wisdom, again and again setting out in a whole smorgasbord of ways the advantage to humans of heeding Lady Wisdom's call in all areas of life. This is the path to blessing, including material prosperity (cf. Prov. 3:9–10). However, it is the very clarity of 1–9's act-consequence motif that has led some to argue that Proverbs teaches a mechanical view of retribution, the crisis of which is embodied in Job and Ecclesiastes. What might better be called the character-consequence structure of Proverbs is clearly set out in 1–9: folly will result in calamity (1:26), whereas wisdom, by comparison, will result in security and preservation (1:33). Wisdom leads to dwelling in the land (2:2), to length of days, years of life, and abundant welfare.

However, the overall picture in Proverbs is more complex than this. The first Solomonic collection (cf. Prov 10:1; 25:1) of Proverbs following 1–9 consists of two sections: 10–15 (see Scoralick 1995) and 16–22. Chapters 10–15 are largely made up of antithetical proverbs with the first line answered by a contrasting second line. Proverbs 10–15 emphasizes the difference between the wise/righteous and the foolish/wicked and the consequences of their chosen paths. The character-consequence structure is emphatic in this section (see, e.g., 11:3, 5, 6, 8, 21, etc.). The righteous are protected, they are saved from evil and established in the land.

However, 16–22 provide nuance to this overarching picture. Van Leeuwen has demonstrated this in an important article on wealth and poverty in Proverbs (Van Leeuwen 1992: 25–36). He notes that there are many sayings that do indeed set out a simple cause–effect relationship by means of which righteousness leads to wealth, and wickedness to poverty. However, he points out that these do not relate to concrete, particular acts and their consequences: "It is the long-term character and direction of a person or group (as 'righteous' or 'wicked') which determines life consequences and 'destiny'" (Van Leeuwen 1992: 27). Furthermore, proverbs are by their very nature partial utterances making the context of proverbs as a whole vital for correct interpretation.

The "better-than" sayings in Proverbs in which the reality that wisdom and prosperity *often do not* accompany one another (cf. 15:16–17; 16:16, 19, etc.) are particularly important in this respect. Van Leeuwen sums up the more complex picture from the whole of Proverbs as follows: "*In general*, the sages clearly believed that wise and righteous behaviour did make life better and richer, though virtue did not *guarantee* those consequences. Conversely, injustice, sloth, and the like generally have bad consequences.... General patterns may be discerned, but many particular events may be unjust, irrational, and ultimately inscrutable" (Van Leeuwen 1992: 32–33). Even before 16–22 we find indications of a nuance to the character-consequence theme in Proverbs. Take 14:11–12, for example:

> ¹¹ The house of the wicked is destroyed,
>   but the tent of the upright flourishes.
> ¹² There is a way that seems right to a person,
>   but its end is the way to death. (NRSV)[7]

Contrary to a simplistic interpretation of the character-consequence structure, here we see that the wicked person lives in a house, i.e. is settled comfortably in the land, whereas the righteous person is living far less luxuriously and vulnerably in a tent. In OT terms it is as though the wicked are established in the land whereas the righteous are still on pilgrimage to the land. Nevertheless, the house is destroyed and the tent flourishes! *Ultimately* the destination of the wicked is death.

---

[7] I am indebted to my friend and colleague David Beldman for drawing my attention to these verses.

However, it is in 16–22 that most of the exceptions to the character-consequence structure are found. In this way the development from 10–15 to 16–22 (and following, see 28:6) embodies a "developmental pedagogy" (Van Leeuwen 1993: 261).[8] Indeed, an element of wisdom in Proverbs is discerning that which fits a particular situation. The wise will learn *when* to use which proverb, as the antithetic juxtaposition in 26:4–5 clearly demonstrates. Wisdom engages the mind fully and always calls for discernment.

The developmental pedagogy of Proverbs climaxes in the extraordinary portrayal of the valiant woman in Prov. 31. This acrostic hymn does in its own way just what 1–9 is doing; it creates a longing for wisdom. As an acrostic the hymn sets out a complete (A–Z) picture of wisdom, and the form of a hymn is that normally reserved for God (Wolters 2001), thereby evoking the extraordinary value in imaging God by becoming wise. In the history of interpretation of this passage scholars have struggled with the fact that this woman is described as one who fears the LORD and is to be praised (31:30), and yet she never engages in overtly religious acts. This is, of course, to miss the point entirely. Just as God builds his wisdom into every area of life so too human wisdom is called to manifest itself in every area of life. We might call this Proverbs' doctrine of the *imago dei*. And this is precisely what the Prov. 31 woman does: she engages in marriage, being a wife, being a mother, homemaking, viticulture, trading in fabrics of the highest quality, charitable works, teaching, etc.

What then is wisdom according to Proverbs. Elsewhere I summarize it in this way. Wisdom is:

- an attribute of Yahweh (Prov. 8:22–31);
- the means by which Yahweh created the world (Prov. 3:19–20);
- built into the fabric of creation and crying out to be heard by humans in all areas of life (Prov. 1:20–21);
- needed by humans in every area of life if they are to flourish (Prov. 3:13–18);
- rooted and grounded in the fear of Yahweh (Prov. 1:7, etc.);
- antithetically opposed to folly;
- developed into a tradition by God's people through the experience of living in God's world. (Bartholomew 2016: 6)

Job and Ecclesiastes in relation to Proverbs

Once the more nuanced picture of Proverbs comes into focus as discussed above, then the view of Job and Ecclesiastes embodying a crisis in a mechanical view of retribution fades away. Proverbs is well aware as a whole that things do not always go well for the righteous and wise and a verse like Prov. 17:3 (cf. 27:21) captures well the content of Job and Ecclesiastes: The crucible is for silver, and the furnace is for gold, "but the LORD tests the heart" (NRSV).[9] Indeed Prov. 17 as a whole is an interesting chapter in this respect. It begins in 17:1 with a better-than proverb, is aware of poverty and disaster

---

[8] On Proverbs' educational pedagogy cf. Ansberry 2011. Ansberry argues that Proverbs' educational agenda is for a young noble of the court.
[9] In the Hebrew לִבּוֹת is plural.

(17:5), and notes that a friend and a brother are born for the time of adversity (17:17).[10] The metaphors of the crucible and furnace are fitting images for Job and Ecclesiastes, and it is hard not to think of Job's friends—albeit negatively—when one reads 17:17.

Ecclesiastes

It is easy to see how Job's profound suffering is like being in a crucible. On the surface this is less obvious with Qoheleth. However, the sort of intellectual quandary that Qoheleth finds himself amidst is in its own way as excruciating as Job's suffering. Indeed, against the backdrop of the Solomon narratives in 1 Kings, nothing prepares the reader for the move from the Solomonic fiction in Eccl. 1:1—even if Qoheleth is not Solomon we are to imagine him as like Solomon—to the shocking summary statement in 1:2 (cf. 12:8 for the inclusio) that "the all" is utterly *hebel*. It has been justifiably argued that the author of Ecclesiastes had the opening chapters of Genesis in front of him and in Gen. 1:31 God sees all that he has made and declares it very good. Qoheleth, by comparison sees "the all" and declares it utterly *hebel* (see Bartholomew, 2020b). Renowned as Solomon was for his wisdom it is beyond belief that he has found his way to *this* conclusion, so that a huge gap is opened up for the reader in the text, a gap that Ecclesiastes as a whole is designed to fill. Qoheleth is literally in a crisis of epic proportions.

Scholars are disagreed as to whether or not Ecclesiastes is overall positive about life. The minority view, which I share, is that he is. The great challenge with Ecclesiastes is how to relate the prologue and epilogue to the main body of the text and how to track Qoheleth's journey as it weaves back and forth. Several points need to be noted in this respect:

1. Time and again scholars try and develop a logical analysis of the book of Ecclesiastes, which it resists. The nature of Qoheleth's struggle is that it meanders backwards and forwards, with a breakthrough on occasion. It circles around and around the tension that is at the heart of the book and leads him again and again to the *hebel* conclusion. It thus has the nature of a meandering, confused journey, and attempts to find a logical order in the book end up flattening out polarities that are intentionally juxtaposed to capture the dilemma he finds himself in. Ecclesiastes thus needs to be read first with a literary sensibility.
2. Secondly, and this is where the background of Proverbs is crucial, there is the issue of Qoheleth's methodology or epistemology. In 1:12–18 Qoheleth describes his quest and his methodology as that of wisdom (1:13] בַּחָכְמָה; cf. 1:16, 17; 2:3]). On the surface, therefore, we expect that Qoheleth's epistemology is the same as that of Proverbs, but it is not. His use of "wisdom" turns out to be ironic. In 7:23–29 the irony is brought out into the open when Qoheleth's "wisdom" lands him in the arms of Lady Folly. The irony of Qoheleth's "wisdom" becomes clearer when we compare it to that of Proverbs. Fox has rightly argued that Proverbs' epistemology is not empirical in the sense of observing and then drawing conclusions on the

---

[10] NRSV translates (וְאָח) "and kinsfolk," but the Hebrew literally reads "and a brother."

basis of observation and reason alone. Rather Proverbs draws from observation to illustrate values the author/s is already aware of and holds to. There *is* an observational aspect to the wisdom of Proverbs but it is observation through the lens of the fear of Yahweh (cf. Brown 2014: 19). Indeed, as von Rad astutely observes, a seminal insight of Proverbs epistemologically is that one can go wrong in the quest for knowledge at the outset and this skews the whole knowing process.

Qoheleth's epistemology, by comparison *is empirical*. It is based on observation, experience, and reason alone, and 7:23–29 exposes such an autonomous epistemology as folly. It is only in Eccl. 12 that Qoheleth finds his way back to beginning with the creator (12:1) before ... before ... before.... Here "Remember your creator" has the same implications as starting with the fear of Yahweh in Proverbs.

3. Thirdly we need to note the contradictory juxtapositions throughout Ecclesiastes. Repetition characterizes the book and major repetitions are the *hebel* conclusions and the so-called *carpe diem* passages. As I have argued elsewhere the *carpe diem* passages are not expressions of a despairing hedonism but are a wonderful affirmation of created life and the activities that constitute it (Bartholomew 2009). Qoheleth is an Israelite and this perspective flows from his immersion in the life of God's people. Juxtaposed with these are the empirical investigations which always lead to *hebel*. The juxtapositions thus embody the profound tension and struggle at the heart of the book, opening up a gap between these antithetical perspectives.

4. The crucial question is whether this dilemma is ever resolved. It is. Partial resolution comes in 5:17 and 7:23–29, and then the fire-fly-like proverb in 11:8 signals a shift from "under the sun" being oppressive to the light (of the sun) being sweet—a metaphor of taste—and pleasant. Resolution comes through the imperatives to rejoice and to remember, leading on to the epilogue.

Job

Job is unusual in that Job is a non-Israelite and the narrative is set outside of Israel. Nevertheless, a dominant name for God in the book, by comparison with Ecclesiastes in which "Yahweh" is never used, is Yahweh (twenty-four times). Thus, there is something universal about Job but the central character is Yahweh, the God of the covenant with Israel. Like Ecclesiastes and Proverbs, Job is predominantly poetic in form, but it also contains narrative sections, and the reader is provided with insight into events in the heavenly court related to God and the Satan that Job does not possess. Far from these characteristics indicating different sources, they are what we would expect in well-crafted literature. Thus, Seow concludes his discussion of the unity of Job by rightly asserting that: "There are all sorts of literary tensions within the book. Hence, instead of performing textual strategies to suit modern preconceptions of coherence, it is necessary to give the ancient narrator-poet the benefit of the doubt and to grapple with those dissonances and asymmetry that may well be part of how the book means" (Seow 2013: 38). Several aspects of Job as a whole need to be taken into account:

1. As with Ecclesiastes there is *irony* at work in Job. In 1:1 Job is described as "blameless and upright, one who feared God and turned away from evil," the quintessential wise man (NRSV). However, in the brief description that follows there is something askew with Job's practice of religion. He performs burnt offerings (1:5) *in case* his children had sinned. Family is the most important thing to Job in the world and his religion is a means to secure that area of his life. Indeed, Job is contained within an inclusio of two sacrifices, namely 1:5 and that of Eliphaz, Bildad and Zophar in 42:7–9. Both are burnt offerings, the one to keep his children safe in case they had sinned, the other an embodiment of repentance for not speaking right of God, as Job had done. In the first, Job acts out of his fear and lack of trust; in the latter, Job intercedes on behalf of his friends and his prayer is accepted.
2. Job, like Ecclesiastes, performs its message through its form. Adversity of the sort Job suffered is long, repetitive, and protracted. And of course this is just like the book of Job, with its long unending speeches. And the speeches of the friends revolve around a view of retribution that lacks the nuance of Proverbs. These are decidedly not the type of friends born for the day of adversity (Prov. 17:17).
3. Things turn out well for Job in the end (42:10–16). As in the beginning (1:2) he ends up with seven sons and three daughters (42:13). In several ways (sacrifice, children, animals) the prologue and the epilogue mirror each other. However, his original children that he sought so hard to protect remain dead. What *has* changed is not just the greater number of sheep, oxen, camels, and donkeys, but Job himself. As a book Job is often dismissed as a theodicy but in my view, this is short-sighted. Resolution comes for Job, not through his final restoration but earlier through his encounter with Yahweh through the speeches out of the whirlwind (38–41). It is this encounter, and no logical explanation, that moves Job from, as it were, having heard of God to having seen him (42:5), from sacrificing to secure his family to praying for the forgiveness of friends who had so misunderstood his predicament.
4. Furthermore, in terms of theodicy, not only does Job exemplify a protest theodicy (Roth 1981: 7–37)—Job spoke right of Yahweh (42:7)—but it shows in narrative and poetic form that evil has a profound tendency to overreach itself. However we understand the Satan, the one thing he did not expect is that Job would undergo the transformation he experienced.

OT wisdom and the OT[11]

In modern OT studies this has been a vexed issue. Historical criticism helpfully identified wisdom as a distinct genre in the OT but, on the whole, unhelpfully came to see law, prophecy, and wisdom as distinct and relatively separate genres, and then

---

[11] Cf. on this issue see Carr (2011) chapters 14 and 15. Carr asserts: "I propose that a plausible option is to explain the lack of Pentateuchal, prophetic, and legal foci in Proverbs as resulting from the fact that the bulk of the book was composed before such foci became prominent" (2011: 407).

swinging to find wisdom motifs all over the place (see Blenkinsopp 1983). The rigid separation of them seems to me inherently unconvincing. "Experts" in ancient Israel may have focused on a particular genre but for the average Israelite it is absurd to imagine torah, prophecy, and wisdom as sealed off from each other.

One might well ask how we have any idea what the average Israelite thought? One answer would be to have a close look at their worship. A cross-section analysis of people's worship reveals a great deal about their worldview and the obvious canonical contender in this respect is the Psalter. The Psalms were central to Israel's worship. The Psalms originated over time but in the form in which we receive them, as noted above, there are clear signs of them being edited into a literary whole. And wisdom plays a significant part in that whole. Psalms 1 and 2 are the introduction to the whole and they clearly set out a doctrine of the two ways for both the individual (Ps. 1) and the nations (Ps. 2), with the kings of the earth advised to "be wise" (2:10). The doctrine of the two ways is, of course, fundamental to OT wisdom. Wisdom language is found scattered around the Psalter and Pss. 37, 49, 73, 112, and 119 have been identified as wisdom psalms.

Psalm 111 has been described as the natural scientist's psalm. Like Pss. 37 and 119 it is an acrostic poem. It refers to the great works of Yahweh, his righteousness, his covenant and his precepts and concludes in v. 10 with the foundational wisdom insight that "The fear of the LORD is the beginning of wisdom." Here, as in many other places, wisdom is integrated into an Israelite worldview with Yahweh and his works in creation and redemption at the center, flowing, in my view, quite naturally and beautifully into v. 10. However, within a historical critical grid verses like v. 10 must be an addition to the original psalm. Westermann, for example, comments: "Among the psalms of descriptive praise, Psalm 111 is usually considered a wisdom psalm. But it is to a greater degree a pure psalm of praise ... Only at the conclusion is a wisdom saying added to the psalm, the same proverb which we find in Proverbs 1:7" (Westermann 1980). As in Prov. 8, there is absolutely no reason why praise and wisdom cannot and should not go together. Indeed, as Brown has pointed out, wonder is central to wisdom in Proverbs. Brown (2014: 20) argues that, "It is the awe-filled and awful wonder of God and creation—the wonder of the Other—that constitutes nothing less than the epistemological foundation and aim of biblical wisdom." And wonder is a close ally to praise. Thus, once the historical critical developmental framework is loosened, it is apparent that torah and wisdom were an integral part of the Israelites' worldview.

Just as wisdom is clearly present in the Psalter so too is law and torah in the wisdom books. Levy, under the evocative heading of "The Educational Theatre of Proverbs" (Levy 2000: 135–42) discerns intertextual echoes from the Torah in Prov. 7:1–27, and argues that the *shema* of Deut. 6:1–4 is clearly alluded to in vv. 1–5. "The father reuses the original Pentateuch text in a sophisticated way" (Levy 2000: 136). For the *shema* God's commandments (cf. "my commandments" of Prov. 7:2) are to be discussed in the home, presumably the same context for the instruction of Prov. 7. They are to be bound on the fingers (cf. Prov. 3:3); in Deut. 6 they are to be bound on the hand. In addition, "the tablet of your heart" alludes to "the heart" of Deut. 6:6 and "tablet" also evokes the tablets of the law.

When it comes to Job, "The law and its themes, concepts, images, and language permeate the Book of Job.... What is surprising is that in the commentaries on Job we rarely find appreciation that the conception of law is central to the book."[12] Similarly in Ecclesiastes knowledge of torah is clearly present, and not just in the epilogue. Ecclesiastes 5:6 concludes the section 4:17–5:6 (Heb.). In 4:17–5:6 we find a restatement of the law of Deut. 23:22–24 in 5:3–4 and the background to 5:5 is Num. 15:22–31. With its allusions to the Torah this section concludes with the exhortation to "fear God" (cf. Lohfink 1990: 633). The awareness of torah should be combined with the presence of vocabulary in the wisdom books that relates to Pentateuchal law, namely "judgment" (Eccl. 3:17; 11:9), "sinner," "sin" (Eccl. 2:26; 5:5 [5:6 EVV]; 8:12), "wicked" and "righteous" (Eccl. 3:17). Job (cf. Job 3) and Ecclesiastes both engage with the opening chapters of Genesis, Ecclesiastes has strong links with Deuteronomy, and so on.

Especially once we grasp that the epistemology of Proverbs is *not* empirical then the question arises of where Proverbs derives its values. Childs argues that in Proverbs, "The superscription thus guards against forcing the proverbs into a context foreign to wisdom such as the decalogue" (Childs 1979: 552, on Proverbs and 1 Kings 1–11 cf. Winkler 2017). However, as I have argued elsewhere, it is precisely in the decalogue that we find enshrined the values assumed and articulated by Proverbs (Bartholomew 2012).

Murphy has proposed that "[t]he problem of the relationship between wisdom literature and other portions of the Old Testament needs to be reformulated in terms of a shared approach to reality" (Murphy 1978: 38). This seems to me quite right; for "shared reality" I would use the term "worldview."

This becomes even clearer when we see that "[a] relationship between religious and secular is not applicable to OT wisdom teaching" (Murphy 1978: 40). Nor is it applicable to *torah*, which orders all aspects of life. How then should we understand the relationship between law and wisdom? The wisdom and legal traditions in the OT are distinct but show an awareness of one another. Both relate to the ordering of the life of God's people in God's world[13] and both are underlain by a theology of creation.

The link between wisdom and creation has long been recognized. What is often not attended to, however, is that the order Proverbs finds in the creation cannot simply be read out of the creation. This is Fox's point about OT wisdom; it is not empirical like that of Qoheleth, but assumes ethical principles or values which it uses observation to support. This is akin to the situation we find in Gen. 1–2. The ordering of creation by Elohim (Gen. 1:1–2:3) and instruction from Yahweh Elohim (Gen 2:4–3:24) go together.

Literary scholars often manifest a refreshing freedom to tread where biblical scholars fear to go. The Canadian literary scholar Northrop Frye, for example, argues that "The conception of wisdom in the Bible, as we see most clearly in some of the

---

[12] Fingarette 2004: 125. See Van Leeuwen 1990: 122, for some of the links between Proverbs and Job and the Pentateuch. Van Leeuwen argues that certain texts in Proverbs and Job presuppose the historical tradition of the gift of the land.

[13] Murphy (1978) is critical of the close association of wisdom with the search for order, arguing that this question is a modern one which focuses on a presupposition of Israel's wisdom approach. However, see Van Leeuwen (1990) for a persuasive defense of taking seriously the tacit presupposition of cosmic order in wisdom literature.

psalms, starts with the individualizing of the law, with allowing the law, in its human and moral aspect, to permeate and inform all one's personal life" (Frye 1982: 121). This seems right to me, although I would nuance Frye's comment by noting that wisdom is not just individual but communal; it is a tradition. Work remains to be done on the relationship between OT wisdom and OT prophecy. In the vision of death in Eccl. 12, for example, there appear to be links with prophetic apocalyptic visions (Bartholomew 2009).

OT wisdom and the New Testament

All strands of the OT, including wisdom, find their fulfilment in the Christ event, and from there radiate out into the new situation ushered in by the coming of the kingdom. Much work remains to be done on the relationship between OT wisdom and the NT (see Witherington 1994; Bauckham 1999; Bartholomew 2014). Indeed, wisdom looms larger in the NT than is often recognized. In the Sermon on the Mount Jesus is clearly depicted as the new Moses but he concludes the Sermon with the story of two houses (Matt. 7:24–27), imagery that appears to come from Proverbs (9; 12:7; 24:3–4). Wisdom is now defined as obedience to Jesus, but as Jesus himself stresses he has not come to abolish the OT but to fulfil it. In the new age believers still require wisdom, and Paul especially, in his letters, locates wisdom in Jesus and prays that believers will be filled with wisdom (1 Cor. 10:30; Col. 1:9; 2:3).

OT wisdom today

Proverbial wisdom has fallen out of favor in modernity, as we will see below. Nevertheless, collections of proverbs continue to be published, and there are journals that specialize in studying them. OT wisdom needs both etic and emic insights, so that both insights from ANE background and contemporary studies of proverbs (for example Mieder 1993) have much to offer.

The great Renaissance scholar Erasmus made his name with his first published book, a collection of proverbs (Erasmus 2001). It is hard to imagine such a situation today. To a major extent modernity has privileged abstraction over lived experience so that the particularity of wisdom has fallen out of favor (see Van Leeuwen 1995). We would need to recover the "biblical worldview" and learn that abstraction, valuable as it is, always emerges out of lived experience, and that its test is whether or not it deepens our lived experience when it returns to it. Such renewed attention to lived experience would revive a sense of the value of wisdom.

OT wisdom relates to all of life. For example, if Qoheleth reaches resolution in his epic struggle, which I think he does, then retrospectively all the areas he attended to are meaningful, and worthy of our attention: horticulture, work, music, politics, law, relationship, eating and drinking, religion, business, etc. Reading OT wisdom canonically falls short if we fail to build a bridge from it right into contemporary life today. Alas, we find far too little of such work. And yet wisdom is so relevant and cries out for such treatment. I am finishing this chapter off as we—hopefully—emerge from the Coronavirus pandemic, a time when great wisdom has been desperately needed in all areas of life. If we are to take OT wisdom seriously as part of God's rule for life then such bridge-building is imperative.

Bibliography

Ansberry, Christopher B. (2011), *Be Wise, My Son, and Make My Heart Glad: An Exploration of the Courtly Nature of the Book of Proverbs*, BZAW 422, Berlin: Walter de Gruyter.

Bartholomew, Craig G. (2009), *Ecclesiastes*, BCOTWP, Grand Rapids: Baker Academic.

Bartholomew, Craig G. (2012), "Hearing the Old Testament Wisdom Literature: The Wit of Many and the Wisdom of One," in C. G. Bartholomew and D. J. H. Beldman (eds.), *Hearing the Old Testament: Listening for God's Address*, 302–31, Grand Rapids: Eerdmans.

Bartholomew, Craig G. (2014), "The Intertextuality of Ecclesiastes and the New Testament," in K. Dell and W. Kynes (eds.), *Reading Ecclesiastes Intertextually*, 226–39, Library of Biblical Studies 587, London: Bloomsbury.

Bartholomew, Craig G. (2016), "Old Testament Wisdom Today," in D. G. Firth and L. Wilson (eds.), *Exploring Old Testament Wisdom: Literature and Themes*, 3–33, London: Apollos.

Bartholomew, Craig G. (2020a), *The God Who Acts in History: The Significance of Sinai*, Grand Rapids: Eerdmans, 2020.

Bartholomew, Craig G. (2020b), "Qohelet as a Master of and Mastered by Metaphor," in D. Verde and A. Labahn (eds.), *Networks of Metaphors in the Hebrew Bible*, 329–346, Leuven: Peeters.

Bartholomew, Craig G. and Heath A. Thomas, eds. (2016), *A Manifesto for Theological Interpretation*, Grand Rapids: Baker Academic.

Bartholomew, Craig G. and Andrew West, eds. (2001), *Praying By the Book: Reading the Psalms*, Carlisle: Paternoster.

Bauckham, Richard. (1999) *James: Wisdom of James, Disciple of Jesus the Sage*, London: Routledge.

Beckwith, Roger. (1985), *The Old Testament Canon of the New Testament Church and its Background in Early Judaism*, London: SPCK.

Blenkinsopp, Joseph. (1983), *Wisdom and Law in the Old Testament: The Ordering of Life in Israel and Early Judaism,* Oxford: Oxford University Press.

Brown, William P. (2014), *Wisdom's Wonder: Character, Creation, and Crisis in the Bible's Wisdom Literature*, Grand Rapids: Eerdmans.

Camp, Claudia V. (1987), "Woman Wisdom as Root Metaphor: A Theological Consideration," in K. G. Hoglund, et al. (eds.), *The Listening Heart: Essays in Wisdom and the Psalms in Honor of Roland E. Murphy O. Carm*, 45–76, JSOTSup 58, Sheffield: JSOT.

Cantwell Smith, Wilfred. (1993), *What is Scripture? A Comparative Approach*, London: SCM.

Carr, David M. (2011), *The Formation of the Hebrew Bible: A New Reconstruction*, Oxford: Oxford University Press.

Childs, Brevard S. (1979), *Introduction to the Old Testament as Scripture*, London: SCM.

Clines, David J. A. (1998), *On the Way to the Postmodern: Old Testament Essays, 1967–1998, Volume II*, Sheffield: Sheffield Academic Press.
Crüsemann, Frank. (1984), "The Unchangeable World: The 'Crisis of Wisdom' in Qoheleth," in W. Schotroff and W. Stegemann (eds.), *God of the Lowly: Socio-historical Interpretations of the Bible*, 57–77, trans. M. O'Connell, Maryknoll: Orbis.
Delitzsch, Franz. (1873), *Das Salomonische Spruchbuch*, Leipzig: Dörffling und Franke.
Dell, Katherine and Will Kynes, eds. (2013), *Reading Job Intertextually*, London: Bloomsbury T&T Clark.
Dell, Katherine and Will Kynes, eds. (2014), *Reading Ecclesiastes Intertextually*, London: Bloomsbury T&T Clark.
Dell, Katherine and Will Kynes, eds. (2020), *Reading Proverbs Intertextually*, London: Bloomsbury T&T Clark.
Erasmus, Desiderius. (2001), *The Adages of Erasmus*, 2nd ed., selected by William Barker, Toronto: University of Toronto Press.
Fingarette, Herbert. (2004), *Mapping Responsibility: Explorations in Mind, Law, Myth and Culture*, Chicago and La Salle, IL: Open Court.
Fox, Michael. (1993), "Wisdom in Qoheleth," in L. G. Purdue, B. B. Scott and W. J. Wiseman (eds.), *In Search of Wisdom: Essays in Memory of John G. Gammie*, 115–31, Louisville: Westminster John Knox.
Frye, Northrop. (1982), *The Great Code: The Bible and Literature*, Toronto: Penguin.
Gese, H. (1983), "The Crisis of Wisdom in Koheleth," in J. L. Crenshaw (ed.), *Theodicy in the Old Testament*, 141–53, Philadelphia: Fortress.
Gressmann, Hugo. (1924), "Die neugefundene Lehre des Amen-em-ope und die vorexilische Spruchdichtung Israels," *ZAW* 42: 272–96.
Gressmann, Hugo. (1925), *Israels Spruchweisheit im Zusammenhang der Weltliteratur*, Berlin: Karl Curtius.
Habel, N. C. (1972), "The Symbolism of Wisdom in Proverbs 19," *Interpretation* 26: 131–57.
Hallo, William W., ed. (1997), *The Context of Scripture, Vol. 1: Canonical Compositions from the Biblical World*, Leiden: Brill.
Heim, Knut M. (2013), *Poetic Imagination in Proverbs: Variant Repetitions and the Nature of Hebrew Poetry*, BBRS 4, Winona Lake, IN: Eisenbrauns.
Keefer, Arthur J. (2020), *Proverbs 1–9 as an Introduction to the Book of Proverbs*, Library of Biblical Studies, London: T&T Clark.
Kynes, Will. (2019), *An Obituary for "Wisdom Literature": The Birth, Death, and Intertextual Reintegration of a Biblical Corpus*, Oxford: Oxford University Press.
Levy, Shimon. (2000), *The Bible as Theatre*, Brighton: Sussex Academic Press.
Lohfink, Norbert. (1990), "Qoheleth 5:17–19: Revelation by Joy," *CBQ* 52 (4): 625–35.
Lim, Timothy H. (2013), *The Formation of the Jewish Canon*, New Haven: Yale University Press.
McCann, J. Clinton. (1993), *A Theological Introduction to the Psalms: The Psalms as Torah*, Nashville, TN: Abingdon.
Melton, Brittany N. (2018), *Where is God in the Megilloth? A Dialogue on the Ambiguity of Divine Presence and Absence*, Oudtestamentische Studiën 73, Leiden: Brill.
Metzger, Bruce M. (1987), *The Canon of the New Testament: Its Origin, Development, and Significance*, Oxford: Clarendon.
Mieder, Wolfgang. (1993), *Proverbs Are Never Out of Season: Popular Wisdom in the Modern Age*, New York: Oxford University Press.
Miller, Patrick D. (1986), *Interpreting the Psalms*, Philadelphia: Fortress.

Morgan, Donn F., ed. (2019), *The Oxford Handbook of the Writings of the Hebrew Bible*, Oxford: Oxford University Press.
Murphy, Roland E. (1978), "Wisdom: Theses and Hypotheses," in J. G. Gammie et al. (eds.), *Israelite Wisdom: Theological and Literary Essays in Honor of Samuel Terrien*, 35–42, Missoula: Scholars Press.
Murphy, Roland E. (1992), *Ecclesiastes*, WBC, Texas: Word.
Mynatt, Daniel S. (2000), "The Poetry and Literature of the Psalms," in H. W. Ballard and W. D. Tucker (eds.), *An Introduction to Wisdom Literature and the Psalms: Festschrift Marvin E. Tat*, 55–66, Macon, GA: Mercer University Press.
Pepper, Stephen C. (1970), *World Hypotheses: A Study in Evidence*, Berkeley, CA: University of California Press.
Pope, Marvin. (1965), *Job*, AB, New York: Doubleday.
Rad, Gerhard von. (1972), *Wisdom in Israel*, translated by J. D. Martin, London: SCM.
Reichenbach, Gregor. (2011), *Gültige Verbindungen: Eine Untersuchung zur kononische Bedeutung der innerbiblische Traditionsbezüge in Sprüche 1 bis 9*, ABG 37, Leipzig: Evangelische Verlagsanstalt.
Roth, John K. (1981), "A Theodicy of Protest," in S. T. Davis (ed.), *Encountering Evil: Live Options in Theodicy*, 7–37, Louisville, KY: John Knox Press.
Sailhamer, John H. (1995), *Introduction to Old Testament Theology: A Canonical Approach*, Grand Rapids: Zondervan.
Schwöbel, Christoph. (1992), *God: Action and Revelation*, Kampen: Kok Pharos.
Scoralick, Ruth. (1995), *Einzelspruch und Sammlung: Komposition im Buch der Sprichwörter Kapitel 10–15*, BZAW 232, Berlin: Walter de Gruyter.
Seow, C. L. (2013), *Job 1–21: Interpretation and Commentary*, Illuminations, Grand Rapids: Eerdmans.
Smith, W. Cantwell. (1993), *What is Scripture? A Comparative Approach*, London: SCM.
Van Leeuwen, Raymond C. (1988), *Context and Meaning in Proverbs 25–27*, SBL Dissertation Series 96, Atlanta, Georgia: Scholars Press.
Van Leeuwen, Raymond C. (1990), "Liminality and Worldview in Proverbs 1–9," *Semeia* 50: 111–44.
Van Leeuwen, Raymond C. (1992), "Wealth and Poverty: System and Contradiction in Proverbs," *Hebrew Studies* 33: 25–36.
Van Leeuwen, Raymond C. (1993), "Proverbs," in L. Ryken and T. Longmann III (eds.), *A Complete Literary Guide to the Bible*, 256–67, Grand Rapids: Zondervan.
Van Leeuwen, Raymond C. (1995), "In Praise of Proverbs," in L. Zuidevaart and H. Luttikhuizen (eds.), *Pledges of Jubilee: Essays on the Arts and Culture in Honor of Calvin G. Seerveld*, 308–27, Grand Rapids: Eerdmans.
Webster, John. (2001), *Word and Church: Essays in Dogmatic Theology*, Edinburgh: T&T Clark.
Westermann, Claus. (1980), *The Psalms: Structure, Content, and Message*, translated by Ralph D. Gerkhe, Minneapolis: Augsburg.
Whybray, Norman. (1995), *The Book of Proverbs: A Survey of Modern Study*, Leiden: Brill.
Winkler, Mathias. (2017), *Das Salomonische des Sprichwörterbuchs: Intertextuelle Verbindungen zwischen 1 Kön 1–11 und dem Sprichwörterbuch*, Herders biblische Studien 87, Freiburg: Herder.
Witherington, Ben. (1994), *Jesus the Sage: The Pilgrimage of Wisdom*, Minneapolis: Fortress.
Wolters, Al. (2001), *The Song of the Valiant Woman: Studies in the Interpretation of Proverbs 31:10–31*, Carlisle: Paternoster.

Wolterstorff, Nicholas. (1995), *Divine Discourse: Philosophical Reflections on the Claim that God Speaks*, Cambridge: Cambridge University Press.

Zabán, Bálint Károly. (2012), *The Pillar Function of the Speeches of Wisdom: Proverbs 1:20–33, 8:1–36 and 9:1–6 in the Structural Framework of Proverbs 1–9*, BZAW 429, Berlin: de Gruyter.

8

The Macro-Structure of the *Megilloth*

Timothy J. Stone

The subject to be examined in this chapter is the macro-structure of the *Megilloth* and the relationship the books within it have to the surrounding books in the collection of the Writings. My method could be labeled a canonical approach, which I prefer,[1] but John Barton has recently labeled it a reader response approach. If one chooses the canonical label, then the compilation of books into collections and the arrangements of these collections is part of the texts' history that bears investigation. Have the books in question been compiled, maybe even written or possibly redacted, with a view to their interrelationship and, if so, to what degree? If one chooses the reader-response label, then it means, according to Barton,[2] that readers find connections and meaning from, in the case of the Writings, an anthology of random books that do "not constitute a unity of any kind." Again, according to Barton, this approach "is like asking about the meaning of the complete plays of Shakespeare. One could order the plays in many ways—chronologically, generically, or thematically—and then find different implications in the various juxtapositions that resulted."[3] I leave it to the reader to decide which label best fits my investigation of the interrelationship of the books of the Writings.

Before this investigation can begin, however, it is important to note that there are many complex historical questions surrounding the formation of the Writings and the various orders for the collection. These issues are omitted here because they are covered elsewhere in some detail (Stone 2013) and because it is helpful to focus on the kinds of connections one sees in the collection. Although this will not be referenced throughout the essay, the various kinds of connections among the books of the *Megilloth* follow patterns seen in the compilation of the collections of the Torah, Former Prophets, Twelve Minor Prophets and Psalms (Stone 2013: 17–33, 88–93). The following investigation takes the arrangement of the Leningrad Codex as its starting point since,

---

[1] While I prefer this label, it must be said that it still needs to be considerably nuanced since it differs from Childs in a few significant ways and because Childs has been badly misunderstood and caricatured by James Barr and John Barton. On this see Driver 2010.
[2] Barton's comments are responding to a collection of essays, in which there are various views. Some more focused on the unity of the collection than others, but my own contribution clearly does not focus on their unity, at least in the way Barton addresses the issue in his response.
[3] Barton 2015: 316.

as I have argued, it is likely the oldest order for the Writings (Stone 2013: 80–212). The order of the *Megilloth* in this codex is Ruth, Song of Songs, Ecclesiastes, Lamentations and Esther.

I will first examine the macro-structure of the *Megilloth* and then its relationship to the surrounding context of the Writings. The following is not an exhaustive, but rather a representative sketch of the big picture.

First, following the sequence of the books in order to see their compilational intent yields few results. Christopher Seitz, for instance, in his exploration of the "instinct towards association" in the *Megilloth*, observes that the "Song of Songs describes the bliss of love and can apply to Boaz and Ruth by juxtaposition" (Seitz 2009: 112). This judgment is made without appeal to any textual connections between the two books. The supposition is based solely on their juxtaposition. The physical appearance of Ruth is never mentioned while the lovers in the Song of Songs seem to never tire of describing the beauty of their beloved's physical form. The prospect of offspring never surfaces in the Song of Songs while the plot of Ruth reaches its climax with the birth of a son.

Julius Steinberg, to take another example, says that the Song of Songs is an illustration of the call to enjoy life with one's wife as mentioned in Eccl. 9:9 (Steinberg 2006: 447). This theme is too general to forge any kind of meaningful connection between the two books and it does not add anything of importance to either book.

No one to my knowledge has tried to make anything of the contiguous relationship of Ecclesiastes and Lamentations.[4] These books are very different from each other in form and meaning.[5] So far Barton seems to be right that these books do not exhibit signs of being connected in any way. Canonical approaches that investigate the possibility that the collections' arrangements could be of significance should also register the presence of dissonance between books. Barton thinks the debate is over the unity of the collection and that canonical approaches find unifying factors because they must. Such a superficial dismissal of one's opponents does not begin to engage with the actual arguments being put forth. The *Megilloth* and the Writings as a whole are extremely diverse in form and content. That is not what is in question. A mosaic makes sense to its viewers precisely because of the differences among the tiles that are, nevertheless, carefully arranged in relationship to one another. Given the fact of the collection's diversity, is there a meaningful way to discuss their arrangement?

First, I propose that the *Megilloth* is more like a spider web than a chain. And this spider web, rather than highlighting the unity of the collection, instead illuminates its textual diversity. The spider web takes the structural shape of a chiasm[6] in which Ecclesiastes forms the center, surrounded by two contrasting pairs. The first pair is the Song of Songs and Lamentation and the second is Ruth and Esther. Both Ruth and the Song of Songs could be described as the positive book to which Lamentations and Esther are the negative counterpart.

---

[4] This situation could now be re-evaluated based on other contributions in this volume.
[5] The prominent role of a female character in all of the books except Ecclesiastes may be an exception and prove to be one factor that unites the collection. For more on this see Stone 2013: 205.
[6] Discovering chiastic structures in the text can be overdone, e.g., Dorsey 2004.

Ruth and Esther share many things in common, but this relationship highlights their differences rather than their similarities. The relationship between these two books has been noticed by a number of scholars.[7]

> Ruth is a Moabitess who marries an Israelite; Esther is a Jew who marries the king of Persia. Each of their national identities play a key role in the way their respective stories unfold. Ruth serves as an emissary between Naomi and Boaz, as does Esther between the king of Persia and Mordecai. Ruth comes from a foreign land to remain in Israel; Esther lives in a foreign land and indicates no intention of returning to Israel. Ruth saves David's line from failure, making his birth possible; Esther saves the Jewish people from genocide ensuring that God's promises to Israel remain unbroken. Both stories share the basic movement of reversal from a tragic and hope- less situation to one of rejoicing and joy. Ruth stands in the line of David, Israel's great king, and Esther becomes queen of Persia. However, in my judgment, their characters could not be more opposite. Ruth is a woman of excellence, who, like Abraham, has left her home, country and parents to seek refuge under the wing of the LORD and is unwavering in her unfailing ḥesed to Naomi.
>
> Stone 2013: 172

By contrast, Esther's character, while often interpreted in positive terms (e.g., Fox, 2001: 196–205), is in my view a pseudo-hero who has assimilated to the Persian culture and forgotten the God of Israel (Stone 2013: 169–73). It is not necessary to agree with this negative appraisal of the character of Esther to allow that she is a foil to Ruth. Within a chiastic structure to the *Megilloth*, the similarities between Ruth and Esther bring into focus the sharp contrast between the two books.

Likewise, the Song of Songs and Lamentations share many features, but remain polar opposites. The books are relatively the same size; they are bigger than Ruth,[8] but smaller than Esther and Ecclesiastes. The Song of Songs contains 1,658 words, 229 columns in the BHS, and 117 verses. Lamentations is similar in size with 2,010 words, 267 columns, and 154 verses. Both books use poetic or stylized language and neither contains a narrative plot. Both feature a dominant female voice in combination with a male voice or voices. More specifically, the phrase "daughter(s) of Jerusalem" occurs seven times in the Song (1:5; 2:7; 3:5, 10; 5:8; 16; 8:4) and twice in Lamentations (2:13, 15), and "daughters of Zion" appears once in the Song (3:11) and eight times in Lamentations (1:6; 2:1, 4, 8, 10, 13, 18; 4:22).[9] Both the Song of Songs and Lamentations employ these phrases synonymously (e.g., Lam. 2:13). These similar features set in relief the way in which the books function as mirror opposites of one another. "The Song celebrates and revels in the love between a woman and a man; in Lamentations

---

[7] Eskenazi and Frymer-Kensky 2011: xxv, compares Ruth and Esther and concludes that they are both heroines but that they are "quite different" and "represent contrast." For more on the relationship between Ruth and Esther, see, Larkin 1996: 10–12; Berg 1979: 146–47, and the works cited there.

[8] Ruth has 85 verses while the Song contains 117 verses and Lamentations 154 verses.

[9] Daughter(s) of Jerusalem occurs fourteen times in the OT and "Daughter(s) of Zion" occurs thirty times. Both phrases appear most frequently in the Latter Prophets.

Lady Zion bemoans her tragic unfaithfulness to the LORD and the abandonment of her supposed lovers. In the Song, the woman is as lovely as Jerusalem (6.4); in Lamentations, the now-wretched Lady Jerusalem is reminded by her enemies that she was once the perfection of beauty (2.15)" (Stone 2013: 207). The arrangement of the *Megilloth* highlights the collection's diversity.

As the center of the chiasm, Ecclesiastes is not paired with any of the other books in the collection. The significant presence of a female voice, which can be found in the rest of the books of the *Megilloth*, does not appear in Ecclesiastes. Ecclesiastes is the odd book out in the collection; it makes no significant connections to other books in the collection nor does it have an opposite.

If one grants that the *Megilloth* is chiastically structured in the Leningrad Codex then it should be noted that this arrangement, while pairing books together, highlights their differences. Unity is the wrong conceptual yard-stick for evaluating the significance of the collection's arrangement.

The associations the books have among the collection of the *Megilloth*, however, are not as strong as the associations they have with those books surrounding them in the Writings. Ruth's strongest connection is to Proverbs, not Esther. The Song of Songs and Ecclesiastes are connected to Proverbs by each book's Solomonic associations and, in the case of Ecclesiastes, by a possible redaction in the book's epilogue, which connect it to Proverbs' prologue. Lamentations' strongest ties are to Esther and possibly to a mini-collection made up of Lamentations, Esther, Daniel, and Ezra/Nehemiah. Esther's strong connection to Daniel 1–6, again to a book outside the *Megilloth*, is well documented. There is not space to look at these in detail, but a few significant examples will suffice.

First, Ruth is linked to Proverbs 31. The acrostic to the woman of excellence or power has several ties to Ruth. Outside of the book of Proverbs, Ruth is the only character in the Hebrew Bible to be called a woman of excellence (*ēšet ḥaîl*). In particular, she is called this by Boaz in Ruth 3:11 where he notes that the people of the gate have given her this label. The last line of the acrostic in Proverbs 31 says that this woman is praised in the gate. In Ruth 3:11, Boaz's words refer to the first and last line of the acrostic in Prov. 31:10–31. In addition, Prov. 31:23 says, "Her husband is known in the gates, when he sits among the elders of the land." This same language describes Boaz as he sits with the elders in the gate to discuss becoming Ruth's husband. The excellent woman language outside of Proverbs is unique to Ruth and the combination of sitting in the gate with the elders is highly unusual in the Hebrew Bible.[10] The acrostic of Proverbs 31 sums up and typifies the ideals of the book of Proverbs as a whole; the excellent woman realizes the ideals of wisdom in the rest of the book and is thus a fitting conclusion to Proverbs. The textual links between Proverbs 31 and Ruth extend this wisdom ideal to the character of Ruth. Here we may have an idea that unifies, at least in part, these two books, but the similarities put into conflict Proverbs' view that the son ought to shun the foreign woman, among others, and embrace Lady Wisdom. The foreign woman is set in parallel to the strange woman (Prov. 2:16; 5:20; 7:5), the

---

[10] This language appears in combination in five other places in the Hebrew Bible besides Proverbs 31 and Ruth: Deut. 21:19; 22:15; 25:7; Josh. 20:4; Lam. 5:15.

evil woman (6:24), and the "prostitute" (23:27), yet Ruth is clearly a foreign woman who also embodies Proverbs' wisdom ideals. The arrangement of these books and their textual associations create a dialogue between the two books, based on common ground, but full of dissonance.

Second, the Song of Songs and Ecclesiastes are often associated with Proverbs regardless of their canonical placement due to the Solomonic associations of each book, though, of course, Ecclesiastes does not mention Solomon by name. In almost every possible arrangement, Ecclesiastes and the Song are near Proverbs and most often follow after it. This ground is well trodden and I will pass over it here (for a summary, see Krüger 2004: 27; cf. Stone 2013: 186–93). Less examined are the textual associations between Proverbs 1–9 and the Song of Songs. Both texts portray a woman as a fountain (Prov. 5:18; Song 4:12, 15) and use deer images for breasts (Prov. 5:19; Song 4:5; 7:4 [Eng 7:3]). There are a number of textual resonances between Proverbs 7 and the adulterous or loose woman and the Song of Songs, in which the same rare Hebrew words are employed in both texts in a similar fashion. To give one example, in both texts there are kisses (compare Prov. 7:13; Song 1:2; 8:1), and a bed perfumed with myrrh, aloes, and cinnamon (compare Prov. 7:17; Song 4:14; 5:5; for more connections between the two texts, see Stone 2013: 188). The many textual associations outlined by Katharine Dell and David Bernat form links between the young wife of Proverbs 5, the loose woman of Proverbs 7, and Lady Wisdom throughout Proverbs 1–9 (Dell 2005: 8–26; Bernat 2004: 327–49). The variety of connections between the two texts does not appear to indicate an intentional link but rather a shared genre of love poetry common in the Ancient Near East (Stone 2013: 192).[11]

Third, it is possible that redaction in the epilogue of Ecclesiastes configures the book in relation to Proverbs' prologue (see the seminal essay of Wilson 1984: 175–92; cf. Fox, 1999: 375–77; Krüger 2004: 209–17). The reasons for this are complex and debated; here I will only summarize the basics of the argument. It appears that Eccl. 12:11–12 places the words of Qoheleth both among *the words of the wise*, which may refer to a collection of wisdom texts, and yet warns against making books beyond these. In other words, the epilogue implies a wisdom collection in which Ecclesiastes is the last and final book. To use the language of Proverbs' prologue and Ecclesiastes' epilogue, the words of the wise *begin* with the fear of the LORD and *end*, when all has been heard, with the fear of God. In this manner, the very beginning of Proverbs and very end of Ecclesiastes form an inclusio around the sayings of the wise. While the differences between these two books can be exaggerated, linking them to each other foregrounds significant differences that both Jewish and Christian readers have almost always recognized (See Seow 1997: 47–60; Fox 1999: 14–26; for more on this see Stone 2013: 193–201).

Fourth, Lamentations' strongest ties are to Esther and conceptually it appears to begin a mini-collection made up of Lamentations, Esther, Daniel, and Ezra/Nehemiah. As the first book in this collection Lamentations introduces themes and, more importantly, questions that are explored in the rest of the collection. Several themes and

---

[11] While this is my current position, the issue needs to be examined more fully since there are other connections, like the language of seeking and finding that do not appear to be the result of sharing a genre.

motifs in Lamentations resonate with Esther, but the most important occur in the last chapter. Many texts are concerned with care of widows and orphans, but Lam. 5:3 is the only place where Israel's exilic state is likened to becoming orphans. Of course, the only book in the Hebrew Bible that contains a major character who is an orphan is Esther, who is also living in exile. Lamentations 5:15 states: "The joy of our hearts has ceased; our dancing has been turned to mourning" (all quotations are taken from the NRSV unless otherwise indicated). This scene of sorrow is reversed in Esth. 9:22, which sums up the book's theme of reversal in the following manner, "as the month that had been turned for them from sorrow into gladness and from mourning into a holiday; that they should make them days of feasting and gladness." In addition to the concept of reversal, both texts use the niphal third person masculine singular of the verb *to turn* (*nēhipak*) and the same word for mourning (*ēbel*). The very last verse of Lamentations, with its implication that the LORD may have utterly rejected Israel, is a haunting and strange way to end a book, but the open-ended nature of this last verse may receive an answer in Esther since the certain survival of the Jews is a prominent theme in Esther. Esther may be a canonical answer to the questions raised at Lamentations' close. If one grants some kind of relationship between these two books, it is not based on their unity, but on the reversal of the themes of sorrow to the time of joy. If there was space, one could examine the way in which the narrative of the mini-corpus moves from the beginning of exile with the destruction of both Jerusalem and the temple in Lamentations, to life in exile in Esther and Daniel 1–6, to the return from exile and the reconstruction of both Jerusalem and the temple in Daniel 7–12 and Ezra/Nehemiah.

Fifth, Esther's links to Lamentations are not as strong as its ties to Daniel 1–6. This has been well documented so I will reserve the discussion to one example (Berlin 2001: xl; Collins 1993: 40; Fox 2001: 146–47). In Daniel 1, the type-scene of a Jew in exile being summoned to the king's court, undergoing intensive preparation and then being presented to the king where the Jew is then exalted to a place of prominence in the court, strongly resembles the story in Esther 2. In both stories, the main characters are described and succeed, at least in part, due to their beautiful appearance (Esth. 2:3, 7; Dan. 1:4, cf. 1:15). Daniel and his friends are the only male characters in the Hebrew Bible to be described thus. Daniel is put under the master of the eunuchs (Dan. 1:8) and Esther is put under the chief of the women (Esth. 2:8). Both find favor (*ḥesed*) before (*l* + *pānēh*) the one overseeing them during their time of preparation. Daniel 1 forms an oblique commentary on Esther 2. This link does not reveal their similarities, but rather their differences. Daniel refuses the food of the court and finds favor because the LORD is with him, while no reason is given for Esther finding favor nor does she refuse the food of the court. Along with Daniel 1, the striking connections between Esther and Daniel 1–6 reveal "that the narrative analogies in Daniel 1–6 provide a *consistent* and *coherent* commentary on Esther where Daniel and his friends serve as a foil to Esther and Mordecai. The issues are never religious in Esther; in Daniel they always are" (Stone 2013: 157).[12] These connections set in relief the differences between Esther and Daniel.

---

[12] If a shared genre were solely responsible for these connections, then it would seem that the relationship would be more like the Song's to Proverbs 1–9, in which the connections reveal no overarching or coherent pattern of relationship.

There are three things to note in conclusion. First, finding unity is the wrong way to understand the goals of a canonical approach to the *Megilloth* or the Writings. These books are diverse and their arrangement highlights this diversity. Second, while the *Megilloth* may be chiastically structured, by far the strongest connections the books have are with other books outside of the sub-collection, which means, in my view, that one should not examine the books of the *Megilloth* in isolation from the Writings as a whole, and that this sub-group of texts, which we now call the *Megilloth*, were compiled in the same process and over the same period of time as the rest of the books of the collection. I do not envision that this was a short or simple process. Third, this paper is only a brief sketch and so I implore the curious and doubtful reader to follow the footnotes.

Bibliography

Barton, John. (2015), "Response," in Julius Steinberg, Tim Stone and Rachel Stone (eds.), *The Shape of the Writings*, 311–16, Winona Lake, IN: Eisenbrauns.

Berg, Sandra. (1979), *The Book of Esther: Motifs, Themes, and Structure*, SBLDS, 44, Missoula, MT: Scholars Press.

Berlin, Adele. (2001), *Esther: The Traditional Hebrew Text With the New JPS Translation*, JPS Bible Commentary, Philadelphia: Jewish Publication Society.

Bernat, David. (2004), "Biblical *Wasfs* Beyond Song of Songs," *Journal for the Study of the Old Testament* 28: 327–49.

Collins, John. (1993), *Daniel: A Commentary on the Book of Daniel*, Hermeneia: A Critical and Historical Commentary on the Bible, Minneapolis: Fortress Press.

Dell, Katharine. (2005), "What is King Solomon Doing in the Song of Songs?" in Anselm Hagedorn (ed.), *Perspectives on the Song of Songs: Perspektiven der Hoheliedauslegung*, 8–26, BZAW, 346, Berlin: W. de Gruyter.

Dorsey, David. (2004), *The Literary Structure of the Old Testament*, Grand Rapids: Baker Academic.

Driver, Daniel. (2010), *Brevard Childs, Biblical Theologian*, FAT, II/46, Tübingen: Mohr Siebeck.

Eskenazi, Tamara Cohn, and Tikva Frymer-Kensky. (2011), *Ruth: The Traditional Hebrew Text With the New JPS Translation*, JPS Bible Commentary, Philadelphia: Jewish Publication Society.

Fox, Michael. (1999), *A Time to Tear Down and a Time to Build Up: A Rereading of Ecclesiastes*, Grand Rapids: Eerdmans.

Fox, Michael. (2001), *Character and Ideology in the Book of Esther*, Grand Rapids: Eerdmans, 2nd edn.

Krüger, Thomas. (2004), *Qohelet: A Commentary*, Hermeneia: A Critical and Historical Commentary on the Bible, trans. O.C. Dean, Minneapolis: Augsburg Fortress.

Larkin, Katrina. (1996), *Ruth and Esther*, Old Testament Guides, Sheffield: Sheffield Academic Press.

Seitz, Christopher. (2009), *The Goodly Fellowship of the Prophets: The Achievement of Association in Canon Formation*, Acadia Studies in Bible and Theology, Grand Rapids: Baker Academic.

Seow, Choon-Leong. (1997), *Ecclesiastes*, The Anchor Yale Bible Commentary, New York: Doubleday.

Steinberg, Julius. (2006), *Die Ketuvim: ihr Aufbau und ihre Botschaft*, BBB, 152, Hamburg: Philo.

Stone, Timothy. (2013), *The Compilational History of the Megilloth: Canon, Contoured Intertextuality and Meaning in the Writings*, FAT, 2, Tübingen: Mohr Siebeck.

Wilson, Gerald. (1984), "'The Words of the Wise': The Intent and Significance of Qoheleth 12:9–14," *Journal of Biblical Literature* 103: 175–92.

9

The Canonical Function of the *Nebi'im*

Christopher R. Seitz

This chapter will undertake a survey of those books which comprise the middle section of the canon of Israel's scriptures. We know this section by the way in which the New Testament refers to it, when it speaks of the "Law and Prophets" or "Moses and the Prophets," that is, the books which follow the Pentateuch or Torah as given to Moses. A third section of books, "the Writings," completes the traditional Hebrew collection, called with reference to these three sub-sections, the Tanak (*Torah*, *Nebi'im*, *Ketuvim*).

In what follows we will discuss the contents of this division and also the logic of its arrangement. The now-familiar ordering of English printed Bibles, which ends with Malachi, is not represented in any list prior to the Reformation. This order, furthermore, has not preserved the tripartite arrangement but has re-cast it, so our discussion will seek to understand what the Hebrew order seeks to communicate in that form.

If one observes the wide variety of orders in translated form in the Christian reception of the Old Testament, the fact of a stable tripartite form stands out by contrast. Vestiges of the form are still very widespread, with the Torah of Moses always standing first and in the five-book form we know well (the Pentateuch) and with books from the Writings bringing up the rear (Daniel, Esther, or Chronicles, for example). But the Writings migrate in a variety of ways. The Minor Prophets may move, but they do so as a collection, not as individual books, and their internal order is fairly consistent. We do know of a different order in Greek dress, though it does not come through in that form in any significant ways in the commentaries and wider reception history in the early Eastern Church.

It has been commented that some differences in the Greek ordering of the Hebrew canon may reflect a desire to place "like with like"—this could explain an order of Hosea, Amos, Micah, followed by Joel, Obadiah, Jonah. The first three books all share a superscription which locates them in the reigns of Kings of Israel and Judah, with the remaining books lacking these. They are also in order of descending length, though that may be an accident. Though now separate in the Hebrew sequence, they are also in this same order.

Of the church fathers in the West, we have Jerome's explanation for a book's date if lacking a chronological notice: date them in relation to their neighbors. No such commentary can be found corresponding to the Greek order being referred to here, and as just noted, it is not obvious that a Greek commentary tradition worked with this order as such, or saw any significance in it as an order. One possibility is that the very fact of an arrangement as having significance, such as is held for the order familiar to us, was not considered to be the case by these early translators/arrangers. Rather, they saw the books as individual works and that was all. Hence the decision simply to re-order them according to "like with like."

The Prophets as a canonical section in the Scriptures of Israel: overview

The Prophetic section of the Hebrew canon comprises what may appear to be an odd combination of substantive narrative chronicle and poetic/oracular material, the latter more instinctively thought of as prophecy: Isaiah, Jeremiah, Ezekiel, and the smaller Twelve prophetic books beginning with Hosea and ending with Malachi. The tradition would in time refer to these two corpuses as "Former Prophets" (the books of Joshua, Judges, Samuel, and Kings) and "Latter Prophets," not highlighting a difference between them—narratives here, poetic oracles there—but collectively referring to them as *Nebi'im* (Prophets).[1]

In time the "former" section would find a fresh affiliation with kindred chronicle/narrative material, whose books exist otherwise in the Writings: Ezra-Nehemiah, Chronicles, Esther. This created something like a "historical" category of books. In my view this occurred due to an instinct to associate "like with like" in early translational versions of an earlier tradition, in an emerging Greek language version of the Hebrew Bible (this argument is defended in Seitz 2009a). The result was to split "former" from "latter prophets," creating? a fresh category of historical writings and allowing the "prophets" to more clearly refer to the Three Major Prophets, the Twelve, and also a relocated Book of Daniel, not now a wisdom writing (Dan. 1:4) but one of the Prophets. The consequence of this, further, was the collecting of the remaining titles under a rubric of "lyrical books" and with it a dismantling of the tripartite arrangement Torah, Prophets, Writings. That said, the lists we have in Christian circles do not have a single four-fold alternative form and frequently give evidence of the Law, Prophets, and Writings conception (that is, with prophetical writings remaining in the center of the list). As noted above, the books that most frequently conclude the Old Testament in Christian circles are Daniel and Esther. We will discuss the variations that appear in Jewish lists here. They are more minor in character.

Former and Latter Prophets: Prophets in history

The Scriptures of Israel in Hebrew dress move from the final book of the Pentateuch (Deuteronomy) into a new, second section, called simply Prophets (*Nebi'im*). English

---

[1] There are some fascinating portions of overlap, as with Isaiah 36–39 and 2 Kings 18–20. See Seitz 1991 and 2007.

printed Bibles replicate this movement partially but include Ruth between Judges and Samuel and then continue on a more historical timeline with Chronicles, Ezra-Nehemiah, and Esther. Prophets is organized otherwise into a Joshua–Kings portion (called in historical-critical parlance "the Deuteronomistic History") and an Isaiah–Malachi portion. In time the first bloc could be called "Former" and the second "Latter" divisions of Prophets. The present MT presents the familiar Isaiah, Jeremiah, Ezekiel order followed by a twelve-book collection. As noted above, the Twelve and Isaiah are most often paired in subsequent lists in Christian circles, usually in that order. They are approximately the same length (on the appearance in lists next to each other of Isaiah and the Twelve, see Trebolle-Barrera, 2000: 94–95, 98).

The Prophets as former and latter represent narrative and classically prophetic material, respectively. That is, the Three Major and Twelve Minor prophetic books consist of proclamation in largely poetic form, going back to the oral speech of the prophets in live time, delivered to Israel by major prophetic figures. Sometimes this is called "writing prophecy" to distinguish it from prophetic activity that was not preserved in the same form of literary presentation.[2] So, Elijah and Elisha find a prominent place in 1 and 2 Kings but their oral speech has not been put in the literary form that we see, for example, in a Hosea or Micah, or any of the other prophetic books. To call these "writing prophets" introduces a possible confusion, however, since none of them produced their own written books. That activity was taken up by others in a manner we will discuss below. The point of the nomenclature was to make a distinction between the prophetic activity recorded in the Deuteronomistic History and what we see in prophetic speech preserved in book form. The distinction is also more keenly felt when Joshua–Kings no longer is followed directly by Isaiah–Malachi, but separated and assigned to new locations such as are found in modern English Bibles, for example.

To place the narrative material of Joshua–Kings next to that of the classical prophetic literature creates some important effects. First, it picks up on the notion of a succession of prophetic activity to follow after Moses, thus insisting that the entire period represented by Joshua–Kings is governed by divine prophetic oversight, via the torah of Moses or by specific prophetic figures so called. Second, it serves the purpose of showing us the scope of the historical season during which the prophets to follow can be located. The loose analogy of Acts and the Pauline Letter collection comes to mind, though by distinction, the Major and Minor Prophets and the Deuteronomistic History provide very little overlap when it comes to locating the former at specific moments on the timeline of the latter (see discussion in Seitz 2014: 193–96, 2011: 157–67, 2009a: 102–3). Only Isaiah and Jonah make an appearance in the history. The superscriptions of the prophetic books function to make clearer from that side of the ledger just when and where the prophets were active. The undated and unlocated books within the Twelve are a special case that needs discussion below (see fuller discussion in Seitz 2007: 113–220). The final three books of the Twelve pick up the timeline after the Exile and so move out beyond the ending of 2 Kings in important ways, leaving us with a sense both of continuity and of horizons to come. The introduction to Zechariah does

---

[2] A standard classification such as we find in textbooks introducing the prophets. Blenkinsopp (1996) is a good recent example.

this quite explicitly, for example (1:1–6), in taking its bearings from the words spoken by prophets previously (see also the references to former prophets in 7:7, 12). The final book Malachi is a special case that requires additional comment, as it appears to introduce a name ("my messenger") that carries the book forward into the future beyond that of prophecy in classical form.

The two-part Prophets section of the canon, then, serves to bridge the giving of the law to Moses forward to generations to come, and assisted by specific agents like Moses for their generations, called prophets. Part one is content to focus on the first dimension while not failing to mention specific prophets as such, while part two concentrates on prophetic speech in its classical guise. It can be possible to theorize that within part two the term "torah" has a less formal meaning than is suggested in the present deuteronomic depiction. Indeed, this aspect had been taken in the source-critical heyday as Exhibit #1, establishing that the prophets really knew nothing of Law except in more ad hoc senses of "instruction" appropriate to their inspired genius and insight. In classic Wellhausian terms, the Law is later than the prophets and by no means its foundation.[3]

Yet whatever we may reconstruct in respect of the term *torah,* the simple fact of juxtaposition of these two major sections under one rubric Prophets implies that the mature torah of Genesis–Deuteronomy is consistent with law as the prophets refer to this on the occasions when they do. The Deuteronomic History (DtrH) returns the favor by simply crediting the proclamation of God's law to every generation under a rubric "by all my servants the prophets" without then stipulating which figure now appearing in part two they have in mind more specifically. The effect of the almost word-by-word appearance of Isaiah 36–39 at a critical juncture in 2 Kings 18–20, whatever else it may mean, leaves no doubt that the DtrH and the classical prophets are seen to be complementary and working in tandem. Similar moves within the second part itself (the appearance of Isaiah 2 in Micah 4) reinforce the "all the prophets" theme as one of consistency to the point of overlap. Jeremiah's reference to Micah and Hezekiah may also be mentioned here (Jer. 26:18, see Seitz 2007: 128, 197, 212 on this point). In sum, introductory courses may be useful in speculating about how something like "law" functioned in more occasional uses in the prophets and only later culminated in the monumental Pentateuchal expression of the same, but the later development deserves to be acknowledged for what it is and its effect considered and appreciated on the terms of the present canonical portrayal. This phase of development deserves the label "historical" every bit as much as reconstructed, earlier, theoretical ones.

Our concern in general is with modern approaches, the character of canonical shaping and association, and the sorts of issues that may arise in one's first critical look at the Old Testament. So it will not be my purpose here to engage in detailed, individual treatment of the three Major and twelve Minor Prophets. I have published previous commentaries and monographs on the Prophets of Israel, and the DtrH.

In one of the (nearly playful) musings of the rabbinic material, the order of the major prophets is declared to be Jeremiah, Ezekiel, and Isaiah, and an explanation for this is given (B. batra 14.b). We are watching an upward curve, from all judgment, to

---

[3] See the Preface to Wellhausen (1885) where he speaks quite personally about having a bad conscience in not seeing evidence of the Law in the Former Prophets and wondering what this might mean.

half-judgment and half-salvation, to all salvation. One might say that this is roughly accurate: Jeremiah predominates with judgment oracles at the end of the period of Judah's existence and provides a sober account of the destruction of Jerusalem and termination of the monarchy (another place of substantial overlap with the last chapters of Kings and the DtrH). Ezekiel's grim pronouncements focus on the same period, in exile, and conclude with hopeful declarations of a new heart, a new spirit, a new rejoined Israel and a new temple. Isaiah soars with the language of salvation, contrapuntally in the first chapters and in sustained notes in the latter. We can also see this order in certain Christian lists, with the Twelve preceding Isaiah.

The three: Isaiah, Jeremiah, Ezekiel

The order with which we are familiar has Isaiah in first position. His is the most historically comprehensive portrayal; if critical theory is correct, stretching over several centuries from seventh to fifth and later. In its present form, traditional exegesis also credited the book with an extraordinary range of coverage and put this down to the marvelous prophetic powers of Isaiah of Jerusalem, who saw into and through the exile and comforted the mourners in Zion (so Ben Sira). Isaiah's sixty-six-chapter shape moves from denunciations in the reign of Ahaz; a figural linking of the outstretched arm of YHWH to include both Assyria and Babylonian agents of judgment; to their eventual demise, within the larger national landscape; with a deliverance of Jerusalem which contrasts Hezekiah favorably with Ahaz previously and serves as a sign of Jerusalem's eventual recovery and pilgrimage center for all the nations previously brought under God's sovereign rule. King and servant combine in the larger movement and bring about, through suffering and death, a means of expiation for Israel that in turn awakens the hearts and wills of all peoples.[4] The signal position of Isaiah serves to guide us as we make our way forward, much in the same way the Letter to the Romans stands in first position and gives us a comprehensive portrayal of creation, justification, sanctification, election and adoption as the lens through which to view the twelve letters to follow.

Jeremiah's presentation is far more chronologically narrowed in coverage. This focus also creates a somber portrayal. Hopeful notes that sound in the opening chapters are directed to a northern kingdom and then held up as an object lesson to Judah for not having learned the lesson of her fate in the previous century. Penitential notes also arise, but these appear to be representative of a later audience who watch the disobedience and register their acknowledgments of the righteousness of God's actions with their forefathers and mothers (Seitz 2004). Jeremiah's own role in the book is crafted to track alongside that of Moses, now as lawgiver of curse and not blessing, given the refusal to heed. I have elsewhere argued that the question of historical Jeremiah's awareness of Deuteronomic traditions ought better to be considered from the angle of his depiction in the book itself, as a prophet like Moses (Seitz 1989). Instead

---

[4] I have written in detail on these matters in Seitz 1991, 1993, 2001, and several journal articles.

of broken tablets we have a burned and reconstituted scroll. Instead of Caleb and Joshua as exempt from death in the wilderness, we have Baruch and Ebed-Melech carrying forward beyond the wholesale judgment over Judah and into a new but uncertain future. Jeremiah must share the fate of Moses and is not exempted, though he sees from afar a new day in the same manner Moses is permitted to look over into the Promised Land before death. The theme of the death of one generation and the birth of a new one, which we see in Numbers, is calibrated so as to be completed within the span of seventy years (Olson 1985).

The influence of Deuteronomy on Jeremiah is obvious and penetrating. The book is a combination of oracles such as we find them in Isaiah; deuteronomic sermons of a "choose this day" and "do this or this will befall you," with the latter frequently presupposing a negative response and so preceding with judgment; and biographical episodes and personal lamentations. Much of the material is specifically dated, also in the manner of the DtrH. The book marches inexorably toward its conclusion, first with exile of king and population in 597 and then with more dramatic results in 587.

Ezekiel opens with an even sharper historical focus (Seitz 1986, especially chapter 3 "The 597 Perspective of Ezekiel Traditions" and Seitz 1985). He is a prophet who accompanied the exiles of the first deportation. He is able to address them and the concrete situation unfolding back in Jerusalem at one and the same time. He is given a terrible scroll to swallow, but unlike Jeremiah offers no lamentation after being given an antacid of divine comfort. And so, declare the terrible judgment he does. Biographical material also pervades his book, including a series of sign acts whereby in his own flesh he enacts the awful fate in store for God's people. Israel has become like Pharaoh or a foreign nation, and even worse. So, the "then you will know that I am the LORD" refrains we recall from Exodus in the confrontation between Moses and Egypt here appear in the form of knowing YHWH God in his judgments and not his deliverances. Then the judgment over city, temple, priesthood, king and false prophet is finally prosecuted, and our prophet can then begin to see a new day. Out of the corpse of a people in a valley of dry bones Ezekiel is given to see the Spirit of God breathe new life. Israel and Judah are rejoined after centuries of division. Good shepherds rule. Prophecy begins to regather strength. A new temple is to be built and the principalities and powers emptied of their awful might, having evacuated themselves in the role of agents of national judgment over God's people.

The three Major Prophets span the horizon of God's work with Israel and Judah and then see into a new future. Comprehensively, they confront all the institutions and manifestations of authority inside God's purposes with his people and expose the dry rot down to the nails and mortar. Isaiah is bold to say that this act of judgment has an expiatory effect that will cleanse the future generations. It will also be the means by which Israel, brought in contact with the nations of the world, will suffer a fate that enables these same peoples to see God at work, in judgment and in salvation, and so come to the knowledge of him via their fate. The diaspora of God's people will remain a fact into the New Testament and provide the synagogue reality into which the prophet Paul will stride centuries later, opening anew the book of Isaiah and declaring that his plan and his secret mystery are being shown forth onto a new day of God's action. The former things are giving way to new things, and did I not say it long ago, says the Lord.

The Twelve

The Twelve smaller prophetic books which follow Ezekiel existed on a single scroll of similar length to that of an individual Major Prophet. The order of the books is as we find it in English Bibles, with some minor exceptions in the history of lists. Some Greek manuscripts place superscripted books together in the first half of the XII and create an order Hosea, Amos, Micah, and then Joel, Obadiah, and Jonah. This tracks with the tendency of the Greek texts to organize like with like, unaware of the significance—if such there is for them—in the Hebrew tradition they have inherited.

Upon inspection it is clear that the movement across the Twelve, if one examines the superscriptions, is roughly chronological. That is, Hosea and Amos are the earliest books and Zechariah and Malachi the latest, with Micah in the middle. Yet half of the books give us no dating reference (Joel, Obadiah, Jonah, Nahum, Habakkuk, and Malachi). The church father Jerome conjectured that undated books were in chronological order due to association with dated neighbors, but the theory is speculative and does not find universal acceptance in the history of interpretation. More recently an alternative notion has found stronger persuasiveness, namely, that undated books are placed where they are for thematic or theological reasons, as they are now found in association with books surrounding them (see most recently the discussion in Seitz 2016). There is certainly a strong argument to be made for seeing Joel, Obadiah, Jonah, and Malachi as late witnesses and as serving this function. Nahum and Habakkuk certainly fit well within the places we now find them, as we will explain shortly.

The superscription of Hosea closely approximates that of Isaiah and may be one reason the two collections are often placed next to each other. Though standard textbooks incline to treat Amos as the first prophet historically speaking, the two prophets are clearly contemporaries and there is good evidence that their respective works were mutually influencing in editorial development (see the very insightful essay of Jeremias 1996). Hosea's superscription, moreover, gives him a more comprehensive feel, by speaking of his activity during the reigns of four Judahite kings and two Israelite rulers. Amos by contrast delivers his strong message into the specific context of the northern kingdom during the reign of Jeroboam.

But the stronger argument in favor of Hosea's signal position is the message he delivers. The passionate YHWH must judge his people but cannot give them up. The marriage of the prophet to Gomer mirrors this theological truth in personal and deeply moving terms as the book opens. And at its close it issues an appeal. Return to the LORD and he will heal and your fruitfulness will again be resplendent (14:1–8). The book ends on this note and in so doing opens onto the history that will follow. Through every prophetic word to be uttered, this divine appeal stands ready to be heeded and acted upon in Israel's favor and blessing (van Leeuwen 1993).

To reinforce this point the book that follows is effectively the words that Hosea said were to be taken so as to approach God in penitence and confession (Hos. 14:2–4), now scripted in the undated book of Joel which follows. A great locust plague serves as the occasion for lamentation and morning, and a concrete worship context for approaching the Holy Lord. The locusts are a natural disaster on the one hand, and figures of the national assaults which we will read about as YHWH's justice descends upon his people. Joel serves to script the penitential words that, if uttered in full voice, will provide for a remnant through any and all judgment to come. The bounty that will again be Israel's is held out as God's promised response. The nation/locusts will be but for a season and then will be gone. God's word of love and devotion, as we heard it ring forth from Hosea, will be the final word through the changes and chances of the history to follow. Amos repeats word for word the refrain of Joel right at the start of his work so as to alert us to the serial character of the presentation to follow (Joel 3:16 and Amos 1:2).

The opening tableau of nations (Amos 1:3–2:16) serves to establish the LORD of Israel as the God over all nations and over all creation. The sins of Edom mentioned at Joel's close (3:19) are here classified more broadly (1:11–12). But now the judgment of the nations serves as a prelude. It is Israel, "the whole family that I brought up out of Egypt" that the prophet means finally to address. The main theme of Hosea (knowledge of YHWH) is here referred to (3:1), with the intention of making sure we read Hosea's critique of cultic abuses and Amos's focus on social crimes as two sides of one coin.[5] Though both prophets address the sins of the Northern Kingdom, one can also see clear evidence that the books wish to warn Judah in no less urgent terms (we see the same movement later in Jeremiah, from the standpoint of Judah itself). Though Amos is viewed as the stern and unmoving prophet of doom that so entranced Wellhausen and early twentieth-century interpreters—the first great prophet, without antecedent, a shepherd called against his will—the center of the book also shows us a man of great compassion and concern (7:2–3, 5–6). Though he receives visions of utter devastation, he begs for mercy. Mercy is then forthcoming.

But unaware of his saving action of intercession, the authorities can only hear haranguing and interference from a professional 'hired gun' from Judah. By silencing him, they cut off the only lifeline being held out to save them.[6] The final visions of the prophet confirm that "the end has come upon my people Israel" and so it has. Amos ends, however, in a way that reinforces the message of Joel. God will purge his people as with fire. He will not destroy them utterly. Those who say "evil will not overtake us" will be doomed. Hosea and Joel and now Amos agree on this fundamental point. The wise are those who walk in the ways of the LORD (Hosea 14:9), in every generation. As Psalm 25 clarifies, the ways of the LORD consist of his character as revealed at Sinai, merciful and gracious, but by no means clearing the wicked. To walk in the ways of the LORD is to understand his character and to come to him with confession and

---

[5] "I can understand these literary connections…only if the pupils of Amos and the pupils of Hosea who handed down the message of the prophets wanted to teach the readers that they could not grasp the central ideas of these prophets by reading their books in complete isolation from one another. By contrast, the readers of the written words of the prophets were supposed to notice the similarity of Amos's and Hosea's message from God…The literary connections between these books show that they should be read in relation to each other. I want to show that the traditionists are on their way to discovering something like a common prophetic theology, not by denying that each prophet lived in singular historical circumstances, but by denying that this fact is decisive for their message" (Jeremias 1996: 171–72).

[6] Jeremias's close reading of the central panel at 7:1–8:3 is brilliant on this point (1996: 32). See my summary in Seitz 2007: 206–7. Jeremias writes, "God's patience ends where the state represented by the priest tries to decide when and where God may speak through the prophet" (32).

penitence. Those who do not know these ways ignore their sin and so also avoid coming to learn of his great mercy as well. We see this very drama play itself out with Amos, Amaziah, and Jeroboam.

Edom plays a specific role in the Twelve, as we have seen thus far. On the one hand this role is familiar from Psalm 137 and elsewhere (Lam. 4:21–22.). Edom stood aloof when Jerusalem fell and even aided Israel's enemies (Obad. 10–14). Special retribution therefore awaits her. But Obadiah makes clear that this specific crime has its focal point in one major flaw: Edom rejected her role as twin brother of Jacob and so with a specific vocation in God's plans. She wanted to be a nation (1–4). She thought to raise herself up above her station, and so God will reduce her and leave her fate in the nations' rapacious hands. As the following book of Jonah opens, we are aware of the "nations" as a major agent in executing God's judgment and of overreaching and so punished in the end. Yet this is not all that can be said about the nations. They are not simply pawns on a great chessboard of God's ways with his own people.

The Book of Jonah rejects that view and resoundingly so—to the point of satire and a humiliating portrait of his own people and the prophetic agent Jonah. Jonah wants to flee from the God who made the heavens and the earth, the seas and dry ground. He rejects his role as prophet of judgment. But he becomes a prophet in spite of himself, when by deduction the sailors know the one hiding must be the one with the True God (1:6–10). They offer sacrifices and become true worshippers in calling on the name of YHWH, as they throw the disobedient one overboard (1:15–16). Yet Jonah is rescued by a great fish and he takes up his distasteful role. He announces judgment and effects a great wave of penitence. We who have been reading the Twelve know this theme and where it will go, and apparently so does Jonah. He tells God this is why he stayed away from his job. God has ways of mercy and justice both. Having marched but a day into a city three days' journey wide he sulks under a booth he has constructed for the purpose (3:3–4). The question hovers in the air as to whether the sackcloth repentance of man and beast will hold. Is it a hungover oath sworn in haste to quit drinking for good? While waiting for his answer God turns to Jonah instead. He makes the shade cease that he had given him by a great plant. God points out that it is a bit odd to care more for a dead plant than for a dead people, and so Jonah suggests it is time then for him to die. Like the parable of the prodigal son when the older brother complains of God's grace, we are left with a question. God reserves the right to have pity and to make merry. So get used to it. Ninevites and prodigals he has come to save.[7]

The ultimate fate of Nineveh—if indeed we are right in how we take the scene outside the city—is not actually given in Jonah. But we know God's mind on the matter. The book of Micah returns us to the landscape of Judah and the history of God's people amongst the nations. He promises a day when nation will not lift up sword against nation but instead will flock to God's holy mountain, asking that they may be taught God's torah (Micah 4:1–4). In this day, God's judgment will cleanse the nations and bring their hostility to an end. As it is now, they walk in the ways of their own gods, but

---

[7] The resemblance of the older brother in Luke 15 and Jonah is unmistakable. Both stories end with a question as well about the character of God's mercy.

Israel knows the God YHWH is their God, and wills to be Lord over all as well. The book ends with the refrain we are beginning to see functioning like a red thread through the books of the Twelve (7:18–20). In doxology God is praised for the mercy that can throw the sins of a people as deep as the sea that held Jonah in its grip.

The appearance of the book of Nahum tells us that the ceaseless iniquity of Assyria won out in the end, leaving a poignant reminder in our mind of a scene of great heartfelt repentance on their part in the days of Jonah. The book opens with the refrain that closed Micah, but now God is great not in mercy but might (1:3). He will by no means clear the guilt. Where Jonah ended with a question, so does Nahum, asking "for upon whom has not come your unceasing evil?" Habakkuk picks up the question and turns in toward God. The one who raised up Assyria as agent of judgment has in turn raised up a more ruthless nation to bring that role to an end. Yet it is unclear how this can be a good plan of action. So the prophet takes his stand on the watchtower to see God's answer to his Jeremiah-like lament. The book of Habakkuk is itself to be a vision of justice that others may read to learn the answer God gives. "He who runs" is the one God has given swift feet and has raised up and strengthened (Isa 40:31).[8] This strengthening comes from reading the vision of Habakkuk, where we learn that God's justice may be slow but it will not delay long. The woes that follow in the present book show God assuredly judging the nations. The final psalm prayer pays tribute to this God of old and gives the reader the language needed to stand strong through a time of waiting (3:1–19).[9] What Joel did following Hosea, Habakkuk does following Nahum and anticipating the great and terrible day of the Lord of Zephaniah.

With the ninth book of the Twelve we reach a crescendo. The prior references to a Day of YHWH from Joel forward here, coalesce, and create a dramatic picture of the entire cosmos wracked in judgment (Zeph. 1:1–6). The prayer of Habakkuk is indeed a necessary support as the movement from Assyria to Babylon reaches a fever pitch. One may suppose that the events of 597 and 587 are being anticipated on the historical plane, but that this entails something yet more penetrating in its cleansing power on the heavenly plane. The final chapter depicts a patient and humble remnant, protected and sustained, and Zion herself rejoicing as all the prior judgments are exhausting their hold. The LORD is in her midst through it all. Her children will be brought home from the places they have been dispersed. Her fortunes will be restored before her very eyes (3:8–20). This is a waiting ("Therefore wait for me, says the LORD," 3:8) that will bear fruit, as Habakkuk has sought to assure us. Haggai then picks up the thread on the other side of judgment and exile as he begins the concrete business of starting anew.

The Book of Haggai is short and entirely in narrative form. Its dating structure is carried over into Zechariah, at least in some measure. Dates seem to be important, and they are provided with a fresh kind of precision (1:1; 2:1, 10, 18, 20). The book poses the

---

[8] See within the larger argument of Francis Watson for the signal role of Habakkuk in the Twelve these important insights on the watchtower scene (Watson 2004); my engagement can be seen in Seitz 2007: 118.

[9] The "feet like hinds feet" (3:19) show a faithful running *a la* 2:2, that is, energized by the vision which is the Book of Habakkuk (1:1 and 2:2–3). Watson's interpretation of the vision scene (2:1–4) in relation to 1:1 and 3:19 is insightful.

central question as to whether Israel's life as before is something that can be re-started, and if so, when exactly. The oracles Haggai receives say with urgency "Yes," but this cannot be a simple thing, given the din and drama of such a total judgment by YHWH. How the house of God could be made clean again, after the assaults of the nations, surely haunted the day. If the reestablishment of the house of God is what assures fertility and spiritual renewal then surely its place must be restored. But how is this to be done properly, as there is no template for its execution. Temple, priesthood, kingship, wisdom—all lie in ruins. Indeed, Haggai and the ensuing books must themselves be questioned when considered from the perspective of whether prophecy is possible, or has its vital force been spent. Who is this Haggai and how is God's word in his mouth to be trusted? These would seem to be the challenges his oracles in the form we have them are addressing. Something is about to happen. It will be a dramatic restoration on the order, even, of the preceding judgment, as Zerubbabel picks up where the destroyed monarchy lay before him in tatters.

Zechariah seconds the word of Haggai, and one may wonder whether a "seconding" is now absolutely critical if Israel is to find its way. The book is highly unusual, consisting of a series of eight (the prefect seven plus yet another) night visions. It is as though the fate of Israel is in middle air and seen not in day but in the shadow land of night. Israel's destiny is "up in the air," moving, but unstable (Halpern 1978). The visions the prophet is given amount to divine reestablishment of Israel's condition: in the face of national forces unleashed by God but now at rest, concerning her religious center, her dispersed peoples, her priesthood and civil authority, her spiritual health and removal of past toxins, and the crowning of king and priest for fresh duty. The words of the prophets preceding are now a kind of category, known to be such: they are former prophets, for now we are in a new age (1:4–6; 7:7, 12). Their words live on and direct the present life of the community. In some ways, they are also the warrant answering the last questions to be resolved: can there be prophecy, and can there be prophets again? The final chapters of the book are replete with quotation and citation from previous prophetic works. The words that Zecharaiah said outlived the ones who spoke them and have an overtaking power continue to seek resolution and final fulfillment. Even a reestablished Israel in the aftermath of national destruction and violent upheaval looks to a final day of the Lord, when a final and permanent cult, priesthood, ruler, and prophet are the lasting standard of God's ways with Israel and the world (14:1–21).

The one crucial thing to note about the strange final book is that its agent of delivery is also at the same time a protagonist active in the work itself (3:1). "My messenger" is sent by God for a great work of preparation, to ready the people with one final prophetic action, so they may stand before the coming final Day of YHWH. Whoever "the prophet Malachi" is within the timeframe and religious context assumed in the opening chapters, he is in that role a figure or type of the messenger to come. His exhortations serve the purpose of modeling what the great messenger to come will be about, yet more dramatically and finally. The final book of the Twelve is then a book in the Twelve and a standard bearer for a future and final encounter with God, unlike anything Israel has experienced and for which there must be a warning bell and a final moment to stop and be ready. Those who heed in Malachi's day are models for the conduct necessary for the future Day (3:16–18). In the time before that day, the law of Moses will serve as guide. Also referred to is a book of remembrance (3:16). A popular interpretation is that this is a book into which are registered the names of the faithful who fear the LORD in Malachi's day. This appears to be the meaning given in most translations. But it has also been argued that the book is a memorial established before the LORD which serves on behalf of those who fear him, and that what is being referred to is the prophetic collection of the Twelve as such (this is the position of Nogalski 2011: esp. 1063). Malachi self-consciously closes that collection and points to a future Malachi and a part memorial at one and the same time. Whether such a reading is to be preferred there can be little doubt that in its present form the book of the Twelve serves to guide and direct the faithful remnant of Israel until the great and terrible day spoken of from Joel to Malachi.

Prophetic inspiration

One of the hallmarks of modern biblical study is attention to an author's intention. Even at the Reformation a general concern to attend to the historical author and the location and specifics of his writing was thought to be critical, and a way to avoid a sense that seemed to float about the human author and which obscured what the Bible wanted to say more efficiently. Yet in this same period appeal to the human author was a far less complicated piece of hermeneutical guidance. Moses and Isaiah and Jeremiah and Solomon and Zechariah were authors whose books were quite directly before us in the canonical form we find them. It might be necessary to think about how Moses wrote Genesis, but this did not amount to positing four sources in the Pentateuch. The rabbis might credit Isaiah's authorship to the men of Hezekiah (B. Batra 14.b), but whatever this might mean, it never prevented the history of interpretation of thinking of him as endowed with a tremendous charism that enabled him to see into the future of exile and return. The author Isaiah's intentions were registered in the book that bore his name.

This appeal to a stable intentionality in the literal sense would soon be asked to bear an additional burden. A history that sat alongside the text and to which it was making reference would soon seem far more realistic in character than the world of Isaiah, book and author both. John Calvin had no book on his shelf called "the history of the world" with which he then correlated the Bible in some way. I choose him because to the early modern readers he more than anyone was sensitive to what we would now call "ostensive reference" and the historicality of the Old and New Testaments. But very soon it would no longer be possible to keep the referentiality of the Bible coordinated with the canonical presentation of its literary givenness. Even the term "literal" would soon come to mean "factual" or "historical."

A theory of inspiration that works very hard to determine a human author's intentions will struggle within battle lines set up by the discipline of biblical studies as this would evolve in the eighteenth century and gather force in the twentieth. Under debate was the prophet Isaiah as the author of the book with which he is associated, and if not, then how much of it and in what concrete setting are we to understand him at work, intending to communicate this or that to this or that audience. In the case of

Isaiah—though any biblical work could be chosen as an example—chapters 40–55 seemed to address a different time and context, and actually did not appear to present themselves as prediction from afar but rather contemporaneous address to an audience other than that of Isaiah of Jerusalem (Seitz 1996). It is difficult to understand what intention of communication there would be for Isaiah's audience at the time of Ahaz and Hezekiah. It seems more likely they would scratch their heads and, like Daniel being given a vision not for his day, need some special reassurance that all would be well (Dan. 8:17, 27; 10:8–12). How do we move from Zechariah 1–8 into 9–14 and not sense a shift of author and context? Or from Galatians to Colossians? Or from Genesis to Exodus? Or from sections of one book to others within the same book? Who as human author intended Isaiah 2:1–5 and Micah 4:1–4 and why are they so similar? Did Jonah borrow from Joel or the other way around?

But there is an additional problem that arises apart from the matter of historical reference and the way the biblical material gives us quite a challenge when it comes to extracting a human author and his intentions in historical context. It is also belied by some of the examples given thus far. For inspiration can also be that act of provision of speech and vision which the prophet is given to declare *whose final purpose and intention is greater than he or she understands or intends.* If this is what divine inspiration really means, then a prophet or inspired author can communicate meaningfully to an audience in time and space and say more than he or they can line up with what God intends to do and say with that selfsame speech as time marches on under his providence (see my final comments on intentionality in the Psalter, Seitz 2017). The biblical text can tell us this with clarity, as when Isaiah is told to bind up his speaking and preserve it, so it can be opened and then address a new day (8:16–20; cf. 29:11–12; 30:8). God will superintend the way a former thing will become a new thing. Inspiration entails obedience in speaking what one is given as chosen agent, not crafting an intentional word according to the canons of ordinary communication (themselves not straightforward when it comes to intention and reception!). The word of God accomplishes things (55:11). It does not stay put under a single intention—though that intention is divinely time-given—and so whoever we say "intended" Isaiah 2 and Micah 4 it is perhaps better to stand before the challenge of God's accomplishing speech as a fact to be considered as such (Seitz 2009b and 2013).

So when it comes to the Book of the Twelve, the standard procedure of determining human authors in time and space gave us a timeline running from Amos to Hosea to Micah, splicing in Isaiah and Jeremiah when able to do so, and moving forward to the latest books as conjectured according to this grid of intentionality (Joel or Jonah or Malachi). The alternative is to deal with intentionality through close reading of the canonical form and seeing if there is another way to understand the communication of God's word. This would be one in which time—accepting there are late works and early works—can double back on itself, seek associations by closer and subsequent reading, offer juxtaposed and inspired speech, as in Joel or Obadiah or Jonah, so as to draw out a meaning that God intends but which becomes available as he accomplishes things in time with a chosen people.

The only way to establish the character of divine intentionality seen through associations is by familiarizing ourselves with the variety of ways the canon invites us to appreciate its character. The Book of the Twelve may convey an intention that arises from the individual witnesses themselves on the one hand, that is, there are twelve books, and their beginnings and endings are carefully marked and the idea of an individual realistically confronting an historical audience is firmly in place. Yet one can also appreciate that alongside this there is another level of intention equally deserving to be called historical that arises when one carefully attends to associations that are now there to be seen and argued for when one takes the canonical form seriously. Yet the case of the three Major Prophets equally establishes that order and sequence may mean not very much at all, as witnessed by the ability of different orders to emerge and not register anything of significance.

Conclusion

It is important to keep this general observation in place as one moves to the third division of the Hebrew Bible. It is also preserved in Jewish and Christian lists in different arrangements, and as we have seen in some places, dissolved altogether so as to give rise to different global arrangements. The Prophets are an amalgam of Deuteronomic History (Joshua-Kings or Former Prophets) plus Three plus the Book of the Twelve. The major connection of Part One (Former) and Part Two (Latter) keeps prophecy within a field of association that is historical but also figural and affiliated in character. Shifting Part One into a single historical timeline, as we find in English printed Bibles is a move that one can easily understand—put like with like—but which ought not run interference for our thinking carefully about the canonical presentation of Prophets such as we find it in the major Hebrew attestation.

Bibliography

Blenkinsopp, Joseph. (1996), *A History of Prophecy in Israel, Revised and Enlarged*, Louisville: Westminster John Knox.
Halpern, Baruch. (1978), "The Ritual Background of Zechariah's Temple Song," CBQ 40: 167–90.
Jeremias, Jörg. (1996), "The Interrelationship between Amos and Hosea," in James W. Watts and Paul House, eds., *Forming Prophetic Literature: Essays on Isaiah and the Twelve in Honor of John D. W. Watts*, JSOTS 235, 171–86, Sheffield: Sheffield Academic Press.
Nogalski, James. (2011), *The Book of the Twelve: Micah–Malachi*, Macon, GA: Smyth & Helwys Publishing.
Olson, Dennis. (1985), *The Death of the Old and the Birth of the New: The Framework of the Books of Numbers and the Pentateuch*, BJS, Atlanta: Scholars.
Seitz, Christopher R. (1985), "The Crisis of Interpretation over the Meaning and Purpose of the Exile," *VT* 35: 78–97.
Seitz, Christopher R. (1986), *Theology in Conflict: Reactions to the Exile in the Book of Jeremiah*, BZAW 176, Berlin: de Gruyter.
Seitz, Christopher R. (1989), "The Prophet Moses and the Canonical Shape of Jeremiah," *Zeitschrift für die alttestamentliche Wissenschaft* 101: 1–15.

Seitz, Christopher R. (1991), *Zion's Final Destiny: The Development of the Book of Isaiah: A Reassessment of Isaiah 36–39*, Minneapolis: Fortress.
Seitz, Christopher R. (1993), *Isaiah 1–39*, IBC, Louisville: John Knox.
Seitz, Christopher R. (1996), "How is Isaiah Present in the Latter Half of the Book? The Logic of Isaiah 40–55 Within the Book of Isaiah," *Journal of Biblical Literature* 115: 219–40.
Seitz, Christopher R. (2001), "Isaiah 40–66," in Leander E. Keck, ed., *The New Interpreters Bible*, vol. 6, Nashville: Abingdon.
Seitz, Christopher R. (2004), "The Place of the Reader in Jeremiah," in Martin Kessler, ed., *Reading the Book of Jeremiah: A Search for Coherence*, 67–75, Winona Lake, IN: Eisenbrauns.
Seitz, Christopher R. (2007), *Prophecy and Hermeneutics: Toward a New Introduction to the Prophets*, Grand Rapids: Baker Academic.
Seitz, Christopher R. (2009a), *The Goodly Fellowship of the Prophets: The Achievement of Association in Canon Formation*, Grand Rapids: Baker Academic.
Seitz, Christopher R. (2009b), "Prophetic Associations," in J. Ahn and S. L. Cook, eds., *Thus Says the Lord: Essays on the Former and Latter Prophets in Honor of Robert R. Wilson*, Library of Hebrew Bible/Old Testament Studies 502, 156–66, London/New York: T&T Clark.
Seitz, Christopher R. (2011), *The Character of Christian Scripture: The Significance of a Two-Testament Bible*, Grand Rapids: Baker Academic.
Seitz, Christopher R. (2013), "Scriptural Author and Canonical Prophet: The Theological Implications of Literary Association in the Canon," in K. Dell and P. Joyce, eds., *Biblical Method and Interpretation: Essays in Honour of John Barton*, 176–88, Oxford: Oxford University Press.
Seitz, Christopher R. (2014), *Colossians*, Brazos Theological Commentary on the Bible, Grand Rapids: Brazos.
Seitz, Christopher R. (2016), *Joel*, ITC, London: Bloomsbury.
Seitz, Christopher R. (2017), "Psalm 2 in the Entry Hall of the Psalter: Extended Sense in the History of Interpretation," in E. Radner, ed., *Church, Society, and the Christian Common Good*, 95–106, Eugene, OR: Cascade, 2017.
Trebolle-Barrera, Julio. (2000), "Qumran Evidence for a Biblical Standard Text and for Non-Standard and Parabiblical Texts," in Timothy H. Lim, ed., *The Dead Sea Scrolls in Their Historical Context*, 89–106, Edinburgh: T&T Clark.
van Leeuwen, Raymond C. (1993), "Scribal Wisdom and Theodicy in the Book of the Twelve," in Leo Perdue, Bernard Brandon Scott, and William Johnston Wiseman, eds., *In Search of Wisdom: Essays in Memory of John G. Gammie*, 31–49, Louisville: Westminster John Knox.
Watson, Francis. (2004), *Paul and the Hermeneutics of Faith*, London: T&T Clark.
Wellhausen, Julius. (1885), *Prolegomena to the History of Israel*, Edinburgh: Adam & Charles Black.

10

Prophetic Intentionality in the Twelve

Don C. Collett

In the tradition of modern biblical interpretation, prophetic inspiration was identified with the original oracles of the prophets (Seitz 2021a: 113–27). Prophetic intentionality was typically conceived in terms of authorial intentionality, where "author" generally meant a single human agent responsible for the original oracles of a given prophet, for example, Hosea or Amos. The larger interpretive matrices and literary structures in which we now encounter these prophets, that is, as books residing within ordered collections such as the Latter Prophets or the Twelve, were typically viewed as the product of editing whose significance was secondary to the main intentions and "authentic" kerygma of the prophets. On this approach, the books of the Twelve were regarded as more or less incidental to the message of its prophets, and its sequencing of the books was typically regarded as an anthology whose order was either wholly driven by chronological concerns (Seitz 2021b: 179–98, and 2021c: 199–210), or a matter of indifference for one's understanding of prophetic intentions in the Twelve.[1]

In keeping with these assumptions, access to prophetic intentionality was made possible by reconstructing the historical biography and life setting of the prophets, insofar as the text provided a set of clues for such a project. As a hermeneutical method, this approach prioritized the importance of recovering the original historical context of the prophets, an enterprise made possible by the *a priori* genre judgment that prophetic texts were essentially historical sources rather than canonical witnesses. Alternatively, access to prophetic intentionality could also be achieved by reconstructing the conscious intentions of the prophets in the books associated with their names. Rather than historicizing the words of the prophets for the sake of linking up with prophetic intentions, this interpretive model psychologizes them (see Collett 2020: 122–31). Applied to the Twelve, this hermeneutical approach subordinates the prophetic intentionality at work in the booked shape of the Twelve to the theological goals privileged by Romantic hermeneutics, placing the literary integrity of each book

---

[1] For recent evangelical example, see the commentary series on the Twelve by McComiskey 1992, 1993, 1998. While much helpful exegesis is to be found in this series, the scope of that exegesis is restricted to the literary relations within a given book, thus suggesting (perhaps unintentionally) that the larger context generated by literary relations between the books in a collection makes no contribution to the meaning of its books *per se.*

in jeopardy. In either case, the meaning of prophetic words is isolated from their booked shape, whether in the name of recovering something called "original" historical context, or "original" authorial intention. The notion that prophetic intentionality was to be sought first of all at the level of the prophetic book received little or no traction in the modern landscape of academic biblical exegesis, whether one speaks of modern historical-critical or evangelical approaches.

Helpful accounts of the move away from these approaches, along with the rise of a canonical model generated by the movement "from prophet to book" in biblical interpretation (see Schart 2016: 244–45), are now available in a number of books and publications and need not be recounted here (Seitz 2007a; 2018: 119–75; 2021d: 291–301; 2021e: 302–14). The issue now calling for further reflection is the significance of the prophetic *book* as a literary feature and medium for communicating the intentions of prophetic voices, along with the implications this has for the way in which readers identify with the Twelve's prophetic witness. As a result of this paradigm shift in prophetic hermeneutics, for example, readers no longer identify with the historical Hosea, but with the canonical Hosea, that is, with the presentation of the historical Hosea in the prophetic book associated with his name.

The following essay will approach the issue of prophetic intentionality in the Twelve from the perspective of canonical hermeneutics. To that end, I will begin by discussing the significance of canonical location for interpreting prophetic intentionality in the Twelve in order to provide readers with a sense of the hermeneutical issues at stake. I will then turn to interpretive issues arising from the booked shape of the Twelve. Here the challenge will be striking the right proportion between the integrity of the twelve witnesses and their booked shape, while also accounting for the reality of integration, or what Christopher Seitz has called the phenomena of cross-reference and association (Seitz 2016: 3–12). Reading the Twelve at the level of books *and* Book inevitably raises the question of the nature of the Twelve's unity and its relation to prophetic intentionality, which is the focus of the third section of this essay. The fourth section will make use of the books of Hosea and Malachi to illustrate the character of prophetic intentionality at work in the Twelve, after which the final section brings matters to a close with some concluding reflections.

Prophetic intentionality and the canonical location of the Twelve

The transfer of prophetic intentions to readers of the Twelve presupposes a context or frame of reference in which the meaning of those intentions is accessed and understood. For this reason, establishing the proper context for reading the Twelve prophets is crucial, because their interpretation will vary according to the particular context in which they are interpreted. The difficulty is that a mixture of debate and confusion continues to reign when it comes to the proper context for interpreting the Twelve, not only in regard to the literary horizon in which they are to be interpreted (books or Book?), but also in regard to their contextual location in the canon. For example, while English Bibles typically follow the sequence of books preserved by the Masoretic Text (MT), the Twelve are positioned at the end of the Old Testament in English versions, with the eschatological horizon at the close of Malachi preceding the gospels in the two-testament Christian Bible. By way of contrast, the tripartite division of the Tanak positions both the Former and Latter prophets in the central panel of the Hebrew Bible (Law, Prophets, and Writings).[2]

What difference, if any, does this make for our understanding of how the Twelve delivers its intentions to its readers? For those who regard the canonical location of a book or collection of books as incidental to the literary means by which it discloses its intentions, the point is of course moot. Reflecting on this question, however, suggests otherwise. Marvin Sweeney observes that "we must address the basic form-critical question to the Bible as whole: What is the form of the Bible, including its structure, genre, setting, and intent?" (Sweeney 1997: 356). In its earlier instantiations, form criticism sought prophetic intentionality on the level of original authors and their historical contexts. Canonical approaches seek to extend form criticism's scope to the final form of prophetic books,[3] while also exploring the intentionality at work in ordered collections such as the Law and the Prophets, the Psalms, and the various sub-collections found in the Writings. On this approach, the question of prophetic intentionality and its character is an extension of Sweeney's question, namely, what contribution does the form of the Bible make to our understanding of prophetic intentions? As we have seen, one answer is that it makes no contribution, and that the material form in which it presents itself as books and ordered collections of books is largely if not completely extraneous to the manner in which Scripture brokers its intentions. The presence of variant canonical orders in the early church is usually cited as supporting evidence for this judgment. Others agree that the form of the canon is part of its intention, while also seeking to negotiate the significance of the range of orders testified to in the manuscript traditions.

The interpretive issues at stake for prophetic intentionality in this debate may be illustrated by tracking a few recent treatments of the Twelve's location in the canon of Scripture. In a recent study (Seitz 2018: 119–29), Christopher R. Seitz notes that in no case do the major Greek codices of the fourth and fifth centuries place Malachi last in the Old Testament canon. The "Malachi last" phenomenon in the English Bible seems to derive from the thirteenth century Paris Bible,[4] a Vulgate ordering that later became the standard for English versions through the advent of the printing press in the

---

[2] The arrangement in the Tanak finds early expression in the anonymous baraita found in the Babylonian Talmud (b. Baba Bathra 14b), which most scholars date to the mid-to-late second century AD, though the reference to "the Law, the Prophets, and the other books" in the Greek prologue to Ben Sira (*ca.* 130 BC) may provide an even earlier attestation for the tripartite division now found in the Tanak. For a discussion of the relevant Greek terms in the prologue, see Orlinsky 1991: 483–90.

[3] Stephen B. Chapman argues that the canonical approach of Brevard Childs is an extension of form criticism's scope to the final form of biblical books. The warrant for this extension was based on the *historical* judgment that "a canonical principle" was at work in the written and redactional extensions of oral tradition in Scripture's formation history. See Chapman 2020: 20–23, cf. esp. 44–45, n. 136; cf. Ackroyd 1987: 13–14, notes 47 and 49; Sanders 1987: 14.

[4] Strictly speaking, the Paris Bible did not end with Malachi, but with 1-2 Maccabees. That said, the Paris Bible positions the Twelve in the final rather than central panel of the Old Testament, as is now typically found in standard English orders of the Old Testament canon.

fifteenth century.[5] But even if Malachi had come last in Greek and Latin orders prior to the thirteenth century, it does not follow that a canonical order with Malachi last would have been accorded significance. As a general rule, early Christian commentators commented on books, rather than the significance of their ordering, unlike rabbinic Judaism, which speculated about why certain orders were in place in the prophets (see b. Baba Bathra 14a–15b). The witness of Christian reception history does not speak of a debate over the orders, nor does commentary on the books engage this issue, though Augustine and Jerome did debate the priority of the Hebrew for the task of biblical translation (Seitz 2018: 123–24).

Over against this assessment, Marvin Sweeney has argued that early Greek and Latin orders for the Christian Old Testament reflect a "distinctive worldview" and rival understanding of the Old Testament, over against the order found in the Tanak. Positioning the Twelve at the end of the Old Testament in the Christian canon recasts their intentionality in an eschatological mode that looks away from Torah and toward the New Testament. As a result, their contribution to the overall perspective of the Christian canon is to eschatologize the whole of the Old Testament and "point to the New Testament," thereby projecting "an eschatological scenario of salvation for the righteous that will be fulfilled in the revelation of Jesus as the Christ" (Sweeney 1997: 361, 364, cf. 358–59). This claim is in no small part based upon the fact that English Bibles place Malachi at the end of the Old Testament canon, a book which ends with a reference to the Day of the LORD and an eschatological Elijah (Mal. 4:5 [3:23]).[6] Given this location for Malachi (so the argument goes), Christians can hardly be blamed for concluding that the Old Testament "organically" unfolds or leans into the New Testament.[7]

By way of response, one might point out that the coda following the end of the last disputation in Malachi 3:15 (3:16–24:6 [3:16–24]) looks back to "the Mosaic ideal" represented in the Torah, and so also shares in the "back to Torah" perspective Marvin Sweeney identifies with the book of Chronicles (Sweeney 1997: 371; cf. Seitz 2018: 120, 122). Moreover, Chronicles and Malachi not only look backward to Torah, but also

---

[5] Seitz 2018: 120–23, 126; cf. Sweeney 1997: 360, who rightly notes that "this [four-part] structure (and the order of books therein) appears to have been set only after the widespread use of printed Bibles in the Western world," though he goes on to add that "it is based on the order of books in the Latin Vulgate, and prior to that, the order of various Greek traditions." As Seitz has demonstrated, the Greek orders in the major codices do not clearly testify to the presence of a fixed and "rival" four-fold order of the Old Testament vis-à-vis the Tanak. Codex Sinaiticus and Codex Alexandrinus both locate the prophets before the majority of Psalms and wisdom books. Codex Vaticanus is arguably the list closest to the so-called four-fold order of law, history, poets, and prophets, though the order of the so-called historical and poetical books differs at a number of points from the English order. Moreover, it places Isaiah, Jeremiah, Ezekiel, and Daniel at the end of the canon *after* the Twelve. See the discussion in Seitz 2009.

[6] References to prophetic texts in the Twelve follow the English numbering, with the numbering found in the MT of *Biblia Hebraica Stuttgartensia* placed in brackets.

[7] See Childs 1970: 122 and 1992: 78. To argue that the Old Testament "leans" into the New Testament not only undermines the independent integrity of the Old Testament's own witness to Christ, but also undercuts the radical newness of the gospel as a surprising and unexpected fulfillment of the Old Testament. The New Testament witness is not simply "the next logical step" after the Old Testament, but a testimony to the Old Testament's surprising fulfillment in Jesus Christ (cf. Paul's use of Habakkuk 1:5 in Acts 13:41).

look toward the future ("let him go up"; "Behold I will send you Elijah"). In lieu of these observations, the judgment that the canonical location of the Twelve bears witness to an eschatologized "Christian" order for the Old Testament, over against a "back to Torah" Jewish order (Tanak), cannot be sustained. Nor for that matter, Sweeney's related claim that when this canonical phenomenon of "Malachi last" is viewed in relation to the New Testament, it becomes clear that "the structure of the [Christian] Old Testament is designed to rehearse the failure of Israel and the Mosaic covenant to achieve God's purposes for the world" (Sweeney 1997: 364).[8] The picture one finds in the coda of Malachi is not simply one in which Israel's disobedience contrasts with the hope for a better future, but one in which the Mosaic ideal represented by Torah finds partial realization in a faithful and obedient remnant who fear the LORD (Mal. 3:16). In sum, the character of prophetic intentionality in the Book of the Twelve is neither a function of the "historical chronology" at work in the Paris Bible and later English versions,[9] nor does it bear witness to a move away from Torah. The prophetic witness and intentionality of the Twelve remains firmly rooted in Torah, as is evident from God's judgment at the outset of the Twelve upon those who forget Torah (Hos. 4:6, cf. 8:12, 14), as well as the command to remember Torah at its close (Mal. 4:4 [3:22]; see Braaten 2003: 129–30).

To be sure, the interpretive construal of the Old Testament identified by Sweeney does not lack modern advocates. The point is that rather than deriving from early Greek and Latin orders, the reading of the Old Testament Sweeney rightly criticizes appears to be a modern phenomenon fostered by the order found in printed Bibles, a reading that has been further enabled and exacerbated by the "the age of eschatology" ushered in by the twentieth century (see Dupré 1993: 145–64). For this reason, it is worth reflecting upon one of the benefits that arises from locating the witness of the prophets between the Torah and the Writings. The Hebrew canon's central panel is not something called the Historical Books, followed by Psalms and Wisdom, but the Prophets, Former and Latter. Breaking up the Prophets by relocating the Latter Prophets at the end of the Old Testament effectively opens the Old Testament to a reading that encourages future-oriented ways of reading the prophets that subsume their intentions under the rubric of "progressive revelation," or construes those intentions in terms of a history driven toward the future through promise. Letting the Latter Prophets remain attached to the Former Prophets in the central panel of the Old Testament canon has the effect of slowing things down (Seitz 2018: 127).

One of the salutary effects of resisting the impulse to interpret prophetic intentionality primarily in terms of forward movement is to allow room for a breathing space or pause (*selah*) that slows the reader down long enough to focus on what the prophets have to say in their own right—to "put the brakes on" the idea of eschatological

---

[8] Although Bultmann famously construed biblical Israel's history as a failure history, that is, an abortion or miscarriage (*Verscheitern*), to my knowledge he did not make the case for this from the canonical order found in modern English Bibles. See the discussion of J. C. K. von Hofmann in Bultmann 1979: 55–58.

[9] As Franz Liere has noted, the Paris Bible reflects "an order that followed closely the historical chronology of biblical history." See Liere 2012: 104.

movement long enough for the reader to stop and listen to them on their own terms, rather than subordinating their *per se* witness to Christ to what they will later mean in the fullness of time inaugurated by Christ's first advent. This is not to argue that the Twelve speak only to their own times, rather than the future. That being said, an approach to the prophets that construes their primary intentions in terms of forward movement or "progress" toward the New Testament inevitably focuses our attention on a history that is coming, rather than the form of the history that is being presented. As a result, the question why the Twelve addresses us through the literary form of books with marked beginnings and endings, as opposed to other options, recedes from the foreground and ceases to constrain our understanding of prophetic intentionality in any meaningful sense.

Prophetic intentionality in the Twelve: books or Book?

The argument of this essay is that it is precisely the booked shape of the Twelve that allows for the sort of pause that has just been described. The literary feature we call "book" is not an artificial canonical division imposed on the biblical text by later interpreters, readers, or so-called "canonizers" on the payroll of the church, but an inherent feature of biblical texts generated by marked beginnings and endings. It offers a more fundamental framework for reading biblical texts than the broadly defined genres of history, story, or narrative. The literary form of the book encloses, orders, and configures the canonical presentation of these genres, rather than vice versa. The mediums of history, story, and narrative, while obviously part of prophetic intentionality, are not properly basic for the way in which prophetic intentions are transferred to readers of the Twelve. If we ask what mediates the oral realities of stories, the historical realities of persons and events, or the literary realities of narrative, the most basic answer is the canonical shape of the Twelve, and that shape is formed by books in the first instance. Stated more broadly, what Israel's Scripture confronts us with is not history, story, or narrative *per se*, but books and collections of books that function on their most basic level as canon, or in a word, authority. When it comes to understanding the function of Scripture, canon is a more basic hermeneutical category than other options, and at the most basic literary level its authority is mediated to readers in the form of books.[10] Thus while the larger unity or order of the canonical Book of the Twelve is also meaningful, the book remains its most basic interpretive unit (see Chapman 2016: 43 and Seitz 2018: 137).

When it comes to the related question how one gains access to prophetic intentions in the Twelve, our point of identification must also be with the Twelve's own way of structuring and ordering the material form of its self-presentation. Arguments for

---

[10] The point may perhaps be demonstrated by asking what comes to mind when one hears words like history, story, or narrative. In most if not all cases, the answer would not be *authority*. Herein lays the problem with elevating categories like history, story, or narrative to a place of fundamental prominence when describing Scripture. It would be better to speak of canonical history, canonical stories, or canonical narratives.

privileging the Masoretic order of the Twelve have been made in a number of places, and the interested reader will do well to consult these arguments (see Schart 2000: 37 n. 17; other advocates of the primacy of the MT order include Steck 1996: 250; Nogalski 1993a: 2 n. 8; Zapff 2003: 295; Seitz 2021f: 165; Watson 2004: 80–88).[11] A case for the Masoretic order may be made by considering the manuscript evidence of Qumran. Though the findings at Qumran do not offer a manuscript of the Twelve that has been preserved in its entirety, the manuscript evidence that is available supports the claim that the Twelve were written on one scroll, along with the claim that insofar as order of the Twelve can be discerned from this evidence, it agrees with the order preserved in the later manuscript tradition of the MT.[12] More pertinent for the purposes of this essay is the question of the Twelve's structure. Why privilege something called the "book" over against other options? After all, is it not the case that what we now call the *book* is an anachronism improperly applied to what is more properly called a *scroll*? A related objection argues that it was not until biblical scrolls were combined in single books or codices in the church during the second and third centuries that the unity and order of prophetic collections were deemed to be meaningful.

With regard to the first objection, it is true that the Hebrew term for scroll (*sēpher*) was not simply identical with what moderns mean when they speak of a book, if by "book" one means a single literary work. While it is generally true that single literary works were written on single scrolls at Qumran, there are exceptions.[13] Yet even in these cases the literary works in question are distinguished from one another by the usual literary means of marked beginnings and endings, which is why the term *sēpher* in ancient Judaism did not simply refer to the physical media of a scroll, but also to its literary content in terms of discrete literary works or books, an identification that would not have been possible if there had not been an original or prior correlation between the *sēpher* and the book (see Chapman 2016: 36–43, esp. 42–43). Translating the term *sēpher* as book is therefore a linguistically legitimate option, especially when we are dealing with literary content that has clearly marked beginnings, along with what Ehud Ben Zvi describes as "highly particular" endings (see Ben Zvi 1996: 141–42).

Later rabbinic tradition also confirms the discrete character of the individual literary works in the Twelve by calling for three spaces to be left between each book in the Twelve (b. Baba Bathra 13b), an early scribal practice that also reinforces the

---

[11] A review of the manuscript evidence can also be found in chapter 5 of Collett 2007.
[12] For a time a few scholars attempted to argue that Qumran bears witness to an order not found in either the MT or LXX tradition in which Jonah followed Malachi. The argument rests upon a reconstruction of a Hebrew manuscript (4QXII^a) that joins together two fragments, one from the end of Malachi and the other from a second fragment containing Jonah 1:1–5. In other words, there is no *single* fragment containing both the end of Malachi and the beginning of Jonah. Moreover, this has been done on the basis of the remnants of three Hebrew letters in the fragment containing the end of Malachi (Waw, He, and Kaph), only one of which is clearly identifiable (He). The argument was never well founded and is now generally recognized to be without merit. See Guillaume 2007: 2–10. For an engagement with Guillaume that affirms his argument while drawing different conclusions, see Pajunen and Weissenberg 2015: 739–42.
[13] While the five books of the Torah were generally written on single scrolls at Qumran, there are three instances in which two books were combined on one scroll (Genesis–Exodus, Exodus–Leviticus, Leviticus–Numbers). See Cross 1998: 229 n. 24.

discrete character of its books.[14] The Masoretic tradition further reinforces these boundaries with the Masora finalis at the end of each book providing the number of verses in each book.[15] However, in the other books found in the Latter Prophets (Isaiah, Jeremiah, and Ezekiel), the midpoint of the books by verses is also noted by the Masoretes (e.g., Isa. 33:21, Jer. 28:11, Ezek. 26:1), while in the Twelve this practice is not followed. Instead, one finds a marker for the midpoint *of the Twelve* at Micah 3:12. Along with the clearly marked beginnings and particular endings, these phenomena invite us to read the prophetic voices in the Twelve as a collection of books within a Book. We may thus say that the Twelve "are" one book, or the Twelve "is" one book, depending on whether we are reading at the level of individual books (reading *per se*), or on the level of association and shared speech within the Book of the Twelve (reading *ad extra*).

Prophetic intentionality and the unity of the Twelve

One's view of the nature of the Twelve's unity tends to determine one's account of prophetic intentions. Addressing the second objection noted above therefore sheds light on the nature of the Twelve's unity and the contribution that makes to our understanding of prophetic intentions. The issue can perhaps be clarified through the following question: Is not the advent of the physical medium of the codex or book responsible for the idea that the Twelve should be read as a unity, that is, on the level of books *and* Book? Answering this question in the affirmative fails to account for the larger intentionality present in the reality of literary cross references and shared speech in the Twelve, literary phenomena, it should be added, that predate the advent of the codex in the first to third centuries AD. Regardless of the particulars involved in their historical origin, these associative literary relations now serve to relate the books of the Twelve with one another. Thus, it is not merely the fact that the Twelve have been written on one scroll or book that justifies reading them as a unified witness, but the intertexual links noted by those who have studied the books (Seitz 2021g: 218–25; cf. Seitz 2007b: 476–78). Reading the Twelve at the level of books and Book implies that the Twelve are not merely a collection of books, but a unified work. At the same time this "associative" context must be understood in a way that brings out the richness of the original and individual voices, rather than erasing the integrity of those booked witnesses for the sake of interpreting them in an alternative context. The hermeneutical issues at stake may be illustrated by engaging with approaches that understand the

---

[14] Ben Zvi regards this rabbinic scribal practice as a "strong marking of each book as a separate book, rather than a chapter within a unified work." Unfortunately Ben Zvi goes further than the evidence warrants when he concludes that b. B. Bat. 13b rules out the possibility that the Twelve should be understood "as integral members of a collection to be understood as a whole (for example, Proverbs, Psalms)." See Ben Zvi 1996: 132. One might argue that the unit formed by Hos. 1:1–1:2a functions in a manner comparable to the examples he cites. See further below.

[15] For a discussion of the Masoretic verse numberings in the books and collections of the Hebrew Bible, see Ginsburg 1966: 68–108. Tabulations of the verses in the threefold division of the Hebrew Bible are found on pages 70 and 106. The verse numbering in the Masora finalis for each book of the Twelve is covered on pages 95–99.

unity of the Twelve in terms of reconstructed editorial contexts, as opposed to the context generated by the booked shape of the Twelve.

Following James Nogalski, Aaron Schart recommends reserving the term "book" for the Book of the Twelve, while speaking of the individual literary works within the Twelve as "writings" rather than books. This distinction is not merely a matter of terminological clarity, but rests upon his judgment that the individual writings "were meant to form a book *only* in combination. Within the collection of the Twelve, the writings were combined in such a way that the meaning of the whole overruled the meaning that a certain text had in its original place. The theological position that was held by the last redactors was inferred into every part of the collection" (Schart 2003: 333, emphasis mine). This approach to the Twelve's unity construes it as a redactional unity generated by editorial moves across the "writings," editorial moves that not only generated their character as books, but also overruled their original integrity as witnesses. While much insight and hard work is to be found in Schart's writings on the Twelve, his comments help illustrate the way in which redactional approaches to the Twelve's unity place undue pressure on the literary integrity of its books.

In more extreme forms, the retrospective editorial moves in redactional approaches not only overrule the original dimensions of prophetic texts, but also effectively undercut their continuing authority. Thus Ehud Ben Zvi finds it impossible to reconstruct redactional processes from the existing text of the Twelve, because "the ongoing process of redaction was *not* bent on *promoting*, or archiving and analyzing itself; instead its function was to shape a series of texts in which the last, if successful, was meant *to supersede and erase* the memory of the previous one" (Ben Zvi 2009: 59, emphasis mine).[16] Such an understanding of the editorial expansion of prophetic texts forms a stark contrast with a canonically oriented approach that not only recognizes a principle of theological authority at work in the formation history of prophetic texts, prior to the later drawing up of canonical lists, but also argues that this authority is basic to their literary coherence and integrity *as books*. On this approach, the basic hermeneutical issue lying at the heart of the concept of canon is the extension of the textual tradition in such a way as to preserve its authority for future generations. If prophetic texts are not the tradent of prophetic authority, but a wholly retrospective literary construct whose continuing vitality derives from future reading contexts, then the original text's ability to speak to future generations is pretty much null and void. Retrospective reading of this kind misunderstands the nature of authority in the religious communities that transmitted the literature as continuation texts (*Fortschreibung*), texts which extend rather than erase the theological reach and vision of their original text in new historical contexts. Extensions of original prophetic texts are made, not just to maintain contact with the past, but to lay authoritative claim upon future generations and point the way into Israel's true future (see Childs 1990: 361–62).

---

[16] For an incisive critique of top-heavy forms of retrospective editing, see Childs 1996: 362–77, esp. 375–76.

Radical forms of redaction criticism also destroy the possibility of any meaningful theological continuity between the original text and its later extensions.[17] The only way to keep the phenomena of *Fortschreibung* in the Twelve from being absorbed into radical forms of redaction criticism is to recognize that the theological authority of canon functioned on a hermeneutical level in the formation history of prophetic books. Instead of viewing editorial extensions as inauthentic or non-genuine, a canonical approach to prophetic intentionality seeks to trace the elements of theological continuity with their "Urtext." This continuity is basic to the unity, coherence, and intentions of prophetic books, and it ultimately arises from the shared theological subject matter that shaped both the original text and the later interpretive matrices which together make up their final form as books. It would be a mistake to regard this as a matter of flattening out tensions between earlier and later perspectives, or to deny that the original text may undergo transformation. The point to be stressed is that the nature of this transformation is not to be conceived in terms of a negation or contradiction that undercuts meaningful theological continuity between original and retrospective intentionality in the prophets. Because of the concern to extend the original text's authority to future generations, the theological function of retrospective editorial moves was not to erase the authority of the original text, but to extend its ongoing authority for later historical contexts and future readers.[18] In like fashion, the shaping of individual prophetic traditions in written book form with marked beginnings and endings reflects "a theological concern to guard the shape of the tradition" in a normative form for future readers.[19]

The reconstruction of editorial contexts and redactional overlays also shifts the interpretive horizon of the Twelve from the context offered by its booked shape to an alternative context supplied by modern scholars. A case in point may be found in James Nogalski's approach to the relation between prophetic intentionality and the redactional character of the Twelve's unity. According to Nogalski, a critical stage in the Twelve's formation history occurred when a "Joel-Related Layer" consisting of the undated writings of Joel, Obadiah, Nahum, Habbakuk, and Malachi was redactionally integrated into a chronological framework formed by two literary precursors.[20] Additional editorial activity also integrated Zechariah 9–14 and Jonah into this corpus on the basis of the

---

[17] Reviewing various models for the editorial adaptation of prophecy to later historical contexts (*Vergegwärtigung, Fortschreibung*, and moderate forms of redaction criticism), Childs offers a penetrating critique of approaches that assign a more autonomous and independent role to later editorial moves vis-à-vis the authority of their "Urtext" (etiology and *vaticinium ex eventu*). The problem is that the "rendering of the biblical text as a purely literary construct runs the danger of undercutting the very rationale for the etiological retrojection of historical material from one age to another" (see Childs 1996: 366). Childs's misgivings with etiological retrospective readings find earlier expression in Childs 1974: 387–97, esp. 396–97.

[18] Childs 1996: 375: "The text is the tradent of authority in establishing a link with specific prophetic figures...The text can certainly be extended beyond the scope of the original prophecy, but the theological link with its origin must be maintained in order to sustain its authority."

[19] See the comments on Deuteronomy in Childs 1979: 223–24, who argues that this shaping "did not destroy, but rather helped to maintain the richness of the tradition, but in such a way as to allow the Mosaic law to be mediated for successive generations who had no direct access to Sinai."

[20] These precursors consisted of a Book of the Four (Hosea, Amos, Micah, Zephaniah) and a combination of Haggai with Zechariah 1–8.

hermeneutical outlook provided by the Joel-Related Layer, resulting in the Book of the Twelve proper.[21] As a result of this redactional activity, and especially the placement of Joel among preexilic books, a broad relationship of promise and fulfillment now obtains between Hosea and the postexilic books of Haggai and Zechariah. Hosea 14:1-3 [2-4] issues a call to repentance that is continued in Joel 1:8-2:17, though these calls do not find fulfillment in Joel. Instead, the *promise* of positive actions on God's part in Joel 2:18-27 finds *fulfillment* in the postexilic repentance of the people described in Haggai 1:12 and Zechariah 1:6. The larger movement from promise in Joel to fulfillment in Haggai and Zechariah forms an interpretive context for the Twelve generated by the Joel-Related Layer. Elsewhere Nogalski describes this interpretive context for the Twelve in terms of a "metahistory" that transcends (but does not replace) the chronological shape of the Twelve (Nogalski 2003: 201, 206; on the concept of metahistory see Steck 2000: 49-50).

It is important to note that in Nogalski's view, the repentance of God's people is *not* actualized in Joel 2:18,[22] but waits until the postexilic period for its fulfillment (Nogalski 2003: 201-202).[23] The difficulty is that his rejection of the actualized character of the repentance in Joel 2 overrides the ordinary sense of the waw consecutive imperfect that introduces Joel 2:18, a verb form that is most often used in contexts which denote temporal succession in the past, rather than the future (Joüon 1991: 390). Nogalski attempts to provide redress for this issue by arguing that when one reads Joel in terms of its literary context among the eighth century prophets of the Twelve, rather than the historical context provided by its postexilic date of composition, the repentance implied in the original temporal sense of Joel 2:18 no longer refers to an actualized historical reality, but is retrospectively transformed into a conditional promise that awaits fulfillment in the books of Haggai and Zechariah.

The question needs to be asked, however, whether the pressure for this reading of Joel's purpose and intention is coming from the text itself, or from his decision to read the Twelve in terms of an alternative context he describes as the Joel-Related Layer. The postexilic prophets bear witness to the reality of repentance among God's people (Haggai 1:12, Zech. 1:6, Mal. 3:16), and so from a historical point of view, the likelihood that Joel's witness also included repentance is historically plausible, as Nogalski himself recognizes. However, this historical reality in Joel's witness is eclipsed by means of a retrospective pressure arising from a redactional theory and editorial overlay. As a result, something called the Joel-Related Layer now stands in the place of the book of Joel itself, the effect of which is to override the original meaning and purpose of repentance in Joel.[24] Here it

---

[21] For a summary of the redaction critical logic undergirding Nogalski's argument for the integration of a "Joel-Related Layer" in the Twelve, see Nogalski 1993b: 275-78.
[22] For a short overview of the history of reception on Joel 2:18 and a brief interaction with Nogalski's reading, see Seitz 2016: 170-79.
[23] Cf. also Nogalski 2000, 97-8: "the promise of YHWH's positive actions appears in 2:18-27, but, as with Hosea 14:5ff., the restoration still lies in the future and the reader is never told explicitly whether the people repent."
[24] A related issue arises from Nogalski's reading of the prologue of Joel in 1:1-4. Do these verses mark a new beginning, or the continuation of a "metahistory" of unfulfilled promise inaugurated by Hosea 14:1-3 [2-4]? The case can be made that reading Joel 1:1-4 in the context of a metahistory generated by a Joel-Related Layer overrides the discrete witness of the book of Joel as a voice *alongside* Hosea, rather than a simple extension and continuation of Hosea 14. See Seitz 2016: 116-17.

would seem that a retrospective editorial move erases a significant aspect of Joel's historical dimension, while at the same time creating an alternative context to the book for accessing its intentions and purpose.

A canonical approach to the Twelve's unity sees oral, written, and redactional phases at work in its formation history, but does not attempt to derive intention from redactional moves *per se* for the simple reason that the intentions that produced the Twelve also included original authors and their tradents. An interpretive focus on the original prophetic oracles naturally tends to grant prominence to that which comes first, whereas an interpretive focus on retrospective editorial pressures tends to grant prominence to that which comes later. On a canonical reading, an appeal to the final form makes room for both original and retrospective pressures, without reducing prophetic intentionality to a function of either one taken in isolation. The delicate balance between the historical and the canonical dimensions of prophecy is threatened when one privileges either original or retrospectively oriented approaches to the book's final form. A better way forward allows the final form of the canon to serve as the final arbiter for determining the semantic level at which original, medial, and retrospective perspectives function, as well as the contribution made by these various levels of intention to the final achievement of prophetic books.

Prophetic intentionality in the books of Hosea and Malachi

What theological difference does the booked shape of the Twelve make for how we understand its unity and intentions, as opposed to other options on offer? Why privilege as hermeneutically basic the marked beginnings and endings of prophetic books over other options, and what difference does this make for the question whether the Twelve should be read as a unity? Because we have books with marked beginnings and endings in the Twelve, it is relatively more difficult to dissolve its unity into a range of external historical sources they share in common (e.g., a common tradition history), or a redactional overlay that subordinates its canonical shape to the latest editorial theory regarding its formation. The same difficulty attaches to approaches which conceive of the Twelve's unity in terms of a storyline, narrative, or metahistory that moves from promise to fulfillment, or from sin through judgment to restoration. The presence of twelve superscriptions remains a stubborn reality that is difficult to overcome, as Ben Zvi has rightly recognized. How shall we then proceed when it comes to the question of reading the Twelve as books that broker their intentions with a Book? A final example may be taken from the book of Hosea and its relation to the book of Malachi.

Ben Zvi rightly recognizes that the superscription of Hosea 1:1, along with the particularized ending provided by Hosea 14:9 [10], constrains its readers to interpret it as a book, though he also argues that those who wrote or edited the Twelve failed to provide the reader with "unequivocal internal evidence" and "accepted discursive markers" for reading the Twelve as a unit. On his view what is needed is a title or incipit at the outset of the Twelve that constrains its readers to read the Twelve, not only as individual books, but as a unified collection of books (Ben Zvi 1996: 137). My argument will be that, given the peculiar use of תחלת in the literary unit formed by Hosea 1:1–2a at the outset of the Twelve, which does not occur elsewhere in a prophetic superscription, this unit offers a unique instance of the kind of header or title Ben Zvi calls for. To be sure, Hosea 1:1–2a does not function as an independent "master title" in its own right. Rather, it demonstrates its signal intentionality in terms of Hosea's character *as a book*, and not apart from that.

Literally translated, Hosea 1:2a reads "The beginning of (that which) the LORD spoke through Hosea," or if one takes the piel perfect as a present perfect, "The beginning of the speaking of the LORD through Hosea."[25] The Hebrew term in 1:2a is תחלת, translated by the LXX as *archē* and rendered in English as "beginning." The MT of Hosea contains an open paragraph marker in the middle of 1:2 that marks the first sentence off as a separate grammatical unit (see Tov 2001: 53–54), while also signaling that the following sentence should start on a new line.[26] This offers one reason among others why Hosea 1:2a should be grouped with the superscription or header that precedes it in 1:1, rather than the narrative beginning or incipit that follows (1:2b: "And the Lord said to Hosea, 'Go, take to yourself a wife of harlotry'"). In its current literary location, Hosea 1:2a functions as an extension of the superscription in 1:1 that introduces Hosea. But just what does the expanded superscription in Hosea 1:1–2a introduce? Hosea 1:2b–9 (Wolff 1974: 12), Hosea chapters 1–3 (Jeremias 1983: 27),[27] the book of Hosea (Vielhauer 2007: 203–205), or the Book of the Twelve?

The answer turns in large part, though not exclusively, on whether one assigns a principial or temporal sense to תחלת. Within the Old Testament itself, the Hebrew term תחלת appears a total of ten times. It is found in Daniel 9:23 at the beginning of the verse, in reference to the beginning of Daniel's prayer. It is also used to describe the beginning of barley harvest (Ru.1:22, 2 Sam. 21:9, 10). Its usage in Amos 7:1 is similar, referring to a time in the agricultural season when "latter growth" begins to sprout. In 2 Kings 17:25 it refers to the beginning of the Assyrian resettlement, and Ezra 4:6 uses the term to speak of the beginning of a Persian king's reign. Notable is the fact that the temporal use of תחלת in Ruth 1:22, 2 Samuel 21:9–10, 2 Kings 17:25, and Daniel 9:23 makes use of the Hebrew preposition *beth*, which is what one expects when it functions in a relative or subordinate clause.[28]

In these seven cases, the sense is clearly temporal rather than principial or foundational. The other two cases outside Hosea 1:2a are found in Proverbs 9:10 and Ecclesiastes 10:13, where the term occurs in the initial position of the verse and it is used in a principial sense to describe the temporal foundations of wisdom (Prov. 9:10) and foolishness (Eccl. 10:13). As noted earlier, תחלת is not used elsewhere in a prophetic

---

[25] For example, this is how Andries Breytenbach renders the clause (Breytenbach 1979: 3). The LXX converts the piel verb in the MT to a noun, rendering the phrase as "The beginning of the word of the LORD through Hosea." Although a similar form to the piel verb in Hosea 1:2a (דִּבֶּר) occurs in Jeremiah 5:13 (הַדָּבֵר), the use of the definite article in Jeremiah 5:13 marks the word as a noun rather than a verb, which is not the case in Hosea 1:2a.

[26] Both the Aleppo Codex and the Leningrad Codex place an open paragraph marker after Hosea 1:2a.

[27] Richtsje Abma argues that since 1:2a properly belongs to 1:1, and 4:1 marks the start of a new unit in Hosea after 1:1 (using the parallel construct phrase "The word of the LORD"), the "beginning" in 1:2a introduces only Hosea 1–3 (Abma 1999: 125).

[28] The Hebrew preposition *beth* plus the infinitive construct usually indicates the presence of a relative or temporal clause, or *beth* plus a time word; for examples, see Job 6:17 and Exodus 6:28.

superscription. If it does function as a wisdom term in 1:2a, as suggested by its usage in these two verses, a principial reading of "beginning" in Hosea 1:2a is to be preferred. On this reading, 1:2a would also anticipate the wisdom coda in Hosea 14:9 [10] and serve to frame the book of Hosea in the language of wisdom. This is not to argue that the principial sense is timeless, or lacks a temporal context, but simply to recognize the priority of the principial sense in Hosea 1:2a, Proverbs 9:10, and Ecclesiastes 10:13 for the temporal reality and pursuit of wisdom. This causal relation between the principial and temporal senses of the term is also reflected in the principial use of בראשית in Genesis 1:1.[29]

The Hebrew word תחלת is a noun in the construct state. One expects it to be followed by a noun, but instead one finds the comparatively rare case of a construct noun followed by a finite verb. In this regard its syntax resembles Genesis 1:1, with the important exception that the noun that opens Genesis 1:1 (ראשית) makes use of an inseparable preposition, thereby opening the possibility that one is dealing with a temporal clause in the first verse of the Bible. While some draw an analogy between תחלת in Hosea 1:2a and בראשית in Genesis 1:1, arguing that both words signal the presence of relative or temporal clauses,[30] the lack of a preposition in Hosea 1:2a argues against this. Andersen and Freedman note that the absence of the preposition in Hosea 1:2a "with such a paragraph-initial time reference is striking" (Andersen and Freedman 1980: 153). This observation weakens the parallel many exegetes draw between Genesis 1:1 and Hosea 1:2a. On the other hand, good arguments can be made for taking Genesis 1:1 as an independent or main clause, rather than a relative clause (Westermann 1984: 93–98 and Eichrodt 1985: 65–73),[31] which makes more sense if one wishes to compare בראשית in Genesis 1:1 with תחלת in Hosea 1:2a. McComiskey rightly observes that תחלת introduces subordinate clauses "when it occurs with a preposition or an implicit prepositional idea (see Ruth 1:22; 2 Sam. 21:9–10; 2 Kings 17:25), but there is no clear linguistic signal that these conditions exist in the context of Hosea 1:2. Thus תְּחִלַּת functions [in Hos. 1:2a] as it does in Proverbs 9:10 and Ecclesiastes 10:13 to introduce an independent [or main] clause" (McComiskey 1992: 11–12).

On the question whether Hosea 1:2a should be translated as a relative clause, the problem is not that one finds a piel verb where a noun is expected, since this phenomenon, though not common, is sufficiently attested in Hebrew. Rather, it is the lack of a preposition in Hosea 1:2a that is unusual for a temporal clause, since relative or subordinate clauses typically make use of a preposition conjoined to an infinitive construct or a time word such as יום. One could argue that the use of a waw consecutive imperfect at the outset of the following clause in 1:2b (ויאמר) implies that 1:2a is a

---

[29] A number of early church fathers argued that both principial and temporal senses for the Hebrew term בראשית are operative in Genesis 1:1. Following Basil of Caesarea, Ephraim Radner argues that while the sense of "beginning" in Gen. 1:1 is principial rather than temporal in the first instance, a temporal beginning is implied. On Basil, see Blowers 2012: 142; cf. Radner 2016: 49 n. 7.

[30] On this reading Hosea 1:2a would be rendered "When in the beginning God spoke by Hosea," and Genesis 1:1 would likewise be translated "When in the beginning God created the heavens and the earth."

[31] John D. W. Watts suggests that Hosea 1:2a should be rendered as a main clause rather than a relative clause, though on analogy with Genesis 1:1 he renders it as "In the beginning Yahweh spoke by Hosea," adding a preposition though the Hebrew lacks one. See Watts 2007: 121 n. 14.

relative or subordinate clause, but this argument fails to convince, because the usual syntactical markers for signaling that 1:2a introduces a dependent clause are absent. It therefore makes better sense to follow the judgment of the later manuscript traditions found in the Aleppo and Leningrad codices, which place an open paragraph marker after Hosea 1:2a, a scribal practice that reinforces the character of 1:2a and 1:2b as independent clauses. In sum, the translation "When the LORD first spoke to Hosea" for 1:2a is not supported on grammatical and syntactical grounds, though this is not the only reason it should be rejected. Reading the function of תחלת in 1:2a according to the principial sense found in wisdom texts like Proverbs 9:10 and Ecclesiastes 10:13 also coheres with the influence of wisdom language elsewhere in Hosea, not only in the coda supplied by 14:9 [10], but also in the book. Comparative evidence from Egyptian wisdom texts also supports this reading (see Breytenbach 1979: 2–4, 366–67; cf. the summary in Boshoff 2005: 176).

With regard to wisdom language in Hosea, C. L. Seow has demonstrated the presence of wisdom language and influence in Hosea 4:7, 11, 14, 7:11, 8:7, 12:1 [2], and 13:13 (Seow 1982: 212–24; see further Breytenbach 1979: 367). The various statements in these verses all give expression to what he styles the "foolish people" motif. According to wisdom texts, foolish people are those who give up their glory and exalt shame (4:7; see Prov. 3:35), who are "without mind" and "simple" (7:11, cf. 4:11; see Job 5:2, Prov. 20:19; cf. Prov. 20:1, 29:3), "without understanding" (4:14),[32] who strive after and inherit the "wind" (8:7, 12:1 [2]; see Prov. 11:29, Job 7:7, Eccl. 1:14), who call the prophet a "fool" (9:7),[33] and who fail to understand the proper time for acting (13:13; see Eccl. 3:1–7, 8:5).[34] The shared grammar and themes in these Hosean texts with Proverbs, Job, and Ecclesiastes makes it clear that the book's wisdom affinities are not limited to the wisdom frame for the book (1:2a, 14:9 [10]), but extend to the book as a whole.[35] Moreover, as many students of Hosea 14:9 [10] have pointed out,[36] the last verse of Hosea is a virtual compendium of wisdom vocabulary and themes found elsewhere in the book.[37] While Hosea's wisdom coda is most probably a later addition, its language

---

[32] Hosea 4:14 makes use of a Hebrew term to describe the fate of foolish people that occurs elsewhere only in Proverbs 10:8, 10 (ילבט). The NASB rightly renders it as "will be cast down" (cf. "stumble" in 14:9 [10]).

[33] The word for "fool" in Hos. 9:7 occurs 26 times in the Hebrew Bible, the majority of which occur in Proverbs (18) and Job (2). See Seow 1982: 221 n. 37.

[34] On "the doctrine of the proper time" in Israelite wisdom traditions, see von Rad 1972: 138–43.

[35] Contra Sheppard, who argues that "The language of the book is suited to the prophet's confrontation with the Canaanite fertility cults and lacks any specialized wisdom vocabulary. Consequently, the last verse is a remarkable exception to this lack of wisdom orientation within the book as a whole" (Sheppard 1980: 129). Aaron Schart also concludes that with the exception of 13:13, the proverbial terminology of Hosea 14:9 [10] is absent from the rest of the book. See Schart 2016: 247.

[36] Breytenbach 1979, 366–67; Macintosh 1997: 582–83; Vielhauer 2007: 184, 201–202, 203–204. Breytenbach contends that the historical Hosea had ties with wisdom circles (367).

[37] Vielhauer helpfully tabulates cross-references with the vocabulary of 14:9 [10] in the rest of the book as follows: חכם 13:13; בין 4:14; ידע 2:8 [10], 20 [22]; 4:1, 6; 5:3, 4, 9; 6:3, 6; 7:9; 8:2, 4; 9:7; 11:3; 13:4, 5; דרך 2:6 [8]; 4:9; 6:9; 9:8; 10:13; 12:2 [3]; 13:7; הלך 1:2, 3; 2:5 [7], 7[9], 13 [15], 14 [16]; 3:1; 5:6, 11, 13, 14, 15; 6:1, 4; 7:11, 12; 9:6; 11:2, 10; 13:3; 14:6 [7]; פשע 7:13, 8:1; כשל 4:5; 5:5; 14:1 [2] (Vielhauer 2007: 184 n. 2). As others have pointed out, the contrast between the "righteous" (צדקים) and "rebels" (פשעים) in the wisdom coda, rather than the expected contrast with the "wicked" (רשעים) is dependent on the usage of פשע in Hos. 7:3 and 8:1.

is clearly built up from the book, an observation that strengthens the contextual case for a principial reading of the header formed by 1:1–1:2a. As noted earlier,[38] this reading also finds support in comparative evidence from the headings or introductions found in Egyptian wisdom texts.[39]

Hypotheses regarding the formation history of 1:1–2a have been offered in most of the commentary literature on Hosea, though their range is more or less limited to a few options. The majority view would seem to be that 1:2a formed the original superscription for the book, to which 1:1 was later added. Andersen and Freedman suggest that the construction in 1:2a "probably marks the original beginning of the prophecy; i.e. the editorial title of the whole work is 1:1 and 1:2a is the beginning of the narrative proper" (Andersen and Freedman 1980: 153). On this reading, 1:2a originally functioned as the narrative beginning of Hosea's prophecies, to which the superscription of 1:1 was later added. The difficulty with this reading of 1:2a lies in the fact that narrative beginnings are typically signaled by the use of the waw consecutive, rather than a construct lacking a preposition. John D. W. Watts therefore argues 1:2b originally functioned as the narrative beginning or incipit of the book, to which 1:2a was later added as an original superscription for the book.[40] At some later stage, Hosea 1:1 was placed over Hosea 1:2ab, resulting in a two-part superscription comprised of 1:1–1:2a. As a result, the original superscription in 1:2a was transformed into a "second superscription" under 1:1, with 1:2b continuing to mark the beginning of the narrative proper, as evidenced by its use of the waw consecutive in the initial position of the clause.

While it remains conjectural, a more likely hypothesis is that 1:1 and the narrative beginning in 1:2b ('And the LORD said to Hosea') formed an original header for the book, to which 1:2a was later added as part of the wisdom framing of the book, in or around the same time as 14:9 [10].[41] Regardless of the time frame, 1:2a was interpolated between the original unit formed by 1:1 and what is now 1:2b. As a result, the phrase "The beginning of" in 1:2a now functions, not as the narrative beginning of Hosea proper (Andersen and Freedman), nor as a second superscription or subscription

---

[38] Breytenbach observes that "The words 'the beginning of the speaking of YHWH' remarkably correspond to the headings or introductions of some Egyptian wisdom instructions" (my translation; Breytenbach 1979: 3 n. 3.

[39] The term glossed as "beginning" in the headers for these texts also signals their dual function as the principial basis and temporal beginning of wisdom (see Pritchard 1969). Examples in Pritchard from collections of Egyptian wisdom instructions are cited by title and headings: *The Instruction of the Vizier Ptah-Hotep*, "The Beginning of the Expression of Good Speech" (412); *The Instruction for King Meri-Ka-Re*, "[The beginning of the instruction which the King of Upper and Lower Egypt:…made] for his son" (414–15); *The Instruction of King Amen-Em-Het*, "The Beginning of the Instruction Which the majesty of the King of Upper and Lower Egypt:…made, when he spoke in a message of truth to his son, the All-Lord" (418); *The Instruction of Prince Hor-Dedef*, "Beginning of the instruction which the Hereditary Prince and Count, the King's Son Hor-dedef, made for his son" (419); *The Instruction of Amen-Em-Opet*, "The Beginning of the Teaching of Life" (421).

[40] Following Gene Tucker's work on prophetic superscriptions, John D. W. Watts writes that "an incipit is a sentence which begins a narrative or a narrative book. A superscription is a title, sometimes expanded, over a book, a portion of a book, or a poem" (Watts 2007: 111 n. 5, citing Tucker 1977: 57). Watts's discussion of Hosea 1:1–1:2 may be found in Watts 2007: 113–14, 120–21.

[41] For an overview of the range of possibilities, see Boshoff 2005: 172–88. Options range from the late eighth century period of Assyrian hegemony through the Babylonian era and into the late Persian period of the fourth century.

(Watts), but as an integral part of an expanded superscription formed by 1:1–2a. Together with Hosea's ending in 14:9 [10], this expanded superscription now functions as a new header or editorial title that interprets the word YHWH spoken by Hosea as the principial beginning or foundation for the prophetic wisdom that follows, both in the book of Hosea and the collection of books formed by the Twelve. Here it is helpful to note that Hosea 14:9 [10] generalizes the call for a wise reading of Hosea's prophecies beyond Israel and Judah, extending their reach to the righteous and wicked of every generation. In keeping with a typical function for wisdom language, this expansion of horizons in Hosea's wisdom coda moves from the historically particular to the recurring realm of a gnomic proverb (Sheppard 1980: 129–30). To these observations we may add that as part of the wisdom frame for the book, 1:2a also constrains prophecy beyond the horizon of Hosea. Thus while Kratz and Vielhauer are right to emphasize that 14:9 [10] opens up a new horizon for the book,[42] it should be noted that the formation of this new horizon is accomplished in conjunction with 1:2a, and not apart from it.

Hosea 14:9 [10] is founded upon the wisdom doctrine of the distinction of the righteous from the wicked.[43] One either "walks after" the LORD's "ways" or stumbles in them, thereby making visible a differentiation between the righteous and the wicked according to the posture they assume toward these ways. This wisdom perspective also finds expression at the end of the Twelve as well, in the coda to Malachi that closes the book in 3:16–4:6 [3:16–24]. Malachi 3:16–18 thus speaks of making visible an eschatological differentiation or distinction between the righteous and the wicked (3:18), between those who fear the LORD and esteem his name (3:16), and those who misread YHWH's providential dealings or ways with Israel in time (3:13–15; cf. 2:17).[44] The combined image presented by 3:16–17 is that of a treasured possession (סגלה) and new priesthood (cf. Ex. 19:5–6) that bear witness to a new beginning in the midst of God's judgment, a "down payment" on and figure of the future described in 3:18. To this end the book of Malachi is given to the faithful in 3:16 as a window that opens onto the future, but also looks back on the Torah for guidance on how to properly negotiate that future.

Though some have argued that the book of remembrance in 3:16 refers to the Book of the Twelve,[45] the thesis that it refers to the book of Malachi is more plausible. At the

---

[42] See Kratz 1997: 18, who argues that the wisdom coda in 14:9 [10] "gives the book of Hosea as a whole a completely new meaning" by providing it with "an orientation similar to that encountered in the late Psalter with Ps 1 as Proömium [introduction to the Psalter]…Here prophecy is everywhere transformed into a wisdom doctrine of life." Cf. also Vielhauer 2007: 184, 200, 203–205. All English translations from original German texts in this essay are mine.

[43] See Kratz 1997: 17: "The knowledge that the author of Hosea 14:9 [10] found in the Book of Hosea, and which he recommends as the hermeneutical key to understanding the book, is the separation of the righteous and the wicked in the ways of God." Cf. Vielhauer 2007: 204, "The book finally received a final reinterpretation with the addition of Hosea 14:9 [10]. A differentiation within Israel into the righteous and the wicked is now decisive for the understanding of the book."

[44] Beth Glazier-McDonald reads Mal. 3:14–15 as a reference to "disgruntled Yahweh fearers" who are the same God-fearers described in 3:16, a reading that finds no support from the context of Mal. 3 (Glazier-McDonald 1987: 262, cf. 260). These voices from Malachi's sixth disputation (3:14–15) represent voices previously identified in 3:5 as those who "do not fear" the LORD and who misread the LORD's ways at the end of the second chapter in 2:17.

[45] Nogalski argues that the book of remembrance in 3:16 refers to the Book of the Twelve (Nogalski 1993b: 206–10; cf. Nogalski 2011: 1061–65 and the nuanced remarks of Seitz 2018: 156).

beginning of the book, Malachi 1:2–3 establishes YHWH's election of Jacob-Israel as the theological frame in which the problem of Jacob-Israel's priesthood is to be understood. As the divinely chosen people of God, Israel was to be YHWH's treasured possession and royal priesthood, an original calling and purpose that stands in stark contrast to the problems with Israel's priesthood described in 1:6–2:9. The end of Malachi returns to the question of Israel's priesthood in the context of hope for Israel's future through the establishment of a new *segullāh* or treasured possession (3:17). Malachi's ministry as YHWH's messenger-prophet results in a partial revitalization of Israel's priesthood through the establishment of a righteous remnant who fear the LORD (3:16), prophetic acts which are then canonically enshrined in a book of remembrance (Malachi) that forms an enduring witness to the distinguishing power of Malachi's prophetic word. The ending of Malachi thus looks back to its beginning, another way in which the integrity of Malachi's witness in the Twelve as a book among other books is distinguished and underscored. At the same time, this book of remembrance serves as a witness to the differentiating wisdom of the LORD's ways found in Hosea's wisdom coda, recontextualizing Hosea's concerns with Israel's unfaithfulness in the realms of the land,[46] Torah, priesthood, and marriage in a postexilic context.[47] Its canonical intentionality not only includes the Torah within its reach (4:4 [3:24]),[48] but also forms a link with the Former Prophets,[49] of whom Elijah is the prophet par excellence.

Conclusion

What do these observations on the books of Hosea and Malachi offer for our understanding of the character of prophetic intentionality at work in the Twelve? We may begin with an observation concerning the relation of prophecy and wisdom that is now relatively non-controversial in the field of late modern biblical studies. By expanding the superscription or header in Hosea 1:1 to include 1:2a, the establishing word God gave Hosea is construed as both prophecy and wisdom from the outset of the Twelve, once again demonstrating that prophecy and wisdom are not hermetically sealed categories in prophetic literature. More controversial is the claim that 1:1–2a functions as a header introducing the Twelve as a collection of twelve books in one book, where the meaning of "one book" is analogous to what we mean when we speak of the two-testament Christian Bible as a single Book comprised of books. The

---

[46] Land is the sphere in which Israel's obedience was to be worked out (Deut. 4:5, 14, 5:31, 6:1, 12:1; cf. 11:31–32), and it is also the sphere in which the whoredom of the priests and people was worked out, as readers learn from the outset of the Twelve (Hosea 1:2b). See Braaten 2003: 131.

[47] Mal. 4:6 [3:24], cf. Hosea 1:2b (land); Mal. 4:4 [3:22], cf. Hos. 4:6, 8:12, 14 (Torah); Mal. 1:6–2:9, cf. Hos. 4:4–11 (priesthood); Mal. 2:10–16, cf. Hos. 2:2–20 [4–22] (marriage).

[48] Wilhelm Rudolph argues that Malachi's call to remember the Torah frames the entire prophetic canon, lest so much attention on the prophets mislead one into thinking the Torah is being left behind (Nogalski 2011: 996, 1067–68; cf. 1006–1007).

[49] On the canon-conscious character of the links between the close of Deuteronomy, Joshua 1, and Malachi 4:4–6 [3:22–24], see Chapman 2009: 343; cf. also his more detailed argument in Chapman 2020: 131–49.

argument made here is that while Hosea's signal character for the Twelve is underscored by the fact that the last book of the Twelve returns to Hosea's concern with the land, Torah, priesthood, marriage, and distinguishing the righteous from the wicked, this is not accomplished by a wholly external interpretive move or retrospective reading imposed upon the witness of the book of Hosea. Rather, as a book of remembrance with its own integrity, Malachi builds upon and extends the founding prophetic wisdom of Hosea that stands at the outset of the Twelve, as marked by the editorial title formed by Hosea 1:1-2a and extended to future readers of the Twelve in the wisdom coda of 14:9 [10]. Stated differently, it is not Hosea 1:1-2a, nor the prologue of Hosea, taken in themselves and interpreted as isolated literary units, that founds prophetic wisdom in the Twelve, but Hosea *as a book* with a beginning and ending framed in terms of language drawn from Israel's wisdom traditions. The book's character as a principial beginning (1:2a) that founds the temporal pursuit of prophetic wisdom in the Twelve is framed by the wisdom coda provided in 14:9 [10], delimiting Hosea's canonical witness as a book while also opening up a window on the books that follow in the book of the Twelve. In sum, Malachi helps make the case for Hosea's signal function, but on terms that presuppose the integrity of Hosea and Malachi *as books*.

The point is worth stressing in a day when the interpretive paradigms for understanding Scripture's unity such as redemptive history, story, and narrative have virtually replaced books and collections of books as the primary horizon for understanding the character of Scripture's unity and its intentions. The story is told that when Calvin was run out of Geneva in 1538, he was in the middle of preaching through the book of Ezekiel. Three years later, in 1541, the town council of Geneva decided that whatever Calvin's faults, he was better than the alternatives on offer. Calvin returned to Geneva at their invitation and promptly took up preaching on the same verse in Ezekiel he left off with three years earlier. The story is interesting, because it bears witness to a book-consciousness and form of *lectio continua* that has almost disappeared in the Christian church of late modernity. The Qur'an famously refers to Christians as "people of the book." One wonders whether today's readers of Scripture might more accurately be described as "people of story," "people of narrative," or "people of history." Perhaps recent interest in reading the Twelve as books *and* Book will help right the ship. One can always hope.

Bibliography

Abma, Richtsje. (1999), *The Bonds of Love: Methodic Studies of Prophetic Texts with Marriage Imagery (Isaiah 50:1-3 and 54:1-10, Hosea 1-3, Jeremiah 2-3)*, Assen: Van Gorcum.

Ackroyd, Peter. (1987), "Continuity: A Contribution to the Study of the Old Testament Religious Tradition," in *Studies in the Religious Tradition of the Old Testament*, 3-16, London: SCM Press.

Andersen, Francis I. and David N. Freedman. (1980), *Hosea*, AB 24, Garden City, NY: Doubleday.

Ben Zvi, Ehud. (1996), "Twelve Prophetic Books or 'The Twelve': A Few Preliminary Considerations," in J.W. Watts and P. R. House (eds.), *Forming Prophetic Literature:*

Essays in Honor of John W. Watts, 125–56, JSOTSup 235, Sheffield: Sheffield Academic Press.

Ben Zvi, Ehud. (2009), "Is the Twelve Hypothesis Likely from an Ancient Reader's Perspective?" in Ehud Ben Zvi and James Nogalski (eds.), *Two Sides of a Coin: Juxtaposing Views on Interpreting the Book of the Twelve/The Twelve Prophetic Books*, 46–96, Piscataway NJ: Gorgias Press.

Blowers, Paul. (2012), *The Drama of the Divine Economy: Creator and Creation in Early Christian Theology and Piety*, Oxford: Oxford University Press.

Boshoff, Willem. (2005), "'Who is wise?' Interpretations of the postscript of the book Hosea (14:10 [English 14:9])," *OTE* 18 (2): 172–88.

Braaten, Lauren. (2003), "God Sows: Hosea's Land Theme in the Twelve," in Paul L. Redditt and Aaron Schart (eds.), *Thematic Threads in the Book of the Twelve*, 104–32, Berlin: Walter de Gruyter.

Breytenbach, Andries. (1979), *Die verband tussen en die ontwikkeling in die profetiese uitsprake in die boek Hosea*, Ph.D. diss., University of Pretoria.

Bultmann, Rudolph. (1979), "Prophecy and Fulfillment" in Claus Westermann (ed.), *Essays on Old Testament Hermeneutics*, 50–75, Atlanta: John Knox Press.

Chapman, Stephen B. (2009), "What are we reading? Canonicity and the Old Testament," *Word & World* 29 (4): 334–47.

Chapman, Stephen B. (2016), *1 Samuel as Christian Scripture: A Theological Commentary*, Grand Rapids: Eerdmans.

Chapman, Stephen B. (2020), *The Law and the Prophets: A Study in Old Testament Canon Formation, with a New Postscript*, Grand Rapids: Baker Academic.

Childs, Brevard S. (1970), *Biblical Theology in Crisis*, Philadelphia: The Westminster Press.

Childs, Brevard S. (1974), "The Etiological Tale Re-Examined," *VT* 24: 387–97.

Childs, Brevard S. (1979), *Introduction to the Old Testament as Scripture*, Philadelphia: Fortress Press.

Childs, Brevard S. (1990), "Analysis of a Canonical Formula: 'It Shall be Recorded for a Future Generation,'" in Erhard Blum, Christian Macholz, and Ekkehard W. Stegemann (eds.), *Die hebräische Bibel und ihre zweifache Nachgeschichte*, 357–64, Neukirchen-Vluyn: Neukirchener.

Childs, Brevard S. (1992), *Biblical Theology of the Old and New Testaments: Theological Reflection on the Christian Bible*, Minneapolis: Fortress Press.

Childs, Brevard S. (1996), "Retrospective Reading of the Old Testament Prophets," *ZAW* 108: 362–77.

Collett, Don. (2007), *Prophetic Intentionality and the Book of the Twelve: A Study in the Hermeneutics of Prophecy*, Ph.D. diss., University of St. Andrews.

Collett, Don. (2020), *Figural Reading and the Old Testament: Theology and Practice*, Grand Rapids: Baker Academic.

Cross, Frank. (1998), "The Stabilization of the Canon of the Hebrew Bible," in *From Epic to Canon: History and Literature in Ancient Israel*, 219–29, Baltimore: Johns Hopkins University Press.

Dupré, Louis. (1993), *Passage to Modernity: An Essay in the Hermeneutics of Nature and Culture*, New Haven: Yale University Press.

Eichrodt, W. (1985), "In the Beginning: A Contribution to the Interpretation of the First Word of the Bible," in Bernhard Anderson (ed.), *Creation in the Old Testament*, 65–73, Philadelphia: Fortress Press.

Ginsburg, Christian D. (1966), *Introduction to the Massoretico-Critical Edition of the Hebrew Bible*, New York: Ktav Publishing House.

Glazier-McDonald, Beth. (1987), *Malachi: Divine Messenger*, SBLDS 98, Atlanta: Scholars Press.
Guillaume, Philippe. (2007), "The Unlikely Malachi-Jonah Sequence (4QXII^a)," *JHS* 7 (15): 2–10.
Jeremias, Jörg. (1983), *Der Prophet Hosea*, ATD 24/1, Göttingen: Vandenhoeck & Ruprecht.
Joüon, Paul. (1991), *A Grammar of Biblical Hebrew*, vol. II, trans. and rev. T. Muraoka, Rome: Pontifical Biblical Institute.
Kratz, Reinhard. (1997), "Erkenntnis Gottes im Hoseabuch," *Zeitschrift für Theologie und Kirche* 94 (1): 1–24.
Liere, Franz. (2012), "The Latin Bible, c. 900 to the Council of Trent, 1546," in Richard Marsden and E. Ann Matter (eds.), *The New Cambridge History of the Bible, Volume 2: From 600 to 1450*, 93–109, Cambridge: Cambridge University Press.
Macintosh, A. A. (1997), *A Critical and Exegetical Commentary on Hosea*, Edinburgh: T&T Clark.
McComiskey, Thomas E., ed. (1992, 1993, 1998), *The Minor Prophets: An Exegetical and Expository Commentary*, 3 vols., Grand Rapids: Baker Books.
McComiskey, Thomas E., ed. (1992), *The Minor Prophets: An Exegetical and Expository Commentary*, Vol. 1: Hosea, Joel, Amos, Grand Rapids: Baker Book House.
Nogalski, James. (1993a), *Literary Precursors to the Book of the Twelve*, BZAW 217, Berlin: Walter de Gruyter.
Nogalski, James. (1993b), *Redactional Processes in the Book of the Twelve*, BZAW 218, Berlin: Walter de Gruyter.
Nogalski, James. (2000), "Joel as 'Literary Anchor' for the Book of the Twelve," in James D. Nogalski and Marvin A. Sweeney (eds.), *Reading and Hearing the Book of the Twelve*, SBLSymS 15, 91–109, Atlanta: SBL.
Nogalski, James. (2003), "The Day(s) of YHWH in the Book of the Twelve," in Paul L. Redditt and Aaron Schart (eds.), *Thematic Threads in the Book of the Twelve*, 192–213, Berlin: Walter de Gruyter.
Nogalski, James. (2011), *The Book of the Twelve: Micah–Malachi*, Macon, GA: Smyth & Helwys Publishing.
Orlinsky, Harry M. (1991), "Some Terms in the Prologue to Ben Sira and the Hebrew Canon," *JBL* 110 (3): 483–90.
Pajunen, Mika S. and Hanne Von Weissenberg. (2015), "The Book of Malachi, Manuscript 4Q76 (4QXII^a), and the Formation of the 'Book of the Twelve,'" *JBL* 134 (4): 731–51.
Pritchard, James B., ed. (1969), *Ancient Near Eastern Texts Relating to the Old Testament*, 3rd edn, Princeton: Princeton University Press.
Radner, Ephraim. (2016), *Time and the Word: Figural Reading of the Christian Scriptures*, Grand Rapids: Eerdmans.
Sanders, James. (1987), "Adaptable for Life: The Nature and Function of Canon," in *From Sacred Story to Sacred Text: Canon as Paradigm*, 9–39, Philadelphia: Fortress.
Schart, Aaron. (2000), "Reconstructing the Redaction History of the Twelve Prophets," in James D. Nogalski and Marvin A. Sweeney (eds.), *Reading and Hearing the Book of the Twelve*, SBLSymS 15, 34–48, Atlanta: SBL.
Schart, Aaron. (2003), "Putting the Eschatological Visions of Zechariah in Their Place: Malachi as a Hermeneutical Guide for the Last Section of the Book of the Twelve," in Mark Boda and Mike Floyd (eds.), *Bringing Out the Treasure: Inner Biblical Allusion in Zechariah 9–14*, 333–43, Sheffield: Sheffield Academic Press.

Schart, Aaron. (2016), "The Concluding Sections of the Writings of the Book of the Twelve Prophets: A Form- and Redaction-critical Study," *PRS* 43 (2): 243–56.
Seitz, Christopher R. (2007a), *Prophecy and Hermeneutics: Toward a New Introduction to the Prophets*, Grand Rapids: Baker Academic.
Seitz, Christopher R. (2007b), review of *Isaiah 56–66: The Anchor Bible*, by Joseph Blenkinsopp, *SJT* 60 (4): 476–78.
Seitz, Christopher R. (2009), *The Goodly Fellowship of the Prophets: The Achievement of Association in Canon Formation*, Grand Rapids: Baker Academic.
Seitz, Christopher R. (2016), *Joel*, London: Bloomsbury T&T Clark.
Seitz, Christopher R. (2018), *The Elder Testament: Canon, Theology, Trinity*, Waco, TX: Baylor University Press.
Seitz, Christopher R. (2021a), "Isaiah and the Search for a New Paradigm: Authorship and Inspiration," in Konrad Schmid, Mark S. Smith, Hermann Spieckermann, and Andrew Teeter (eds.), *Essays on Prophecy and Canon: The Rise of a New Model for Interpretation*, FAT 149, 113–27, Tübingen: Mohr Siebeck.
Seitz, Christopher R. (2021b), "The Book of the Twelve: New Horizons for Canonical Readings, with Hermeneutical Reflections," in Konrad Schmid, Mark S. Smith, Hermann Spieckermann, and Andrew Teeter (eds.), *Essays on Prophecy and Canon: The Rise of a New Model for Interpretation*, FAT 149, 179–98, Tübingen: Mohr Siebeck.
Seitz, Christopher R. (2021c), "The Unique Achievement of the Book of the Twelve: Neither Redactional Unity Nor Anthology," in Konrad Schmid, Mark S. Smith, Hermann Spieckermann, and Andrew Teeter (eds.), *Essays on Prophecy and Canon: The Rise of a New Model for Interpretation*, FAT 149, 199–210, Tübingen: Mohr Siebeck.
Seitz, Christopher R. (2021d), "Prophetic Associations," in Konrad Schmid, Mark S. Smith, Hermann Spieckermann, and Andrew Teeter (eds.), *Essays on Prophecy and Canon: The Rise of a New Model for Interpretation*, FAT 149, 291–301, Tübingen: Mohr Siebeck.
Seitz, Christopher R. (2021e), "Scriptural Author and Canonical Prophet: The Theological Implications of Literary Association in Canon," in Konrad Schmid, Mark S. Smith, Hermann Spieckermann, and Andrew Teeter (eds.), *Essays on Prophecy and Canon: The Rise of a New Model for Interpretation*, FAT 149, 302–14, Tübingen: Mohr Siebeck.
Seitz, Christopher R. (2021f), "What Lesson Will History Teach? The Book of the Twelve as History," in Konrad Schmid, Mark S. Smith, Hermann Spieckermann, and Andrew Teeter (eds.), *Essays on Prophecy and Canon: The Rise of a New Model for Interpretation*, FAT 149, 153–78, Tübingen: Mohr Siebeck.
Seitz, Christopher R. (2021g), "The Prophetic Division of the Scriptures of Israel," in Konrad Schmid, Mark S. Smith, Hermann Spieckermann, and Andrew Teeter (eds.), *Essays on Prophecy and Canon: The Rise of a New Model for Interpretation*, FAT 149, 218–25, Tübingen: Mohr Siebeck.
Seow, C. L. (1982), "Hosea 14:10 and the Foolish People Motif," *CBQ* 44 (2): 212–24.
Sheppard, Gerald T. (1980), *Wisdom as a Hermeneutical Construct: A Study in the Sapientializing of the Old Testament*, BZAW 151, Berlin: Walter de Gruyter.
Steck, Odil H. (1996), "Zur Abfolge Maleachi-Jona in 4Q76 [4QXIIa]," *ZAW* 108: 249–53.
Steck, Odil H. (2000), *The Prophetic Books and their Theological Witness*, trans. James Nogalski, St. Louis: Chalice Press.
Sweeney, Marvin A. (1997), "Tanak versus Old Testament: Concerning the Foundation for a Jewish Theology of the Bible," in Henry T. C. Sun and Keith L. Eades (eds.), *Problems in Biblical Theology: Essays in Honor of Rolf Knierim*, 353–72, Grand Rapids: Eerdmans.
Tov, Emanuel. (2001), *Textual Criticism of the Hebrew Bible*, 2nd rev. edn, Minneapolis: Fortress Press.

Tucker, Gene. (1977), "Prophetic Superscriptions and the Growth of the Canon," in George W. Coats and Burke O. Long (eds.), *Canon and Authority: Essays in Old Testament Religion and Theology*, 56–70, Philadelphia: Fortress Press.

Vielhauer, Roman. (2007), *Das Werden des Buches Hosea: Eine redaktionsgeschichtliche Untersuchung*, BZAW 349, Berlin: Walter de Gruyter.

von Rad, Gerhard. (1972), *Wisdom in Israel*, trans. James D. Martin, Harrisburg, PA: Trinity International.

Watson, Francis. (2004), *Paul and the Hermeneutics of Faith*, London: T&T Clark.

Watts, John D. W. (2007), "Superscriptions and Incipits in the Book of the Twelve," in James D. Nogalski and Marvin A. Sweeney (eds.), *Reading and Hearing the Book of the Twelve*, SBLSymS 15, 110–24, Atlanta: SBL.

Westermann, Claus. (1984), *Genesis 1–11: A Commentary*, trans. John J. Scullion, S.J., Minneapolis: Augsburg Publishing House.

Wolff, Hans Walter. (1974), *Hosea: A Commentary on the Book of the Prophet Hosea*, trans. G. Stansell, Philadelphia: Fortress Press.

Zapff, Burkard. (2003), "The Perspective of the Nations in the Book of Micah as a 'Systematization' of the Nations' Role in Joel, Jonah, and Nahum? Reflections on a Context-Oriented Exegesis," in Paul L. Redditt and Aaron Schart (eds.), *Thematic Threads in the Book of the Twelve*, 292–312, Berlin: Walter de Gruyter.

11

The Book of the Twelve in the Septuagint

W. Edward Glenny

This chapter is unique in this volume because its topic is the Septuagint (LXX) version of a canonical collection known as the Twelve or the Minor Prophets. Often discussion of Old Testament (OT) is limited to the Hebrew Bible. But in this essay I will attempt to demonstrate the importance and value of also considering the Septuagint in the discussion, especially for studying the Christian canon. In our attempt to accomplish that we will briefly introduce LXX Twelve, trace the historical evidence for the unity of the Twelve, present the order and location of the Twelve in Greek and Hebrew Bibles, summarize the early textual evidence concerning the Twelve, and attempt to demonstrate the literary coherence in the Twelve in the LXX.

LXX Twelve

The translation units of the LXX were translated by various translators over three or four centuries, beginning in the third century BCE, and in various places, including Egypt and Palestine (see Aitken 2015: 1–12, for a concise introduction to the LXX). Some books have more than one translation, and changes and copyists' mistakes would have been introduced into the text from the time of translation. Thus, there is no such thing as "the Septuagint" *per se*. However, used in a general way like one might speak of the English Bible, the term refers to the Greek translation of the Hebrew Bible and some apocryphal and pseudepigraphal books that were included in the collection, as in the Rahlfs-Hanhart edition. This is the way the term is being used in this chapter (see Glenny 2016: 263–5; McLay 2003; Jobes and Silva 2015: 13–17).

The Greek translation of the Twelve is generally a close rendering of a Hebrew consonantal text similar to the MT, although the translator demonstrates "considerable flexibility, with word choices often reflecting context and style," and there are important differences between the two versions (Dines 2015: 440; see also Glenny 2009; Tov and Polak 2009). It is commonly believed that the LXX Twelve was translated into Greek mid-second century BCE in Egypt (Dines 2015: 441).

Reading the Twelve as a unit

The evidence that the Twelve Prophets were considered to be a unit, or collection, goes back to Ben Sirach 49:10 about 180 BCE ("May the bones of the twelve prophets send forth new life from where they lie," NRSV) and is confirmed by the manuscripts from the Judean desert, dating back to as early as the second century BCE, that give evidence of these books being placed together on a scroll (Fuller 1996). The collection of the Twelve Prophets is also counted as one of the twenty-four (or twenty-two) books comprising the Hebrew Scriptures. Josephus counts the Twelve as one book when he refers to the twenty-two books Jews believed to be divine (*Ag. Ap.* 1.8), and it must have been one of the twenty-four books Ezra made public (2 Esd. 14:44–45). Also, the instructions in the Babylonian Talmud "stipulate leaving four lines between canonical books, but only three between the prophets of the Twelve," indicating these books were connected in a special way (Redditt 2003: 1; see Lim 2013: 23-25 for other proof of the unity of the Twelve). The Masoretic Text (MT) from medieval times marks the midpoint of every book, but it does not mark the midpoint of each of the books of the Twelve; instead, it marks the midpoint of the collection at Mic. 3:12.

The Twelve are often "counted as a single book in patristic lists" (Gallagher and Meade 2017: 81 n. 42), and it is not until Augustine (354–430) that the Twelve are counted individually when totaling the number of books in the canon (*On Christian Teaching* 13.28; Gallagher and Meade 2017: 228). His is also the earliest attested use of the term "Minor Prophets" to refer to these twelve books (*City of God* 18.29; see also Gallagher and Meade 2017: 191). Earlier, Gregory of Nazianzus and Amphilochius of Iconium (both fourth century) had listed all twelve prophets in their canon lists, following the LXX order, but they did not count them individually; Gregory still counted twenty-two OT books, and Amphilochius did not report a total number (Gallagher and Meade 2017: 145–47, 152–55, 200–1 n. 128).

Another important detail that supports the fact that the Twelve were from earliest times considered a unit, or collection, is the strong evidence and scholarly consensus that they were translated into Greek by one translator, and thus considered a unit in the mid-second century BCE when the Septuagint translation of these books apparently took place (Dogniez 2021: 309–10). Furthermore, they were always treated as a single book or collection of books in the Greek tradition.

Thus, from as far back as we have evidence of these books, the Twelve have been counted as and considered to be one collection, one book. They are twelve books that comprise one book in the Jewish canon (often called "the Book of the Twelve"). They were sometimes read individually, as the *Pesharim* show (see especially the *Pesharim* on Habakkuk and Nahum; Fuller 1996: 87 n. 3 lists the others). NT authors also give evidence of reading them individually (e.g., "the prophet," Matt 2:5–6, 15; "Hosea," Rom 9:25–26), but references like "the book of the prophets" in Acts 7:42, referring to Amos 5:25–27, also suggest they read them as a collection; see also Lim 2013: 24–25). The Twelve are a unit or collection made up of individual works, and in their canonical contexts the meaning of each contributed to the meaning of the whole, while the meaning of the whole was the context for interpreting each work. These books were judged canonical at an early stage in the process of canonization, and some of them, who may not have been included otherwise, made their way into the canon as part of the collection, contributing to the cumulative and collective message of the whole.

Two different orders

Although there are a few different orders of the Twelve in the canon lists and manuscripts (see Fuller 1996 on 4QXII[a] and Swete 1914: 202, on Codex Venetus), two are predominant. We will call these orders the LXX or Greek order and the MT or Hebrew order, which is the order found in English Bibles. The LXX or Greek order is Hosea-Amos-Micah-Joel-Obadiah-Jonah, and then the last six are the same as in the Hebrew (see Swete 1914: 227; Muraoka 2002: IV–VI). Thus, the first book (Hosea) and the last six are in the same position in both orders, but books two to five are arranged differently.

Hebrew Order (MT)	**Greek Order (LXX)**
Hosea	Hosea
Joel	Amos
Amos	Micah
Obadiah	Joel
Jonah	Obadiah
Micah	Jonah
Nahum	Nahum
Habakkuk	Habakkuk
Zephaniah	Zephaniah
Haggai	Haggai
Zechariah	Zechariah
Malachi	Malachi

The LXX Twelve has its own consistent, unique order (see the lists in Gallagher and Meade 2017: 70–173 and Swete 1914: 201–14), with few variations (see Dines 2012: 364–66). Although the LXX manuscripts and Greek Christian lists evidence several differences in the order of books in the Poetry (including Writings) and Prophetic sections, there is a consistent order of the Greek Twelve. This suggests both that the Twelve was an established and fixed collection when it was included in the LXX and that those who edited the LXX did not feel they had the liberty to rearrange the books in the Twelve in the same way that they rearranged other books.

For several reasons most scholars believe the MT order is original (see Lim 2013: 28; Nogalski 2011: 3–4). It is the order found in the Hebrew manuscripts at Qumran. Also, there is a tendency in the LXX to arrange books chronologically (e.g., Ruth, Chronicles, Ezra, Nehemiah), and placing Hosea, Amos, and Micah first in the Twelve would fit such a pattern of chronological reordering and help provide a basis for the origin of the LXX order. Similarly, it is argued this pattern of attempting to improve on the order in the MT is seen in the LXX in giving more prominence to Amos and Micah, perhaps due to their length, significance, and links to Hosea (Watson 2004: 83), and less to Joel and Obadiah. Thus, it is argued there is no rationale to explain the development of the MT order from the LXX, but there is rationale to explain development in the other direction (see Schart 2000: 37). Furthermore, some feel there are more word links between books in the MT order than in the LXX (Nogalski 2011: 4), although the force of this argument is questionable, especially if themes of books are also included in the discussion (see the discussion of LXX connections below and the work of Dines 2012).

In contrast, Jones and Sweeney believe the LXX order preceded the one in the MT. Key to Jones's argument is the "literary and thematic affinity" shared by Joel and Obadiah (Jones 1995: 194–95), which was previously developed by Bergler (1988). Jones sees the verbal connections between these two books as evidence that they would have entered the collection at the same time, together as in the LXX arrangement, and not in the positions they have in the Hebrew arrangement (Jones 1995: 198–99). He also argues the interest in foreign nations in Joel is developed in Obadiah, Jonah, and Nahum, and is one reason for the arrangement of these books in the LXX (Jones 1995: 201–3). Sweeney, building on Jones, offers further support for the logic of the LXX order. He feels the Hebrew order evidences concern for both Israel and the nations from the beginning, at the same time focusing on Jerusalem throughout, and this order would have been appropriate in the time of Ezra and Nehemiah when concern had shifted away from the north to Jerusalem. While with the LXX order the collection begins with a focus on Israel, northern and southern kingdoms, in Hosea, Amos, and Micah, and then it shifts to the nations in the next four books and comes back to Jerusalem's judgment and restoration in Zephaniah, Haggai, and Zechariah; then Malachi concludes the collection with prophecy about the future (Sweeney 2000: 57; 2003: 152–53). In the first three books in the LXX order, Israel's situation with the Assyrians serves as a pattern for the situation of Judah and Jerusalem with the Babylonians, and then in Joel the focus turns to Jerusalem's fate relative to the nations. Interest in Israel's role as a type or pattern for Judah and Jerusalem reflects concerns of the late sixth and early fifth centuries BCE (Sweeney 2003: 152–54).

Others theorize that the source of the alternative order of the books of the Twelve in the LXX was the translator's *Vorlage*. This is supported by several facts: (1) the translator's pattern of following the word order in his *Vorlage* closely suggests he would not change the book order (Dines 2012: 356); (2) the early manuscript evidence for the LXX *Vorlage*; and (3) the sequence differences in Hebrew manuscripts contemporaneous with the LXX *Vorlage* of the Twelve (see Jones 2020: 293). However, the last two points could also be used to argue for a change in order at the time of the translation or very shortly thereafter, which could have been influenced by the differences from the *Vorlage* in the translation. Furthermore, although the translator closely followed the order of the text in his source, he did make other changes in meaning, and he may have felt free also to make changes in the order of books to enhance the different meaning he found at places in the *Vorlage* and to augment the relevance of the collection for the faith community at the time it was translated or shortly thereafter. Dines (2012: 368) concludes that since the LXX translator "could occasionally put his own mark on the translation," his reordering of the books is "not out of the question." And Sweeney (2000: 64) suggests the LXX version's "concern with Israel, the nations, and the restoration of the nations in Jerusalem fits well with Christian theology and its understanding of the role of prophecy as a means to predict the fulfillment of Israel's destiny in the revelation of Christ to the nations."

The location of the Twelve in Hebrew and Greek Bibles

The placement of the collection of the Twelve in the Septuagint differs from its location in the Hebrew Bible. The Hebrew Bible has three divisions: Torah, Prophets (Former and Latter), and the Writings (see the Prologue to Ben Sirach; Sir 38:24–34; Luke 24:44; 4QMMT; see the essay by Dempster, Chapter 2 in this volume). The Septuagint can have 3–5 sections, arranged according to more specific literary genre (see the essay by Meade, Chapter 3 in this volume). The dominant Greek order of the divisions of the Old Testament is found in Vaticanus (Torah–History–Poetry and Writings–Prophets), and it is also found in "the great majority of authorities, both Eastern and Western (Melito, Origen, Athanasius, Cyril, Epiphanius (I, 3), Gregory, Amphilochius, the Laodicene and 'Apostolic' canons, Nicephorus, Pseudo-Chrysostom, the Cheltenham list, the African canons of 397, and Augustine)" (Swete 1914: 219).

In most Greek manuscripts the order of the Major and Minor Prophets in the LXX also differs from their order in the Hebrew Bible. In three of the Greek codices (Vaticanus, Alexandrinus, and Venetus; see discussion of these below), as well as in most Patristic lists, the Twelve precede the Major Prophets in what is the most common LXX order (see Swete 1914: 201–14). Sinaiticus (S) varies from this more common LXX order in that the so-called Major Prophets (Isaiah, Jeremiah, and Ezekiel) as well as Daniel precede the Twelve in that codex. The location of the Prophets in Sinaiticus is the traditional place of these Prophets in Judaism (i.e., the Hebrew order), giving prominence to the Major Prophets, and it is already seen in the discussion of the Prophets in Ben Sira, who considers the Three in 48:20–49:9 and then summarizes the Twelve in one verse (49:10, referring to "the Twelve Prophets"). However, whether the Twelve were placed before or after the so-called Major Prophets, they were always together, as one unit. They were never separated (Tov 2015: 23–24).

Early textual evidence for the Twelve

The textual evidence for the Twelve comes from three main sources: the Judean Desert, the early Greek Christian manuscripts, and the Hebrew Masoretic tradition. The evidence from the Judean Desert and the early Greek manuscripts is especially relevant to our discussion. Fuller (1996) believes there is evidence of eight Hebrew scrolls containing books of the Twelve from Qumran (4QXII[a-g] and 5QAmos). The earliest two (4QXII[a, b]) are from the middle of the second century BCE, about the time these books were translated into Greek; it appears that in the oldest of these (4QXII[a]) another book may follow Malachi, and Fuller argues it is Jonah because a portion of Jonah was found that seems to fit at the end of Malachi in 4QXII[a]. He contends all the other witnesses to the Twelve from the Judean desert follow the normal Hebrew order of the books. Some of these reconstructed manuscripts contain more than one book, but 4QXII[d] only contains Hosea 1:6–2:5 and 5QAmos contains only the remains of Amos 1:2–5. Fuller's analysis of the contents of these manuscripts is disputed to varying degrees by (1) Tov (2002: 142; 2012: 96–97), who concludes only 4QXII[b, g] contain more than one book (i.e., the Twelve; Fuller 1996: 92, writes that in these two cases "certain transitions between 'books' are preserved"), (2) Brooke (2006), who feels 4QXII[c, d, e, g] contain evidence of the Twelve, and (3) Guillaume (2007), who questions whether any of these manuscripts should be designated "XII." Furthermore, the texts in these Qumran manuscripts are not uniform; some of these MSS are very close to the MT, some are unaligned, and some have readings that align with the LXX (like 4QXII[c]; see Jones 2020: 287–88). They give "evidence that both the proto-MT text and texts like the *Vorlage* of LXX were in use in the mid-second century BCE" (Jones 2020: 287). The *Vorlage* of LXX Twelve would have come from this period of textual diversity. Lim (2013: 26-28) helpfully summarizes the discussion:"Despite the variation in classification by scholars, it appears that manuscripts containing the Twelve in the MT order did exist at Qumran and its surrounding environs. But given the sparse evidence, it is not clear whether books of the Twelve always appeared as parts of a collection or individually." He also suggests that because claims for a manuscript of the Twelve at Qumran are based on reconstruction and also because some of the manuscripts have non-MT text types, it is impossible to rule out the possibility of different sequences of the Twelve in the Qumran evidence. However, if there were different sequences of the Hebrew books of the Twelve at Qumran, there is no evidence that later copyists accepted the variant sequences. The Masoretic order was stable in later Hebrew manuscripts.

The Greek scroll from Naḥal Ḥever (8ḤevXIIgr) contains parts of Jonah, Micah, Nahum, Habakkuk, Zephaniah, and Zechariah, including the seam between Jonah and Micah. It is from the second half of the first century BCE, and its revised translation appears to be corrected to reflect a Hebrew text closer to the proto-MT; this development shows not only an interest in the proto-MT text but also an interest in using the Twelve in Greek. Interestingly this Greek manuscript follows the Hebrew order of the Twelve, perhaps further evidence of a correction toward the proto-MT, which was apparently gaining status at that time as the preferred Hebrew text. The last and most complete Hebrew manuscript from the Judean desert that contains portions of the Twelve is Mur88 from Wadi Murabbaʿat. It is comprised of portions of Joel through Zechariah, and it was probably produced late first century or early second century CE. Its consonantal text is very close to the MT, and it also follows the order of the books found in the Hebrew manuscripts from Qumran.

The oldest Christian Greek witnesses to the Twelve are the codices Vaticanus (B, fourth century), Sinaiticus (א or S, fourth century), and Alexandrinus (A, fifth century), and the earliest papyrus codex of the Twelve is the Freer Twelve Minor Prophets Codex (W, third century; see De Troyer and Choat on W). B is the oldest complete text of the Twelve in any language, but W has portions of all the books; S has Joel to Malachi in the LXX order, and A contains all twelve books (Swete 1914: 201–2). All of these Greek manuscripts have what is called the Greek or LXX order of the Twelve (see Swete 1914: 227; Muraoka, BdA, 23.1, IV–VI). Codex Venetus (V eighth century) has the order Hosea, Amos, Joel, and then the Hebrew order for the rest of the books (Swete 1914: 202), but otherwise the order of the Twelve is consistent in the ancient Greek manuscripts, suggesting that "their sequence functioned in a normative manner" (Lim 2013: 21; Gallagher and Meade 2017: 70–173). No Hebrew manuscript has the LXX order of the Twelve.

There is some other early evidence of the Greek order in early Christianized pseudepigrapha (see Dines 2012: 355). This order is found in the list of the leaders of Israel in *4 Ezra* 1:39–40 (this portion of the work from the third century CE), and aberrant arrangements of the basic LXX order are found in *Martyrdom of Isaiah* 4:22 and *Lives of the Prophets* 6–16, both likely from the first century CE. Thus, as Dines (2012: 355) concludes, "Despite uncertainties about origin and dating, these passages point to at least the possibility that the [LXX] sequence predates its appearance in Christian manuscripts."

From the time LXX Twelve was translated, about the middle of the second century BCE, it would have existed and been used alongside the Hebrew (see the evidence in Dines 2012: 363–68). Jones (2020: 288) summarizes that from the first century BCE on, while "proto-MT was emerging as the dominant text form within pre-rabbinical Judaism in Palestine, the Old Greek translation continued to be read, transmitted, altered, and revised, surviving as the textual base in the Greek Christian Bible and developing a complex transmission history of its own." This is consistent with the evidence from Qumran of multiple textual forms existing in the second century BCE.

Literary coherence in LXX Twelve

Especially important when considering the literary coherence of LXX Twelve is the distinctive sequence of the books in this version (see above). According to Jones (2020: 295), "The separate identity of LXX Twelve can be assessed in the coherence of its unique sequence of books." And on the basis of his analysis of the sequence of the Twelve in the LXX, Sweeney (2000) argues that the LXX Twelve is a distinctive and coherent literary whole. What is the rationale for the LXX sequence and the evidence for such coherence in it?

Chronology, length of books, addressees, and provenance

It is sometimes suggested that the order of LXX Twelve was an attempt to arrange the books more chronologically (Swete 1914: 227). Only Isaiah, Hosea, and Amos date themselves to the "days of Uzziah" in their superscriptions; Micah dates to the subsequent king of Judah, Jotham. (Most today would date the ministry of Amos before Hosea's [Stuart 1987: 283; Seitz 2007: 185, 202], but it is possible that the book of Hosea was written before Amos.) Jewish tradition interpreted Hosea 1:2 ("The beginning of the word of the Lord by Hosea") to mean that among the four prophets who prophesied during the same period, Hosea, Isaiah, Amos, and Micah, the Lord spoke first to Hosea, and hence Hos 1:2 was also understood to reflect Hosea's place of priority in the Twelve (see b. Baba Bathra 14b–15a). Jerome understood this verse as a reference to the beginning of the writing prophets' prophetic activity (Bons et al. 2002: 24).

According to Jewish tradition there is a well-ordered chronology of the books in LXX Twelve: the first six books were thought to come from the second half of the eighth century BCE; the next three books, Nahum, Habakkuk, and Zephaniah were considered to be from the second half of the seventh century BCE; and the last three books (Haggai, Zechariah, and Malachi) were reckoned to be from the sixth/fifth centuries BCE, or the post-exilic period (Macintosh 1997: lii; Jones 1995: 240–41). However, Joel, Obadiah, and Jonah do not have any chronological information in their superscriptions, and today few, if any, would date them to the eight century, although the events described in Jonah, could be dated to that period. Thus, it is unlikely that the date of the first six books in LXX Twelve is the sole influence on their arrangement, which differs from the order of the same six books in the Hebrew (Sweeney 2000: 55).

The length of the books is also a possible explanation for the order of the first six books in LXX Twelve, which begin with the longest book and move by order of length to the shortest of the six, with the exception of the last book, Jonah, which is longer than Obadiah. Jonah may have been placed at the end of the first six because it contains prophetic narrative rather than prophetic oracles, as the other books do. In this regard, Fuller understands Jonah to be at the end of the Twelve, after Malachi, in 4QXII[a], and it could have been the last book added to the collection and placed at the end of the first six in the LXX sequence (Jones 1995: 129–69, 199–200).

The order of the first three books in LXX Twelve may be influenced not only by their early date and length but also by their addressees and provenance. Hosea and Amos are early and the two longest books of the six, and both also address the northern kingdom. The prophet Hosea is from the north and addresses his own people, and Amos is from the south and addresses the north. Micah is from the south and addresses his own people. Thus, I have argued elsewhere that in the LXX Twelve "there is a sequence in the home countries of the first three prophets in the Twelve as they relate to their ministries to the north and south" (Glenny 2013: 7). Hosea's superscription provides the framework for these first three books, because the kings of Israel and Judah named in that superscription are the kings named in the superscriptions of the other two books. Jones observes that, "The information contained within the superscriptions unites and organizes the three books under the rubric of chronology and also explains the position of Hosea at the head of the collection" (Jones 1995: 192). He also comments (193) that the book of Micah has a complementary relationship to Hosea and Amos, applying the historical lessons of the destruction of Samaria (Mic. 1:1, 5–7) to Jerusalem and Judah (Mic. 1:5, 9; 3:9–12). A distinctive LXX reading that ties the three books together is the mention in LXX Amos 1:1 that the book contains the words he saw "concerning Jerusalem," whereas in the Hebrew it is "concerning Israel." Although the contents of Amos address the northern kingdom, Israel, the translator has Jerusalem on his mind and perhaps sees Israel as the north and south with Jerusalem as its legitimate capital (Karrer and Kraus 2011: 2345–46). Whatever the reason for the different reading in LXX Amos 1:1, the address to Jerusalem in a book focused on Israel forms a bridge between the clear message for Israel in Hosea and the message for Judah and Jerusalem in Micah.

Although the date and length of the books in LXX Twelve may have been factors in their arrangement, neither of these features is a completely satisfactory explanation of their order. The factors considered in this section provide further possible explanation for the sequence of the books in the LXX arrangement.

Catchwords and literary themes

The discussion of catchwords and literary themes in this section is not meant to prove the LXX sequence of the Twelve is superior to the Hebrew or to argue that one was the original order. The purpose of this section is to show that there are many literary connections between the twelve prophets in the Septuagint arrangement. Some of these connections are only found in the Greek text and the LXX sequence, and where a catchword or thematic connection in Greek does not work with the Hebrew text or arrangement or where a connection in the Hebrew is not found in the LXX, that is called negative evidence for literary coherence in the LXX.

1. Hosea–Amos

Seitz (2007: 215) suggests the epilogue in Hosea 14:10 is intended to be "a motto for the whole collection [the Twelve], functioning as Psalm 1 does for the Psalter." In the LXX it reads "Who is wise and will understand these things or prudent and will comprehend them? For the ways of the Lord are straight, and the righteous walk in them, but the ungodly will fall in them." The wisdom motifs in the verse universalize its warning as well as the message of Hosea and the Twelve. In the LXX the adjective "ungodly" (ἀσεβής) in Hos 14:10 also prepares the reader for the Oracles against the Nations in Amos 1:3–2:16, each of which contains the words "on account of the three ungodly acts ... and on account of four I will not turn away," employing the noun "ungodly act" (ἀσέβεια). Dines (2012: 357) summarizes that the oracles in Amos 1–2 "particularize Hosea's general warning. The effect is lost when, as in Masoretic ordering, Joel intervenes."

There is also some negative evidence, or lack of evidence in the LXX for the Joel–Amos order in the MT. The words "the Lord roars from Zion and from Jerusalem gives his voice" (ויהוה מציון ישאג ומירושלם יתן קולו) in Joel 4(3):16 and Amos 1:2 are identical, except for the waw at the beginning in Joel, and they link Joel to Amos in the Hebrew. But the Greek has two different verbs for "roar": ἀνακράζω in Joel 3:16 and φθέγγομαι in Amos 1:2, showing no concern to connect the two similar phrases. Furthermore, the most common translation equivalent for שאג ("roar") in the LXX is ὠρύομαι, which is employed seven of the twenty-one times the Hebrew verb occurs in the OT. The fact that these are the only two times these Greek words (ἀνακράζω and φθέγγομαι) are used to render שאג in the LXX further emphasizes the lack of connection in the translator's mind between these two books and is consistent with the fact that Joel does not precede Amos in the LXX tradition. To argue for stylistic literary variation here (as Dines does 2012: 360–61) seems to be inconsistent with the repetition of the same Greek phrase ("he gave his voice") in both verses in the LXX. Furthermore, in LXX Joel the verbs are future tense, rendered as *yiqtols* and suggesting future actions, while in LXX Amos both are aorist, suggesting the prophecy, which in LXX Amos concerns Jerusalem (1:1; Hebrew has "concerning Israel"), was in the past. Thus, in LXX Amos the message about the northern tribes, which was given in the past in the Hebrew text, is concerning Jerusalem in the LXX, and Israel's experiences served as a pattern for Judah and Jerusalem.

2. Amos–Micah

There is also negative evidence supporting the LXX order in LXX Amos 9:12. In the Hebrew the clause "that they may possess the remnant of Edom" forms a strong link with Obadiah's prophetic word against Edom, which follows Amos in the Hebrew. As is well known, this clause is rendered differently in Greek: "that the remnant of mankind may seek." The translator apparently reads ירש ("possess") as דרש ("seek") and אדום ("Edom") as אדם ("man, mankind"). The very words that are read differently in the two versions are the words that form the connections with the following books in the Hebrew and Greek versions. In Hebrew there are strong links between Amos and Obadiah with the words "possess" (ירש; Obad. 17, 19 [3x]) and "Edom" (אדום; Obad. 1, 8); in fact, seven of the nine times "Edom" occurs in the Hebrew of the Twelve are in Amos (five times) and Obadiah (two times; see also Joel 4:19 and Mal. 1:4). "Edom" (Greek Ἰδουμαία) is not found in the Greek or Hebrew versions of Micah, the book following Amos in the LXX, and the verb "possess" (ירש) is only found once in Micah (1:15) in the form of a substantival participle, which the translator renders as a noun (κληρονόμος), not as a verbal. These links connect these books in the Hebrew, and in fact, one could view the book of Obadiah as a commentary on the Hebrew text of Amos 9:12 (Seitz 2007: 183). The links connecting Amos 9:12 to Obadiah in the Hebrew are so striking that Jones (1995: 190) has suggested "the MT of Amos 9:12 is a redactional alteration of the [different] Hebrew text that is preserved in the LXX [translation]," and the MT alteration of the original reflected in the Greek creates a link between Amos and Obadiah in Hebrew. However, since "Edom" does not occur in Micah, there is no connection in the Hebrew between Amos 9:12 and Micah, and the connection with the verb "possess" is very remote in the Hebrew text of Micah.

Interestingly, the Greek text of Amos 9:12, which reads "that the remnant of mankind may seek [me]," has strong positive thematic and linguistic connections with Micah, which follows Amos in the LXX. The word "remnant" (κατάλοιπος), which is an important word in LXX Amos (1:8; 6:9; 9:1; and esp. 9:12), is not found in LXX Obadiah. But it does occur four times in LXX Micah (2:12; 3:1, 9; 7:18; see also ὑπόλειμμα three times in Mic. 4:7 and 5:6). Also, several other themes in the promises of restoration in LXX Amos 9:11–15 are also developed in LXX Micah. The theme of the salvation of the "nations" (ἔθνη) in Amos 9:12 ("and all the nations upon whom my name has been called might seek me") is also important in Micah where this word occurs eleven times (see esp. 4:2–3; 5:6–8; 7:16); it does occur four times in Obadiah also, but there it is always in the context of the judgment of Idumea and the nations (1:1–2, 15–16). The mention of the tent of "David" in Amos 9:11 has thematic connections with the reference to the ruler who will come from Bethlehem in Mic. 5:2, and both LXX Amos and LXX Micah offer hope of a future restoration of a united people of Israel around a restored Davidic ruler (Amos 9:11–12; Micah 5:1–5). Also, the language describing the restoration of the people and land of Israel in Amos 9:11–15 is similar to passages in Micah, like 4:4–7; 7:14–17 (note the phrase καθὼς αἱ ἡμέραι τοῦ αἰῶνος in Amos 9:11 and Mic. 7:14). Furthermore, the reference to the God of

Israel as παντοκράτωρ ("Almighty") in the LXX plus in Amos 9:15 and in LXX Micah 4:4 (but nowhere in Obadiah) further supports the picture that emerges from these two LXX books that the Lord is God over all peoples, including the other nations.

If one could say that Obadiah is a commentary on the Hebrew text of Amos 9:12, then one could also say that Micah is a commentary on LXX Amos 9:11-15, and perhaps on the whole book of Amos. The mention in LXX Amos 1:1 that the book contains the words the prophet saw "concerning Jerusalem" indicates that the LXX translator felt there was a message for all Israel, the nations, and especially Jerusalem, in Amos, similar to that found in Micah. The experience of the northern kingdom was apparently understood to be a lesson for Jerusalem. The sequence in the LXX supports this understanding.

3. Micah–Joel

The Zion tradition also forms a connection between Micah and Joel, the book following Micah in the LXX. The image of Zion in the last days in Mic. 4:1-4 (parallel with Isa. 2:2-4) shares themes with Joel (3:3, 16; see also Jerusalem in Joel 2:1, 15; 3:17, 21; Jones 1995: 210), and in both books the nations gather at Jerusalem. However, the reasons they gather are different in the two books. In Micah they gather in peace to learn of the Lord's ways and to hear his law (4:1-4), but in Joel they are gathered at Jerusalem to make war and be judged (3:2-21). Here the connection between the books is based on the juxtaposition of contrasting depictions of the gathering of nations at Jerusalem, which complement each other (Jones 1995: 210, 219; Glenny 2013: 9; see also many other connections between LXX Joel and Obadiah in Jones 1995: 194-99). The same kind of complementary imagery is found in the depiction of Nineveh in Jonah and Nahum (see below). Also, it is worth noting that the description of the Lord's blessing on the land in the Day of the Lord in Joel 3[4 MT]:18 is very similar to Amos 9:13.

4. Joel–Obadiah

There is what Dines calls a "striking transition" between Joel and Obadiah in the LXX; Idumea/Edom is singled out from the other nations in Joel 3[4 MT]:19 and then becomes the whole focus of Obadiah (see esp. Obad. 1, 8; Dines 2012: 357). As we have seen elsewhere in this survey, in this arrangement it is common for a book to develop a theme found in the preceding book. There are also several other verbal ties between Joel and Obadiah in the LXX (see Glenny 2013: 9-10, and Jones 1995: 195-99): (1) the phrase "in [on] Mount Zion" in Joel 2:32 and Obad 17; the similar phrases referring to "holy mountain" in Joel 3:17 and Obad. 16; the phrase "they cast lots" in Joel 3:3 and Obad. 11; and the similar phrases referring to turning back retribution on your head[s] in Joel 3:4, 7 and Obad. 15. The "Day of the Lord" theme is also important in both of these books; "in both books the Day of the Lord is imminent and a time of judgment against the all the nations (Joel 3:14; Obad. 15)" (Glenny 2013: 9). LXX Joel also has some connections with LXX Amos, most notably the use of the same phrase in Amos 9:13 and Joel 3:18, "the mountains will drip [with] sweetness" (ἀποσταλάξει τὰ ὄρη γλυκασμόν). Finally, it is worth noting that the superscription to LXX Joel ("The word of the Lord that came to Joel, the son of Pethuel") is more similar to the superscriptions of Hosea-Amos-Micah, which precede it in the LXX than the superscription to Obadiah is ("The vision of Obadiah"), and the superscription to Obadiah is similar to Nahum (referring to the author's "vision"), which follows after Jonah in the LXX.

5. Obadiah–Jonah

The sequence Obadiah-Jonah is the only seam between the first six books of the Twelve that is the same order in the LXX and the Hebrew. Dines (2012: 358, 362) found no special thematic or verbal connections between these books. Jonah's connection with the first five books of the collection may be based on the fact that the events described in it are from the eighth century and Jonah is usually connected with the prophet in 4 Kgdms 14:25–27 who ministered prior to the fall of the northern kingdom. However, it also differs from the first five books in that Jonah resembles historical narrative, and the first five books are presented as the words of a prophet or as oracles from the Lord through a prophet. This may be the reason Jonah was placed after the first five.

Jonah has several literary links with the first five books, including the linguistic tie of the descriptions of the attributes of God based on Exod. 34:6 in Joel 2:13 and Jonah 4:2 (see also Mic. 7:18 and Nah. 1:3). In Joel 2:13 and Jonah 4:2 the description of the Lord's attributes is expanded by the phrase "repent concerning evils" (from Exod. 32:12, 14), further uniting those two passages. Joel and Jonah are also connected by the question: "Who knows whether he will turn and repent?" in Joel 2:14 and Jonah 3:9 (see Glenny 2013: 10–11). Furthermore, these books have a connection in their description of the repentance of both beasts and humans (Joel 1:20; Jonah 3:8).

Jonah also has a thematic relationship with Joel and Obadiah which provides balance and contrast to the themes of Israel and the nations in the Twelve. Jones (1995: 217) comments that in Joel and Obadiah "the salvation of Israel is brought about through the judgment of the nations. In Jonah, the salvation of the heathen people of Nineveh restores hope for the possibility of salvation for the similarly penitent Israel." In addition, while in Joel 3 [4 MT] and Obadiah the reason the nations are judged by the Lord is because of their treatment of God's elect nation, Israel, according to the book of Jonah God's election of Israel does not limit his exercise of his sovereign mercy on behalf of the nations.

6. Jonah–Nahum

Another possible reason Jonah was placed where it is in the LXX collection is because of its relationship to Nahum. Jonah qualifies and balances the message of Nahum, which follows Jonah in the LXX order (see Glenny 2013: 11). The description of the Lord as "slow to anger" (μακρόθυμος) in Nah. 1:2-3 connects Nahum with the descriptions of the attributes of God based on Exod. 34:6 in Joel 2:13 and Jonah 4:2, both of which contain this attribute. Thus, there is a link to Jonah, as well as Joel. More importantly, the juxtaposition of Nahum and Jonah contrasts the Lord's divine mercy toward Nineveh in the book of Jonah with the limits of his patience and his divine justice toward the Assyrians in Nahum. Jones (1995: 213–24) explains, "Jonah teaches that the sovereignty of divine mercy may permit a reprieve to be extended even unto a people as wicked as the legendary city of Nineveh. Nahum, on the other hand, reflects the belief that God's universal justice will not be stayed, but rather will be fully executed against the enemies of God and God's elect." The contrast between God's judgment of the nations in Joel, Obadiah, and Nahum with his mercy on Nineveh in the book of Jonah "creates literary tension" and "initiates a dynamic play of perspectives that intensifies the respective messages of each book" (Jones 1995: 219).

A theological theme in LXX Twelve?

"The Day of the Lord" is sometimes suggested as a theme for the Twelve (see Glenny 2013: 12). This phrase, which occurs thirteen times in the Twelve, only occurs twice elsewhere in the OT. It is explicitly mentioned in every book in the LXX and MT versions of the Twelve, with the exception of Hosea ("day of the feast of the Lord" in 9:5 may refer to it; note 9:6–7), Jonah, and Nahum (1:2–6 is probably a description of it). Especially important are the extended prophecies concerning the day of the Lord in Joel and Zephaniah, because these books are programmatic for the message of the Twelve, particularly in the LXX, by virtue of their position in the LXX order (see below), enclosing the four books addressing the specific nations. The texts in LXX Twelve that directly refer to "the Day of the Lord" are Amos 5:18–20; Mic. 2:4 ("that day"); Joel 1:15; 2:1; 3:4; 4:14–21; Obad. 15; Hab. 3:16 ("day of affliction"); Zeph. 1:7–16; Hag. 2:23 ("that day"); Zech. 14:1 ("days of the Lord"); and Mal. 4:1, 5–6. Each of the Twelve ends with a message of hope (Watson 2004: 137; Ben Sirach 49:10, cf. 46:12), and the hope is connected to a future time when the Lord will intervene in a direct way and punish Israel's enemies and deliver the remnant of Israel and the elect among the nations. That day is called "the Day of the Lord."

The books of Hosea and Malachi, at the beginning and end of the collection, unite the books in a unique way. The themes of "marriage and divorce, love and election, [and] false worship" are important in both books (Seitz 2007: 213). Furthermore, in both books marriage and divorce are related to the Lord's covenant with Israel, but in different ways. In Hosea (esp. Hos. 1–3) the prophet's marriage illustrates and represents the covenant relationship of the Lord with Israel, but in Malachi (esp. LXX Mal. 2:14–16) divorce is condemned and the faithfulness of God's people, Israel, in their marriages is emphasized as a vital component of their covenant with the Lord.

An important feature in Malachi is the colophon found in the last three verses (4:4–6 [MT 3:22–24]), which corroborates Malachi's position at the end of the Twelve and in the Hebrew signals the end of the Prophets or the "time of the prophets" (Fuller 2012: 373; see also van der Toorn 2009: 253–56). In the Hebrew that postscript reads,

> Remember the law of my servant Moses, the statutes and rules that I commanded him at Horeb for all Israel. Behold, I will send you Elijah the prophet before the great and awesome day of the LORD comes. And he will turn the hearts of fathers to their children and the hearts of children to their fathers, lest I come and strike the land with a decree of utter destruction.
>
> Mal. 4:4–6 ESV

But there is a difference in the sequence of these verses in the LXX (see esp. Fuller 2012). In the LXX the Elijah passage (4:5–6 in the MT) precedes the statement about Moses (4:4 in the MT). The text of the LXX also differs from the Hebrew in the Elijah verses primarily in its description of Elijah as "the Tishbite" rather than "the prophet" in the Hebrew and in the phrase "restore ... the heart of a person to his neighbor" rather than "turn ... the hearts of children to their fathers." Thus, the Greek text puts less emphasis on Elijah as a prophet and it broadens the description of reconciliation and restoration beyond the family. There are no significant differences between the Hebrew and Greek in the verse regarding Moses. What is most important for our purposes is that the Hebrew order, with the verses about Elijah at the end in the emphatic position for forming an inclusio, seems to signal a conclusion of prophetic activity and an anticipation of the fulfillment of the prophecies, especially those concerning the Day of the Lord (the Twelve are the last of the Prophets in the Hebrew order; see Baba Batra 14b). The LXX arrangement, with the verse about Moses at the end of Malachi, ends with an emphasis on the "law of Moses" with its "ordinances and statutes for all Israel." The Moses verse at the end of Malachi in the LXX seems to tie together the Twelve, connecting with the emphasis in Hosea at the beginning of the collection on covenant fidelity (esp. 1:2; 4:1, 6) and on promises of Israel being united in covenant faithfulness (1:10–11; 2:18–23; 3:4–5). Fuller (2012: 376–77) suggests this was the older arrangement of these verses, perhaps going back to the LXX *Vorlage*, since the LXX translator closely followed the order of his *Vorlage* in all matters; consequently, the MT is a "rearrangement" that occurred after the translation of the Twelve, perhaps made by temple scribes "as the authoritative form of the scroll." Thus, the original, LXX arrangement, enclosed the Twelve prophets, and the revised MT arrangement brought the Hebrew Prophets to a conclusion, emphasizing their covenant fidelity. The LXX reading, "Elijah the Tishbite," rather than "Elijah the prophet" in the MT supports this understanding.

LXX Twelve as a tripartite work

There seems to be a growing consensus that the organization of the Twelve in the LXX is best seen as a "tripartite division" with a transition book between the different parts (see Glenny 2013: 12–16; Harl et al. 1999, 86; Jones 2020). The first section includes the eighth century prophets Hosea, Amos, and Micah. These books address Israel and Judah. The first two books are especially focused on the Lord's judgment of northern Israel and Samaria, although both of these prophets show concern for Judah and Jerusalem. In Micah, and to some degree in Amos, the prophesied judgment of Samaria is a warning for Jerusalem and Judah.

The third well-defined section includes the post-exilic books Haggai, Zechariah, and Malachi, and it is characterized by promises of restoration for the nation of Israel. The prophet Haggai exhorts the returned exiles to rebuild the Temple, so the Lord can also return and fill it with his glory. The prophet Zechariah prophesies of an eschatological Davidic king, called the Branch; this agent of the Lord will redeem and purify the people, rescue and cleanse the holy city, and judge the other nations. When this new king appears "the cosmos is transformed, and the nations defeated as YHWH establishes sovereignty at Zion" (Sweeney 2000: 61). The book of Malachi concludes the collection with a return to the call to covenant fidelity heard in Hosea, the first book in the collection. It also picks up several other themes found in the Twelve, such as Edom's destruction, the Day of the Lord, and observance of the Mosaic law; the last two themes are emphasized by their presence in the conclusion to the collection (4:4–6).

The most interesting division of the Twelve, as far as its arrangement and themes, is the second and middle division, Obadiah, Jonah, Nahum, and Habakkuk, which is bracketed and enclosed by the transitional books Joel and Zephaniah. The books in this second division are united by the fact that each of them addresses a specific nation: Obadiah addresses Edom; Jonah and Nahum address Nineveh/Assyria; and Habakkuk addresses Babylon. The two middle books address the same nation, and they complement each other with the focus on the Lord's mercy toward the Assyrians in Jonah and his justice in Nahum. The two transitional books, Joel and Zephaniah, which enclose the four "oracles to the nations" in the middle section, both contain lengthy prophecies about the Day of the Lord, and the contents of each of them summarizes the overall message of the Twelve. Joel prophesies that the Lord will use other nations to judge Judah (and Jerusalem) on the Day of the Lord. But the Lord will then return to Mount Zion, judge the other nations, and restore and bless his people by pouring out his Spirit on them in fulfillment of his new covenant. The lack of historical specificity, emphasis on the Day of the Lord, and use of other texts from the Twelve in Joel make the book programmatic for the whole collection (Sweeney 2000: 58; see Bergler 1988 on the use of other Scripture in Joel). Nogalski (2011: 211) writes that, "In Joel one encounters the recurring theological motifs of the Book of the Twelve. These recurring elements all run through Joel, making it the literary anchor of the larger corpus." Zephaniah is similar in summarizing the message of the Twelve, with its focus on the Lord's judgment of the nations of the earth as well as Judah and Jerusalem on the Day of the Lord; at that time the Lord will purify Israel and the nations and restore a remnant of Israel in Jerusalem to a position of honor among the nations. Thus, as Joel turns the topic from the Lord's judgment of Israel and Judah to his concern for the nations, Zephaniah follows Habakkuk in turning the focus back to Judah and Jerusalem (see Glenny 2013: 13–14 for development of the books in the second division). There is an obvious emphasis on the nations in the center of the LXX Twelve collection. This emphasis is also seen in other thematic and textual changes, most notably the use of the term παντοκράτωρ, referring to Israel's God as a universal god. (Of the 180 times this title occurs in the LXX, 110 are in the Twelve where it closely corresponds to the Hebrew title צבאות; see Glenny 2009: 186–89). It is also seen in the important difference between the LXX rendering of Amos 9:12 "so that the remnant of mankind may seek [me]" instead of the Hebrew, "so that they [Israel] may possess the remnant of Edom" and in more subtle indicators, like Jonah's self-description in Jonah 1:9 as "a slave of the Lord" rather than the MT's "a Hebrew."

Sweeney summarizes that the LXX version of the Twelve is organized first to address the Lord's concerns with Israel and Judah and then with the nations, but in the MT version these concerns are mixed; furthermore, two programmatic books, Hosea and Joel, are placed first in the MT, but in the LXX one introduces the Lord's concerns with Israel and Judah, and the other introduces his concerns with the nations (Sweeney 2000: 59). In the LXX the Lord's concerns and dealings with the nations are enclosed in his dealings with Israel. God's concerns begin and end with Israel, but they include the nations and ultimately his work with Israel and the nations depends on his intervention on the great and final Day of the Lord.

In summary, the evidence suggests the Greek Twelve "developed as a literary tradition with a history of transmission and reception all its own" (Jones 2020: 286). The Greek translation differs from its Hebrew counterpart; it constitutes a distinct and autonomous literary collection in which the individual works and the collection have a communicative function and outlook that are independent of the Hebrew collection (Sweeney 2000: 51–52, 56); and it deserves attention as a work on its own. Furthermore, the evidence of literary coherence found in the content and order of the books in LXX Twelve supports reading them as a "coherent literary whole" (Sweeney 2000: 49).

LXX Twelve and a Christian reading of Scripture

From all we know about the Scriptures employed by the authors of the NT, we can summarize that they drew on a diverse textual tradition, which included Aramaic, Hebrew, and Greek texts of the Scripture of Israel (Tov 2012: 179–90). However, the main Scriptural text that they employed was the Septuagint, which is natural for people who spoke Greek, among other languages, and were also writing in Greek for Greek speakers (Porter 2019). There are approximately thirty quotations from the Twelve in the NT, and Menken and Moyise (2009: 4) conclude, "New Testament authors usually employ the LXX version of the Minor Prophets, but in some cases there are indications for the use of the Hebrew text or of another Greek translation." The use of LXX texts of the Twelve is especially characteristic of Matthew, Luke-Act, the Gospel of John, Paul, Hebrews, 1–2 Peter, and James (Menken and Moyise).

Jewish writers from the time of Christ and the Apostles also valued and used the LXX (Lim 2013: 33–34). In his description of the translation of the LXX, Philo (ca. 20 BCE–ca. 50 CE) considered the LXX translator's to be "prophets," producing a translation that was so close to the Hebrew that if Jews and Greeks could read both "they would admire and reverence them both as sisters, or rather as one and the same both in their facts and in their language" (*Mos.* 2.40). It is no surprise he primarily used and referred to the LXX, rather than the Hebrew, in his writings. Josephus (37–ca. 100 CE) did the same. In this regard it is noteworthy that several times they both refer to the LXX by calling it the "sacred writings" (Philo, *Mos.* 2.290, 292; Josephus, *Ant.* 1.13; 10.210 and *Ag. Ap.* 1.54, 127), using the same phrase Paul uses to describe the OT Scriptures, when he tells Timothy that from a child you have known the "sacred writings" (ἱερὰ γράμματα).

The Church Fathers also employed the LXX. Origen is well known for his work on the *Hexapla*. Jerome, although well-known for preferring the Hebrew text as the basis for his Latin translation, continued to employ the LXX in his exegesis and teaching (Lim 2013: 35). It is also well-known that Augustine defended the Greek version. For these and other Church Fathers the Greek version was part of the ecclesiastical tradition, and it had catholic and apostolic support. It was received in the early church as Scripture. It is canonical not because Augustine and "Jerome read it *per se*; rather, because it was canonical, the apostles and fathers read it as a witness to Christ" (Lim 2013: 36; see 30–36).

Early Christians read LXX Twelve as normative Scripture that was relevant for them and for their communities. They believed that the canonical form of these writings, which included the LXX, continued to speak to them over the centuries. These books, many of which were connected explicitly by their superscripts to Israel's canonical history, were read with a canonical hermeneutic (see Watson 2004: 129–38 on MT; see Glenny 2009 for examples of theological interpretation in the LXX).

"The LXX Twelve ought to be read for its theological contribution, because it, like the MT Twelve, possesses its own thematic logic, catch-words between books, and history of reception that acknowledges its unity" (Lim 2013: 36). And if LXX Twelve ought to be read for its theological contribution to Christianity, it must also somehow be included along with MT Twelve in the reckoning of the Christian canon. How to do this is not so clear (see Glenny 2012), but a first step must at least involve including the LXX version not only in the discussion of the text of the Twelve, but also in the interpretation, theology, and canonical history of the Twelve.

Bibliography

Aitken, James A. (2015), "Introduction," in James A. Aitken (ed.), *T&T Clark Companion to the Septuagint*, 1–12, London: Bloomsbury T&T Clark.
Bergler, Siegfried. (1988), *Joel als Scriftinterpret*, New York: Peter Lang.
Bons, Eberhard, Jan Joosten, and Stephan Kessler. (2002), *La Bible d'Alexandrie. 23.1. Les Douze Prophètes: Osée*, BdA 23, 1, Paris: Cerf.
Brooke, George. (2006), "The Twelve Minor Prophets and the Dead Sea Scrolls," in André Lemaire (ed.), *Congress Volume: Leiden 2004*, VTSup 109, 19–43, Leiden: Brill.
Choat, Malcolm. (2006), "The Unidentified Text in Freer Minor Prophets Codex," in Larry W. Hurtado (ed.), *The Freer Biblical Manuscripts: Fresh Studies of an American Treasure Trove*, TCSt 6, 87–121, Atlanta: SBL Press.
De Troyer, Kristin. (2006), "The Freer Twelve Minor Prophets Codex – A Case Study: The Old Greek of Jonah, Its Revisions, and Its Corrections," in Larry W. Hurtado (ed.), *The Freer Biblical Manuscripts: Fresh Studies of an American Treasure Trove*, TCSt 6, 75–85, Atlanta: SBL Press.
Dines, Jennifer M. (2004), *The Septuagint*, London: T&T Clark.
Dines, Jennifer M. (2012), "Verbal and Thematic Links between the Books of the Twelve in Greek and their Relevance to the Differing Manuscript Sequences," in Rainer Albertz, James D. Nogalski, and Jacob Wöhrle (eds.), *Perspectives on the Formation of the Book of the Twelve*, 355–70, Berlin: Walter de Gruyter.
Dines, Jennifer M. (2015), "The Minor Prophets," in James K. Aitken (ed.), *T&T Clark Companion to the Septuagint*, 438–55, London: Bloomsbury T&T Clark.
Dogniez, Cécile. (2021). "The Twelve Minor Prophets," in Alison G. Salvesen and Timothy M. Law (eds.), *The Oxford Handbook of the Septuagint*, 307–20, Oxford: Oxford University Press.

Fuller, Russell. (1996), "The Form and Function of the Book of the Twelve: The Evidence from the Judean Desert," in J. W. Watts and P. R. House (eds.), *Forming Prophetic Literature: Essays on Isaiah and the Twelve in Honor of John D. W. Watts*, JSOTSup 235, 86–101, Sheffield: JSOT Press.

Fuller, Russell. (2012), "The Sequence of Malachi 3:22–24 in the Greek and Hebrew Textual Traditions: Implications for the Redactional History of the Minor Prophets," in Rainer Albertz, James D. Nogalski, and Jacob Wöhrle (eds.), *Perspectives on the Formation of the Book of the Twelve*, 371–79, Berlin: Walter de Gruyter.

Gallagher, Edmon L. and John D. Meade. (2017), *The Biblical Canon Lists from Early Christianity: Texts and Analysis*, Oxford: Oxford University Press.

Glenny, W. Edward. (2009), *Finding Meaning in the Text: Translation Technique and Theology in the Septuagint of Amos*, VTSup 126, Leiden: Brill.

Glenny, W. Edward. (2012), "The Septuagint and Apostolic Hermeneutics: Amos 9 in Acts 15," *BBR* 22: 1–26.

Glenny, W. Edward. (2013), *Hosea*, SEPT, Leiden: Brill.

Glenny, W. Edward. (2016), "The Septuagint and Biblical Theology," *Them* 41: 263–78.

Guillaume, Phillippe. (2007), "A Reconsideration of Manuscripts Classified as Scrolls of the Twelve Minor Prophets (XII)," *JHS* 7 (16): 1–12.

Harl, Marguerite, et al. (1999), *La Bible d'Alexandrie. 23.1. Les Douze Prophètes 4–9: Joël, Abdiou, Jonas, Naoum, Ambakoum, Sophonie*, BdA 23, 4–9, Paris: Cerf.

Jobes, Karen H. and Moisés Silva. (2015), *Invitation to the Septuagint*, 2nd edn, Grand Rapids: Baker Academic.

Jones, Barry A. (1995), *The Formation of the Book of the Twelve: A Study in Text and Canon*, SBLDS 149, Atlanta, GA: Scholars Press.

Jones, Barry A. (2020), "The Book of the Twelve in the Septuagint," in Lena-Sofia Tiemeyer and Jacob Wöhrle (eds.), *The Book of the Twelve*, VTSup 184, 286–304, Leiden: Brill.

Karrer, Martin and Wolfgang Kraus, eds. (2011), *Septuaginta Deutsch: Erläuterungen und Kommentare zum griechen Alten Testament*, 2 vols, Stuttgart: Deutsche Bibelgesellschaft.

Lim, Bo H. (2013), "Which version of the Twelve Prophets Should Christians Read? A Case for Reading the LXX Twelve Prophets," *Journal of Theological Interpretation* 7 (1): 21–36.

Macintosh, A. A. (1997), *Hosea*, ICC, Edinburgh: T&T Clark.

McLay, R. Timothy. (2003), *The Use of the Septuagint in New Testament Research*, Grand Rapids: Eerdmans.

Menken, Maarten J. J. and Moyise, Steve (eds.). (2009), *The Minor Prophets in the New Testament*, LNTS 377, London: T&T Clark.

Muraoka, Takamitsu. (2002), "Introduction aux Douze Petits Prophètes," in Eberhard Bone, Jan Joosten, and Stephan Kessler (eds.), *La Bible d'Alexandrie. 23.1. Les Douze Prophètes: Osée*, BdA 23, 1, I–XXIII, Paris: Cerf.

Nogalski, James D. (2011), *The Book of the Twelve: Hosea – Jonah*, Macon GA: Smith and Helwys.

Porter, Stanley E. (2019), "Paul and His Use of Scripture: Further Considerations," in Stanley E. Porter and Christopher D. Land, *Paul and Scripture*, PAST 10, 7–30, Leiden: Brill.

Redditt, Paul L. (2003), "The Formation of the Book of the Twelve: A Review of Research," in Paul L. Reditt and Aaron Schart (eds.), *Thematic Threads in the Book of the Twelve*, 1–26, Berlin: Walter de Gruyter.

Schart, Aaron. (2000), "Reconstructing the Redaction History of the Twelve Prophets," in James D. Nogalski and Marvin A. Sweeney (eds.), *Reading and Hearing the Book of the Twelve*, SBLSymS 15, 34–48, Atlanta: Society of Biblical Literature.
Seitz, Christopher R. (2007), *Prophecy and Hermeneutics: Toward a New Introduction to the Prophets*, STI, Grand Rapids: Baker Academic.
Stuart, Douglas. (1987), *Hosea – Jonah*, WBC 31, Waco, TX: Word Books.
Sweeney, Marvin A. (2000), "Sequence and Interpretation in the Book of the Twelve," in James D. Nogalski and Marvin A. Sweeney (eds.), *Reading and Hearing the Book of the Twelve*, SBL Symposium Series 15, 49–64, Atlanta, GA: SBL Press.
Sweeney, Marvin A. (2003), "The Place and Function of Joel in the Book of the Twelve," in Paul L. Reditt and Aaron Schart (eds.), *Thematic Threads in the Book of the Twelve*, 133–54, Berlin: Walter de Gruyter.
Swete, Henry Barclay. (1914), *An Introduction to the Old Testament in Greek*, 2nd edn, 1989. Reprint of the 1914 Cambridge University Press edition, Peabody, MA: Hendrickson.
Tov, Emanuel. (2002), "The Biblical Texts from the Judean Desert: An Overview and Analysis of the Published Texts," in Edward. D. Herbert and Emanuel Tov (eds.), *The Bible as Book: The Hebrew Bible and the Judean Desert Discoveries*, 139–66, London: Oak Knoll.
Tov, Emanuel. (2012), *Textual Criticism of the Hebrew Bible*, 3rd edn, Minneapolis, MN: Fortress.
Tov, Emanuel. (2015), "The Septuagint in Codex Sinaiticus Compared with Other Sources," in Scott McKendrick, et al. (eds.), *Codex Sinaiticus: New Perspectives on the Ancient Biblical Manuscripts*, 21–29, London: The British Library.
Tov, Emanuel and Frank Polak. (2009), *The Revised CATSS Hebrew/Greek Parallel Text*, 2nd edn., Jerusalem.
van der Toorn, Karel. (2009), *Scribal Culture and the Making of the Hebrew Bible*, Cambridge, MA: Harvard University Press.
Watson, Francis. (2004), *Paul and the Hermeneutics of Faith*, London: T&T Clark.

Section Three

New Testament Canonical Sub-Units

12

The Four-Fold Gospel Collection

Gregory R. Lanier

The traditional Gospels ascribed to Matthew, Mark, Luke, and John present unique challenges within the Christian canon, for they are formally anonymous (unlike most of the epistles), four in number (unlike Acts, Revelation, or most OT books), but singular in topic (covering the same basic story of Jesus' life). Key questions about this pluriform collection go back at least as early as Irenaeus and continue to dominate NT scholarship (see Stanton 2004: 63): Why did the church receive four Gospels, instead of one? Who picked *these* four and excluded the others?

To sketch the four-fold Gospel sub-canon, I will proceed in three steps. First, I will outline the state of research: providing an introduction to other "Gospel" writings, describing the two main operating paradigms that prevail in Gospels scholarship, and articulating the methodological concerns and research questions that drive the field. Second, I will set forth eight aspects of the historical development of the Gospels collection, focusing on the various ways in which the four-fold Gospel coalesced while also paying attention to the broader stream of writing in which the canonical four are situated. Third, I will reflect on implications of a four-fold Gospel for today's reader.

State of research

Every standard work on NT canon covers the Gospels at length, for it is generally recognized that they, along with the Pauline Corpus, formed the canonical nucleus from an early stage. The process by which this situation came to be is, however, immensely debated. Space does not permit covering every issue or perspective in detail, let alone the staggering amount of research over the past two centuries. I will sketch the main fault lines and generally refer the reader to research that is more recent, which, in turn, can point to older scholarship.

Extra-Biblical "Gospels"

Discussing the Gospels immediately requires defining what counts. When speaking of the traditional four Gospels, I will refer to their final forms as attested in the manuscript tradition. While there are non-trivial differences among, say, the Byzantine text-form, the so-called Western text-form, and the critical reconstructions (e.g., NA28/UBS5), the overall textual situation is stable enough for our purposes.

At present there is no generally accepted canon of the other "Gospel"-like writings that were roughly contemporary with the four-fold Gospel and share a focus on the teachings of or events surrounding the life of Jesus. I will focus on the twenty that receive the most attention, even if the label "Gospel"—which I will use for convenience—is not always a perfect fit (for texts and details, see Robinson 2002; Kraus et al. 2009; Ehrman and Pleše 2011).

Major examples

Some of the most well-known "Gospels" are often pseudepigraphically attributed to major Christian figures and emerge fairly early; most but not all have survived in near-complete form (Table 12.1). (Dates reflect the consensus for the *composition*, not the surviving manuscript[s]).

Fragments

Several lack known titles but appear to derive from what were originally longer "Gospel" writings, surviving to the present only in fragmentary form (Table 12.2). (Dates reflect the consensus for the manuscripts; composition dates would be earlier but are debated.)

Table 12.1 Dating and description of extra-Biblical "Gospels"

Title	Est. dating (century)	Description
Infancy Gospel of Thomas	Mid/late 2	Recounts the exploits of Jesus as a miracle-working child; well-known up through Middle Ages
Protevangelium of James	Late 2	Tells the backstory of Mary up to the birth of Jesus; influenced the doctrine of Mary's perpetual virginity
Gospel of Thomas	Early/mid 2	Presents 114 "sayings" (*logia*) of Jesus, many of which have Synoptic parallels, with perhaps a proto-Gnostic flavor
Gospel of Peter	Mid/late 2	Provides an alternate version of the passion and resurrection of Jesus, particularly vilifying the Jews
Gospel of Judas	Mid 2	Retells the passion week with a particular emphasis on secret revelations given to Judas
Gospel of Mary	Mid/late 2	Records Jesus' Gnosticized dialogues with his disciples about the nature of the material world
Apocryphon of John	Late 2	Gives heavily Gnosticized teachings of the resurrected Jesus to John on cosmology
Gospel of Philip	Early 2	Presents a mixture of Gnostic sayings of Jesus on creation, marriage, sacraments, and other topics
Gospel of Truth	Mid 2	Describes Jesus' cosmic descent to bring salvation via gnosis and features various Gnostic teachings

Table 12.2 Dating and description of "Gospel" fragments

Manuscript designation	Est. dating (century)	Description
P. Egerton 2 (+ P. Köln 255)	2	Records four episodes of Jesus (two controversy scenes, healing of a leper, and a miracle on the Jordan) with partial parallels to the canonical Gospels
P. Oxy. 840	3/4	Describes a dispute between Jesus and a priest over issues of purity
P. Oxy. 1224	3/4	Contains six sayings of Jesus with partial Synoptic parallels (but appear to be independent)
P. Oxy. 4009	2/3	Contains various fragmentary, mission-related sayings of Jesus (that resemble sentences in Matthew/Luke)
P. Oxy. 5072	2/3	Records an exorcism story and sayings of Jesus to a disciple, with partial Synoptic similarities
P. Vienna G. 2325	3	Records a variation of Jesus' "strike the shepherd" saying; also known as the Fayyum fragment

Attested but no surviving manuscripts

Finally, a handful are referenced and/or quoted by various church fathers, but specific manuscripts of them have not been discovered (Table 12.3). Other candidates could be mentioned, but these figure the most in scholarship on the Gospel canon. Their very existence reveals extensive early Christian interest in the sayings and stories of Jesus and his associates. Their quantity and circulation raise key questions about the formation of the canonical collection, to which we turn.

Operating paradigms

With four traditional Gospels on one side and over twenty "Gospel"-like writings on the other, it is natural to ask, *how* and *why* the canonical divide was drawn the way it is. Could it have been otherwise? The scholarly landscape is divided (though not 50/50) into two basic paradigms or models for understanding how Matthew, Mark, Luke, and John became privileged within mainstream Christianity while none of the others gained equal traction. One paradigm can be labeled "intrinsic," holding that the differentiation emerged naturally as the writings were recognized to be inherently scriptural, given by God himself through the apostolic circle (e.g., Hill 2010; Kruger 2012, 2013). The other paradigm can be labeled "extrinsic," holding that the canonical vs. non-canonical distinction was arrived at and ultimately enforced through a process of ecclesiastical debate (e.g., Gamble 1985; Metzger 1997; McDonald 2017). Some scholars attempt to balance aspects of both (e.g., Bruce 1988; Schröter 2013; Bokedal 2014).

One can discern which paradigm is at play through the language used to answer certain questions regarding canonical development (Table 12.4). Within both paradigms the standard assumption is that, for better or worse, the Gospels canon is "closed" (by divine inspiration, church-historical decision, or some combination).

Table 12.3 Dating and description of other attested "Gospels"

"Gospel" of	Est. dating (century)	Description
Marcion	2	Shortens the Gospel of Luke (e.g., lacks birth narrative and genealogy), though some argue it pre-dates Luke's final form
the Egyptians	2	Contains various discussions of child-bearing and celibacy (not to be confused with a Nag Hammadi text with the same title)
the Ebionites	2/3	Presents various scenes that apparently harmonize Matthew, Mark, and Luke; its identity is debated, as patristic sources are inconsistent in describing it
the Hebrews	2/3	Presents (Gnostic-leaning) versions of various episodes of Jesus' life and describes the Spirit as his "mother"
the Nazarenes	2	Contains accounts of Jesus' baptism, teaching, healings, and passion that may derive from Matthew; it is also occasionally connected to the so-called "Zion Gospel" and/or the "Jewish Gospel" (attested in medieval scholia of Matthew as *To Ioudaikon*)

Table 12.4 Questions at play for intrinsic vs. extrinsic canon paradigms

Question	Intrinsic canon	Extrinsic canon
How was the church involved in canon formation?	The church "received" or "recognized" the Gospels	The church "chose" or "authorized" the Gospels
Why were the four Gospels, and only these four, included?	These four were self-authenticating	These four met criteria for canonicity: apostolic, pre-100 CE, orthodox, and widely used
When did this four-fold canonical distinction emerge?	Early and organically, beginning as soon as the Gospels were recorded	Later and non-organically, imposed by informal or formal ecclesiastical decision
Why were the other "Gospels" excluded from the canon?	They were not actually "excluded," for they were not up for consideration anyhow (and it could not have been otherwise)	They failed to meet the criteria for canonicity (and it could have been otherwise)

However, in recent years some proponents of the extrinsic paradigm have developed a more "open" stance on the boundaries of the Gospels canon. That is, in the earliest stages (late first to early second century) Matthew, Mark, Luke, and John were merely part of a broader cottage industry of "Gospel"-writing alongside *Thomas*, *Peter*, the Egerton Gospel, and so forth. None were necessarily better or worse than the others but equally part of a rich environment of the early reception of Jesus. It was only decades or even centuries later that the battles over heresy and orthodoxy required lines to be drawn between Gospels that were "in" or "out"; up until then, there were no inherent qualitative differences (Watson 2013; see critiques by Bauckham 2019; Bockmuehl 2019).

Unsurprisingly the actual history of the emergence of a four-fold (and only four-fold) Gospel was more complex than an intrinsic–extrinsic binary can accommodate—

to which I will turn in 'Development of the Gospel canon'. Before doing so, I will outline key research issues.

Methodological concerns and questions

Regardless of operating paradigm, scholars who study the Gospel canon do not adopt any monolithic method but, rather, employ a hybrid approach drawing from the standard tools of NT criticism. Three are most important.

(i) *Textual criticism*. The text of the four Gospels and other "Gospel"-writings must first be reconstructed before any detailed work can be done with them; and inevitably one must have a perspective on whether the longer readings at Mark 16:9–20, Luke 22:43–44, John 7:53–8:11 and others belong in the canonical text of their respective Gospels. Other manuscript-related lines of inquiry are vital: i.e. the adoption of the codex versus the roll; the use of *nomina sacra*; the nature of scribal handwriting; and the respective quantities of apocryphal versus canonical manuscripts.

(ii) *Source and redaction criticism*. Though typically more at home in pure studies of the Synoptic Problem, these related sub-fields are also relevant for the topic of canon. The use of one Gospel by another evangelist may have canonical implications. Moreover, the basic toolset is crucial for detecting if/when a church father is using a written Gospel in a known form rather than oral tradition (Koester 1994; Gregory and Tuckett 2005). And applying source and redaction criticism to non-canonical "Gospel" writings themselves—especially where they may be drawing on the four canonical Gospels—has become an important part of the picture.

(iii) *Reception history*. Finally, the critical study of early church reception is of obvious importance to the canon question, including patristic citations/quotations of Gospel texts (canonical and non-canonical), explicit discussions of Gospel authorship and apostolicity, debates about permissible Gospel usage within the church, early Gospel commentary efforts, and publication of canon lists.

Perhaps more important than critical methods—which themselves are fairly standard—are the questions that drive how these methods are employed. Underlying the operating paradigms and methodological toolbox are core questions that guide the research:

- To what degree was early Christianity shaped by theological unity or diversity (or both)? How did the orthodoxy/heresy conflict impact canonical development? Were the four Gospels "chosen" as an expedient response to a contingent situation of theological controversy?
- To what extent can we take the writings of early church fathers at face value? Are Papias, Justin, and Irenaeus (to pick three) trustworthy historical sources—and when they are not, how can we tell? And how confidently can we ascertain their direct use of the canonical form of the Gospels?

- How should we factor in the circumstantial (and, thus, incomplete) nature of the artifactual record? Given the lengthy timeline, climate issues (especially in Judea), and randomness of archaeological preservation, how should we think about the relative number of manuscript remains? Does respective quantity of papyri—mostly limited to one region (Egypt)—accurately reflect early readership?
- Should the field move beyond the canonical/non-canonical (or orthodox/heterodox) way of thinking and instead conceptualize the field as one of Gospel production—where every "Gospel"-writing is given its own fair shake? And even if the distinction is retained, how should non-canonical "Gospels" factor into research on the canonical four?

I will not endeavor to answer each question. Of course, each deserves a monograph in its own right, but elements of them will run throughout the discussion that follows.

Development of the Gospel canon

In this section I will trace eight key features of the historical emergence of a four-fold Gospel consciousness and situate it against the broader production of "Gospel" writings. At certain points the developmental storylines of canonical and non-canonical writings come across as fairly similar (e.g., manuscript attestation), which may give the impression that they should not be differentiated. But on the whole, it will be clear that the privileging of Matthew, Mark, Luke, and John appears to have coalesced early and organically. None of these eight features is the "smoking gun" for or against a four-fold Gospel collection. Of more importance is their cumulative force (see the survey of some of these in Gamble 2019).

Early circulation and readership

There is extensive evidence that both canonical Gospels and non-canonical "Gospel" writings were in circulation among Christian readers well before any kind of ecclesiastical decision.

The earliest evidence are telltale signs of intracanonical awareness of the Gospels. Paul's epistles may allude to phrasing from Jesus' Sermon on the Mount (Romans 12–14), Olivet Discourse ("thief in the night," 1 Thess. 5:2; Matt. 24:42–43), divorce instructions ("Not I, but the Lord," 1 Cor. 7:10–11; Mark 10:2–12), and mission instructions ("eat what is set before you," 1 Cor. 10:27; Luke 10:8). First Timothy (1 Tim) 5:18 refers to "the worker deserves his wages" in writing (*graphē*) that is elsewhere found in Luke 10:7. Second Peter (2 Peter) 1:16–18 refers to and partially quotes the transfiguration account. And 1 John 1:1–4 shows obvious familiarity with John 1:1–18 (possibly due to shared authorship). Some of these may have arisen via oral or pre-Gospel written traditions—but the possibility remains that some indicate a burgeoning literary access to written Gospels within the apostolic circle. There is no comparable evidence on the non-canonical side of the ledger.

Manuscripts, particularly papyri from the 100s to the 400s, are another indication of the extent to which these Gospel writings circulated during the early period. The majority of early findings are fragmentary and come from the dry climate of Egypt, thus raising intractable questions about the degree to which they represent all of early Christendom. Numbers may give a skewed picture, particularly if Egypt happened to be more (or less) inclined to heterodox traditions than, say, Judea or other parts of the Mediterranean. Nevertheless, the findings are relevant indicators of some degree of early readership of both canonical and non-canonical Gospels (Tables 12.5 and 12.6). If one limits the window to the second century, there are six to fourteen papyri of the Gospels, compared with two to five of non-canonical "Gospels" (depending on dating) (Hill 2013). While the attested manuscript findings for both broader and narrower timeframes skew in favor of Matthew, Mark, Luke, and John, it is nevertheless true that non-canonical texts were in circulation.

Turning lastly to patristic sources, I will summarize the earliest evidence of church fathers directly referring to these writings by name or using wording that appears to derive from them at a literary level (not just via oral tradition, though some examples are debated). The lists are not exhaustive but suffice to establish the point (Tables 12.7 and 12.8).

The evidence shows that early documentation of Jesus traditions included but was not solely limited to the four-fold Gospel, as non-canonical "Gospels" had some measure of circulation. Early usage, therefore, is relevant to but does not by itself predetermine the canon question.

Table 12.5 Early Greek papyri of the canonical Gospels (2–5 century)*

Gospel	Manuscript number (Gregory-Aland)	Total
Matthew	$\mathfrak{P}^1$ $\mathfrak{P}^{19}$ $\mathfrak{P}^{21}$ $\mathfrak{P}^{25}$ $\mathfrak{P}^{35}$ $\mathfrak{P}^{37}$ $\mathfrak{P}^{45}$ $\mathfrak{P}^{53}$ $\mathfrak{P}^{62}$ $\mathfrak{P}^{64+67}$ $\mathfrak{P}^{70}$ $\mathfrak{P}^{71}$ $\mathfrak{P}^{77}$ $\mathfrak{P}^{86}$ $\mathfrak{P}^{101}$ $\mathfrak{P}^{102}$ $\mathfrak{P}^{103}$ $\mathfrak{P}^{104}$ $\mathfrak{P}^{105}$ $\mathfrak{P}^{110}$	20
Mark	$\mathfrak{P}^{45}$ $\mathfrak{P}^{88}$ $\mathfrak{P}^{137}$	3
Luke	$\mathfrak{P}^4$ $\mathfrak{P}^7$ $\mathfrak{P}^{45}$ $\mathfrak{P}^{69}$ $\mathfrak{P}^{75}$ $\mathfrak{P}^{82}$ $\mathfrak{P}^{111}$	7
John	$\mathfrak{P}^5$ $\mathfrak{P}^6$ $\mathfrak{P}^{22}$ $\mathfrak{P}^{28}$ $\mathfrak{P}^{39}$ $\mathfrak{P}^{45}$ $\mathfrak{P}^{52}$ $\mathfrak{P}^{66}$ $\mathfrak{P}^{75}$ $\mathfrak{P}^{80}$ $\mathfrak{P}^{90}$ $\mathfrak{P}^{93}$ $\mathfrak{P}^{95}$ $\mathfrak{P}^{106}$ $\mathfrak{P}^{107}$ $\mathfrak{P}^{108}$ $\mathfrak{P}^{109}$ $\mathfrak{P}^{119}$ $\mathfrak{P}^{120}$ $\mathfrak{P}^{121}$ $\mathfrak{P}^{122}$ $\mathfrak{P}^{134}$	22

* Compiled using the *Kurzgefasste Liste* (Institut für neutestamentliche Textforschung).

Table 12.6 Early manuscripts of select non-canonical "Gospels" (2–5 century)

"Gospel"	Manuscripts	Total
Infancy Gospel of Thomas	None (all are later, multiple languages)	0
Protevangelium of James	Greek (P. Bod. 5)	1
Gospel of Thomas	Greek (P. Oxy. 1; 654; 655); Coptic (Nag Hammadi 2)	4
Gospel of Peter	None (earliest is from Akhmim, 8/9 century)	0
Gospel of Judas	Coptic (Codex Tchacos 3)	1
Gospel of Mary	Greek (P. Oxy. 3525; P. Ryl. 463); Coptic (BG 8502)	3
Apocryphon of John	Coptic (BG 8502; Nag Hammadi 2, 3, 4)	4
Gospel of Philip	Coptic (Nag Hammadi 2)	1
Gospel of Truth	Coptic (Nag Hammadi 1, 12)	2
"Gospel" fragments	P. Egerton 2; P. Oxy. 840; 1224; 4009; 5072; P. Vienna G. 2325	6

Table 12.7 Early references to canonical Gospels

Writer	Approx. date	Source	Reference to...
Unknown	100s–130s	*Barn.* 4.14	Matt. 22:14
		Did. 8.2–3	Matt 5:6–13
Unknown	140s	*Ep. Apost.*	Matthew & John (multiple)*
Polycarp	140s	*Phil.* 2.3	Luke 6:20
Justin Martyr	150s	*Dial.* 103.8–9	Luke 22:43–44
		Dial. 106.3	Mark 3:17
Athenagoras	170s	*Leg.* 11	Matt. 5:44–45 or Luke 6:27–28
		Leg. 32	Matt. 5:28
		Leg. 33	Mark 10:12
Theophilus	180s	*Autol.* 2.13	Luke 18:27
		Autol. 2.22	John 1:1
		Autol. 3.13–14	Matt. 5:28, 32, 44, 46; 6:3
Clement of Alexandria	190s	*Quis. div.* 1.5	Mark 10:17–31
		Stromata	All four Gospels (multiple)

* See Hannah 2008 for extensive discussion.

Table 12.8 Early references to non-canonical "Gospels"

Writer	Approx. date	Source	Reference to...
Unknown	140s	*Ep. Apost.* 4	*Infancy Gospel of Thomas*
Irenaeus	180s	*Haer.* 1.20.1	*Infancy Gospel of Thomas*
		Haer. 1.31.1	*Gospel of Judas* (possibly)*
		Haer. 3.11.9	*Gospel of Truth*
Clement of Alexandria	190s	*Strom.* 2.9	*Gospel of the Hebrews*
		Strom. 3.63; 3.93	*Gospel of the Egyptians*
		Strom. 7.16	*Protevangelium of James*
Serapion	190s	Eusebius, *Hist. eccl.* 6.12	*Gospel of Peter*
Tertullian	200s	*Adv. Marc.* 4.4–7	*Gospel of Marcion*
Hippolytus	210s	*Haer.* 5.2	*Gospel of Thomas*
		Haer. 5.2	*Gospel of the Egyptians*
Origen	230s–240s	*Hom. Luke* 1.2	*Gospel of Thomas*
		Hom. Luke 1.2	*Gospel of the Egyptians*
		Comm. Matt. 10.17	*Protevangelium of James*
		Comm. Matt. 10.17	*Gospel of Peter*

* It is not yet settled that this is the same as the Coptic *Gospel of Judas*.

Narrative formation

Apostolic Christianity placed great weight on an emplotted understanding of Jesus' life. The simplest formulation is found in the tradition "received" and passed along by Paul in 1 Cor. 15:3–7: Jesus died for sins, was buried, rose again, and appeared to many (cf. 1 Tim. 3:16). A more extensive plotline is attributed to Peter in Acts 10:36–41: baptism by John, Galilean ministry of healing/teaching, Judean ministry, crucifixion in Jerusalem, resurrection on the third day, post-resurrection appearances. The Pauline corpus shows familiarity with additional narrative details of Jesus' life: birth to a woman (Gal. 4:4), descent from Abraham and David (Rom. 1:3; Gal. 3:16), brothers (Gal. 1:19), temptation (Heb. 2:18), betrayal (1 Cor. 11:23a), Last Supper (1 Cor. 11:23b–25), trial before Pilate (1 Tim. 6:13), crucifixion (Phil. 2:8), and ascension (Rom. 8:34). Enormous value was placed on the narrative of Jesus' life within the apostolic circle (cf. John 20:30).

When we turn to the four-fold Gospel, we see each of these plot elements reflected. All four Gospels begin in different ways, but they share the same basic storyline for the ending of Jesus' life. They also have numerous touchpoints along the way: the Synoptic Gospels are not only substantially similar to each other but overlap with John at various points, such as the ministry of John the Baptist, the feeding of the 5,000, Jesus walking on water, the role of Mary and Martha, and the triumphal entry. In short, the major events of Jesus' life seemed to form an implicit rule of faith that shaped the four-fold narrative and gave it tremendous unity—which, of course, was never imposed from outside.

The situation is different for non-canonical "Gospels." Among the few that have a narrative (rather than a string of sayings/dialogues), their narratives do not generally overlap with each other. Some fill in gaps before the childhood of Jesus or after the resurrection—which may imply that the in-between details of Jesus' ministry itself were already seen as adequately attested (Hill 2013). Paul's letters and other non-Gospel NT writings do not mention narrative details of Jesus' life that are *only* covered in non-canonical sources. Even when church fathers signal familiarity with these "Gospels," they show little interest in the added details they have to offer. Rather, they tend explicitly to reject them.

In short, there appears to be a kind of centripetal force among the four Gospels that, despite their known differences in details, converge on a vastly similar narrative form shaped by the early Christian preaching of Jesus' life and deeds. By contrast there appears to be a centrifugal force that gives extra-biblical "Gospels" large-scale diversity, not unity.

Literary connections

Moving from narrative shape to literary formation, one of the most well-documented results of source and redaction criticism is that one or more evangelist(s) made direct use of the written work of his predecessors at some level. Any given hypothesis of literary interdependence (e.g., Two Source, Neo-Griesbach, Augustinian, Farrer, etc.) points in the same basic direction in terms of canonical development: use of one Gospel by another implies some level of authoritative sanctioning.

Consider one potential scenario. The prevailing view is that both Matthew and Luke make use of Mark, to such a degree that at the pericope level Mark has very little content that is not accounted for somewhere in the other two. Both seem to be augmenting the basic Markan narrative. Though it could be argued that the later evangelists sought to replace Mark, they are still treating it as accurate and normative—and the reality is that Mark survived as a standalone Gospel regardless. The same cannot be said for the hypothesized other source shared by Matthew and Luke, known as "Q," which has not survived independently.

The foundations of the "Q" hypothesis have been increasingly challenged in recent years, as the possibilities that Luke used Matthew (Goodacre 2002; Watson 2013) or Matthew used Luke (MacEwan 2015) have received renewed attention. Either way a later evangelist would be adopting not only one but two prior Gospels.

Lastly, it is possible that the author of John interacted with at least one Synoptic Gospel. Internally there are plausible points of contact with Mark (Bauckham 1998b), Luke (especially in the passion; Matson 2001, who proposes Luke's use of John but the arguments are reversible), and even Matthew (Barker 2015) (see further Frey 2013). Externally, Clement of Alexandria was the first to suggest that John was produced in direct consultation with the prior three (Eusebius, *Hist. eccl.* 3.24.11–12).

Stepping back, the lines of evidence (even if drawn differently) suggest a kind of early momentum even among the evangelists, as the use of one Gospel by a successor, and then the use of both by a third, and then the use of all three by a fourth evangelist generated a four-fold shape of the burgeoning Gospel collection (see Schröter 2013; 2018).

Extra-biblical "Gospels" fit into this picture in two ways. First, some hypothesize that the canonical Gospels make use of earlier forms of writings now considered apocryphal: i.e. John's use of *P. Egerton* 2; Luke's use of an earlier form of Marcion's "Gospel" or a sayings collection that later coalesced as the *Gospel of Thomas* (e.g., Klinghart 2008; Watson 2013). Such hypotheses remain disputed, and the overwhelming majority of scholars draw the direction of influence the other way, whereby non-canonical "Gospels" stand downstream, not upstream, of the four-fold Gospel, explicitly drawing upon their wording and/or concepts (see numerous examples in Watson and Parkhouse 2018; also Gathercole 2012; Goodacre 2002; Zelyck 2019). Second, there is sparse evidence that non-canonical "Gospels" drew on each other as sources; rather, textual parallels are mediated through the four-fold Gospels. There is no real sense that they gravitated toward one another literarily.

In sum, the literary interconnections among the four-fold Gospel—combined with the literary usage of them *by* non-canonical "Gospels" but lack of such activity *among* the same—seem to imply some kind of mutual privileging of the four from the start.

Scribal assimilation

From the earliest recoverable stages of the transmission of the text of the Gospels, scribes sometimes knowingly or unknowingly imported wording from another Gospel into a given Gospel they were copying—a process called scribal assimilation (see Royse 2007; Pardee 2019). This tendency becomes common in late antiquity but is already happening earlier, as illustrated by a few examples from $\mathfrak{P}^{45}$ and $\mathfrak{P}^{75}$ (Table 12.9).

The presence of inter-Gospel assimilation suggests that early scribes read them together to such an extent that they could easily, even unknowingly, slip from one to another and back while copying. Conceptually the four were a kind of mutually-reinforcing repository of Jesus tradition. In fact, the most vivid example of this assimilating activity might be the disputed ending of Mark (16:9–20). Those who argue that it was a later addition often suggest that it resulted from a scribe's weaving various phrases from Matthew, Luke, and John together to give Mark a fuller ending (see, e.g., Kelhoffer 2000).

Table 12.9 Examples of scribal assimilation

Verse	Papyrus	Apparent assimilation
Matt. 20:31	𝔓⁴⁵	Insert *pollō* from Mark 10:48 and Luke 18:39
Luke 3:22	𝔓⁷⁵	Omit "the" before "Holy" in agreement with Matt. 3:16
Luke 11:12	𝔓⁴⁵	Replace "egg" with "bread" from Matt. 7:9
Luke 12:24	𝔓⁴⁵	Insert "birds of the air and" from Matt. 6:26 before "the ravens"
John 1:17	𝔓⁷⁵	Replace *axios* with *hikanos* from Matt. 3:11, Mark 1:7, and Luke 3:16
John 6:5	𝔓⁷⁵	Replace "we buy" with "they buy" from Matt. 14:15 and Mark 6:36

Importantly, such scribal assimilation does not extend to the extra-biblical "Gospels." It is true that certain scribes, as they copied a Gospel, sometimes inserted sayings of Jesus that are of unknown origin (e.g., Codex Bezae at Mark 9:49; Luke 6:4). Sayings of Jesus doubtless circulated outside the bounds of the canonical Gospels (Acts 20:35). However, it is significant that, so far as the manuscript record reveals, no scribe inserted wording from *known* non-canonical "Gospels" into a Gospel manuscript. The impulse toward assimilation appears confined to the four-fold Gospel collection. Considering how early Christianity certainly knew about and had access to non-canonical "Gospel" writings (covered above), it is notable that scribes resisted the temptation to assimilate material from them even where germane (e.g., in the Lukan childhood narrative).

Cross-Gospel assimilation among early scribes has received comparatively little attention in the study of canon formation (e.g., one sentence in Hill 2019), but the pattern contributes to a bigger picture of early Christian four-Gospel consciousness.

Authorial ascription and titles

It is well-known that the canonical Gospels are *formally* anonymous, in that their texts do not directly identify any names unlike, say, Rom. 1:1 and Rev. 1:1. Traditionally this fact has been used to argue that the Gospels were *actually* anonymous: that is, no one knew or cared about authorial ascription (perhaps even the evangelists themselves) until a much later period when the church imposed apostolic criteria in selecting the orthodox Gospels (see summary in Gathercole 2018). However, the question has been reopened in recent years, with several lines of evidence suggesting that the ascription of named authors to the four Gospels goes back much earlier than typically assumed.

(i) *Papyri and other early NT translations* (recently catalogued in Gathercole 2013) show early and widespread evidence for formal Gospel titles, typically in the form *euangelion kata matthiaon* etc. (or the simpler form *kata matthiaon*). These ascriptions can occur in the vertical margin before or after the actual Gospel text, in running headers, in the scribal colophon, or on a cover page (flyleaf). In terms of papyri, one finds "Matthew" in 𝔓⁴ (2nd/3rd century) and 𝔓⁶² (early 4th), "Luke" in 𝔓⁷⁵ (early 3rd), and "John" in 𝔓⁶⁶ (2nd/3rd) and 𝔓⁷⁵ (early 3rd); and "Mark" is not (yet) attested, largely due to its fewer surviving papyri. Thereafter, all four have named titles across the majuscule and minuscule traditions. And the earliest witnesses for every major version (Old Latin, Coptic, Syriac) contain the traditional attributions. Thus, not only do some of the papyri place the use of Gospel titles in the second century, but the cumulative evidence suggests that the practice must have been well-established and widespread in that period.

(ii) *Patristic references* to named authors of the four Gospels (not just the content of the Gospels, see "Early circulation and readership" above) do not simply emerge at the end of the second century (e.g., Irenaeus) but go back earlier. The earliest is likely Papias (early 100s), who is reported to have ascribed Gospels to "Mark" and "Matthew" (Eusebius, *Hist. eccl.* 3.39.15–16) and possibly "John" (frag. 19, Holmes 2007). Claudius Apollinarius (170s) makes reference to "Gospels" and specifically names "Matthew" (*Peri Pascha*). Hegesippus (170s) reportedly refers to an evangelist named "John" (Eusebius, *Hist. eccl.* 3.17.1–3.18.1). Theophilus (180s) ascribes a Gospel to "John" (*Autol.* 2.22). The Muratorian Fragment (170s–190s, possibly later) ascribes a third Gospel to "Luke" and a fourth to "John"; presumably "Matthew" and "Mark" were named earlier, but that part of the fragment has not survived. And Clement of Alexandria (190s) refers to the names of all four Gospel authors ("Matthew," *Strom.* 1.21.147; "Mark," *Quis. div.* 5.1; "Luke," *Paed.* 2.1.15; "John," *Protr.* 4.59.3). Among the church fathers the association of written Gospels with the traditional authors goes back very early. Importantly, the church fathers never dispute the Gospels based on indecision about the authors' identities (versus, say, Hebrews).

(iii) *Circulation of multiple Gospels* may imply yet earlier authorial associations, even if formal titles come later. It is likely that the Gospels were not limited merely to local communities but had broader readership in mind (Bauckham 1998a). As early as 125 CE (Aristides, *Apol.* 15–16), multiple Christian books were in circulation. And Luke 1:1 implies multiple Gospel-like narratives already in play. Thus, it stands to reason that as soon as multiple Gospels were in circulation beyond their authors' immediate vicinities, it was necessary to distinguish them at least with informal authorial ascriptions that would travel orally with the Gospels, later becoming formalized in the manuscripts themselves (Hengel 2000: 48–56). Moreover, it seems possible that when the authors of Matthew or Luke received a copy of Mark ("Literary connections", above), they would have raised questions about the trustworthiness of the author before using it (Gathercole 2018). While this line of argument cannot be proven decisively, it explains why and how the authorial associations became solidified already at the start of the second century.

From a canon perspective, these early roots of Gospel titles point to an inherent recognition that there were *multiple* Gospels in use that required differentiation. The longer form of the title itself is intriguing: "Gospel according to X" suggests there is a singular "Gospel" of Jesus but from multiple perspectives (*kata*). The four belong together as one *thing*. The authorial ascriptions, then, may be another indicator of a burgeoning recognition of the four-fold Gospel (though see Petersen 2006).

The situation is somewhat different on the non-canonical side. Though names of apostles (Thomas, Philip, etc.) are attached to several of them—perhaps imitating the convention that had already evolved for the canonical four (Bauckham 2019)—only two adopt the "Gospel according to" formula (Table 12.10). There is little sense of cohesiveness among these titles. Moreover, it is worth pointing out that "apocryphal" ("hidden") is not a pejorative later imposed upon non-canonical documents to

Table 12.10 Titles of non-canonical "Gospels"

"Gospel"	Title in the text or paratext of extant manuscripts
Infancy Gospel of Thomas	"[The stories of Thomas the Israelite] concerning the childhood deeds of the Lord" (manuscripts vary)
Protevangelium of James	"The birth of Mary—the revelation of James" (*P. Bod.* 5)
Gospel of Thomas	First lines: "The hidden sayings that the living Jesus spoke and Didymus Judas Thomas wrote down" (Coptic)
	Postscript: "Gospel according to Thomas" (Coptic)
Gospel of Peter	Not extant
Gospel of Judas	"The hidden word of revelation Jesus spoke with Judas Iscariot"
Gospel of Mary	Not extant
Apocryphon of John	First lines: "The teaching of the Savior, and the revelation of the mysteries and the things hidden in silence, things he taught his disciple John"
	Postscript: "Apocryphon of John"
Gospel of Philip	Postscript: "Gospel according to Philip"

undermine them but was used by at least three authors themselves (*Gospel of Thomas, Gospel of Judas,* and *Apocryphon of John*). Such self-awareness may suggest that they stood distinct from and supplemented a nucleus of normative, non-"hidden" Gospels already circulating in the church (Hill 2013).

Navigation of plurality

The way the early church navigated the tension of a plurality of Gospel writings is also significant for understanding incipient canonical awareness. Two responses are instructive.

Harmonizing

Some church fathers attempted to create a harmony of the Gospels that would yield one comprehensive, linear narrative out of pieces drawn from the singular Gospels. Jerome mentions that Theophilus of Antioch (180s) compiled such a harmony (*Epist.* 121.6; *Vir. ill.* 25), but nothing of it survives. The *Gospel of the Ebionites* may very well have been a partial harmony of the Synoptics (Gregory 2005, 2017). Justin Martyr's tendency to conflate Gospel quotations may suggest he was using an early, partial harmony (see arguments for and against in Verheyden 2012).

But of most importance is the work of Justin's student Tatian: the so-called *Diatessaron* (160s–170s). Tatian's harmony survives chiefly in a Greek fragment from Dura-Europos, the Syriac commentaries of Ephrem and Aphrahat, a Latin translation by Victor of Capua (Codex Fuldensis), and various Arabic recensions. The traditional name "through four" (*dia + tessarōn*) was first recorded by Eusebius (*Hist. eccl.* 4.29.6) and reflects Tatian's efforts at producing a single work that draws extensively from all four Gospels, even Mark. Though he likely knew and may have even used non-canonical sources at the margins, the preponderance of evidence shows Matthew, Mark, Luke, and John to be his near-exclusive sources, though tracing his editorial work back to the Greek is challenging (Baarda 2012).

That said, "*Diatessaron*" was not its only designation. Victor refers to the work as *Diapente* ("through five"), though he explicitly emphasizes Tatian's *four* sources. The Syriac translator of Eusebius translates *diatessarōn* as "Of the Connected" (*d-mechallethe*), while the Old Syriac Gospels refer to it as "Gospel of the Separated" (*ewangelyon d-mepharreshe*). Ephrem and Aphrahat—and the broader Syrian church, to some degree—treat Tatian's final product simply as "the Gospel," not as a harmony. On top of this, Tatian's procedure of drawing from prior Gospels has analogies with the redactional work of, say, Matthew and/or Luke. Such considerations lead some scholars to argue that Tatian's production was not really a harmony but a "Gospel"-writing in its own right, circulating alongside the others in the early stream until it was relegated to "harmony" status due to Tatian's suspected heterodoxy (Crawford 2016; Watson 2016b). Whatever the case, it is clear Tatian privileged the four-fold Gospel in his editorial work, and even if he were self-consciously creating a competitor, that objective itself implicitly recognizes that the church was already, by the mid- to late-100s, using four Gospels (Hill 2019).

Importantly, no such harmonizing is attested for the non-canonical "Gospels." It would be nearly impossible to accomplish anyhow.

Comparative mapping

The major tradeoff of a Gospel harmony is the sacrifice of the integrity of each, as they are broken up and reassembled into a new singularity. An alternative approach to navigating Gospel plurality is modeled first by Ammonius and then Eusebius, which focuses on comparison instead of consolidation.

Early in the third century, Ammonius of Alexandria purportedly created a way of lining up the contents of the four Gospels known today as the "Ammonian Sections" (see Crawford 2014). Manuscripts no longer remain but his work can be partly reconstructed through Eusebius, who described its methodology and made use of it as a starting point for his own work (*Ep. ad Carp.*). Ammonius started with Matthew and lined up parallel passages from Mark, Luke, and John in columns to the right. Some argue that Ammonius left columns blank for unique Matthean material, and then included non-Matthean material from the other three as a kind of appendix—there is no clear evidence either way. The result was a helpful way of navigating some Gospel parallels while retaining Matthew's sequence as the backbone. However, Mark, Luke, and John were rent asunder. A better solution was needed.

In the fourth century, Eusebius of Caesarea built on Ammonius's work and developed what is known as the "Eusebian Canons" (or "Canon Tables"). It was apparently the first literary cross-referencing system of any kind, and it is a standout example of the use of tables to organize data in antiquity (see Coogan 2017; Crawford 2019). The Canons consist of two main features. Eusebius first divided the text of each Gospel into comparable segments and assigned sequential numbers: 1–355 for Matthew, 1–235 for Mark, 1–343 for Luke, and 1–232 for John. He then devised ten tables that reflect the various possibilities for tracking the same episodes across sources:

- Canon I   Material found in all four Gospels
- Canons II–IV   Material found in three Gospels (e.g., Matthew, Mark, and Luke)
- Canons V–IX   Material found in two Gospels (e.g., Matthew and Luke)
- Canon X   Material found in only one Gospel.

For example, the first entry in Canon I, dealing with Isaiah's prophecy of John the Baptist, lines up Matt. 3:3 (#8), Mark 1:3 (#2), Luke 3:3–6 (#7), and John 1:23 (#10).

Importantly, Eusebius's system was paratextual: the canon tables appeared at the beginning of a Gospel codex, and the indexing numbers were placed at the margin of each section. Each Gospel's text was thereby retained, unlike with Tatian or Ammonius. But the system gave readers the tools needed to navigate the immensely complex data and discern the harmony of the Gospels without forcing them into a singular harmonization. The tradeoff was that Eusebius did not offer a comprehensive, linear chronology.

Canons I–IX in particular reinforced how the Gospels correlate with each other in various ways as wholes. Moreover, the system only works if all four Gospels are present (e.g., in a codex) and intact—otherwise the coding system falls apart. Though Eusebius was aware of non-canonical "Gospels," he used none of them in his apparatus—nor is there any similar cross-referencing tool for said writings. The Eusebian Canons, then, reified the interconnectedness of the Gospels that was already developing, drawing us to read the Gospels *together* while respecting their individuality.

Though harmonization and comparative mapping were divergent means of navigating plurality that involved various tradeoffs, the underlying impulse of both further illumines the unique four-foldness of the Gospels in early Christianity.

Materiality

Having examined scribal handling of the wording of the Gospels (see "Scribal assimilation" above), a few broader manuscript features of the Gospels are also relevant to this topic.

The use of abbreviated forms of key words like "Jesus" or "God" (*nomina sacra*) appear in Christian copies of both canonical and non-canonical texts but tend to be more frequent and consistent in the former. The adoption of certain handwriting styles, standardized page sizes and layout, and paragraph segmentation (*paragraphos, ekthesis*, etc.) is more common among canonical Gospel manuscripts and suggest they were often geared towards public reading, not just private. This notion is corroborated by Justin Martyr's statement that, by the mid-100s, the Gospels were read as part of public worship (*1 Apol.* 67).

So-called *diplae sacra* (˃ markings) appear in the margins beginning in the fourth century as a means of identifying quotations of Scripture. While typically reserved for OT references, these same markings are used to mark *NT quotations* of Matthew in *P. Oxy.* 405 and Luke in $\mathfrak{P}^7$—perhaps implying some kind of scriptural awareness (Hill 2013).

The margins of Gospel manuscripts from late antiquity are often filled with scholia containing early commentary from fathers such as Chrysostom. The same is not true for the non-canonical "Gospels," for which there are essentially no extant commentaries until modern times.

Finally, the Gospels were with rare exception transmitted in codex/book form (rather than roll/scroll form) from the earliest period—and by the third century were even gathered into multi-Gospel codices (e.g., 𝔓⁴⁵; 𝔓⁷⁵; possibly 𝔓⁴⁺⁶⁶⁺⁶⁷). By contrast, non-canonical "Gospels" from the same period appear almost equally divided between roll and codex forms (Hill 2013). While the rationale for the Christian preference for the codex over the roll continues to be debated, the data suggest that Christians overwhelmingly preferred the codex for writings deemed scriptural (Hurtado 2006: 43–93; also Trobisch 2000). Moreover, no codex has been found that mixes canonical Gospels with non-canonical ones, and only rarely have they been found co-located together (namely, *P. Oxy.* 1 of *Thomas* and *P. Oxy.* 2 [=𝔓¹] of Matthew at Oxyrhynchus; see Epp 2004). The only substantive examples of grouping multiple non-canonical "Gospels" into a single codex is Nag Hammadi II (*Apocryphon of John, Gospel of Thomas, Gospel of Philip*; 3rd/4th century) and *P. Berolinensis* (BG) 8502 (*Gospel of Mary* and *Apocryphon of John*; 5th century).

While the inclusion of a set of writings in a codex does not imply "canon" in a straight-line fashion (i.e. Codex Alexandrinus includes *1 Clement*), the early use of the codex for the Gospels—alongside other manuscript/scribal features—reinforces the sense that the early church saw the four-fold Gospel as inherently special.

Conceptualization as a Four-Fold Gospel

Finally, there are various ways the church conceptualized and, eventually, codified a pluriform Gospel collection. Subtle indicators appear quite early, where some fathers not only refer to a singular "Gospel" (*Did.* 15.3–4; *2 Clem.* 8.5) but collectively call them "Gospels" (Justin, *1 Apol.* 66.3; Theophilus, *Autol.* 3.12; *Ep. Diogn.* 11.6), reflecting how they were known as a plurality. Hippolytus develops this instinct further with the phrase "four-fold Gospel" (*Comm. Dan.* 1.17), and Origen flatly states that "the Gospels are four" (*Comm. Jon.* 1.6). This pattern contrasts with some heretical movements that tended to prefer a single Gospel—i.e. Ebionites (Matthew), Marcionites (a form of Luke), Valentinians (John) (Irenaeus, *Haer.* 3.11.7)—which may indicate they were aware of and thereby consciously deviated from the orthodox norm of multiple Gospels.

Another interesting conception of the Gospels is how Justin Martyr refers to them also as plural "memoirs" (*apomnēmoneumata*) of the apostles (*1 Apol.* 33.5; 66.3; 67.3; *Dial.* 100.4; 101.3; 102.5; 103.6, 8; 104.1; 105.1.5–6; 106.1.3–4; 107.1). Not only is this terminology relevant for understanding *what* the Gospels are, but it shows how Justin already in the second century thought of these writings as deriving from a plurality of apostles (or associates) and containing their diverse recollections of Jesus.

The most vivid conceptualization of a four-fold Gospel was pioneered by Irenaeus. Apparently the four-fold collection already existed, so he simply tried to justify *why* "the Gospels can neither be more nor fewer in number than four" by developing analogies with the four winds, the four covenants of God, and the four faces of the cherubim in Rev. 4:7 (echoing Ezek. 1:10) (*Haer.* 3.11.8). Just as the four cherubim uphold the glory of God that, in Ezekiel, appears in man-like form, so also the four evangelists uphold the glory of Christ. Pointing especially to the Gospel openings,

Table 12.11 The *Tetramorph* of Irenaeus

Creature	Gospel	Rationale
Lion	John	Conveys Jesus' glory and power
Calf/ox	Luke	Begins with Zechariah's priestly sacrifice in the temple
Man	Matthew	Begins with the genealogy of Jesus
Eagle	Mark	Begins with the prophetic spirit in quoting Isaiah

Irenaeus reasoned that just as "the creatures are four-fold" (*tetramorpha*), so also the "Gospel" (note: singular) is "four-fold" (*tetramorphon*), with the parallels shown in Table 12.11. These parallels would be tweaked by various church fathers, but the overall sense remains the same regardless of configuration: there is, per the *Tetramorph*, an inner-biblical logic for why *four* Gospels belong together as one.

A final indicator of the solidification of a four-fold Gospel is the development of canon listings that specify the NT books acknowledged within the church. While some lists exclude various writings (like Jude), *all* known lists include four and only four Gospels: i.e. the Muratorian Fragment; Origen (*Hom. Josh.* 7.1); Eusebius (*Hist. eccl.* 3.3.5); Cyril of Jerusalem (*Catech.* 4.36); the Mommsen Catalogue; Epiphanius (*Pan.* 76.22.6); the Apostolic Canons; the Gelasian Decree; and others (Gallagher and Meade 2017). No comparable canon list of apocryphal "Gospels" is attested apart from orthodox *rejections* of them. With the exception of Serapion's temporary confusion about whether the *Gospel of Peter* could be read at Rhossus (Eusebius, *Hist. eccl.* 6.12), no extra-biblical "Gospel"-writings were ever considered contenders, nor was the status of Matthew, Mark, Luke, or John ever in doubt, it seems. They were included in canon lists and discussions as a set, not individually.

Summary

The above survey of the development of the four-fold Gospel suggests two important conclusions. First, it is true that a variety of Gospel-related writings circulated in the early church, even in the second century before any canonical/non-canonical division crystallized. There was immense interest in setting forth the story of Jesus. Second, the cumulative evidence suggests that there was indeed an early privileging of the four Gospels in distinction from non-canonical peers at essentially every point—narrative shaping, literary connections, scribal behavior, titles, harmonization, manuscript/codex features, etc.

As early as Clement of Alexandria we read that the "four Gospels have been handed down" (*Strom.* 3.13.93); at the end of the relevant period (367 CE), Athanasius likewise describes the Gospels as "handed down and confirmed as divine" (*Ep. fest.* 39.4). Early Christians were not, it appears, awaiting formal ecclesial sanctioning of a four-fold Gospel collection. Momentum for a plural Gospel had developed long before. No one, it seems, *decided* to treat the four as special. They were simply "handed down" that way.

Implications of a Four-Fold Gospel

The centripetal gravitation of the early church towards a four-fold Gospel presents readers with intriguing challenges and prospects.

First, the plural unity of Matthew, Mark, Luke, and John might shape how one thinks of the genre of the Gospels and their literary production as a whole. The four focus on a *bios*-like, orderly presentation of the life of Jesus, with emphasis on his moral and eschatological teaching and his death/resurrection. Other "Gospels" often cover different stories altogether (e.g., birth of Mary in *Protevangelium of James*), lack any sort of coherent narrative or even sequencing (e.g., *Gospel of Philip*), or focus only on (largely esoteric) sayings of Jesus with little reference to the cross (e.g., *Gospel of Thomas*). Given the extensive genre similarities of Matthew, Mark, Luke, and John—and the lack of such family resemblance among the others—the notion that they were equal competitors in a stream of "Gospel"-writing becomes strained (Burridge 2019; similar assessment of Nag Hammadi "Gospels" in Robinson 2004). Rather, the emergence of the Gospel genre becomes yet another glue that binds the four together.

Second—and somewhat balancing out the prior point—the early circulation of additional "Gospel"-writings beyond the four presents an opportunity to study each writing within a broader process of reception. Though traditional scholarship tends to be siloed, there is much to be gained from comparing, say, Lukan parables with their comparanda in the *Gospel of Thomas*, or the Christology of *P. Egerton* 2 with that of John. Not only do the upstream canonical Gospels illumine downstream writings source- and redaction-critically, but the later "Gospels" also provide important points to compare/contrast the ways in which Jesus was interpreted by diverse Christian communities.

Third, the four-foldness of the Gospels *necessitates* differences (otherwise they would be identical) and, thus, requires readers to navigate certain well-known tensions (Watson 2016a: 77, 104). Did Jesus cleanse the temple at the beginning of his ministry (John), at the end of his ministry (Synoptics), or both? How might the genealogies of Matthew and Luke be reconciled (and should they be)? Is Jesus' lament over Jerusalem midway through his journey (Luke) or during his temple week (Matthew)? When did Jesus visit Capernaum? Do the Gospels differ on the day of Jesus' crucifixion? The list goes on. No such problems would arise if the church had simply embraced only one Gospel. Early Christians were aware of these tensions and developed different ways of handling them (Origen's historicity/theology distinction; Augustine's *Harmony*)—and the same issues face today's readers.

Finally, the four-fold Gospel invites us amid all the complexity to read the Gospels not only as individual works (vertically) but also in conversation with one another (horizontally) (Stanton 2004: 90). To do so is simply to follow the lead of Eusebius, whose tables offer a crash course in canonical reading (see Crawford 2014, 2018; Coogan 2017). For example, in Canon III (material shared by Matthew–Luke–John) he makes the intriguing decision to align the genealogies of Matt. 1:1–16 and Luke 3:23–38 with the *Logos* passages of John 1:1–5, 9–10, 14. None of them, of course, are identical pericopes. Yet he treats them as parallel ways of grasping the origins of Jesus, both in his humanity (Matthew/Luke) and divinity (John)—a fascinating christological move. As another example, Eusebius aligns Luke 22:32 (Jesus' pre-resurrection prediction that Peter will "return" after stumbling) with John 21:15–17 (Jesus' post-resurrection threefold restoration of Peter); both are unique to their Gospels but, per Eusebius, should be read in a mutually illuminating way.

A canonical reading of the four-fold Gospel, in short, attempts to balance two objectives. The distinctives of each Gospel's testimony to Jesus should be respected, so as to avoid forcibly imposing, say, Matthew on a reading of Mark. Yet, the meaning of each member of the collection cannot be fully understood apart from the whole. The living portrait of Jesus is by necessity a composite of four painters. Studying a story in Luke, such as the rejection at Nazareth, requires us to navigate its local Lukan context and trace out if, where, and how a similar account factors into other Gospels with potentially different literary contexts. While the single-Gospel commentary tradition remains a strong force in Gospels scholarship, more works are being undertaken that explore what it means to pursue a more comprehensive reading of the four-fold Gospel (e.g., Burridge 2007; Adams 2011; Watson 2016a; DelHousaye 2020).

Bibliography

Adams, Edward. (2011), *Parallel Lives of Jesus: Four Gospels—One Story*, London: SPCK.
Baarda, Tjitze. (2012), "Tatian's Diatessaron and the Greek Text of the Gospels," in Charles E. Hill and Michael J. Kruger (eds.), *The Early Text of the New Testament*, 336–49, Oxford: Oxford University Press.
Barker, James. (2015), *John's Use of Matthew*, Minneapolis: Fortress.
Bauckham, Richard, ed. (1998a), *The Gospels for All Christians: Rethinking the Gospel Audiences*, Grand Rapids: Eerdmans.
Bauckham, Richard. (1998b), "John for the Readers of Mark," in Richard Bauckham (ed.), *The Gospels for All Christians: Rethinking the Gospel Audiences*, 147–71, Grand Rapids: Eerdmans.
Bauckham, Richard. (2019), "Gospels before Normativization: A Critique of Francis Watson's *Gospel Writings*," in Catherine Sider Hamilton and Joel Willitts (eds.), *Writing the Gospels: A Dialogue with Francis Watson*, LNTS 606, 17–39, London: T&T Clark.
Bockmuehl, Markus. (2019), "Fourfold Gospel Writing," in Catherine Sider Hamilton and Joel Willitts (eds.), *Writing the Gospels: A Dialogue with Francis Watson*, LNTS 606, 40–60, London: T&T Clark.
Bokedal, Tomas. (2014), *The Formation and Significance of the Christian Biblical Canon: A Study in Text, Ritual and Interpretation*, London: T&T Clark.
Bruce, F. F. (1988), *The Canon of Scripture*, Downers Grove, IL: IVP Academic.
Burridge, Richard A. (2007), *Four Gospels, One Jesus? A Symbolic Reading*, rev edn, London: SPCK.
Burridge, Richard A. (2019), "Ancient Biography and the Development of the Canonical Collection," in Catherine Sider Hamilton and Joel Willitts (eds.), *Writing the Gospels: A Dialogue with Francis Watson*, LNTS 606, 63–80, London: T&T Clark.
Coogan, Jeremiah. (2017), "Mapping the Fourfold Gospel: Textual Geography in the Eusebian Apparatus," *JECS* 25: 337–57.
Crawford, Matthew R. (2014), "Ammonius of Alexandria, Eusebius of Caesarea and the Origins of Gospels Scholarship," *NTS* 61: 1–29.

Crawford, Matthew R. (2016), "The Diatessaron, Canonical or Non-Canonical? Rereading the Dura Fragment," *NTS* 62: 253–77.

Crawford, Matthew R. (2018), "Rejection at Nazareth in the *Gospels of Mark, Matthew, Luke*—and *Tatian*," in Francis Watson and Sarah Parkhouse (eds.), *Connecting Gospels: Beyond the Canonical/Non-Canonical Divide*, 97–124, Oxford: Oxford University Press.

Crawford, Matthew R. (2019), *The Eusebian Canon Tables: Ordering Textual Knowledge in Late Antiquity*, Oxford: Oxford University Press.

DelHousaye, John. (2020), *The Fourfold Gospel, Volume 1: A Formational Commentary on Matthew, Mark, Luke, and John: From the Beginning to the Baptist*, Eugene, OR: Pickwick.

Ehrman, Bart D., and Zlatko Pleše. (2011), *The Apocryphal Gospels: Texts and Translations*, New York: Oxford University Press.

Epp, Eldon Jay. (2004), "The Oxyrhynchus New Testament Papyri: 'Not without Honor except in Their Hometown'?" *JBL* 123: 5–55.

Frey, Jörg. (2013), "Das vierte Evangelium auf dem Hintergrund der ältern Evangelientradition: zum Problem: Johannes und die Synoptiker," in Juliane Schlegel (ed.), *Die Herrlichkeit des Gekreuzigten: Studien zu den Johanneischen Schriften I*, WUNT 307, Tübingen: Mohr Siebeck.

Gallagher, Edmon L., and John D. Meade. (2017), *The Biblical Canon Lists from Early Christianity: Texts and Analysis*, Oxford: Oxford University Press.

Gamble, Henry Y. (1985), *The New Testament Canon: Its Making and Meaning*, Philadelphia: Fortress.

Gamble, Henry Y. (2019), "The New Testament Canon: Recent Research and the Status Quaestionis," in Lee Martin McDonald and James A. Sanders (eds.), *The Canon Debate*, 267–94, Grand Rapids: Baker Academic.

Gathercole, Simon J. (2012), *The Composition of the Gospel of Thomas: Original Language and Influences*, SNTMS 151, Cambridge: Cambridge University Press.

Gathercole, Simon J. (2013), "The Titles of the Gospels in the Earliest New Testament Manuscripts," *ZNW* 104: 33–76.

Gathercole, Simon J. (2018), "The Alleged Anonymity of the Canonical Gospels," *JTS* 69: 447–76.

Goodacre, Mark. (2002), *The Case Against Q: Studies in Markan Priority and the Synoptic Problem*, New York: T&T Clark.

Goodacre, Mark. (2012), *Thomas and the Gospels: The Case for Thomas's Familiarity with the Synoptics*, Grand Rapids: Eerdmans.

Gregory, Andrew. (2005), "Prior or Posterior? The Gospel of the Ebionites and the Gospel of Luke," *NTS* 51: 344–60.

Gregory, Andrew. (2017), *The Gospel According to the Hebrews and the Gospel of the Ebionites*, Oxford: Oxford University Press.

Gregory, Andrew, and Christopher Tuckett. (2005), "Reflections on Method: What Constitutes the Use of the Writings That Later Formed the New Testament in the Apostolic Fathers?" in Andrew Gregory and Christopher Tuckett (eds), *The Reception of the New Testament in the Apostolic Fathers*, 61–82, Oxford: Oxford University Press.

Hannah, Darrell D. (2008), "The Four-Gospel 'Canon' in the *Epistula Apostolorum*," *JTS* 59: 598–633.

Hengel, Martin. (2000), *The Four Gospels and the One Gospel of Jesus Christ: An Investigation of the Collection and Origin of the Canonical Gospels*, Harrisburg, PA: Trinity.

Hill, Charles E. (2010), *Who Chose the Gospels? Probing the Great Gospel Conspiracy*, Oxford: Oxford University Press.

Hill, Charles E. (2013), "A Four-Gospel Canon in the Second Century? Artifact and Arti-Fiction," *EC* 4: 310–34.

Hill, Charles E. (2019), "Diatessaron, Diapente, Diapollon? Exploring the Nature and Extent of Extracanonical Influence in Tatian's Diatessaron," in Matthew R. Crawford and Nicholas J. Zola (eds.), *The Gospel of Tatian: Exploring the Nature and Text of the Diatessaron*, 25–53. Edinburgh: T&T Clark.

Holmes, Michael W. (2007), *The Apostolic Fathers: Greek Texts and English Translations*, 3rd edn, Grand Rapids: Baker Academic.

Hurtado, Larry W. (2006), *The Earliest Christian Artifacts: Manuscripts and Christian Origins*, Grand Rapids: Eerdmans.

Kelhoffer, James A. (2000), *Miracle and Mission: The Authentication of Missionaries and Their Message in the Longer Ending of Mark*, WUNT 2/112, Tübingen: Mohr Siebeck.

Klinghardt, Matthias. (2008), "The Marcionite Gospel and the Synoptic Problem: A New Suggestion," *NovT* 50: 1–27.

Koester, Helmut. (1994), "Written Gospels or Oral Tradition?" *JBL* 113: 293–7.

Kraus, Thomas, Michael J. Kruger, and Tobias Nicklas, eds. (2009), *Gospel Fragments*, Oxford Early Christian Gospels Texts, Oxford: Oxford University Press.

Kruger, Michael J. (2012), *Canon Revisited: Establishing the Origins and Authority of the New Testament Books*, Wheaton, IL: Crossway.

Kruger, Michael J. (2013), *Question of Canon: Challenging the Status Quo in the New Testament Debate*, Downers Grove, IL: Intervarsity.

MacEwan, Robert K. (2015), *Matthean Posteriority: An Exploration of Matthew's Use of Mark and Luke as a Solution to the Synoptic Problem*, LNTS 501, London: T&T Clark.

Matson, Mark. (2001), *In Dialogue with Another Gospel? The Influence of the Fourth Gospel on the Passion Narrative of the Gospel of Luke*, SBLDS 178, Atlanta: Society of Biblical Literature.

McDonald, Lee Martin. (2017), *The Formation of Biblical Canon*, 2 vols, London: Bloomsbury.

Metzger, Bruce M. (1997), *The Canon of the New Testament: Its Origin, Development, and Significance*, Oxford: Oxford University Press.

Pardee, Cambry. (2019), *Scribal Harmonization in the Synoptic Gospels*, NTTSD 60, Leiden: Brill.

Petersen, Silke. (2006), "Die Evangelienüberschriften und die Entstehung des Neuetestamentlichen Kanons," *ZNW* 97: 250–74.

Robinson, J. M., ed. (2002), *The Coptic Gnostic Library: A Complete Edition of the Nag Hammadi Codices*, 5 vols, Leiden: Brill.

Robinson, J. M. (2004), "The Nag Hammadi Gospels and the Fourfold Gospel," in Charles Horton (ed.), *The Earliest Gospels: The Origins and Transmission of the Earliest Christian Gospels—The Contribution of the Chester Beatty Gospel Codex P45*, JSNTSup 258, 69–87, London: T&T Clark.

Royse, James R. (2007), *Scribal Habits in Early New Testament Papyri*, NTTSD 1, Leiden: Brill.

Schröter, Jens. (2013), "Jesus and Canon: The Early Jesus Tradition in the Context of the Emergence of the New Testament Canon," in *From Jesus to the New Testament: Early Christian Theology and the Origin of the New Testament Canon*, trans. Wayne Coppins, 249–71, Waco, TX: Baylor University Press.

Schröter, Jens. (2018), "Jesus and Early Christian Identify Formation: Reflections on the Significance of the Jesus Figure in Early Christian Gospels," in Francis Watson and Sarah Parkhouse (eds.), *Connecting Gospels: Beyond the Canonical/Non-Canonical Divide*, 233–55, Oxford: Oxford University Press.

Stanton, Graham. (2004), *Jesus and Gospel*, Cambridge: Cambridge University Press.

Trobisch, David. (2000), *The First Edition of the New Testament*, Oxford: Oxford University Press.

Verheyden, Joseph. (2012), "Justin's Text of the Gospels: Another Look at the Citations in *1 Apol*. 15.1–8," in Charles E. Hill and Michael J. Kruger (eds.), *The Early Text of the New Testament*, 313–35, Oxford: Oxford University Press.

Watson, Francis (2013), *Gospel Writing: A Canonical Perspective*, Grand Rapids: Eerdmans.

Watson, Francis. (2016a), *The Fourfold Gospel: A Theological Reading of the New Testament Portraits of Jesus*, Grand Rapids: Baker Academic.

Watson, Francis. (2016b), "Towards a Redaction-Critical Reading of the Diatessaron," *EC* 7: 95–112.

Watson, Francis, and Sarah Parkhouse, eds. (2018), *Connecting Gospels: Beyond the Canonical/Non-Canonical Divide*, Oxford: Oxford University Press.

Zelyck, Lorne. (2019), *The Egerton Gospel (Egerton Papyrus 2 + Papyrus Köln VI 255): Introduction, Critical Edition, and Commentary*, TENTS 13, Leiden: Brill.

13

Corpus Apostolicum

Darian R. Lockett

It is clear that Acts and the Catholic Epistles (CE) were eventually associated as a canonical sub-collection. Evidence for this exists especially in the form of canon lists and manuscript remains. We will consider this evidence in what follows. First, however, we must consider what to call this NT collection unit. David Trobisch has argued, based upon the *Novum Testamentum Graece* (NA27) using the siglum "a" to refer to manuscripts containing Acts + CE, that such manuscripts were given the name "Praxapostolos." Yet the manuscripts designated as "a" in NA27 merely contain a portion of Acts and/or the CE and do not necessarily suggest a coherent collection unit (see Parker 2008: 284–85, who lists the contents of manuscripts to the ninth century). Thus, one should be cautious because, as we shall see below, the association between Acts and the CE before the fourth century (or seventh according to Grünstäudl 2021: 20) is difficult to establish.

In the Byzantine period there was a tradition of creating Praxapostoloi, but these manuscripts did not appear before this time. According to Gibson, these manuscripts (called "Praxapostolos") always contained Acts and the CE along with the Pauline corpus and would sometimes include appendices with lectionary materials (Gibson 2018: 10). It is in this Byzantine tradition where the first and most confident use of the term Praxapostolos occurs. In the subsequent tradition the term Apostolos is used to describe a lectionary codex or manuscript that contained readings (*anagnosmata* or *pericopae*) from the NT epistles used later especially in the Byzantine tradition. It seems that the Apostolos manuscripts are closely related to those of the Praxapostolos in that the Apostolos lectionary readings were derived from the Praxapostolos manuscripts (Gibson 2018: 10–15). This much is clear in the later Byzantine tradition.

The discussion of Acts and the CE is greatly complicated when Aland and Aland use the siglum "a" for manuscripts containing Acts and/or the CE and use the term Apostolos to describe them (1989: 92 n. 1). As noted above, Trobisch labels the same set of manuscripts as Praxapostolos which unnecessarily confuses the issue. Neither Praxapostolos nor Apostolos seems suitable as a description of the early canonical associate of Acts and the CE. Parker laments this noting, "The term Praxapostolos is sometimes used more carelessly to include Revelation as well ... or for Acts and the Catholic epistles alone (it would be helpful to have a term which unequivocally described these eight texts [Acts and the CE] together)" (Parker 2008: 283). Not wanting to confuse the early canonical association between Acts and the CE with the later Byzantine tradition and in the absence of any better terminology, this essay will use the label Corpus Apostolicum (see Niebuhr 2016 who hints at such a title) both to refer to the specific manuscripts containing Acts and the CE and more generally the tradition of associating Acts and the CE together as a sub-unit of the NT canon.

If not already apparent, the history and hermeneutical significance of the Corpus Apostolicum is a difficult story to tell—this is the case for four central reasons. First, one must untangle the issue of whether or not these two units (Acts and the CE) constitute one or two discrete sub-units within the NT canon. Second, the story of the Corpus Apostolicum is hard to tell because the development of the CE as a seven-letter collection within the NT canon is itself a fragmentary story on account of the paucity of early evidence. Third, the earliest and most important evidence for the Corpus Apostolicum comes exclusively from the manuscript tradition and early canon lists. To my knowledge there is no discussion of this collection unit in the early fathers. Finally, any conclusions regarding early NT canonical sub-collections must be established from a limited pool of fragmentary evidence, namely comments from early church leaders, canon lists, and manuscripts. This final challenge is one that faces any attempt to give an account of the early development of the NT canon and therefore necessarily complicates the description of the Corpus Apostolicum in particular.

In light of the first two difficulties, this chapter will first consider the formation of the CE as a NT sub-collection. Second, the essay will discuss the association between Acts and the CE. It will be important throughout both of these sections to bear in mind the other two challenges listed. The image that emerges of both a discrete CE collection and a Corpus Apostolicum will necessarily be composite, brought together by the cumulative evidence gathered from church fathers, canon lists, and manuscripts. The final section of the essay will offer some reflections on the function of the Corpus Apostolicum within the NT canon as a whole. The formation of the Catholic Epistle collection will be considered first before moving on to discuss its association with Acts.

Catholic Epistles as a collection[1]

Though perhaps the least recognized canonical sub-collection of the NT, there is a growing body of literature that argues the CE (James, 1–2 Peter, 1–3 John, and Jude) was a coherent letter collection which formed toward the latter stages of the development of the NT canon (see especially, Niebuhr, 2003, 2013; Schlosser, 2004; Nienhuis 2007; Norelli, 2011; Lockett 2017).

The term "Catholic Epistle"

The seven letters of James, 1–2 Peter, 1–3 John, and Jude are traditionally called the Catholic Epistles or the General Letters. The interchangeability of the terms "catholic"

---

[1] The following section is an abbreviated and reworked version of Lockett 2017, chapter 3, and Lockett 2018.

and "general" suggests that they were eventually collected together due to shared genre—namely, they belonged to the same sub-genre of letter addressed to a non-specific audience. Some ancient precedent for this understanding is found in Apollonius's (196/197) description of the Montanist Themiso, who dared "in imitation of the apostle [John] to compose a catholic epistle [καθολικήν...ἐπιστολήν]" (Eusebius *Hist. eccl.* 5.18.5). Though Clement of Alexandria (150–215) might have known that the term Catholic Epistle was used for the seven NT letters (Niebuhr 2013: 1087), he also referred to the letter sent by the elders in Acts 15:23-29 as "the catholic epistle of all apostles [ἐπιστολήν ... καθολικήν]" (*Strom.* 4.15.97). In addition, Eusebius reports that Dionysius of Alexandria (*ca.* 190–264) was "most useful to all in the catholic epistles [καθολικαῖς ... ἐπιστολαῖς] which he drew up for the churches," namely to Sparta, Athens, and Nikomedia among others (*His. eccl.* 4.23.1). Origen (*ca.* 185–254) seems to have had this understanding of at least 1 John and perhaps 1 Peter (for 1 John, *Comm. Jo.* 1.22.137; 2.23.149; and 1 Pet., *Comm. Jo.* 6.35.175; cf. Eusebius, *Hist. eccl.* 6.25.5). Later in the tradition, Leontius of Byzantium (first half of the sixth century) argues that these letters "are called catholic because they were written not to one single people like Paul's, but in general to all" (*De Sectis*, act 2.4).

However, the term "catholic epistle" was eventually used to refer to a discrete collection of letters within the NT canon. Harry Gamble argues that, "Although the description 'catholic' was sometimes used for individual letters in the second century ... we do not see this term applied to a group of letters until the fourth century, when Eusebius speaks of 'the seven [letters] called catholic' (*Hist. eccl.* 2.23.25)" (Gamble 2002: 287). Raymond Brown notes an alternative meaning of Catholic Epistle: in "the West another interpretation appears whereby 'universal, catholic,' refers not to the general character of the audience but to the general acceptance of these epistles." This can be

> seen in the designation *epistulae canonicae*, e.g., Junilius (PL 68, 19C) [and] may be interpreted to say that to the books that were called 'canonical' (I Peter, I John) may be added five more (James, II Peter, Jude, II and III John). Cassiodorus (*De institutione divinarum Litterarum* 8; PL 70, 1120B) understood 'canonical' as an epithet for all seven epistles.
>
> Brown 1982: 4

As we will see in the following survey, the label Catholic Epistles eventually came to be used of the seven NT letters James through Jude as a collection.

The Catholic Epistles in the early church

We know from Eusebius that Papias (c. 150) "used quotations from the first Epistle of John, and likewise also from that of Peter" (*Hist. eccl.* 3.39.15). Irenaeus (130–200) mentions the four-fold Gospel canon (*Adv. Haer.* 3.11.8) and Paul's letters and thus is aware of these sub-collections, yet he does not mention the CE. Irenaeus does clearly refer to 1 Peter (*Adv. Haer.* 4.9.2, see also 5.7.2; 4.16.5; 4.34.2), and 1 John by name (*Adv. Haer.* 3.16.3, 5–8). Furthermore, Irenaeus's use of 1 and 2 John suggests that the two letters were very closely associated. Quoting from 2 John 11, Irenaeus says the text is from John the disciple of the Lord (*Ad. Haer.* 1.16.3). He then places 2 John 7-8 in the midst of a quotation from 1 John (*Ad. Haer.* 3.16.5-8). Though it is possible that Irenaeus could have received 1 and 2 John as a single letter (Lieu 1986: 19; Nienhuis 2007: 35; Painter 2009: 243), this explanation seems unlikely (so Grünstäudl 2021: 14 n. 37).

In the West, Tertullian (160–223) knew and used 1 Peter, 1 John, and Jude (*Cult. Fem.* 1.3.1-3), directly quoting 1 Peter (*Scorp.* 12.2 and 14.3). He refers to James of Jerusalem and is careful to demonstrate the consistency between Paul and the Pillar apostles, yet he never refers directly to the letters of James, 2 Peter, or 2–3 John. The combined testimony of Irenaeus and Tertullian indicates that 1 Peter and 1 John were widely used in the West during the early third century. In addition, Tertullian accepts Jude, but indicates no awareness of 2 Peter, while Irenaeus uses 2 John but not Jude (Nienhuis 2007: 44).

Clement of Alexandria makes clear reference to 1 Peter (*Strom.* 3.18.110.1; 4.20.129.3; *Paed.* 3.11.53.3), 1–2 John (*Strom.* 3.4.32.2; 2.15.66.4), and Jude (*Stom.* 3.2.11.2; *Paed.* 3.8.44.3-45.1). However, there is significant debate over whether Clement knew of James (see Allison 2013: 15). According to Eusebius, Clement had written in his *Hypotyposeis* "concise explanations [outlines] of all the Canonical Scriptures, not passing over even the disputed writings [ἀντιλεγομένας], I mean the Epistle of Jude and the remaining Catholic Epistles ... [καθολικὰς ἐπιστολὰς]" (*Hist. eccl.* 6.14.1). This commentary is now only preserved in Latin (the *Adumbratioines in epistluas canonicas*). Much later Cassiodorus (*ca.* 485–ca. 585) offered a summary of Clement's commentary noting specifically his expositions *in epistula sancti Petri prima, sancti Ioannis prima et secunda et Iacobi* (a mistake for *Iudae*?). Eusebius claims that Clement commented on the CE, but was this the term Clement himself used for these texts? And, can we be sure which specific texts Clement commented upon and did they include James? Both Nienhuis (2007: 48–50) and Grünstäudl (2013: 273) argue that we cannot be confident that Clement commented on all seven of the NT letters (yet for a different view see Norelli 2011: 458–59, 484). Does this suggest that there was a CE collection singled out with other NT texts for commentary at the time of Clement? It is difficult to answer this and the other questions raised above with any degree of confidence.

With Origen we have the first patristic witness to cite all seven letters (though Nienhuis argues "it is doubtful he accepted [2 Pet. and 2–3 Jn] as authentic," 2007: 54). Specifically, he referred to both 1 Peter and 1 John (and possibly Jude) as a "catholic epistle" (1 Pet., *Sel. Ps.* 3; *Comm. Jo.* 6.175.9 and 1 John, *Comm. Jo.* 1.138, 2.149). However, Origen also refers to the Epistle of Barnabas as a "catholic epistle" (*Cels.* 1.63), thus it is unclear whether Origen refers to these letters as part of a Catholic Epistle collection, or if he was referring to their general audience. Nienhuis notes that because Origen used the term primarily of 1 John, this suggests he understood "catholic" as a reference to a general audience and thus a genre distinction (2007: 53). Eusebius records a passage from Origen's commentary on Matthew where he refers to 1 Pet. 5:13: "Peter acknowledged ... in the catholic epistle [ἐν τῇ καθολικῇ ἐπιστολῇ]," (*Hist. eccl.* 6.25.5). Furthermore, in his *Comm. Rom.* (preserved only in Latin), he refers to Jude as an *epistula catholic*. Whereas Origen does refer to both 1 Peter and 1 John as a "catholic epistle" in his writings that survive in Greek, it is hard to know whether or not the use of "catholic epistle" in those texts that survive in Latin translation and in Eusebius are evidence that Origen understood these seven letters as part of the CE collection or if those references might be later interpolation.

Origen is a key witness as Nienhuis observes: "Of greatest importance is the fact that Origen is the first witness to use the world 'catholic' in association with some of the proto-CE" (2007: 53). However, Nienhuis concludes, although in possession of all seven letters, "Origen shows no awareness of a discrete canonical collection called the CE" (2007: 63). If Origen operated within an earlier tradition that accepted the seven letters as a collection called the CE, he would not have needed to state explicitly that he received them this way. It is true that there is some later fluidity in the CE, especially in order; however, whether not Clement and Origen stand as witnesses for or against an early CE collection is notoriously hard to determine with confidence. Nienhuis might overstate the evidence against Origen's knowledge of a CE collection, the truth is we just do not know.

This situation changes with Eusebius (*ca.* 260–339) where we find what many consider the first reference to the "Catholic Epistles" considered a technical designation for a discrete collection (Neibuhr 2013: 1088; Norelli 2011: 510; Nienhuis 2007: 66). Following an elaborate record of the martyrdom of James, the Lord's brother, Eusebius notes:

> Such is the story of James, whose is said to be the first of the Epistles called Catholic [ὀνομαζομένων καθολικῶν ἐπιστολῶν]. It is to be observed that its authenticity is denied, since few of the ancients quote it, as is also the case with the Epistle called Jude's, which is itself one of the seven called Catholic; nevertheless we know that these letters have been used publicly with the rest in most churches.
> *Hist. eccl.* 2.23.24–25

Leaving to one side the comments regarding traditions of authenticity, upon which he does not elaborate, clearly Eusebius not only received a tradition of using these letters, "as in most churches," but that tradition also included referring to these seven letters starting with James and likely concluding with Jude with the label "Catholic Epistles." John Painter suggests the fact that Eusebius mentions James and Jude is significant: "James and Jude, the brothers of Jesus, form an inclusion around the collection," that is, the two brothers of Jesus "form ... the bookends of this collection." He continues: "To name the first and the last was to identify this collection. This might have been necessary, given that reference to a catholic epistle was used in a nonspecific way in earlier sources" (Painter 2009: 458 n. 11).

It will be helpful to note in passing the commentary tradition and what light it might shed on the situation. Following Clement's *Hypotyposeis* mentioned above, we find fragments of commentary on all the CE (except 2 Peter) in Pseudo-Didymus (Didymus the Blind, 313–398) in the form of catena and fragments on the letters from John Chrysostom and Cyril of Alexandria. In the fifth century, Euthalius of Alexandria (*ca.* 458) mentions the "the seven Catholic Epistles" in his prologues to the Pauline Epistles and the Apostolos (Niebuhr 2013: 1089; see also von Soden 1911: 668). The tradition of commenting on the CE together continues with Bede's *Commentary on the*

Seven Catholic Epistles (679), Walafrid Strabo's *Glossa Ordinaria* (*ca.* 842, partially dependent on Bede), the commentaries of Isho' Dad of Merv (*ca.* 850, in Syriac), and Pseudo-Oecumenius (tenth century, in Greek).

From the time of Eusebius, it became common to refer to these seven letters as a discrete sub-collection within the NT canon using the title of "Catholic Epistles." How much earlier than Eusebius these letters were considered a discrete collection is a question that remains unanswered. It is clear that Eusebius records the traditions which he received, and thus it stands to reason that the collection formed sometime before him.

The Catholic Epistles in the early canon lists

Karl-Wilhelm Niebuhr suggests that the Muratorian Fragment (perhaps second century; for debate over early and late dating of the Fragment see Hahneman 1992; 2002; Verheyden 2003) possibly refers to the CE (2013:1087), while Joseph Verheyden argues that the Fragment's information "regarding the Catholic Epistles is hopelessly confusing" (2003: 528). Lines 68–69 read: "the epistle of Jude and two of the above-mentioned [bearing the name of] John are used [counted] in the catholic [church/epistles]" (*epistola sane iude et superscrictio Iohannis duas in catholica habntur*, translation in Gallagher and Meade 2017: 18, material in brackets added). It is not clear what *in catholica* refers to—most suppose it refers to these letters being "used" in the "catholic church," however the reading "counted" in the "catholic epistles" is possible (see the reconstruction by Katz 1957: 273, rejected by Metzger 1987: 197 but accepted by Moule 1981: 266). At any rate, the Fragment only refers to Jude and two of the Johannine letters. Hahneman suggests that the "absence of 1 Peter (and James) is extraordinary, and most probably implies omissions in the Fragment. The letters found in the Fragment, namely 2 (and 3?) John and Jude, are elsewhere found only in larger collections of the catholic epistles" (Hahneman 1992: 181). Though there are many unknowns regarding the Fragment (including its date), Hahneman is likely correct to suggest that it has for some reason omitted reference to at least 1 Peter and 1 John and perhaps James as well.

Eusebius provides a kind of canon list. After mentioning the Gospels and Paul's letters, Eusebius writes:

> Following them the Epistle of John called the first, and in the same way should be recognized the Epistle of Peter. ... These belong to the Recognized Books [ἐν ὁμολογου]. Of the Disputed Books [ἀντιλεγομένων] which are nevertheless known to most are the Epistle called James, that of Jude, the second Epistle of Peter, and the so-called second and third Epistles of John which may be the work of the evangelist or of some other with the same name.
>
> *Hist. eccl.* 3.25.1–5

Reading this passage along with *Hist. eccl.* 2.23.24–25, it seems clear that Eusebius is aware of the CE collection. Nienhuis concludes that Eusebius "is the first witness to the existence of a seven-letter collection known as the Catholic Epistles, headed by James and including letters of Peter, John, and Jude" (2007: 66). Nienhuis is certainly correct that at least by the time of Eusebius the collection includes our seven NT texts and is called the CE; however, as Eusebius is commenting on tradition he received from earlier times, it is difficult to know how much earlier the collection formed.

From the time of Eusebius onward, the CE was comprised of all seven letters mostly in their traditional ordering: James, Peter, John and Jude (Parker 2008: 285–86; Norelli 2011: 508). Cyril of Jerusalem (*ca.* 350) lists "the seven Catholic Epistles of James, Peter, John, and Jude" (*Catech.* 4.36, translation in Gallagher and Meade 2017: 115). In canon 59 of the Synod of Laodicea (between 342 and 381, likely before 380, see Gallagher and Meade 2017: 129–30), they are listed after the four Gospels and Acts and before the Pauline letters. In 367, Athanasius lists the "Acts of the Apostles and seven letters, called catholic [ἐπιστολαὶ καθολικαὶ], by the apostles, namely: one by James; two by Peter; then three by John; and after these, one by Jude" (*Ep. fest.* 39.18, translation in Gallagher and Meade 2017: 123). Though without the label CE, the Apostolic Canons, a series of canons in book 8 of the Apostolic Constitutions, lists all seven letters yet in the order of James, 1–3 John, Jude, and 1–2 Peter. Gregory of Nazianzus (*ca.* 330–390) calls them "the seven catholic [ἐπιστολαὶ ἑπτὰ ... καθολικαὶ]" epistles (*Carmina Theologica*, 1.1.12). Similarly, Epiphanius (*ca.* 376) calls the letters "catholic epistles [καθολικαῖς ἐπιστολαῖς]" (*Panarion* 76.22.5). Though listing the seven in a different order, Amphilochius (*c.* 380) seems to be working within the same tradition which receives these letters as the CE: "Of the catholic epistles some say we must receive seven; others only three is it necessary to accept: the one of James, and one of Peter, and those of John, one. But some receive three [of John], and in addition to them the two of Peter and that of Jude, the seventh" (*Iambi ad Seleucum*, 310, translation in Gallagher and Meade 2017: 154). Finally, the Latin Mommsen Catalogue (or the Cheltenham List) omits James and Jude, while in the canon list *Breviarium Hipponsense* (canon list 36) the CE are listed in the order 1–2 Peter, 1–3 John, Jude, James. However, Jerome and Augustine included the CE in their traditional order.

All this suggests that the CE originated somewhere in the eastern church sometime during, but some argue more likely after, the time of Origen and before Eusebius writes in the early fourth century (Nienhuis and Wall 2013: 29). The eastern origin and especially the traditional order of James, Peter, John, and Jude is supported in the manuscript tradition.

The Catholic Epistles in the early manuscript tradition

It must be said at the outset that the manuscript history of the CE is extremely fragmentary. There is some evidence of association between the texts of the CE before the major fourth and fifth century codices.

Perhaps the earliest manuscript evidence of some association between letters that were eventually collected into the CE collections is P72. This third or early fourth century papyrus codex includes the complete text of Jude and 1–2 Peter along with several other ancient Christian texts. The eclectic nature of the texts included suggests that this was for private use (rather than for public reading). In an attempted reconstruction, Tommy Wasserman (2005) argues that 1–2 Peter and Jude were actually written by the same hand. Stan Porter notes that, "If this is true, it indicates that by as early as the third century, 1 Peter, 2 Peter, and Jude were considered a subcorpus and copied together, even if they were bound with other manuscripts for particular theological purposes" (2013: 123). In addition, David Horrell argues that it is "interesting to note … that the linking of 1–2 Peter with Jude [in P72] … [hints] as to the early stages in the clustering of 'catholic epistles'" (Horrell 2009: 512). In the end, it is difficult to conclude with confidence that such evidence suggests that 1–2 Peter and Jude were considered a sub-corpus; however, this evidence is suggestive.

The papyrus manuscript P100 contains Jas 3:13–14:4 and 4:9–5:1 and consists of a single page from a codex of "26 fragmentary lines of text on both the front and reverse sides. Pagination from both the front and reverse are preserved in the upper margin, and the pages are numbered sequentially ς and ζ (6–7). This would indicate a codex that began with James and that could have included other texts following James" (Blummell and Waymet 2015: 134). Porter suggests that these page numbers "indicate, that page 1 was the beginning of the Epistle of James. Since Hebrews probably was included with the Pauline Epistles, it is possible either that P100 was a manuscript of just the Epistle of James or that it was the first book in a collection of the Catholic (or General) Epistles" (Porter 2013: 123). James 1:25–27 is preserved in a nearly complete leaf from a parchment codex that has been dated to the fifth century (0173). Again, the pagination of the manuscript (17–18) suggests that this miniature codex began with the Epistle of James. It is possible that if these manuscripts did begin with James, they could have contained a collection of writings which may have included the CE.

The fragmentary parchment codex 0232 (P.Ant.12) contains a portion of 3 John 1–9 and Larry Hurtado speculated that it "may have originally contained a collection of writings ascribed to the apostle John, a 'Johannine Corpus'" (Hurtado 2006a: 39). This is partially based on the fact that the fragment contains page numbers (164, 165) that suggest the codex was large enough to contain several texts. However, based on his revised calculation, Kruger argues "this manuscript likely contained the book of Hebrews and a full collection of the Catholic Epistles" (Kruger 2012: 265).

Up to this point the evidence is scant, though perhaps suggestive. The situation improves with the major majuscule codices of the fourth and fifth century. Codex Vaticanus (B or 03; *ca.* 300–325) Sinaiticus (ℵ or 01; *ca.* 330–360) and Codex Alexandrinus (A or 02; *ca.* 400–440) all place the seven CE in the order of James, 1–2 Peter, 1–3 John, and Jude. What is even more suggestive is that all three codices connect Acts and the CE placing the unit either before (Vaticanus and Alexandrinus) or after (Sinaiticus) the Pauline corpus. In the following section we will consider the connection between Acts and the CE further, but what is of interest here is that when this larger collection unit moves around within the NT canon, the CE move as a unit. This seems to suggest not only that Acts + CE was a larger collection unit (again more on that below), but more that the seven CE were understood as a discrete collection.

Some have suggested that the sequence of the CE, at least James–Peter–John, is dependent upon Paul's account in Gal. 2:9: "when James and Cephas and John, who seemed to be pillars" (Lührmann 1981). Some manuscript evidence that might support this theory is found in the bilingual, Greek-Latin, codex Claromontanus (D or 06; sixth century). This codex preserves a table of contents in Latin between Philemon and

Hebrews which lists the seven CE in the order: 1–2 Peter, James, 1–3 John, and Jude.² This somewhat unusual ordering of the letters corresponds to the order of the "pillar apostles" in the *varia lectio* of Gal. 2:9 in the Greek part of the codex.³ In Paul's list of the "pillar apostles" we find Peter (rather than Cephas) mentioned followed by James and John.⁴ Not only is this further evidence of a somewhat discrete collection of CE, but it might further suggest their arrangement, at least in some segments of the tradition, was influenced by Gal. 2:9.

In the Syriac versions of the New Testament there are two trajectories. The Peshitta includes only James, 1 Peter, and 1 John, or the major CE, while the remaining four CE, the minor, are found in the Philoxenian and Harklean editions.

The manuscript evidence indicates that the CE eventually entered the NT canon as a collection possibly after circulating individually and as smaller groups. Harry Gamble notes:

> The history of the Catholic Epistles holds significance for larger conceptions of the history of the canon. Since they found inclusion in the canon not individually but precisely as a group, since that collection did not take shape until late in the third century at the earliest, and since that collection came to constitute, along with the Gospels and the Pauline Letters, one of the three major sub-units of the canon, it is very difficult to speak of a New Testament canon ... prior to the fourth century.
>
> Gamble 2002: 288

One might quibble with Gamble's dates as it is plausible that the Catholic Epistle collection took shape in the early third century, perhaps 225 or earlier if Clement is aware of the collection. Also, one might disagree with his assessment that we cannot speak of a New Testament canon before the fourth century. This largely depends on how one defines canon. Yet Gamble's observation that the CE came into the New Testament canon as a collection and that they constitute one of the three major sub-units of the New Testament canon is surely correct.

The association between Acts and the Catholic Epistles

As noted above, to my knowledge, there are no references to the specific collection unit of Acts + CE (Corpus Apostolicum) in the surviving patristic record. This means all the more that evidence of a larger collection unit containing Acts and the CE will come from the fragmentary evidence of the surviving canon lists and manuscripts. In what

---

² Greek/Latin diglot, with the Greek and Latin in stichometric lines on facing pages (the image can be viewed at: http://www.csntm.org/manuscript/View/GA_06 [CSNTM Image Id: 275955 and 275956]).
³ Image can be viewed at: http://www.csntm.org/manuscript/View/GA_06 (CSNTM Image Id: 275589).
⁴ The substitution of Πέτρος for Κηφᾶς along with moving Πέτρος in front of Ἰάκωβος is attested in D F G d f g Vg. *Syr.* [psh. harcl.] Tert. Hier. al. The papyrus manuscript P46 reads Πέτρος for Κηφᾶς but retains the order of James, Peter, John.

follows, rather than tracing the reception of the Book of Acts individually, focus will concentrate on the evidence of the connection between Acts and the CE.

The association between Acts and the CE in the early canon lists

There is clear evidence of the association of Acts and the CE in the later canon lists of the East: Cyril of Jerusalem, Athanasius, the Synod of Laodicea, and Epiphanius.

Cyril mentions: "the four Gospels.... Receive also the Acts of the Twelve Apostles; and in addition to these the seven Catholic Letters of James, Peter, John, and Jude; and as a seal upon them all, and the last work of the disciples, the fourteen Letters of Paul" (*Catech.* 4.36, translation Gallagher and Meade 2017: 115–16). Cyril's order reflects the same order of Vaticanus and Alexandrinus, and interestingly he notes Paul's fourteen letters constitute the "last work of the disciples." Nienhuis argues that Cyril's limitation of Acts to "the twelve Apostles" in fact "explicitly excludes the work of Paul" and suggests that this might emphasize the narrative flow of Acts which begins with the Jerusalem apostles and moves out from that geographic center (2007: 77–78).

Athanasius's Easter letter of 367 lists the "Acts of the Apostles and seven letters, called Catholic, by the apostles, namely one by James, two by Peter, then three by John, and after these, one by Jude" (*Ep. Fest.* 39.18, Gallagher and Meade 2017: 123). Once again, Acts and the CE are listed in succession and again there is an emphasis upon these being texts "by the apostles" which might be a way of emphasizing the Jerusalem apostles as they are portrayed in Acts and their letters contained in the CE.

The Synod of Laodicea lists: "four Gospels of Matthew, of Mark, of Luke, of John; General [Πράξεις καθολικαὶ] Acts of the Apostles and the seven general epistles [ἐπιστολαὶ καθολικαὶ ἑπτὰ] are thus: one of James, first and second Peter, first, second, and third John, one of Jude" then goes on to list the fourteen letters of Paul (Canon 59, Gallagher and Meade 2017: 133). It is interesting that the term καθολικαὶ is used to describe both Acts and the seven letters which suggests an association.

Finally, Epiphanius lists "the four holy gospels" then the fourteen epistles of Paul and then "the general epistles [καθολικαῖς ἐπιστολαῖς] of James, Peter, John, and Jude" but then notes "before these [and] with Acts of the Apostles in their times" (*Panarion* 76.22.5, Gallagher and Meade 2017: 169). Though Paul's letters are mentioned before Acts and the CE, it seems clear that Epiphanius understands both that Acts and the CE precede Paul in the canonical order and that they go "with" each other "in their times."

The canon lists here show a consistent preference, especially in the East, to link Acts with the CE, and furthermore, this unit most often follows the Gospels and precedes the Pauline Corpus (with Codex Sinaiticus being the one exception).

The association between Acts and the CE in the early manuscript tradition

Furthermore, one finds suggestions of the association between Acts and the CE in the manuscript tradition. Though Trobisch vigorously presents the manuscript support for the association between Acts and the CE, his data is somewhat misleading. According to Trobisch's chart outlining the distribution of collection units in the NT manuscripts, there are 655 manuscripts of the "Praxapostolos" (Trobisch's terminology, 2000: 26).

However, on the subsequent page he indicates that there are 622 manuscripts containing Acts and the CE (however, when adding all the instances of "a" in the chart he provides, these manuscripts total only 511). The most misleading element of Trobisch's discussion is the fact that these manuscripts merely contain portions of Acts and/or the CE, thus it is not clear that every one of these manuscripts is a witness for the association of Acts and the CE (see Parker 2008: 284–85, who lists the contents of all these manuscripts).[5]

Though Trobisch's presentation of the evidence is less than clear, there are hints within the manuscript tradition that suggest early association between Acts and the CE. Schröter notes that whereas several manuscripts associate Acts and the CE the "compilation of Gospels + Acts or Acts + Letters of Paul are not found" (with the exception of P45 and P 53). Therefore, he argues, "For this reason Acts and the Catholic Letters could also be united together into one group of writings by the editors of the *Novum Testamentum Graece*" (Schröter 2013: 289; however, note his dependence upon Aland's numbers which are similar to Trobisch's, 289 n. 75). Telling readers n. 75 is on pages 289 of Schröter. Adding to this, Parker notes that in the later manuscript tradition "Acts and the Catholic letters were generally copied together" either in copies of the entire NT, partial fragments, or in manuscripts that contain just Acts + CE (Parker 2008: 283).

Whereas their eventual association is clear, it is difficult to determine with confidence how early Acts and the CE were related in the manuscript tradition. It might be safest to say this association became more uniform starting from the seventh century. This is because the oldest copy of a manuscript containing *only* Acts and the CE dates to the seventh century (P74). It is possible such a manuscript existed before this time. The fifth century parchment 048 includes portions of Acts, the CE, and Paul; furthermore, in 0166 (the Heidelberg Fragment, fifth century) the verso has the end of Acts (28:30–31) and the recto contains a text from James (1:11). Parker notes that 0166 could have contained Acts and all of the CE but that its fragmentary state precludes confidence (2008: 285). Furthermore, 093 (sixth century) contains fragments from Acts and 1 Peter.

Despite these examples, Parker concludes (regarding P74) that it is in "the seventh century we have the first certain example of a manuscript containing Acts and the seven letters together" (2008: 285). Regarding the specific association of Acts and the CE in the manuscript evidence he argues:

> The evidence overall suggests a lack of fixed practice before the seventh century at the earliest. On the other hand, the order of the seven Catholic letters is very uniform, especially among Greek manuscripts. The stage at which the eight writings were first counted together is, so far as the manuscripts attest, the fourth century. The fact that both 01 and 03, the two great Bible codices, treat them as a unity (manifest by the fact that they disagree as to the order of the larger blocks) is our earliest example.
>
> Parker 2008: 285–86

---

[5] I am grateful to Wolfgang Grünstäudl for sharing his helpful insights regarding the manuscript evidence discussed here.

Though Grünstäudl challenges Parker's assessment that Sinaiticus and Vaticanus treat Acts + CE "as a unity" (Grünstäudl 2021: 21), this evidence at least demonstrates a clear association between Acts and the CE from the fourth century.

It seems plausible to argue that the association can be seen in the fourth and fifth century majuscule codices. The observation made by Parker to the effect that whereas the larger collection unit of Acts + CE (Corpus Apostolicum) appears in different locations within the NT canon in Sinaiticus and Vaticanus, yet when moved it does so precisely as a unit, is significant (this is not diminished even when acknowledging Grünstäudl's argument that in these codices Acts + CE should not be seen as "a firmly entrenched unity," 2021: 22).

Codex Alexandrinus contains a further clue to the association of Acts + CE. After the subscripted title, "Epistle of Jude," there follows a colophon: "The Acts of the Holy Apostles and Catholics [ΠΡΑΞΕΙΣ ΤΩΝ ΑΓΙΩΝ ΑΠΟΣΤΟΛΩΝ ΚΑΙ ΚΑΘΟΛΙΚΑΙ]."[6] Both πραξεις and καθολικαι appear in the nominative case which likely indicate that they refer to the Book of Acts and the "Catholics" (the CE as a group) respectively. This suggests that the entire colophon, or "*subscriptio*," intentionally "combines Acts and the General Letters to a single collection unit" (Trobisch 2000: 33; see also Childs 1984: 495 and Lockett 2017: 112–13).

There is a similarly intriguing colophon that draws together Acts and the CE found in the so-called Euthalian Apparatus (181 Gregory-Aland, eleventh century). The colophon placed at the end of the CE reads: "The Book of Acts and the Catholic Epistles was corrected on the basis of the exact transcript in the library of Eusebius Pamphili [ἀντεβληθή δὲ τῶν πράξεων καὶ καθολικῶν καθολικῶν ἐπιστολῶν τὸ βιβλίον πρὸς τὰ ἀκριβῆ ἀντίγραφα τῆς ἐν Καισαρείᾳ βιβλιοθήκης Εὐσεβίου τοῦ Παμφίλου]. The grammar suggests Acts and the CE were considered one book (the Grandville-Sharp rule applies to the substantives πράξεων and καθολικῶν). Grünstäudl is likely correct to suggest caution in drawing any conclusions from this colophon—he argues that all "one can gain from it is that 'at some time, some codex'... containing the Praxapostolos was corrected on the basis of a copy in the library at Caesarea" (2021: 17–18, it should be noted Grünstäudl's original German reads "Apostelgeschichte und Katholische Briefe" and does not use the term "Praxapostolos"). Though we cannot say with confidence that there was an exemplar copy of Acts and the CE in Eusebius's library (as Carriker 2003: 232), the presence of such a colophon, especially as it conveys the idea the Acts + CE is a single book, is further evidence of the traditional association of these texts. If such an exemplar existed in the library at Caesarea, which had ties to Origen himself (see Carriker 2003 and Grafton and Williams 2006), this could constitute intriguingly early evidence for both the canonical association between Acts and the CE and also the CE as a discrete collection.

The manuscript tradition indicates that from the fourth century Acts and the CE were associated. Nienhuis (2007: 79) concludes: "The evidence clearly suggests that Acts + CE were considered in the East to be a discreet [sic] canonical unit" which was followed by the Pauline Corpus.

---

[6] Folio 84 verso; found at http://www.bl.uk/manuscripts/Viewer.aspx?ref=royal_ms_1_d_viii_fs001r.

The function of the Corpus Apostolicum in the New Testament canon

Whereas one could focus just on the canonical function of the discrete seven-letter collection of CE within the NT canon (see Nienhuis and Wall 2013; Lockett 2017; 2021; Grünstäudl 2021), this final section briefly discusses the placement and function of the Corpus Apostolicum in the NT canon.

The discussion above has already noted there is evidence for two locations for the Corpus Apostolicum in the NT canon: either following the Pauline Corpus (Sinaiticus) or between the four Gospels and the Pauline Corpus (Vaticanus and Alexandrinus). The later placement is almost uniformly represented in the East while in the West the CE are often detached from Acts and placed after the Pauline Corpus and Acts in between the four Gospels and Paul. An example of drawing hasty conclusions based upon one particular order of the NT may be found in Wall: the "Pauline corpus followed by the non-Pauline corpus—indicates that the non-Pauline letters play a subordinate role, keeping Pauline letters in proper check-and-balance" (Wall 1992b: 176-77). Such a conclusion can only be supported by the wrong assumption that the Western order is the only canonical order. It is thus wrong to argue that the canonical logic of the NT is one which "recognizes the triumph of Pauline Christianity (or the canonical interpretation of it) within the catholicizing church" (Wall 1992b: 176). Rather, the fact of these two orders of the NT canon should indicate that neither can be given ultimate priority—both have a logic guiding the associations made by intentional placement of the texts (Bauckham 1999: 116). While acknowledging both orders, for the purposes of this essay we will focus on the placement of Acts + CE between the Gospels and the Pauline Corpus because it is this tradition that more uniformly understands Acts + CE (Corpus Apostolicum) as a discrete collection unit.

A majority of scholars acknowledge the literary role Acts plays in providing a narrative backdrop for the NT epistles generally. Karl-Wilhelm Niebuhr appreciates the narrative function of Acts and argues for reading the CE in light of the narrative framework provided by Acts, which in turn draws together the apostolic personalities from across the collection units of the NT (Gospels and Pauline Corpus). Even the titles of the CE, in naming the apostolic author of the text, intentionally connects each letter back to that author's narrative introduction in Acts. Through these connections, Niebuhr argues, "all information about the authors from the Gospels and Acts appear as guidelines for reading their letters. One of Acts' decisive guidelines that arises from the readers of the canon is the apostles' community with each other" (Niebuhr 2009: 51). Thus, Acts provides the narrative structure which offers the character development and emplotment of the authors of the CE and Pauline Corpus. In this way the book of Acts functions as "a hinge" for the entire NT canon because it "allows the inclusion of all apostolic writings into a single narrative context" (Niebuhr 2003: 583, author's translation).

Furthermore, Niebuhr argues that the cohesive narrative context created by reading the epistles through the narratival development of Acts creates a kind of apostolic harmony. Therefore, the interactions between the apostles in Acts serve "as model cases to resolve conflicts among themselves and [serve] as models of unity" (Niebuhr 2003:

583, all citations from this work are my own translation). Even the conflict between Paul and James is resolved by the narrative structure of Acts: "There was no hint of a conflict between the apostles ... not even in the Epistle of James. Instead, the letters of the apostles are now the protagonists themselves, together peacefully joining hands in the canon as in Gal 2:9" (Niebuhr 2003: 574). Therefore, through the narrative of Acts conflicts between apostles, as they are seen in Paul's letters, are in this way "canonically resolved" (Niebuhr 2003: 584).

Similarly, David Trobisch argues that "the main function of Acts is to fill in the gaps in the story as it is told through the two New Testament letter collections: the Letters of Paul and the Catholic Epistles" (2010: 119). Evidence that supports his claim includes the first half of Acts, which takes up the story of the apostles and Jesus' family as they are introduced immediately after the account of the ascension (Acts 1:13–14); whereas the second half of the book focuses on Paul. Thus, he concludes: "The overall design of Acts is quite clear. Jerusalem dominates the first part of the story, Paul dominates the second part of the story, and in the middle (Acts 15) both parties shake hands" (Trobisch 2010: 120). This overall structure is supplemented by Trobisch's excellent narrative analysis of the two halves of Acts.

From this narrative function of Acts Trobisch argues that the canonical function of the book is to resolve the conflict between Paul and the Jerusalem leadership. A kind of narrative balance is struck in how Acts portrays those deeds accomplished by Peter as finding mirror accomplishment by Paul. Though Niebuhr also mentions the way Acts resolves conflict between the apostles, Trobisch, along with Nienhuis (2007: 77–78) and Wall (1992a), make the theological conflict between the Pauline and CE letter collections the focus of Acts' canonical function.

Wall argues that this later canonical function of Acts is in conflict with the historical meaning of Acts. He argues that one should "relocate the hermeneutical center for the study of the Acts of the Apostles from its *historical* to its *canonical* moment" (Wall 1992a: 110, emphasis added). Thus, the intention of the text's historical author, Luke, is different from the canonical function of the text of Acts within the NT—that is, "biblical Acts" versus "canonical Acts." For Wall, Acts therefore functions as "a 'canonical bridge' between the four-fold Gospel and the multiple letter [sic] of the Second Testament" (Wall 1992a: 112, see also 121). In Schröter's estimation, Harnack also understood this conflict between the historical and canonical meaning of Acts: "the canonization of Acts would have to be traced back less to its *content* than to the church-political constellations at the end of the second century" (Schröter 2013: 275).

Furthermore, Wall argues that the canonical role Acts played was to authorize the letter collections of the NT. This authorizing function of Acts is accomplished by supplying "a narrative introduction for the entire epistolary canon, Pauline and Catholic" (Wall 1992a: 128–29). As noted above, Wall argues that "Pauline Christianity had triumphed ... and it was now the Jewish apostolate of James, Cephas and John which needed legitimating" (Wall 1992a: 120). And while authorizing, Acts also brokers conflict between Paul and the apostles, yet not so much as historical figures, but more by quelling the conflict that might be detected between the Pauline Corpus and the CE as letter collections: "Acts performs an interpretive role, not so much to temper the diversity envisaged by the two different collections of letters, but to prompt impressions of their rhetorical relationship within the New Testament" (Wall 1992a: 131).

Three critical observations of Wall's work in particular are worth noting. First, similar to Harnack, Wall argues that the historical content and intention of Acts is at odds with its eventual canonical function within the New Testament (Wall denies this [Wall, 2010: 190 n. 23] in a comment aimed at Childs' critique [Childs 2008: 225–26], but this still seems the correct evaluation, see Lockett 2017: 131 n. 151). Second, Wall understands that Luke and Acts as "two halves of a single narrative" were "divided during the canonizing process, only to follow different canonizing paths and to play different canonical roles" within the New Testament (Wall 1992a: 114). Wall's argument that the church divided the once united work of Luke–Acts is incorrect (Wall 1992a: 114; see Schröter 2013: 293, see also 295–99). Finally, Wall argues that Acts functions to connect the two letter collections in terms of legitimating either Paul ("Luke's defence of Paul was to present him as a legitimate apostolic witness," Wall 1992a: 121) or the CE (for the "canonizing community ... it was now the Jewish apostolate of James, Cephas and John which needed legitimating," Wall 1992a: 121). However, neither the Pauline Corpus nor the CE depended on Acts for their authority—though Acts certainly functioned to draw together the composite (Pauline and Catholic) apostolic witness in the epistles.

A different perspective—one that does not understand Acts as authorizing other NT collections nor necessarily brokering a conflict between Paul and the CE collection—can be seen in Schröter and Childs. Brevard Childs notes "at the beginning of the second century ... the book of Acts served to establish the legitimacy of the Pauline interpretation of the gospel, *along with the other apostles*, as the truthful apostolic witness to the crucified and resurrected ... Lord" (Childs 2008: 226). Following Jens Schröter, Childs rejects Harnack's view that Acts was part of the church's political agenda at the end of the second century "to shape its traditions toward the goal of early Catholicism." Rather, appreciating the *Wirkungsgeschichte* of Acts, "the Gospels and the Pauline letter corpus present two *simultaneous* stages of the development of the New Testament canon independently of each other, and each acknowledged early as authoritative" (Childs 2008: 230; following Schröter 2003, English translation, 2013). Furthermore, "none of the early Church Fathers assigned Acts the role of buttressing the authority of Paul that had long since been accepted. Rather, the expansion of Pauline tradition to all the apostles allows a combination of the Lukan Pauline traditions with the substantive contents of Acts to occur without a sense of undue friction" (Childs 2008: 230–31). Thus, for Childs, the Gospels and the Pauline Corpus simultaneously were received into the NT canon independent of each other, and therefore Acts was never pressed into any kind of authorizing duty for either collection. Furthermore, rather than quelling a conflict between apostolic voices regarding the gospel, Acts endorses the *equally authoritative witnesses* of both canonical epistle collections *without a sense of friction* (contra Nienhuis and Wall 2013: 61, 64, 66).

For Childs, Acts presented "the apostles as the legitimate guardians of the Jesus traditions, strengthened by the connection with the catholic letters of Peter, James, and John, and the portrait of Paul in Acts as in agreement with that of the letters. This orientation toward legitimating the apostolic proclamation is thus constitutive for an understanding of the New Testament canon" (Childs 2008: 231).

Similarly, Jens Schröter argues that Luke's gospel was authorized via its connection to Paul *independent* from Acts. Therefore, there existed two authoritative canonical collection units—the Gospels and Pauline Corpus—before Acts and the CE (Schröter 2013: 293). Acts, then, enjoyed the support of the already authorized tradition of Paul and thus Acts belonged to neither Gospels nor Pauline Collection as the manuscript evidence clearly demonstrates. Schröter argues, "Acts provided the church with the possibility of relating the already existing collections to one another and thus grounding their canon on the witness of Jesus and the apostles, with which the witness of Paul was then also in agreement" (Schröter 2013: 294; see also 276–302). So, the function of Acts was not so much to authorize as to coordinate the composite apostolic witness to Jesus Christ. Acts thus

> presents itself not only as the second part of the Gospel of Luke but *also* as a conceptually and literarily independent presentation of the history of early Christianity insofar as it describes the unfolding of the Christ witness through his [sic, "its"] witness. That with this linking of the Jesus story with the activity of the apostles and Paul it lent itself to the emergence of the New Testament canon precisely as an integration writing is obvious.
>
> Schröter 2013: 294

Schröter argues that Harnack rightly emphasized Acts' connections to the three major corpora of the New Testament, namely the Gospels, Letters of Paul, and CE. Harnack argued:

> The Acts is in a certain way the key to understanding the idea of the New Testament of the Church, and has given it the organic structure in which it stands before us. By taking its place at the head of the "Apostolus" the Acts first made possible the division of the Canon into two parts and justified the combination of the Pauline Epistles with the Gospels. It is also possible to speak of a threefold division, in which the Acts (together with the Catholic Epistles and Revelation) formed the central portion.
>
> Harnack 2004: 67

Schröter notes that "The canonical meaning of Acts can be captured well from this perspective. In the first place, it consists in presenting the apostles as the legitimate preservers of the Jesus tradition (a function that was then strengthened through its compilation with the Catholic Letters) and to show the Paul image of Acts to be in agreement with that of the letters" (Schröter 2013: 300). However, Schröter emphasizes, against Harnack, that this canonical function is not contrary to the historical-critical meaning of Acts—especially as he exaggerated the antithesis between the historical and Lukan (Acts) versions of Paul. Rather than a later imposition upon Acts, "the exclusive binding of the Jesus witness to the circle of the Twelve can be regarded precisely as a characteristic feature of Acts' conception of history" (Schröter 2013: 301).

Schröter and Childs are surely correct in resisting the sharp distinction between the historical and canonical intention of the Corpus Apostolicum. They are also likely correct in that Acts functioned less to legitimate either Gospels or Paul, but rather as the consensus clearly demonstrates, in its narrative portrayal of the apostolic mission Acts is to draw the letter collections and their apostolic authors together into a canonical whole.

Though much more needs to be done in order to fully understand the canonical function of the Corpus Apostolicum, it can be claimed initially that it likely formed because of the narrative role Acts played in introducing and connecting the apostles and Paul as authors of the epistles that followed. Just as Acts moves from the pillar apostles to Paul, so too the CE follow directly after Acts and then are followed by the Pauline Corpus, at least in the Eastern ordering of the NT canon.

Bibliography

Aland, Kurt and Barbara Aland. (1989), *The Text of the New Testament: An Introduction to the Critical Editions and the Textual Criticism*, Grand Rapids: Eerdmans.

Allison, Dale C. (2013), *The Epistle of James: A Critical Commentary*, ICC, London: Bloomsbury.

Bauckham, Richard J. (1999), *James: Wisdom of Jesus, Disciple of Jesus the Sage*, London: Routledge.

Blumell, Lincoln H. and Thomas A. Waymet. (2015), *Christian Oxyrhynchus: Texts, Documents, and Sources*, Waco: Baylor University Press.

Brown, Raymond E. (1982), *The Epistles of John*, Anchor Bible 30, New York: Doubleday.

Carriker, A. J. (2003), *The Library of Eusebius of Caesarea*, SVigChr 67, Leiden: Brill.

Childs, Brevard S. (1984), *The New Testament as Canon: An Introduction*, Philadelphia: Fortress.

Childs, Brevard S. (2008), *The Church's Guide for Reading Paul: The Canonical Shaping of the Pauline Corpus*, Grand Rapids: Eerdmans.

Gallagher, E. L. and J. D. Meade. (2017), *The Biblical Canon Lists from Early Christianity: Texts and Analysis*, Oxford: Oxford University Press.

Gamble, Harry Y. (2002), "New Testament Canon: Recent Research and the *Status Quaestionis*," in L. M. McDonald and J. A. Sanders (eds.), *The Canon Debate*, 267–94, Peabody: Hendrickson.

Gibson, Samuel James. (2018), *The Apostolos: The Acts and Epistles in Byzantine Liturgical Manuscripts*, Piscataway, NJ: Gorgias Press.

Grafton, Anthony and Megan Williams. (2006), *Christianity and the Transformation of the Book: Origen, Eusebius, and the Library of Caesarea*, Cambridge, MA: Harvard University Press.

Grünstäudl, Wolfgang. (1992), *The Muratorian Fragment and the Development of the Canon*, Oxford: Clarendon.

Grünstäudl, Wolfgang. (2013), *Petrus Alexandris: Studien zum historischen und theologischen Ort des zweiten Petrusbriefs*, WUNT 2/353, Tübingen: Mohr Siebeck.

Grünstäudl, Wolfgang. (2021), "The Wait is Worth it: The Catholic Epistles and the Formation of the New Testament," in Darian R. Lockett (ed.), *The Catholic Epistles: Critical Readings*, 9–24, London: Bloomsbury.

Hahneman, Geoffrey. (2002), "The Muratorian Fragment and the Origins of the New Testament Canon," in L. M. McDonald and J. A. Sanders (eds.), *The Canon Debate*, 405–15, Peabody: Hendrickson.

Harnack, Adolf von. (2004), *The Origin of the New Testament: And the Most Important Consequences of the New Creation*, trans. J. R. Wilkinson, 1925, reprint, Eugene, OR: Wipf and Stock.

Horrell, David G. (2009), "The Themes of 1 Peter: Insights from the Eariels Manuscripts (the Crosby-Schøyn Codes ms 193 and the Bodmer Miscellaneous Codex containgin P72)," *NTS* 55: 502-22.

Hurtado, Larry W. (2006a), *The Earliest Christian Artifacts: Manuscripts and Christian Origins*, Grand Rapids: Eerdmans.

Hurtado, Larry W. (2006b), "The New Testament in the Second Century: Text, Collections and Canon," in Jeff Childres and David Parker (eds.), *Transmission and Reception: New Testament Textual-Critical and Exegetical Studies*, Text and Studies: Contributions to Biblical and Patristic Literature 4, 3-27, Piscataway, NJ: Gorgias.

Katz, Peter. (1957), "The Johannine Epistles in the Muratorian Canon," *Journal for Theological Studies* 8: 273-74.

Kruger, Michael J. (2012), "The Date and Content of P. Antinoopolis 12 (0232)," *New Testament Studies* 58: 254-71.

Lieu, Judith. (1986), *The Second and Third Epistles of John: History and Background*, Edinburgh: T &T Clark.

Lockett, Darian R. (2017), *Letters from the Pillar Apostles: The Formation of the Catholic Epistles as a Canonical Collection*, Eugene: Pickwick.

Lockett, Darian R. (2018), "Why Have We Stopped Reading the Catholic Epistles Together? A Reception History of an Early Collection," in Stanley E. Porter and Andrew W. Pitts (eds.), *Christian Origins and the Establishment of the Early Jesus Movement*, ECHC 4, 393-411, Leiden: Brill.

Lockett, Darian R. (2021), *Letters for the Church: Reading James, 1-2 Peter, 1-3 John, and Jude as Canon*, Downers Grove: IVP Academic.

Lührmann, Diter. (1981), "Gal 2.9 und die katholischen Briefe: Bemerkungen zum Kanon und zur regula fidei," *Zeitschfift für die neutestamentliche Wissenschaft* 72: 65-87.

Metzger, Bruce M. (1987), *The Canon of the New Testament: Its Origin, Development, and Significance*, Oxford: Oxford University Press.

Moule, C. F. D. (1981), *The Birth of the New Testament*, London A & C Black.

Moule, C. F. D. (2003), "Exegese im kanonischen Zusammenhang: Überlegungen zur theologischen Relevanz der Gestalt des neutestamentlichen Kanons," in J.-M. Auwers and H. J. De Jong (eds.), *The Biblical Canons*, 557-84, Leuven: Leuven University Press.

Moule, C. F. D. (2009), "James in the Minds of the Recipients," in Karl-Wilhelm Niebuhr and Robert W. Wall (eds.), *The Catholic Epistles and Apostolic Tradition*, 43-54, Waco, TX: Baylor University Press.

Niebuhr, Karl-Wilhelm. (2013), "Catholic Epistles," *Encyclopedia of the Bible and its Reception* 7: 108-92.

Niebuhr, Karl-Wilhelm. (2016), "Die Apostel und ihre Briefe. Zum hermeneutischen und ökumenischen Potential des Corpus Apostolicum im Neuen Testament," in H. Omerzu and E. D. Schmidt (eds.), *Paulus und Petrus. Geschichte – Theologie – Rezeption*, 273-92, ABG 48, Leipzig: Evangelische Verlagsanstalt.

Nienhuis, David R. (2007), *Not By Paul Alone: The Formation of the Catholic Epistle Collection and the Christian Canon*, Waco: Baylor University Press.

Nienhuis, David R. and Robert W. Wall. (2013), *Reading the Epistles of James, Peter, John, and Jude as Scripture: The Shaping and Shape of a Canonical Collection*, Grand Rapids: Eerdmans.

Norelli, Enrico. (2011), "Sulle origini della raccolta delle Lettere Cattoliche," *Rivista Biblica* 2: 453–521.
Painter, John. (2009), "The Johannine Epistles as Catholic Epistles," in K.-W. Niebuhr and R. W. Wall (eds.), *The Catholic Epistles and Apostolic Tradition*, 239–305, Waco: Baylor University Press.
Parker, D. C. (2008), *An Introduction to the New Testament Manuscripts and Their Texts*. Cambridge: Cambridge University Press.
Porter, Stanley E. (2013), *How We God the New Testament: Text, Transmission, Translation*, Grand Rapids: Eerdmans.
Schlosser, Jacques. (2004), "Le Corpus Épîtres des Catholiques," in J. Schlosser (ed.), *The Catholic Epistles and the Tradition*, Bibliotheca Ephemeridum Theologicarum Lovaniensium, 3–41, Leuven: Leuven University Press.
Schröter, Jens. (2003), "Die Apostelgeschichte und die Entstehung des neutestamentlichen Kanons," in J.-M. Auwers and H. J. De Jong (eds.), *The Biblical Canons*, 395–429, Leuven: Leuven University Press.
Schröter, Jens. (2013), *From Jesus to the New Testament: Early Christian Theology and the Origin of the New Testament Canon*, Baylor-Mohr Siebeck Studies in Early Christianity 1, translated by Wayne Coppins, Waco, TX: Baylor University Press.
Soden, Hermann F. von. (1911), *Die Schriften des Neuen Testaments*, vol. 1, Göttingen: Vandenhoeck and Ruprecht.
Trobisch, David. (2000), *The First Edition of the New Testament*, Oxford: Oxford University Press.
Trobisch, David. (2010), "The Book of Acts as a Narrative Commentary on the Letters of the New Testament: A Programmatic Essay," in Andrew F. Gregory and C. Kavin Rowe (eds.), *Rethinking the Unity and Reception of Luke and Acts*, 43–127, Columbia: University of South Carolina Press.
Verheyden, Joseph. (2003), "The Canon Muratori: A Matter of Dispute," in J.-M. Auwers and H. J. De Jonge (eds.), *The Biblical Canons*, 487–556, Leuven: Leuven University Press.
Wall, Robert W. (1992a), "The Acts of the Apostles in Canonical Context," in Robert W. Wall and Eugene E. Lemcio (eds.), *The New Testament as Canon: A Reader in Canonical Criticism*, JSNTSup 76, 110–28, Sheffield: JSOT Press.
Wall, Robert W. (1992b), "The Problem of the Multiple Letter Canon," in Robert W. Wall and Eugene E. Lemcio (eds.), *The New Testament as Canon: A Reader in Canonical Criticism*, JSNTSup 76, 129–83, Sheffield: JSOT Press.
Wall, Robert W. (2010), "A Canonical Approach to Acts and Luke's Gospel," in Andrew F. Gregory and C. Kavin Rowe (eds.), *Rethinking the Unity and Reception of Luke and Acts*, 172–91, Columbia: University of South Carolina Press.
Wasserman, Tommy. (2005), "Papyrus 72 and the Bodmer Miscellaneous Codex," *New Testament Studies* 51: 137–54.

14

The Pauline Corpus

E. Randolph Richards

The Pauline Canon (or Corpus Paulinum) is defined as the traditional thirteen letters of Paul, plus the letter to the Hebrews. The majority of modern Pauline scholars argue some or most of those letters were actually penned by the Apostle. A minority of Pauline scholars argue all thirteen sans Hebrews are from Paul (e.g., Donald Guthrie, Luke T. Johnson). A much smaller minority on the other side argue few of the letters are from Paul or that only pieces of some of the letters are from Paul (e.g., Walter Schmithals). Many scholars argue those not from Paul were penned by one or more disciples of Paul and were not intended to deceive but rather to represent what their master would have written were he still alive (e.g., Bruce Metzger, Armin Baum). At least one scholar, Bart Ehrman (2012: 17 n. 19), posits such letters not from Paul must be considered forgeries regardless of the motive. I agree that there are no innocent apostolic pseudepigrapha; such pseudepigrapha were written to deceive (Richards 2018: esp. 11–14 and 129–30).

Arguments for or against Pauline authorship of four, seven, ten, thirteen or even fourteen letters are for another day. We will use the ancient definition of the Pauline Canon: the thirteen letters attributed to Paul, plus the letter to the Hebrews for reasons noted later. Evidence for a Pauline Canon can be seen in three ways: early lists, early writers, and manuscripts. While each type of evidence has strengths and weaknesses, taken together the evidence suggests a stable Pauline Canon by at least the third century. But this same evidence raises questions about the inclusion of Hebrews in the Pauline Canon, and it legitimately raises the question of how letters dispatched across the Roman empire came to be a collected set. We will conclude by listing a few questions that need further research.

Early Lists

There is at least one and possibly two lists of Paul's letters which predate our earliest manuscript (P46, *ca.* 200). First, Marcion (writing *ca.* 130–140) is said by his opponents to hold to a Pauline canon of ten letters: Galatians, 1–2 Corinthians, Romans, 1–2 Thessalonians, Laodiceans (seemingly Ephesians), Colossians, Philippians, and Philemon. Schmid (1995: 1:294–319) argues Marcion inherited a ten-letter collection, but Scherbenske (2013: 94–112) re-argues that Marcion "corrected" the texts to fit his hermeneutic. Given Marcion's demonstrated willingness to edit Scripture, we cannot be confident what was his original list nor what being on his list meant. Are these all the letters he knew or only those he approved?

Second, the Muratorian Fragment or Canon is a canon list, *possibly* from the second century. This list of twenty-two New Testament books in a Latin manuscript from the seventh century is thought to be a translation of an earlier Greek original. The relevant section is:

> It is necessary (47) for us to discuss these one by one, since the blessed (48) apostle Paul himself, following the example of his predecessor (49–50) John, writes by name to only seven churches in the following sequence: To the Corinthians (51) first, to the Ephesians second, to the Philippians third, (52) to the Colossians fourth, to the Galatians fifth, (53) to the Thessalonians sixth, to the Romans (54—5) seventh. It is true that he writes once more to the Corinthians and to the Thessalonians for the sake of admonition, (56–7) yet it is clearly recognizable that there is one Church spread throughout the whole extent of the earth. For John also in the (58) Apocalypse, though he writes to seven churches, (59–60) nevertheless speaks to all. [Paul also wrote] out of affection and love one to Philemon, one to Titus, and two to Timothy; and these are held sacred (62–3) in the esteem of the Church catholic for the regulation of ecclesiastical discipline. There is current also to (64) the Laodiceans, another to the Alexandrians, forged in Paul's (65) name to the heresy of Marcion, and several others (66) which cannot be received into the catholic Church (67)— for it is not fitting that gall be mixed with honey. (68) ... (73) But Hermas wrote the *Shepherd* (74) very recently, in our times, in the city of Rome, (75) while bishop Pius, his brother, was occupying the chair (76) of the church of the city of Rome.
>
> English translation and line numbers from Metzger 1987: 306–7

The value of the list depends upon its dating. Initially, scholars (e.g., Grant 1965: 301; cf. Metzger 1987: 124) dated the Greek exemplar about AD 170, because, among other reasons, it seems to refer to Pius I (140–155) as "recent." If so, it would represent a known collection of Paul's letters in Rome by the middle of the second century, listing the thirteen Pauline letters, but not mentioning Hebrews. Sundberg (1973) countered, arguing for a fourth century date in the eastern regions of the empire. Everett Ferguson (1982) responded to Sundberg, reasserting the early date. Metzger (1987: 193) felt Ferguson "sufficiently refuted (not to say demolished)" Sundberg's arguments. Hahneman (1992: 3) considered Metzger's rebuttal to be "brief and dismissive," arguing, e.g., the Fragment uses *catafrygum*, a fourth century Latinized form of a Greek nickname for the Montanists (Hahneman 1992: 211–12), a point Ferguson (1993: 696) vigorously disputes as an emendation (see Hill). More recently, Clare Rothschild (2018) suggests the Fragment is a fourth or even ninth century Roman fake, but Christophe Guignard (2019) aggressively disagrees. In other words, at the moment, the matter has not been resolved, with strong opinions for both a second and fourth century date.

Early writers

Also predating extant manuscripts, references by first- and second-century Christian writers can demonstrate awareness of one or more of Paul's letters but are less suitable for demonstrating the existence of a collection, much less a complete canon.

First-century witnesses

The author of 2 Peter refers to "letters" of Paul: "So also our beloved brother Paul wrote to you according to the wisdom given him, speaking of this as he does in all his letters. There are some things in them hard to understand, which the ignorant and unstable twist to their own destruction, as they do the other scriptures" (2 Pet 3:15–16, NRSV). This passage is not as helpful as may first appear, since it is largely dismissed as a second-century pseudepigrapon, but there may be elements of circular reasoning involved. One argument for 2 Peter as pseudonymous is that there were no collections of Paul's letters in Rome in the early 60s and thus 2 Peter must be from the second century when such collections did exist. Bauckham (1983: 131–35, 158–62) reasons 2 Peter is an innocent pseudepigraphal Testament, but this is not so clear (Richards and Boyle 2020: 404–9). On the other hand, if the letter is Petrine, then it becomes the earliest known reference to a collection of Paul's letters; yet, it would still not speak as to the size of the collection.

Clement, an early bishop of Rome (*ca.* 96), is the only other first-century witness to Paul's letters. Ralph Martin (2000 [1975]: 227) thinks that Clement "at best knows only four Pauline letters." Robert Grant (1965: 81–83) sees in Clement references to Romans, 1 Corinthians, Galatians, Ephesians, and Philippians. Tim Johnson (1999: 3–4) sees an allusion to Hebrews in 1 Clem. 36:1–5. Art Patzia (1993: 90) though, cautions, "We need to remember that Clement may have been aware of more letters than he utilized in his correspondence." We are left with Clement providing evidence of *a* collection but not of its size. For those of us who accept 2 Peter as Petrine, it provides similar evidence (see Richards 1998: 160–62).

Second-century writers (c. 100–200)

Ignatius (writing *ca.* 105–115 in Asia Minor) refers or alludes to all but 2 Thessalonians, 1–2 Timothy, Titus and Philemon, while Polycarp (writing *ca.* 110–140 in Asia Minor) alludes to all fourteen letters except Colossians, 1 Thessalonians, Titus, and Philemon. Also, it is noteworthy that Polycarp refers to a collection of Paul's letters in the hands of the Philippians (Pol. *Phil.* 3.2). Tatian (writing *ca.* 160–170 in Syria) also appears to reject 1–2 Timothy, but McDonald (2007: 279) reminds us Tatian demonstrated a "willingness to change or correct the four canonical gospels." Both Irenaeus (writing ca. 175–185 in Lyons) and Clement of Alexandria (writing c. 182–202 in North Africa) mention all but Philemon. Tertullian (writing *ca.* 197–220 in North Africa) and Origen (writing *ca.* 203–250 in North Africa) seem to agree with subsequent church fathers in seeing a collection with thirteen letters and Hebrews. Thus, even though Papias (writing *ca.* 110–140 in Asia Minor), Barnabas (writing *ca.* 80–120 in Alexandria), and Justin (writing c. 150–160 in Italy) show no evidence of familiarity with Paul's writings (see the detailed analysis in Grant 1965: 62–107), we may still maintain the second century demonstrates a growing familiarity with Paul's letters.

Manuscript evidence

Although Paul's letters were dispatched individually at different times to different churches, manuscripts containing Paul's collected letters are remarkably uniform in sequence. With the few exceptions we will discuss, all extant manuscripts containing Paul's letters have the same letters in the same order: Romans, 1–2 Corinthians, Galatians, Ephesians, Philippians, Colossians, 1–2 Thessalonians, 1–2 Timothy, Titus, Philemon, and Hebrews. Before examining the exceptions, let us consider why they might have been arranged in this sequence. David Trobisch (1994: 25, 52–53) suggests we can discern two "principles" that seemed to influence the arrangement of Paul's letters. First, letters addressing the same community (1–2 Corinthians, 1–2 Thessalonians) or individual (1–2 Timothy) are set together. Second, letters to churches (Romans–2 Thess.) are listed first, then letters to individuals (1 Timothy–Titus). Within these groupings, the letters are organized by length, from longest to shortest, with the exception that Galatians precedes Ephesians. According to Murphy-O'Connor (1995: 124), Galatians has only 92 percent of the characters of Ephesians. Ancient scribes, however, counted lines (*stichoi*) not characters. Codex Sinaiticus listed both letters as having 312 *stichoi* each, leading Murphy-O'Connor (ibid.) to conclude placing Galatians first was "an insignificant error." Trobisch (1994: esp. 52–53) posits a more elaborate theory, suggesting Galatians was the last of the group of letters begun by Romans and Ephesians begins a new grouping.

Additionally, Hebrews complicates the sequence of letters. Hebrews is found in several locations. Some manuscripts append Hebrews to the end of the grouping of letters to churches (2 Thessalonians). In Byzantine manuscripts (as in modern English versions), Hebrews follows all the letters of Paul, i.e., after Philemon. One manuscript (P46) places Hebrews between Romans and 1 Corinthians—its proper position according to Trobisch's organizing principles of destination and length.

Papyrus 46

The earliest extant copy of any of Paul's letters is the papyrus codex P46, often dated about AD 200 (e.g., NA28). Recently, it has become fashionable to resist dating any early papyri narrowly; thus, P46 is listed as "early third century" (e.g., the University of Michigan library). Ancient codices were usually made by stacking four sheets (folios) and stitching them together down the middle. Folding the sheets created eight leaves and thus sixteen pages (one quire). Multiple quires were then stacked and bound together to create a codex. This allowed a scribe to add quires if additional space was needed and to replace a damaged quire. Unlike most manuscripts, however, P46 is made of a single quire. The scribe stacked fifty-two papyrus sheets to form 104 leaves and 208 pages. We know we have eighty-six of the original 104 leaves, because the original scribe also numbered the pages—another very unusual custom. A single quire had at least two disadvantages. First, the scribe needed to calculate how many pages would be needed for the task, at least by the midway point, since after the midpoint the number of pages were then fixed. Second, a single thick quire when folded caused the interior pages to extrude. When the codex's edges were trimmed to be even (as was custom), the interior pages became narrower. So with P46, scholars have noted the pages become narrower each page until leaf 53, and then the pages incrementally become wider. The single quire was, though, an advantage to modern scholars. As Dan Wallace (2013) noted from his personal examination of the manuscript, "Since the first extant page is numbered 17 (folio 8), and starts with Romans 5:17, we can extrapolate that the manuscript began with Romans 1 and is missing the outer seven double leaves." Wallace concludes seven folios are missing, thus fourteen pages (seven leaves) at the beginning and another fourteen pages at the end (suggesting the extant numbering was on folio 9).

The manuscript, though partial and damaged, appears to be our earliest manuscript of Paul's letters and is quite early. The Chester Beatty Library and the University of Michigan each have some folios. Combined, the surviving manuscript contains (in sequence) the rest of Romans, Hebrews, 1–2 Corinthians, Ephesians, Galatians, Colossians, and 1 Thessalonians (through 5:28, but the last folio is quite fragmentary). By estimating there were seven remaining leaves, F. G. Kenyon (1934: vi–vii), the original examiner of the manuscript, concluded there was sufficient space for 2 Thessalonians and 1 Timothy but not enough space for the others. Kenyon calculated that 2 Timothy, Titus, and Philemon would need about ten leaves and thus he concluded it more likely that they were excluded, leaving the last four to five leaves blank. Kenyon's conclusions are oft cited as evidence that the Pastorals were not originally included with Paul's letters, such as I. H. Marshall's (2004: 10) dismissive comment, "As is well-known, P46 lacks the Pastoral Epistles."

Kenyon's conclusion has some challenges. First, if the scribe planned only through 2 Thessalonians, then he already knew he had more than enough space. Ancient scribes typically calculated the lines (stichometry) needed for a book and then the required number of pages. Scribes were paid by the line, so they kept count. Here, yet another peculiarity of P46 comes into play. Jeremy Duff (1998: esp. 583–84) claims there are 50 percent more letters per page in the last leaves than are on the middle leaves, suggesting the scribe became concerned about space as he progressed. Why would the scribe compress, if he already knew he had plenty of space? Duff suggests rather that the scribe knew he was running out of room for what he planned to include. Trobisch (1994: 16) concludes: "After he had filled more than half the book, he realized there would not be enough room for all the text he planned to copy. He started to write more characters in each line and gradually increased the 26 lines per page in the first half of the codex to 28, then to 30, and in the end to 32 lines per page." Dan Wallace (2013) tempers by noting that the compression is not as severe as Duff implies: "[The compression] is partially due to the fact that the outer leaves are wider than the inner leaves. Nevertheless, there are more letters in the back outer leaves than the front outer leaves, showing that at least some compression did take place. And this seems to suggest that the scribe was aware of the problem he had created for including the pastorals and began to compensate upon realizing his mistake." Either reconstruction (Kenyon or Duff) requires a scribe that miscalculated, but Kenyon's theory does not explain the compression. In a response perhaps to Wallace, David Inglis (2014) argues the scribe was perhaps responding to Marcion and built the codex but then decided to add Hebrews making compression necessary, but the scribe "never intended to include the Pastorals." Edgar Ebojo (2014) provides a more detailed analysis and suggests P46 did not include the Pastorals (pp. 204–35), but it is not clear if the issues with P46 are fully resolved. Wallace's cautious assessment still seems justified: whether or not P46 "originally contained the Pastorals is yet to be seen." For the purposes here, the peculiarities of P46 should caution us against citing it as evidence of a Pauline collection without the Pastorals.

The sequence in P46 is also unusual among manuscripts of the Pauline corpus in its placement of Hebrews between Romans and 1 Corinthians as well as in its reversal of Ephesians and Galatians. The sequence can be seen clearly on the manuscript images provided by the Center for the Study of NT Manuscripts. (Unless otherwise noted, all references to digital images of manuscripts refer to those at csntm.org.) We can see the end of one letter and the beginning of the next, since the manuscript does not begin a new page when it starts a new letter. Thus, for example, the end of Hebrews and the beginning of 1 Corinthians are on one sheet (GA_P46, image 134547) as are the end of Galatians and the beginning (title and first line) of Philippians (GA_P46, image 134798). Stan Porter (2008: 200) suggests that P46 retains the original order of a first Pauline canon. Trobisch (1994: 16–17) makes a more compelling argument that P46 "corrected" the inversion of Galatians and Ephesians and placed Hebrews after Romans according to the organizing principle of length. Trobisch's explanation seems quite reasonable, although we recognize the challenge of asserting the motivations of ancient scribes. At a minimum we can maintain that at least one early scribe felt the freedom to rearrange the "letters of Paul" to what seemed to him a better sequence.

Codex Vaticanus

Codex Vaticanus (B 03) is usually considered one of our best early manuscripts. In Vaticanus, Hebrews follows 2 Thessalonians, but the original manuscript breaks off at Heb. 9:14 with ΚΑΘΑ-, "purify".[1] The codex begins at Gen. 46:28 and the text after Heb. 9:14 is minuscule, indicating the original codex was damaged and repaired. The repaired text is dated paleographically to the fifteenth century, according to Versace (2018: 295–96). When repaired, the remainder of Hebrews was finished and then James followed, lacking the Pastorals and Philemon. This has led some scholars to conclude the original manuscript did not include the Pastorals (and presumably Philemon). It is more likely the later scribe who repaired Vaticanus did not copy the Pastorals and Philemon after Hebrews (where the Pastorals and Philemon would have originally been in B), because as Grenz (2018: 17 n. 79) reasons, almost all available fifteenth century manuscripts had the Pastorals and Philemon before Hebrews (69 of 74 mss in NTVMR). Therefore, many Vaticanus scholars (e.g., Skeat 1984: 465) think the

---

[1] See https://digi.vatlib.it/view/MSS_Vat.gr.1209, slide 1518.

omission of the Pastorals was accidental. At the least, however, Vaticanus indicates an inclusion of Hebrews and positioned after 2 Thessalonians.

Codex Vaticanus has another peculiarity involving the sequence of Paul's letters. It has often been suggested that its exemplar (or an even earlier one) had Hebrews in yet another location. The Greek section numbers (usually dated to the fourth century) are continuous through all the letters of Paul; however, when we get to Ephesians the number jumps from 58 to 70. Section numbers 59–69 are found in Hebrews, even though it is located after 2 Thessalonians. This suggests whatever exemplar Vaticanus used for the section numbers probably had Hebrews between Galatians and Ephesians—a position that is not found in any other manuscript or lectionary. If this is the case, then the scribe of Vaticanus relocated Hebrews to a location known in the three other major manuscripts of the time period: Codex Sinaiticus (ℵ 01) dated to the fourth century, Codex Alexandrinus (A 02) dated to the fifth century, and Codex Ephraemi Rescriptus (C 04) dated to the fifth century. It is commonly thought these four major uncial manuscripts are independent of each other; yet all four present the same sequencing: Romans, 1–2 Corinthians, Galatians, Ephesians, Philippians, Colossians, 1–2 Thessalonians, Hebrews, 1–2 Timothy, Titus, and Philemon, placing Hebrews after 2 Thessalonians and before the Pastorals.

Codices Claromontanus, Augiensis, Boernerianus

Whether or not Paul wrote Hebrews—and I do not think he did—our earliest witnesses suggest that ancients considered Hebrews to belong *in some way* with the letters of Paul. David Trobisch (1994: 25–26) contends Hebrews was *added* (albeit very early) to the Pauline Corpus, pointing to three manuscripts of Paul's letters that did *not* include Hebrews: Codex Claromontanus (D^P 06), Codex Augiensis (F^P 010), and Codex Boernerianus (G^P 012). Codex Claromontanus has Greek on the left and Latin on the right and begins with Rom. 1:7b.[2] It has a *nearly* traditional sequence of Pauline Letters, retaining Hebrews at the end of the Corpus Paulinum. Colossians and Philippians are reversed in sequence. Only the late fourteenth-century minuscule MS 5 shares the peculiarity of reversing the order of Colossians and Philippians[3]. This minuscule also has Hebrews after 2 Thessalonians and before the Pastorals, as do MSS 01, 02, 03, and 04. Claromontanus (codex D^P is not to be confused with the better-known Codex Bezae, D^{ea} or 04) has one other notable oddity. After Philemon and before Hebrews, a Latin list of Old and New Testament books (with stichometry), termed *Catalogus Claromontanus*, was later inserted.[4] The actual Codex Claromontanus, other than reversing the sequence of Colossians and Philippians, supports the traditional sequence of Paul's letters, followed by Hebrews. The catalog differs from the actual contents of the codex having its own unique variations. It lacks Philippians, 1–2 Thessalonians and Hebrews and includes some non-canonical books: "Epistles of Paul: to Romans, to Corinthians 1, to Corinthians 2, to Galatians, to Ephesians, to Timothy 1, to Timothy 2, to Titus, to

---

[2] See https://gallica.bnf.fr/ark:/12148/btv1b84683111.
[3] See https://gallica.bnf.fr/ark:/12148/btv1b110002532/f157, with Colossians on the left and Philippians on the right.
[4] See https://gallica.bnf.fr/ark:/12148/btv1b84683111/f866.

Colossians, to Philemon, to [sic] Peter 1, to [sic] Peter 2, of James, of John, of John 2, of John 3, of Jude, of Barnabas, Revelation of John, Acts of the Apostles, Shepherd, Acts of Paul, Revelation of Peter" (Latin text in Westcott 1896: 574–76).

Since Hebrews is found in Codex Claromontanus (and in its traditional location), why does Trobisch discuss this manuscript when arguing Hebrews was not part of the Pauline corpus? After Philemon, the manuscript originally had three blank pages, which a later scribe used for the *Catalogus Claromontanus*. Trobisch (1994: 13) suggests these blank pages functioned as some sort of divider between Paul's letters and Hebrews: "The evidence suggests that Hebrews was not part of the manuscript that was copied to produce the Codex Claromontanus, but was added later." By "later," Trobisch cannot mean after the writing of Codex Claromontanus, since Hebrews is in the original hand. This is easily seen by comparing Philemon and Hebrews (GA_06, images 275950 and 275958), noting, e.g., the smooth breathing marks and the distinctive φ, ω, and ζ. Trobisch is saying that in the exemplar of Claromontanus, Hebrews was not a part of the Pauline Canon and that the scribe of Claromontanus put the blank pages there to indicate a canonical division. I suggest an alternative explanation by looking at the other two related manuscripts.

The other two manuscripts, Codex Augiensis (F^p 010) and Codex Boernerianus (G^p 012), clearly contain Paul's letters and do not include Hebrews. Hatch (1951) has argued convincingly these two manuscripts are related to each other, sharing a common ancestor, but not exemplar. They both contain the same omissions and unusual readings. Moreover, these two manuscripts share enough in common with Codex Claromontanus that Trobisch (1994: 20–22) is convinced, as am I, that all three are related. In both Augiensis and Boernerianus, when the scribe was aware of an omission, he left sufficient blank space for the missing material, e.g., 1 Cor. 3:8–16 (GA_012; image 5031). In Augiensis, the corresponding column of Latin contains the missing text. Codex Augiensis is a ninth century Greek-Latin diglot (in parallel columns with Greek always in the interior column of the codex). This codex lacks the beginning of Romans (beginning with λαλει at 3:19) and the *Greek* text ends after Philemon 1:20, leaving a space for verses 21–25 (GA_010; image 148151). The corresponding Latin column has the remaining verses of Philemon in Latin. The leaves that follow contain the book of Hebrews in Latin but no corresponding Greek text (GA_010; image 148152). I found no commentator who noted the missing end of Philemon in Greek and the inclusion of Hebrews in Latin. It is possible its Greek exemplar was fragmentary since the Greek text breaks off before the ending of Philemon, ending in the middle of the page with the end of Phlm 1:20, leaving the remainder of the column blank. The Latin in the adjoining column contains the remainder of Philemon with a concluding "Amin."

Codex Boernerianus is also a ninth century Greek-Latin diglot (with the Latin written interlinear above the Greek text). The parchment codex, comprising ninety-nine leaves, contains the letters of Paul, and also ends after Philemon 1:20 at precisely the same word as Codex Augiensis, again leaving a space for verses 21–25 (GA_012; image 5183). A distinctive of Codex Boernerianus is that it finishes each letter by noting the letter ends and then adding another line listing the next letter. Thus, 1 Timothy ends (GA_012; image 5167) with:

επληριωθη επιστολη προς τιμοθεον A
αρχεται προς αυτον B

Codex Boernerianus makes no comment, however, about the ending of Philemon, although the scribe seems aware there is missing text. The Latin in this codex is interlinear (like a translational gloss) so there is no supplied Latin for any missing Greek text anywhere in the codex. After sufficient space for the rest of Philemon, the manuscript has: προς λαουδακησας αρχεται επιστολη (GA_012; image 5183), suggesting that the letter to the Laodiceans followed. The remainder of the page is blank. Did its exemplar originally contain the Letter to the Laodiceans? Would Hebrews have followed next? We cannot know. In any case, the truncated ending of Philemon suggests its exemplar lacked the final verses. Thus, while the codex in its current state does not have Hebrews, we can be less certain about why. Because both codices truncate Philemon (in the same place), it seems more likely the exemplar was fragmentary. It is difficult to *conclude* either Augiensis or Boernerianus is *evidence* of a Pauline collection intentionally without Hebrews. Finally, as for Codex Claromontanus, the reason for the blank pages is less clear. The three manuscripts are likely related, probably tracing back to a common exemplar. If so, then the subsequent letter may well have been the Letter to the Laodiceans. The scribe was unwilling to copy it and so left the pages blank before the next letter, Hebrews. It is difficult to conclude that any of these three manuscripts provide *evidence* of a collection of Paul's letters circulating without Hebrews. Along with these three manuscripts, a fourteenth century minuscule is sometimes suggested to be related to the other three by sharing many of the same readings, with Rom. 12:11 often cited as the example. Although the UBS 3 cited it as parallel, an examination of the passage shows it is not.[5]

The manuscript also has an unusual sequence: Acts, General Epistles, Pauline Epistles, Gospels, and no Revelation. Hebrews is found after 2 Thessalonians and before the Pastorals. Colossians is located after Ephesians and before Philippians. The many peculiarities of this manuscript make it hard to draw any conclusions, but we may at least note it does contain Hebrews within the Pauline letters.

So, to summarize the case against Hebrews, Trobisch (1994: 20, 22) maintains three manuscripts contain the thirteen letters of Paul but lack Hebrews, concluding the evidence "can easily be explained by the assumption that Hebrews was added later to a collection of thirteen letters of Paul. This thirteen-letter collection is still extant in Codex Boernerianus (G 012) and Codex Augiensis (F 010)" (22). As attractive as I find this conclusion, the evidence is too weak to support it. We are debating possibilities in an *exemplar* and that particular scribe's motives. Codex Claromontanus contains Hebrews in the original hand. The blank pages could signify some distinction from Paul's letters, but it would not be clear what kind of distinction. On the other hand, we must note the scribe chose to *include* Hebrews in a manuscript containing only Paul's letters, placing it after Philemon, the traditional location. With respect to Codices Augiensis and Boernerianus, one may only conclude that the Greek exemplar *perhaps* lacked Hebrews, but it is more likely its Greek exemplar was fragmentary since it breaks off the Greek text before the ending of Philemon.

[5] See https://gallica.bnf.fr/ark:/12148/btv1b110002532/f105.

Conclusions about evidence for the Corpus Paulinum

Three conclusions seem justified from the manuscript evidence. First, all manuscripts of Paul's letters that are not fragmentary contain all thirteen letters of Paul *and* Hebrews. Second, the location of Hebrews was less fixed. Lastly, and perhaps most significantly, the sequence of the thirteen letters of Paul is nearly fixed even in our earliest manuscripts with only two variations: Eph–Gal are flipped in P46 as are Col–Phil in Claromontanus (and MS 5). The bedrock of thirteen Pauline letters is well stated by Trobisch (1994: 22):

> There is no manuscript evidence to prove that the letters of Paul ever existed in an edition containing [only] some of the thirteen letters ... To retain the view of an independent grouping of the letters of Paul at different Christian congregations, one must assume that the collectors not only ordered the letters the exact same way but also had access to exactly the same number of letters— thirteen.

Perhaps in the earliest stages, a publisher may have perceived some freedom with the *sequencing* of the letters. P46 seems to "correct" the sequence of some letters. The four great majuscules placed Hebrews after 2 Thessalonians as the last of the letters to congregations, before the letters to individuals. In the case of the section numbers in Vaticanus, it appears a later scribe felt the freedom to relocate Hebrews to what seemed to him the appropriate location. Nonetheless, all manuscripts are letter *collections* with at least thirteen (arguably fourteen) letters. The evidence is thorough and quite early. There is no extant evidence for any singular letter of Paul circulating independently. In fact, there is no evidence of smaller collections of Paul's letters, such as a set of Corinthian letters. This lack of evidence for anything other than a full collection, though, has not prevented scholars from conjecturing that individual letters of Paul and subsets of letters did in fact circulate, as we will discuss below.

Earlier evidence from canon lists and church fathers is consonant, suggesting some knowledge of multiple letters of Paul, a potential collection, but no clear indication of the size of the collection. Marcion was purported to have ten letters, including Laodiceans (which was probably Ephesians) and excluding the Pastorals and Hebrews (although it is not clear if he knew of them). The Muratorian Fragment (Canon Muratori) provides evidence of a thirteen-letter collection of Paul's letters, but its import depends on its origin. If the Fragment originated in Rome in the second century, then it is perhaps evidence of the thirteen-letter Pauline corpus before Hebrews was added. If the Fragment belongs to the fourth century in the Eastern empire, its value is less clear. It might reflect an earlier, pre-Hebrews corpus, or it might simply reflect that region's opinion of Hebrews. Given the uncertainties surrounding Marcion and Canon Muratori, one can conclude only that their evidence is no more helpful than the manuscript evidence: Paul's letters were known by at least some, but they provide no evidence for or against a collection of Paul's letters until the late second or early third century, which corresponds with our manuscript evidence. Scholars are left to speculate how the collection arose between Paul and P46.

Hebrews and the Corpus Paulinum

Before we discuss how the collection may have arisen, we need to address the question of Hebrews. The manuscript evidence has Hebrews within or adjacent to the letters of Paul. This has led many scholars to conclude that ancients considered Hebrews to be a letter of Paul. While churches in the Eastern empire were more accepting of Pauline authorship, as Ellingworth (1993: 5) observes, "the canonical status of Hebrews was more uncertain there [Rome] than in the East." It may be more accurate to state that ancients at least considered Hebrews to be "with" the letters of Paul.

Hebrews as non-Pauline

First, this essay is not attempting any argument for Pauline authorship of Hebrews. Even allowing for excessive freedom on the part of an amanuensis, the differences between Hebrews and the other Pauline letters seem too foundational. Hebrews is not even clearly a letter, appearing better as a sermon ("a word of exhortation"; Heb. 13:22), with perhaps an epistolary postscript (Heb. 13:20–25), which could easily have been appended to a dispatched copy of the sermon. While we might imagine Paul liking the essay, I would not want to argue Paul wrote those arguments, particularly related to the Law. Ellingworth (1993: 6–12) presents a convincing case against Pauline authorship.

Hebrews as part of the ancient Corpus Paulinum

While modern scholarship overwhelmingly favors that Paul did not author the letter to the Hebrews, the ancient manuscript evidence must be explained. Clearly, Hebrews was considered "part" of Paul's letter collection. Hebrews is consistently within the collection, often at the end of the Corpus Paulinum, but also in other locations *within* the Corpus. One might best describe it as "restless" within the Pauline collection, eventually coming to rest at the end.

Another very persuasive point is how Hebrews is identified, both in the opening and how the earliest editors titled Hebrews. It is not identified by the author/sender. Greco-Roman letters in general as well as the other non-Pauline letters in the New Testament are identified by the sender. Additionally, in biblical manuscripts, non-Pauline letters are identified by the sender not by recipient, e.g., 3 John (John C), not "To Gaius" (3 Jn 1:1). We speak of the Letter of James, not the Letter to the Twelve Tribes (Jas 1:1). Of all the New Testament letters, *only* the letters of Paul are identified by the recipient rather than by the sender. Paul's letters follow the common Greco-Roman pattern for identifying letters *in a collection*, where the author is not named but only the recipient is; e.g., the letters of Cicero are identified and grouped by recipient (Atticus, Brutus, Quintus, etc.) and then numbered. Likewise, the letters of Seneca the Younger are "Letters to Lucilius" and then numbered (Richards 2017). This suggests the Pauline letters were always (or very quickly) part of a set, which needed not the identification of the author but merely of the recipient to distinguish one from another. Hebrews is titled, then, not in the pattern of other New Testament letters, but in the unique manner of Paul's letters, suggesting Hebrews was part of the collection very early if not at the earliest stages. The fact that Hebrews floated a bit within the fixed canon of thirteen letters suggests that ancients did not debate *if* it belonged but only *how* it belonged. The inconsistent placement of Hebrews likely indicates an original thirteen-letter collection of Paul's letters, but the consistent inclusion of Hebrews *somewhere* within the canon likely indicates that Hebrews was added very early or perhaps even at the onset of the collection.

Collection theories

How did Paul's letters become a collection? Robert Wall (2004: 29) asserts, "We know, for instance, that the ancient church circulated various versions of the Pauline letter canon, differently formed and arranged according to theological, stichometric and chronological principles." Wall (5) even suggests this is the consensus view: "Virtually all scholars now also agree that either a nine-letter (consisting of letters to 'the seven churches') or a ten-letter collection of the sort that Marcion evidently knew was in wide circulation in the early catholic church of the second century." Evidence is otherwise.

Traditionally discussions of the rise of the Pauline collection begin with a discussion of someone(s) desiring to have a copy of Paul's letters. Since Paul wrote to at least nine different locations, how does one acquire copies? In Col. 4:16, Paul encourages the church in Colossae to acquire a copy of his letter to the church in Laodicea. It is not surprising, therefore, that scholars suggested that if a church treasured their own letter(s) of Paul, they would begin to collect copies of his letters written to other churches. Thus, scholars such as Zuntz (1963: 278–79) surmised, partial collections arose in various regions (e.g., Asia Minor, Macedonia, Achaia), perhaps in the early second century, leading finally to more complete collections in the early third century, such as P46, and eventually to complete collections that we find represented in the majuscules of the fourth and fifth century. Harry Gamble (1985: 36) calls this approach "the snowball theory" and Porter (2004b: 99–103) calls it the "gradual collection or Zahn-Harnack theory." Despite the attractive logic, the manuscript evidence, as Trobisch (1994) has demonstrated, does not support it, lacking any evidence for partial collections. The snowball approach fell out of vogue, and scholars began building upon an older theory by Edgar J. Goodspeed (1927: 1–64), who suggested that after the publication of Acts, someone decided to collect copies of the dispatched letters of Paul from the various churches. Goodspeed's reconstruction, even when modified by Knox (1953 [1935]), had not prevailed, but as Porter (2004b: 103–7) noted, the underlying approach remained attractive. Subsequent theories on the formation of the Pauline corpus retained the idea of "an occasion, an agent and a motive" (Gamble 1985: 39). C. F. D. Moule (1962), Hans Conzelmann (1966), Walter Schmithals (1972), and H. M. Schenke (1975) suggested clever theories which all share that an individual (or an individual school) took the initiative to collect the dispatched letters of Paul.

In 1991 and more fully in 1998, I noted that the idea of "collection" often suggests an active process, i.e., that someone "collected" the dispatched letters. "Collection" theories are often built upon two presuppositions. First, they assume no collection existed until someone desired to *publish* the letters. Thus, Paul's letters would need to be esteemed (by someone) before a collection could exist. Second, collection theories assume the published set arose from making copies of the *dispatched* letters. In contrast, I suggested our collection arose originally from Paul's personal set. Porter (2004b: 125) acknowledges and supports my reconstruction, although he later seems to claim the idea as his own (beginning 2011: 30–35; and recently 2016: 175–78). There is much to commend the idea that our collection arose from Paul's own set of copies. Ancient letter writers commonly kept copies of their letters. Harry Gamble (1985: 101) notes, "In antiquity, collected editions of letters were nearly always produced by their author or at their author's behest, often from copies belonging to the author." Suetonius knew three sets of Caesar's letters and he seems to suggest (*Vit. Jul.* 56.6) that the *Epistulae ad senatum* were published by Caesar himself: "Some letters of his to the senate are also preserved, and he seems to have been the first to reduce such documents to pages and the form of a note-book." We can find evidence of letter writers retaining personal copies among the Roman aristocratic elite: "I am jotting down a copy of this letter in my notebook" (see Cic. *Fam.* 7.25.1; 9.26.1; *QFr.* 2.10.4). Examples are also found in Egyptian papyri, on tablets in Roman Britain, as well as in the letters of Ignatius and other early Christian writers. Lastly, we may add that in some references to making such copies, ancients mentioned they were copied into *membranae* (Latin), that is, notebooks made from parchment (rather than wax tablets), a fairly recent innovation in the first century. In 2 Tim. 4:13, Paul, imprisoned in Rome, asks Timothy to bring him his cloak, his books, and especially his notebooks, τας μεμβρανας, using what appears to be a Hellenized form of the Latin. Since other ancient letter writers retained copies of their own important letters in *membranae*, plausibly Paul did as well. Thus, the first (and perhaps the only) collection of Paul's letters may have been Paul's own copies. And if Timothy did in fact bring Paul's *membranae* to him in Rome, this might explain how first-century Christian authors writing from Rome were familiar with Paul's letters.

It may be critiqued that Paul was no Cicero or Seneca. Certainly since Adolf Deissmann (1910), scholars have noted the gap between the epistolary essays of the Roman aristocratic elite and the popular papyrus letters, with Paul's letters falling somewhere in-between. The argument here is not that Paul's letters compare to the aristocratic elite but rather that letter writing in general shared some basic commonalities. John White (1978) and others have noted that Paul used common epistolary rhetoric and formulae, which are also found in the letters of Cicero, Seneca and other Roman elite. Most of what separates the letters of the elite from the common letters are differences of degree, not of substance. Letter writers used secretaries (Cic. *Fam.* 9.26.1; Richards 1991). Those used by the elite like Cicero and Seneca were more skilled. Letter writers used papyrus, tablets, leafbooks, and notebooks, but those of the elite were finer quality (Cic. *Att.* 13.21, 25). Likewise, those who troubled to write significant letters retained their own copies (Cic. *Fam.* 7.25.1); after Cicero heard a letter to Caesar was damaged under transport, Cicero noted, "Later on I sent Caesar an exact duplicate of my letter" (Cic. *QFr.* 2.12.4). There is no evidence to suggest that Paul would have deviated from custom. He likely retained copies. Thus, it is not as unlikely as commonly suggested that a collection of Paul's letters existed in Rome during his imprisonment.

I suggest the (original) collection fell into the hands of disciples upon Paul's death and was not initially esteemed but merely retained. Craig Evans (2019) has argued that papyrus survived much longer than is commonly thought. In the second century, as Paul's popularity grew, churches began to request copies. Initial copies retained the codex format of the original set, perhaps more from inertia than any practical or theological reason. Very early on, a copy organized the letters by length, first to churches and then to individuals, grouping those which shared a common destination. Subsequent inertia retained the practice of the codex and the sequence until it became tradition. Whether Paul or a later disciple urged the publication, the manuscript evidence makes a compelling case that Paul's letters from the onset were published as a collection.

Ongoing research questions

The Pauline Canon discussion has several areas for further research. I will suggest three.

The manuscript tradition

Dan Wallace (2013) has indicated our most important manuscript, P46, needs further study. High quality digital photos available online afford the opportunity for someone to make a stronger case as to whether or not the scribe was planning to include the Pastorals. Also, the dating of the Canon Moratori has not yet been resolved. The later date may be gaining popularity, but is this from better reasoning or because dating manuscripts early is currently out of fashion?

The place of Hebrews: a home for the homeless epistle?

According to manuscript tradition, Hebrews belonged "in some way" with the thirteen letters of Paul yet did not have a fixed location. P46 seems to include it as a letter of Paul, listing it second by length after Romans. The major majuscules appear to consider it a letter to a congregation yet in some way distinct from the others, being positioned last instead of by length. Other manuscripts seem to consider it in some way as belonging with Paul's letters but, again, in some way distinct, being placed at the end of the collection instead of by audience and length. Is it possible to build a reconstruction that better explains "in what way" the early church considered Hebrews to be a part of the Pauline corpus? Perhaps first we need to ask, Why was Hebrews included in the Pauline corpus? Attridge (1989: 1–6) suggests Hebrews was included in the Corpus Paulinum in order to provide the anonymous work an apostolic pedigree. This theory requires such motives as early as AD 200 (P46). Perhaps Hebrews was part of the inherited collection, part of Paul's "notebooks." We have examples of ancient writers appending a copy of another person's letter to the end of one's own; Cicero did it in a letter to Atticus (*Att.* 3.9), Atticus did it in a letter to Cicero (*Att.* 1.17), and other papyrus letters do it (PZen 10). Furthermore, the younger Pliny noted his uncle kept notebooks full of excerpts from works he liked (Pliny *Ep.* 3.5.15–16). More research could be done.

Canonical criticism and canonical order

Canonical criticism explores how texts within a particular canon or sub-canon interpret one another, often by examining how a text refers/alludes to another. Paul sometimes references other letters he wrote, but he only refers to non-canonical letters (unless the Laodicean letter is Ephesians; Col. 4:16) and only when writing to a church that had received the earlier letter (e.g., see 1 Cor. 5:9; 2 Cor. 2:4). Thus, Paul never assumes his readers had a collection. Yet modern scholars find it useful to read "horizontally" in Paul, i.e., using one Pauline text to shed interpretive light on another, even if the letters were not originally connected.

Canonical criticism also explores the interpretive significance of the order of books in a particular canon. While it seems likely Paul's letters were arranged merely on a pragmatic basis, sectioning those to congregations and then those to individuals, and then by length in each section, nevertheless, once a sequence is established, does the canonical order begin to drive theology? For example, scholars are sometime smitten with the idea that the letter at the head of a set functions in some way as the summary for the set, as John Knox (*Philemon,* 10) proposed for Ephesians as the head of the collection of letters by Onesimus (noting Ign. *Eph.* 12.2). Romans is often argued as the center of Paul's theology. How much influence did its location at the "head" of the Pauline collection have? The ramifications are serious. If Romans is the "key," then "justification by faith," arguably a major theme in Romans, becomes a—if not the—key for understanding Paul, as has been argued since the days of the Reformation, even though the concept occurs in only two letters of Paul. One could suggest the recurring themes of unity in Ephesians and Colossians might demonstrate a—if not the—central theme in Paul. First Timothy as a later letter could make a compelling argument to represent more mature thought in Paul. Yet, the place of Romans as "first" in theology remains largely unquestioned. How much has the canonical order of Paul's letters influenced this thought? In what other ways might the sequence of Paul's letters affect interpretation?

Bibliography

Attridge, H. W. (1989), *Hebrews,* Hermeneia, Philadelphia: Fortress.
Bauckham, R. (1983), *Jude and 2 Peter,* WBC, Nashville: Thomas Nelson.
Baum, Armin D. (2017), "Content and Form: Authorship Attribution and Pseudonymity in Ancient Speeches, Letters, Lectures, and Translations—A Rejoinder to Bart Ehrman," *JBL* 136 (2): 381–403.
Conzelmann, H. (1966), "Paulus und die Weitsheit," *NTS* 12 (3): 231–44.
Deissmann, A. (1910), *Light from the Ancient East: The New Testament Illustrated by Recently Discovered Texts of the Graeco-Roman-World,* trans. L. R. M. Strachan, New York and London: Hodder and Stoughton.
Duff, J. (1998), "P46 and the Pastorals: A Misleading Consensus?", *NTS* 44 (4): 578–90.
Ebojo, Edgar Battad, (2014), "A Scribe and His Manuscript: An Investigation into the Scribal Habits of Papyrus 46" (unpublished thesis), University of Birmingham.
Ehrman, B. D. (2012), *Forgery and Counterforgery: The Use of Literary Deceit in Early Christian Polemics,* Oxford: Oxford University Press.

Ellingworth, P. (1993), *The Epistle to the Hebrews,* NIGTC, Grand Rapids: Eerdmans.
Evans, C. A. (2019), "Longevity of Late Antique Autographs and First Copies: A Postscriptum," in C. A. Evans and J. J. Johnston (eds.), *Scribes and Their Remains,* London: T&T Clark.
Ferguson, E. (1982), "Canon Muratori: Date and Provenance," in E. A. Livingstone (ed.), *Studia patristica* 17.2, Oxford: Pergamon, 677–83.
Ferguson, E. (1993), "Review of Geoffrey Mark Hahneman, *The Muratorian Fragment and the Development of the Canon*," *JTS* 44: 696.
Gamble, H. (1985), *The New Testament Canon: Its Making and Meaning,* GBS, Philadelphia: Fortress.
Goodspeed, E. J. (1927), *New Solutions to New Testament Problems,* Chicago: University of Chicago Press.
Grant, R. M. (1965), *The Formation of the New Testament,* New York: Harper & Row.
Grenz, Jesse R. (2018), "Textual Divisions in Codex Vaticanus," *TC: A Journal of Biblical Textual Criticism* 23: 1–22.
Guignard, C. (2019), "The Muratorian Fragment as a Late Antique Fake? An Answer to C. K. Rothschild," *Revue des Sciences Religieuses* 93: 73–90.
Guthrie, Donald. (1990), *New Testament Introduction.* 4th edn., Downers Grove, IL: InterVarsity Press.
Hahneman, Geoffrey Mark (1992), *The Muratorian Fragment and the Development of the Canon,* Oxford: Clarendon Press, 1992.
Hatch, W. H. P. (1951), "On the Relationship of Codex Augiensis and Codex Boernerianus of the Pauline Epistles," *HSCP* 60: 187–99.
Hill, C. E. (1995), "The Debate Over the Muratorian Fragment and the Development of the Canon," *WTJ* 57: 437–52.
Inglis, David. (2014), "The Contents of P46," available online: https://sites.google.com/site/inglisonmarcion/Home/paul/what-did-p46-originally-contain (accessed June 22, 2020).
Johnson, L. T. (1999), *The Writings of the New Testament: An Interpretation,* rev. edn, Philadelphia: Fortress.
Kenyon, F. G. (1934), *The Chester Beatty Biblical Papyri Descriptions and Texts of the Twelve Manuscripts on Papyrus of the Greek Bible: Fasciculus III: Pauline Epistles and Revelation,* London: Emery Walker.
Knox, J. (1953 [1935]), *Philemon among the Letters of Paul,* rev. edn, London: Collins.
McDonald, L. M. (2007), *The Biblical Canon: Its Origin, Transmission, and Authority,* Peabody, MA: Hendrickson.
Martin, R. P. (2000 [1975]), *New Testament Foundations,* rev. edn, vol. 2, Eugene, OR: Wipf & Stock.
Marshall, I. H. (2004), *The Pastoral Epistles,* ICC, Edinburgh: T&T Clark.
Metzger, B. (1987), *Canon of the New Testament: Its Origin, Development, and Significance,* Oxford: Oxford University Press.
Moule, C. F. D. (1962), *The Birth of the New Testament,* 3rd edn, London: A & C Black.
Murphy-O'Connor, J. (1995), *Paul the Letter Writer,* Collegeville, MN: Liturgical Press.
Patzia, A. (1993), "Canon," in G. F. Hawthorne, R. P. Martin, and D. G. Reid (eds.), *DPL,* 85–92, Downers Grove: IVP.
Patzia, A. G. (2011), *The Making of the New Testament: Origin, Collection, Text and Canon,* 2nd edn, Downers Grove: IVP.
Porter, S. E., ed. (2004a), *The Pauline Canon,* Leiden: Brill.
Porter, S. E. (2004b), "When and How was the Pauline Canon Compiled? An Assessment of Theories," in idem (ed), *The Pauline Canon,* 95–127, Leiden: Brill.

Porter, S. E. (2008), "Paul and the Process of Canonization," in C. A. Evans and E. Tov (eds.), *Exploring the Origins of the Bible: Canon Formation in Historical, Literary, and Theological Perspective*, 173–202, Grand Rapids: Baker Academic.

Porter, S. E. (2011), "Paul and the Pauline Letter Collection," in M. F. Bird and J. R. Dodson (eds.), *Paul and the Second Century*, LNTS 412, 19–36, London: T&T Clark.

Porter, S. E. (2016), *The Apostle Paul*, Grand Rapids: Eerdmans.

Richards, E. R. (1991), *The Secretary in the Letters of Paul*, WUNT 2/42, Tübingen: Mohr Siebeck.

Richards, E. R. (1998), "The Codex and the Early Collection of Paul's Letters," *BBR* 8: 151–66.

Richards, E. R. (2012), "Pauline Prescripts and Greco-Roman Epistolary Convention," in S. E. Porter and A. W. Pitts (eds.), *Christian Origins and Greco-Roman Culture: Social and Literary Contexts for the New Testament*, Early Christianity in its Hellenistic Context 1, 497–514, Leiden: Brill.

Richards, E. R. (2017), "Some Observations on Paul and Seneca as Letter Writers," in J. R. Dodson and D. E. Briones (eds.), *Paul and Seneca in Dialogue*, 49–72, Leiden: Brill.

Richards, E. R. (2018), "Was Matthew a Plagiarist? Plagiarism in Greco-Roman Antiquity?" in S. E. Porter and A. W. Pitts (eds.), *Christian Origins and the Establishment of the Early Jesus Movement*, ECHC 4, TENTS 12, 108–33, Leiden: Brill.

Richards, E. R. and K. J. Boyle (2020), "Did Ancients Know the Testaments Were Pseudepigraphic? Implications for 2 Peter," *BBR* 30.3: 403–30.

Rothschild, C. K. (2018), "The Muratorian Fragment as Roman Fake," *NovT* 60 (1): 55–82.

Schenke, H. M. (1975), "Das Weiterwirken des Paulus und die Pflege seines Erbs durch die Paulusschule," *NTS* 21 (4): 505–18.

Scherbenske, E. (2013), *Canonizing Paul: Ancient Editorial Practice and the Corpus Paulinum*, Oxford: Oxford University Press.

Schmid, U. (1995), *Marcion und sein Apostolos*, ANTF 25, Berlin: de Gruyter.

Schmithals, W. (1972), "On the Composition and Earliest Collection of the Major Epistles of Paul," in idem, *Paul and the Gnostics*, trans. J. Steely, 239–74, Nashville: Abingdon.

Skeat, T. C. (1984), "The Codex Vaticanus in the Fifteenth Century", in *JTS* 35 (2): 454–65.

Stevens, C. S. (2020), *History of the Pauline Corpus in Texts, Transmissions, and Trajectories: A Textual Analysis of Manuscripts from the Second to the Fifth Century*, TENT 14, Leiden: Brill.

Sundberg, A. C., Jr. (1973), "Canon Muratori: A Fourth Century List," *HTR* 66: 1–41.

Trobisch, D. (1994), *Paul's Letter Collection*, Minneapolis: Fortress.

Versace, P. (2018), *I Marginalia del Codex Vaticanus*, StT 528, Vatican: Biblioteca Apostolica Vaticana.

Wall, R. W. (2004), "The Function of the Pastoral Letters within the Pauline Canon of the New Testament: A Canonical Approach," in S. E. Porter (ed.), *The Pauline Canon*, 27–44, Leiden: Brill.

Wallace, D. B. (2013), "Some Notes on the Earliest Manuscript of Paul's Letters." Available online: https://danielbwallace.com/2013/06/08/some-notes-on-the-earliest-manuscript-of-pauls-letters/ (accessed February 26, 2020).

Westcott, B. F. (1896), *General Survey of the History of the Canon of the New Testament*, 7th edn, London: Macmillan.

White, J. L. (1978), "Epistolary Formulas and Cliches in Greek Papyrus Letters," *SBLSP* 14: 289–319.

Zuntz, G. (1963), *The Text of the Epistles: A Disquisition upon the Corpus Paulinum*, Oxford: Oxford University Press.

15

Revelation as the Ending of the Canon

Külli Tõniste

The primary purpose of this chapter is to survey the historical process and circumstances by which Revelation came to be included in and placed at the end of the Christian canon. But it is not just history that I am interested in, I am also curious regarding the purpose and contribution of this book for the canon as a whole.

Although some question its belonging in the canon *per se*, in practice, the book of Revelation has often been treated as an appendix. Revelation certainly is one of a kind in the New Testament, and therefore it does not fit into any particular sub-collection. Because of its distinctiveness, Revelation finds itself shuffled about within New Testament theologies. Authors have not reached a consensus about where it belongs theologically. Should it be treated among the Johannine materials? But what, if anything, holds Johannine materials together? Perhaps it should be read in the context of non-canonical apocalyptic literature? But none of these other writings were considered a part of Scripture; how then could they provide an interpretive lens for Revelation?

Accordingly, it will be helpful to survey the historical process and circumstances by which Revelation came to be included in the Christian canon and which placed Revelation at the end. And then it will also be beneficial to look at how this book forms an ending to the biblical canon (literarily and theologically). I suggest that this book forms an ending to the canon as a whole and, therefore, suggest that we should remove it from the category of utopias and rather understand it as practical theology instructing Christians how to live under a hostile government. I argue historically and theologically that the editorial choice to place Revelation at the end was not a marginalizing decision and it was not placed there randomly. Revelation is not an appendix, but a calculated, intentional, and culminating ending to a long story, and therefore it has spiritual, theological, and practical implications.

Why canon formation was necessary

The early church was concerned with preserving the Scriptures, and not the record of the process of selecting them. The historical records concerning the process are fragmented and the sources are limited. We mainly have three types of sources that prove helpful for reconstructing the canonization process: the writings of the early fathers, the earliest canon lists, and the earliest codex-style manuscripts of the Bible. The last two are particularly valuable because they also provide insight into the canonical ordering of the writings.

During the first Christian centuries, the church had many Scriptures but no firm canon (Gamble 2003: 410). All the writings comprising the NT were first recognized as Scriptures and, only then, included within the canon. Some writings that were held in the same high esteem as Scripture did not eventually make it into the canon (e.g., Shepherd of Hermas). When the canon of the NT was formalized perhaps as late as the fourth century, the Scriptures that did not make the final cut fell out of use in worship and also did not have the benefit of the continued mass production those reckoned to be Scripture did. Over time such writings were no longer considered Scripture.

In the first four centuries we can discern a movement away from having a loose collection of Scriptures and toward compiling a defined (and closed) canon. While many Christian writings were regarded as Scripture from early on (cf. 2 Pet. 3:15–16), it took time for the church to realize the need for canon. In his classic book, *The Canon of the New Testament*, Bruce M. Metzger deals with the following influences on the development of the canon: Gnosticism, Montanism, persecution of Christians, changes in ancient book-making technique, and development of other collections and lists of "canonical" books in Jewish and pagan cultures (Metzger 1997 75–112).

Canon formation was a complex process and there would have been other influences such as: the influence of the authoritative theologians (Origen, Athanasius, Jerome and Augustine); the political and cultural differences; different theological orientations of the great ecclesiastical centers (Rome, Alexandria, and Antioch); and the influence of the early ecclesiastical councils (Gamble 2003: 65–67). There was no one single reason to formalize the twenty-seven-book collection called New Testament. But due to many circumstances it was necessary for the church to come to an agreement about an authoritative collection of Scriptures to support Christian faith and practice.

Inclusion of the Book of Revelation into the canon

The earliest available witnesses to the use of Revelation as Scripture are the apostolic fathers and patristic authors. Comparing their use of Revelation with that of Old Testament texts sheds light on their understanding of the text's function and authority. However, the challenge is that the apostolic fathers simply allude to texts rather than gave explicit references with quotation formulas. Often it is hard to determine whether they were citing from a book or simply representing an oral tradition. However, because the Apocalypse is so distinctive in its language, style, and content, we can usually be rather certain that the actual book was used in the apostolic fathers. Another difficulty is that the writings of the apostolic fathers do not discuss the canonicity of the materials that they cite or allude to. What we get is a testimony that a certain book was known, used, and valued by some theologians early on. The actual discussions regarding the canon fall to a later time, mostly to the third and fourth centuries.

Nevertheless, from the fact that the early theologians cited the Apocalypse, alluded to it, or commented on it, we gather that their readers would have recognized and valued that source. Moreover, if references to Revelation are presented in a manner similar to when an author is citing the OT Scriptures (e.g., by prefacing it with "it is written" or any other citation formula customary for citing Scriptures, by using it to refute heretics, and/or by defending it against the criticism of heretics), we can assume that Revelation was considered to be of the same status as those OT Scriptures. If it is used to refute other writings and correct ideas it means it was considered authoritative. Also, Revelation's use in worship liturgy as well as the use of its imagery in decor of early churches and catacombs would show its elevated status. The following is a survey of early witnesses to the book of Revelation. Although sparse and rather fragmented these witnesses serve as evidence that Revelation was an integral part of Christian theology and preaching as early as in the second century.

Early Eastern witnesses to the Book of Revelation

The early church can be divided by culture and language into the Greek-speaking East and the Latin-speaking West. I will first consider the early Eastern witnesses to the book of Revelation as that is closer to its birthplace in Asia Minor.

Papias (*ca.* AD 116), bishop of Hierapolis and friend of Polycarp and, according to some accounts, also of the apostle John, affirmed, according to Andreas of Caesarea, Revelation as inspired Scripture and also commented on part of it.[1] Dionysius, bishop of Corinth (*ca.* AD 170), made a possible reference to the "woe" of Rev. 22:18–19 as he complained that people have distorted his letters by "taking away some things and adding others" (*Hist. eccl.* 4.23.12).

Tatian (*ca.* AD 172), the author of the lost *Diatessaron*, probably alludes to the Apocalypse in his only existing work *Address to Greeks* when showing that the present heaven and earth are finite and in the new superior world there is no disease and there is perpetual daylight (Rev. 21:4 and 22:1–6). He may have John in mind when attributing this thinking to "the teaching of the prophets" (Tatian, *Orat.* 20). Clement of Alexandria (*ca.* AD 194) also explicitly references the Apocalypse as he explains that the righteous "will sit down on the four-and-twenty thrones, judging the people, as John says in the Apocalypse" (Clement, *Strom.* 6.13).

According to Eusebius, Theophilus, the bishop of Antioch *ca.* AD 180, quoted from the Revelation of John in his writing titled *Against the Heresy of Hermogenes* (*Hist. eccl.* 4.24.1). Eusebius also knew of a work by Melito, bishop of Sardis (d. AD 190), a respected and well-travelled theologian. The title of Melito's work was either *On the Devil and the Apocalypse of John* or simply *The Apocalypse of John* (*Hist. eccl.* 4.26). Eusebius also preserved what Melito thought to be the books of the OT, which may suggest that Eusebius considered him a reliable early witness in the question of Scripture (*Hist. eccl.* 4.26). Furthermore, Melito travelled to Palestine in order to gather information regarding the true Christian Scriptures, which makes his witness in favor of the Apocalypse all the more significant.

---

[1] This fragment is preserved through Andreas, bishop of Caesarea in Cappadocia: "With regard to the inspiration of the book (Revelation), we deem it superfluous to add another word; for the blessed Gregory Theologus and Cyril, and even men of still older date, Papias, Irenaeus, Methodius, and Hippolytus, bore entirely satisfactory testimony to it" (*ANF* 1:155).

Adversus Cataphrygas is an anonymous fragment from Asia preserved by Eusebius. It condemns the Montanists who created new Scriptures. This document from the beginning of the third century appears to allude to Rev. 22:18–19 as a reason why there should be no new Scriptures or prophecies created (*Hist. eccl.* 5.16). Apollonius, who according to some accounts was a bishop of Ephesus (*ca.* AD 210), is recorded by Eusebius to have made use of the Apocalypse in his controversy with the Montanist sect that claimed that their center in Phrygia was the heavenly Jerusalem of which John had written (*Hist. eccl.* 5.18; also see Westcott 1896: 389).

Origen (*ca.* AD 230) accepted the book of Revelation as Scripture (though he had reservations concerning James, 2 Peter, and 2–3 John). Origen regarded the Gospel of John, the Apocalypse, and 1 John (possibly also 2 and 3 John) as having been written by the same person, the one "who leaned on Jesus' breast, namely John" (*Comm. Jon.* 5.3 [*ANF* 9:346–47]). Origen's testimony reaches us via Eusebius, and while Eusebius sets his remark in the context of a canon list, Origen's comment is focused upon the issue of authorship of those accepted scriptural writings. Origen is also cited by Rufinus as listing John's Apocalypse as one of the Lord's trumpets alongside the other NT authors in his *Homilies on Joshua* (Rufinus, *Orig. Hom. Jos.* 8.1). Finally Methodius, bishop of Lycia and of Tyre (d. AD 311), received the Apocalypse as a work of "the blessed John" and had no doubts about its authority as Scripture (Methodius, *Res.* 3.2.9).

It is significant that the writers who originated from Asia Minor (Papias, Melito, Irenaeus [originally from Smyrna], Apollonius, and Methodius), whose churches would have been among the original recipients of the book of Revelation (or in the close geographic region), all recognized it as authoritative and attributed it to John (presumably the apostle). This acceptance is all the more significant because the churches of Asia Minor appear to have a tendency to limit the boundaries of canonical Scripture rather than expand it.[2]

In addition to the church fathers, some heretical movements also testify to the early knowledge and use of the Apocalypse in the East. For example, a gnostic heretic Cerinthus (*ca.* AD 100), possibly a contemporary of the apostle John from the Roman province of Asia, used it extensively. Later when chiliasm fell out of favor in Eastern Christianity and the book of Revelation with it, Dionysius of Alexandria (*ca.* AD 247) mentions that some attributed Revelation to a gnostic called Cerinthus. He mentions such while he himself disagreed and attributed it to a different, but also godly and inspired, John (Eusebius, *Hist. eccl.* 7.25). In this long segment cited by Eusebius, Dionysius does not provide any historical evidence to show that John could not have been the author. Instead, he argues, on the basis of the differences of vocabulary, style, and quality of Greek, that the Gospel and the Epistles come from a single author, while the Apocalypse comes from a different author. He appears to dislike the book because so many heretical movements used it, and he concludes that it could not have originated from apostolic authority (Eusebius, *Hist. eccl.* 7.25.7). Later in the fourth century, Epiphanius objects to Dionysius's arguments and defends the book's apostolic origins

---

[2] Westcott knows only one instance where an Asiatic author appears to give authority to an uncanonical book–namely, Irenaeus' reference to the Shepherd of Hermas (Irenaeus, *Haer.* 4.20.2). Hebrews, James, 2 Peter, and Jude were viewed as uncertain in Asia Minor (Westcott 1896: 395).

by engaging the criticisms of Dionysius directly (Epiphanius, *Haer.* 51.35). Other branches of proto-Gnosticism and Gnosticism also used the Apocalypse: the Ophite sectarians (*ca.* AD 100) quoted from it, and the Marcosians (early second century), against whom Irenaeus argues, appear to have used Revelation and its symbolic interpretations (*Haer.* 1.14.6; 15.1).

The early consensus about the authority of Revelation in the East gave way to general suspicion because of the widespread misuse of the book by heretical movements. At the key era of canon formation in the fourth century, we will see that Revelation will be at the center of controversy in the East. It takes some time for Revelation to recover from the misuse and the consequent marginalization. However, the theology of Revelation had already been firmly incorporated into the theology of the church during the first three centuries.

Early Western witnesses to the Book of Revelation

I now turn to the early Western witnesses to the book of Revelation. Here we find that as early as at the turn of the century we have Hermas (*ca.* AD 100), in the *Visions* section of his *Shepherd*, making frequent allusions to the Apocalypse. Much of the imagery in the Shepherd is directly derived from Revelation: such as, the church as a woman/bride (Herm. *Vis.* 2.4; 4.2; Rev. 12:1; 21:2), the beast as her enemy (Herm. *Vis.* 4.1; Rev. 12:4), Books of Life with the names of the righteous in them (Herm. *Vis.* 1.3; Rev. 20:15), and mention of the great tribulation (Herm. *Vis.* 2.2; 3.2; Rev. 7:14; also 2 Thess. 2:3).

Justin Martyr, a philosopher and an early Christian apologist who converted around AD 130, considers the Apocalypse both a prophetic and an apostolic work. In his *Dialogue with Trypho the Jew* he writes,

> [T]here was a certain man with us, whose name was John, one of the apostles of Christ, who prophesied, by a revelation that was made to him, that those who believed in our Christ would dwell a thousand years in Jerusalem; and that thereafter the general, and, in short, the eternal resurrection and judgment of all men would likewise take place.
>
> *Dial.* 81.4

The unknown author of *The Epistle of the Churches at Lyons and Vienne* testifies to knowledge of the book of Revelation in southern France around AD 177, demonstrating how widespread the book was already in the second century. A modified version of Rev. 22:11 is cited (see Eusebius, *Hist. eccl.* 5.1.61) with more of the work preserved by Eusebius in *Hist. eccl.* 5.1.1–2.

Though serving in the Western church, Irenaeus of Lyons, as a disciple of Polycarp of Smyrna, is a representative of Eastern thought quoting from Revelation more than thirty times in his *Adversus Haereses* (according to the index of *ANF* 1:602). The largest number of these references, including direct quotes from Rev. 20 and 21, appear toward the end of the book where Irenaeus uses these as evidence to argue for the physical resurrection of the dead and the coming of the New Jerusalem on earth. He also considered it to be written by John the disciple of Jesus (*Haer.* 4.20.11). Even as early as AD 178, Revelation appears to be well-integrated into the theological writings of Irenaeus as he cites from it alongside Isaiah, Paul's letter to Galatians, and the gospel of Matthew. Irenaeus had no hesitations about its scriptural status.

Tertullian from Carthage who converted about AD 195, defended the Christian Scriptures against Marcionite heretics in his *Against Marcion* and mentions the Apocalypse of John that Marcion rejects. Tertullian accepts it as an authoritative and apostolic work (Tertullian, *Adv. Marc.* 4.5).

Hippolytus of Rome (d. AD 235) was possibly a pupil of Irenaeus. According to Eusebius he had a debate with a learned Roman presbyter, Gaius (or Caius), over the Johannine authorship of the book of Revelation (Eusebius, *Hist. eccl.* 4.20). Gaius challenged Johannine authorship so as to undermine the authority of Revelation for his anti-Montanist polemics. In response Hippolytus wrote a treatise titled *On the Gospel of John and the Apocalypse*. The treatise was directed against the group he called the Alogi that rejected the two books (Florovski 1987). The work itself has not been preserved (Metzger 1997: 150).

Cyprian, bishop of Carthage (d. AD 258) used Revelation abundantly with other Scriptures (although he never mentioned Hebrews). He frequently prefixes it with the phrase "it is written" and cites it in the same paragraph with the other NT Scriptures without any subordinating distinctions (for example, Cyprian, *Epistle* 13.1 and *Epistle* 36.1). Commodius, a North-African clergyman, wrote *Instructions for the Christian Life* (ca. AD 240) and *Apologetic Poem against Jews and Gentiles* (AD 249). Both works appear to include catechetical instructions, and in these he elaborated on the contents of Revelation. He speculated on the end of the world and the millennium and developed a view that there would be two antichrists, based on the two beasts of Revelation. The first antichrist is based on Nero and the second and more powerful one comes from the Jews. Pope Gelasius classified Commodius as an apocryphal writer due to his borderline heretical views (Commodius, *Instr.* 1.41, see also Shaff 1907–1910).

Victorinus, bishop of Pettau (*ca.* AD 290) knew and cited abundantly from the Apocalypse. He wrote several commentaries on both OT and NT books, as well as a commentary on the Apocalypse. His commentary is the oldest commentary on Revelation in existence. In it Victorinus proposed a chiliast interpretation.[3] Pamphilus was a presbyter of Caesarea (d. AD 309) and a friend of Eusebius. He was a learned man and had great love for the Scriptures. He collected and copied several manuscripts of biblical books that were preserved in the once-famous library of Caesarea and of which fragments remain. Following the judgments of Origen, he supported John the apostle as the author of the Apocalypse (Pamphilus, *Apol.* 7; cf. Rev. 20:13, 6).

Against Dice-Players (*Adversus aleatores*) is a pastoral text against gambling. The author is unknown but is probably a bishop from North Africa. The document dates around AD 300 and the author cites Scripture abundantly, including Revelation, but also the Shepherd and *Didache* (Metzger 1997: 163–64). Lactantius, born in either Africa or Italy, was a teacher of rhetoric who converted in old age. In about AD 315 he

---

[3] For the *Commentary on the Apocalypse* by Victorinus, see *ANF* 7:344–60.

settled in Gaul and was chosen by Emperor Constantine to be the teacher of his son Crispus. In his *Divine Institutes* he cites prophecies of Revelation and elaborates on them upon numerous occasions (Lactantius, *Inst.* 7.16–17; 7:27; *Epit.* 42). In addition to the Eastern and Western Fathers, the *Sibylline Oracles* and *Testaments of the Twelve Patriarchs* contain numerous references to the Apocalypse. These mimic the genre of the Apocalypse and thus testify to the popularity of this book (Westcott 1896: 410).

The above examples document that the apostolic and early church fathers both from the East and West knew and used Revelation and attributed to it scriptural status alongside other NT writings. The majority considered it apostolic in origin and it was known and used in a wide geographic area. On many occasions Revelation was cited on a par with OT Scripture (as is evident from the writings of Cyprian). Its author John was called both an apostle and a prophet (as in the writings of Justin Martyr). Revelation was used to refute and correct the teachings of the heretics (as in the works of Irenaeus and others), which speaks of its status and authority. The majority of the fathers seemed to assume its apostolic authorship, and Revelation was defended when someone attacked either its authenticity or authorship (as in the works of Hippolytus against Gaius and later Epiphanius against Dionysius).

Although any one of these witnesses in isolation does not provide conclusive evidence, together they suggest that Revelation was regarded as Scripture from very early on, alongside the Gospels, the Pauline Epistles, and the Catholic Epistles, and that Revelation was indeed better known and accepted than some of the Catholic Epistles. Objections to its status as Scripture or its apostolic authorship seem to have risen later as the book becomes fashionable among heretical movements. What seemed like an early consensus in the church fell apart when the time came to ratify this informal "canon" of Scripture. In the fourth century many questions arose concerning the authority and origin of Revelation. It almost seems that the book was hijacked by the sectarians which caused the churches to question its origin. And what should have been disputes between various interpretations of Revelation had escalated into disputes about the origin and authority of Revelation and its author.

Early canon lists as witnesses of the canon formation

Canon lists are important because they represent larger Christian communities and churches rather than just the preferences of individual authors who may or may not have had access to all the early manuscripts. Therefore, we should take seriously whatever light they can shed upon the issues of the acceptance of Revelation as Scripture. Lists by leaders and bishops, such as Eusebius, Athanasius, Augustine, Amphilochus, and Gregory of Naziansus, express a general consensus of the church of their areas. Personal opinions, where they sometimes differed from the consensus, can be discerned in their writings. For example, Eusebius had access to multiple sources, and as a historian he presented the general consensus, but he was not shy at times about inserting his personal opinion (see for example, *Hist. eccl.* 3.25.1–7; 7.25.1–27).

Whereas some canon lists date to the second century, the vast majority come from the fourth century. By the end of the fourth century the NT canon began to be crystallized as evidenced by the fact that most of the later canon lists do not even bother to name the contents of the Pauline corpus, they simply state either thirteen or fourteen Pauline Epistles assuming that the readers would know which epistles were meant. They also state that there were seven Catholic Epistles, and it is assumed that the readers knew which ones were meant. Athanasius' *Festal Letter* (AD 367) has been traditionally considered the date of fixing the NT canon in the Western Church. But some consider it "a minor point" which did not settle anything for the wider church (Gallagher and Meade 2017: 30). Debates over the canon continued in the East where the Catholic Epistles and the book of Revelation remained contested.

I discuss the following canon lists more or less chronologically. Marcion is the author of the first known canon list. His canon included only ten Pauline Epistles and a revised version of Luke. It did not include Revelation or any other book that would have exhibited Jewish or OT influences. He considered Paul to be the only true apostle and rejected Jerusalem authorities like Peter, John and Jude (Trobisch 2000: 77). His theological premise was that the Father of Jesus was a God of love, and as such was rather different from the OT Creator that he called a demiurge. As Tertullian stated: "Marcion expressly and openly used the knife, not the pen, since he made such an excision of the Scriptures as suited his own subject-matter" (*On Prescription Against Heretics*, 38). The Marcionite canon and teachings of Gnosticism were widespread in the early church, and most of the church fathers of that time wrote against his teachings (Cross and Livingstone 1997: 1034).

The Muratorian Canon is dated not long before AD 200 and belongs to the Western church (Campenhausen 1972: 243–44). Williams suggests Hippolytus as the possible author; however, nothing can go beyond a hypothesis in this matter (Williams 1969: 50–51). The Muratorian Canon accepts the Revelation of John. It also accepts the Revelation of Peter, with a side note that some were not willing that the latter should be read in the church.

Vetus Latina is not really a canon list, but refers to the Old Latin versions of the Bible that circulated in the churches, especially in North Africa and southern Gaul, before Jerome composed his Vulgate. There is evidence for Latin translations of Scripture from as early as the second century. Scholars have reconstructed most of it through citations found in the writings of the church fathers. The content of the Vetus Latina is a reconstruction by Westcott, who believes it to be akin to the Muratorian Canon. The book of Revelation was certainly part of the Vetus Latina, although it is unknown from how early on. *The Acts of the Scillitan Martyrs*, from the otherwise unknown village of Scillium in North Africa, is probably the oldest dated document in the history of the Latin church and one of the oldest pieces of evidence for the Vetus Latina. It shows that at least the Pauline Epistles, but quite likely other parts of the NT, were circulated in Latin around AD 180. We do not know if Revelation was included at that early date (Metzger 1997: 156–57).

The Clermont List (Codex Claromontanus) has been preserved for us as an insert into a sixth-century manuscript and it is hard to date with accuracy. Some authorities believe that it represents the accepted usage of Scripture in Egypt around AD 320 (Zahn 1890: 157–72 and Harnack 1904: 84–88). It includes Revelation, as well as *Barnabas*, Shepherd, *Acts of Paul*, and the *Apocalypse of Peter*. It looks like an error that a scribe has omitted Philippians, 1 and 2 Thessalonians, and probably also Hebrews. There is a short horizontal line before *Barnabas*, Shepherd, *Acts of Paul*, and the

Apocalypse of Peter, which Metzger suggests is to distinguish them from the titles that the scribe considered authoritative. Williams records that there is also a line before the Catholic Epistles, Acts, and Revelation, which may suggest change of authorship (see Metzger 1997: 230; Williams 1969: 52).

Eusebius, bishop of Caesarea and the author of the first church history, wrote around AD 324. He classified the book of Revelation under universally acknowledged books, but was quick to add that some dispute it and some reject it (*Hist. eccl.* 3.3.4; 3.38.2). On the basis of the great lengths to which Eusebius went to explain and substantiate what seemed to be his personal preference (that the status of Revelation is disputed and therefore it is a lesser of the NT books), one can deduce that the wider church had welcomed the Apocalypse as part of the canon. Eusebius acknowledged that fact and was aware he represented a minority view. The Montanist abuse of the Apocalypse gave him reason to lessen the status of Revelation, so he emphasized that some did not consider it genuine (*Hist. eccl.* 7.25.18–27).

Cyril of Jerusalem (*ca.* AD 350) reveals that the use of Revelation was discouraged in the Eastern church. Cyril, the bishop of Jerusalem, lists the Scriptures to be read in a document called *Catechetical Lectures*, but does not include Revelation (*Catech.* 4.36, see also Metzger 1997: 210). The criteria appear to have been that if a book is not read in churches, it should not be read in private devotion either. It is possible that the book's excessive use by Montanists had caused Eastern church leaders like Cyril to shy away from Revelation.

The Cheltenham List (Mommsen Catalogue), discovered in 1885 by Theodor Mommsen, is believed to represent the canon of North Africa and is dated to AD 359. It includes Revelation, but excludes Hebrews, James, and Jude (Williams 1969: 53). The Catalogue also lists the Gospels in an unusual order: Matthew, Mark, John, and Luke. The so-called Canon 60 (59) of the Synod of Laodicea (*ca.* AD 363) lists the present-day NT, but omits Revelation. Almost nothing is known of the Synod of Laodicea, and the document seems to give subject headings of the canons issued by the earlier councils. According to Zahn, the document is a later appendix to an original set of 59 ecclesiastical laws and not an original (Zahn 1890: 193–202).

Athanasius' Festal Letter 39 from AD 367 may be the first canon list that corresponds exactly to the present-day NT canon. Athanasius writes, after having listed the canonical books:

> there are other books besides these not indeed included in the Canon, but appointed by the Fathers to be read by those who newly join us, and who wish for instruction in the word of godliness ... But the former, my brethren, are included in the Canon, the latter being [merely] read; nor is there in any place a mention of apocryphal writings. But they are an invention of heretics, who write them when they choose, bestowing upon them that so, using them as ancient writings, they may find occasion to lead astray the simple.
>
> *Ep. fest.* 39.7

Despite the witness of Athanasius, the issue of the canon was clearly not settled yet. There continued to be differences in both the content and the order of the canon.

Epiphanius, contemporary and countryman of Cyril, and the bishop of Salamis in Cyprus (*ca.* AD 368), in writing against false teachers, includes a list of Scriptures that coincides with our present NT. Elsewhere he notes that some have doubts concerning the Apocalypse, but he appears not to share them. He considers the Apocalypse to be of apostolic origin (Epiphanius, *Haer.* 51.35). But he also includes the *Wisdom of Solomon* and the *Wisdom of the Son of Sirach* and calls them "divine writings" too (*Haer.* 76.5).

The Apostolic Canons (AD 380) was one of many additions made by the final editor of an ancient Syrian book of church order called *The Apostolic Constitutions*. The document appears to represent the views of the Syrian churches toward the end of the fourth century. It was added to an earlier document. This canon omits Revelation, probably under the same objections as we found in Cyril of Jerusalem. Gregory of Nazianzus (d. AD 389) agrees with Athanasius in his canon list when it comes to the OT, but differs with respect to the NT. He places the Catholic Epistles after the Pauline Epistles and omits Revelation. However, he knew about its existence and, on a handful of occasions, quoted from it (*Or.* 29.7; 42.9).

Another list of biblical books from the same period comes from Amphilocius (d. AD 394), the bishop of Iconium in Lycaonia (Asia Minor). To his friend Seleucus he wrote in poetic form a list of both Old and New Testament books (*Iambi ad Seleucum*). He includes Revelation at the end, but notes that most consider it spurious. He also records that some say there are three Catholic Epistles (James, Peter, and John), while others say that there are seven. He still concludes his list with these words: "This is perhaps the most reliable [literally, the most un-falsified] canon of the divinely inspired scriptures."[4]

The Carthaginian Catalogue preserves the endorsement of twenty-seven books that constitute the NT canon by the Third Council of Carthage in AD 397 (the whole council lasted from the Synod of Hippo in AD 393 to 424). Augustine of Hippo (*ca.* AD 397), in his book *Christian Instruction*, provides his selection of the canonical books and it coincides with our NT canon, with the exception of the book order, which is different in the case of the Catholic Epistles and Acts. He also provides the following criteria for determining canonicity:

> to prefer those that are received by all the catholic churches to those which some do not receive. Among those, again, which are not received by all, he will prefer such as have the sanction of the greater number and those of greater authority, to such as are held by the smaller number and those of less authority. If, however, he shall find that some books are held by the greater number of churches, and others by the churches of greater authority (though this is not a very likely thing to happen), I think that in such a case the authority on the two sides is to be looked upon as equal.
>
> *Doctr. chr.* 2.8

---

[4] Amphilocius, Ap. Gregor. Nazianz. *Carm. Sect.* 2.7. Metzger comments on the hypothetical form of Amphilocius' statement. He finds it noteworthy that "here we have a bishop in Asia Minor a colleague of the Gregories and of Basil, and yet he seems to be uncertain as to the exact extent of the canon!" (Metzger 1997: 213).

The Peshitta, is not a canon list but a Syriac version of the Bible. The Peshitta is valued among Eastern Orthodox and Assyrian Christianity to this day as *the* Scriptures. Their tradition holds that most of the NT and parts of the OT were originally written in Aramaic, the native tongue of Jesus and the apostles. Only later was the NT translated into Greek. The Peshitta is dated to the early fifth century, and possibly even earlier. It did not originally include Revelation and some of the Catholic Epistles: 2 Peter, 2 and 3 John, and Jude. Revelation was added to the Peshitta as late as the eleventh century.

The Decree of Gelasius (*Decretum Gelasianum*) is attributed to Popes Damasus, Gelasius, and Hormisdas. It may originate from a council held, probably, at Rome in AD 382, although many scholars argue that it is a private compilation from the sixth century (Dobschütz 1912). It lists the books included in the Old and New Testaments, and then includes a list of sixty-two apocryphal books and thirty-five names of heretical authors. Interestingly, the document does not include the Revelation of John among the NT canon.

The study of these early canon lists is confusing. At times their particular purpose and the extent of authority are hard to determine (as in the case of the Muratorian Fragment). At other times their very authenticity is under question (as is the case with Canon 60). At still other times, the lists are difficult to date (as in the case of Codex Claromontanus and the decree of Gelasius). From what we can tell, it seems that the Eastern canons are more restricted and either doubt or reject Revelation along with some of the Catholic Epistles, while the Western canons are more likely to include both as well as some additional writings that were later rejected.

Early codex manuscripts as the primary witnesses of the canon formation

The earliest codices of the Bible. Sinaiticus, Vaticanus, Alexandrinus, and Ephraemi, provide another witness to the canon formation process.

Codex Sinaiticus (א), is the only complete uncial manuscript of the NT to date and, together with Codex Vaticanus, is the earliest copy of the whole Greek Bible. It has been dated to around AD 340. Both are the work of skilled professional scribes. According to James Bentley, Tischendorf believed the handwriting of one of the scribes of Codex Sinaiticus and one of the scribes of Codex Vaticanus was the same.[5] Scholars theorize that both codices were produced after the decree of Constantine the Great, who in AD 331 commissioned Eusebius of Caesarea to provide him with fifty complete and professional manuscripts of the Christian Bible on fine parchment. Codex Sinaiticus is an important witness to the acceptance of Revelation to the canon from very early times; however, it also includes the *Epistle of Barnabas* and Shepherd of Hermas at the end.

Codex Vaticanus (B), dated to the middle of the fourth century, was long kept a secret as it was locked behind the walls of the Vatican. It was through the writing of Tischendorf in 1867 that it was first brought to the public eye. A year later Roman Catholic scholar Carlo Vercellone published the official edition (Bentley 1986: 126). Two great Cambridge scholars, Brooke Foss Westcott and Fenton John Anthony Hort,

---

[5] Sinaiticus has a couple of interesting spelling mistakes, providing further evidence that the place of their origin may have very well been Caesarea, see Bentley 1986: 119.

used Codex Vaticanus and Codex Sinaiticus as the primary basis for their Greek text of the NT. Codex Vaticanus does not technically include Revelation, as the manuscript breaks off at Heb. 9:14, but there are very few scholars who doubt that it originally included Revelation.

Codex Alexandrinus (A) is an early fifth-century manuscript of the Greek Bible, written in two columns on vellum. Its history is unknown, but it may have been brought from Constantinople to Alexandria in 1308. Sometime in the seventeenth century, Cyril, patriarch of Constantinople, gifted the manuscript to King James I in England. Codex Alexandrinus corresponds in order to the Codex Vaticanus. It includes the book of Revelation, followed by the two Clementine Epistles.

Codex Ephraemi (C) is a fifth-century palimpsest; the original pages have been washed, scraped, written over with writings of St. Ephraem Syrus, and rebound (Trobisch 2000: 25). Many pages are therefore illegible. Scholars have, however, deciphered fragments of every NT book except 2 Thessalonians and 2 John. It contained Revelation, but due to its fragmentary nature, it is impossible to restore the original ordering of the books.

David Trobisch has proposed an hypothesis that Codex Sinaiticus, Codex Vaticanus, Codex Alexandrinus, and possibly also Codex Ephraemi, preserve something that he calls a Canonical Edition of the NT. He proposes that such edition was published perhaps as early as the middle of the second century. It started with the Gospels and ended with the book of Revelation and became the archetype of all the other NT collections (Trobisch 2000: 3). Trobisch builds his argument on the uniform use of titles, *nomina sacra*, and other textual phenomena that did not come from the authors of the various NT writings, but that indicate careful editorial work in compiling this collection of Scripture.

What can be concluded based on the study of these earliest manuscripts is that sometime during the fourth century the matters of the NT canon began to stabilize. As far as we can tell, the present twenty-seven NT books were firmly included in all four major codices, and they are arranged in a somewhat unified order.[6] Additional writings appear in Codex Sinaiticus and Codex Alexandrinus where they are placed at the end. The inclusion process of these additional writings is uncertain. This placement may indicate that they are considered to be of a lesser importance (or "disputed"), or perhaps we can hypothesize, based on ancient book-making practices, that the additional writings could have been added by customers' requests as each ancient manuscript was copied and bound for a particular client.

Acceptance, status, and use of Revelation

What can be said by way of summary about the historical processes that included Revelation into the Christian canon? We have observed a general consensus in the

---

[6] Trobisch believes that all of the major codices included the twenty-seven NT books, see Trobisch 2000: 25.

church about the authority of Revelation during the first three centuries. That consensus continued in the church in the West throughout the fourth century and was fixed by Athanasius' Festal Letter in AD 367 in a manner that today is considered a norm. However, the Eastern churches pushed Revelation to the margins some time during the fourth century. Indeed, it appears that the church in the East held a more restrictive line concerning the boundaries of Scripture: it disputed not only Revelation, but also some of the Catholic Epistles. So, while Augustine and the Synod of Carthage recognized the minor Catholic Epistles and Revelation, several Eastern theologians (following the tradition of the Peshitta) and the Synod of Laodicea omitted them.[7]

Westcott provides the following progression of witnesses. Chrysostom, a presbyter of Antioch and later patriarch of Constantinople (d. AD 407), who also gave the Bible its present name (*ta biblia*), never cited the Apocalypse as Scripture, though Westcott believes that he was familiar with it (Westcott 1890: 450). Also, Westcott does not know of more than just one citation from the Apocalypse in the works of Ephraim Syrus, a Syrian deacon (d. AD 378; Westcott 1890: 452). Likewise, Basil, bishop of Caesarea in Cappadocia (AD 330–379), refers to the Apocalypse only once (Basil, *Adv. Eunom.* 2.14). Perhaps after Gregory of Nyssa, the brother of Basil, who refers to the Apocalypse twice as part of Scripture while making no allusions to disputed Catholic Epistles, the suspicion toward the Apocalypse was starting to dissipate (Gregory of Nyssa, *Adv. Apoll.* 37; Westcott 1890: 454). Finally, Gregory's successor, Andrew, bishop of Caesarea at the end of the fifth century, shows no reservation with accepting the Apocalypse as Scripture; he wrote a commentary on it. Andrew also lists the testimony of Papias, Irenaeus, Methodius, Hippolytus, and Gregory of Nazianzus in support of its authority as inspired Scripture (Andreas, *Fragments of Papias*, 8). With Andrew, the Eastern church was beginning to return to its original judgment about the Revelation as Christian Scripture and as an authoritative part of the canon. Yet later, Arethas, the successor of Andrew in the See of Caesarea in the early tenth century, also wrote a commentary on the Apocalypse (Westcott 1896: 455). Sometime in the eleventh century Revelation was also included in the Peshitta. The acceptance of Revelation coinciding with commentaries written on Revelation suggests for me that perhaps hesitancy concerning Revelation was less the matter of origin or authority and more the matter of finding an acceptable interpretation.

Even after formally accepting Revelation into its canon, the Eastern Church has been shy in using the text of the Apocalypse in liturgy and it has never been included in the Byzantine lectionary. This is perhaps because the liturgical arrangements had already developed before the formal acceptance of Revelation in the east, and no changes were made to incorporate Revelation. Although not frequently read, Revelation is visibly incorporated into Eastern worship through church architecture. Traditional Orthodox cathedrals seek to imitate, via their décor, the new Jerusalem and God's heavenly throne room, as portrayed in Revelation.

---

[7] Might the fact that Revelation was critical of the Laodicean church (Rev. 3:15–19) have played a role in the rejection of the book in the Synod of Laodicea?

Canonical order: historical issues and theological significance

Finally, the significance of the canonical order of the New Testament remains to be discussed. One could observe that there was a tendency in the early church to put agreed-upon books to the front and the disputed toward the end of the canon lists. If this was the standard, then this could imply that the people who ordered the Bible and placed Revelation at the end considered it as the least of the biblical books. Can we show that, although last, Revelation is not the least among the NT writings?

In the second century there was a significant change in ancient book-making craft: codices emerged and gained in popularity, and they eventually replaced scrolls. We know that the church accepted codices from the very beginning (the oldest codex fragment of a NT dates to the second century, see Trobisch 2000: 19–20). It was by far the preferred book form in the early church and practically all NT writings preserved to our day are in the form of codices. However, it was not until the fourth century that bookbinders were able to make codices big enough to contain all the NT writings in a single volume. It may not be a coincidence that this is simultaneous with the canon debates. The church had to decide the canon and also face the issue of canonical ordering. What criteria did the church use for organizing the NT writings into a canonical collection?

Sub-collections that formed the canon

It is more than probable that before the canon as we know it was published, sub-collections of Scripture emerged. Very early on Gospel collections and collections of Pauline letters were available. The canon lists and some other literary sources give evidence of this.[8] It is also likely that the Catholic Epistles first followed Acts, and at some point, they together formed a collection: the so-called Praxapostolos (Trobisch 2000: 38–39, 103). Revelation, however, has always stood alone and not as part of a collection. Both its substantial size and different genre set it apart from other NT materials. There is no evidence of its ever having been grouped with other books in canon lists, not even with the other apocalypses that occasionally appeared in some canon lists (*Apocalypse of Peter*, *Apocalypse of Paul*, and Shepherd of Hermas). The Muratorian Canon is the only catalog that lists the *Apocalypse of Peter* following the book of Revelation, but with a note that some do not allow it to be read at church, which seems to make a qualifying distinction between the two books. Codex Claromontanus includes many additional books, but the ordering is the following: *Barnabas*, Revelation, Acts, Shepherd of Hermas, *Acts of Paul*, and *Apocalypse of Peter*. The Revelation is, therefore, separated from the other apocalypses by *Barnabas*, which precedes it, and Acts which follows it. There is no evidence that Revelation would have belonged into a collection with the other apocalypses. There were other writings that

---

[8] In *The Acts of the Scillitan Martyrs* a person is asked what is in his suitcase. He answers: "books and Pauline epistles" or alternative translation: "books, that is Pauline epistles." This document seems to indicate that Pauline letters were circulating as a collection at a very early age. See Gamble 1995: 131 (also n. 138).

occasionally appeared on the margins of the canon, such as *Wisdom of Solomon, 1–2 Clement, Psalms of Solomon, Sirach,* and *Constitutions,* but there is no identifiable collection of "dubious books" either. Revelation is sometimes set apart from these books by a separating remark. All the evidence suggests that Revelation stood by itself and not as part of any sub-collection.

External order between the sub-collections that formed the canon

Once the collections (Gospels, Acts, Pauline Epistles, Catholic Epistles) were formed, their external order remained flexible for some time. Beckwith has observed the same phenomena in the development of the ordering of the OT books: the various collections change places for quite some time while their internal ordering is more or less fixed (Beckwith 1986: 184). Over time, the ordering of collections became more tradition-bound.

Other essays in this volume specifically take up the canonical sub-collections of the Gospels, Pauline Epistles, and Acts and the Catholic Epistles, therefore we will only consider the sub-collection of Revelation. The Apocalypse represents both a change in genre as well as some continuation. It is also chronologically a later book.[9] Speaking from this side of the canon formation, in Revelation we meet the churches that have already received the instructions in forms of letters (e.g Ephesians), and in the form of the book of Revelation they receive in some sense the final letter. Revelation also reveals what happens when churches refuse to follow the apostolic instruction given in the epistles. We see struggles with heresy and apostasy in some churches. It is interesting that Revelation is sequentially separated from the rest of the Johannine literature by Jude, which suggests that narrative sequence and genre were of higher importance than presumed authorship in forming canonical collections. (There may have been separate unknown reasons why James, Peter, John, and Jude were given in this way.) Such ordering does not state anything concerning authorship, for the same is true with Luke and Acts that are canonically separated. It is left up to the reader to draw conclusions concerning the authorship, and, at times, the attributed titles by Bible editors attempt to guide them. The authorship of Revelation was a matter of debate in the early church and until this day it remains an open question.

Possible criteria for canon ordering

We should remember that Revelation was not the most disputed book accepted into the canon. In the Western church Hebrews and 2 Peter received a much cooler welcome. Yet, the church included those two works into the canon according to their logical place considering the genre and authorship; they were not simply pasted to the end of the NT. Similarly, the Russian Orthodox Church that follows the traditions of the

---

[9] Most scholars date Revelation to the reign of Domitian around AD 95, although there are some who argue that it was written prior to the destruction of Jerusalem in AD 70 (for example, Robinson 1976: 221–53; Rowland 1982: 403–13.

Eastern Church (that had the most trouble with accepting Revelation) today uses a canon that has Revelation *preceding* the Catholic Epistles. They used different criteria to order their canon, but the location of Revelation once it was accepted does not reveal any intent to marginalize that book.

Accordingly, I conclude that there was no essential connection between the difficulties that Revelation had in being accepted as canonical and its position at the end of the collection. The placement given for Revelation does not indicate it had lesser authority (its authority was established during the first three centuries), but rather it is thoughtfully placed there because of its genre (concluding the collection of epistles) and its theological message that brings the NT to closure. The latter is the most important reason why Revelation is placed to the end: Revelation concludes the story of Christ as told in the NT. It is showing the resurrected Christ ruling his church in glory and looking forward to the Parousia. As F. C. Evans appropriately writes concerning the position of Revelation at the end of the canon:

> there is a certain fitness in the position of Revelation in the Canon, despite the intense antipathy it aroused for long periods in certain quarters, and the melancholy history of its use and interpretation in the Church. It brings together into a single whole a number of separate concerns which are to be found in other New Testament writings, such as the threat of heresy in the last days, the danger of apostasy, the necessity of persecution, the tension between present and future, the coexistence of judgement and salvation, Christ as a figure of conflict, and the suffering but exalted Lord addressing his Church and ruling it until the parousia.
>
> Evans 1970: 282

Revelation "fits" at the end. I would go even further and argue that Revelation functions to form a conclusion not only for the NT writings, but also the entire biblical canon. There are other writings that dedicate a substantial amount of material to eschatology, for example, Isaiah in the OT, but they do not see themselves as *being* the end in the way that Revelation does. It is hardly an option that the author of Revelation knew he was writing the final book of the collection called the Bible; however, as the following Christian generations read his book, they were convinced that it was the suitable ending. Readers, not authors, created the canon, but the authors through their writings created the kind of readers that formed this canon with Revelation as the end.

The blessing and curse included in Revelation (originally intended by the author to secure the appropriate copying and preservation of the text of Revelation only) may also have been an argument among the editors that Revelation should form an ending of the canon. A blessing is promised to whoever reads it (Rev. 1:3) and a curse to those who either add or subtract from its message (Rev. 22:18–19).[10] Adding other writings

---

[10] This blessing-curse structure of Revelation is similar to Deuteronomy, which forms the end of the Pentateuch (Deut. 27-28; 30:15–20). Gamble argues that this curse is an authorial note for the Apocalypse only and should not be made a statement for canon because it was just the author's way of saying that his book should be published and multiplied without any changes (Gamble 1995: 105). In the ancient world scribal accuracy could not be assumed, so the remark functioned like today's copyright.

beyond this statement would have raised questions. The church interpreted this statement to be applicable to the entire canon, indicating the completion of it: nothing is to be added, nothing is to be subtracted, and blessed is everyone who reads it.[11]

Implications arising from Revelation as the canon ending

It took some time for the boundaries of the canon to solidify. Some canon lists included books following in order after Revelation. For example, the *Apocalypse of Peter* follows Revelation in the Muratorian Canon and Codex Claromontanus had Acts, *Shepherd*, *Acts of Paul* and the *Apocalypse of Peter* following it, and there were other odd lists, but no two such lists would agree. Also, there are manuscripts including additional books (Codex Alexandrinus includes *1 and 2 Clement* and *Psalms of Solomon*), but usually there were visual separations to set other books apart. Parchment was too expensive to leave pages empty. Admittedly the Eastern canon which added Revelation later does not end with it.

Being an ending, Revelation is where the full meaning of the canonical story is revealed and where its theological culmination is to be found. The image of a tree of life was already planted in the reader's mind in Genesis 3:22, but in Revelation 22:2 it bears fruit. The fact that Revelation portrays the culmination of the canon has significant spiritual, doctrinal and practical implications.

First, the spiritual implications. Though the New Testament records messianiac prophecy regarding the birth, life, cross and resurrection of Jesus, Revelation adds more. It shows Jesus as present and intimately involved in the life of the church: saving, instructing through his Spirit, preserving through sufferings, and finally judging and rewarding. In Revelation, history moves toward Christ's coming in final victory. The road to the victory involves doing battle with internal and external temptations and various beasts and hellish forces, but the outcome is certain: in Christ those who believe are conquerors. Revelation focuses on the task of the church to carry out worship of the Triune God and to witness of Christ to the world continually, in all places and at all times. It deals with the sin and judgment of all evil forces. This book contains solid spiritual nourishment for believers, in addition to encouragement, discipline, comfort, hope and reward. It resolves the crises of sin and death introduced in Genesis with the perfect new Creation as the last chapter in God's book.

Second, doctrinally, eschatology cannot be treated as an obscure appendix to systematic theology. Enlightenment theologians pushed the Apocalypse into the category of utopias, a place of escape from a difficult world. Far from being a utopia, Revelation is a battle plan for the church living in a hostile Empire. It shows God as actively involved in the church. It portrays Christ not as a victim of Roman crucifixion, but as the resurrected and enthroned ruler of the universe. It portrays the church not as a minority culture struggling to survive (although they struggle) but as the ultimate

---

[11] This curse was already cited by a third-century author of the *Fragment Adversus Cataphrygas* as a warning to heretics who created new Scriptures. This may suggest that Revelation was viewed very early on as the book that closes the canon.

victors that endure and outlive all oppressive political and economic structures. It unmasks the true and unnatural face of evil, describing it through many monsters and brings order out of chaos through the word of God. The symmetry and orderliness of the new creation is stunning.

Third, practically speaking, it is a book to live by. It injects energy and expects a rapid response from readers. "Speedily" is one of the key terms John uses. It captures imagination and sends us forth toward an end that is constantly delayed. It leaves room for choices and imagination. Who are the nations of the earth? Will they perish or will they repent? Who will respond to the Spirit and the Bride who call "Come!" The book brings closure but also has some openness in it.

The placement of the book of Revelation at the end of the canon is editorially wise. It is a complex book that is not suitable for a quick reference or mining for catchy quotes. The book requires familiarity with the canonical story for its interpretation. Readers who have read the canon from left to right have the vocabulary and framework to comprehend its narrative. Readers must have filled their minds with Scriptures of the Old and New Testaments to appreciate fully the imagery of the Apocalypse. Reading through the whole canon is a challenging task requiring discipline and commitment, taking on average a year or more to accomplish. But in most cases, it is even a much longer process accompanied by instruction received from preaching and liturgy. Much like climbing a mountain to reach the peak one cannot skip any stages of the path. There are no shortcuts. The greater the effort the more one appreciates the view from the top.

John wrote in the beginning: "Blessed is the one who reads and those who hear" (Rev. 1:3a). But at the end he writes "blessed is the one who keeps" 22:7 and 12. At the end one must put the book down and act. Beyond treasuring the Bible as an artifact and witness of a two-thousand-year-old community and beyond just preserving it, its authors and editors hope that readers put it down and follow its instruction in action for the glory of God.

Reading the canon, the word of God, in its full measure from cover to cover is a great privilege. I speak as one from a country where the Bible was for many years forbidden literature that had to be smuggled into the country, risking a jail sentence. Christians need Scripture to keep and practice their faith. And Christians need the *entire* Scripture to practice and live their faith correctly.

Bibliography

Beckwith, Roger. (1986), *The Old Testament Canon of the New Testament Church and Its Background in Early Judaism*, Grand Rapids, Eerdmans.

Bentley, James. (1986), *Secrets of Mount Sinai: The Story of Finding the World's Oldest Bible – Codex Sinaiticus*, New York: Doubleday.

Campenhausen, Hans von. (1972), *The Formation of the Christian Bible*, Philadelphia: Fortress.

Cross, F. L. and E. A. Livingstone, eds. (1997), *The Oxford Dictionary of the Christian Church*, New York: Oxford University Press.

Dobschütz, Ernst von. (1912), *Das Decretum Gelasianum, De Libris recipiendis et non recipiendis*, TUGAL 38.4, Leipzig: Walter de Gruyter.

Evans, F. C. (1970), "The New Testament in the Making," in P. R. Ackroyd and F. C. Evans (eds.), *The Cambridge History of the Bible: From the Beginnings to Jerome*, 232–84, New York: Cambridge University Press.

Fee, Gordon D. (1989), "The Formation of the New Testament Canon," Review of *The Canon of the New Testament: Its Origin, Development, and Significance* by Bruce M. Metzger, *Int* 43 (4): 410–12.

Florovski, Georges. (1987), *The Byzantine Fathers of the Fifth Century*, The Collected Works of George Florovsky, vol. 8, Vaduz, Europa: Büchervertriebsanstalt.

Gallagher, Edmon L. and John D. Meade. (2017), *The Biblical Canon Lists from Early Christianity: Texts and Analysis*, Oxford: Oxford University Press.

Gamble, Harry Y. (1995), *Books and Readers in the Early Church: A History of Early Christian Texts*, New Haven: Yale University Press.

Gamble, Harry Y. (2003), "The Formation of the New Testament Canon and Its Significance for the History of Biblical Interpretation," in A. J. Hauser and D. F. Watson (eds.), *A History of Biblical Interpretation: The Ancient Period*, 409–29, Grand Rapids: Eerdmans.

Harnack, Adolf von. (1924), *Marcion: Das Evangelium vom fremden Gott*, 2nd edn, TU 45, Leipzig: J. C. Hinrichs.

Harnack, Adolf von. (1904), *Chronologie der altchristlichen Literatur*, vol. 2, Leipzig: J. C. Hinrichs.

Hays, Richard B. (1989), *Echoes of Scripture in the Letters of Paul*, New Haven: Yale University Press.

Kenyon, F. G. (ed.). (1915), *British Museum: The Codex Alexandrinus: (Royal Ms 1 D V-VIII)*, Oxford: Oxford University Press.

Lake, K. (ed.). (1911), *Codex Sinaiticus Petropolitanus: The New Testament, the Epistle of Barnabas, and the Shepherd of Hermas*, Oxford: Clarendon.

Martini, C. M. (ed.). (1968), *Novum Testamentum e Codice Vaticano Graeco 1209 (Codex B)*, 3rd edn, Rome: Vatican.

Metzger, Bruce M. (1997), *The Canon of the New Testament: Its Origin, Development, and Significance*, Oxford: Clarendon.

Milne H. J. M. and T. C. Skeat. (1938), *Scribes and Correctors of the Codex Sinaiticus*, Oxford: Oxford University Press.

Robinson, John A. T. (1976), *Redating the New Testament*, Philadelphia: Westminster.

Rowland, Christopher. (1982), *The Open Heaven*, New York: Crossroad.

Schaff, Philip. (1907–1910), "History of the Christian Church: Volume II Ante-Nicene Christianity A.D. 100–325" n.p. [cited July 30 2021]. Available online: http://www.ccel.org/ccel/schaff/hcc2.v.xv.xliii.html?highlight=commodian#highlight.

Tischendorf, Konstantin von (ed.). (1843), *Codex Ephraemi Syri Rescriptus: sive fragmenta utiusque testamenti e codice graeco parisiensi celeberrimo quinti ut videtur post christum saeculi*, 2 vols, Leipzig: Taubnitz.

Trobisch, David. (2000), *The First Edition of the New Testament*, New York: Oxford University Press.

Westcott, Brooke Foss. (1896), *A General Survey of the History of the Canon of the New Testament*, London: Macmillan.

Williams, C. S. C. (1969), "The History of the Text and Canon of the New Testament to Jerome," in G. W. H. Lampe (ed.), *The West from the Fathers to the Reformation*, vol. 2 of *The Cambridge History of the Bible*, 27–53, New York: Cambridge University Press.

Zahn, Theodor. (1890), *Geschichte des neutestamentlichen Kanons*, vol. 2, Erlangen: A. Deichert.

Section Four

Hermeneutical Considerations of Canon

16

Hermeneutical Reflections on Canonical Sub-Collections: Retrospect and Prospect

Ched Spellman

The nature and role of canonical sub-collections represent an area of study that is hermeneutically significant. Sometimes the debate about the formation of the canon either focuses on grand macro-level issues (like the shape of the two-testament witness as a whole) or granular contextual issues (like the meaning of references to a particular writing in the earliest churches). In this scenario, a gulf often opens up between theory and practice. What is the exegetical payoff of my understanding of the macro-structure of the Hebrew Bible? Why would it be important to know the position of the book of Acts in the New Testament if I am examining Paul's letter to the Corinthians?

Reckoning with the formation and function of canonical sub-collections can more closely connect the historical questions about canon formation and the theological and hermeneutical issues that arise when considering the subject matter of Scripture and when closely reading individual biblical texts. When considering the unique place of sub-collections in the broader biblical canon, several concepts native to canon studies are relevant: the context of canon, the coherence of canonical intentionality, the notion of canon-consciousness, and the relevance of the biblical canon to the task of biblical theology. In this chapter, I briefly examine each of these areas and seek to articulate the strategic function of canonical sub-collections.[1]

Relating history, theology, and hermeneutics in canon studies

In this discussion, a canonical approach aims to distinguish but rightly relate the historical investigation of canon formation and the textual examination of biblical writings. Here, an interpreter seeks to organically connect the *formation* of the canon to the *function* of the canon. Accordingly, historical and hermeneutical modes of

---

[1] Within canon studies, there is diversity in the methods and conclusions among various scholars who treat these issues. In the current volume, each contributor has a shared belief in the strategic significance of the biblical canon and the importance of canonical sub-collections while also navigating issues of method and approach in different ways. The reflections offered here, therefore, do not *speak for* but rather *dialogue with* this wide-ranging scholarship.

analysis are required. How does a historical approach to biblical interpretation relate to a canonical approach? In short, many who affirm the importance of canon for biblical interpretation would argue that historical investigation is *necessary* but not *sufficient* for a fully orbed understanding of biblical texts (e.g., see Lockett 2017b, 2017c, Seitz 2018: 21–34, 271–79).

The first part of this formulation affirms that historical investigation is *necessary* in order to understand the contours and setting of an ancient literary text. A further concern in this line of thinking is to problematize any facile account of a strictly linear development between distinct phases of composition, collection, canonization proper, and consolidation within particular communities. Reckoning with points of overlap among these categories remains an important feature when studying discrete writings within the context of a collection. In this account, historical work remains *necessary* as one pursues an author's textual intention and also the formation of the collection in which biblical books find a home.

A canonical approach, though, asks several critical questions about the scope of the historical-critical project and concludes that it is not *sufficient* as a comprehensive program. Here the issue is not whether historical analysis is used but rather the manner in which it is utilized. It is *integral* to specific research steps, but not *adequate* for a full understanding of this literature. Speaking in this manner immediately raises the question, sufficient or adequate for what? The answer to this issue relates to the question, "What is the Bible?" and assumes a particular theological account of Scripture's ontology. These interlocking areas of inquiry can be illustrated by a brief definitional interlude. When we define the Bible, there are historical, theological, and hermeneutical dimensions to this understanding.

A working definition of Scripture as "God's Word to his people" can serve to highlight each of these aspects of the nature of the biblical canon. That it is *God's* Word to his people points to the "dogmatic location" of the canon in the economy of salvation (cf. Webster 2003: 95–126; Ward 2009: 49–95). This theological emphasis accounts for the way God uses Scripture in his action of revelation and redemption. That it is God's *Word* to his people highlights the verbal aspects of canon as a collection of literary writings (i.e. words) that require skillful reading and interpretation. That it is God's Word *to his people* points to the historical location of the canon and its gradual development among a believing community of authors and readers. The fullest definition of the scriptural canon will incorporate all three elements—authors, texts, and readers.

Though this approach challenges a standard historical-critical method, the use of historical analysis described here should demonstrate that a canonical approach cannot rightly be labeled "ahistorical," nor can one say that it has an aversion to history or a historical-critical examination of the relevant evidence. Indeed, even directly historical-critical tools serve an indispensable purpose in providing the "depth dimension" that is necessary for a reader to perceive the guiding and governing function of a canonical collection. Seitz articulates this concern, stressing that a canonical approach does not reject or neglect historical investigation but rather seeks a proper "proportion" in the use of this data: "Proper proportion must be weighted to what is said. There is nothing especially theological or holistic or unhistorical in such an approach. The text is honored for what it chooses to communicate in the form it chooses to say that, and historical judgments are kept in proportion to this reality" (2014: 51, 28–56; cf. Seitz 2011: 27–39; Gignilliat 2019: 19–40; and Childs 1992: 211–17 who develop this notion of "depth dimension" in relating a canonical approach to historical investigation).

This posture toward the historical, theological, and hermeneutical dimensions of the biblical canon represents a distinct scholarly position but also involves a relatively modest claim. In this scenario, there is something of a give and take relationship between the interpretation and reception history of these texts. The meaning (much less the authority) of these writings is not repositioned or relegated to a subsequent phase of canonization. Likewise, the historical-critical analysis of a text's origin and pre-history is not rendered meaningless. Rather, historical analysis is seen here as the starting point rather than the culminating apex of the interpretive task. This procedure is modest because it does not involve the exclusion of historical analysis *per se* but rather relegates the pre-history of a text to the preliminary phase of investigation. The historical occasion of the writing or a historically reconstructed background of the author and recipients can play a requisite role here but not a governing one.

The formation and function of canonical sub-collections

A preliminary step in canonical analysis seeks to outline the process by which an individual text becomes associated with smaller and larger literary collections. The critical role of historical analysis includes identifying and examining the recontextualization of these historically conditioned writings within a canonical sub-collection and ultimately within the context of the Old and New Testaments broadly conceived. Along these lines, Chapman cautions that "to disregard or reject the biblical text's discourse is inevitably to replace the Bible's own contextualization of its traditions with a contextualization derived from somewhere else" (2020: 79). Again, historical investigation is necessary here, but that necessity relates to properly locating the individual writing and also perceiving its recontextualized role within a collection alongside other biblical writings. The smaller groupings and larger sections begin to be read in relatively consistent ways across time. As this process develops and matures, more and more communities and individuals begin to share a common order of reading.

In light of this reception history, there is a strong probability that sub-collections figured into the understanding of the earliest readers of the biblical collections. The presence of trends in the way biblical documents are grouped together in the manuscript evidence demonstrates that they were in some way seen in light of one another from an early phase of reception. Indeed, the presence of writings grouped together likely indicates at least a minimal cognitive judgment that these writings are related conceptually and should thus be related materially. As Larry Hurtado argues, this "practice of combining more than one text in the same manuscript" is an "artifactual feature" that historians of the New Testament canon should not neglect (2006: 35). In view of this development, the context of the biblical canon should be understood to be a "collection of collections" that takes on an increasingly discernable shape (cf. Harry

Gamble's characterization of canon formation as "a history of smaller collections," 2002: 267–95). Biblical texts "enter" the biblical canon, in other words, by way of groupings ("collection units") rather than as individual compositions. Lockett summarizes this historical observation by concluding that "the process of canonization" should be viewed "as the compilation of collections" (2017a: 97, cf. 60–62, 87–90, 96–100).

Accordingly, the meaningful content of the concept of canon consists of these groupings and their organic relationship to one another. The collection of the collections or grouping of the groupings indicates a decisive moment in the formation of the biblical canon and also represents a critical touchpoint between the way the canon formed and the way it continues to function for the earliest and latest readers of the biblical canon. This important mediating step is sometimes missing in accounts of the relationship between the *history* of the canon and the *hermeneutics* of the canon. Sub-collections provide an important step toward discerning the historical particularities involved in the formation of the canon as a whole. Focusing on this grouping of individual texts within a broad understanding of the canon formation process will influence the way that one speaks about the effect of the canonical context of the interpretive task.

"Tracing" the role of sub-collections in the biblical canon requires both historical investigation and textual analysis. Thus, driving too thick of a wedge between external historical evidence and internal literary evidence when considering the question of canon appears to be unnecessarily disruptive. The value of sub-collection as an analytical concept, too, is its relative flexibility. Historically, a sub-collection is a group of biblical writings that circulates together in some form. This grouping could also be physically stored or housed in a particular way. Hermeneutically, a sub-collection is a group of biblical writings that conceptually function in relation to one another. So, as a mental construct, a "canonical context" could hold for a particular set of texts even if a book was produced across several different scrolls or if there was no codex that "contained" the entire collection. Considering the relationship between these two material and conceptual realities forms a key part of this discussion. If a group of texts consistently circulates together, a natural consequence would be that readers of these writings associate them with one another. The grouping itself, then, would function as a hermeneutical matrix within which a reader accesses and relates a particular work to all other texts.

The canonical location of the book of Acts is an instructive example of this feature of the discussion. The way in which you relate the book of Acts to the Gospel narrative of Luke will influence the way you view this book in relation to both the four-fold Gospel corpus and also the New Testament letters (i.e., as Luke–Acts or Luke and Acts). Moreover, whether or not one relates the Catholic Epistles directly to the composition and canonization of the book of Acts, for example, would re-frame how any historical reconstruction is envisioned. What might seem like a re-location of the Catholic Epistles to a place after Acts for readers of contemporary English Bibles would be a restoration of a reading order familiar to a reader of many ancient Greek manuscripts (cf. the order of Acts followed by the Catholic Epistles in the *Tyndale House Edition* of the Greek New Testament).

Moreover, one of the critical points in the formation of the New Testament canon that has relevance for the Catholic Epistles would not only be the moment when each of the individual letters joined the New Testament collection broadly conceived. Rather, the relevant question would be the nature of the Catholic Epistles collection itself on the one hand, and its connection to the book of Acts on the other. In relation to the broad shape of the New Testament canon, the further question would then be about the nature of the relationship of the Acts + Catholic Epistles unit (*praxapostolos*) to the grouping of the four-fold-Gospel, the Pauline Letters and Hebrews, and finally the Revelation.

Regardless of your answers to these specific historical questions, the point here is the established legitimacy of noting a link between history and hermeneutics in this area. If this is how the canon formed, it will certainly affect how the canon functions (or at the least might function for the reader that takes canonical realities into account). As Lockett notes, "holding canon and Scripture together allows for understanding the entire canonical process, from composition to canonization as a historically interrelated and hermeneutically significant process" (2017a: 232). Noting the way these discrete and discernible units are associated with one another shows that issues of arrangement and design were active from the very beginning of the canon formation process.

Sub-collections and canonical contextuality

A core concept in the study of biblical literature is "context." What does context consist of and in which direction should interpreters gaze as they seek to orient themselves to the biblical text? More to the point, what is the "default context" within which study of a given biblical writing will take place? As mentioned above, historical investigation is necessary in order to study the biblical writings and understand the dimensions of the canon formation process. The role of history for the purpose of biblical interpretation typically relates to identifying the relative value of reconstructed settings for understanding the social, intellectual, and theological milieu of an ancient writing and also the relationship between narrative portrayal and a historically reconstructed sequence of events. A canonical approach to reading the Scriptures would argue not only for the helpfulness but also the necessity of the final form of the canonical texts being taken into account when discerning meaning. The canonical context, in this approach, is an appropriate and necessary further context for reading the biblical narratives, poems, prophecies, and epistles.

Though it is certainly possible to conceive of biblical books independent of the collections where they are located within the biblical canon, this conceptual re-orientation can have a significant effect on one's ability to articulate the message of the Bible and navigate both its unity and diversity. The concept of canon in general allows for a study of "contextuality" that notes the generation of meaning produced by juxtaposing *just these works* in *just this fashion*. The believing community not only received and treasured the biblical writings, they also handed them down to later generations in a way that would maintain their compositional shape and extend their literary legacy.

The phrase "canonical contextuality" has the benefit of emphasizing the notion of *context*. The study of contextuality is the study of a writing's textual or literary context.

Where an individual writing is positioned in relation to other writings in a collection (either materially or conceptually) has significant hermeneutical ramifications. This type of study seeks to uncover the "semantic effect of a book's relative position" within the biblical canon (Sailhamer 1995: 213). In this sense, "context" is now "context within the literary shape of the final form of the canon" (Seitz 2007: 179). Any time a physical or conceptual reading sequence has been established, the study of contextuality is both instructive and worth pursuing (cf. Spellman 2014: 101–41).

At this point of the discussion, we shift from primarily historical modes of inquiry to hermeneutical modes of analysis. After establishing the *fact* of canon, we are asking now about the *function* of the canon. A physical grouping of biblical books or a stated arrangement of biblical books can influence the way each of those individual texts within that grouping is understood in general terms. Oftentimes a grouping or arrangement of texts implies and encourages a rough order of reading that assigns implicit priority to certain texts and draws individual texts into one another's orbit. Indeed, a clearly delineated collection requires a consideration and communication of the relationship between compositional units. The members of a unit have at least one clear common characteristic, namely, that they are present within this particular collection. Given this canonical association, the lingering follow-up question is often whether *clearly delineated* collections have also been *carefully crafted*. If the Old and New Testament represent large carefully crafted collections of several smaller carefully crafted collections, then a study of the ordering principle or associative logic at work in the formation and function of the collection seems not only warranted but imperative.

Rather than isolate the dynamics of groupings as an outlier to the more central notion of the "canon as a whole," it may be more fruitful to revise our understanding of the canonical context in order to account for the contours of a carefully curated collection of carefully curated sub-collections. Reckoning with the form and function of canonical sub-collections can generate fruitful insight for both historical investigation in the canon formation process and also the hermeneutical effect of canonical collections on the reading process.

Mere and meant contextuality

The level of analysis that observes these contextual effects without dealing with the issue of intention might be described as "mere contextuality." Mere contextuality is the effect that arises in the mind of the reader when writings are seen in relation to other writings. This level of analysis focuses on the connections produced by a broader literary context. Moreover, studies of mere contextuality are not necessarily concerned with how individual writings come to be included in a collection, associated with certain groupings, or positioned in a specific manner. Instead, the focus is deliberately on the result of that physical placement or conceptual location. The concern is more on the meaning generated by the juxtaposition rather than giving an account of how an ordering or a grouping came to be. In sum, here the goal is to demonstrate and observe the meaningful effect that an order of reading has on our understanding of the biblical books. One might note the textual and theological fittingness of Revelation and its vision of "the end" as the final word of the New Testament canon, for example, regardless of whether or not this position was designed by an author or compiler.

On one hand, a study of contextuality that restricts itself to analyzing the effect that the broader context of the biblical collection has on an individual writing without recourse to intention (i.e. mere contextuality) has been solidly established and can bear hermeneutical fruit. On the other hand, there are also ways to ask whether the shape of the biblical canon has been intended in some way. This analysis moves from "mere contextuality" to "meant contextuality." Indeed, the location of a particular writing in a collected group of writings demonstrates that someone has *already* deemed the works to be connected in some way. In some cases, at least, the order of reading itself represents an interpretive move. As John Barton notes, "Collecting books together is potentially an interpretive process" (1997: 34). To give a standard example, the position of the Law and the Gospels at the beginning of the Old Testament and New Testament, respectively, indicates their perceived foundational role. Seitz observes further that "order and association precede lists, and they are accomplishments of a deeply theological nature to begin with" (2009: 45). In this regard, the concept of canonical shaping and canon-consciousness among the believing community seems to allow for the possibility of an intended contextuality.

The study of mere contextuality recognizes the often unacknowledged impact that sequence and ordering have on readers. The study of meant contextuality considers the ways in which the content of the biblical writings and the direction of the biblical authors themselves have shaped the very canonical context in which we access and read the Scriptures. The meaning of biblical writings initially *influences* and is subsequently *influenced by* the canonical context in which they then circulate. Contributing to a profile of meant contextuality, biblical authors make intertextual references to other biblical books and also to broader canonical sections and sub-collections. For example, Paul discusses the "the law" (Rom. 3:21a) in light of texts from individual Psalms (3:10–18) and also the Genesis narratives that feature Abraham (Gen. 4:1–25). Alongside these intertextual references, he also refers to "the Law and the Prophets" that bear witness (Rom. 3:21b). Paul thus develops his theological argument in light of the meaning of specific texts and also the cumulative message of named canonical sections.

To give another example, through compositional strategy and canonical shaping, the book of Deuteronomy forms the last part of the Pentateuch followed by Joshua, the first book in a sequence of prophetic histories. The end of Deuteronomy depicts Moses composing and completing "a book of the Law" (Deut. 31:24–29) and the beginning of Joshua refers to the "book of the Law" that is to be remembered and revered (Josh. 1:7–8; cf. Ps. 1.1–2; Mal. 4:4). Examining the placement of Deuteronomy beside Joshua would require examining local and global compositional strategy (passage-level and book-level meaning) and also local and global canonical shaping (association of Deuteronomy with a Prophetic History sequence and also the possible force of a "Law–Prophets" construct). This pattern can also be seen in the reception history when those in the believing community refer not only to individual texts and biblical books but also groups of biblical books and distinct sub-collections (see Chapman 2015: 281–304).

Book ordering and canonical grouping as complementary concepts

Observing this feature of the canonical context also recognizes the multi-faceted nature of the biblical canon itself. The composite shape of the broader canonical collection is formed by the various groupings of the individual sections and also strategic texts that connect these corpora. Reckoning with the material and mental category of sub-collections can allow for a more textured understanding of "canonical context." Conceiving of the canonical context as the "grouping of the groupings" can help a reader gain a better grasp on just what is meant by the "context of the canon."

There is sometimes a justifiable concern at this point that the "canonical context" can sometimes function as an overly theoretical construct that flattens out the particularities of individual writings. The framework of a canon as a collection of collections, though, can re-locate the intensity and direction of the guidance that the canon provides. The associative unity generated or suggested by a canonical collection is multifaceted and multilayered. A sub-collection connects individual writings within the purview of a circumscribed number of texts gathered together based on a local set of criteria (e.g., genre, authorship, narrative continuity, theological compatibility). This scenario represents an organic process of recognition rather than an external and arbitrary up or down application of a categorical label or status.

A common objection to the study of book order as a factor for interpretation is the presence of different orderings within the lists and manuscripts of various communities. In one way this is an important historical situation that must be taken into account. If the canonical context requires a sequence that is static, then a canonical approach would be threatened by even minor differences in the order of books. However, the categories of mere and meant contextuality can account for the way that order and arrangement manifest within a collection. Variation in sequence sometimes indicates an interpretation of a biblical book's function in relation to other biblical books. Far from discounting the meaningful role of a canonical context, this example seems to demonstrate it. Variations in ordering among books within the biblical canon is certainly present but should be understood in light of the historically demonstrable and readily discernible patterns of stability that can be detected on a small scale and a large scale across the collection.

Both book ordering *and* book grouping then would be hermeneutically significant. They contribute to the effect that the canonical context can and does have for early and later readers. Connecting these two concepts (ordering and grouping) is another means by which a reader can find the canonical context meaningful even in the presence of diverse variations in ordering. This interpretive framework also opens up an avenue to recognize both "close" and "distant" pairing within the context of a collection (i.e., books right beside one another and also books that are clearly connected but with a number of works between them).

Here the meaningful force of a linear sequence functions *within* the associative pressure of a gathered collection. The crux of the issue relates directly to the hermeneutical effect of "grouping" and not *only* in the syntagmatic relations of proximity and juxtaposition. Sub-collections generate an effect through both discernible arrangement and the "achievement of association" (Seitz 2009) that occurs within a canonical grouping. Book ordering and broader grouping units are not mutually exclusive but are factors that can be analyzed in tandem. Thinking about the "shape" of the canonical context with sub-collections as orienting starting points allows a reader to recognize the meaningful effect of both ordering (which prompts questions about the implications of arrangement) and grouping (which prompts questions about the implications of association).

The metaphors we read canonical collections by

In their now classic study, *Metaphors We Live By*, Lakoff and Johnson observe the prevalence of metaphor in everyday speech and also the influence that metaphors have on how a person or group perceives a concept or issue. In this way, the metaphorical language we utilize partially structures "what we do and how we understand what we are doing" (see Lakoff and Johnson 1980: 5, 3–24; cf. Vanhoozer 2016). There are also what we might call "metaphors we *read* by" when considering the shape of the biblical canon. The controlling metaphor that is used when describing the nature of canonical contextuality will likely both highlight and hide certain features of the concept. Some elements will be explained but other elements will be obscured. To illustrate the above discussion of the hermeneutical effect of the canonical context, we can consider two extended analogies: the nature of montage within a film and the model of planets within a solar system.

When considering the arrangement of biblical books within a collection, and in particular focusing on the effect of books that appear side-by-side in a sequence or list, there is an effect similar to the "montage effect" in film (Sailhamer 1995: 213–15 develops this analogy). In a cinematic montage, there are generally distinct scenes or images juxtaposed in quick succession. Montage sequences also usually incorporate a dramatic musical score or a voiced narration that offers commentary on the voiceless images or clips. In these instances, the viewer is strongly encouraged to understand the discrete scenes or images in light of one another. The meaning of the individual units is influenced by what comes before and after. The effect of contextuality is similar to this film technique. The analogy can help a reader of the biblical canon conceptualize the hermeneutical effect that juxtaposition has when reading a collection of literary texts. Just like a film encourages viewers to synthesize scenes that follow one another, a canonical collection encourages readers to view texts in particular arrangements as part of a meaningfully shaped whole. This hermeneutical effect is particularly prominent for readers committed to sequential reading of biblical texts within a collection.

The analogy of the montage effect in film highlights the importance of arrangement and the impact of linear sequence on a reader encountering a literary collection. A possible objection to the value of this effect relates to variations in these arrangements. If different orderings of biblical books within a sequence are utilized in different communities across time, then how can this meaningful effect have any bearing on the interpretive task of reading these books? An initial general response to this challenge is that the hermeneutical "montage effect" of juxtaposed works within a literary collection would still apply to each of these various orderings. Each sequence would adjust the hermeneutical effect that might be generated by the literary neighborhood a given writing might have when it takes up residence within a material or conceptual order of reading. The fundamental insight that juxtaposition within a sequence generates a hermeneutical effect, though, is actually not impacted by variation within an order of reading (especially when those variations are measured and exhibit detectable rationale).

Another analogy for the way that books relate to one another in a canonical collection is the gravitational pull among planets within a solar system (Stone 2015: 6–8 develops this analogy). In our solar system, there are a number of planets that rotate around the sun at varying distances. Many of these planets also have one or more smaller moons that rotate within their orbit. In this way, we might conceive of a literary compilation of books that have general but also specific relational profiles. This analogy helps a reader recognize that certain books "gravitate" toward one another when they are included within the same collection or sub-collection. They tend to circulate together and when they appear in lists, they are typically close or clearly related in some way to one another.

This way of conceptualizing the relationship between biblical books also helps demonstrate that variation in a list or linear sequence does not automatically negate any hermeneutical influence. Rather, even in multiple diverse orderings, certain books can maintain a direct or indirect relation to one another within a discrete collection. Planets within a solar system may not always align along strict coordinates or stay the exact same distance apart at every moment but they nevertheless maintain their place within the solar system as a whole and retain their relative locations within that geometrically complex space. So too, biblical books may vary in sequence (by "moving around") yet remain part of the biblical canon as a whole and often within discernible proximity to a common profile of texts within a canonical sub-collection. The letter to the Hebrews, for example, migrates across but never departs from the Pauline corpus in New Testament manuscript groupings. The book of Genesis, by contrast, is planted firmly in the beginning of the Pentateuch.

Both of these metaphors help articulate and conceptualize a particular function of canonical contextuality for biblical readers. The montage effect helps illustrate the linear aspect of an established sequence of biblical books. The gravitational pull of planets helps illustrate the complexity and balanced stability that accompanies "movement" within and across sub-collections. If we diversify the metaphorical concepts we use to describe and illustrate the hermeneutical effect of canonical context, our measured assessment will have more explanatory power and gain the ability to account for historically diverse ordering patterns.

Sub-collections and canonical intentionality

A corollary point of discussion that arises particularly when we begin to speak of the pressure put upon interpreters who read individual writings within the context of a canonical collection relates to the viability of the notion of "canonical intention." If the mode of analysis shifts from *mere* to *meant* contextuality, what are the parameters within which we can meaningfully speak of "intention" at the level of the biblical canon as a whole? Which theological confessions fund and underpin a canonical approach to studying the Bible in general and to reading individual biblical texts in particular? In other words, is the appeal to intentionality at the level of a collection or a sub-collection a way of speaking about the motives of the communities that gather biblical texts into collections, a way of referring to general theological categories like divine inspiration and providence, or a reference to the workings of biblical authors as they compose their texts? Even if we answer, "all of the above," there is still a need to account for the unique profile this purpose bears in these domains. To pursue this underlying question, we can briefly examine the historical, theological, and hermeneutical categories which are necessary for the notion of "canonical intentionality" to function in a coherent and cohesive way.

In terms of history, we can ask, are there any historical factors that might indicate whether or not the various collections were formed and shaped intentionally? Did the individuals and communities that read, preserved, and circulated biblical writings self-consciously think in terms of a collection that had boundaries and a profile of coherent criteria for inclusion? Or, was this process more of a logistical necessity that did not factor into their perception and commitment to this literature? As an initial response to this question, we can note that the existence of collected biblical writings indicates the presence of a believing community that gathered and passed along just these writings *in just this way*. The manner in which groups of individuals collected and transmitted these writings can indicate both an awareness of a writing's legitimacy as an included member of a collection and also sometimes the perceived role that a particular writing has within a collection.

Paratextual features of biblical manuscripts can indicate something of the intended use and role that a particular writing was to have. These paratextual elements include titles given to individual compositions, abbreviation patterns in the text such as the *nomina sacra*, or the choice of the codex as a means of publication (cf. Bokedal 2014: 83–194; Goswell 2008: 160–74). While these features must be carefully assessed and are not self-interpreting, paratextual elements such as these can indicate that the communities that passed along these writings had a certain degree of collection-consciousness that influenced how they perceived whether or not a particular writing belonged within a given collection.

The evidence for a collection-consciousness among the believing community also points to intentional steps taken by these groups as they gathered biblical writings for the purpose of preservation and publication. The notion of collection-consciousness, then, is a legitimate concept that has some explanatory power for understanding the historical and hermeneutical dynamic at work among the community of early readers who receive, collect, and pass along the biblical literature (see section on canon-consciousness below).

In terms of theology, we can ask, what confessional commitments are required for the notion that a gathered collection of individual writings might bear a divine purpose that is naturally complex but profoundly coherent? When considering the dogmatic location of the concept of canon, which theological realities ground the condition and possibility of intention at the level of the biblical canon? In this regard, a robust understanding and articulation of divine providence undergirds an account of canon formation that seeks to account for both the inspired textual witness and the divine subject matter of biblical texts. Indeed, these theological categories are necessary for an analysis of texts that implicitly and explicitly make statements about God's being and actions in the world.

A crucial component of a confessional account of canon formation is a notion of history governed by God as creator and covenant-maker. In the framework of providence, inspired texts from across disparate time-periods and social situations can speak truly with a unified theological coherence because they speak of the selfsame God at work in the world. This theological framework further accepts that God is a communicative being who has sovereignly chosen to reveal himself and his will through written texts and by divinely commissioned biblical authors (cf. Sailhamer 2009: 59–99; Vanhoozer 2012: 296–386; Kira 2019: 180–207). Providence, revelation, and inspiration are thus some of the orienting categories that ground the profile of theological realities that must be true for God to design the scriptural canon to speak as a unified and coherent whole (cf. Gignilliat 2019: 41–56; Collett 2020: 9–23). Canonical intentionality relies upon these theological concepts to maintain its cohesive center.

In terms of hermeneutics, we can ask, what role does the textual intention of biblical authors play in the notion of canonical intentionality? In canon studies, this question is often pursued in light of the distinct phases of the canon formation process. How does the composition phase of biblical books relate to the canonization by which they are associated and collected with other works?

This question has several dimensions. We can ask how the discrete purpose of a biblical author relates to the associations and meaning generated by a reader considering one writing in view of another. Further, we can ask about an author's purpose in making intertextual use of an already established authoritative text. We can also ask how the purpose of a biblical author relates to subsequent intertextual connections that utilize a portion of that author's text. Finally, we might ask how biblical authors themselves understood and contributed to the canon formation process. Were there any ways that biblical authors influenced or guided the earliest phases of the association and arrangement that happened during canonization? Answering these questions can be pursued by considering the possibility that canon-consciousness was a factor for biblical authors and also early and later generations of readers (see below).

Speaking broadly, each of these categories of individuals can be said to have some connection to the "intentional" activity at work in the shaping of the final form of the biblical canon: the readers of a collection, the shapers of a collection, and the authors of biblical books within that collection. Especially if a broad understanding of canon is utilized, this network of assumptions and "intentions" can form the matrix in which we speak meaningfully about "canonical intentionality."

Sub-collections and canon-consciousness

As mentioned above, one way to further explore the relationship between the composition and the canonization phase of the biblical canon is to examine canonical intentionality in light of the notion of canon-consciousness. Put differently, the idea of canon-consciousness has the potential to address some of the questions raised by the issue of canonical intentionality. What is canon-consciousness? Put simply, canon-consciousness is a basic awareness of a canonical collection (a "consciousness" of a canon). The scholarly discussion about canon-consciousness orbits around three complex definitional questions: What is a canon? What does "consciousness" of a canon entail? And, finally, who are the ones said to possess a canon-consciousness?

Recognizing that these definitional components are fraught with debated issues, a working definition of each can help illustrate the value of the notion of canon-consciousness in the study of the biblical canon. A *canon* can be characterized as an authoritative collection of authoritative writings (on the challenges and implications of defining canon along these lines, see Chapman 2010; Kruger 2012; and Spellman 2014: 8–45). The concept of canon communicates both the notion of collection and also normative authority. The biblical canon is thus an authoritative collection of biblical writings. These distinctions help explicate the significance of a phrase like "the canon of Scripture." It is a collection that contains a set of normative writings that are recognized by a particular community to be set apart from all other writings.

A *consciousness of canon* refers to a basic or developed awareness of such a collection. This involves an awareness of the fittingness of a group of writings to belong together within the scope of a collection. A "concept of canon" also involves understanding the nature and authority of the larger whole of the canonical collection conceptually. In other words, the developing framework of connected groupings of biblical literature functions as a kind of "mental construct" that guides an author's or a reader's sense of the Bible as a whole. In this "mind"-set, an individual (author or reader) is aware or conscious of a broader theological and literary context. The makeup of this mindset includes an awareness of togetherness (*Zusammen–Denken*) and a consciousness of a broader canonical context (*Kanonbewußtsein*) when reading individual writings (on these terms see Childs 1992: 71–79; 1996: 362–77; Balla 1997: 98–106; Driver 2010: 171–84; Dempster 2009: 47–77; Shepherd 2016: 1–37).

Acknowledging the viability of this possibility lends legitimacy to the notion that an individual or group of readers might be able to conceptualize a distinct reading context. Even without a definitive list, someone could still conceive of an inter-related body of literature as a distinct and coherent entity. In relation to the formation of the biblical canon, the notion of canon-consciousness entails an awareness of the authority and inter-relatedness of the biblical literature. In the historical process of composition and canonization, in other words, there is an awareness both of the authority of certain traditions (either oral or written) and also a sense of the inter-related nature of those traditions.

The wide-ranging literary texts, contexts, meanings, and messages found within the biblical literature are bound together by a reader's sense of the "big picture" of the canonical context. Accessing "consciousness" here does not involve an attempt to reconstruct the mental processes of an individual author or reader. Rather, the evidence of canon-consciousness would be drawn from historical and textual indicators of this awareness.

Who, then, are we talking about when we refer to this concept? Who has a canon-conscious mindset? For this question, the answer may be an author who is aware of a larger literary collection. The answer may also be a reader who is aware of an individual writing's place within that larger literary collection. Utilizing these working definitions, we can see how this concept might apply in biblical and theological studies.

Canon-consciousness can refer to the idea that as the earliest *biblical readers* gathered individual biblical writings together, they did so with an awareness of a broader literary collection of authoritative writings. If canon-consciousness was a factor in their thinking, they could have associated one writing with another writing and circulated certain writings as a gathered group. These circulation patterns would then form the literary and theological framework by which later generations of readers received and passed along this biblical literature (cf. also the discussion above on "collection-consciousness"). Canon-consciousness can also refer to the notion that *biblical authors* were directly aware of an authoritative collection of biblical literature (or, a stable collection of authoritative writings). If canon-consciousness was a factor in their thinking, in other words, the biblical authors could write their books in light of a larger literary and theological context.

How might one determine whether or not an individual author had a "canon-conscious" mindset? At this point, we are not attempting to reconstruct an author's internal motivation, mental state, or even larger goal as an end in itself apart from the writing itself. Rather, we are seeking to discern an author's textual intention. What has an author actually done in the composition of his text? In this way, the canon-consciousness of a biblical author would be discerned by paying close attention to the way he has positioned his words and his overall compositional strategy. Textual features, in other words, are at the center of this area of study. A canon-conscious composition would be a text written in light of the context of a canonical collection or sub-collection. In this instance, there would be some element of an author's textual work that showed an awareness of a canonical context.

What type of evidence would demonstrate a form of canon-consciousness at work among both the biblical authors who were writing the texts of Scripture and also the believing community that was copying, preserving, and treasuring those texts as they passed them on to later generations? There seem to be at least three primary indicators of canon-consciousness at the compositional level. These relate to the literary location, perceived authority, and intended scope of a given composition. A canon-conscious author might show (1) an awareness of a broader literary (and authoritative) collection; (2) an awareness of the way his own writing functions in relation to that collection (with the same normative authority of, in continuity with, or in contribution to those texts); or (3) an intended audience for his writing that is purposefully broad both in terms of geography and longevity (i.e., "for future generations" of readers).

Why is the notion of "canon-consciousness" important for the study of the biblical canon? In short, if canon-consciousness was a factor in biblical composition, and if it was also a factor in biblical canonization, then it can also factor into biblical interpretation. In other words, if biblical authors had a form of canon-consciousness, if the earliest readers have a form of canon-consciousness, then contemporary readers have a warranted and legitimate incentive for maintaining a canon-conscious mindset as well. The notion of canon-consciousness also relates to other strategic concepts in biblical and theological studies (such as canonical shaping, intentionality, and exegesis).

These considerations make the appeal to canon (in all its multifaceted connotations) not arbitrary but rather fitting.

Sub-collections and biblical theology

Another question that haunts the methodological discussion of canonical interpretation regards the impact these distinctions have or do not have on the hermeneutical task: What tangible difference does this approach make at the interpretive level? What is the exegetical payoff of reading these biblical books in light of one another? An initial answer to these questions involves grasping and articulating the meaning and message of biblical books and canonical sub-collections. When grappling with book-level meaning, the relationship to other books is a natural concern in light of the theological confession that biblical texts speak of the same divine subject matter. The historical givenness of distinct canonical collections and sub-collections also encourages this mode of analysis.

Because part of the biblical theology task is to consider the theological message of the whole Bible on its own terms, to trace central themes carefully across the canon, and to reflect upon the relationship between the testaments, the question of canonical contextuality is a significant one (cf. Spellman and Kimble 2020: 15–21; Klink and Lockett 2012: 13–25). At the very least, the question of book ordering is worth considering when describing the message of a particular section of the canon or a particular grouping within the Old Testament or New Testament. In other words, the ordering of biblical books, their relationship to one another within groupings, the groupings of those groupings, and any effects this might have on the Bible's overarching theological message are all of interest to the biblical theologian.

To give a few small-scale examples, we can briefly consider the canonical location and function of the Old Testament books of Ruth and Chronicles as well as the New Testament books of James and 1 Peter. The canonical location of Ruth, who can find? There are three primary locations of Ruth in the ordering traditions: between Judges and Samuel (LXX), prior to the Psalter at the head of the Writings (Baba Bathra 14b), and after the book of Proverbs (MT). Given this pattern within lists and manuscripts of the Old Testament, a study of mere contextuality would note the effect of the book of Ruth in these three positions.

In addition to discerning any textual links among books, a canonical study of Ruth would ask how the central themes of the narrative (e.g., providence, redemption, the nations, etc.) intersect with the writings in its textual proximity in the collection (cf. Dempster 2015; Stone 2015; and Goswell 2019). For example, Ruth might provide a contrast to the confusion and wickedness of Israel devoid of godly leadership (after Judges). With its final genealogy ending with David, it might introduce a collection of David's Psalms (as first in the Writings). And, it might provide a narrative illustration of God-fearing wisdom (after Proverbs). Moreover, a study of meant contextuality might seek to sort out the priority in these three positions whether the primary criterion is external evidence (i.e., the most ancient ordering) or internal evidence (textual or thematic links with surrounding books). Both lines of inquiry are possible and profitable when considering the "big picture" of these sub-collections.

We can also consider the compilational dynamic between Ezra–Nehemiah and the book of Chronicles (cf. Gallagher 2014; Koorevaar 2015; and Steins 2015). The book of Chronicles also has three primary positions within ancient lists and manuscript traditions: directly following the book of Kings (LXX), as the first book of the Writings (MT), and as the final book in the Writings (Baba Bathra 14b). In the ordering where Chronicles comes first, the book of Ezra–Nehemiah typically comes last. In the ordering where Chronicles comes last, the book of Ezra–Nehemiah immediately precedes this work. The "montage effect" metaphor reminds us that this arrangement for the book of Chronicles influences its perceived purpose within the collection. As the final book of the Writings and therefore of the Hebrew Bible, the book appears to function as a retrospective narrative commentary on the entirety of redemptive history (beginning with Adam and ending with Cyrus's decree). If one considers the other ordering options, though, does Chronicles lose this function when somewhere other than the final position? Here, the solar system analogy can help conceptualize this movement. In both major Hebrew ordering traditions, Chronicles appears in the last major sub-collection in the Old Testament (the Writings). Thus, in this model, Chronicles maintains its retrospective function in contradistinction to its juxtaposition with the similar narrative flow of the book of Kings.

Further, in orderings where Chronicles and Ezra–Nehemiah appear side-by-side, Ezra–Nehemiah invariably comes first followed by Chronicles. This arrangement is out of chronological order and points to a literary or theological ordering principle. Accordingly, even in this variation for Chronicles (being the first or last word of the Writings), the book maintains its position within the orbit of the Writings grouping and also has a gravitational pull to a non-chronological juxtaposition with Ezra–Nehemiah. In terms of biblical theology, seeking to understand the overall message of the Writings corpus would involve reckoning with the meaning of the message of these books. Ezra–Nehemiah may be understood to recount a joyful return that marks the end of exile (emphasizing the fulfillment of Ezra 1; cf. Steinberg and Stone 2015: 43–47) or also as a narration and interpretation of Israel's failure to maintain obedience even after the return from physical exile (emphasizing the lament of Nehemiah 13; cf. Spellman 2018). Just how the purpose and message of Ezra–Nehemiah is understood, then, will affect how one views its relation to a book of Chronicles that emphasizes the reign and dynasty of King David and stops just shy of a return from exile.

In each of these cases, a grasp of the biblical book on its own terms is needed in order for the consideration of its function within a canonical context to be pursued. Each biblical book has been carefully composed and generates a discrete center of gravity. As a gathered collection, then, these books form an intensely interwoven network of distinct theological directions within a web of mutual associations. In this way, compositional strategy and compilational logic can be brought into a dialogue that does not dissolve one mode of analysis into the other.

In the New Testament canon, there are also distinct but multifaceted sub-collections that prompt similar questions. One example is the relationship between the book of James and 1 Peter. As the Catholic Epistles unit forms in the later development of the New Testament, James and 1 Peter maintain a relatively consistent relationship with one another at the head of the collection. In addition to general theological connections between these letters, the openings of both texts contain several striking verbal and specific thematic connections. These include their broad audience, the mention of exile as a geographic and theological descriptor, the treatment of endurance through trials, and the use of Leviticus 19 and the command to love one's neighbor as a central plank in their opening argument (for these connections see Lockett 2017a: 141–55; Nienhuis and Wall 2013: 74–81, 114–19).

In light of our discussion here, what would be the best way of describing the nature of these textual connections? Does the ordering of James, then 1 Peter *generate* this connection, *amplify* independently established patterns, or does it represent a happy coincidence of arbitrary positioning? In one sense, the verbal, thematic, and structural connections between the openings of James and 1 Peter are "suggestive of an intentional juxtaposition of the two texts" by the community of first readers (Lockett 2017a: 177). Moreover, the striking profile of textual features within these two writings provides a baseline warrant for a compilational coordination. In this way, the relationship between James and 1 Peter is not only *fitting* (via textual links) but they have also been *fitted* into this relationship by means of the canonical process (via physical and conceptual juxtaposition).

Moreover, this "fittingness" would likely have been recognized by close readers who would have received and assessed these two texts. In this way, the notion of collection-consciousness represents a thick account of "mere contextuality." In this reading, seeing the connection brought into view by the canonical context of a Catholic Epistles collection is not only *valid*, but also *vital* for a full understanding of these New Testament letters.

How would this framework affect not only the meaning of individual compositions but also the way in which these writings interface with the rest of the New Testament? In other words, if James and 1 Peter are understood to be members of a canonically significant sub-collection, would this affect the way they might resonate with the wide-ranging literary and theological trajectories within the New Testament? Thinking of the broader horizon of New Testament theology in this vein, these letters would organically engage in a textual dialogue with one another but would also interface with other New Testament theological trajectories *as a group* rather than as literary lone rangers.

What is at stake here can perhaps be seen if we consider the analogy of the school yard game of Red Rover: If a reader of Paul were to say, Red Rover, Red Rover, let *Jude* come over, the postcard epistle of Jude would almost always be dwarfed and perhaps enveloped by Paul and his formidable letter collection. However, if a reader of Paul were to say Red Rover, Red Rover, let *the Catholic Epistles* come over, the textual and theological playing field would shift and the interactive nature of the game would be modified. Jude would then dialogue with broader features of New Testament theology alongside James, Peter, and John. Paul, in other words, would find himself on the playing field with someone his own size. In this scenario, the letters of Paul would find a complex but complementary dialogue partner in the letters of the Pillar Apostles. Writings like James and 1 Peter would function as individual compositions in their own right but when these letters dialogue with the broader New Testament canon, they would do so in the company of their respective sub-collections.

It is worth noting that within the New Testament there is already the expectation for this kind of complementary dialogue without conflict between the meaning and purpose of apostolic writings. In 2 Peter's well-known comment about those who might twist the teachings of Paul, the dialectic framework for New Testament theology is outlined (see 2 Pet. 3:1–2, 14–16). These texts present not only the relational dynamic between the apostles Peter and Paul, they also explicitly refer to the letters of Paul and the letters of Peter. Peter himself frames his current composition in light of a previous literary text (2 Pet. 3:1) and then speaks of the teaching of Paul himself (3:15, "our beloved brother Paul") in light of a single letter of Paul (3:15, "wrote to you") as well as a gathered collection of other Pauline epistles (3:16, "as he does in all his letters") that are directly characterized as scriptural texts (3:16, "as they do the other Scriptures"). This distinctly canon-conscious statement encourages readers of the New Testament epistles to navigate the message of Paul and Peter by means of their written texts. While there are many exegetical details that need analysis here, the canonical portrayal of 2 Peter encourages readers of the New Testament to pursue the task of New Testament theology in light of letter collections.

Maintaining an awareness of canonical context also brings into dialogue texts and theological trajectories that might otherwise remain unnoticed. This phenomenon might move in several directions. Reckoning with the critical consensus on the chronology of composition might inform a theology of the Gospels where Matthew is followed by Mark (which is written first on Markan priority). In light of the clear literary connections between Luke and Acts, the sequence Luke–John–Acts might draw you to consider the theological significance of John 14–17 (on the Holy Spirit's identity and relationship with the Father and Son) in light of the account of the Spirit's work in the ministry of Jesus in Luke and among the apostles in Acts. Considering the Pauline corpus as a whole will bring the letters to Timothy, Titus, and Philemon into a bookended relationship with Paul's larger letter to the Romans. The beginning and end of the Catholic Epistles collection further brings into focus possible connections between James and Jude. Noting the beginning and end of most New Testament orders might prompt a reflection on the relationship between Matthew's "book of the genealogy of Jesus, the Christ" (1:1) and Revelation's call to read and heed "the words of the prophecy of this book" (1:3; 22:18).

These inner-biblical reflections are certainly possible in a historical approach or a reading that does not take canonical considerations into account, though they will likely seem less warranted when individual writings are analyzed independently of their received collection or within the conceptual parameters of a reconstructed setting. However, the point here is that these types of connections are made possible (and even prompted) by the canonical context of the New Testament itself. As an established avenue for reflecting upon the message of the New Testament as a whole, then, this area of study helps show the natural and fruitful relationship that canon studies can have with the discipline of biblical theology.

Closing reflection

As a final point of discussion, I simply note that the argument and approach(es) to the biblical writings in this volume and broached in this essay demonstrate the enduring relevance of the concept of "collection" and "sub-collection" as legitimate and warranted categories of analysis. Trobisch argues that the interpretation of the New Testament writings necessitates a consideration of the groupings and ordering patterns that appear in the earliest manuscripts of these writings (2000: 26–28, 102–6). The chapters of this volume illustrate the merit of this observation and represent the kinds of historical, theological, and hermeneutical fruit that can come from this type of careful analysis.

A canonical approach to biblical interpretation will both answer some questions and prompt others beyond its purview. The reflections in this chapter have sought to articulate some of the ways one might see canonical sub-collections as an appropriate hermeneutical framework for reading the two-testament biblical canon. In this sense, the path forward is the road that has already been shaped and contoured by previous generations of readers who had future generations in mind as they collected, treasured, and passed along biblical literature.

Further research is needed in order to realize the full yield of this approach to the biblical canon. Tracing canonical sub-collections provides a blueprint for navigating a fresh entryway onto well-worn paths and also shines a light on several genuinely new textual trajectories. In my view, the canonical approach in general and the analysis of canonical sub-collections in particular have a strategic role to play within the broader field of Old and New Testament studies.

Bibliography

Balla, Peter. (1997), *Challenges to New Testament Theology: An Attempt to Justify the Enterprise*, Tübingen: Mohr Siebeck.

Barton, John. (1997), *Holy Writings, Sacred Text: The Canon in Early Christianity*, Louisville: Westminster John Knox.

Bokedal, Tomas. (2014), *The Formation and Significance of the Christian Biblical Canon: A Study in Text, Ritual and Interpretation*, London: Bloomsbury.

Chapman, Stephen B. (1996), "Retrospective Reading of the Old Testament Prophets," *ZAW* 108: 262–77.

Chapman, Stephen B. (2008), *The Church's Guide for Reading Paul: The Canonical Shaping of the Pauline Corpus*, Grand Rapids: Eerdmans.

Chapman, Stephen B. (2010), "The Canon Debate: What It Is and Why It Matters," *JTI* 4 (Fall): 273–94.

Chapman, Stephen B. (2015), "Interpretation by Canonical Division in Early Judaism and Christianity," in Julius Steinberg and Timothy J. Stone (eds), *The Shape of the Writings*, Siphrut: Literature and Theology of the Hebrew Scriptures 16, 281–309, Winona Lake, IN: Eisenbrauns.

Chapman, Stephen B. (2020), "The How as Well as the What: Canonical Formatting and Theological Interpretation," in Don Collett, et al. (eds.), *The Identity of Israel's God in Christian Scripture*, 65–80, Atlanta: SBL Press.

Childs, Brevard S. (1992), *Biblical Theology of the Old and New Testaments*, Philadelphia: Fortress Press.

Collett, Don C. (2020), *Figural Reading and the Old Testament: Theology and Practice*, Grand Rapids: Baker.

Dempster, Stephen. (2009), "Canons on the Right and Canons on the Left: Finding a Resolution in the Canon Debate," *JETS* 52.1 (March): 47–77.
Dempster, Stephen. (2015), "A Wandering Moabite: Ruth—A Book in Search of a Canonical Home," in Julius Steinberg and Timothy J. Stone (eds.), *The Shape of the Writings*, Siphrut: Literature and Theology of the Hebrew Scriptures 16, 87–118, Winona Lake, IN: Eisenbrauns.
Driver, Daniel R. (2010), *Brevard Childs, Biblical Theologian: For the Church's One Bible*, Tübingen: Mohr Siebeck.
Gallagher, Edmon L. (2014), "The End of the Bible? The Position of Chronicles in the Canon," *TynBul* 65.2: 181–99.
Gamble, Harry. (2002), "The New Testament Canon: Recent Research and the *Status Quaestionis*," in Lee M. McDonald and James A. Sanders (eds.), *The Canon Debate*, 267–94, Peabody: Hendrickson Publishers.
Gignilliat, Mark S. (2019), *Reading Scripture Canonically: Theological Instincts for Old Testament Interpretation*, Grand Rapids: Baker.
Goswell, Gregory. (2008), "What's in a Name? Book Titles in the New Testament," *Pacifica* 21 (June): 160–74.
Goswell, Gregory. (2019), "The Ordering of the Books of the Canon and the Theological Interpretation of the Old Testament," *JTI* 13.1: 1–20.
Hurtado, Larry W. (2006), *The Earliest Christian Artifacts: Manuscripts and Christian Origins*, Grand Rapids: Eerdmans.
Kira, Joshua Ryan. (2019), *Between Speech and Revelation: An Evangelical's Dialogue with Farrer, Jüngel, and Wolterstorff*, Eugene: Pickwick.
Klink, Edward W. and Darian R. Lockett. (2012), *Understanding Biblical Theology: A Comparison of Theory and Practice*, Grand Rapids: Zondervan.
Koorevaar, Hendrik J. (2015), "Chronicles as the Intended Conclusion to the Old Testament Canon," in Julius Steinberg and Timothy J. Stone (eds.), *The Shape of the Writings*, Siphrut: Literature and Theology of the Hebrew Scriptures 16, 207–36, Winona Lake, IN: Eisenbrauns.
Kruger, Michael J. (2012), "The Definition of the Term 'Canon': Exclusive or Multi-Dimensional?" *Tyndale Bulletin* 63 (1): 1–20.
Lakoff, George and Mark Johnson. (1980), *Metaphors We Live By*, Chicago: University of Chicago Press.
Lockett, Darian. (2017a), *Letters from the Pillar Apostles: The Formation of the Catholic Epistles as a Canonical Collection*, Eugene: Pickwick.
Lockett, Darian. (2017b), "Limitations of a Purely Salvation-Historical Approach to Biblical Theology," *HBT* 39.2: 211–31.
Lockett, Darian. (2017c), "'Necessary but not sufficient': The Role of History in the Interpretation of James as Christian Scripture," in Robbie Castleman, et al. (eds.), *Explorations in Interdisciplinary Reading: Theological, Exegetical, and Reception-Historical Perspectives*, 69–89, Eugene: Pickwick.
Nienhuis, David R. and Robert W. Wall. (2013), *Reading the Epistles of James, Peter, John, and Jude as Scripture: The Shaping and Shape of a Canonical Collection*, Grand Rapids: Eerdmans.
Sailhamer, John H. (1995), *Introduction to Old Testament Theology: A Canonical Approach*, Grand Rapids: Zondervan.
Sailhamer, John H. (2009), *The Meaning of the Pentateuch: Revelation, Composition and Interpretation*. Downers Grove: IVP.

Seitz, Christopher R. (2007), *Prophecy and Hermeneutics: Toward a New Introduction to the Prophets*, Grand Rapids: Baker.

Seitz, Christopher R. (2009), *The Goodly Fellowship of the Prophets: The Achievement of Association in Canon Formation*, Grand Rapids: Baker.

Seitz, Christopher R. (2011), *The Character of Christian Scripture: The Significance of a Two-Testament Bible*, Grand Rapids: Baker.

Seitz, Christopher R. (2014), *Colossians*, Grand Rapids: Brazos.

Seitz, Christopher R. (2018), *The Elder Testament: Canon, Theology, Trinity*, Waco: Baylor University Press.

Shepherd, Michael B. (2016), *Textuality and the Bible*, Eugene: Wipf and Stock.

Spellman, Ched. (2014), *Toward a Canon-Conscious Reading of the Bible: Exploring the History and Hermeneutics of the Canon*, Sheffield: Sheffield-Phoenix Press.

Spellman, Ched. (2018), "Nehemiah's New Shadow: Reading and Rereading the Ezra–Nehemiah Narrative," *STR* 9.1 (Spring): 3–22.

Spellman, Ched and Jeremy Kimble. (2020), *Invitation to Biblical Theology: Exploring the Shape, Storyline, and Themes of the Scriptures*, Grand Rapids: Kregel.

Steinberg, Julius and Timothy J. Stone. (2015), "The Historical Formation of the Writings in Antiquity," in Julius Steinberg and Timothy J. Stone (eds.), *The Shape of the Writings*, Siphrut: Literature and Theology of the Hebrew Scriptures 16, 11–58, Winona Lake, IN: Eisenbrauns.

Steins, Georg. (2015), "Torah-Binding and Canon Closure: On the Origin and Canonical Function of the Book of Chronicles," in Julius Steinberg and Timothy J. Stone (eds.), *The Shape of the Writings*, Siphrut: Literature and Theology of the Hebrew Scriptures 16, 237–80, Winona Lake, IN: Eisenbrauns.

Stone, Timothy J. (2015), "The Search for Order: The Compilational History of Ruth," in Julius Steinberg and Timothy J. Stone (eds.), *The Shape of the Writings*, Siphrut: Literature and Theology of the Hebrew Scriptures 16, 175–86, Winona Lake, IN: Eisenbrauns.

Trobisch, David. (2000), *The First Edition of the New Testament*, Oxford: Oxford University Press.

Trobisch, David. (2012), *Remythologizing Theology: Divine Action, Passion, and Authorship*, Cambridge: Cambridge University Press.

Vanhoozer, Kevin J. (2016), "The Discarded Imagination: Metaphors by Which a Holy Nation Lives," in *Pictures at a Theological Exhibition*, 17–48, Downers Grove: IVP.

Ward, Timothy. (2009), *Words of Life: Scripture as the Living and Active Word of God*, Downers Grove: IVP.

Webster, John B. (2003), "A Great and Meritorious Act of the Church? The Dogmatic Location of the Canon," in John Barton and Michael Wolter (eds.), *Die Einheit der Schrift und die Vielfalt des Kanons*, 95–126, Berlin: Walter de Gruyter.

Contributors

Craig G. Bartholomew (Ph.D., University of Bristol) is the Director of the Kirby Laing Centre for Public Theology in Cambridge, UK. Amongst other areas his current research relates to Old Testament origins and the question of God. The first in a four-volume series in this area is due out in 2022, namely *The Old Testament and God*. Craig is the author of numerous books, most recently *God Who Acts in History: The Significance of Sinai* (2020), and co-authored with Bruce R. Ashford, *The Doctrine of Creation: A Constructive Kuyperian Approach* (2020).

Tomas Bokedal (Th.D., Lund University) is Associate Professor at NLA University College, Bergen, Norway, and Lecturer in New Testament at King's College, University of Aberdeen, Scotland. He previously taught Greek and theology at the Lutheran School of Theology in Gothenburg, Sweden. His primary fields of research concern Christian origins and the relation of "Scripture and Theology." He is the author of *The Formation and Significance of the Christian Biblical Canon: A Study in Text, Ritual and Interpretation* (Bloomsbury T&T Clark, 2014) and *Christ the Center: How the Rule of Faith, the* Nomina Sacra *and Numerical Patterns Shape the Canon* (forthcoming 2022). Among his present projects are a study on Scripture in the Second Century (forthcoming 2023) and a monograph on Papias of Hierapolis (forthcoming).

Stephen B. Chapman (Ph.D., Yale University) is Associate Professor of Old Testament at Duke University. He is the author of *1 Samuel as Christian Scripture* (2016) and *The Law and the Prophets* (2020), as well as co-editor (with Marvin A. Sweeney) of the *Cambridge Companion to the Hebrew Bible/Old Testament* (2016). His work focuses on the formation of the biblical canon, scriptural hermeneutics, the literary dynamics of biblical narrative, and the history and use of the Bible within the Christian tradition and Western culture.

Don C. Collett (Ph.D., University of St. Andrews) is Professor of Old Testament at Trinity Episcopal School for Ministry. He received the B.A. in philosophy and history from Montana State University in Bozeman, MT, and the M.Div. from Westminster Seminary in California. In addition to published journal articles, chapters in books, and reviews, he is the author of *Figural Reading and the Old Testament: Theology and Practice* (2020), and co-editor of *The Identity of Israel's God in Christian Scripture: Essays in honor of Christopher R. Seitz*, ed. Don Collett, Mark Elliott, Mark Gignilliat, and Ephraim Radner (2020).

Nancy L. deClaissé-Walford (Ph.D., Baylor University, Waco, Texas) is the Carolyn Ward Professor of Old Testament and Biblical Languages at Mercer University's

McAfee School of Theology. She is also a Research Associate in the Department of Old Testament Studies at the University of Pretoria in South Africa and the Old Testament Editor for the Word Biblical Commentary Series. Her major research work is in the book of Psalms, with the following book publications: *Reading from the Beginning: The Shaping of the Hebrew Psalter* (1997); *Introduction to the Psalms: A Song from Ancient Israel* (2004); *The Book of Psalms*, The New International Commentary on the Old Testament (2014); and *Psalms, Books 4–5*, The Wisdom Commentary Series (2020). Her current writing project is a reworking of the commentary on Books 1–2 of the Psalter for the Word Biblical Commentary Series.

Stephen G. Dempster (Ph.D., University of Toronto) is Professor Emeritus at Crandall University and Adjunct Professor at Toronto Baptist Seminary. His research concentrates on Biblical Theology, Old Testament Canon formation, and Biblical Hebrew. He is currently researching commentaries on Genesis, Jeremiah and Isaiah, and a monograph on the Kingdom of God. In addition to many essays, he has written a biblical theology of the Old Testament (*Dominion and Dynasty*, 2003) and *Micah: A Theological Commentary* (2017).

Matthew Y. Emerson (Ph.D., Southeastern Baptist Theological Seminary) is Dean of Theology, Arts, and Humanities and Professor of Religion at Oklahoma Baptist University. His research interests include the Old Testament's use in the New Testament, early Christian interpretation, and theological method. He serves as co-Executive Director of the Center for Baptist Renewal, co-editor of the *Journal of Baptist Studies*, steering committee member of the Scripture and Hermeneutics Seminar, and Senior Fellow for the Center of Ancient Christian Studies. Publications include "*He Descended to the Dead*": *An Evangelical Theology of Holy Saturday* (2019) and *Christ and the New Creation: A Canonical Approach to the Theology of the New Testament* (2014).

W. Edward Glenny (Th.D., Dallas Theological Seminary; Ph.D., University of Minnesota) is Professor of New Testament and Greek at University of Northwestern – St. Paul (MN) where he has taught for the past twenty-three years. He has published on Septuagint translation technique (*Finding Meaning in the Text: Translation Technique and Theology in the Septuagint of Amos*, 2009) and on the Greek Twelve Prophets (volumes on *Hosea, Amos*, and *Micah* in the Brill Septuagint Commentary Series and *Amos: A Handbook on the Greek Text* in the Baylor Handbook on the Septuagint, 2022), and he is co-editor of the *T&T Clark Handbook of Septuagint Research* (2021).

Gregory R. Lanier (Ph.D., University of Cambridge) is Associate Professor of New Testament at Reformed Theological Seminary, Orlando, FL. He is the author of *Corpus Christologicum: Texts and Translations for the Study of Jewish Messianism and Early Christology* (2021); *The Septuagint: What It Is and Why It Matters* (with William A. Ross; 2021); *Studies on the Intersection of Text, Paratext, and Reception* (ed. with J. Nicholas Reid; 2021); *Septuaginta: A Reader's Edition* (with William A. Ross; Hendrickson, 2018); and *Old Testament Conceptual Metaphors and the Christology of Luke's Gospel* (Bloomsbury T&T Clark, 2018).

Darian R. Lockett (Ph.D., University of St. Andrews) is Professor of New Testament at Talbot School of Theology, Biola University. He is the author of several books and articles, including *Understanding Biblical Theology: A Comparison of Theory and Practice* (2012), *Letters from the Pillar Apostles: The Formation of the Catholic Epistles as a Canonical Collection* (2017), *Letters for the Church: Reading James, 1–2 Peter, 1–3 John, and Jude as Canon* (2021), and is editor of *The Catholic Epistles: Critical Readings* (Bloomsbury T&T, 2021).

Lee Martin McDonald (Ph.D., University of Edinburgh) was president and now Emeritus Professor of New Testament at Acadia Divinity College. He is the author of *The Formation of The Christian Biblical Canon* (1995), *The Biblical Canon: Its Origin, Transmission, and Authority* (2007), *The Formation of the Biblical Canon* (two vols., Bloomsbury, 2017), and is co-editor of *The Canon Debate* (2002) with James A. Sanders and *Jewish and Christian Scriptures: The Function of "Canonical" and "Non-Canonical" Religious Texts* (T&T Clark, 2010) with James H. Charlesworth.

John D. Meade (Ph.D., The Southern Baptist Theological Seminary) is Associate Professor of Old Testament and Director of the Text & Canon Institute at Phoenix Seminary. He authored *The Biblical Canon Lists from Early Christianity* (2017; with Edmon Gallagher) and *A Critical Edition of the Hexaplaric Fragments of Job 22–42* (2020).

E. Randolph Richards (Ph.D., Southwestern Seminary) is the Research Professor of New Testament, Palm Beach Atlantic University. He is currently co-editor of *Inscriptions, Papyri and Other Artifacts*, Ancient Literature for New Testament Studies 10 (2022). He is the author or co-author of nearly a dozen books and dozens of articles on a range of subjects from Gospels and Paul to intercultural hermeneutics. He is currently writing the two-volume commentary on the Gospel of John in the Word Biblical Commentary and an introduction to the New Testament.

Christopher R. Seitz (Ph.D., Yale University) is Senior Research Professor of Biblical Interpretation, Wycliffe College in the University of Toronto. His recent publications include: *The Character of Christian Scripture: The Significance of a Two Testament Bible* (2011); *Colossians: The Brazos Theological Commentary Series* (2014); *Joel: International Theological Commentary* (Bloomsbury T&T Clark, 2016); *Elder Testament: Canon, Theology, Trinity* (2018); *Convergences: Canon and Catholicity* (2020); *Essays on Prophecy and Canon: The Rise of a New Model for Interpretation* (2021).

Ched Spellman (Ph.D., Southwestern Baptist Theological Seminary) is Associate Professor of Biblical and Theological Studies at Cedarville University. He is the author of *Toward a Canon-Conscious Reading of the Bible: Exploring the History and Hermeneutics of the Canon* (2014) and co-author of *Invitation to Biblical Theology: Exploring the Shape, Storyline, and Themes of Scripture* (2020).

Timothy J. Stone (Ph.D., University of St Andrews) is an independent researcher. He is the author of *The Compilational History of the Megilloth: Canon, Contoured*

Intertextuality (2013) and *Meaning in the Writings* (2013) as well as the co-editor of *The Shape of the Writings* (2015).

Külli Tõniste (Ph.D., London School of Theology, Brunel University) is Associate Professor of Bible and Theology and Rector of the Baltic Methodist Theological Seminary in Tallinn, Estonia. She is author of *The Ending of the Canon: A Canonical and Intertextual Reading of Revelation 21–22* (Bloomsbury T&T Clark, 2016) and is currently awaiting the publication of her a commentary on the Book of Revelation in the Central and Eastern European Bible Commentary series (forthcoming).

Index of Biblical/Extra-Biblical References

Old Testament

Genesis
1	47
1:1	196
1:1–5	44
1:28	107–8
1:31	149
2–3	112
3:15	38
3:22	305
4:1–25	317
6:3	111
6:13	112
12:1–3	38
12:10–20	111
15:12–16	111
18:22–33	112
20	112
37–50	112
49:8–12	38
50	107
50:24	111

Exodus
1:6	107
1:7	107
7–11	112
13:19	107
14:31	111
19:5–6	199
32:12	218, 130
32:14	218
34:6	218
40:33	107
40:34–39	107

Leviticus
1:1	107
26	44
27:34	107

Numbers
1:1	107
11–12	112
15:22–31	153
35:13	107

Deuteronomy
1:1–5	108
6:1–4	152
6:4–9	44
18	112
18:15	108
24:10–12	44
31:7–8	108
31:24–29	317
34:7	111
34:10–12	108
34	108

Joshua
	317
1	47
1:1	108
1:7–8	317
1:7–9	108
1:8–9	44
18:1	108
24:32	107

Ruth
1:22	195–6
3:11	162
4:17–22	45

1 Samuel
19:11	128
29:1	128
31:1	128

2 Samuel
3:1	128
5:22	128

15:6	128	1:2–3	44
15:10	128	2	42, 45
20:1	128	2:10–11	128
21:9–10	195–6	25	174
		72	45, 128
1 Kings		72:17	42
1:24–25	128	72:20	128
		73	128–9
2 Kings		78:1	109
2:12	39	88	129
12:14	39	89	45, 129–30
17:25	195–6	90:13	130
18–20	170	105	130
		107	130
4 Kingdoms		108	130
14:25–27	218	110	45
		111	152
1 Chronicles		137	175
6:31–37	128	145	131
9:19	128	151 (LXX)	133
2 Chronicles		Proverbs	
29:25	109	1:7	145, 148
36:22–23	42, 44, 47	1:20–21	148
		1:26	146
Ezra		1:33	147
4:6	195	2:2	147
9:10–11	109	2:16	162
		3:9–10	146
Esther		3:13–18	148
2	164	3:19–20	145, 148
2:3	164	3:35	197
2:7	164	5:18	163
2:8	164	5:19	163
9:22	164	5:20	162
		6:24	163
Job		7:1–27	152
1:1	145, 151	7:5	162
1:2	151	7:13	163
1:5	151	7:17	163
5:2	197	8:22–31	146
7:7	197	9	154
42	151	9:10	195–7
		11:29	197
Psalms		12:7	154
1	47	14:11–12	147
1–2	125, 152	17:1	148
1:1–2	317	17:3	148
1:2	128	17:5	149

17:17	149, 151	7:3	163
20:1	197	8:1	163
20:19	197	8:4	161
23:27	163		
24:3–4	154	Isaiah	
26:1–12	145	2	170
29:3	197	2:1–5	179
31	148, 162	8:16–20	179
31:23	162	11	40
31:30	145	29:11–12	179
		30:8	179
Ecclesiastes		33:21	190
1:1	149	36–39	170
1:2	149	40–48	40
1:12–18	149	40:31	176
1:14	197	55:11	179
2:26	153		
3:1–7	197	Jeremiah	
3:17	153	18:18	42
5:3–4	153	25	44
5:5	153	26:4–5	109
5:6	153	26:18	170
5:17	150	28:11	190
7:23–29	149–50	31:31–33	40
8:5	197		
8:12	153	Lamentations	
9:9	160	1:6	161
10:13	195–7	2:1	161
11:8	150	2:4	161
11:9	153	2:8	161
12:8	149	2:10	161
12:11–12	163	2:13	161
12:13–14	145	2:15	161–2
		2:18	161
Song of Songs		4:21–22	175
1:2	163	4:22	161
1:5	161	5:3	164
2:7	161	5:15	164
3:5	161		
3:10	161	Ezekiel	
3:11	161	7:26	42
4:5	163	26:1	190
4:12	163	37	40
4:14	163		
4:15	163	Daniel	
5:5	163	1–6	162, 164
5:8	161	1:4	164, 168
5:16	161	1:8	164
6:4	162	1:15	164

8:17	179	3:14	217
8:27	179	3:16	174, 217
9	42, 44	3:17	217
9:10	109	3:18 (LXX)	217
9:23	195	3:19 (LXX)	217
10:8–12	179	3:19	174
		3:21	217
Hosea		4:14–21	219
1:1	194	4:16	215
1:1–2	194–5, 198–201	4:19	216
1:2	196–7, 213, 220		
1:10–11	220	Amos	
2:18–23	220	1:1	214
3:4–5	220	1:2	174, 215
4:1	220	1:3–2:16	174
4:6	187, 220	1:8	216
4:7	197	1:11–12	174
4:11	197	3:1	174
4:14	197	5:18–20	219
7:11	197	6:9	216
8:7	197	7:1	195
8:12	187	7:2–3	174
8:14	187	7:5–6	174
9:5	219	8:2	112
9:7	197	9:1	216
12:1	197	9:11–15	216–17
13:13	197	9:12	216, 221
14:1–3	193		
14:1–8	173	Obadiah	
14:2–4	173	1	216–17
14:9	174, 194, 196–9, 201	1–2	216
		1–4	175
14:10	215	8	216–17
		10–14	175
Joel		11	217
1:8–2:17	193	15	217, 219
1:15	219	15–16	216
1:20	218	16	217
2:1	217, 219	17	216–17
2:13	218	19	216
2:14	218		
2:15	217	Jonah	
2:18	193	1:6–10	175
2:18–27	193	1:15–16	175
2:32	217	3:3–4	175
3:3	217	3:8	218
3:4	217, 219	3:9	218
3:7	217	4:2	218

Index of Biblical/Extra-Biblical References

Micah
1:1   214
1:5   214
1:5–7   214
1:9   214
2:4   219
2:12   216
3:1   216
3:9   216
3:9–12   214
3:12   190, 208
4   170
4:1–4   175, 179, 217
4:2–3   216
4:4–7   216
5:1–5   216
5:6–8   216
7:14–17   216
7:16   216
7:18   216
7:18–20   40, 176

Nahum
1:2–3   218
1:3   176

Habakkuk
3:1–19   176
3:16   219

Zephaniah
1:1–6   176
1:7–16   219
3:8   176
3:8–20   176

Haggai
1:1   176
1:12   193
2:1   176
2:10   176
2:18   176
2:20   176
2:23   219

Zechariah
1:1–6   170
1:4–6   177
1:6   193

7:7   170, 177
7:12   109, 170, 177
14:1   219
14:1–21   177

Malachi
1:2–3   200
1:4   216
1:6–2:9   200
2:14–16   219
2:17   199
3:1   177
3:15   186
3:16   178, 187, 193, 200
3:16–18   177
3:16–4:6   186, 199
3:17   200
4:1   219
4:4   187, 200, 317
4:4–6   44, 219
4:5   186
4:5–6   219

Apocrypha or Deutero-Canonical Books

2 Esdras
14:44–45   208

4 Ezra
1:39–40   213
14:44–47   54

Sirach
Prologue   67
39:1–5   36
44–49   35, 40
49:10   36

2 Maccabees
2:1–15   43rev
2:13–15   67
15:9   109

New Testament

Matthew
1:1   328
1:1–16   246
3:3   243

7:24–27	154	3:21	317
23:35	68	8:34	237
24:15	37	12:11	279
24:42–43	234		

1 Corinthians

Mark		3:19	37
1:3	243	5:9	285
10:2–12	234	7:10–11	234
16:9–20	233	10:27	234
		10:30	154
Luke		11:23	237
1:1–4	7–8	11:23–25	237
2:20	7	15:3–7	236
3:3–6	243		
3:23–38	246	2 Corinthians	
7:22	7	2:4	285
10:7	234		
10:8	234	Galatians	
10:16	8	1:19	237
10:24	7	2:9	91, 258–9
11:51	68	3:16	237
22:32	247	4:4	237
22:43–44	233		
24	36	Philippians	
24:25–27	7, 9	2:8	237
24:27	x		
24:44	x, 67	Colossians	
		1:9	154
John		2:3	154
1	246	4:16	10, 282, 285
1:23	243		
7:53–8:11	233	1 Thessalonians	
20:30	237	5:2	234
20:30–31	104		
21:24–5	104	2 Thessalonians	
22:15–17	247	2:3	293

Acts		1 Timothy	
1:1–3	8	3:16	236
1:13–14	264	5:18	234
10:36–41	236	6:13	237
15	91		
17:3	9	2 Timothy	
20:35	239	3:14–17	10
		4:13	283
Romans			
1:1	239	Hebrews	
3:10	37	2:18	237
3:10–18	317	12:5–6	37

13:20–25	281	22:11	293
13:22	281	22:12	306
		22:18	328
1 Peter	326–7	22:18–19	10, 304
5:13	254		

Miscellaneous Early Jewish and Christian Literature

2 Peter			
1:16–18	234		
1:19–21	10	1 Clement	
3	328	36:1–5	273
3:15–16	8–10, 273		
		2 Clement	
1 John		2:4	9
1:1–4	7, 234		
		Gospel of Thomas	
3 John		52	54
1	281		
		Protevangelium of James	
Revelation			
1:1	239	1:1	281
1:3	10, 304, 306, 328		
1:4	13	**Pseudepigrapha**	
2:3–3:22	13		
4:7	244	4 Maccabees	
7:14	293	18:10	109
12:1	293		
12:4	293	Lives of the Prophets	
20:15	293	6–16	213
21:2	293		
22:2	305	Martyrdom of Isaiah	
22:7	10, 306	4:22	213

Index of Ancient Sources

Africanus 60
Ammonius of Alexandria 242–3
Amphilochius of Iconium 13, 69, 74, 208, 257, 295, 298
Andrew of Caesarea 291, 301
Apollinarius, Claudius 240
Apollonius 253, 292
Athanasius 16, 27, 33, 60–1, 69–71, 74, 245, 257, 260, 295, 297
Atticus 284
Augustine of Hippo 64, 141, 186, 208, 222–3, 257, 295, 298, 301

Baba Batra 35, 39, 53–4, 68, 73, 113, 170, 178, 186, 189, 213, 220, 325–6
Barnabas 273–4
Basil the Great 27, 301
Bede 255–6
Ben Azzai 113
Bryennios 69

Cassiodorus 253–4
Cerinthus 292
Cicero 283–4
Clement of Alexandria 11–12, 238, 240, 245, 253–4, 273, 291
Commodius 294
Cyprian 294
Cyril of Jerusalem 61, 71–2, 245, 257, 260, 297

Dionysius of Alexandria 292
Dionysius of Corinth 291

Epiphanius 61, 69, 72–5, 245, 257, 260, 292–3, 298
Eusebius of Caesarea 14, 71–2, 242–3, 245–7, 253–6, 291–2, 294–5, 297
Euthalius of Alexandria 255

Gregory of Nazianzus 61, 72, 208, 257, 295, 298
Gregory of Nyssa 301

Hegesippus 240
Hermas 293
Hilary 61
Hippolytus 244, 294

Ignatius of Antioch 8–9, 23, 273, 283
Irenaeus of Lyons 7–13, 244–5, 253–4, 273, 293–4
Isho'Dad of Merv 256

Jerome 36, 40–1, 53, 60–1, 66, 70, 73–4, 167, 173, 186, 213, 222, 241, 257
John Chrysostom 14, 301
John of Damascus 60–1, 73–4
Josephus x, 14, 36, 41, 54, 68, 110, 208, 222
Junilius 253
Justin Martyr x, 109–10, 241, 243–4, 273–4, 293

Lactantius 294–5
Leontius of Byzantium 253

Manuscripts
048 261
093 261
0137 258
0166 261
0232 (P.Antinoopolis 12) 258
1QIsa 19
1QS 66
4QM 133
4QMMT 36–7, 54, 67, 133, 211
4QpaleoGen-Exod 66
4QPs 132–3
4QXII 66, 209, 211–12, 214
5QAmos 211–12
5/6 HavPs 132

8HevXIIgr 212
11QPs 132–5
GA 260 19
GA 534 19
GA 828 19
GA 1443 19
GA *Lect* 1627 19
GA 2252 19
GA 2437 19
GA 2563 19
Mur88 212
Muratorian Fragment 12, 13, 240, 245, 256, 272, 280, 296, 299, 302, 305
MS 5 277, 280
MS 01 277
MS 02 277
MS 03 277
MS 04 277
Nag Hammadi II 244
P1 244
P4 239, 244
P7 243
P45 238–9, 244, 261
P46 274–6, 280, 282, 284
P53 261
P62 239
P66 239, 244
P67 244
P72 257–8
P74 261
P75 238–9, 244
P100 258
P. Berolinensis (BG) 8502 244
P. Egerton 2 246
P. Oxy. 1 244
P. Oxy. 2 244
Ra46 65
Ra68 65
Ra106 65
Ra122 65
Aleppo (A) 34, 40–1, 46, 197
Alexandrinus (A) 18–19, 21, 65, 75–6, 211–12, 244, 258, 260, 262–3, 277, 299–300, 305
Augiensis (F) 277–9
Bezae (D) 239
Boernerianus (G) 277–9

Cairensis (C) 34, 40, 46
Claromontanus (D) 258–9, 277–80, 296–7, 299, 302, 305
Ephraemi Rescriptus (C) 277, 299–300
Leningradensis (L) 19, 34, 40–1, 46, 70, 159–60, 162, 197
Sinaiticus (S) 18, 21–2, 65, 74–6, 211–12, 258, 260, 262–3, 277, 299–300
Vaticanus (B) 19, 21, 65, 75, 211–12, 258, 260, 262–3, 276–7, 280, 299–300
Venetus (V) 65, 211–12
Washingtonianus (W) 18, 212
Marcion 271, 296
Melito of Sardis 10, 37, 60–1, 64, 69–70
Methodius 292

Nicephorus 60–1, 69

Origen 60–1, 64, 69, 222, 244–6, 253–5, 262, 273, 290, 292, 294

Pamphilus 74, 294
Papias 240, 273–4, 291
Philo of Alexandria 55, 222
Pliny the Younger 284
Polycarp 273
Pseudo-Athanasius 60–1, 69
Pseudo-Didymus 255
Pseudo-John Chrysostom 60, 72
Pseudo-Oecumenius 256
Pseudo-Tertullian 110

Rufinus 61, 292

Serapion 245
Strabo, Walafrid 256
Suetonius 283

Tatian 241–2, 273, 291
Theophilus 240, 291
Tertullian 64, 254, 273, 294, 296

Victor of Capua 242
Victorinus 294

Index of Modern Authors

Aland, B. 251
Aland, K. 251
Albertz, R. 101
Andersen, F. I. 196, 198
Attridge, H. W. 284

Barone, F. P. 60–1
Barr, J. 81
Bartholomew, C. G. 141, 148, 150, 153
Barton, J. 54, 124, 159–60, 317
Bauckham, R. 273
Beckwith, R. T. 34, 41, 303
Ben Zvi, E. 189, 191, 194
Bentley, J. 299
Bergler, S. 210
Bernat, D. 163
Bokedal, T. 19–20, 22–3
Brodie, T. L. 83–4
Brooke, G. 212
Brown, R. E. 253
Brown, W. P. 152

Camp, C. V. 146
Chapman, S. B. 40, 313
Childs, B. S., 1, 8, 46, 84–5, 88–90, 105–6, 111, 125, 128, 139, 142–4, 153, 265
Clines, D. J. A. 38, 143
Conzelmann, H. 282
Craigie, P. C. 131
Crüsemann, F. 142

Delitzsch, F. 141
Dell, K. 163
Dines, J. M. 210, 213, 215, 217–18
Dorival, G. 67
Duff, J. 275

Ebojo, E. B. 276
Ehrman, B. D. 271
Ellingworth, P. 281
Elliott, J. K. 13
Epp, E. J. 13
Evans, C. A. 284
Evans, F. C. 304

Ferguson, E. 272
Flint, P. W. 133
Fox, M. 143, 149–50, 153
Freedman, D. N. 196, 198
Frye, N. 153–4
Fuller, R. 211, 214, 220

Gamble, H. Y. 79, 81–2, 253, 259, 282–3
Gibson, S. J. 251
Glenny, W. E. 214
Goodspeed, E. J. 282
Goswell, G. 82, 88
Goulder, M. 125
Grant, R. M. 273
Grenz, J. R. 276
Gressmann, H. 141
Grünstäudl, W. 254, 262
Guignard, C. 272
Guillaume, P. 212
Gunkel, H. 123–4, 141

Habel, N. C. 146
Hahneman, G. 256, 272
Haran, M. 35
Harnack, A. von 266
Hatch, W. H. P. 278
Hill, C. E. 13
Horrell, D. G. 258
Hurtado, L. W. 12–13, 258, 313

Inglis, D. 276

Janowitz, N. 109
Johnson, L. T. 273
Johnson, M. 319
Jones, B. A. 210, 213–14, 216, 218–19
Joosten, J. 60

Kenyon, F. G. 275
Knox, J. 282, 285
Kratz, R. G. 199
Kraus, H.-J. 128
Kruger, M. J. 87–8, 258

Laird, B. P. 13
Lakoff, G. 319
Lange, A. 64-5
Lemcio, E. E. 88
Levy, S. 152
Lim, B. H. 212
Lockett, D. R. 89, 314-15
Luther, M. 121

McComiskey, T. E. 196
McDonald, L. M. 273
Margolis, M. L. 41-2
Marshall, I. H. 275
Martin, R. P. 273
Menken, M. J. J. 222
Metzger, B. M. 8, 12, 80-1, 272, 290, 297
Morgan, D. F. 41
Moule, C. F. D. 282
Moyise, S. 222
Murphy, R. E. 142, 153
Murphy-O'Connor, J. 274

Niebuhr, K.-W. 256, 263-4
Nienhuis, D. R. 87, 254-7, 260, 262, 264
Nogalski, J. 192-3, 221
Noth, M. 102

Painter, J. 255
Parker, D. C. 251, 261-2
Patzia, A. G. 81, 273
Polzin, R. E. 124
Pope, M. 142
Porter, S. E. 258, 276, 282-3
Preuss, H. D. 142

Rad, G. von 150
Rahlfs, A. 74
Rendtorff, R. 102-3
Richards, E. R. 282-3
Römer, T. 108
Rothschild, C. K. 272

Sailhamer, J. H. 88
Sanders, J. A. 125, 133-4
Sarna, N. M. 121
Schart, A. 191
Schenke, H. M. 282
Scherbenske, E. 272

Schiffman, L. H. 109
Schmid, K. 101, 110-12
Schmid, U. 271
Schmithals, W. 282
Schröter, J. 1, 261, 264-6
Schwöbel, C. 141
Seitz, C. R. 1, 106, 160, 171, 184-5, 215, 312-13, 317
Seow, C. L. 150, 197
Sheppard, G. T. 125
Skeat, T. C. 12
Skehan, P. 134
Spellman, C. 83, 89-91
Stanton, G. 13
Steinberg, J. 41, 160
Stone, T. 41, 46, 160
Sundberg, A. C. 64, 272
Sweeney, M. A. 68, 75, 185-7, 210-11, 213, 221-2

Talmon, S. 134
Tov, E. 134, 212
Trebolle Barrera, J. 67
Trobisch, D. 83, 87, 89-90, 251, 260-1, 264, 274-80, 282, 300, 329

VanderKam, J. C. 54
Van Leeuwen, R. C. 145-7
Verheyden, J. 256
Versace, P. 276
Vielhauer, R. 199

Wallace, D. B. 275-6, 284
Wall, R. W. 88, 91, 263-5, 282
Wasserman, T. 257-8
Watts, J. D. W. 198
Webster, J. 140-1
Westcott, B. F. 296, 301
Westermann, C. 113, 125, 127, 152
White, J. L. 283
Williams, C. S. C. 296-7
Wilson, G. H. 125, 127-8, 133, 135
Wolterstorff, N. 140-1

Yarkin, W. 134

Zahn, T. 8, 297
Zuntz, G. 282

www.ingramcontent.com/pod-product-compliance
Lightning Source LLC
Chambersburg PA
CBHW052141300426
44115CB00011B/1466